America's Historically Black Colleges & Universities

America's Historically Black Colleges and Universities series examines the varying role of these important institutions throughout the Civil Right struggle and American history as a whole.

Previously Published

Harry Lefever, *Undaunted by the Fight: Spelman College and the Civil Rights Movement, 1957-1967*

Bobby L. Lovett, *America's Historically Black Colleges & Universities: A Narrative History from the Nineteenth Century into the Twenty-First Century*

Bobby L. Lovett, *"A Touch of Greatness": A History of Tennessee State University*

F. Erik Brooks, *Tigers in the Tempest: Savannah State University and the Struggle for Civil Rights*

America's Historically Black Colleges & Universities

A Narrative History from the Nineteenth Century into the Twenty-first Century

Bobby L. Lovett

Mercer University Press
Macon, Georgia

MUP/P509

1400 Coleman Avenue
Macon, Georgia 31207

First Paperback Edition

Books published by Mercer University Press are printed on acid-free paper that meets the requirements of American National Standard for Information Sciences—Permanence of Paper for Printed Library Materials.

ISBN 978-0-88146-534-1
Lovett, Bobby L.
America's historically Black colleges & universities : a narrative history from the nineteenth century into the twenty-first century / Bobby L. Lovett. -- 1st ed.
p. cm.
Includes bibliographical references and index.
ISBN 978-0-88146-215-9 (hardcover : alk. paper)
1. African American universities and colleges--History. I. Title.
LC2781.L68 2011
378.73'08996073--dc23
2011017402

With wearied hope we have been waiting the moment of our sacred freedom.

—*Alexander Pushkin*

This book is dedicated to all those who gave me help along the way, especially my children, grandchildren, wife, and other family members, who have continuously encouraged me.

Contents

Acknowledgments

This research project began as part of a 2004 project sponsored by the Education Testing Service in Princeton, New Jersey. The purpose of the ETS-HBCU Scholars project was to develop presentations showing the valuable contributions of the historically black colleges and universities. As part of the three-person team, including Beverly Guy-Sheftall of Spelman College and Howard Simmons of Morgan State University, my responsibility was to research and write a twenty-page historical narrative. Thanks to financial support from ETS, each of the three of us was able to hire a graduate assistant for one year to help with the individual parts of the project. It was that stimulus, which truly was so motivating to me, that I was able to continue to gather sources. Most social science researchers—especially at HBCUs—must conduct research and write with little or no funding or reduction in class load. Faculties at HBCUs carry heavy teaching loads and usually work without graduate assistants. Nonetheless, to be good teachers they must create, organize, write, and publish new information.

The problem this book seeks to solve is the lack of a treatise that synthesizes available sources into a narrative history of the HBCUs, 1837–2009. During the extensive research process, I found that no one had written a narrative on historically black colleges as a whole. Individual narratives on specific black colleges were scarce. I found short articles in journals, newspapers, and magazines; graduate theses and dissertations; institutional websites and book length manuscripts (both published and unpublished)—some of which satisfied internal needs (self-study, alumni brochures, centennial celebrations, etc.). Other materials pursued the motives of those who either were defending HBCUs or criticizing their existence based on statistical data, student performance, faculty characteristics, and alumni outcomes. Many scholarly articles on HBCUs and black higher education appeared in journals.

I am grateful to the Fisk University Library's Special Collections, Tennessee State University Special Collections, Atlanta University Woodruff Library's Special Collections, and US Department of Education's National Center for Education Statistics, the Library of Congress, the Tennessee State Library and Archives, Nashville Public Library's Civil Rights Collection, The Educational Testing Service, and the websites of 105 HBCUs. I also had Internet access to the reports, statistics, and published documents of the Southern Education Foundation; the American Council on Education; and the higher education boards and commissions of Alabama, Arkansas, Delaware, Georgia, Kansas, Kentucky, Louisiana, Maryland, Mississippi, Missouri, North Carolina, New

Jersey, Ohio, Pennsylvania, South Carolina, Tennessee, and Texas. I am also grateful to other agencies, libraries and archives that have digitized many sources, including items from the missionary societies and the philanthropic agencies' nineteenth- and twentieth-century reports. These electronic sources made this four-year research and writing process less expensive and less time consuming. I spent a year less working on this book than on my last major book. For every article, dissertation, master's thesis, monograph, book, and photograph and Internet source used in this book, I extend my sincere appreciation to the authors, editors, compilers, and writers for their work that related to HBCUs and the history of American higher education.

Bobby L. Lovett

Preface

This book presents a brief narrative history and development of the historically black colleges and universities (HBCUs) since 1837, their contributions and uniqueness, including the evolution of the HBCUs from grammar and high schools to fully accredited colleges and universities. The book ends with the portrait of the HBCUs, including statistics, as they encounter twenty-first-century complexities.

Higher education advanced in the North with the establishment of Harvard in 1636. By the time of the American Revolution, nine institutions of higher education existed in the country. They emphasized religion and the liberal arts. Religious denominations sponsored most of these institutions. In 1833, the Society of Friends founded Haverford College, which still emphasizes the Quaker spiritual democracy and liberty of conscience. Many Quakers in the seventeenth century believed the advantages of a free education should be available to Negroes, too, so among several Northern institutions, the Quaker schools admitted a few Negro students.[1]

The South had a few colleges, universities, and military academies. But, a few were in development despite the anti-intellectual stance of the ruling class. Maryville College, Berea College, and Franklin College admitted blacks prior to the Civil War. In each case these institutions were religiously based, and their founders professed human equality. By 1860, 90 percent of four million slaves and half of America's 488,000 free Negroes were illiterate; 44 percent of free Negroes and practically all the slaves lived in Southern states.[2]

The specific history of the HBCUs began in northern territory with the establishment of Cheyney, Lincoln, and Wilberforce Institutes. These institutions were founded by northern, anti-slavery and religious groups, and they survive today.

The number of HBCUs remained at a total of three until the Civil War years. They increased in number partly because of the Morrill Land Grant Act (1862), which helped create about four public HBCUs by setting aside millions of acres of public land to support public colleges. The former eleven Confederate states, among the post-1860 fifteen former slave states, did not organize land-grant colleges until restoration to the Union. To maintain white supremacy and

---

[1] See Greg Kannerstein, ed., *The Spirit of the Intellect: Haverford College, 1883–1983* (Haverford PA: Haverford College, 1983); "Histories of the College," www.haverford.edu.

[2] John Hope Franklin and A. A. Moss Jr., *From Slavery to Freedom: A History of Negro Americans*, 6th ed. (New York: Knopf, 1988) 137.

Jim Crow (racial segregation by law), they created seventeen land-grant HBCUs.[3] All but three of the land-grant HBCUs began after the 1890 Morrill Land Grant Act, which gave money instead of land and said the states had to admit all students to the land-grant institutions or establish separate colleges for blacks and whites. The Morrill Land Grant Act used federal land allocations to fund a public college in each of the states. Congress authorized three more land-grant HBCUs in 1972. The Morrill Act eventually fostered sixty-nine land-grant colleges and universities, including land-grant HBCUs. The heyday of the birth of American institutions of higher education, nearly 150 colleges and universities, occurred between 1880 and 1900.[4] Except for the exceptions mentioned above, Negroes were confined to the early freedmen schools and HBCUs.

There existed in the late nineteenth century some fundamental questions about how to treat Negro Americans, whether to educate them at all, and what kind of education was best suited for blacks. For decades after the 1865 emancipation of the slaves, black and white Americans debated how to reconstruct the nation and how to handle "the Negro questions." Some solutions to social Reconstruction, such as the idea of "forty acres and a mule" proposed for former slaves, challenged the notion held by European Americans that the land was exclusively theirs. Many European Americans desired no socio-economic competition, including equal education, from non-whites, and especially from the Negro, mostly former slaves. They confined the Native Americans to "reservations," and between 1882 and 1934, took their land and their human rights. Upon the emancipation (1865), the question thus was what should be done with the Negro.

European Americans did not place the former slaves on reservations as they did the Native Americans; they did not colonize former slaves out West, in Mexico, and Central America as presidents Abraham Lincoln and Andrew Johnson had proposed. Instead, the radical wing of the Republican Party controlled the Congress and granted the freedmen constitutional citizenship through the Civil Rights Bill of 1866. Through reconstruction acts, they granted black adult males the right to vote and hold public offices in the former slave

---

[3] The term "Jim Crow" refers to state and local laws that mandated segregation in public facilities. These laws resulted in the systematic legalization of social, educational, and economic inequalities for African Americans. See C. Vann Woodward, *The Strange Career of Jim Crow* (New York: Oxford University Press, 1966) 13–26; Joel Williamson, ed., *The Origins Segregation* (New York: D.C. Heath and Co., 1968) v–ix.

[4] Robert A. Devine, T. H. Breen, George M. Frederickson, and R. Hal Williams, *America Past and Present*, 6th ed. (New York: Longman, 2002) 503.

states in 1867. The radical Republicans gave constitutional guarantees of these rights through the 14th Amendment (1868) and 15th Amendment (1870). The federal Congress also gave former slaves and other Negroes protection from discrimination in accessing public accommodations under the Civil Rights Act of 1875. However, whites in the North and the South often refused to accept the idea of "black equality." The US Supreme Court in *Civil Rights Cases,* 109 US 3 (1883) declared the 1875 act unconstitutional. White intellectuals and others then employed scientific racism to justify white supremacy in ruling America, and they condoned whites' treatment of blacks as inferior citizens.

Jean Louis Agassiz, professor and chair of natural history and science at Harvard University, helped to crystallize in the minds of European Americans the notion of race—the idea of "whites" and "blacks," the inferiority of Negroes, and the justification for lesser human and civil rights for these non-Europeans. His racial views, a reflection of the ethnic separatism in his native Europe, influenced the development of white supremacy ideas, Jim Crow regulations, and policies of discrimination and exclusion for American citizens of African descent.[5] As a result, the whites reinforced Jim Crow with state legislation, municipal codes, and judicial interpretations. Even in the North, *de facto* racial segregation and discrimination practices became acceptable, especially as more and more Southern whites relocated there. Historian Carol Berkin said, "At the end of the Civil War, the nation held conflicting *expectations* and faced difficult *choices* regarding the future of the defeated South and the future of the freed people.... White Southerners expected to keep African Americans in a subordinate role through black codes and violence."[6] They exported racist practices to the North, reinforcing the negative ways Northern whites already viewed their fellow citizens of African descent.

This Jim Crow legacy helped prevent HBCUs and their constituents—mostly located in the former slave South—from entering fair and equal competition in American higher education in the late nineteenth and the early twentieth centuries. Even within a century gone by, these barriers, visible and invisible, slowed the evolution of HBCUs into fully developed institutions; their progress could not compare to that made by colleges and universities for white Americans.

---

[5] L. A. to S. G. Howe, 9 August 1863, in Elizabeth Cary Agassiz, ed., *Louis Agassiz: His Life and Correspondence* (Boston: E. C. Agassiz, 1885) 56–57. This book is online at http://www.gutenberg.org/ebooks/6078 (accessed 24 November 2010).

[6] Carol Berkin, Christopher L. Miller, Robert W. Cherny, and James L. Gormly, *Making America: A History of the United States* (Boston: Houghton Mifflin, 1995) 472.

During the Civil War and Reconstruction periods of American history, the most brutal effects of Jim Crow were softened by the generosity and humanitarian efforts of wealthy American philanthropists—almost all of them white—and by the federal US Freedmen's Bureau, which helped build schools for former slaves. Equally important were the assistance and encouragement of Negro churches and black education associations. These combined efforts resulted in the establishment of nearly 800 schools for Negroes forty-five years after slavery.

This growing number of freedmen's schools, however, required order, standards, and controls. Indeed, in the 1880s and 1890s, white Americans formed associations to set standards, controls, and order for schools, colleges, and universities serving whites. Negro education was left out of this reform movement.

However, in 1914–1943, Northern philanthropic agencies and the Commission on Interracial Cooperation (CIC) pressured these regional accreditation associations, the state governments, and the federal government to conduct studies of conditions of "Negro education." Northern philanthropists funneled grants to Southern state education departments to initiate self-studies at the nearly 250 HBCUs. Although most of their benefactors and founders meant them to be schools of higher education, they were not "real" colleges according to standards set for white colleges. In response to the studies, the philanthropic groups gave matching grants to selected HBCUs to build facilities fit for the four-year collegiate level. This movement by the philanthropic agencies especially reached a feverish pitch during the 1920s and 1930s. Northern philanthropic agencies, especially the General Education Board based in New York, also funded fellowship programs to help HBCU faculty members go north to study for graduate degrees. Columbia University in New York City educated and trained many of these Negro students.

To improve the secondary education base for HBCUs, the Northern sponsors and Negro education leaders persuaded Southern state governments to create "Negro divisions" within the state departments of education. To feed the HBCUs a higher quality student, the philanthropic agencies, including the Julius Rosenwald Fund of Chicago, also built hundreds of elementary and high schools. The northern education reformers pushed Southern states to create more high schools for Negro citizens. They did this without disturbing Jim Crow mores in the South; however, the result was to help bring Southerners out of educational darkness and include them, including Negroes, in America's growing higher education movement.

However, in response to the self-studies sponsored by Northern philanthropic agencies, there was the "great purge" of HBCUs in 1917–1930. Many HBCUs downgraded their collegiate claim to the status of normal (teacher education) two-year colleges (some accredited, and some unaccredited). After all, nearly two generations since slavery, there were more Negro preachers than Negro teachers. Some HBCUs could not meet even the "normal school" status and thus confined their missions to high school curricula; others simply shut down. Approximately 119 of about 240 Negro institutions of higher education counted by the studies in 1910 became four-year colleges. Again, with the help of Northern philanthropic agencies, about forty-four of the surviving 119 HBCUs had some variation of approval/accreditation by 1938. By 1943 ten HBCUs offered graduate work. Several HBCUs advanced to university status after 1947. In 1955, Howard University became the first HBCU to offer the doctorate. Several HBCUs offered PhDs by 2010.

HBCUs not only served an educational function for all of American society, these institutions served important social and political roles that helped transform American society into a more humanitarian place. The Declaration of Independence, the US Constitution, and the Bill of Rights gained more truthfulness through the changes forced in American society through the Negro's civil rights movement; HBCUs had direct involvement in these dramatic political and social American changes. Through the leadership and support of their graduates, their students and former students, faculty and staff members (whites and blacks), the HBCUs positively affected the modern version of the American civil rights movement.

Beginning in 1935, the National Association for the Advancement of Colored People (NAACP) helped advance the HBCUs toward equal status with the nation's traditionally white institutions (TWIs), and much of this beginning was affiliated with Howard University. At a time when only one HBCU had a law school, only two of them had a medical school, only three offered some graduate degrees, and no HBCU had an engineering program, the NAACP-affiliated lawyers filed lawsuits to force the states to upgrade public HBCUs or admit graduate and professional Negro students into the TWIs. They based their arguments on *Plessy v. Ferguson*, 163 US 537 (1896) that ordered "separate but equal" facilities, but the fifteen former slave states were not complying with *Plessy v. Ferguson*. The NAACP and their plaintiffs filed many such cases from 1935 to 1950, winning most of the decisions, until the US Supreme Court announced a more definitive and sweeping decision through the *Brown v. Board of Education*, 347 US 483 decision on 17 May 1954. *Brown* declared "separate but equal" was inherently discriminatory and unconstitutional.

This civil rights activity that begin in the 1930s involving Negro education influenced the most activist of the Civil Rights Movement during the 1960s. The events of the 1960s directly affected the HBCUs and their future development.

While many of the administrators at the black colleges tried to ignore the Civil Rights Movement and keep the lid on campus activism, many students, alumni, and faculty members (black and white) became the Civil Rights Movement's "foot soldiers." Their success in sit-in demonstrations, freedom rides, civil disobedience, Christian nonviolence, and political action influenced Congress to pass effective civil rights bills during 1964 and 1968. This seemed to bring the Civil Rights Movement to a close, but the movement continued to unfold.

Beginning in 1968, the NAACP and other plaintiffs sued the federal and state governments for not desegregating higher education in the nineteen Jim Crow states. Remnants of Jim Crow higher education existed within these nineteen states including points in the North including Delaware, Maryland, Ohio, and Pennsylvania. Key federal court cases such as *Geier v. Governor Ellington* US (1968–2005), *Adams v. Richardson* US (1970–1987), and *Ayers v. Governor Fordice* US (1977–2002) compelled nineteen states and the federal government to develop long-range plans for desegregation of higher education. Some states, such as Texas and Kentucky, developed a series of five-year plans for desegregation of higher education with the approval of the Office of Civil Rights (OCR) through 2007. OCR guidelines required the states to enhance qualitatively the public HBCUs and not close or merge them except under strict OCR scrutiny. Only one of the HBCUs, Tennessee State University, merged with a TWI in 1979 but continued battling the Geier court case in the face of white conservative attacks until 2005. In the 1970s, US presidents, including Richard Nixon, Gerald Ford, and Jimmy Carter, regardless of party affiliation, increased federal budgetary support of the HBCUs. Although some HBCUs, (e.g., Tennessee State University, Texas Southern University, Florida Agricultural and Mechanical University, and Grambling University) would experience complex problems of leadership, governance, and accreditation by 2010, the desegregation of higher education between 1968 and 2005 greatly benefitted HBCUs and blacks in general through expanded access to higher education, expanded graduate program offerings, higher numbers of accredited programs, and increased enrollments and graduation rates.

The number of blacks enrolled in America's colleges and universities exceeded 2.3 million (12.6 percent) out of 18.2 million-college students by 2007–2010. The graduation rates for blacks completing bachelor's degrees at HBCUs and TWIs improved since 1965, but by 2008 racial gaps in American college graduation rates remained. Some 57 percent of freshmen in 2001–2002 completed bachelor's degrees by 2008.[7] Some 13.6 percent of blacks—who made up 14 percent of American college students—hold a bachelor's degree. Enrollment has grown at HBCU campuses; a quarter of a million students attended these minority institutions.

However, there was a downside to America's desegregation of higher education. The HBCU share of black college students fell from 95 percent (pre-*Brown*) to 16 percent. Moreover, mainly because of "white flight" from the inner cities, the HBCUs found themselves competing with predominantly black colleges and universities (PBCUs). These city colleges, state community colleges, and urban institutions had predominantly minority students. The PBCUs, too, began to demand federal, state, and local funds to help educate their predominantly impoverished and poorly educated high school students. Thus, a few more HBCUs closed their doors, or merged with another institution. The HBCU attrition rate slowed to 11 percent, 1955–2009, compared to 54 percent, 1918–1954. Nevertheless, in 2010 there were fewer HBCUs than existed in 1921, and many of the surviving HBCUs, especially the private ones, had financial problems by 2010.

The profile of the HBCUs changed dramatically over the last 110 years. By 2007, among 108 surviving HBCUs listed in this book, 91 percent were four-year institutions; forty-nine were public institutions. There was a time when private HBCUs outnumbered the public ones three to one. By 2007, because of the Civil Rights Movement and desegregation of American society, the HBCUs averaged 20 percent or more non-black students. By 2010, four of the surviving HBCUs enrolled a majority of white students. HBCUs averaged 27.8 percent white faculty and 14.2 percent other race faculty, while America's traditionally white institutions (TWIs) averaged a mere 6 percent black faculty. Although some 84 percent of the country's black college students attended TWIs, the surviving 103 HBCUs still produced 20 to 30 percent of America's black college graduates. Yet, the HBCUs made up only 2.5 percent of US institutions of higher education at the turn of the twenty-first century and represented 23.4 percent of the 465 minority institutions of higher education listed by the US Department of Education. Also on the brighter side, in 2009–2010, Carnegie Corporation listed

---

[7] Asian/Pacific Islander students had the highest graduation rates (67 percent), followed by whites (60 percent), Hispanics (48 percent), African Americans (42 percent) and American Indians/Alaska natives (40 percent).

eight HBCUs under the Carnegie Groupings of Research Level Universities offering doctorate degrees.[8]

[8] Generally, my statistics and calculations are based on the National Center for Education statistics and tables on faculty, enrollment by race, and budgets; US Department of Education, Digest of Education Statistics, Institute of Education (Washington DC: NCES 1996–2010); NCES, *Digest of Education Statistics: 2009*, "Fall enrollment, degrees conferred, and expenditures in degree-granting HBCUs: 2006, 2006–07; 2007, and 2007–08," Table 240; *List of HBCUs—White House Initiatives on Historically Black Colleges and Universities* (2008); "History's Milestones of African American Higher Education," *Journal of Blacks in Higher Education* 1995): 86–90; United Negro College Fund (UNCF), *Historically Black Colleges and Universities: Past, Present, and Future* (Fairfax VA: UNCF, 1994) 1–19; UNCF, *Roots that Run Deep: An Historical Look at the Impact of the United Negro College Fund and Its Member Colleges in American History* (Fairfax VA: UNCF, 2010) 1–20.

HBCU Photographs Captions and Credits

1. Daniel Payne, First Black College President, Wilberforce University, 1862 (Courtesy of Ohio Historical Society, Isaac & Lenora Lane Collection)
2. Second US Colored Light Artillery Regiment, Battery A, 1864 (Courtesy of Chicago Historical Society)
3. John Mercer Langston (W. J. Simmons, *Men of Mark*; Courtesy of University of North Carolina Chapel Hill)
4. Booker T. Washington (This and the remaining photographs are courtesy of the Library of Congress)
5. Center: Margaret and Booker T. Washington, and Andrew Carnegie at Tuskegee Faculty Institute, 1906
6. Black and White Students at Berea College 1900
7. Classroom Activities at the A. & T. College in North Carolina 1900
8. Claflin University Musical Band 1899
9. A Howard University Class 1900
10. Roger Williams University Students
11. Howard University 1900
12. Hampton Institute Native American Orchestra 1900
13. Hampton Normal and Agricultural Institute Bible Class
14. Stone Hall, Morris Brown College
15. Negroes Serve in America's Wars, Company D, 18th Illinois 1899
16. Cadets at Haines Normal and Industrial Institute
17. Julius Rosenwald
18. John D. Rockefeller
19. Students at Fisk University 1900
20. Junior Preparatory Class of Fisk University 1900
21. Fisk University Theological Hall 1900
22. Fisk University Choir in the Chapel
23. Shaw University Hospital & Medical School 1900

Daniel Payne, First Black College President, Wilberforce University, 1862

Courtesy of Ohio Historical Society, Isaac & Lenora Lane Collection

Second US Colored Light Artillery Regiment, Battery A, 1864
Courtesy of Chicago Historical Society

John Mercer Langston

W. J. Simmons, Men of Mark; Courtesy of University of North Carolina Chapel Hill

Booker T. Washington
Courtesy of the Library of Congress

(above) Center: Margaret and Booker T. Washington, and Andrew Carnegie at Tuskegee Faculty Institute, 1906; (below) Black and White Students at Berea College, 1900
Courtesy of the Library of Congress

(above) Classroom Activities at the A. & T. College in North Carolina, 1900
(below) Claflin University Musical Band, 1899
Courtesy of the Library of Congress

(above) A Howard University Class, 1900; (below) Roger Williams University Students

Courtesy of the Library of Congress

Howard University, 1900
Courtesy of the Library of Congress

Hampton Institute Native American Orchestra, 1900

Courtesy of the Library of Congress

Hampton Normal and Agricultural Institute Bible Class

Courtesy of the Library of Congress

Stone Hall, Morris Brown College
Courtesy of the Library of Congress

(above) Negroes Serve in America's Wars, Company D, 18th Illinois, 1899
(below) Cadets at Haines Normal and Industrial Institute
Courtesy of the Library of Congress

Julius Rosenwald
Courtesy of the Library of Congress

John D. Rockefeller
Courtesy of the Library of Congress

Students at Fisk University, 1900
Courtesy of the Library of Congress

(above) Junior Preparatory Class of Fisk University, 1900
(below) Fisk University Choir in the Chapel
Courtesy of the Library of Congress

Fisk University Theological Hall, 1900
Courtesy of the Library of Congress

Shaw University Hospital & Medical School, 1900
Courtesy of the Library of Congress

1

Antebellum Times through Reconstruction

A federal report, The Traditionally Black Institutions of Higher Education (1985), partly reads,

> The black colleges were founded and evolved in an environment unlike that of any other group of colleges—one of legal segregation and isolation from the rest of higher education. The population from which these colleges drew their students lived under severe legal, educational, economic, political, and social restrictions. The origin and development of the traditionally black institutions cannot be fully understood except in the context of the educational and socioeconomic status of the black population....[1]

Indeed, the development and direction of the historically black colleges and universities (HBCUs) depended greatly on the status of the black population and dynamics of African-American society. The larger historical events, too, constantly affected the development of the HBCUs.

European Americans did not admit African Americans into the nation's schools, academies, and colleges during the colonial period of American history (1607–1780). This was a time when Americans began developing views on the concept of race. A push for the abolition of slavery and for equal treatment of free Negroes occurred during and after the Revolutionary War (1776–1783). In the 1790 census, Negroes (blacks) made up 19.27 percent of Americans. Ten percent of them were free persons. Negroes constituted a third of Southerners.

During the "new nation" period of American history, America's first national government passed ordinances in 1784, 1785, and 1787 to sell and settle land in the Northwest Territory. This legislation led to the creation of the states of Indiana, Illinois, Michigan, Ohio, and Wisconsin. It also prohibited slavery in those new states and set aside some of the land to be sold to support public education. Northerners relished the idea of beating the Southerners into the territory because they viewed white Southerners as lazy and dominated by the slave-owning class. New Englanders and Easterners gladly populated the

---

[1] Susan T. Hill, *The Traditionally Black Institutions of Higher Education, 1860–1982* (Washington DC: US Department of Education [USDOE], National Center for Education Statistics [NCES], 1983) xii–xix.

Northwest Territory, carrying with them the ideas of civil rights for the citizens (whites), but they wanted no socio-economic competition from slaves, free Negroes, or Native Americans.

When the founding fathers decided to meet in Philadelphia in May–September 1787, the divide between Northern capitalism and the interest of the Southern slaveholders helped shape the new Constitution and structure American society along lines of class, race, slavery, and color (i.e., mulattoes). South Carolina made slavery a political issue because slaves outnumbered the white South Carolinians; an estimated half of North American slave imports entered the port of Charleston, and about half the white families in South Carolina owned slaves. Since the Stono Rebellion (1739), when a slave from Angola, Africa, led a rebellion, white South Carolinians feared Negro rebellion and domination. With leadership from South Carolina delegates, the Southerners easily gained most of their demands in the Constitution of 1787. Through a series of compromises, they could count three-fifths (60 percent) of the slaves in computing representation in the House of Representatives. They gained provisions for strong fugitive slave laws to force other states to give up runaway slaves. South Carolina lost 30 percent of its slaves during the Revolution, and in Georgia two-thirds of the slaves deserted their owners. Indeed, the "underground railroad" had been in place since the Revolutionary War years. Another compromise over slavery in the new Constitution meant the federal government could not restrict the Atlantic slave trade for another twenty years (1787–1807), but the slave states agreed to accept a tax of $10 per imported slave. To gain these concessions, the Southerners inadvertently admitted, however, that the slaves were human beings as well as property, and the Northerners unfortunately accepted the Southern argument that slaves were property. Essentially, the new Constitution intentionally left the slavery issue unresolved, and this would prove to be a bloody mistake.

Many Americans considered the enslavement of fellow human beings as evil. This was a time when many Europeans suffered bondage in America as indentured servants through redemption contracts, and criminals shipped from England were held to convict labor contracts. The anti-slavery society, headed by Benjamin Franklin, presented an anti-slavery petition to the Constitutional Convention delegates. Pennsylvania delegate Gouverneur Morris said slavery "was the curse of heaven on the States, where it prevailed." "Misery and poverty" characterized the Southern states. In compromising with the Southern states over slavery, the Northern states sacrificed "every principle of right of every impulse of humanity," said Morris. James Madison advocated freeing blacks that had served in the Continental Army.[2]

In the earliest post-Revolutionary War decades, the antislavery movement centered in the South where most slaves were held. In the 1790s, Quakers and other antislavery men began an organized reaction against the issue of American slavery. Racially speaking, the new state of Tennessee (founded 1796) recognized Free Negroes as citizens and allowed them to vote and participate in the militia until 1834. Some of the "founding fathers" worried about the problem of slavery, its tendency to politically divide the new nation, and the moral implications of America holding nearly 20 percent of its people in slavery.[3] In 1799, the will and estate of former president George Washington freed some 124 of his slaves, but other slaveholding presidents did not follow his example over the next sixty years.[4]

Kenneth Morgan said, "America entered the nineteenth century with slavery expanding throughout the South, with racial lines becoming more hardened in the South and with a slow, gradual approach to abolitionism in the northern states."[5] However, between 1780 and the 1820s, in the North, several of the original thirteen states gradually abolished slavery. At the same time, when America expanded into land west of the Appalachian Mountains and south of the Ohio River, several new slave states entered the Union. Negro leaders saw the handwriting on the wall; American slavery was not ending as Washington had hoped; this peculiar institution was steadily expanding. In 1829, David Walker, a free Negro, issued his militant *Appeal to the Coloured Citizens of the World* against slavery.[6] In 1831, an enslaved Negro named Nat Turner heeded Walker's appeal with a slave rebellion in Virginia that left sixty whites dead and several slaves hanged. Southern manumission and anti-slavery leaders had to

---

[2] Lawrence Goldstone, *Dark Bargain: Slavery, Profits and the Struggle for the Constitution* (New York: Walker and Company, 2009) 1–7.

[3] Ibid., 157–58.

[4] Kenneth Morgan, *Slavery and Servitude in Colonial America: A Short History* (New York: New York University Press, 2000) 110–111, 116–20, 125; See Gordon S. Wood, *The Americanization of Benjamin Franklin* (New York: Penguin Books, 2004) 226–29, 245; Francois Furstenberg, *In the Name of the Father: Washington's Legacy, Slavery, and the Making of a Nation* (New York: Penguin Books, 2007) 72–74, 78, 83, 84–86, 87, 225, 227; Willard S. Randall, *Alexander Hamilton: A Life* (New York: Perennial/Harper Collins, 2003) 14, 15, 25, 54, 291–94, 394, 404; Andrew Levy, *The First Emancipator: The Forgotten Story of Robert Carter, the Founding Father Who Freed His Slaves* (New York: Random House, 2005) 17, 32, 49, 124.

[5] Morgan, *Slavery and Servitude*, 126.

[6] David Walker, *Walker's Appeal…to the Coloured Citizens of the World* (Boston: D. Walker, 1830), available on the University of North Carolina's *Documenting the American South*, http://docsouth.unc. edu/nc/ walker/walker.html.

flee north, when the slavocracy reacted by banning anti-slavery literature and persecuting local abolitionists. By then, white bondage, including indentured servitude, had come to an end in America.

The shift of the antislavery movement to the North had something to do with the acceptance of Negroes into colleges in 1837–1855. The antislavery movement affected the establishment of the first black colleges; indeed, education became a central focus and a liberating force in the abolitionist movement. Horace Mann led the common school movement against ignorance and against the argument that school taxes violated property rights—an argument the white ruling class, the planters, and other Southern land owners used to impede the educational advancement of the Southern US for nearly a hundred years.[7] Mann argued that education saved citizens from poverty and vice, and prepared them for the adequate performance of their social and civic duties.[8] He became head of the Massachusetts public board of education, the first one in America, in 1837. Throughout the 1850s, mostly in the North, there was a significant expansion of public schools that taught reading, writing, arithmetic, and the "Protestant ethic" of industry, punctuality, sobriety, and frugality.[9] Many New Englanders and some other Northerners believed education could improve the quality of life for people of all races. However, by 1861, most white Southerners outside the upper classes were illiterate. Few universities existed in the South, and whites prohibited Negroes from attaining education beyond what was required to be a laborer.[10]

White Southern opposition to blacks' equal access to formal education was violent. In 1837, white vigilantes whipped a free Negro named Alphonso Sumner nearly to death and exiled him from Nashville for operating a school in the back of his barbershop. They also accused him of writing letters to runaway slaves on behalf of the slaves' relatives. Sumner fled to Cincinnati, opened a school in a Negro church, joined the Ohio antislavery society, helped form the Ohio Colored Men's Convention, and served on the Cincinnati Board for Colored Public Schools. In Cincinnati, "a gateway to the Underground Railroad," people of

---

[7] In many slave states, the slavocracy owned the majority of the best cultivable land.

[8] Horace Mann, "Thoughts for a Young Man: A Lecture" (Boston: Ticknor, Reed & Fields, 1850) 1–84.

[9] Robert A. Devine, T. H. Breen, George M. Frederickson, and R. Hal Williams, *America Past and Present*, 6th ed. (New York: Longman, 2002) 318–19.

[10] Leon Litwack, *North of Slavery: The Free Blacks in the Free States, 1790–1860* (Chicago: University of Chicago Press, 1961) 318–19; Carter G. Woodson, *The Education of the Negro Prior to 1861* (Brooklyn NY: A&B Books, 1998) 1–30; Francis D. Adams and Barry Sanders, *Alienable Rights: The Exclusion of African Americans in a White Man's Land, 1619–2000* (New York: HarperCollins, 2003) 191–226.

European descent (including immigrants) protected their white status and socioeconomic privileges by rioting against free Negro residents between 1829 and 1861. In Philadelphia, several riots against the Negro community took place during that time.[11] Simply put, many whites feared and prevented Negroes, slave or free, from equal access to education. At least half of America's 500,000 free Negroes were illiterate by 1860. Fewer than four thousand Negroes had attended formal schools by then. Only 5 to 10 percent of the slaves seemed literate.[12]

Again, religion had much to do with the antislavery movement and the acceptance of blacks into higher education. The Society of Friends (Quakers) professed enlightened ideas about the family of man and the need for education. Quakers, who considered slavery "a covenant with hell," had challenged the wording of the Declaration of Independence; slave owner Thomas Jefferson had omitted the statement about the evils of the slave trade. As early as 1789, the annual meetings of the Quakers in New York and Pennsylvania, submitted petitions asking Congress to stop the slave trade. The Pennsylvania Society for the Abolition of Slavery under Benjamin Franklin submitted a petition. Despite the Quakers' efforts, Congress took no action. The Society of Friends later published the *Declaration of Sentiments* (1833), which read in part,

> We further believe and affirm—that all persons of color, who posses the qualifications which are demanded of others, ought to be admitted forthwith to the enjoyment of the same privileges, and the exercise of the same prerogatives, as others. And that the paths of preferment, of wealth and of intelligence, should be opened as widely to them as to persons of a white complexion.[13]

Within this early nineteenth-century milieu, a few colleges admitted and matriculated Negroes. The American Baptist Free Mission Society operated New York Central College (1819–1858) in McGrawville. Courses taught at New York

---

[11] Bobby L. Lovett, *The African American History of Nashville, 1780–1930: Elites and Dilemmas* (Fayetteville: University of Arkansas Press, 1999) 24, 34–35, 37, 44; John Hope Franklin and Alfred A. Moss Jr., *From Slavery to Freedom: A History of Negro Americans*, 6th ed. (New York: Alfred A. Knopf, 1988) 152–53.

[12] See Edward A. Johnson, *A School History of the Negro Race in America from 1619 to 1890* (New York: Isaac Goldmann, 1911); Henry Gannett, *Statistics of the Negroes in the United States* (Baltimore: John F. Slater Fund Trustees, 1894) 6, 32, 33, 25, 26.

[13] See Howard H. Brinton, *Friends for 300 Years: The History and Beliefs of Friends since George Fox Started the Quaker Movement* (Philadelphia: Pendle Hill, 1965); Hugh Barbour and J. William Frost, *The Quakers* (Westport CT: Greenwood Press, 1988); Kenneth Morgan, *Slavery and Servitude in Colonial America: A Short History* (New York: New York University Press, 2000) 5-31.

Central College included Christianity and vocational skills, and the college admitted blacks and whites, males and females. Negroes William G. Allen, George B. Vashion, and Charles R. Reason taught there. In 1849, Reason opened Avery College in Pennsylvania. James Hall, a Negro, completed the Medical College of Maine in 1822. Beginning in 1848, Dartmouth College (founded 1789) admitted students regardless of color.[14] The Western Reserve College (founded 1826) in Cleveland, Ohio, admitted Negroes in the 1830s. Antislavery societies flourished in that part of the country. Otterbein College in Ohio (founded 1841) admitted Negroes early on, and continues to be a diverse institution. Antioch College in Yellow Springs, Ohio (founded 1852), based its mission on a commitment to social justice. Harvard University (founded 1636) began to admit Negroes in 1848. Amherst (Massachusetts), Rutland (Vermont), Oneida Institute (New York), Union College (New York), Princeton (New Jersey), and various medical colleges and seminaries admitted some Negro students.[15]

The matriculation of black students at some of these biracial religious colleges affected the development of HBCUs, the institutions specifically designed to educate black Americans, because they educated the faculty members of the early black schools and colleges. Abolitionist Calvin Stowe was a student at Bowdoin College in Maine in 1824, when the first Negro, Edward Mitchell, enrolled there. Stowe became a professor at Bowdoin. His wife, Harriet Beecher Stowe, wrote *Uncle Tom's Cabin* (1852)—a novel that pricked America's conscience to view slavery as an evil, moral problem. Oliver O. Howard became head of the Freedmen's Bureau in 1865. He served as founding president of Howard University, 1867–1869, and then became president of Bowdoin College.[16]

Oberlin

Oberlin College, originally named Oberlin Collegiate Institute, opened in 1833. In 1835, Oberlin admitted Negroes, and graduated a Negro around 1844. Oberlin College built the Negro student enrollment to nearly 4 percent by 1855.

---

[14] Lerone Bennett Jr., *Before the Mayflower: A History of Black America*, 6th ed. (New York: Penguin, 1988) 172, 173.

[15] Carter G. Woodson and Charles H. Wesley, *The Negro in Our History* (Washington DC: Associated Publishers, 1922, 1972) 320, 321–22; George A. Wheeler and Henry W. Wheeler, *History of Brunswick, Topsham, and Harpswell, Maine* (Brunswick ME: Alfred Mudge and Sons, 1878) 498–519, available online at http://www2.curtislibrary.com/history/wheeler/index.html.

[16] Many of the institutions' websites include historical backgrounds: "About Bowdoin: The History of the College," www.bowdoin.edu; "Dartmouth: A Brief History," www.dartmouth.edu; "A Brief History of Berea College," www.berea.edu; Case Western, "Visiting Case: A Brief History," www.case.edu.

Oberlin College began under Asa Mahan, John Morgan, and others who seceded from Lane Theological Seminary in Cincinnati, where Southern students and others convinced the trustees to stop the heated discussion of abolitionism. But antislavery societies flourished in the Oberlin area, and the town included integrated public schools. James Bradley was the first black man to enroll at Oberlin in 1835. Two years later, the first black woman, Harriet Hunter, enrolled in the Lady's Department.

John Mercer Langston, born of a slave mother and her white owner (and common law husband) in Virginia, became one of Oberlin College's early students. When he was young, his parents, a white planter and his Negro wife, sent him to Ohio to live with his free brothers. He completed his degree at Oberlin College in the late 1840s. After law programs refused his admission because of race, Langston completed his private study of law under a local judge, and upon court order became the first Negro to gain admission to the bar in Ohio in 1854. In that year he married Oberlin graduate Caroline Wall, also a mulatto. Two years later, near Oberlin, he became the township clerk—the first elected Negro official. Langston often recommended (and funded) Negro students to enroll in Oberlin College, and some of them lived in his home.

Langston became a recruiter of US Colored Troops during the Civil War, president of the blacks' first national civil rights organization, the National Equal Rights League in October 1864, and staff member of the federal Freedmen's Bureau. He joined the Howard University law department as founding dean, 1869–1876. Langston also served as vice president and acting president of Howard University for two years as well as the president of Virginia Normal and Collegiate Institute. President U. S. Grant appointed him to the DC Board of Health, and President Rutherford B. Hayes appointed him minister to Haiti in 1877–1885. He was elected to the United States House of Representatives (Virginia) by 1892, and he wrote his autobiography, *From the Virginia Plantation to the National Capitol* (1894).

The land-grant program moved from Hampton Institute to Virginia Normal and Collegiate Institute in 1920. In 1923, the four-year college program started. They changed the name to Virginia State College in 1930. It became Virginia State University in 1979.[17]

---

[17] James M. Colson, "History of Virginia State College," unpublished manuscript, Virginia State University, Special Collections; "Historical Profile" of Virginia State University, VSU Library and Media Services, 2005; F. W. Nicholas, "The Black Land-Grant Colleges: An Assessment of the Major Changes between 1965–66 and 1970–71" (EdD dissertation, University of Virginia, 1973) 1–31; Grace Vernell-Hill Norbrey, "A Study of the Development of the Land-Grant Program at Virginia State University, 1920–1983" (EdD

Most of the free Negroes attending Oberlin originated from Northern states, especially Ohio, but some Southern Negroes, such as Marion I. Lewis of Tennessee, attended Oberlin. The Philadelphia-based African Methodist Episcopal Church (AMEC) supported some of Oberlin's black students, such as Fanny Jackson Coppin. She became the head of Philadelphia's Institute of Colored Youth, 1869–1902, and the wife of AME Bishop Levi Coffin, formerly a leading abolitionist. Oberlin had an outstanding school of music that trained several blacks. Langston's daughter, Nettie DeElla, and other black women studied in that program. At least sixty-two black women of color engaged in collegiate studies at Oberlin before the Civil War.

The majority of Oberlin's black students, like Caroline Wall Langston, matriculated in preparatory and female departments that focused on music and domestic science. Two of every three Negro students during the entire antebellum period completed no more than one year at Oberlin College. "Of the one hundred blacks enrolled in the college from 1840 through 1865 thirty-two of them (17 men, 15 women) earned degrees," said historian William Cheek. That was understandable, given Negroes' lack of access to primary and secondary schools. However, by 1900 Oberlin College claimed 128 of the 301 Negroes that had graduated from white colleges and universities. In 2004, Oberlin College's website reported enrollment of 547 minority students (19.3 percent) in a total enrollment of 2,827 students, with African Americans constituting 4.4 percent of total enrollment and 23.4 percent of Oberlin's minorities. Cleveland, thirty miles away, was predominantly black by then.[18]

---

dissertation, George Washington University, Washington DC, 1983) 1–10; J. W. Davis, "The Negro Land-Grant College," *Journal of Negro Education* 2/1 (1933): 1–15.

[18] See H. N. Frost, ed., *Register of the Members of Both Graduate and Non-Graduate of Phi Delta Literary Society, Oberlin College* (Oberlin OH: Oberlin College, 1891) 18, 31, 34; W. E. Bigglestone, "Oberlin College and the Negro Student, 1865–1940," *Journal of Negro History* 56 (1971): 198–219. E. N. Lawson and M. Merrill, "The Antebellum 'Talented Thousandth': Black College Students at Oberlin before the Civil War," *Journal of Negro Education* 52/2 (Spring1983): 142–55; C. L. Waite, *Permission to Remain among Us: Education for Blacks in Oberlin, Ohio, 1880–1914* (Westport CT: Greenwood, 2003) 1–21; J. O. Horton, "Black Education at Oberlin College: A Controversial Commitment," *Journal of Negro Education* 54/4 (Autumn1985): 477–89; Juanita D. Fletcher, "Against the Consensus: Oberlin College and the Education of American Negroes, 1835–1865" (PhD dissertation, American University, 1974) 1–23; William E. B. Du Bois, in *The College-Bred Negro* (Atlanta GA: Atlanta University, 1900) 29, makes estimates of Oberlin black graduates. Robert S. Fletcher, *A History of Oberlin College: From Its Foundation through the Civil War*, 2 vols. (Oberlin: Oberlin College, 1943) 1–10; Woodson, *The Education of the Negro Prior to 1861*, 219, 220, 224–225; Wanda F. Jackson, "John Mercer Langston: Troubled African American Leader," *The Griot* 23/1 (Spring 2004): 61–72; William Cheek and Aimee Cheek, *John Mercer Langston and the Fight for Black Freedom, 1829–65* (Urbana: University of Illinois Press, 1996)

Berea College

Berea College of Kentucky (founded 1855) was founded by anti-slavery men, including John Fee, editor of the *Antislavery Manual*, J. A. R. Rogers, and E. Henry Fairchild (an Oberlin professor), for the education of black *and* white students. Berea had founders who believed "God has made of one blood all peoples of the earth." The writings of antislavery editor Cassius M. Clay influenced Berea College leaders. They held fast to the radical vision of a college and a community committed to interracial education; as well, they dedicated Berea College to uplift Appalachian people and to promote the belief in the equality of women and men from all "nations and climes."[19]

However, Berea suspended operations after John Brown's raid on an arms depot in Harpers Ferry, Virginia, in October 1859.[20] Negrophobia swept across the South, and pro-slavery sympathizers drove the school's faculty out of the county. Berea supporters and the antislavery families fled across the river to Ohio. When the Civil War ended with a Northern victory, Berea College reopened in 1866 with ninety-six Negro and ninety-one white students. Some Negro students had served in the US Colored Troops (USCT), and Kentucky was among the top three states furnishing the most USCT to the Union Army. The 13th Amendment (1865) ended slavery, and the 14th Amendment (1868) extended citizenship and protection of civil rights to Negro citizens.

Nonetheless, from 1867 through 1871, Democrats, neo- and former Confederates started a movement to "redeem" the Southern states from Republican control. White supremacists in Kentucky became violently opposed to equal rights for former slaves and other blacks. Fee, Rogers, and their families remained targets of local thugs; consequently, the teachers patrolled the campus each night. The children slept on the first floor in case of arson. When Willard W. Wheeler left Lexington after recruiting Negro students to attend Berea, a mob ambushed him.

Berea's founders meant for the school to maintain an equal ratio of black and white students, but Berea had 177 Negroes and 157 white students by 1877. Some white students left in protest of too many Negroes at Berea. The administration of William G. Frost, in 1892–1908, yielded to the pressures and

---

34–35, 84–85, 88, 87, 89, 90, 97–98, 110, 170, 177–78, 187; William E. B. DuBois, *The College-Bred Negro: A Study Made under the Supervision of the 5th Atlanta University Conference* (Atlanta: Atlanta University, 1900) 29–31.

[19] Ralph T. Jans, "Racial Integration at Berea College, 1950–1952," *Journal of Negro Education* 2/1 (Winter 1953): 26–37.

[20] See Robert E. McGlone, *John Brown's War against Slavery* (New York: Cambridge University Press, 2009) 1–20.

assured white applicants they would not have to share rooms with Negroes. The blacks suffered segregation in all aspects of campus social life. Many white students viewed Negro students as inferior. Negro students protested to Frost, but to no avail. Through the use of racial accommodation, Berea's administration tried not to attract the attention of race radicals, but a Kentucky state legislator responded to the concerns of the white students. He secured the "Day Law" for Kentucky colleges in 1904, saying that blacks and whites could not attend the same institutions of higher learning. Berea College trustees challenged the law—some say to save face for Frost. *Berea College v. Commonwealth of Kentucky*, 211 US 45 (1908) upheld Kentucky's Day Law. In 1909, the Negro students had to leave Berea College. Berea trustees helped establish Lincoln Institute, an HBCU, near Louisville for Negro students.

Berea College produced some outstanding Negro graduates. Julia Britton Hooks, born in Frankfort in 1852, attended Berea, moved to Memphis in 1876, taught school there, founded a school, and served as the philanthropic "Angel of Beale Street." Her descendants became prominent politicians and judges in Memphis. Carter G. Woodson, who became the second Negro to earn the PhD in history at Harvard, attended Berea. He seldom mentioned his Berea background, but Woodson did outline the beginning of Berea College in his book, *The Negro in our History* (1922). W. E. B. Du Bois recruited Berea College graduates and other HBCU graduates to study Negro problems in various cities during his involvement with the Atlanta University Annual Conferences on Negro problems. Berea College integrated after *Brown v. Board of Education* (1954), and enrolled 17 percent black students by 2005.

Maryville College

Maryville College (founded 1819) in Tennessee was one of the first colleges to educate Negroes. Isaac L. Anderson and other leaders of the Presbyterian reformed tradition organized the Southern and Western Theological Seminary (near Maryville, Tennesee) to bring education and enlightenment into the frontier area west of the Appalachian Mountains and in the Southwest Territory, for men and women. George Erskine, a former slave, was among the first students in 1819, and under the sponsorship of the Manumission Society of Tennessee, he graduated and became a Presbyterian minister.

In February 1861, east Tennessee counties (where only 10 percent of Tennessee slaves resided compared to 70 percent in west Tennessee) voted against state secession. The east Tennesseans petitioned the General Assembly to secede from Tennessee. The minority Confederate faction arrested, suppressed, and exiled pro-Union citizens. Maryville College remained closed during 1861–1866.

Upon reopening, Maryville College again admitted students regardless of race and color. Therefore, the federal Freedmen's Bureau, philanthropists William Thaw of Pittsburgh, and John C. Baldwin New York helped finance the rebuilding of the facilities in 1869. Other philanthropists from New York and Chicago, as well as the students, helped build facilities. William J. Hale, the black man who in 1911 became the first president of Tennessee Agricultural and Industrial State Normal School for Negroes, was a former student of Maryville College. Maryville College continued to educate Negro students until *Berea College v. Commonwealth of Kentucky*, 211 US 45 (1908) affirmed that states could require racial segregation even in private institutions. Maryville College funded the Negro students' education in a nearby HBCU, Swift Memorial College.[21]

Franklin College

Founded by Tolbert Fanning and his English-born wife, Franklin College (1842–1862), on the eastern outskirts of Nashville, Tennessee, trained and educated a few Negroes. The couple believed working-class Southerners needed formal education. The school affiliated with the Christian Church (Disciples of Christ) and emphasized Christian education, agricultural science, and manual labor instruction. The Tolbert couple quietly admitted three free Negroes to work at the school, receive private tutoring, and attend manual labor classes. Franklin College closed during the Civil War. The Union Army occupied Nashville in February 1862, and Franklin College re-opened briefly, but soon closed for good. A former student wrote a proud history of the institution, but did not mention the Negroes[22] who became teachers and founders of freedmen's schools.

Cheyney College

The first antebellum higher education institutions established *exclusively* for Negroes started in the North. Abolitionism and religion influenced the start of these three institutions.

---

[21] "History," www.maryvillecollege.edu (2007); C. Van West, "Maryville College," in Carroll Van West, ed., *Tennessee Encyclopedia of History and Culture* (Nashville: Rutledge Hill Press, 1998) 576–77; Harold M. Parker Jr., "A School of the Prophets at Maryville," *Tennessee Historical Quarterly* 34/1 (Winter 1975): 72–90; see Ralph W. Lloyd, *Maryville College: A History of 150 Years* (Maryville TN: Maryville College, 1969) 1–23.

[22] James Scobey, *Franklin College and Its Influences* (Nashville, 1906) 148–57. A rare and fragile copy exists in the Special Collections of Nashville Public Library, Church Street, Nashville TN.

Cheyney College, the Institute for Colored Youth, was founded in Philadelphia on 25 February 1837. Richard Humphreys, a Quaker philanthropist, bequeathed $10,000 to establish the school for Negroes. Humphrey's will specified that the school was "to instruct the descendents of the African Race in school learning, in the various branches of the mechanic arts, trades and agriculture, in order to prepare and fit and qualify them to act as teachers." The school moved from Philadelphia to George Cheyney's farm twenty-five miles west of the city in 1902. The Institute for Colored Youth became Cheyney Training School for Teachers in 1913. It became State Normal School at Cheyney in 1921. In 1959, it became Cheyney State College. Cheyney joined the State System of Higher Education as Cheyney University of Pennsylvania in 1983.

In 2003, Cheyney State University had a diverse student body and continued to cherish "its legacy as America's oldest historically black institution of higher education."[23]

Lincoln University of Pennsylvania

Located in Chester County, Pennsylvania, Lincoln University for Negroes gained a charter in April 1854 as Ashmun Institute. The Pennsylvania Presbyterians chartered it, and like the Presbyterians who founded Maryville College, they believed college-educated Negroes could help spread the gospel among their dark-skinned brothers and sisters. After admitting the first students in 1856, the institution claimed to be "the first institution anywhere in the world to provide a higher education of arts and sciences for male youth of African descent."[24] Abolitionist John Miller Dickey and others sustained the school. In 1866, Ashmun Institute was renamed Lincoln University to honor the late president.

By 1900, Lincoln University graduated 600 students, many times more than any of the 33 degree-granting HBCUs. The institution achieved the Middle States Association of Colleges and Schools (MSACS) accreditation in 1922. Horace Mann Bond left as head of another HBCU, Fort Valley State College in Georgia, and became Lincoln's first black president, 1945–1957. Lincoln University became associated with the Commonwealth of Pennsylvania in 1972 as a state-

---

[23] There is evidence of another college founded for Negroes. Charles Avery donated money to establish Avery College for Negroes near Pittsburgh in 1849. The school flourished. Within a few years, this HBCU did not survive, and not much is know of its detailed operations. *Cheyney Facts,* Cheyney University of Pennsylvania, 2004, www.cheyney.edu.

[24] Horace Mann Bond, *Education for Freedome: A History of Lincoln University, Pennsylvania* (Princeton: Princeton University Press, 1976) 1–10, 11–40.

related, coeducational university. Lincoln University had an enrollment of 2,343 students by 2006.[25]

The Civil War (1861–1865), more than any prior event in American history, facilitated eventual freedom, cultural and social progress for most of America's blacks. More important to our discussion, hundreds of freedmen's schools and many new HBCUs were established during the Civil War.

Abraham Lincoln's Emancipation Proclamation, which took effect 1 January 1863, made *de jure* what fugitive slaves escaping into the Union Army lines had been doing *de facto* since the war began in 1861. What did this historic event mean for Negro Americans? In a speech on 14 April 1876, the centennial year of the Declaration of Independence, Frederick Douglass reflected upon the Emancipation Proclamation:

> I shall never forget that memorable night when at a public meeting ["Watch Care night services"], in a distant city, with three thousand others not less anxious than myself, I waited and watched for the word of deliverance which we have heard read today. Nor shall I ever forget the outburst of joy and thanksgiving that rent the air when the lightning brought to us the emancipation proclamation....[26]

Although it was a jubilant event, emancipation was a difficult time for slaves freed without food, housing, clothes, or education. The whites kept the houses, tools, animals, crops, land, and the money the slaves' labor had helped produce. Freedmen desperately needed help.

A Union Army general in South Carolina, on 9 February 1862, asked Northerners to send help for the destitute freedmen. The bulk of social services provided to the freedmen depended heavily on missionary groups who answered General Thomas Sherman's call. Northern missionaries, blacks and whites, raised money and provided clinics, hospitals, cemeteries, church services, and schools for the freedmen. When thousands more fugitive slaves fled into Union-occupied areas, northerners and some local blacks established classes in

---

[25] George W. Williams, *History of the Negro Race in America, 1619–1880* (New York: G. P. Putnam Sons, 1883) 178, 388, 392, 393.

[26] David W. Blight, *Frederick Douglass' Civil War: Keeping Faith in Jubilee* (Baton Rouge: Louisiana State University Press, 1989) 198; *Nashville Union and American*, 16–23 September 1873; Frederick Douglass, *Autobiographies, Narrative of the Life, My Bondage and My Freedom, Life and Times* (New York: New American Library, 1999) 915–935; Bobby L. Lovett, "Black Adult Education during the Civil War, 1861–1865," in Harvey G. Neufeldt and Leo McGee, eds., *Education of African American Adult: An Historical Overview* (Westport CT: Greenwood Press, 1990) 27–43.

the contraband camps.[27] This process began the establishment of freedmen's schools and HBCUs.

The Boston Educational Commission formed on 4 February 1862 to aid freedmen in their "industrial, social, intellectual, moral and religious improvement."[28] The National Freedmen's Relief Association formed in New York on 22 February 1862. In 1863, the Northwestern Freedmen's Aid Commission began in Chicago, and the Friends Freedmen's Relief Association started in Philadelphia. The US Commission for the Relief of the National Freedmen passed a resolution in December 1863, asking President Lincoln to give the freedmen "a legal and quiet possession of adequate land for their residence and support, as rapidly and as early as possible." Lincoln was the product mostly of self-education; however, he responded and sent the matter to Congress. He said the subject of the letter "is one of great magnitude and importance."[29]

The American Baptist Home Mission Society, other Baptist agencies, the Wesleyan Methodist Church, and the Reformed Dutch Church sent aid to the slaves. The American Freedmen's Aid Union displaced the US Commission in March 1865 in order to support all measures and institutions aimed at helping the colored man.[30] In late 1865, the American Freedmen's Aid Union united the agencies in Pittsburgh, Cincinnati, Chicago, and Boston-New York. They would send two thousand teachers, prevent the ill-treatment of Negroes, secure their citizenship rights, and place them "in a condition in which further help shall not be needed."[31]

The American Missionary Association (AMA) began in 1846 as a nondenominational Christian agency to protest against comparative silence of other missionary societies with regard to slavery. The groups that united into the AMA originated out of successful legal efforts to free slaves who had mutinied

---

[27] US Bureau of Education, *A Study of Private and Higher Education for Colored People in the United States*, Bulletin No. 38 (Washington DC: General Printing Office, 1917) appendixes; Franklin and Moss Jr. *From Slavery to Freedom*, 185–86.

[28] "The Freedmen's Societies," in US Bureau of Education, *Negro Education, A Study of Private and Higher Education Schools for Colored People in the United States*, Bulletin No. 39 (Washington: GPO, 1917) 1–20, 270–77.

[29] Abraham Lincoln, "Message to Congress Regarding Freedmen's Aid Societies," 17 December 1863 in *The American Presidency*, www.presidency.uscb.edu/ws/index, University of California Santa Barbara, online project.

[30] "The Freedmen's Societies," 277.

[31] US Bureau of Education, *Negro Education: A Study of the Private and Higher Schools for Colored People in the United States*, Bulletin No. 39 (Washington DC: GPO, 1917) 270–77, Fisk University, Special Collections.

and taken control of the *Amistad* slave ship in August 1839. The enslaved Africans landed this Spanish slave ship in American waters. The Constitution had forbidden the importation of slaves since 1808. After successfully defending these slaves and gaining their freedom, the *Amistad* Committee and other missionary societies merged to form the AMA in Albany, New York, on 3 September 1846, to conduct Christian missionary and education work. One of the *Amistad* captives, Sarah Kinson, studied at Oberlin College and joined the AMA staff. AMA worked in the South in the 1850s and by 1865 was raising hundreds of thousands of dollars to expand freedmen's education. By 1868, the AMA had 532 personnel.[32]

In 1867–1904, the AMA aided sixty-three Negro schools in eleven states, including three theological seminaries, three colleges, twenty-five secondary, seven elementary, four schools affiliated with the AMA, and twenty-one ungraded schools, totaling 13,023 students and 479 teachers and administrators. The AMA sponsored ten schools for 1,983 white students, and twenty-nine schools in other countries. In 1888, Daniel Hand of Guilford, Connecticut, gave the AMA a million dollars for "The Daniel Hand Educational Fund for Colored People."

The AMA operated Lincoln Normal School (Marion), Emerson Normal and Industrial Institute (Mobile), Burrell Normal School (Talladega), Trinity School (Florence), Cotton Valley School (Fort Davis), Cottage Grove Industrial Academy (Cottage Grove) in Alabama; Fessenden Academy and Industrial School (Fessenden), and Orange Park Normal and Manual Training School (Orange Park) in Florida. Ballard Normal School (Macon), Albany Normal School (Albany), Knox Institute and Industrial School (Athens), Howard Normal School (Cuthbert), Forsyth Normal and Industrial School (Forsyth), Dorchester Academy (McIntosh), Beach Institute (Savannah), and Allen Normal and Industrial School (Thomasville) existed in Georgia. Chandler Normal School operated in Lexington (KY). The AMA operated Straight University in New Orleans. Tougaloo College, Mount Hermon Seminary (Clinton), Lincoln School (Meridian), Girl's Industrial School (Moorhead), and Mound Bayou Normal Institute existed in Mississippi. The AMA schools in North Carolina included Joseph K. Brick Agricultural and Normal Institute (Enfield), Washburn Seminary (Beaufort), Lincoln Academy (Kings Mountain), Douglas Academy (Lawndale), Peabody Academy (Troy), and Gregory Normal Institute (Wilmington). In South

---

[32] Richard B. Drake, "The American Missionary Association and the Negro, 1861–1866" (PhD dissertation, Emory University, 1957) 1–31; Clifton Johnson, "The American Missionary Association, 1846–1861: A Study in Abolitionism" (PhD dissertation, University of North Carolina, 1959) 1–21.

Carolina, Avery Normal Institute was located in Charleston, and Brewer Normal School operated in Greenwood. In Tennessee, the AMA supported LeMoyne Normal Institute (Memphis) and Fisk University (Nashville). Additionally, the AMA operated Tillotson College in Austin, Texas, and Gloucester High and Industrial School in Cappahosie, Virginia. These schools enrolled 11,884 students.[33] Between 1888 and 1908, the AMA raised $10.2 million. They consolidated thirty schools, 1890 and 1910, and continued support for fifteen HBCUs.[34]

Anti-slavery societies in Cincinnati organized the Freedmen's Aid Society of the Methodist Episcopal Church (MEC) in August 1866. They borrowed $8,000 to finance their efforts. By 1908, they supported 8,319 students and employed 507 teachers in thirteen states. They helped 22 institutions in Alabama, Arizona, Florida, Georgia, Louisiana, Maryland, Missouri, Mississippi, and South Carolina, Tennessee, Texas, and Virginia. Forty-five percent continue today.

In *Christian Education of the Negro* (1909) report, the MEC also reported 164 of the students preparing for the ministry, 319 in medicine, 116 in dentistry, and fifty-four in nursing programs.[35] Many students studied industrial subjects, taking printing, carpentry, sewing, housekeeping, and dressmaking courses. The MEC Freedmen's Aid Society received more than $9.2 million between 1866 and 1907 to support freedmen's education. Some twelve of the twenty-two schools were college level; six of them had black presidents, and the others had Northern-born white presidents. The board said on 4 November 1908, "While giving, as far as possible, an opportunity to educate and consecrate the young men and women to serve their own people in this capacity, our policy will be to retain our white teachers, and when vacancies occur to fill their places by other Northern (white) teachers as an indispensable feature in these schools."[36] The

---

[33] US Bureau of Education, *Negro Education: A Study of the Private and Higher Schools for Colored People in the United States*, Bulletin No. 39 (Washington DC: GPO, 1917) 170–77; C. J. Ryder, James Cooper, and H. P. Douglass, *The Christian Education of the Negro by the American Missionary* (Cincinnati: MEC, 1909) 133–34; MEC Freedmen's Aid Society Report, 1908, and similar reports for each of the agencies appear in William N. Hartshorn and George W. Penniman, ed., *An Era of Progress and Promise, 1863–1910: The Religious, Moral, and Educational Development of the American Negro since his Emancipation* (Boston: Priscilla Publishing Co., 1910) 26–27, includes a report of the five Clifton Conferences, 1901–1908, www.statelibrary.dcr.stat.nc.us, State Library of North Carolina.

[34] Joe M. Richardson and Maxine D. Jones, *Education for Liberation: The American Missionary Association and African Americans, 1890 to the Civil Rights Movement* (Tuscaloosa: University of Alabama Press, 2009) 1–37.

[35] Ibid., 170.

[36] Ibid., 170–72.

Society also supported twenty-two schools among the white people in five states to help raise literacy across the region.

The Presbyterian Church, North, also made a report of *The Christian Education of the Negro* (1909). This agency had freedmen's committees in Indianapolis, New York, Philadelphia, and Pittsburgh. They began mission work among blacks in 1865; a faction of the southern Presbyterian Church joined the Confederate effort in 1861.

On 16 September 1882, the Presbyterian Church North united their freedmen aid societies and humanitarian efforts as the Board of Missions for Freedmen of the Presbyterian Church in the United States of America. The Board of Missions aimed to build churches, schools, colleges, and seminaries for the freedmen. Between 1867 and 1904, the board founded and supported more than twenty-two HBCUs, which enrolled 4,470 students by 1908. These schools included Barber Memorial Seminary (Anniston, Alabama), and Cotton Plant Academy (Cotton Plant, Arkansas), Arkadelphia Institute (Arkadelphia, Arkansas), Monticello Institute (Monticello, Arkansas), and Richard Allen Institute (Pine Bluff, Arkansas). They also sponsored Haines Normal and Industrial Institute (Augusta, Georgia), Fee Memorial Institute (Camp Nelson, Kentucky), and Mary Holmes Seminary (West Point, Mississippi). They supported seven freedmen schools and colleges in North Carolina, one in Oklahoma, five in South Carolina, and one in Tennessee. They founded five boarding schools for girls and thirteen coeducational boarding schools. All but eight Presbyterian schools had all Negro faculty and staff. Some 14,580 students by 1908 were "under religious influence and are being trained in the ways of the Presbyterian Church."[37]

The American Catholic Church did little for freedmen's education until the turn of the twentieth century. Impoverished Irish immigrants, who entered the country in large numbers in the 1840s due to famine in Europe, were primarily Catholic. Irish Catholics were not as heavily involved in slavery as other European Americans. The Irish competed with free blacks and slaves for jobs in the North and the South. In the South, the Catholic Church had a few Sunday classes for Negroes before 1860, and the Catholics organized a few black congregations and minor schools in the US after 1899. In heavily black New Orleans, the Catholics established Xavier University in 1915, and Xavier is the only Catholic HBCU among hundreds of Catholic colleges in the United States.

Just before the end of the nineteenth century, other church denominations, black and white, joined the movement to support schools for Negroes. The Christian Church (Disciples of Christ) eventually supported a dozen black

---

[37] Ryder and Douglass, *The Christian Education of the Negro*, 1–10, 250–300.

schools, and Jarvis Christian College (Hawkins, Texas) became their flagship. The Episcopal Church's American Church Institute for Negroes established four freedmen schools, including St Phillip's College in San Antonio, Texas.

The *Christian Education of the Negro* (1909) report included a "list of 259 Institutions for the Education of the Negro." The US Bureau of Education *Bulletin* (1917) said among the schools and colleges for Negroes, the Negro churches maintained 153 schools, 828 teachers, and 17,299 students by 1915.

The American Baptist Home Mission Society (ABHMS), based in New York City, played a major role in the development of HBCUs. The ABHMS began in 1832 to spread the gospel into the frontier and help the poor. However, the national denominational conventions split over the issue of slavery in 1844–1861. These divisions created the Southern Baptist Convention (SBC), Methodist Episcopal Church South, and Presbyterian Church in the South. Many white Southern Christians had no qualms about supporting human enslavement.

It wasn't until 1924 that the SBC directly supported a Negro college, American Baptist Theological Seminary in Nashville. Many of the returning Confederate soldiers, former slave owners, vigilantes, arsonists, nightriders, neo-Confederates, and others often destroyed freedmen schools, scattered the students back to the farms, and denounced black education as Northern meddling in Southern racial affairs. Seldom did individual pastors and churches in the South speak out in outrage, and the SBC almost never did so until after the Civil War. The SBC also failed to support the black's Civil Rights Movement, 1954–1968. Baptists supported no specific black college or university by 2009.[38]

The African Methodist Episcopal Church (AMEC), which began out of protest led by Richard Allen and other free Negroes against the racially prejudiced policies of the Methodist Episcopal Church in Philadelphia, played a major role in the expansion of black education during and after the Civil War. The AMEC had no churches in the Deep South prior to the Civil War, but President Lincoln gave his blessings in the winter of 1863 for the AMEC to evangelize and educate former slaves in the Union occupied areas. AME Bishop Daniel A. Payne arrived in Nashville on 5 December 1863 and organized two AME churches and Sunday schools. AME bishops fanned out and focused on organizing the Negroes and attempting to make Reconstruction work.[39]

---

[38] Paul Harvey, *Redeeming the South: Religious Cultures and Racial Identities among Southern Baptists, 1865–1925* (Chapel Hill: University of North Carolina Press, 1997) 169, 185–186.

[39] Robert E. Morrow, *Northern Methodism and Reconstruction* (East Lansing: Michigan State University Press, 1956) 1–30; David O. Moore, "The Withdrawal of Blacks from Southern Baptist Churches Following Emancipation," *Baptist History and Heritage* 16 (1981):

In 1890, the AMEC financially supported twenty-three schools, colleges, and seminaries. In 1916, the number declined to thirteen major schools including ten colleges and three seminaries. These included Shorter Junior College (Little Rock, Arkansas), Campbell College (Edwards, Mississippi), Daniel Payne College (Birmingham, Alabama), Kittrell College (Kittrell, North Carolina), Western University (Quindaro, Kansas), Allen University (Columbia, South Carolina), Edward Waters College (Jacksonville, Florida), Morris Brown (Atlanta, Georgia), Paul Quinn College (Dallas, Texas), Wilberforce University (Xenia, Ohio); and Jackson (Little Rock, Arkansas), Payne (Wilberforce, Ohio), and Turner (Atlanta, Georgia) theological seminaries. AMEC schools taught crafts, manual labor courses, liberal arts, and religion (particularly the role of persons of African descent in the formation of western Christianity).[40]

Wilberforce University

The Methodist Episcopal Church (MEC) conference of Ohio founded Wilberforce University, near Xenia in Greene County, Pennsylvania in 1855. The MEC Ohio conference also cooperated with the African Methodist Episocopal Church (AMEC) to raise money for this college meant to train and educate Negro students. The name honored William Wilberforce, the noted English abolitionist. The MEC conference in Ohio already had founded the Union Seminary in 1844, and later used funds from the closed seminary to aid Wilberforce University. Wilberforce University enrolled some 207 students, many of them former slaves, by 1859.

The AMEC bought Wilberforce University for $10,000 from the MEC of Ohio and newly incorporated the institution on 10 July 1863. Wilberforce president and AMEC Bishop Daniel Payne became America's first Negro college president. He had started a secondary school for Negroes in Philadelphia in the 1830s, but he had to flee after whites who opposed educated Negroes exerted pressure against him. Payne later made education a requirement among AMEC clergy. Payne, the AME Church, Wilberforce University, and pro-Unionists drew opposition from local Southern transplants and some other whites who opposed the abolition activity and the education of Negroes.[41]

12–18; Lawrence S. Little, *Disciples of Liberty: The African Methodist Episcopal Church in the Age of Imperialism, 1884–1916* (Knoxville: University of Tennessee Press, 2000) 68.

[40] Du Bois, *The College-Bred Negro*, 28.

[41] "History," www.wilberforce.edu; see also Horace Talbert, *The Sons of Allen: Together with a Sketch of the Rise and Progress of Wilberforce University, Ohio* (Xenia OH: Aldine Press, 1906); *Documenting the South*, e-book, University of North Carolina at Chapel Hill, 2000; Daniel A. Payne, *The History of the Origin and Development of Wilberforce University* (Xenia OH: Wilberforce University Library and Archives, 1999) 1–31.

Negroes and other Unionists in the Wilberforce community traveled to nearby Xenia to celebrate the 9 April 1865 surrender of the Confederates. President Lincoln and General Grant had permitted some of the twenty-five thousand US Colored Troops in the Army of the James to have the honor of being among the first of Union troops to enter the nearby Confederate capital, Richmond, Virginia. Southern sympathizers were angry about the defeat and the use of black troops. However, black and white Unionists were euphoric about the turn of events.

Just after their return to the Wilberforce community, the group of Negroes and other Unionists received bad news: someone had shot and killed President Lincoln. Wilberforce's main building including classrooms and dining hall had burned down, perhaps related to the racial animosity in the area. The AMEC rebuilt the school. Daniel A. Payne remained president until 1875. Benjamin F. Lee served as president from 1876 until 1884. In 1887, the state operated the Department of Normal and Industrial Education on the Wilberforce campus. The department (today's Central State University) trained teachers and taught vocational arts.

This administrative and curricular arrangement created division, constant conflict, and campus politics among AME church personnel. William E. B. Du Bois accepted his first teaching position at Wilberforce University in 1894, and he confirmed the tense political-religious environment on campus. That was the year Payne Theological Seminary incorporated into Wilberforce and the military training program got started. The political and religious intrigues on campus infuriated the scholarly Du Bois. Because Du Bois thought religion and college campuses did not mix, he left Wilberforce to teach at Atlanta University.[42]

The North Central Association of Colleges and Schools (NCACS) granted Wilberforce provisional accreditation in 1939. In 1943, the NCACS granted full accreditation, but revoked accreditation in 1947 with separation of Wilberforce University from the industrial education program, which became Central State University of Ohio. The NCACS restored accreditation to Wilberforce University in 1956. The institution continued to expand as a four-year college and erected new buildings. In 1974 a tornado destroyed part of the city of Xenia and the campus. Rembert E. Stokes served as president from 1956 until 1977. Wilberforce University had several short-term presidents over the next twenty-five years.

Floyd H. Flake, formerly a representative in the US House of Representatives, became president in July 2002 and served through 2008 to

---

[42] Kenneth R. Janken, *Walter White: Mr. NAACP* (Chapel Hill: University of North Carolina Press, 2003) 189–91, 330, 345; David L. Lewis, *W. E. B. Du Bois: The Fight for Equality and the American Century, 1919–1963* (New York: Henry Holt, 2000) 537–38.

stabilize and advance the institution. In his resignation letter, dated 24 January 2008, he said in part,

> The world of higher education had changed markedly over several decades and the University had not kept pace with these tectonic shifts. The University environment that I inherited, one of instability, risk, and lingering questions about financial and academic performance, has been replaced by a more optimistic, productive, and predictable operating climate. We have experienced an awakening to the renewed possibility of a stronger, more effective University in its third century of operation....[43]

Student enrollment exceeded 1250 in 2008. There were new computer labs, and an Engineering, Mathematics and Aerospace Academy sponsored by NASA. The federal government helped with some $9 million in grants. The number of academic majors was reduced from fifty-four to seventeen, and a master's degree began. Wilberforce students originated from Ohio, thirty-one states, and three foreign countries. Eighty percent of them resided on campus.[44]

Lincoln University

Lincoln University of Missouri was another Negro initiative in early higher education. The 62nd and 65th US Colored Troops (USCT) donated thousands of dollars to start Lincoln Institute in January 1865. The school opened on 17 September 1866 under an officer of the 62nd USCT. The institution moved to the present site in Jefferson City, Missouri, in 1869. The institution was designed for the special benefit of the freed slaves.[45]

Lincoln Institute received state aid by 1871 and included preparatory and normal (teacher training) departments. It became a state school, Lincoln University, in 1879. Lincoln University became Missouri's first black Morrill Land Grant institution in 1891 by adding agricultural and industrial curricula. NCACS accredited the institution in 1934. Lincoln got a Civil Pilots Training program and graduate programs in 1940. In 1942, when a Negro student sued for

---

[43] "President's Message," http://www.wilberforce.edu, Wilberforce University, 2008.

[44] Lewis, *W. E. B. Du Bois: The Fight for Equality and the American Century,* 26, 27, 56, 162, 184, 537–38; W. E. B. Du Bois, *Black Reconstruction in America, 1860–1880* (New York: Atheneum Books, 1977) 637, 665–67; Woodson and Wesley, *The Negro in Our History*, 319; Elliott M. Rudwick, *W. E. B. Du Bois: Propagandist of the Negro Protest* (New York: Atheneum, 1978) 41; W. E. B. Du Bois, "The General Education Board," *Crisis* 37/1 (January 1930): 177; Payne, *History of the African Methodist Episcopal Church,* 149–5, 186–87, http://www.docsouth.unc.edu/church/payne; D. A. Payne, *The History of the Origin and Development of Wilberforce University* (Xenia: Wilberforce University Archives, 1999) 4, www.wilberforce.edu/library.

[45] "History of Lincoln University," http://www.lincolnu.edu, Lincoln University, 2010.

admission into the School of Journalism at the University of Missouri, the state granted Lincoln University a journalism program. Lincoln's enrollment totaled nearly 800 students when former president Harry S. Truman visited the campus in 1954. By 1965, Lincoln had 1,652 students and has produced some five thousand graduates since 1871. The website reports, "Lincoln University serves a diverse clientele, both commuter and residential, engages in a variety of research projects, and offers numerous programs in addition to providing an array of academic programs."[46]

Again, the nineteenth-century curricula for HBCUs mostly reflected the religious and educational philosophy of Northern missionaries: religion, moral living, working with the hands, liberal arts, civic education, and loyalty to America. HBCUs focused on training teachers, artisans and industrial workers, and ministers. Black teachers at the HBCUs infused the curricula with lessons on race. Textbooks included Lydia Maria Child *The Freedmen's Book*, which consisted of short biographies on black heroes. Most of the early Negro institutions of higher education, however, prepared few students for actual college or university work. Du Bois's 1900 study counted about 726 students enrolled in college programs "specially designed for them" at some 30 HBCUs, including 135 at Lincoln of Pennsylvania, 42 at Howard University, and only 2 at Branch Normal College in Pine Bluff, Arkansas.[47]

Meanwhile, political turbulence during the Reconstruction affected the history of HBCUs. These disturbances adversely affected black American educational history in general. Three days after Andrew Johnson succeeded President Lincoln, John Mercer Langston and a delegation of blacks met with Johnson. They requested "complete emancipation, and secondly, full equality before American law." Johnson said he believed blacks should accept colonization (moving to another country) to prevent clashes with the whites. On 10 October 1865, Johnson said to a regiment of US Colored Troops, "This country is founded upon the principle of equality.... The institution of slavery made war against the United States...and the [US] has decided that the institution of slavery must go. It is for you to establish...you are fit and qualified to be free."[48]

---

[46] Ibid., Lincoln University was recognized in 2007 for enrolling many international students.

[47] Darlene Clark Hine, William C. Hine, and Stanley Harrold, *African Americans: A Concise History*, 2nd ed. (Upper Saddle River NJ: Pearson Prentice Hall, 2006) 234; Du Bois, *The College-Bred Negro*, 28–29.

[48] Cheek and Cheek, *John Mercer Langston and the Fight for Black Freedom*, 448; William Scott, "Johnson," *Nashville Colored Tennessean*, 14 October 1865, p. 1.

In March 1865, Congress approved the US Bureau of Refugees, Freedmen, and Abandoned Lands (the Freedmen's Bureau) to take over functions heretofore carried out by the Army and the missionaries. The Bureau became *de facto* the first federal social work agency. It allocated more than $500,000, and helped support freedmen's schools. This federal agency helped create Atlanta University, Fisk University, Storer College, Biddle Memorial Institute, Howard University, and Saint Augustine's Normal and Collegiate Institute. Frederick Douglass, among prominent Negro leaders, applauded the educational efforts of the Bureau, but he believed the Congress was under-funding the agency. Douglass refused an appointment to the Bureau.[49]

In early 1866, the National Colored Men's Convention sent a delegation to speak to Johnson about Negro rights and male suffrage. Johnson repeated his position that the Negroes should accept emigration. Douglass replied in the *Washington Chronicle* (7 February 1866):

> Even if it were true, as you allege, that the hostility of the blacks toward the poor whites must necessarily project itself into a state of freedom and that this enmity between the two races is even more intense in a state of freedom than in a state of slavery, in the name of Heaven, we reverently ask, how can you, in view of your professed desire to promote the welfare of the black man, deprive him of all means of [defense], and clothe him whom your regard as his enemy in panoply of political power?[50]

After white mobs rioted and massacred dozens of freedmen in New Orleans and Memphis in May 1866, in June the Congress proposed the 14th Amendment to guarantee equal protection of the laws, due process of the law, and that all persons born in the United States were citizens. President Johnson had said the bill discriminated against white immigrants who had to endure a lengthy process to become American citizens.[51] Since slavery days, he said, there was too much conflict between poor whites and blacks. It was best to colonize the blacks elsewhere. On 16 May 1868, Congress failed, by a single vote, to impeach him. On 28 July 1868, the US Secretary of State reported the states ratified the 14th Amendment: "All persons born or naturalized in the United States, and subject to the jurisdiction thereof, are citizens of the US and of the

---

[49] Luther P. Jackson, "The Educational Efforts of the Freedmen's Bureau and Freedmen's Aid Societies in South Carolina, 1862–1872," *Journal of Negro History* 8/1 (January 1923): 1–40.

[50] Frederick Douglass, "Reply of the Colored Delegation to the President," *Washington Chronicle*, 7 February 1866, in Philip S. Foner, ed., *Frederick Douglass: Selected Speeches and Writings* (Chicago: Lawrence Hill Books, 1999) 589.

[51] Ibid.

State wherein they reside and are guaranteed equal protection of the laws and due process of the laws."

Ulysses S. Grant (R) became president on 4 March 1869. He supported the 15th Amendment to give Negro male citizens the right to vote and hold public office. In March 1870, the required number of states ratified the 15th Amendment. Grant said, "It became an absolute necessity, however, because of the foolhardiness of the President [Johnson] and the blindness of the Southern people to their own interest." Grant called the amendment the "most important event…since the nation came into life.... We have washed color out of the Constitution." He urged Congress to promote education "to make their [blacks'] share in the government a blessing and not a danger."[52]

However, the Northern missionaries began ending their massive efforts to aid the freedmen. Northerners were turning their attention to rapidly transforming the base of the American economy from agriculture to industry. In 1869–1872, the Congress began phasing out the Freedmen's Bureau. In 1874, the Freedman's Bank and Trust Company and its thirty-three branches went bankrupt. This agency was "morally and practically" part of the Freedom's Bureau, said W. E. B. Du Bois, who further praised the Freedman's Bureau by saying, "Up to June 1869, over half a million patients had been treated by Bureau physicians and surgeons, and sixty hospitals and asylums had been in operation.... Such was the dawn of Freedom; such was the work of the Freedmen's Bureau."[53] Many Southerners and neo-Confederates filled the vacuum with a war of terror against the Negro and whites who helped him. Federal troops headed southward. The courts indicted many racists, white supremacists, neo-Confederates and terrorists.

Grant served his last term and left office in March 1877. His successor, President Rutherford B. Hayes (R) agreed to the Compromise of 1877 that broke the tie in the Electoral College, gave Hayes the White House, but began the end of progressive Reconstruction. In his 5 March 1877, inaugural address, Hayes said, "Let me assure my countrymen of the Southern States that it is my earnest desire to regard and promote their truest interest…and forever wipe out in our political affairs the color line and the distinction between North and South." Hayes promised to uplift the Negroes through federal support for their education. He agreed to establishment of schools for Indians and benefits from the Homestead Act but made no similar effort to benefits the blacks.[54] Historian

---

[52] Ulysses S. Grant, *Personal Memoirs of U. S. Grant* (New York: Webster, 1885) 25, 437.

[53] W. E. B. Du Bois, *The Souls of Black Folk* (New York: Penguin Books, 2003) 31.

[54] William A. DeGregorio, *The Complete Book of U.S. Presidents: From George Washington to George Bush* (New York: Barricade Books, 1991) 186.

Rayford Logan of Howard University named Hayes "the principal presidential architect of the consolidation of white supremacy in the South" because he failed to enforce federal law against those who terrorized Negro citizens.[55]

Nevertheless, under some federal protection, from 1870 to 1905, Negroes became city council members, county magistrates, state representatives, US senators (two), and congressional representatives (twenty-two). All came from Southern states. Even though the 15th Amendment had given Negroes voting rights in all the Northern states, the Northern black population was insufficiently concentrated in districts to gain any political power before 1928.

Despite the "nadir of Reconstruction," as Rayford Logan phrased it, the Morrill Land Grant Act (1862) aided the establishment of public land-grant HBCUs by setting aside millions of acres of public land to support public colleges. Justin Smith Morrill (1810–1895) of Vermont introduced the Morrill Land Grant bill, which passed Congress in 1859, but during sometimes violent slave debates in Congress, President James Buchanan, a Pennsylvania Democrat, sympathized with the pro-slavery South. He favored the *Dred Scott v. Sanford* (1857) Supreme Court decision that sided with the South, supported slavery, and declared Negroes non-citizens of the United States. Buchanan sided with the South again, and vetoed the 1859 land grant legislation. However, the Civil War came in 1861, and eleven of the fifteen slave states left the Union and formed the Confederate States of America. President Lincoln signed the land grant legislation on 2 July 1862. Northern states created land grant colleges, and admitted black students and women. After Congress re-admitted the former Confederate states, they, too, began receiving Morrill funds but refused to admit blacks into the land grant colleges.

Tennessee became the first former Confederate state readmitted into the Union in July 1866, and thus became eligible for Morrill Land Grant appropriations. However, Tennessee had no public college, and so, the state assigned the money to a private institution, the East Tennessee University in 1869. The election to the Tennessee General Assembly of some fourteen Negro state legislators took place in 1872–1886, and they demanded that black Tennesseans, too, benefit from federal land grant funds. The General Assembly set aside a few Morrill scholarships for Negroes, who applied to the white institution, now named the University of Tennessee. The Negroes, 26.4 percent of Tennesseans, could use the funds to attend Fisk University and other private HBCUs. In response to the 1890 Morrill Land Grant Act, which included stronger

[55] Rayford W. Logan, *The Betrayal of the Negro: from Rutherford B. Hayes to Woodrow Wilson* (Toronto: The Macmillan Company, 1965) 23–28.

language that required equal treatment of the races or loss of the money, Tennessee granted a portion of the money to establish a "Negro Department" at nearby Knoxville College where student recipients farmed and did some minor industrial subjects at that Presbyterian- supported HBCU.[56]

Alcorn College

In 1871–1873, state legislators authorized the first black land-grant HBCU, Alcorn College in Alcorn, Mississippi. The University of Mississippi was for whites but had closed during the Civil War when students and faculty members mostly joined the Confederate Army. The president since 1856, F. A. P. Barnard, although a participant in enslavement of Negroes, opposed the Confederate rebellion. Barnard went back North and became president of Columbia University. The University of Mississippi reopened in September 1870, but the chancellor and the professors refused to enroll Negroes even though the state constitution now prohibited racial discrimination. The chancellor and seven professors signed a statement "that should the applicant belong to the Negro race, they would, without hesitation, reject him, and as the university was established exclusively for the white race, they would instantly resign if the trustees should require them to receive Negro students." According to the reports, no Negroes applied for admission.[57]

In 1871, Mississippi created Alcorn Agricultural and Mechanical College for Negroes, using 1862 federal land scrip. Governor James L. Alcorn (R) persuaded the legislature to establish the school on the site of the former Oakland College, where the whites had left to join the Confederate Army. State House speaker John R. Lynch, a Negro, signed the bill.

Hiram R. Revels gained the presidency of Alcorn. Born in North Carolina in 1822, he attended a Quaker seminary in Indiana and graduated from Knox College in Illinois. Revels helped form black regiments in Maryland during the Civil War and then taught school in Missouri and Vicksburg. He accompanied the Union Army to Jackson as a USCT chaplain and AME minister. Revels located in Natchez and became a political leader. Revels favored the removal of all disqualifications on ex-Confederates. He believed in racial accommodation, and thus won favor with white Republicans that dominated the legislature. Negroes, however, outnumbered whites in the Mississippi Republican Party and made up 57 percent of the population. Revels gained election to fill Jefferson Davis's former seat in Congress, after the Negroes in the legislature insisted that

---

[56] Bobby L. Lovett, *The Civil Rights Movement in Tennessee: A Narrative History* (Knoxville: University of Tennessee Press, 2005) 117, 136, 336–37, 346, 347.

[57] Editor, "Ole Miss," *Jackson Clarion*, 11 October 1870, p. 1.

a black man occupy one of the two appointments to partial terms or gain election to the full term US Senate seat. The whites agreed to the partial term (25 February 1870–3 March 1871) for Hiram Revels.[58]

Hiram Revels became president of Alcorn in 1871 with an annual salary of $500 a year and eight faculty members. However, politics led to Revels' demise. In 1874, the governor removed Revels, causing sixty students to withdraw from Alcorn College in protest. James W. Garner, author of *Reconstruction in Mississippi* (1968) said, the Radical Republicans, "...by their alliance with the colored race against the native whites finally brought on [a white] revolution."[59] Democrats and former Confederates redeemed the state government in 1876 through violence and war against Negro and Radical Republicans. The state Republican Party ceased operations. The legislature reduced the appropriations to Alcorn College, which then suffered neglect for more than a quarter century. John R. Lynch, speaker of the house, secretary of state and then three-term Congressmen, wrote *The Facts of Reconstruction* (1913). Lynch said Alcorn educated blacks helped increase black political representation in Mississippi.[60] Indeed, it did, but only for a very short time. In 1878, Alcorn A&M College met the 1862 Morrill Act requirements; the first of the HBCUs to be so designated a land grant institution. The curriculum included agriculture and military tactics. The school had two departments: Academic Department, and College Preparatory Department. Alcorn was an all-male secondary-trades school.

A college-trained man, John H. Burrus became president in 1883. Born a mulatto slave in Texas, upon the Confederate defeat, he, his mother, and two brothers moved to New Orleans. John ended up in Memphis as a cook on a steamboat. He moved to Nashville to work as a waiter at a hotel. He studied at night under two hotel tenants. He saved $300 and entered Fisk Free School in summer 1867. That fall, the institution received a charter as Fisk University. John Burrus continued the academic program, the college course, and graduated in 1874 in Fisk University's first college class. Burrus became a principal at a school near Nashville, a delegate to the National Republican Convention (1876), and secretary for the Tennessee State Republican Party (1878), taught mathematics at Fisk (1877–1883), and received the AM degree in 1879 from Dartmouth. After Tennessee began receiving the federal Morrill Land Grant funds in 1869, the

---

[58] John Hope Franklin and A. A. Moss Jr., *From Slavery to Freedom: A History of Negro Americans*, 6th ed. (New York: Knopf, 1988) 220; John R. Lynch, *The Facts of Reconstruction* (Indianapolis: Bobbs-Merrill, 1970) 44–45, 93.

[59] James W. Garner, *Reconstruction in Mississippi* (Baton Rouge: Louisiana State University Press, 1968) 124, 107, 180, 355, 369.

[60] Lynch, *The Facts of Reconstruction*, 39–43.

money was given to the private East Tennessee University (today's University of Tennessee) that admitted no blacks. Burrus led a committee to petition the Tennessee General Assembly. The committee also included HBCU representatives John Braden of Central Tennessee College, H. S. Bennett of Fisk University, L. B. Teft of Roger Williams University, and others. The General Assembly appropriated $25,000 for two years to allow state senators to nominate Negro students to East Tennessee University, giving each student $50, which they could use to enroll at Fisk, Roger Williams, or Central Tennessee, the black schools. Burrus studied law, gained admission to the bar in 1881, and served on the local board of education in 1878–1883.

With his vast political and educational experiences, Burrus convinced the Mississippi legislature to appropriate $11,000 for a library, equipment, and campus repairs. He upgraded the faculty by hiring his brother James and other Negro college graduates. James also had graduated from Fisk University in 1874 and taught there as well. The enrollment doubled to 216 students by 1887. The 1890 Morrill land grant amendment helped get more funding for Burrus to build better facilities at Alcorn A. & M. College.

However, Mississippi in 1890 adopted the Confederate emblem as the state flag along with the slogan "Ethnic supremacy—For the Right" of white people. The whites, a minority population, placed that slogan on the Democratic Party's state ballot. After the neo-Confederates "redeemed" Mississippi and began a reign of racial terror, John Burris and his brother James left Alcorn in 1893–1894 and headed back to Tennessee.[61]

Around the turn of the twentieth century, Alcorn began to show progress once more. Alcorn College had 339 students, seven graduates, sixteen teachers by 1900 and admitted women in 1903. By 1910, Alcorn had 170 females and 445 males. Alcorn had 750 students by 1927, and with the help of the northern philanthropic agencies, particularly the General Education Board (GEB), and through the issuance of state bonds Alcorn College was able to construct buildings fit for collegiate status. Alcorn began a four-year college curriculum by 1928, and by 1934 structured itself into divisions of agriculture, liberal arts and sciences, home economic, and mechanical industries. New Deal agencies gave $50,909 to build a girls' dormitory. SACS accredited the high school in 1936, and awarded the college department a "B" rating in 1940.

A keenly defined white supremacy policy ruled nakedly in Mississippi for more than a century. Negro citizens had no real socioeconomic influence. Even the white native Republicans (scalawags) and white Northern opportunists

---

[61] "John H. Burrus," in William J. Simmons, *Men of Mark: Eminent, Progressive and Rising* (Cleveland OH: G. M. Rewell Company, 1887) 87, 363, 365, 367, 799.

(carpetbaggers) helped local whites keep land out of the hands of black Mississippians. Negroes long endured a new kind of slavery. Seldom did they transcend widespread illiteracy, ignorance, and the lowly economic status of tenants, day laborers, and sharecroppers. They were prevented from voting and holding state, county, and local public offices; and Mississippi developed a criminal injustice system that placed thousands of blacks on crude, brutal prison farms where life expectancy was short. Mississippian James W. Garner, a social scientist trained at Columbia University and author of *Reconstruction in Mississippi* (1901), defended white Mississippi. Garner said,

> When the [Republicans] surrendered the government to the democracy [Democrats], in 1876, the public school system, which they had fathered, had become firmly established, its efficiency increased, and its administration made somewhat less expensive than at first. There does not seem to have been any disposition upon the part of the Democrats to abolish it or impair its efficiency.... They kept their promise to the Negroes [*sic*].... The system of public education...is destined to be the chief means of solving the great problem which the Civil War left as a legacy to the white race.[62]

Garner, who resented the way Northern whites blamed American white racism on the white Southerners, believed Republicans "had an over-confidence in the mental and moral ability of the black race, so far as their ability to govern them selves was concerned." Whites, Garner believed, were "the dominant race" because of "tradition, education, and superior economic and legal advantages."[63] Thus, Mississippi officials viewed Negro higher educational progress as undesirable. Lynch recognized this, and said Mississippi only kept Alcorn operating at a minimal, because "the State might otherwise forfeit and lose the aid it now receives from the national government for the support of agricultural institutions."[64] But Lynch and other once-influential black Republicans fled north, and left Alcorn College to suffer for another century.

South Carolina's black Morrill land grant program began in 1872 as a high school-like institution called Colored Normal, Industrial, Agricultural, and Mechanical College of South Carolina. South Carolina assigned the Negro land-grant funds to a Methodist Church freedmen's school, Claflin University (founded 1869), originally located in Charleston. The founders organized Claflin

---

[62] Garner, *Reconstruction in Mississippi*, 296, 336, 408.

[63] Ibid.

[64] Lynch, *The Facts of Reconstruction*, 53; Josephine Posey, *Against Great Odds: The History of Alcorn State University* (Jackson: University Press of Mississippi, 1994) 4, 11, 14–23, 25, 50.

around the Baker Theological Institute, which merged with Claflin in 1870. They transferred Claflin from Charleston to Columbia, and with help from Lee Claflin of Massachusetts, the school purchased the old Orangeburg Female College in Orangeburg, South Carolina. Historian Asa H. Gordon said, "The Negro's acquisition of education and a fair degree of intelligence, like his acquisition of freedom, would have been an impossibility without his own efforts." Claflin College added a normal department in 1877, a college program by 1879, and a law department in 1881. The Colored Normal, Industrial, Agricultural, and Mechanical College of South Carolina existed in the Claflin University industrial department until 1896.[65]

Meanwhile, in 1873, University of South Carolina (USC) became a racially integrated university. Blacks made up a majority of the delegates to the constitutional convention, and they and white Republicans changed the state constitution to prohibit racial discrimination in 1869. They provided a scholarship for Negro students to attend USC. Secretary of State Henry E. Haynes, a former sergeant in the Union Army, became the first Negro to attend and graduate from the medical school. Black politician Francis L. Cardozo served on the board of trustees and enrolled in the law department. Whites left USC, leaving white Northern missionaries and one black, Richard T. Greener, a graduate of Harvard, to reconstitute a faculty. Ninety percent of the students were black. USC remained open with fewer than 200 students, mostly in pre-college classes. Blacks held the majority on the board of trustees.

Some outstanding Negro students emerged from the integrated USC. Johnson C. Whittaker, became the second Negro at West Point Military Academy on 23 August 1876, joining Henry O. Flipper—the first Negro to graduate from West Point (1877). George W. Murray enrolled in the University of South Carolina in the fall of 1874. He gained election to the US Congress in 1893. Former slave William A. Sinclair attended Claflin before entering USC. Sinclair continued at Howard University, earning three degrees. He worked for the AMA in Nashville and earned a medical degree from Meharry Medical College.

The experiment in racial integration at USC came to an abrupt end in 1876—the same year Reconstruction collapsed in Mississippi. Wade Hampton (D) convinced some Negro leaders, including former black Union Army Major

---

[65] Asa H. Gordon, *Sketches of Negro Life and History in South Carolina* (Columbia: University of South Carolina Press, 1929) 81, 95, 105, 107, 111; "About Claflin," http://www.claflin/about, Claflin University, 2010; "History of SC State University," http://www.scsu.edu, South Carolina State University, 2010; J. G. Marszalek, *A Black Congressman in the Age of Jim Crow: South Carolina's George Washington Murray* (Gainesville: University of Florida Press, 2006) 7–8, 159.

Martin Delaney, to aid his election as governor. This racial accommodation gesture was a mistake. Some white race radicals began a riot at the mostly black town of Hamburg on 4 July 1876 and spread the violence throughout the state. Juries later acquitted seven white men indicted for murder.[66] The rebels proclaimed white supremacy, became "Red Shirt"-wearing supporters for Hampton, and dared Republicans to show at the polls. Hampton won by a 1,134-vote margin. One historian said, "Certainly enough Negroes did vote for Hampton to give him a majority."[67] Hampton, a former Confederate Army general, had allowed the murder of Union soldiers who foraged for food and supplies near Columbia in February 1864. When the Union contacted him about the incidents, Hampton seethed with hatred. He said Southerners had a right to shoot a Union forager down, "as he would wild beast." He promised to be "fair and equal" toward black interests. Hampton dismissed the board of trustees at USC and appointed new members. They expelled all the Negro students.[68]

State Democrats argued that although whites were in the minority (43 percent), "white men of intelligence and wealth" must rule the government. After 1882, the threat of the Negro majority in the state ceased to exist. As it had done to force the protection of slavery into the Constitution of 1787 and led the Confederate rebellion in 1861, South Carolina remained a center of white supremacy. The state Democratic Party refused to give equal protection of the law to Negro citizens. The white minority condoned general war on the Negro majority. South Carolina white officials disregarded the Constitution but took advantage of the blessings and benefits of the United States.

Rod Andrew wanted to create a paternalistic arrangement to bring blacks into the South Carolina Democratic Party, but whites decisively rejected his vision. The ferociously racist political machine of Benjamin R. "Pitchfork" Ben Tillman defeated him. He led the revision of the state constitution to exclude as many of the remaining black voters as possible. Tillman later gained election to the US Senate. There, he said in 1900, "We shoot [blacks] in South Carolina when they come in competition with us [whites] in the matter of elections."[69] Only 10 percent of eligible black voters registered to vote. The state officials instituted

---

[66] Steven E. Woodworth, *Nothing but Victory: The Army of the Tennessee, 1861–1865* (New York: Knopf, 2005) 626–27.

[67] Hampton M. Jarrell, *Wade Hampton and the Negro: The Road not Taken* (Columbia: University of South Carolina Press, 1969) 125–27, 148–49, 99, 159.

[68] Alrutheus A. Taylor, *The Negro in South Carolina during the Reconstruction* (Washington DC: Association for the Study of Negro Life and History, 1924) 312.

[69] Sidney Andrews, *The South since the War* (Boston: Houghton Mifflin, 1971) 1–10, 386; Rod Andrew, *Wade Hampton: Confederate Warrior to Southern Redeemer* (Chapel Hill: University of North Carolina Press, 2008) xv, 3.

education requirements, literacy tests, and property qualifications as well as intimidation to disenfranchise blacks. They oppressed blacks *and* poor whites, and through the electoral laws by the landholding-class diminished the overall size of the state electorate. Historian Sidney Andrews said, "Nine of every ten white men in South Carolina had almost as little to do with even state affairs as the Negroes."[70]

Under the rule of the white supremacists, South Carolina became one of the poorest states in America. State officials shifted the majority of public education funds to the minority white population, yet white South Carolinians fell below the national level of education achievement. Many white South Carolinians remained very poor compared to Northern whites. The wealthiest city in the state, Charleston, was almost half-black, but that city lacked institutions of higher education for Negroes.[71]

However, with help from Northern white missionaries and philanthropists, blacks delivered education to other black South Carolinians. Avery Institute in Charleston, South Carolina, was "unique and exemplary in black-white race relations."[72] Avery Institute did almost all the local Negro high school education in Charleston, enrolling 200 high school and 300 normal school students. Francis L. Cardozo, a native of Charleston, with the help of the American Missionary Association (AMA), started Avery Institute after expanding the Saxton freedmen's school in October 1865. Cardozo had received his education in Charleston's free Negro schools before going to Scotland in 1844 to study at the University of Glasgow. He headed a church in Connecticut before returning to Charleston to work with the AMA. Charles Avery of Pittsburgh, Pennsylvania, gave the initial funding for the new school. By 1880, Avery Institute enrolled 448 students, and employed eight teachers—mostly Northerners. The first black principal was hired in 1915. The school became public in 1947 and closed in 1954 with the *Brown v. Board of Education* decision. In 1978, the original building became the Avery Institute of Afro-American History and Culture. It was renovated and opened as a research facility, conference center, and museum in

---

[70] Andrew, *The South since the War*, 386; Joel Williamson, *After Slavery: The Negro in South Carolina during Reconstruction* (Chapel Hill: University of North Carolina Press, 1965) 231–39.

[71] Edward A. Miller Jr., *Gullah Statesman: Robert Smalls from Slavery to Congress 1839–1915* (Columbia: University of South Carolina Press, 1995) 215; see W. E. B. Du Bois, *Black Reconstruction in America, 1860–1880* (New York: Atheneum Books, 1977) 1–30.

[72] "Avery Institute," http://www.nps.gov/history, Charleston Historic Sites, 2010.

1990. Avery became the "best school for blacks in the entire state" and "attracted the children of upper-class blacks."[73]

The Northern missionaries established other schools to serve the huge black population. The Quakers started Laing Normal and Industrial School at Mount Pleasant. Then there was Browning Industrial and Mather Academy at Camden; Brewer Normal and Industrial and Agricultural Institute at Greenwood; and Elizabeth E. Wright's Voorhees Normal and Industrial School at Denmark. Former slave Alexander Bettis founded Bettis Institute at Trenton. The American Baptist Home Mission Society (ABHMS) named Shaw Memorial Institute for Colonel Robert G. Shaw, commander of the 54th USCT of Massachusetts. Bathsheba A. Benedict of Rhode Island and the ABHMS established the Benedict Institute to educate young men of the Baptist faith for the ministry, to prepare efficient teachers for the colored, and to train all the students in the essentials of Christian essentials of Christian citizenship. The AMEC established Payne Institute through the leadership of Bishop W. F. Dickerson. Payne began in Cokesbury in 1871, but moved to Columbia in 1880 to become the center of Allen University (founded 1870), an AMEC school.[74]

Meanwhile, the Colored Normal, Industrial A. & M. State College remained a department at Claflin University, where a board of trustees appointed by the legislature cooperated with the board of Claflin University. The industrial and agricultural department had a 250-acre experimental farm, shops for training carpenters and blacksmiths, its own faculty, and an annual state appropriation. In 1896, the state legislature, in its response to the requirements of the 1890 Morrill Land Grant amendment, approved the Colored, Normal, Industrial, and A&M College to start classes separate from Claflin in 1896. Thomas E. Miller and six trustees headed the land-grant institution, which opened on 27 September 1896. Miller was an opponent to outspoken George Washington Murray, the last black to represent South Carolina in the US Congress. Murray believed Miller got

---

[73] Bernard E. Powers Jr., *Black Charlestonians: A Social History, 1822–1885* (Fayetteville: University of Arkansas Press, 1994) 153; see Edmund L. Drago and Eugene C. Hunt, *A History of Avery Normal Institute from 1865 to 1954* (Charleston: Avery Research Center, 1891) 1–10; W. J. Gaboury, "George Washington Murray and the Fight for Political Democracy in South Carolina," *Journal of Negro History* 62 (1977): 258–69; Gordon, *Sketches of Negro Life and History in South Carolina*, 95, 107, 268, 269; Edmund L. Drago, *Initiative, Paternalism, and Race Relations: Charleston's Avery Normal Institute* (Athens: University of Georgia Press, 1990) 1–15.

[74] "Historical Background," http://www.allenuniversity.edu, Allen University, 2010; Williamson, *After Slavery*, 231–33; Miller, *Gullah Statesman*, 223–24.

the job because he was a conservative Negro, "forced on the colored people."[75] Miller, who had attended Lincoln University in Pennsylvania, and served two terms in the US Congress, did not challenge white power, and thus he served as the president of South Carolina State until 1911.

No doubt South Carolina's Negro land-grant institution was *not* equal in respect to the US Supreme Court decision of *Plessy v. Ferguson* (1896), which said separation of the races was all right as long as facilities remained equal. But the facilities were not equal, and South Carolina officials thus violated the equal protection clause of the 14th Amendment (1868). The classes began in eight small buildings, including log cabins, a barn, with a small diary herd, 135 acres of land, and a few small farm animals. The school enrolled about 1,000 students not of collegiate level in the first year. In 1911, the institution began to make progress under President Robert S. Wilkinson, a alumnus. South Carolina State granted the bachelor's degree in 1924. It included sixty faculty members and a state appropriation of $150,000 by 1927. Northern philanthropic funds assisted the institution in its quest toward real college status.

One of South Carolina State's notable graduates was Ernest Everett Just. He entered South Carolina State at the age of thirteen in 1896. His examination scores were good enough to place him in the Classical Preparatory Department. He advanced quickly through the normal department and graduated as a licensed teacher in 1899. He entered Kimball Union Academy in Vermont, did some remedial work to catch up with the northern students, and finished the four-year classical course in three years. He then attended Dartmouth College, majoring in biology and science, and became the only Negro graduate in 1907. Howard University hired Just to teach literature and rhetoric, among other subjects, and in 1901 included him in the newly organized department of biology, which he later came to head. In 1922, South Carolina State offered him the honorary doctorate. He recommended his graduate students for faculty positions at South Carolina State College and gained the support of northern philanthropic agencies, including the General Education Board, Rosenwald Fund, and Rockefeller Foundation for faculty fellowships and research grants. In its new building (built in1910), Howard's science program excelled, and by 1940, Ernest Just published seventy-five research articles and two books: *The Biology of*

---

[75] "History of SC State University," http://www.scsu.edu/about scstate, South Carolina State University, 2010; John F. Marszalek, *A Black Congressman in the Age of Jim Crow: South Carolina's George Washington Murray* (Gainesville: University of Florida Press, 2006) 33, 100, 119.

the Cell Surface (1939) and *Basic Methods for Experiments on Eggs of Marine Animals* (1939).[76]

In 1920, Charleston had 35,582 whites and 32,326 Negroes. Charleston County had 44,214 whites and 64,236 Negroes. Some 22 percent of the local Negroes were illiterate. In 1923–1924, South Carolina spent $11.4 million in public funds on white education and $1.4 million on education for Negro citizens, who still outnumbered whites. From 1919 through 1929, the General Education Board persuaded South Carolina to hire a state agent for Negro education. Rosenwald funds built 381 Negro schools in South Carolina by 1929 to house 57,105 students, 34 percent of the rural Negro school population. This expansion of access to secondary education for Negroes in South Carolina helped advance the state's HBCUs, including Allen University, Benedict College, Claflin College, Clinton Junior College, Denmark Technical College, Morris College, South Carolina State University, and Voorhees College. The HBCUs now had a more qualified student pool from which to recruit new students. Under a state white supremacy government, the University of South Carolina continued to bar black citizens until the Civil Rights Act of 1964 forced South Carolina to begin racial desegregation.

The white South Carolinians, still "fighting the Civil War," however, as were other predominantly white state colleges, minimized black enrollment by setting higher admissions standards despite the crippling educational effects their Jim Crow practices, laws, and regulations had imposed on four generations of black South Carolinians. On the other hand, like other Southern colleges that could not compete nationally after the integration of 1964, USC readily enrolled black athletes to help win athletic contests. Still, USC enrolled only a small percentage of the state's African American citizens in the regular curricula. Coming from mostly one-race, *de facto* re-segregated and poorer quality public schools, indubitably, black South Carolinians continued to have a hard time competing socio-economically with the whites. Migration to the industrial Northern cities caused the state's black population to decline from 58.9 percent in 1860 to 30 percent by 2008. By 2010, South Carolina State University still could not compete equally with the state's white state colleges and universities.

Virginia State College began as a black Morrill land-grant program in 1872. Like South Carolina State College, this public institution began as a department at a private HBCU, Hampton Institute. Negro Republicans and other black politicians

[76] Kenneth R. Manning, *Black Apollo of Science: The Life of Ernest Everett Just* (New York: Oxford University Press, 1983) 18, 19, 130, 137, 234, 266.

enjoyed near full political participation in Virginia, 1871–1898, when about 85 of them held public offices. However, most of them were racial accommodationists, who feared white power. Thus, though blacks represented 42 percent of the people, they received no comparable consideration from the whites.

On 6 March 1882, the Virginia legislature chartered Virginia Normal and Collegiate Institute for Negroes. They later located the school in Chesterfield County across the Appomattox River from Petersburg. A legislator sponsored a hostile lawsuit, delaying the opening until 1 October 1883. The Virginia Normal and Collegiate Institute had 126 students and seven faculty members, one building, thirty-three acres, a 200-book library, and a $20,000 budget. Tuition was $3.35 plus room and board. The first normal (two-year) department class graduated in 1886: Lucretia Campbell, Carrie Bragg, Willie Davis, Susie Douglass, Robert Green, Jerry Lucas, James Shields, and Fannie Walker. The class photograph showed four black teachers and president John M. Langston.[77]

The advancement of education for the former slaves and other Negroes, as well as the establishment of higher educational institutions for them was a slow but a definite movement. By 1870, a few hundred American Negroes had received various levels of higher education, including twenty-eight collegiate degrees, while 10,000 white Americans had college degrees. None of the HBCUs offered a bachelor's degree by 1870. By the 1880s, Negro school attendance increased from five to more than 40 percent, while white attendance increased from 20 to more than 60 percent. Negroes and American philanthropists had created high schools, normal schools, and sixteen colleges for twelve thousand students. A quarter of all Negroes could read and write by 1880. Eight of the HBCUs had an extensive college curriculum by 1885 and thirty-three offered collegiate training by 1900.[78]

The former slaves and their descendants needed more wide spread access to higher education by the 1880s. By mid-1880, no one really knew in what directions the hundreds of black schools would evolve, while the number of schools and colleges for blacks continued to increase. Negro leaders, concerned northern industrialists and philanthropists, and others continued to debate Negro curricula issues. Some of them argued whether Christian education, trades and manual labor, industrial arts, teacher-education training, and few liberal arts courses should continue to dominant Negro education, while white Americans were busy reforming their system of education. They were seeking to

---

[77] "About VSU," http://www.vsu.edu, Virginia State University, 2010.

[78] Irwin Unger, *These United States: The Questions of Our Past* (New York: Prentice Hall, 1989) 431; Du Bois, *The College-Bred Negro*, 12, 13, 14, 15. Du Bois estimated 2,331 Negro college graduates between 1826 and1899 (37).

improve American institutions along the lines of centuries-old European universities. Many black leaders wanted their white benefactors, friends, and supporters to help Negroes equal the pace of white educational advancement. Negro leaders wanted to train blacks for the new industrial economy, produce black professionals and educated leaders. Once-enslaved Negroes were trying to catch up and realize the American dream after slavery had held them back.

Among the late nineteenth-century black leaders pushing for expanded Negro education was Booker T. Washington, who had recently founded the Tuskegee Institute in rural Alabama. He spoke on "The Educational Outlook in the South" to the National Education Association (NEA) meeting in Boston in 1884. He focused on whites helping blacks and Negroes helping themselves to improve their access to secondary and industrial education. He said, "Brains, property, and character for the Negro will settle the question of civil rights."[79] He acknowledged white missionaries and philanthropists. However, Washington said,

> Any movement for the elevation of the southern Negro in order to be successful must have to a certain extent the cooperation of the southern whites. They control government and own the property—whatever benefits the black man benefits the white man. The proper education of all the whites will benefit the Negro as much as the education of the Negro will benefit the whites.[80]

As the debate about the quality and direction of Negro education became louder, northern philanthropic men and the agents of a rapid developing American industrial capitalism sent, in January 1885, an envoy, Henry Brown of Oberlin, to address Negro leaders attending the World Exposition in New Orleans. The wealthy industrialists wanted to test their recent ideas about focusing on industrial education for educating Negro youth. The northerners wanted to further the use of education to bring civility and progress to the southern region. As well, if they could tap southern raw resources and the region's cheap labor, the northern industrialists could make American capitalism a world power and a real moneymaking machine. However, they had to tranquilize the southern region, and do this carefully without threatening the southern Bourbon and planter-classes with any pretense of "racial equality." The wealthy and well-traveled Americans knew about the ethnic conflicts and racial separatism in Europe. Therefore, they opted for domestic tranquility and

---

[79] Hugh Hawkins, *Booker T. Washington and His Critics: Black Leadership in Crisis* (Lexington MA: D. C. Heath and Company, 1974) 3–17.

[80] Ibid.

development of a post-Civil War society where American blacks and whites would *coexist* within a thriving economy—all for the betterment of American capitalism.

Mifflin W. Gibbs, author of *Shadow and Light: An Autobiography* (1902), to which Washington wrote the introduction, reported the results of the New Orleans meeting. The Negro delegates said they wanted schools to prepare Negro youth for "some useful and profitable means of livelihood, considering the restrictions engendered by the trades unions, and the obstacles of race prejudice."[81] Gibbs, Blanche K. Bruce, Frederick Douglass, P. B. S. Pinchback, W. G. Simmons, T. Thomas Fortune, and others had signed "A Call for a Conference on 'Schools of Trade'" for Negroes:

> Emancipated, turned loose, poor, ignorant and houseless, continually surrounded by difficulties and embarrassments sufficient to appall and retard, by commendable effort on their part, sustained by the generous aid of philanthropists friendly to education, our race in the South has made gratifying advance, mentally and morally. But with this progress of mind and morals, we are confronted with the need of opportunity to qualify ourselves for those activities and industries necessary to make a people prosperous and happy.... In view of this vital necessity the undersigned do hereby call a conference, without distinction, of delegates appointed by mass meetings in cities and counties; presiding officers of colleges, principals of schools, bishops, and leading ministers; editors and publishers friendly to the movement are also invited to meet at New Orleans, Louisiana, January 15, 1885, for expression on this subject.[82]

Gibbs believed "the conference ... to promote industrial education ... failed to be fruitful," because the religious organizations wanted the movement of race advancement "launched under some particular denominational control." Yet, Gibbs believed they had to be involved because churches were "our largest organizations;" they had "the ear of the [Negro] masses." He believed the annual "industrial fairs ... held by the colored people in different southern states" also reached the Negro masses that attended these several-days fairs to see the military drill by the Negro militia companies, like the Douglass Guards in Nashville.

T. Thomas Fortune, who studied at Howard University before settling in New York and starting newspapers including the *Globe*, the *Freeman*, and the New York *Age*, said, "I simply maintain that the sort of education the colored

---

[81] Mifflin W. Gibbs, *Shadow and Light: An Autobiography* (Lincoln: University of Nebraska Press, 1995) 201–203, 203–219; Du Bois, *The Souls of Black Folk*, 89–90.

[82] Gibbs, *Shadow and Light*, 201–203, 203–219; Du Bois, *The Souls of Black Folk*, 89–90.

people of the South stand most in need of is elementary and industrial. They should [receive instruction] for the work to be done.... Education is the preparation of the mind for future work."[83] On 17 September 1883, Fortune had testified before the US Senate Committee about the conditions of the Negro population. The 1880 US Census said blacks had increased to 6.5 million compared to 757,208 in 1790, and the Negroes now owned 140,000 farms, homes and industries. Fortune said,

> The greatest misfortune which the government inflicted upon us up to the close of the war was the almost universal illiteracy of the masses—illiteracy which was designed and made irrevocable the most stringent of statutory enactments. Our intellectual and material poverty, absolute bankruptcy, was caused by the government, which closed the book of knowledge to us and denied us the common right to accumulate [wealth]. We are not responsible even today for the widespread poverty ... among us. We have not the facilities and aptitude to amass large fortunes by speculation and peculation, but we are learning to emulate the virtuous example or our white fellow citizens in this regard.... Aside from the vastly inadequate work being done in the South by the states, it should not be omitted here that northern churches and organizations and individuals contribute annually to the education of the freedmen quite as much as the states; but the contributions from these sources are uncertain and fluctuating.... We need a national board of education, adequate compensation for black labor, stoppage of chain gang labor, and respect of black rights.[84]

Prominent at the New Orleans meeting was William J. Simmons (1849–1890), a Baptist minister and founder of an HBCU. He wrote *Men of Mark: Eminent, Progressive and Rising* (1887),[85] because he was afraid younger Negroes had no knowledge about great black men and the importance of education. He filled the book with photographs and biographies of these men. He said, "I admire these men. I have faith in my people. I wish to exalt them. I want their lives snatched from obscurity to become household... conversation."[86] Simmons recognized black women by saying "To the women of our race," especially to the devoted, self-sacrificing mothers" who gave birth to great black men.[87] Simmons

---

[83] Gibbs, *Shadow and Light*, 210–11.

[84] Ibid., 367; see David H. Jackson, *Booker T. Washington and the Struggle against White Supremacy: The Southern Educational Tours, 1908–1912* (New York: Palgrave Macmillan, 2008) 1–31.

[85] Simmons, *Men of Mark*, preface, 1–23, 64–65, 144, 512, 1026.

[86] Ibid., 1–62, 50.

[87] Ibid., 1–62, 55.

believed Negro girls need education in domestic economy, cookery, photography, printing, nursing, poultry-raising, stenography, type-writing, artistic painting, dairying, etc. He attended Rochester University in New York before completing his studies at Howard University in 1873. After serving as a school principal in Washington, DC, Simmons headed south and became pastor of the First Colored Baptist Church in Lexington, Kentucky. In September 1880, the General Association of Colored Baptists of Kentucky selected him president of the new Normal and Theological Institute ("Simmons University"), and in 1882 he became editor of the *American Baptist* newspaper. Simmons chaired the Kentucky State Colored Men's Convention, and served on the committee on education and labor for the 1883 National Colored Men's Convention. The delegates petitioned Congress to set aside unclaimed bounty money of Negro soldiers to support colored high schools. On 25 August 1886, Simmons' call for the Negro Baptists to unite their efforts led to formation of the American National Baptist Convention. Simmons and other black leaders protested the railroad companies selling first-class tickets to blacks and then placing them in dirty smoking cars. Simmons protested racial lynching and the whites' denial of meaningful government positions to Negro citizens. "We are the ruled class and have no share in government," he said.[88] Simmons disagreed with leading Negro men about focusing on industrial education. Simmons said to fellow blacks, "If the Industrial craze be not watched our literary institutions will be turned into workshops and our scholars into servants and journeymen. Keep the literary and industrial apart.... We need scholars."[89]

The seventy-three-year-old Frederick Douglass also attended the New Orleans meeting. Douglass said, "The real problem, which this nation has to solve, and the solution of which it will have to answer for in history, were better described as the white man's problem.... The question is whether the white man ever can be elevated to that plane of justice, humanity and Christian civilization which will permit Negroes, Indians and Chinamen, and other darker colored races to enjoy an equal chance in the race of life."[90] Douglass had no formal education, but the old former slave and former abolitionist leader maintained considerable influence in black affairs until he died in 1895. In the 1870s and the1880s, Douglass was a popular visitor to the Negro colleges, and the books authored by Douglass were read by many Negro students.

Indeed, as exhibited by the leadership of the 1880s, many Negro leaders benefited from having access to higher education. George H. White of North

---

[88] Ibid., 49, 87, 363, 365, 367, 799.

[89] Ibid., 52–53.

[90] Ibid.

Carolina, a graduate of Howard University, was the last black Reconstruction congressional representative. Henry P. Cheatham, educated at Shaw University, became Recorder of Deeds for District of Columbia. Judson W. Lyons, a graduate of Howard became Register of the US Treasury. Joseph A. Booker, a student at Arkansas Branch Normal and a graduate of Roger Williams University, helped found Arkansas Baptist College. George Washington Williams, a USCT veteran, attended Howard University, and published *History of the Negro Race in America from 1619–1880* (1882) and *A History of the Negro Troops in the War of the Rebellion* (1887).[91]

The development of Negro leadership by northern institutions and the rising HBCUs was crucial to the overall development and advancement of all black Americans. Though few in number, college-educated Negroes continued to protest and petition against the rising tide of white supremacy in America and the unchecked tendencies of southern Jim Crow to become absolute in its brutal and inhumane behavior. Educated blacks also provided an important liaison with the northern philanthropists who continued to develop programs to uplift Negro education, secondary, and higher education. Some 240 Americans received PhD degrees in 1900; one American Negro, Du Bois, held a PhD degree.[92] Northern missionaries, the Union Army, the Freedmen's Bureau, philanthropists, Negro leaders, churches, and religious denominations could take the credit for this educational progress in America,[93] which to some observers seemed very little. Yet, Negro Americans had made educational progress in the face of great white resistance, especially in the southern United States. Over the next generation, Negro men and women educators worked with the northern philanthropists to advance as many of the so-called HBCUs to real collegiate status. This advancement was for the benefit of the entire American nation. Indeed, the period of 1890–1945 would be a complex, feverish one for the history of America's black colleges and universities.

---

[91] George Washington Williams, *The Negro Race in America from 1619 to 1880: Negroes as Slaves, as Soldiers, and as Citizens* (New York: G.P. Putnam Sons, 1882); G. W. Williams, *A History of the Negro Troops in the War of the Rebellion, 1861–1865* (New York: Harper and Brothers, 1887); John Hope Franklin, *George Washington Williams: A Biography* (Chicago: University of Chicago Press, 1998) 1–30.

[92] Unger, *These United States*, 597.

[93] Gibbs, *Shadow and Light*, 217.

2

"The Strange Career of Jim Crow"

The creation of artificial categories of "race," especially as defined in the nineteenth century, led to defining the quantity and quality of education for "whites" and for "blacks." For many American leaders, there simply was no logic in having racial categories at all while also proclaiming racial equality; after all, ethnic equality was not a fact in turbulent Europe. The creation of the American concepts of "white" and "black" had grown out of the need for many European Americans to bolster the ideal of ethnic supremacy in America, just as ethnic rivalry and wars characterized Europe. Europeans in America developed a racial system based on skin color and geographical origin for the three major groups of Americans: European Americans (whites), African Americans (blacks), and Native Americans (Indians). Concepts of ethnicity and race emphasized "us" against "them."[1]

Many persons believed Native Americans and the former slaves would die out, leaving the rich North American continent to Europeans only. Negro leader Frederick Douglass said, "We are kept back by prejudice and the idea the Negro, like the Indian, will die out.... How absurd. Die Out? Never! We survived slavery and new laws to prevent our intermarriage. Our destiny is in our hands." The whites, who have been free of European tyranny, enslavement, and ethnic oppression for many generations, should not criticize blacks about slow progress. "The wonder is, not that the freedmen have made so little progress, but, rather, that they have made so much—not that they have been standing still, but that they have been able to stand at all," said Douglass.[2]

The debates about ethnicity and race affected how the dominant white Americans in the late nineteenth and early twentieth centuries viewed African Americans' desire to access public and private education equally. However, despite concerns expressed by black leaders, including B. T. Washington, T. Thomas Fortune, and Frederick Douglass, at the Colored Men's Convention at

---

[1] See C. Vann Woodward, *The Strange Career of Jim Crow* (New York: Oxford University Press, 1966) for discussion of the origins of the Jim Crow system.

[2] Waldo E. Martin Jr., *The Mind of Frederick Douglass* (Chapel Hill: UNC Press, 1984) 73; Frederick Douglass, *Life and Times of Frederick Douglass* (Boston: The Library of America, 1994) 503; F. Douglass, "Self-Made Men," *Nashville Union and American*, 18 September 1873, p. 1.

New Orleans, while struggling to realize the American dream for their own kind, whites had little desire to truly make America a racial melting pot complete with real, equal opportunities. Most white Americans were not "prepared to spend more money on institutions for blacks to enable them to graduate students who could compete effectively with whites.... Northern philanthropists and missionary associations were not prohibited from developing private black colleges so long as these institutions would accommodate the dominant/subordinate relationship between whites and blacks in the South," said Tilden J. LeMelle."[3]

Fortunately, after 1890, a number of moderates and liberals, especially among American industrialists and the plutocracy, believed America needed to eradicate the most brutal aspects of Jim Crow (racial segregation) and bring tranquility to American society in order to enhance the possibility of America economically dominating an ethnically turbulent old Europe. Yet, they, too, believed in subtle expressions of white supremacy in America, and some forms of ethnic separatism, but these wealthy Americans accepted the moral idea of giving blacks the opportunities to develop educationally along lines *parallel* to whites though remaining socially *separate* as two distinct racial groups in America.

This moral concession to human rights and black initiative helped create several more HBCUs.

Lincoln Institute (1910–1970), Swift Memorial College (1883–1955), and Manual Labor University (1868–1874) exemplified the birth and death of many nineteenth-century HBCUs. All three of these institutions of higher education focused on secondary education, training teachers, manual labor, and agricultural and industrial education. They illustrated how Negro access to higher education through the early integrated colleges could give African Americans a head start in developing a small cadre of Negro educators who, in turn, could help establish, lead, and maintain post-Civil War HBCUs. However, these institutions also exemplified how dependent the post-Emancipation Negroes were upon white resources that were so badly needed to operate quality institutions of higher education in America.

Daniel Wadkins and Samuel Lowery, free Negroes who had studied at Franklin College, helped to establish a freedmen's school—Tennessee Manual Labor University. Daniel Wadkins, born free in Nashville at the age of nineteen,

---

[3] Tilden J. LeMelle, "The HBCU: Yesterday, Today and Tomorrow," *Education* 123 (2000): 1, 190. Ina C. Brown, *The Story of the American Negro* (New York: Friendship Press, 1938) 11; Ina C. Brown, *National Survey of Higher Education of Negroes*, 3 vols. (Washington DC: US Department of Education [USDOE], 1942) 1:1–6, 55.

headed a school in 1839 and operated it until 1857 when white vigilantes entered the room and ordered him to shut the school down. After Union Army occupation, Wadkins reopened the classes. He teamed with local white Republicans and won election to the Nashville city council in 1867. Samuel Lowery, another of Manual Labor's founders, was born in 1836, about twelve miles from Nashville, to a Negro and a free Cherokee woman. Samuel joined the Christian Church (Disciples of Christ) in 1849 and attended Colored Christian Church headed by his father, Peter. In 1858, Samuel went to Cincinnati to pastor the Harrison Street Christian Church. He left for Canada, headed a church or two nearby in New York State, and remained in the area until 1861. He returned to farm in Ohio, made his way back to Nashville in 1863, and served as chaplain and teacher for the 9th US Colored Heavy Artillery.

In December 1867, Wadkins, Lowery, and others in the Colored Christian (Disciples of Christ) Church formed Tennessee Manual Labor University on the eastern outskirts of Nashville. They modeled the curricula after the white Franklin College (1855–1862), which had taught agriculture, manual labor courses, trades, and reading, writing, arithmetic, and some classics. The Annual Tennessee Colored Agricultural and Mechanical Fair (1866–1882), promoted this kind of freedmen's education. Tennessee Manual Labor University enrolled the first class of a hundred students the following January. The white Vine Street Christian Church, from which the Colored Christian Church originated, gave them neither sanction nor support. None of the Southern Christian denominations helped the freedmen establish schools between 1865 and 1924.

Moreover, many Northern whites seemed to prefer to give donations to HBCUs operated by Northern missionaries and educators. In 1868, because so many men claimed to raise money for infant HBCUs that the Northern churches were inundated, Wadkins solicited a letter of support from Frederick Douglass, who responded in a letter, saying, "I consider you an entirely trustworthy man, and your mission highly important, not only to the colored people as a class, but of the first importance to the whole country."[4] Negro founders of black schools often had little success raising money among whites in either the North or the South. Tennessee Manual Labor University suffered financial trouble, but in November 1872, a Negro—Sampson W. Keeble—gained election to the Tennessee General Assembly, and in 1873 submitted a money bill for Manual Labor University. The bill failed to pass, and the school closed a few years later.

---

[4] D. Wadkins to the Benevolent Citizens of New York, Nashville, a printed appeal, December 1867, American Missionary Association Papers, Tennessee files, Amistad Research Center, Tulane University, New Orleans LA.

The General Assembly gave funds to two white private schools in Tennessee, 1869–1905.

Samuel Lowery then formed another freedmen's school and taught nearby until local Klansmen broke it up. Some whites in Middle Tennessee claimed education ruined the Negro so that he no longer wanted to work the farms and plantations—at least for the slave wages they wanted him to accept. Some whites talked of bringing in Chinese laborers, but that movement collapsed when Congress passed the Chinese Immigration Exclusion Act (1882). Lowery moved to Alabama and formed another freedmen's school, the Industrial Academy for Negroes. With the help of local white businesspersons, he started Lowery Industrial Silk Culture and Manufacturing Company.[5] Lowery's venture, and the effort by all-black groups to establish schools and colleges, often failed to attract much capital from whites in the late nineteenth century, and even in the Northern states, the development of schools and colleges for blacks had a difficult time without white support.

Central State University began in 1887 as an Ohio state-funded industrial department of private Wilberforce University. However, in fear of Jim Crow advancing north, some upper-class blacks objected to granting a separate state program for Negroes. In a gesture of racial accommodation, the state of Ohio supported the Department of Normal and Industrial Education alongside the private program at Wilberforce University. After all, Cincinnati had a public school program and separate board for Negroes by the mid-1850s. The dual program at Wilberforce was troublesome. In 1941, the state of Ohio changed the name to the College of Education and Industrial Arts, and North Central Association of Colleges and Schools (NCACS) granted accreditation in 1943, but then withdrew approval in 1947 because of continued administrative problems. The state court chartered the College of Education and Industrial Arts separately from Wilberforce University. Finally, in 1951 it became Central State College, then gained university status in 1965, and took the name Central State University by 1986—counting among its 10,045 graduates 204 that had earned doctorate degrees.[6]

---

[5] William K. Pendleton, "Tennessee Manual Labor University," *Millennial Harbinger* 30 (1868): 25–27; David Mills and B. Lovett, "Samuel Lowery," in Bobby L. Lovett and Linda T. Wynn, eds., *Profiles of Africans in Tennessee* (Nashville: Local Conference on Afro-American Culture and History, 1996) 80–81; George W. Hubbard, *The Colored Schools in Nashville, Tennessee* (Nashville: G. W. Hubbard, 1868) 1–15.

[6] Lathardus Goggins, *Central State University: The First One Hundred Years, 1897–1987* (Wilberforce: Central State University, 1987) 1–81; http://www.centralstate.edu, Central State University, 2010.

Jim Crow legislation peaked in the South by 1890, and lynching saw a dramatic rise. Biracial colleges expelled Negroes, but two of them, Berea and Maryville Colleges, defiantly created HBCUs for displaced black students. Indeed, despite the brutality of Jim Crow and white supremacy, humanitarianism and the principle of brotherhood had not died in the hearts of all Americans.

After *Berea College v. Commonwealth of Kentucky*, 211 US 45 (1908) upheld Kentucky's Day Law (1904), the Negro students had to leave Berea College, and efforts to establish a Negro college nearby began immediately. Local whites opposed the move. With $200,000 seed money from northern steel magnate Andrew Carnegie's foundation, Berea trustees purchased three farms in Simpsonville, east of Louisville and near a black population center. They planned to establish Lincoln Institute, but local white residents secured a state law requiring voter approval for a school established in the county. The Kentucky courts declared the act unconstitutional; however, the effort to establish a college for Negroes moved elsewhere.

Berea trustees opened Lincoln Institute in Lincoln Ridge, near Louisville, on 1 October 1910. By 1914, the institution had enrolled 104 students in elementary, secondary, normal, industrial, manual labor, and agricultural courses. In the 1930s, the institution had eight white and seven black teachers and offered high school to junior college curricula. Unfortunately, a lack of resources forced this black school to drop the junior college department. Whitney M. Young, Sr., served as the first Negro president. Despite Young's building the curriculum in vocational education, economics, nursing, agriculture, religion, and building and maintenance trades, black Kentuckians still had no access to a four-year college, except for public Kentucky State College. The most famous graduate, Whitney M. Young, Jr., graduated from Lincoln Institute at age fourteen, completed a bachelor's degree at Kentucky State College, and graduate studies at the University of Minnesota. He taught at Atlanta University and eventually became head of the National Urban League.

After the US Supreme Court issued the *Brown v. Board of Education* (1954) decision, enrollment at Lincoln Institute steadily declined because Negroes now had educational opportunities at integrated public schools. The final graduation occurred in June 1966, and Lincoln Institute completely closed in 1970. Its remnant became a boarding high school under the Lincoln Foundation and continued serving socio-economically disadvantaged youth in grades seven through twelve. Thirty-two high school students graduated in 2005, all of them receiving college scholarships. The Lincoln Institute Alumni Foundation established the Whitney M. Young Scholarships.[7]

In 1901, a Tennessee Jim Crow law forced Maryville College to expel Negro students. Again, *Berea College v. Kentucky* (1908) approved such state Jim Crow laws. However, Maryville College trustees transferred a quarter of the endowment to Swift Memorial College.

William H. Franklin, a graduate of Maryville College and a Negro pastor of a local Presbyterian congregation, founded Swift Memorial College in 1883 in Rogersville, Tennessee. The Presbyterian Board of Missions for Freedmen supported this HBCU, including the building of dormitories in 1903 and the start of a four-year college curriculum in 1904. By 1909, the Board of Missions for Freedmen of the Presbyterian Church in the USA continued supporting the institution, which by then had 208 students, ten teachers, and a budget of $12,000. In 1916, the US Bureau of Education recommended that Swift Memorial could only achieve junior college status with such limited resources. Almost 83 percent of the budget came from the Presbyterian Board of Freedmen's Missions. Franklin retired in 1926, but Swift Memorial Junior College continued expanding until the Presbyterian Board of Missions ended its support in 1952. Soon after *Brown v. Board of Education* (1954), Maryville College once again admitted black students, and Swift Memorial Junior College closed in 1955.[8]

Negro Americans not only struggled to gain educational funds from the coffers of wealthy white America, but blacks struggled to gain a fair share of public funding for their higher education. Shortly after emancipation, former slave states Delaware and Maryland had to confront the issue of higher education for freedmen, but their response was to do as little as possible.

In Delaware, white hostility toward free Negroes caused the black population to decline from 22 percent in 1840 to 18 percent by 1860. Whites closed admission of free Negro citizens to all the tax-aided schools. The 1860 US Census reported 112,216 blacks living in Delaware, compared to the 275,000 Negroes living in the slave state of Tennessee. The latter state, approved the proposed 13th Amendment by March 1865, but Delaware, a border state, retained slavery until ratification of the 13th Amendment on 18 December 1865. Thereafter, "the classification of Delawareans by race was left to the intuitive

---

[7] Lincoln Institute Alumni Website, www.lincolninstitutealumni.com, 2005.

[8] "History," www.maryvillecollege.edu, Maryville College, 2007; Linda T. Wynn, "Swift Memorial College (1883–1955)," in Lovett and Wynn, eds., *Profiles of American Americans in Tennessee*, 118–119; "Maryville College," in Carroll Van West, ed., *Tennessee Encyclopedia of History and Culture* (Knoxville: University Press, Tennessee Historical Society, and Rugledge Hill Press, 1998) 76–77.

judgment of whites," said W. H. Williams.[9] Unlike Tennessee, Delaware had no *legal* racial definition that distinguished blacks from whites. By 1865, private funds supported seven schools for black Delawareans, yet only three percent of black Delawareans attended school. About half of the state's Negroes were still illiterate as late as 1890. Williams wrote, "intense racism became part of the heritage of twentieth-century Delaware and provided the rationale for the ongoing mistreatment of African Americans."[10]

Delaware State University (founded 1891) grew out of such post-emancipation experiences of blacks. As a white supremacist state, Delaware sought to prevent the integration of large numbers of Negroes into existing traditionally white institutions (TWIs). Thus, on 15 May 1891, the Delaware General Assembly authorized Delaware State College for Colored Students—a quarter of a century after the emancipation. With this decision, Delaware whites meant, in part, to satisfy federal requirements of the 1890 Land Grant amendment. The school began with a mere seven students. The preparatory department began in 1893, and the three-year normal school (teacher training) curriculum began in 1897. The institution granted its first normal school degrees in 1898.

By 1912, Delaware State had extended its college program to four years, and it phased out the preparatory program in favor of a high school diploma in 1916. Model school and junior college divisions existed by 1923. The faculty and staff extended the college curricula into arts and sciences, elementary education, home economics, and industrial arts in 1932, and the first college class graduated in 1934. Delaware State received MSACS provisional accreditation in 1945; the name became Delaware State College in 1947. However, MSACS revoked accreditation for failure to maintain required standards in 1949 but restored it in 1957. In 1993, this HBCU became Delaware State University. DSU had four hundred acres, six colleges, and 3,722 students from twenty-eight states and thirty-one countries, 168 faculty members (83.3 percent doctorates), programs in instruction, service, and research, and more than 3,756 undergraduate and graduate students in 2005–2006. By 2010, DSU offered 55 undergraduate, 23 masters, and 5 doctoral degrees.[11]

Like Delaware, Maryland, was one of the original thirteen English colonies. After President Lincoln's Emancipation Proclamation of 1863, slaves left Maryland in large numbers. Many of them fled to nearby Washington, DC,

---

[9] William H. Williams, *Slavery and Freedom in Delaware, 1639–1865* (Wilmington DE: SR Books, 1996) 238, 243.

[10] Ibid.

[11] "About DSU," www.dsu.edu/history, 2010.

where Congress had abolished slavery in the district in June 1862. Although the Emancipation Proclamation did not apply to the border states, one of them—Maryland—(through Lincoln's nurturing) abolished slavery in 1864.

Former Maryland slaves converted to wage labor, tenancy, and sharecropping, yet still had no citizenship rights. In December 1865, the delegates at the Maryland State Colored Men's Convention demanded, "Manhood rights which are enjoyed by the white citizens of this state," said Richard P. Fuke. Like Delaware next door, Maryland, by 1865, had only seven private schools for Negroes. The public school system included Negroes in 1867. However, most education for black Marylanders remained privately funded until 1872. Fuke also wrote, "Black Marylanders neither enjoyed total freedom nor suffered absolute coercion, but their struggle made two things clear: much of whatever they might accomplish, they would have to do by themselves; and such efforts would remain confined by white attitudes determined to regulate them."[12]

Bowie State University (founded 1854) exemplified educational initiatives by Maryland Negroes, and is an example of how some HBCUs founded by blacks survived by gaining public funding. Bowie State began on 9 January 1865, founded by the Baltimore Association for the Moral and Educational Improvement of Colored People, which had existed since 28 November 1864. Bowie State is the oldest HBCU in Maryland as a school operated in the African Baptist Church. The Freedmen's Bureau provided some support, and after 1870, the institution occasionally received financial support from the city of Baltimore. Philanthropist Nelson Wells gave money to help educate the freedmen at Bowie, and, after 1872, the state of Maryland assisted, too. The school became a normal school to train teachers in 1883, and Negro protest forced Baltimore to hire Negro public schools teachers in 1888. The state board of education assumed control in 1908, and relocated Bowie College to a 187-acre site in Prince George County.

The name became Maryland Normal and Industrial School at Bowie in 1914. Maryland State Teachers College at Bowie became a three-year-college for training teachers in 1925, adding the bachelor's program in 1935, and becoming Maryland State Teachers College at Bowie in 1951. The National Council for Accreditation in Teacher Education (NCATE) approved Bowie in 1958. MSACS accredited Bowie in 1961. Full secondary education began in 1961, the liberal arts college program began in 1963, and Bowie State College began offering graduate degrees in education in 1970. The faculty and staff organized the Adler-Dreikurs

---

[12] Richard P. Fuke, *Imperfect Equality: African Americans and the Confines of White Racial Attitudes in Post-emancipation Maryland* (New York: Fordham University Press, 1999) 238, 250.

Institute of Human Relations in 1975. The institution became Bowie State University and part of the University System of Maryland on 1 July 1988, and in 1994, the Maryland Higher Education Commission affirmed Bowie's mission, heritage, and special commitment to the African American community and for identifying a special focus on computer and technology applications and teacher education.

By 2005, the institution was offering twenty-one undergraduate and eighteen graduate programs, a dual degree in engineering and dentistry, and the first HBCU satellite program overseas in partnership with the University of Maryland. Also in 2005, the first doctoral recipients earned the EdD. Bowie State programs aimed "to enable students to think critically, value diversity, become effective leaders, function competently in a highly technical world, and pursue advanced graduate study."[13]

Another Maryland HBCU, Coppin State College (1900–) began as a teacher-training department in the "Colored High School," later called Douglass High School, in Baltimore. The department became a two-year normal program in 1902 and separated from the city high school in 1909. In 1926, this facility became the Fanny Jackson Coppin Normal School. A three-year college curriculum was added in 1931, and extended to four years by 1938. The institution became a part of the Maryland higher education system in 1950, was renamed Coppin State Teachers College, and moved to a 38-acre campus in 1952. MSACS accredited the institution in 1962. Coppin expanded beyond teacher education in 1963, became Coppin State College, and granted its first Bachelor of Arts degree in 1967. In 1972, Coppin was renamed Coppin State University, moved to a new location in 1974, and became part of the University System of Maryland on 1 July 1988. Collaborative arrangements with other institutions allowed Coppin students to pursue majors in four other areas including engineering, pharmacy, and dentistry. CSU developed unique programs in the Community Nursing Center to provide a medical clinic in affordable health care for local residents. The institution included the Coppin Academy public charter high school, grades nine through twelve. CSU became "a model urban, residential liberal arts university."[14]

---

[13] The *Bowie State University Fact Book, 2006–2007* (Bowie MD: Bowie State, 2007) 3; "About Bowie State," http://www.bowie.edu, 2010; Juan Williams and Dwayne Ashley, *I'll Find a Way or Make One: A Tribute to Historically Black Colleges and Universities* (New York: HarperCollins, 2004) 17, 333; Jessie C. Smith, ed., *Notable Black American Women* (Westport CT: Greenwood Press, 1992) 217, 224–228, 459, 461, 1095, 1097.

[14] "Welcome to Coppin State," http://www.coppin.edu/about, Coppin State University, 2010.

Morgan State University (1867–), an MEC school, was called the Centenary Biblical Institute before being renamed Morgan College in 1890 in honor of the Reverend Lyttleton (Littleton) Morgan, who donated land for the school. Morgan College awarded its first college degree in 1895. It became part of the University of Maryland system in July 1988 with a new mission to designate the institution as the state's public urban university with undergraduate and master's programs in engineering, business, architecture, and teacher education, and doctoral programs in a dozen areas.

The University of Maryland Eastern Shore (founded1886) began as Delaware Conference Academy, with a mere thirty-seven students, and was sponsored by the Delaware Conference of the Methodist Episcopal Church. By 1890, many knew the institution as Princess Anne Academy. Maryland assumed control in 1919 to satisfy the 1890 Morrill Land Grant Act, and named the institution the Eastern Shore Branch of the Maryland Agricultural College. The Negro land-grant institution became a state school outright in 1926, and was upgraded to a four-year college program in 1927. MSACS accredited the institution in 1937. In 1948, the school became Maryland State College. On 1 July 1970, Maryland State College became the University of Maryland Eastern Shore. Today, Eastern Shore offers master's degrees in at least twelve areas, and PhD programs in education, toxicology, marine-estuarine, environmental sciences, and applied computer science.

Despite a slow start, the four public HBCUs in the former slave state of Maryland gained the public and private resources needed to build accredited collegiate programs earlier than most public HBCUs. Across most of the former Confederate states, the expansion of higher education was painfully slow, especially in regards to Southern Negro cities, where the Jim Crow system limited the expansion of the HBCUs from 1900 to 1925. Because Jim Crow state governments withheld from Negro children the equal access they needed to gain quality secondary, college preparatory, and college education, the HBCUs had to fill the vacuum—often with limited resources. According to the writer A. L. Evans, "the HBCUs were not designed to succeed; rather they were established to appease black people or to serve as 'holding institutions' so that black students would not matriculate in historically white colleges and universities."[15]

---

[15] See histories for Coppin State, Eastern Shore, and Morgan State on http://www.coppin.edu/about, Coppin State University, 2010; http://www.umes.edu, "2009 UMES Annual Report," University of Maryland Estern Shore, 2010; http://www.morgan.edu, Morgan State University, 2010; see Toni H. Kennard, *The Handbook of Historically Black Colleges and Universities* (Wilmington DE: Jireh and Associates, 1994); A. L. Evans, "Historically Black Colleges and Universities (HBCUs)," *Education* 123/1

Still, the number of HBCUs continued to increase, and the 1890 Morrill Land Grant Act was a tremendous stimulus for the creation of public HBCUs, whose numbers of land-grant colleges increased from three to seventeen. Half these Negro schools existed before 1890, but without land-grant funds. On 30 August 1890, President Benjamin Harrison (R) signed an amendment to the 1862 Morrill Land-Grant Act:

> No money shall be paid out under this act to any State or Territory for the support and maintenance of a college where a distinction of race or color is made in the admission of students. But the establishment and maintenance of such college separately for white or colored students shall be held in compliance with the provisions of this act if the funds received in such State or Territory be equitably divided as hereinafter set forth.

West Virginia State College began as the West Virginia Colored Institute in 1891, but became predominantly white after integration in the 1960s. The West Virginia Board of Education surrendered the institution's land-grant status, but the college's black president Hazo W. Carter worked to get land-grant status restored by act of Congress by 2001. Kentucky State Normal and Industrial Institute, opened in October 1887 to train Negro teachers, became Kentucky State Industrial College in 1926 and received SACS approval in 1933. Florida A&M or State Normal and Industrial College for Colored Students opened 18 March 1891, included a college farm directed by former black US Congressman Josiah T. Walls, graduated its first students in 1921, and gained state recognition for four-year college status in 1927. Oklahoma recognized HBCU land grant Langston University (1897–) as a four-year institution in 1926.

Fort Valley State College began as the local Negro high school in 1895. It was designated the Teachers and Industrial College of Forsyth, and became Fort Valley College in 1939, with Horace Mann Bond as president. Bond published *The Education of the Negro in the American Social Order* (1934), and in 1936 completed his PhD at the University of Chicago. He improved on Fort Valley's two-year college into a four-year institution before leaving in 1945. In 1949,

---

(Fall 2002): 3–15. Evans's tables list HBCUs and founding dates. See also Walter R. Allen and Joseph O. Jewell, "A Backward Glance Forward: Past, Present, and Future Perspectives on Historically Black Colleges and Universities," *The Review of Higher Education* 25/3 (Spring 2002): 241–61; C. S. Person, "Revitalization of a Historically Black College: A Maryland Eastern Shore Case" (EdD dissertation, Virginia Polytechnic State University, 1998) 1–21.

Georgia designated Fort Valley the Negro land-grant school, and gave university status in 1996.[16]

The University of Arkansas at Pine Bluff (1875–) illustrates an intriguing story about the history of HBCUs within the era of Jim Crow. Joseph Carter Corbin, who was born in 1833 of free Negro parents in Virginia and moved to Chillicothe, Ohio, obtained his education in the local schools. At age fifteen, he taught in Louisville, Kentucky, before going to study at Ohio State University. Corbin returned to Louisville to work as a clerk, and in 1872 traveled to Little Rock, Arkansas, to edit the *Arkansas Republican*—governor's official newspaper. Under the Republican Party, Corbin became state superintendent of education, which made him ex-officio president of the board of trustees for the new Arkansas Industrial University (University of Arkansas) in 1872. The institution included access for Negroes, after some northern missionaries from Little Rock complained to the Republicans; however, no Negroes attended classes, and a separate branch of the university for Negroes did not start until 1875.

After the Reconstruction government was overthrown, Corbin lost his position. He left Arkansas to teach for two years at Lincoln Institute in Missouri. After Lincoln graduated its first class of students, Corbin returned to Little Rock, and in 1875, Governor Augustus H. Garland sent him to establish the Branch Normal College in Pine Bluff for Negroes; again, since most Negroes could not access the University of Arkansas in Fayetteville in the Ozark Mountains.

On 27 September 1875, the Branch Normal School for Negroes began in an old frame house on Lindsay Street in Pine Bluff. The city was about forty-four miles from Little Rock, and near predominantly black areas of the state. Corbin became founder, principal, teacher, and janitor for seven students. Enrollment rose to seventy-five students in 1875–1876, mostly in the elementary grades, and required no tuition. The school admitted any Negro resident of Arkansas if he or she could read at fourth grade level, and do some writing, arithmetic, and a little geography.

After Corbin petitioned the Arkansas legislature, they appropriated funds to construct a building and a hand-dug well on twenty acres on the western streets of Pine Bluff. Branch Normal new campus opened on 30 January 1882.

---

[16] C. S. Person, "Revitalization of a Historically Black College: A Maryland Eastern Shore Case" (EdD dissertation, Virginia Polytechnic State University, 1998) 1–20; F. W. Nicholas, "The Black Land-Grant Colleges: An Assessment of the Major Changes between 1965–66 and 1970–71" (EdD dissertation, University of Virginia, 1973) 1–20; Grace Vernell-Hill Norbrey, "A Study of the Development of the Land-Grant Program at Virginia State University, 1920–1983" (EdD dissertation, George Washington University, 1983) 1–11; Whittington B. Johnson, *Black Savannah, 1788–1864* (Fayetteville: University of Arkansas Press, 1996) 3–10, 25.

Corbin charged fees, including $1 a month to out-of-state students, and used the money to hire more personnel including a second teacher in 1885. In 1887, the boys boarded out in the homes of local citizens, but the school built a girls' dormitory. There were 250 students and five graduates.

Corbin was a learned man. He published articles on mathematics in northern education journals. He was "certainly one of the most scholastic men of the race," said the Arkansas *Weekly Gazette*.[17] After Corbin joined the losing side of state politics in 1893, the white supervisor of the industrial shops gained control of admissions, fees, and reports to the board of trustees of the University of Arkansas. There were five teachers and 206 students, but still no custodian. Enrollment dropped as the supervisor demanded more cash from students at Branch Normal. He reportedly took his orders from a trustee who lived in Pine Bluff, and they finally got Corbin dismissed in 1902. Corbin became principal of the local black public school.

Branch Normal hired another principal, Isaac Fisher, although the two local white men maintained control. Fisher, a graduate of Tuskegee Institute, tried to impose Booker T. Washington's model of industrial education upon Branch Normal. Corbin and local black leaders fought attempts to "downgrade" the state's only public HBCU. Branch Normal did not progress to the four-year level even by Corbin's death in 1911. The institution had about 130 elementary and forty secondary students, including twelve in the teacher education normal (two-year college) courses. A frustrated Fisher returned to Tuskegee, Alabama.

While whites enjoyed access to a full-fledged University of Arkansas, the Arkansas Branch Normal made progress as a junior college (normal school). In 1927, Arkansas appropriated $275,000 as matching funds to philanthropic funds to build new facilities, and the institution became Branch Normal College. The governor appointed seven whites and two blacks as trustees for the Negro college, and, as late as March 1967, two blacks and five whites posed for a photograph as the board of trustees. Meanwhile, in 1929, the state certified Branch Normal as a four-year college. Under the leadership of John Brown Watson, the institution completed the construction of collegiate buildings on the current site (Highway 79) in 1929, and moved to the new campus on 15 December. The new facilities consisted of the president's home, administration building, and brick dormitories. The college conferred the first two Bachelor of Arts degrees in 1930. The Watson administration built eight faculty cottages and a gymnasium in 1932, and two dormitories and a brick library in 1939 with financial help from philanthropic agencies, federal agencies, and state

[17] J. C. Corbin to the editor, *Arkansas Weekly Gazette* 28 October 1886, p. 1.

appropriations. By 1942, the institution became Arkansas Agricultural, Mechanical, and Normal State College.

Much of the Arkansas AM&N collegiate growth came under Lawrence A. Davis Sr., president from 1943 to 1973. A building program from 1950 to 1965 doubled the campus facilities. In 1967, forty-five of the graduates had earned doctorate degrees. President Davis said,

> The College had to set about its task limited by a rigidly economic, political, and social context. It functioned for more than eighty years of its history as a 'Negro' college with all the inherent and inevitable deficiencies and disadvantages incident to that status.... In the years ahead the College will be viewed and appraised within the emerging social context which it is at once helping usher in and which it is preparing young people.

On 1 July 1972, as result of the state's plan to desegregate higher education, Arkansas AM&N State College became the University of Arkansas at Pine Bluff. UAPB offered graduate degrees in the 1990s on a campus of 56 buildings, 318 acres, and a research farm of 871 acres.[18]

Tennessee offers another story of how Jim Crow practices decisively impeded the growth of Negro access to higher education. After passage of the 1890 amendment, the state of Tennessee allowed the University of Tennessee to establish a "Negro Department" at nearby Knoxville College (1875–)—a freedmen's school operated by the Board of Freedmen's Mission of the United Presbyterians. The university's "Negro Department" worked the students on a small Knoxville College farm, and the president and faculty ordered admission standards "lenient to the colored man" and modified courses "to suit the requirements of the students of this race," including shop work, manual labor courses and work on the Knoxville College farm "for pay." The university president said, "we believe that this College now provides the 'brother in black' the kind of education which he needs most." The University of Tennessee financed sixteen students at Knoxville College in 1891, expending $3,526.64 (5.2 percent of the federal land grant money), while the University of Tennessee was receiving $67,640 in federal land grant funds. In 1911, the University of Tennessee received $68,960 in federal funds, and gave Knoxville College $10,350

---

[18] S. L. Recken, "Rags to Respectability: Arkansas and Booker T. Washington," *Arkansas Historical Quarterly* (hereafter abbreviated *AHQ*) 57 (2008) 54–71; E. L. Wheeler, "Isaac Fisher: The Frustrations of a Negro Educator at Branch Normal College, 1901–1911," *AHQ* 41/1 (Summer 1982): 3–11; T. Rothrock, "Joseph Carter Corbin and Negro Education in the University of Arkansas," *AHQ* 30/4 (Winter 1971) 277–314; William H. Martin, "The Education of Negroes in Arkansas," *Journal of Negro Education* 16/3 (Summer 1947): 317–24.

(15 percent of the federal land grant money that was allocated to Tennessee) for Negroes.[19] The increase in money to Knoxville College was the result of Negro complaints that black citizens did not receive equal access to higher education funds in Tennessee under *Plessy v. Ferguson* (1896), the US Supreme Court decision that decreed a "separate but equal" principle.

In 1909, the state of Tennessee authorized the creation of four public normal schools—one each for whites in east, middle, and west Tennessee, and one, Tennessee Agricultural and Industrial State Normal School, for Negroes. The school for Negroes was added to the 1909 State Normal School bill after Negro leaders formed a black educational association and lobbied state officials to grant public higher education also to Negro citizens. Tennessee A&I State Normal School for Negroes opened in June 1912 with 250 students. In 1913, the state designated it the recipient of land-grant funds, which ended the arrangement between the University of Tennessee and Knoxville College. The HBCU land grant did not receive an equal portion according to the percentage of black Tennesseans, and this discrimination over the next half century reduced public help for rural black Tennesseans and Negro farmers. The under-funded Tennessee A&I was, like most HBCUs called a "land-grant institution," could not engage all three land-grant functions: teaching, research, and extension services.

While the Jim Crow system was careful to deny American Negroes equal access to higher education, America's black population (14 percent) increased 13.5 percent between 1880 and 1890. Negro percentages remained moderate to large in most of the former slave states, but white population growth increased 26 percent because of a large influx of European immigrants. American immigration quota acts excluded persons from Africa, Asia, and South America. The Negro Americans numbered 9,827,830 in 1910. Immigrants totaled 13 million, and the influx of Europeans diminished the Negro population's percentage from 20 percent in 1890 to 11 percent by 1910. Even so, Negroes still comprised 32.3 percent of the southern population; 50 percent in Mississippi and

---

[19] Samuel H. Shannon, "Agricultural and Industrial Education at Tennessee State University during the Normal Phase, 1912–1922: A Case Study" (doctoral dissertation, George Peabody College for Teachers, 1978) 1–31; S. H. Shannon ("Land-Grant College Education and Black Tennesseans: A Case Study in the Politics of Education," *History of Education Quarterly* 22/2 [Summer 1982] 139–57) quotes the University of Tennessee president; Lester C. Lamon, "The Tennessee Agricultural and Industrial Normal School: Public Education for Black Tennesseans," *Tennessee Historical Quarterly* 32/1 (Spring 1973) 42–58; Evelyn P. Fancher, "Tennessee State University, 1912–1974: A History of an Institution with Implications for the Future" (PhD dissertation, George Peabody College for Teachers, 1975) 1–37; Lois C. McDougald, *A Time Line Chronology of the Tennessee A. & I. State College Campus, 1909–1951* (Nashville: TSU Print Shop, 1981) 1–41.

South Carolina, and 40 percent in Florida, Georgia, Louisiana, and Alabama. White Americans turned their attention away from helping former slaves and their descendants make the long, painful transformation from slavery to freedom—their attention to equalizing educational opportunities for the Negro took second place to the white European immigrants and their quest to achieve education, training, and the American dream. W. T. Williams, a field agent for Slater Fund, surveyed the black schools in 1912 and found that only twenty-three of them required fourteen Carnegie units of high school work for admission; thirty-two HBCUs did college work, mostly private HBCUs; of 13,474 students, only 1,131 students studied in college classes.[20] The Negro's struggle to access higher education continued through the twentieth century.

Alabama Agricultural and Mechanical University (founded 1875) ended up in a political struggle against Tuskegee Institute over who most deserved HBCU 1890 land-grant status. Alabama gave its federal land-grant funds to all-white Auburn University, which had little or no provision to service black Alabamians. The state raised the budget for the Huntsville State Normal School for Negroes (founded 1875) to $2,000 in 1878. After moving into a two-story house on Clinton Street in 1885, the school had its name changed by the state to State Normal and Industrial School for Negroes.

Founding President William H. Council fought a constant battle against Tuskegee Institute and Booker T. Washington over land-grant status. Both institutions had classes and performed extension work among the Negro farmers who operated 42 percent of Alabama's farmland. The governor eventually appointed a committee to resolve the impasse, and it voted to give both institutions some funds. Council argued that, "Tuskegee was a private institution," and Alabama A&M won the land grant funds in 1891. Alabama A&M then developed a new campus outside Huntsville.

The state legislature authorized the bachelor's degree on 9 December 1896 and changed the name of the institution from State Normal and Industrial Institute for Negroes to Alabama Agricultural and Industrial College for Negroes. Four students, mostly out-of-state residents, received the Bachelor of Science degree in 1901. The Carnegie Foundation gave $12,000 to build a library in 1906. There were eight college graduates by 1908. Alabama A&M was mostly a

---

[20] Edward T. Ware, "Higher Education of Negroes in the United States," *Annals of the American Academy of Political and Social Science* 49/1 (September 1913): 209–213. Ware presided over Atlanta University. Thomas J. Jones, "Negro Population in the United States," *Annals of the American Academy of Political and Social Science* 49/1 (September 1913): 1–9. W. T. B. Williams, *Report of Negro Universities of the South: Occasional Papers* No. 13 (New York: Slater Fund, 1913, 1922) 1–10.

teacher preparation institution, and between 1901 and 1909, about 183 students graduated from the normal department. Council enhanced his influence across the region by granting honorary master's and doctorate degrees to powerful members of the black elite class. By 1915, the indebted institution was downgraded to the Alabama A&M Institute and could not continue a four-year curriculum.

The recovery of Alabama A&M State College depended mostly on tuition, fees, philanthropic contributions, and federal funds. Mrs. M. French Sheldon of England, Virginia McCormack, the Slater Fund, and the Peabody Fund in particular helped save the institution. The institution included a practice school, junior high school and high school for Negroes in Madison County. In 1924, the Rosenwald Fund financed construction of a campus high school, which SACS approved in 1932. Alabama only had six approved high schools for Negroes, and Alabama officials made it worst by moving funds from black schools to help white schools and teachers survive the Depression. They diverted land-grant funds to help the white land grant, Auburn University. Alabama A&M received a state budget of $17,500 in 1932, but was denied $34,000 in appropriations in 1934. The General Education Board (GEB) gave $140,000 to upgrade Alabama A&M to college level. The faculty added the third and fourth years of college work in 1939 and 1940. The awarding of bachelors degrees resumed in 1941, when thirty-five students completed the four-year college course. The institution had 647 students, forty-two at college-level, fifty-two staff and faculty members holding twelve master's degrees and one doctorate in 1942. Alabama A&M State College achieved SACS approval in 1947.[21]

Tuskegee Normal and Industrial Institute (1881–) began with thirty students on 4 July 1881, as a state-authorized institution. It had no land, no buildings, and little else but a $2,000 appropriation for salaries. Booker T. Washington, a graduate of Hampton Institute, organized the first classes in a barn and a hen house. He said in *Up from Slavery* (1901),

> From the very beginning, at Tuskegee, I was determined to have the students do not only the agricultural and domestic works, but to have them erect their own buildings.... During the now nineteen years' existence of the Tuskegee school, the plan of having the buildings erected by student labor has been [continued]. In this time, forty buildings ...have

---

[21] Richard D. Morrison, *History of Alabama A. & M. University, 1875–1992* (Huntsville AL, 1993) 1–37, 51, 60, 75–77, 132, 329–35; *Walking in the Wilderness, An Autobiography of Richard David Morrison* (Huntsville AL, 1993) 1–21; "History of Alabama A&M: Past Presidents," http://www.uapb.edu, Alabama A&M University, 2010.

> been built, and all except four are almost wholly the product of student labor.

The students made their own bricks and furnished the nearby community with bricks. They failed three times to build a successful brick kiln, but with $15 they met success the fourth time.

Once again, northern agencies were more likely to help whites to establish freedmen's schools and colleges than to give money to Negroes to do the same thing, and here, Washington, who well knew this, had to build a relationship with northern agencies to help fund Tuskegee.

> In the summer of 1882, Miss Davidson and I both went north and engaged in the work of raising funds for the completion of our new building. On the way [n]orth I stopped in New York to try to get a letter of recommendation from an officer of a missionary organization who had become somewhat acquainted with me a few years previous. This man not only refused to give me the letter, but [also] advised me most earnestly to go back home at once, and not attempt to get money.[22]

Washington continued his journey, finding help in Massachusetts. He concluded,

> When our old students return to Tuskegee now, as they often do, and go into our large, beautiful, well-ventilated, and well-lighted dining room, and see tempting, well-cooked food—largely grown by the students themselves—and see tables, neat tablecloths and napkins, and vases of flowers upon the tables, and hear singing birds, and note that each meal is served exactly upon the minute, with no disorder, and with almost no complaint coming from the hundreds that now fill our dining room, they, too, often say to me that they are glad that we started as we did, and built ourselves up year by year, by a slow and natural process of growth.[23]

B. T. Washington and George Washington Carver built Tuskegee into a powerful force of public service and outreach to eliminate poverty, illiteracy, and disease in rural Alabama. In 1892, the year that Tuskegee became totally private, Washington sponsored a Negro Conference for farmers, mechanics, schoolteachers, and ministers that expanded into two days, including the Worker's Conference on the second day. When Carver joined the Tuskegee faculty in 1897, the US Department of Agriculture began giving Tuskegee free garden seeds for local farm families. With help from Morris K. Jesup, a New York philanthropist, Carver and Tuskegee began operating a movable classroom,

---

[22] Booker T. Washington, "Making Bricks without Straw," in *Up from Slavery* (New York: Oxford University Press, 1995) 55, 98–107.

[23] Ibid.

"the Jesup Wagon," which took farming and housekeeping demonstrations to the people in the countryside—forerunner of agriculture extension programs.

George Washington Carver became the first Negro to graduate from Iowa State University in 1894, and received his master's degree there. He and other black students could not live on campus, but in later years, in order to facilitate Carver's research visits, Iowa State built a cottage on campus for him. When Carver's fame as a scientist grew across the country, there were personality clashes with Booker T. Washington, although the two men enjoyed a relatively mutual appreciation of each other until Washington's death in 1915. Thereafter, Carver devoted more time to agricultural research, and developed hundreds of agricultural products (such as peanut brittle and peanut butter) that benefited America. He wrote dozens of agricultural bulletins and articles for farmers, including *How to Grow the Peanut and 105 Ways of Preparing it for Human Consumption* (1918), and articles based on his expertise on sweet potatoes as an alternative to the cotton crop.[24]

As an American inventor, Carver became a member of the Royal Society of Arts in England, received the Spingarn Medal from the NAACP and the Roosevelt Medal for Outstanding Contribution to Southern Agriculture. He was honored with the George Washington Carver National Monument (built in 1943 in Missouri), featured on a US postage stamp in 1948, and elected to the Hall of Fame for Great Americans in 1977. Carver devoted his life to science; his gravestone read in 1943, "He could have added fortune to fame, but caring for neither, he found happiness and honor in being helpful to the world."[25]

Some observers considered Tuskegee a center of social, religious, economic, and urban reform despite its rural setting. Strangely, elite- and middle-class blacks seemed to share the white rhetoric that the blacks practiced low morals, which led to their higher incidents of disease, crime, poverty, and social exclusion from the larger society, and Tuskegee, therefore, began the Phelps Hall Bible Training School.

In 1900, Washington, with the help of W.E.B. Du Bois and others organized the National Negro Business League. He even offered Du Bois a position at Tuskegee, but Du Bois remained at Atlanta instead of moving to rural Alabama.

---

[24] G. W. Carver, *How to Grow the Peanut and 105 Ways of Preparing It for Human Consumption* (Tuskegee AL: Experimental Station, Tuskegee Normal and Industrial Institute, 1918) 1–29.

[25] John H. Franklin and Alfred A. Moss Jr., *From Slavery to Freedom: A History of African Americans*, 8th ed. (New York: McGraw-Hill, 2000) 455, 588.

Booker T. Washington said Southern whites often opposed providing any kind of higher education to Negroes because they considered an educated Negro as "a dangerous Negro."

> The white people, as well as the colored, were greatly interested in the starting of the new school, and the opening day was looked forward to with much earnest discussion. There were not a few white people in Tuskegee who looked with some disfavor upon the project. They questioned its value to the colored people, and had a fear that it might result in bringing about trouble between the races. Some had the feeling that in proportion as the Negro received education, in the same proportion would his value decrease as an economic factor in the state.... These people feared the result of education would be that the Negroes would leave the farms, and that it would be difficult to secure them for domestic service. The white people who questioned the wisdom of starting this new school had in their minds pictures of what was called an educated Negro, with a high hat, imitation gold eye-glasses, a showy walking-stick, kid gloves, fancy boots, and what not—in a word, a man who was determined to live by his wits. It was difficult for these people to see how education would produce any other kind of a colored man.

Tuskegee, in 1915, was one of the largest HBCUs: 1,338 in attendance, all boarders, from Alabama, thirty-two other states, and nineteen foreign countries, 184 teachers, all colored, 122 of them men and sixty-two women. Tuskegee had a budget of $277,914, including $134,094 in donations, $91,598 from endowment funds, tuition, fees, grants from Slater and GEB, and sales of some of the thousands of acres of land owned by Tuskegee Institute. Tuskegee began offering the bachelor's in 1921.[26]

Since the late eighteenth century, European Americans had initiated a movement to retain America completely under European-American rule. European Americans culminated their efforts in the 1890s. At last, they achieved

---

[26] Washington, *Up from Slavery*, 55; also see R. Norrell, *Reaping the Whirlwind: The Civil Rights Movement in Tuskegee* (New York: Random House, 1985) 1–20; M. Thrasher, *Tuskegee: Its Story and Its Works* (Manchester NH: Ayer Co., 2000) 1–10; Addie L. J. Butler, *The Distinctive Black College: Talladega, Tuskegee, and Morehouse* (Metuchen NJ: Scarecrow Press, 1977) 1–21; Felix James, "Booker T. Washington and George Washington Carver: A Tandem of Adult Educators at Tuskegee," in Harvey G. Neufeldt and Leo McGee, eds., *Education of African American Adult: An Historical Overview* (Westport CT: Greenwood Press, 1990) 61–74; Adam Fairclough, "Tuskegee's Robert R. Morton and the Travails of the Early Black College President," *Journal of Blacks in Higher Education* 31 (2001): 94–105. Tuskegee became a land grant college in 1972.

white solidarity and intellectualized the idea of American white nationalism.[27] More than 80 percent of Negro voters suffered disenfranchisement by poll taxes, ballot box laws, and whites-only Democratic Party primaries. The 15th Amendment (1870) had forced many of the northern states to remove obstacles to Negro voting; however, in many American towns and cities the whites used widespread corruption of politics, mob violence, race riots and lynching to deny civil rights to black Americans. The last Negro left Congress in 1905, after Negroes mostly lost the right to vote, and there were white-led race riots in North Carolina. In places where Negroes still had political power, race radicals attacked and disposed of them.[28] By the end of the nineteenth century, American society became more unjust, more unequal, and less democratic—characteristics that reflected the concepts of white supremacy. The nation's highest court turned a deaf ear to racial justice in Louisiana and approved white supremacy through *Plessy v. Ferguson*, 163 US 537 (1896):

> Legislation is powerless to eradicate racial instincts or to abolish distinctions based upon physical differences, and the attempt to do so can only result in accentuating the difficulties of the present situation. If the civil and political rights of both races [were] equal one cannot be inferior to the other civilly or politically. If one race be inferior to the other socially, the Constitution of the U.S. cannot put them upon the same plane.

The dissenting opinion by Justice Marshall Harlan said, "I am of opinion that the statue of Louisiana is inconsistent with the personal liberty of citizens, white and black, in the State, and hostile to both the spirit and letter of the Constitution of the United States." The federal court again affirmed Jim Crow in *Cumming v. County Board of Education*, 175 US 528 (1899), in which Negro citizens in Georgia had protested because the county shut down their only high school but allowed two white high schools to continue operating. This time, Harlan joined the unanimous *Cumming* decision in favor of white defendants. In southern states, it became acceptable to pool from several counties the black students to be sent to another county's high school. A 1901 Tennessee law read, "It shall be unlawful for any school, academy, college, or other place of learning to allow white and colored persons to attend the same school, academy, college,

---

[27] Ware, "Higher Education of Negroes in the United States," 209–13.

[28] H. Leon Prather Sr., *We Have Taken a City: Wilmington Racial Massacre and Coup of 1898* (Rutherford NJ: Farleigh Dickinson University Press, 1984) 1–30. The late H. Leon Prather was a longtime professor of history at Tennessee State University. He was among HBCU scholars who struggled to publish several books while teaching heavy class loads.

or other place of learning." Tennessee had penalties of $50 fines and imprisonment.[29]

With the US Supreme Court on their side, popular writers reinforced the white solidarity movement, and used "scientific racism" to justify the concept of white supremacy. They used sociological and biological treatises to illustrate blacks were inferior to whites, and they infused these ideas into the curricula of American education.[30] A Negro weekly newspaper said that Thomas Dixon's book, *The Clansman*, which later became the racist film, *The Birth of a Nation*, presented blacks as white American society's worst enemies.[31] The *Globe* said, "It is absolutely false to say that the new Negro's aspiration is to mix with the whites."[32] Sutton E. Griggs, an 1890 graduate of Bishop College, countered white supremacist arguments. In *Imperium in Imperio: A Study of the Negro Race Problem*, Griggs concludes, "When will all races and classes of men learn that men made in the image of God will not be the slaves of another image?" [33] Griggs formed a publishing company with financial backing from the National Baptist Publishing Board headed by Richard H. Boyd, a former student of Bishop College. Griggs argued that Negro colleges could create black leaders capable of leading the race to real freedom. Griggs published more than thirty books, essays, and pamphlets before his death in 1933.[34]

In 1900, in another attempt to counter the conditions that impeded Negro progress, the fifth conference convened at Atlanta University to discuss the

---

[29] Supreme Court cases in Alfred H. Kelly and Winfred A. Harbison, *The American Constitution: Its Origins and Development*, 4th ed. (New York: W. W. Norton, 1970) 1161–65; Charles Warren, *The Supreme Court in United States History*, 2 vols. (New York: Little, Brown and Company, 1926) 807–808; Harold J. Spaeth, *The Warren Court: Cases and Commentary* (San Francisco CA: Chandler Publishing Company, 1966) 395–99.

[30] "Scientific racism" is propaganda about "differences between the races" written as if it were scientific. See Rugledge M. Dennis, "Social Darwinism, Scientific Racism, and the Metaphysics of Race," *Journal of Negro Education* 62/3 (Summer 1995). See also Thomas Dixon, *The Clansman: An Historical Romance of the Ku Klux Klan* (New York: Doubleday, Page & Co. 1905); Robert W. Shufeldt, *The Negro: A Menace to American Civilization* (Boston: Graham Press, 1907); Madison Grant, *The Passing of the Great Race, Or, The Racial Basis of European History* (New York: Charles Scribner's Sons, 1916); Sutton E. Griggs, *Imperium in Imperio: A Study of the Negro Race* (Nashville: National Baptist Publishing Board, 1899; repr. New York: Modern Library, 2003); S. E. Griggs, *Pointing the Way* (Nashville: Griggs Publishing, 1908).

[31] *The Nashville Globe*, 1 February 1907; Henry Gannett, *Statistics of the Negroes in the United States* (Baltimore: John F. Slater Fund, 1894) 32, 33, 25, 26.

[32] *The Nashvillle Globe*, 1 May 1907.

[33] Griggs, *Imperium in Imperio* (2003), 177.

[34] Lovett, *The African-American History of Nashville*, 241, 245–47.

Negro's social, economic, and education problems. Fourteen annual conferences resulted in *The Atlanta University Conference Publications*. These conferences had begun with ideas of W. E. B. Du Bois at Atlanta University and Booker T. Washington at Tuskegee Institute. The 1900 reports estimated that 1,304 Negroes, including 252 women, had received bachelor's degrees from Harvard, Yale, Oberlin, seventy other northern colleges, and thirty-four HBCUs. There were 28,560 Negro teachers in 1900, and 1.5 million Negro children in school. The bulk of Negro children attended inferior schools, and only a third of eligible black children attended secondary schools at all. Some 27 percent of the sixty-four public high schools for southern Negroes did not include the twelfth grade. Some had no English composition course.[35] A conference attendee, Du Bois said in his book, *The Souls of Black Folk*,

> The Negro race in America, stolen, ravished, and degraded, struggling up through difficulties and oppression, needs sympathy and receives criticism; needs help and is given hindrance, needs protection and is given mob violence; needs justice and is given charity, needs leadership and is given cowardice and apology, needs bread and is given a stone....This nation will never stand justified before God until these things are changed.... The problem of the twentieth century is the problem of the color-line—the relation of the darker to the lighter races of men....[36]

The *Nashville American* newspaper declared Du Bois's book "dangerous for the Negro to read."[37]

The Atlanta University annual conference also responded to the "scientific racism" movement, citing statistics to show the conditions of Negroes in America. John Hope, another conference attendee, later reported in the *Voice of the Negro* that Atlanta University, Clark College, Morehouse, Morris Brown, and Spelman colleges enrolled 2,104 students, but only 126 of them were studying

---

[35] Gary B. Nash, J. R. Jeffrey, J. R. Howe, P. J. Frederick, A. F. Davis, and A. M. Winkler, *The American People: Creating a Nation and a Society*, 6th ed. (New York: Pearson-Longman, 2004) 562–63, 626; Franklin and Moss Jr., *From Slavery to Freedoms*, 8th ed., 405–406; Gannett, *Statistics of the Negroes in the United States*, 26; Gary B. Nash, et al., *The American People: Creating a Nation and a Society*, 6th ed. (New York: Pearson, Longman, 2004) 626; W. L. Jenkins, "The Formation of Black Colleges and Universities," in Wilbert L. Jenkins, *Climbing up to Glory: A Short History of African Americans during the Civil War and Reconstruction* (Wilmington DE: Scholarly Resources, Inc., 2002) 177–284.

[36] W. E. B. Du Bois, *The Souls of Black Folk* (New York: Penguin Books, 2003) 36–50.

[37] "Souls of Black Folk," *Nashville American*, 26 September 1903, p. 2.

college subjects. Six persons sat for the Atlanta University class of 1904.[38] The US Bureau of Education said that, by 1910, 35 percent of blacks fourteen years of age and older could not read and write, at a time when only 27.3 percent of the Negro population was urban. This changed to 43.7 percent urban by 1930. By 1912, 54 percent of Negroes ages five to eighteen enrolled in schools, and black illiteracy decreased to 27.5 percent by 1914. Some 5,997 students attended historically black schools, colleges, and universities by 1914.[39]

The HBCUs continued to enroll thousands of students in preparatory, secondary grades, and campus high schools. Although HBCUs had to struggle to move to the next stage of development, Northern philanthropists, churches, benevolent societies, former slaves and descendants, Negro churches, black church state conventions, and public agencies further decreased the illiteracy rate for the Negro population.

These agencies included the John F. Slater Fund, General Education Board, Carnegie Foundation, Anna T. Jeanes Fund, Phelps-Stokes Fund, Julius Rosenwald Fund, and George Peabody Fund. The Peabody Fund assisted education of the common people in the more destitute portions of the post-Civil War South. Congress presented him a gold medal for helping to rebuild the war torn southern states, and establishment of Peabody Normal College for whites in Nashville. The Peabody Fund, along with the Virginia Randolph Fund, became part of the John F. Slater Fund in 1914.

The General Education Board began in 1902, and was chartered by Congress in 1903. John D. Rockefeller began the GEB with $50,000 and increased the amount to $180 million by 1914, by which time the GEB had contributed a total of $650,105 to Negro schools.[40] The gifts promoted practical farming, establishment of public high schools in the southern states, promotion of institutions of higher education, and schools for Negroes. The GEB funded the Homemakers' Clubs for Negro girls, including the ones funded through Hampton Institute throughout Virginia. The GEB sponsored white supervisors of

---

[38] *Voice of the Negro* 1/1 (January 1904): 1–10; Louis R. Harlan, "Booker T. Washington and the *Voice of the Negro*, 1904–1907," *Journal of Southern History* 45/1 (February 1979):45–62. *Voice of the Negro* moved to Chicago after the September 1906 race riot but ceased publication in 1907; Jones, "Negro Population in the United States," 9.

[39] Jones, "Negro Population," 34, 13; Dwight O. W. Holmes, *The Evolution of the Negro College* (College Park MD: McGrath Publishing, 1969) 105–106; Fred McCuston, *Graduate Instruction for Negroes* (Nashville TN: George Peabody College, 1939) 1–10; US Bureau of Education, *Negro Education: A Study of the Private and Higher Schools for Colored People in the United States*, Bulletin No. 39 (Washington DC: GPO, 1917) 1–40.

[40] *The General Education Board: An Account of Its Activities, 1902–1914* (New York: General Education Board, 1915).

Negro education in nine southern states, and helped establish 912 high schools in eleven southern states. GEB gave nearly $41 million for Negro education by 1940.

In 1907, Anna T. Jeanes, the wealthy daughter of a northern industrialist summoned Booker T. Washington and Hollis B. Frissell to her room in a Quaker home for the aged in Philadelphia to receive a deed of trust for her wealth. The two men became sole trustees for "The Fund for Rudimentary Schools for Southern Negroes." Frissell and Washington had power to appoint a board of trustees, several of whom—Abraham Grant, Robert R. Moton , James C. Napier, and Robert L. Smith—were black. The Jeanes Fund Negro Rural School Fund supported Negro master teachers, modeled after methods by Virginia Randolph, a Negro teacher. They assisted or supervised rural schools, supervised the training of other teachers, met with the local community, and taught teachers how to improve the children's lives by canning and preserving food, building septic tanks and toilets, learning new teaching techniques, and implementing home economics techniques like personal care, sewing and making clothing, and raising money for education. B. C. Caldwell said,

> The Jeanes work, now in its fifth year…aimed to reach…the remote country school for Negro children, out of sight in the backwoods, down the bayou, on the sea marsh, up in the piney woods, or out in the gullied wilderness of abandoned plantations. Nearly all these schools [meet] in shabby buildings, mostly old churches, some in cabins and country stores, a few in deserted dwellings. I have seen one in Alabama held in a saw-mill shed, one in Arkansas in a dry kiln, one in Louisiana in a stranded flatboat, and one in Texas in a sheepfold. For the most part untrained teachers [teach] these schools without any sort of supervision. The equipment is…meager, the pay small and the term short. Jeanes…undertook to send trained industrial teachers into this field.[41]

By 1913, there were 120 Jeanes teachers in 120 counties in eleven southern states. The Jeanes Fund employed supervising teachers in 163 counties in the southern states, affecting 100,000 students. Almost all Jeanes teachers were from HBCUs, earning $40 to $70 per month. The Jeanes Fund merged into the Southern Education Foundation in 1937.

Caroline Phelps Stokes established the Phelps-Stokes Fund from 1911 to 1913. Phelps-Stokes donated money for improvements at Negro schools, administrative reorganization, buildings, and HBCU community involvement projects. Her nephew, Anson Phelps Stokes directed the fund, and worked closely with Booker T. Washington, James H. Dillard, John D. Rockefeller, Julius

---

[41] B. C. Caldwell, "The Work of the Jeanes and Slater Funds," *Annals of the American Academy of Political and Social Science* 49/1 (September 1913): 173–76.

Rosenwald, and Frederick Keppel of Carnegie Foundation, and others through 1946. Stokes planned fellowships for persons at southern white institutions to do research on the Negro problems. Anson Stokes advocated matching grants to extend the foundation's work as widely as possible. Thomas Jessie Jones, formerly on the staff at Hampton Institute, directed the program in Negro education.[42]

In 1912, the Rosenwald Fund focused on education, health, fellowships, race relations, and books for Negro college libraries. Julius Rosenwald was a partner in the Sears, Roebuck and Company, a retail and mail order department store in Chicago in 1895. He began his aid to black education in 1912 through contacts with Washington at Tuskegee. The fund erected ninety-two schools in Alabama alone, and nineteen others in Arkansas, Georgia, Mississippi, North Carolina, Tennessee, and South Carolina by 1915. Rosenwald expanded the endeavor into a foundation in 1917, called the Rosenwald Rural School Building Fund. The Rosenwald Fund helped construct 4,977 schools, 217 teachers' homes, and 163 shop buildings in fifteen states before Julius Rosenwald died in 1932. The fund donated over $70 million dollars to schools, colleges, universities, museums, Jewish charities, and other causes before closing in 1948.

The John F. Slater Fund (1882–1937) directed its attention to higher education for Negroes in training teachers to work in the primary schools. The Slater Fund helped build and establish country training schools and gave $500 a year for three years for industrial teaching. The fund supported Atlanta University, Fisk, Hampton, Spelman, Tuskegee, other HBCUs, summer normal school at HBCUs for teachers, and academic and industrial training for country teachers. Slater Fund became a part of the Southern Education Foundation by 1937.

One of the most influential leaders of the early twentieth-century philanthropic groups that aided the HBCUs was James Hardy Dillard, who was born in Virginia and was a teacher at several southern schools including Tulane University in New Orleans. Dillard was director of the Jeanes Foundation (1907–1931), director of the Slater Fund (1910–1917), member of the Southern Education Board (1908–1913), and a member of the GEB after 1917. He communicated often with Booker T. Washington and William H. Taft about board matters and things

---

[42] Edward T. Ware, "Higher Education of Negroes in the United States," *Annals of the American Academy of Political and Social Science* 49/1 (September 1913): 209–218; J. M. Stephens Peeps, "Northern Philanthropy and the Emergence of Black Higher Education—Do-Gooders, Compromisers, or Co-conspirators?" *Journal of Negro Education* 50/3 (Summer 1981): 251–69; D. O. W. Holmes, "Twenty-five Years of Thomas Jessie and the Phelps-Stokes Fund," *Journal of Negro History* 7/4 (October 1938): 475–85.

affecting HBCUs and other black American education issues. Dillard organized the Commission on Southern Race Questions during a meeting of the Southern Sociological Congress, which met in Nashville on 7–10 May 1912, to gain more involvement of southern state universities in improving education. This effort involved the YMCA that started "systematic study of the Negro problem in all its phases" through courses at southern schools, and fellowships sponsored by Phelps-Stokes Fund.[43]

Philanthropic agencies tried to remedy America's racial paradox, while simultaneously trying not to invoke retaliation from southern white supremacists. Writers such as J. M. S. Peeps illustrated that some Northerners were more interested in exploiting the Southern states' resources than in helping the Negroes, and that humanitarianism was always secondary to the capitalists' economic aims. Indeed, many Northern philanthropists pushed Washington's promotion of industrial, manual labor education for Negroes. Liberal arts education helped transform HBCU students into the image of European culture.[44] This was good for the transmittal of white values but did not always give value to Negro and African culture and values. Thus, the early staffs, boards, and decision-making of the northern philanthropic organizations involved few Negro staff members. The Freedmen's Aid Society of the MEC had two corresponding secretaries, one white and one black. Negroes were presidents of half the collegiate grade freedmen's institutions sponsored by the

---

[43] Caldwell, "The Work of the Jeanes and Slater Funds," 173–76. Data on the philanthropic agencies in the above paragraphs see J. E. Fisher, *The John F. Slater Fund: A Nineteenth Century Affirmative Action for Negro Education* (Lanham MD: University Press of America, 1986) 1–10; W. E. B. Du Bois, "The General Education Board," *Crisis* 37 (1930) 1–20; Lance G. E. Jones, *The Jeanes Teacher in the United States, 1908–1933* (Chapel Hill NC: University of North Carolina Press, 1937) 1–32; E. R. Embree and J. Waxman, *Investment in People: The Story of the Julius Rosenwald Fund* (New York: Harper and Brothers, 1949) 1–10; M. R. Werner, *Julius Rosenwald: The Life of a Practical Humanitarian* (New York: Harper and Brothers, 1939) 1–10; J. Rosenwald Fund Papers, Special Collections, Fisk University Library, Nashville TN; Fred McCuistion, *The South's Negro Teaching Force* (Nashville: Rosenwald Fund, 1931) 1–28; J. M. McPherson, "White Liberals and Black Power in Negro Education, 1865–1915," *American Historical Review* 75/5 (June 1970): 1357–86; "The Tradition of White Presidents at Black Colleges," *Journal of Blacks in Higher Education* 16 (30 June 1997): 93–99; Joe M. Richardson, *Christian Reconstruction: The American Missionary Association and Southern Blacks, 1861–1890* (Athens: University of Georgia Press, 1986) 1–30; *General Education Board: An Account of Its Activities*, 1–20.

[44] J. M. S. Peeps, "Northern Philanthropy and the Emergence of Black Higher Education—Do-Gooders, Compromisers, or Co-Conspirators," *Journal of Negro Education* 50 (1981): 251–69; see W. A. Nielsen, *The Big Foundations* (1972) 1–21; Walter B. Weare, *Black Business in the New South: A Social History of the North Carolina Mutual Life Insurance Company* (Durham: Duke University Press, 1993) 214–15.

Methodists. Charles C. Spaulding, head of the North Carolina Mutual Life Insurance Company, became the first Negro elected to the Slater Fund's board of directors. Spaulding's company served as regional broker for Rosenwald Fund money and scholarships in North Carolina. Five blacks sat on the Jeanes board.

Negro assistant state agents, including Robert E. Clay in Tennessee, had no primary decision-making authority in the Negro division of the state department of education. They often sat in state board meetings, saying nothing, even when the discussion was offensive to blacks because they feared being fired. They often did the fieldwork, meeting with Negro school officials in urban and rural areas, relaying the wishes of the state director of Negro education, helping complete the building of Rosenwald schools, and occasionally introducing the white boss to Negro community leaders. R. E. Clay was a barber, businessperson, and headed the National Negro Business League in Bristol, Tennessee, before joining Washington's triumphant Tennessee tour in September 1909.

Philanthropic agency officials used diplomacy and funding to persuade southern officials to do this or do that for Negro education. James Dillard cautioned Booker T. Washington: "My main feeling was that we should, as far as possible, work through the organized [Southern state] school authorities."[45]

The Slater Fund financed goodwill tours by Booker T. Washington that were also a means to assess the progress of Negro education. The great Southern tours influenced ideas and educational approaches to prescribing the kind of curriculum departed to blacks. Historian David H. Jackson provided historical analysis of these tours. In his book, Jackson writes of a speech given by Washington, where he said,

> Our greatest danger is that in the great leap from slavery to freedom we may overlook the fact that the masses of us are to live by the productions of our hands, and fail to keep in mind that we shall prosper in proportion as we learn to dignify and glorify common labor and prosper in proportion as we learn to draw the line between the superficial and the substantial, the ornamental gewgaws of life and the useful. No race can prosper until it learns that there is as much dignity in tilling a field as in writing a poem.[46]

---

[45] J. Dillard to B. T. Washington, 1 June 1907, and A. Jeanes to BTW, 25 February 1905, in Louis R. Harlan and Raymond W. Smock, eds., *The Booker T. Washington Papers*, 11 vols. (Urbana: University of Illinois Press, 1972-) 9.285, 8.201–202; Louis R. Harlan, *Booker T. Washington: The Wizard of Tuskegee, 1901–1915* (New York: Oxford University Press, 1983) 201–202, 195–98, 263, 425, 448.

[46] David H. Jackson, *Booker T. Washington and the Struggle against White Supremacy: The Southern Educational Tours, 1908–1912* (New York: Palgrave Macmillan, 2008) 142;

Washington served on the Fisk University board of trustees (1909–1915), enrolled his son in the university, and gained a Howard University trustee seat for cohort James C. Napier.

Booker T. Washington made his influences felt in Arkansas, and wrote the foreword to Mifflin W. Gibbs, *Shadow and Light*. Gibbs headed Washington's National Negro Business League in Arkansas. In 1905, Washington spoke at Arkansas Branch Normal College, and when he toured the area, the HBCU presidents, and of course Tuskegee graduates played leading roles. Washington and his associates designed these tours to spread the "Tuskegee machine's" message, crown Washington "the leader of the Negro people," and paint a more positive and progressive picture of blacks, said David Jackson. The men accompanying Washington represented what Du Bois called "the Talented Tenth." Meanwhile, Isaac Fisher, now the head of Arkansas Branch Normal College returned to Tuskegee as a frustrated man because the former president of the college and local black leaders fought attempts to turn the HBCU into "another Tuskegee." In 1920, Tuskegee student Floyd Brown arrived in Arkansas and established the Fargo Industrial School near Brinkley. Although Fargo Industrial closed in 1949, Booker T. Washington's former students established twenty-three "little Tuskegees" said Monroe N. Work, director of research at Tuskegee Institute and editor of the *Negro Yearbook*. [47]

Booker T. Washington toured Mississippi in 1908, speaking at every major black town and at Negro colleges. However, the outspoken white supremacist governor of Mississippi believed education was a waste on Negro workers, and he shut down the State Normal School for Negroes and did not allow Washington to include state institutions on his speaking tour. Nevertheless, Washington scheduled speeches at an HBCU recently opened in Utica. Former Tuskegee student William H. Holtzclaw established Utica Normal and Industrial Institute in 1902–1903, starting the classes under a tree and teaching about twenty students. The townspeople built a small frame schoolhouse outside Utica on a former plantation, about twenty-five miles from Jackson, and the twelve-person faculty began teaching farming and industrial subjects. Holtzclaw published *The Black Man's Burden*, organized a choir to raise money, and held

---

Washington, *Up from Slavery*, 144; B. L. Lovett, "James Carroll Napier (1845–1940): From Plantation to the City," in Randy Finley and Thomas A. DeBlack, eds., *The Southern Elite and Social Change: Essays in Honor of Willard B. Gatewood Jr.* (Fayetteville: University of Arkansas Press, 2002) 73–94; Stephen J. Wright, "The Development of the Hampton-Tuskegee Pattern in Higher Education," *Phylon* 10/4 (Fourth quarter, 1949): 334–42.

[47] S. L. Recken, "Rags to Respectability: Arkansas and Booker T. Washington," *Arkansas Historical Quarterly* 57 (2008): 54–71.

conferences on farming techniques, health care, and improved nutrition.[48] After Holtzclaw died in 1943, the high school section of Utica Normal and Industrial Institute became the Hinds County Agricultural High School; the other part became Utica Institute Junior College in 1952, Utica Junior College in 1958, and Hinds County Community College in 1987, offering associate degrees and certificates to about 950 students. By 2007, the Hinds County Agricultural High School was all that remained on the college's 236-acre site.

When Booker. T. Washington toured Florida and then Texas in 1912, many of those who had been educated at HBCUs graced the trains and podiums. Perhaps this was another indication of the growing influence of the "Tuskegee model of education," but more likely it was an indication of the respect many black leaders had for "the wizard of Tuskegee."[49] Among the guests was Texas's Robert L. Smith, who attended Avery Institute, University of South Carolina, and Atlanta University, was a businessperson, teacher, state representative, and board member of the Jeanes Fund. His presence showed Washington's influence with philanthropic agencies. Washington spoke at the Robert Hungerford Normal and Industrial School in all-black Eatonville and was entertained at the Daytona Educational and Industrial School for Girls, operated by Mary M. Bethune, who also proudly exhibited the Tuskegee model in practice.[50] Northern newspapers covered the tours, showing Washington's influence as a Negro leader.

By the start of the First World War in Europe, the philanthropic agencies needed to separate out the elementary, secondary, high schools, normal schools, and the four-year colleges in order to focus on upgrading the best of Negro collegiate institutions. Next, they needed to determine those Negro colleges capable of gaining accreditation as four-year institutions offering bachelor's degrees. This was not easy, because anyone could start an institute, college, or school. Often, the "college" was a one-room abode under the tutelage of a stern proprietor with no college training.

In 1913, several HBCUs formed the Association of Colleges for Negro Youth (ACNY) to lobby the federal government for help to improve the HBCUs, and help petition the all-white regional accrediting agencies to give collegiate

---

[48] William H. Holtzclaw, *The Black Man's Burden* (New York: Neale, 1915).

[49] Louis R. Harlan, *Booker T. Washington, The Wizard of Tuskegee, 1901–1905* (New York: Oxford University Pres, 1983) vii–xiv.

[50] See Shirley Hopkins-Davis, *History of the Utica Campus* (Utica MS: Utica College, 2007) 1–10; Jackson, *Booker T. Washington and the Struggle against White Supremacy*, 1–50; David Jackson Jr., *A Chief Lieutenant of the Tuskegee Machine: Charles Banks of Mississippi* (Gainesville: University of Florida Press, 2002) 75, 104; Jackson, *Booker T. Washington*, 66, 70–71, 89–90.

recognition to qualified HBCUs. Statistical research expert, George E. Haynes, a Fisk graduate with MA and PhD degrees from Yale and Columbia universities, led the effort. He was founding executive director of the National Urban League, secretary of ACNY, and a faculty member at Fisk (1911–1918), before leaving to serve as director of Negro economics for the US Department of Labor. He published several books and studies and his early efforts helped influence Congress to direct the US Department of Interior, Bureau of Education, to complete *Negro Education: A Study of the Private and Higher Education Schools for Colored People in the United States,* Bulletin No 38. The study included site visits in 1913–1915 and confirmation of facts in 1916 to determine the number of Negro schools and their condition. The bulletin concluded, "Many of them [are] pitiable shambles of poor buildings, inadequate support, and low standards."[51] Too many HBCUs had too few resources, too large a burden of educating Negro citizens, and too little help from local funds. They also over-taxed their resources with a mixture of students in elementary, high school, normal, and college levels.[52]

The study said 294 of all 747 Negro schools seemed exceptional, but fewer than 100 of them offered any college curriculum. In many ways, the report seemed accusatory, condescending, and paternalistic. It was not in favor of elevating most HBCUs to full college status. The report recommended either closing and/or downgrading status for several HBCUs. The recommendation was to strengthen the public schools and existing college-level HBCUs "without starting new ones at this time." Bulletin No. 38 also said, "Rules of sanitation and

---

[51] US Bureau of Education, *Negro Education: A Study of the Private and Higher Education Schools for Colored People in the United States,* Bulletin No. 38 (Washington DC: Bureau of Education, 1917).

[52] Nina Mjagkij, ed., *Organizing Black America: An Encyclopedia of African American Associations* (New York: Garland Publishing, 2001) 78; see Association of Colleges and Secondary Schools for Negroes (ACSSN) collection at Atlanta University in the Southern Education Foundation Records, 1882–1979, Archives and Special Collections, Robert Woodruff Library, Atlanta University Center, Atlanta GA; Leland S. Cozart, *A History of the Association of Colleges and Secondary Schools, 1934–1965* (Charlotte NC: Heritage Printers, 1967) 1–19; S. P. Fullinwider, *The Mind and Mood of Black America: twentieth Century Thought* (Homewood IL: Dorsey Press, 1969) 94–95. In 1934, the Association of Colleges for Negro Youth (ACNY) became the Association of Colleges and Secondary Schools for Negroes (ACSSN). A year after passage of the Civil Rights Act (1964), the ACSSN disbanded. See also US Bureau of Education, *Negro Education: A Study of the Private and Higher Education Schools for Colored People in the United States,* Bulletin No. 38 (Washington DC: Bureau of Education, 1917) 1-35.

fire protection have been disregarded and many pupils are in serious danger" because of the cheap, random erection of facilities for some Negro schools.[53]

Some of the recommendations and other unfortunate events at HBCUs took effect after the end of World War I. Roger Williams University lost American Baptist Home Mission Society support after mysterious fires devastated the campus next to Vanderbilt University in the midst of a white streetcar suburban development being built in 1907; the American Baptist Home Mission Society sold the property and withdrew further support; Roger Williams reopened two years later on the black side of town under the Tennessee Missionary Negro Baptist Convention, but closed in 1929, and the students merged with Lemoyne College 210 miles west in Memphis; Walden University once had an African mission school, law, pharmacy, nursing, industrial engineering, and medicine, but never recovered financially from lawsuits and a dormitory fire that killed several students in the first decade of the twentieth century. Walden's medical department gained a separate charter as Meharry Medical College in 1915, but Walden was downgraded to junior college status and eventually closed in 1929.

From 1900–1910, the education reform movement swept the southern states. Again, many Southern churches, however, when compared with the Northern religious denominations, did little to help with the higher education of Negroes. Even so, white Christians, including Amory D. Mayo and Atticus G. Haygood, started discussions about the poor condition of southern education. Conferences between white Southerners and northerners began in 1898 and continued through 1915. However, "The beneficent effects of these conferences ... are more apparent in what they done for the white people than in advantages accruing to the Negroes," said George Dickerman.[54] Between 1870–1913, Southern states spent $166 million on Negro education. Of this amount, the Negro paid "a fair proportion.... However, there are four well-defined retarding forces to the fullest economic development of the Negro in the South, and to these evils this commission should give thoughtful and earnest consideration—the tenant system, the on crop system, the abuse of the credit system, and rural isolation," wrote Charles H. Brough, Southern Universities Commission Chair and a professor at the University of Arkansas in 1913. Brough reminded the readers that Negro education had been "shamefully neglected." He, however, yielded to the idea of white supremacy: "As the sons of proud Anglo-Saxon sires, we of the South doubt seriously the wisdom the enfranchisement of an inferior

---

[53] D. O. W. Holmes, "The Beginnings of the Negro College," *Journal of Negro Education* 3/2 (April 1934): 163–93.

[54] G. S. Dickerman, "History of Negro Education," in US Bureau of Education, *Negro Education*, Bulletin No. 38 (Washington DC: General Printing Office, 1917) 267.

race. We believe that reconstruction rule was 'a reign of ignorance, mongrelism, and depravity.'"[55] US Bulletin No. 38 quoted an open letter from the Southern Universities Race Commission: "The South cannot realize its destiny if one-third of her population is undeveloped and inefficient.... The inadequate provision for the education of the Negro is more than an injustice to him; it is an injury to the white man." In his transmittal of Bulletin No. 38, the secretary of the interior said, "The effective education of the Negroes of the US is essential to the welfare of the entire nation."[56]

The appeal for progressive education that included all races in the South went unheeded and most Southern authorities seemed intent on designing public schools for Negro citizens that were inferior to those for whites. Southern states continued to increase the high schools for whites, but for Negro children, they created "county training schools." Historian H. Leon Prather said, "The county training schools were the origin of public high school opportunities for southern rural blacks. Their course of study consisted of seven elementary grades, in addition to the state's high school course of study in the eighth and ninth grades." The Slater Fund required that instruction should extend through a minimum of eight years.[57]

Therefore, many HBCUs had to maintain high school departments into the 1920s and 1930s. This reduced their image as a college, and sometimes caused accreditation problems,—because high school and college courses were often cross-listed and taught in the same classroom at the same hour. Thus, the Northern agencies sponsored the establishment of additional county training schools for Negroes as a way to take the burden off the HBCUs and feed better-prepared students to them. Northern agencies financed training for teachers at these schools in order to extend the HBCU curricula to include higher subjects. By 1928, the Slater, Peabody, GEB, Jeanes, Phelps-Stokes, and Rosenwald funds had spent $26.3 million to expand, maintain, and influence black higher education. Between 1914 and 1930, the Slater Fund helped establish county training schools in thirteen states, and of the 3,048,289 Negro schoolchildren in fifteen southern states, 71 percent (2,165,147) were enrolled in school. By 1930, there were 47,426 certified Negro teachers, and Negroes had received 1,707

[55] Charles H. Brough, "Work of the Commission of Southern Universities on the Race Question," *Annals of the American Academy of Political and Social Science* 49/1 (September 1913): 47–57.

[56] US Bureau of Education, *Negro Education*, 267–69.

[57] US Bureau of Education, *A Study of Private and Higher Education for Colored People in the United States*, Bulletin No. 38, 41; H. Leon Prather Sr., *Resurgent Politics and Educational Progressivism in the New South, North Carolina, 1890–1913* (Cranbury MS: Fairleigh Dickinson University Press, 1979) 260–61.

bachelor's degrees, 289 professional degrees, seventy-six master's degrees, and several doctorate degrees. Slater Fund estimated the need for 6,310 additional teachers and a more rapid expansion.[58]

Texas exemplified the proliferation of Negro colleges, and illustrated the reason why Negroes so desperately needed their own colleges and universities. One reason for the peculiarities of black society in Texas was the isolationism suffered by black Texans from slavery in the 1840s through freedom in June 1865. Texas, an American state born in 1845 out of foreign conquest and founded by militant pro-slavery leadership including Southerners such as US President James K. Polk, an owner of four slave plantations in Mississippi and Tennessee. Polk, who had headed the US House of Representatives when the hated Gag Rule (1836) prevented anti-slavery petitions from being read on the floor, was determined to expand the cotton kingdom and strengthen the institution of human bondage. When Polk made his bid for the presidency in April 1844, blacks already constituted 27 percent of Texas's population—including 27,000 slaves. Texas was on the American frontier, and in this wilderness, communication was difficult and slave rebellions and the intervention of eastern abolitionists was not a factor in the manumission of any significant number of black Texans. Texas was expansive, yet the Negro population was concentrated and near-perfectly controlled in the slave holding areas of east Texas and the neighboring western counties of Louisiana and Mississippi.

Texas Confederates committed to rebellion and treason against the US in February 1861, however, few battles or skirmishes occurred on Texas soil. In the vast expanse of Texas, most slaves did not know of Lincoln's Emancipation Proclamation of 1 January 1863 and were unaware that approximately two hundred thousand Negroes officially served as soldiers and sailors in the Union Army, with some twenty-five thousand of them being among the first Union Army troops to occupy Richmond, Virginia—the Confederate capital—when the Rebels surrendered in April 1865. It wasn't until 25 June 1865, upon the arrival of

[58] Slater Fund Reports, 1930, in the Southern Education Foundation Records, 1882–1979, Archives and Special Collections, Robert Woodruff Library, Atlanta University Center, Atlanta GA; US Office of Education, *National Survey of the Higher Education of Negroes* (Washington DC: GPO, 1942) 1–30, and tables 1–10; Henry A. Bullock, *A History of Negro Education in the South, from 1619 to the Present* (New York: Praeger, 1970) 1–53; Ina C. Brown, "The National Survey of Negro Higher Education and Post-war Reconstruction: The Place of the Negro College in Negro Life," *Journal of Negro Education* 11/3 (July 1942): 375–81.

a Union Navy gunboat to Galveston, that most of the slaves in Texas learned that they were now freemen.[59]

Historian C. Vann Woodward said "The determination of the Negro's 'place' took shape gradually under the influence of economic and political conflicts among divided white people—conflicts that were eventually resolved in part at the expense of the Negro." "Black Colleges," The *Handbook of Texas Online*, said

> After the Civil War, black Texans discovered that the abolition of slavery did not carry with it any guarantee of social, political, or economic equality. This became evident during the course of Reconstruction as many white Texans refused to accept African Americans as equals, and worked systematically to keep them in a segregated, second-class status as near to slavery as possible.... Laws [kept] blacks from voting, holding public office, and serving on juries. Laws segregating public facilities ... also appeared....[60]

Former slaves had none of the wealth their labor had accumulated on Texas land, and Congress and the Texas government made no appropriate response to this problem. Black Texans had to engage their meager resources and abilities to establish a higher education system. Unlike arriving European immigrants, the former slaves had the stigma of enslavement by whites and continuing discrimination on account of their skin color and African blood. From 1865 to 1869, the Freedmen's Bureau helped establish more than one hundred freedmen's schools, and, again, northern missionary groups aided black educational efforts. However, many white Texans remained resentful of the Negro's emancipation, his effort to acquire land and wealth, and his quest to provide higher education for his children. Prior to the emancipation, only a few hundred of the 58,558 black Texans were free in 1850, and only 217 were believed to be literate. With a lack of financial resources, many HBCUs never reached collegiate status. By 1935, the Texas department of education recognized thirteen HBCUs near collegiate quality. SACS rated two senior-level HBCUs "A," and recognized five Texas HBCUs with "B" rating. At the time, SACS gave a Jim

---

[59] William Dusinberre, *Slavemaster President: The Double Career of James Polk* (New York: Oxford University Press, 2003) 131.

[60] Quotes in K. M. Hamilton, "White Wealth and Black Repression in Harrison County, Texas: 1865–1868," *Journal of Negro History* 84/4 (Autumn 1999): 340–59; *The Handbook of Texas Online*, www.tshaonline.org/handbook, 2008, 1–11; Texas State Historical Society, "African Americans in Reconstruction," www.pqc.edu/history; Henry A. Bullock, "Negro Higher and Professional Education in Texas," *Journal of Negro Education* 17 (1948): 365–373; C. Vann Woodward, *The Strange Career of Jim Crow*, 6.

Crow designation of "approval" ("A" or "B") but not equal accreditation to Negro colleges.[61]

Mary Allen College opened in 1866 under the Presbyterian Board of Missions for Freedmen of the Presbyterian Church in Crocket, Texas. Industrial courses and crafts, along with the rudiments of reading and writing dominated the curricula, but these curricula required few teachers with bachelor's degrees.

Wiley College (1873–) began in Marshall, Texas, under the MEC Freedmen's Aid Society. In 1892, the institution reorganized with the first black president and received support from philanthropic agencies to help build facilities. At the end of World War II, Wiley had nearly five hundred students. Wiley received "A" rating approval from SACS before 1954. Wiley remained affiliated with the United Methodist Church, which supported the institution through their Black College Fund (1972–). Wiley remained committed to providing students with a broad liberal arts and career-oriented education in a Christian environment, promoting teaching and learning excellence, and improving the quality of human experience.[62]

Tillotson College began in 1876–1877 in Austin under the American Missionary Society and George J. Tillotson of Connecticut. Samuel Huston College began in 1900 under the Freedmen's Aid Society. In 1934, this institution received "A" rating from SACS. The two schools merged on 24 October 1952, and the institution became Huston-Tillotson University on 28 February 2005, offering bachelor's degrees in business, humanities, education, social sciences, natural science, and technology.

Negro Baptists established Centennial College, an institution of high-school caliber, in Marshall in 1875, but the school merged with Bishop College in 1881, and the college—which trained ministers—then offered high school courses, and lower-level college courses. In 1929, the high school department was discontinued, and the state department of education recognized Bishop as a senior college. Bishop College received "B" rating from SACS in 1931 and "A" rating in 1948. The institution developed a master's degree program and a junior college branch located in Dallas. Financial difficulties nearly closed it in 1972. Unfortunately, Bishop lost SACS accreditation in December 1986, filed for bankruptcy in 1987, closed, and sold the campus in 1988.

---

[61] Anna Wilson, "Education for African Americans," Cecil Harper Jr., "Freedmen's Bureau," *The Handbook of Texas*, http://www.tshaonline.org, 2010; William R. Davis, *The Development and Present Status of Negro Education in East Texas* (New York: Teachers College Press, 1934) 1–26.

[62] "The Place Where Every Student Can Succeed," http://www.wileyc.edu, Wiley College, 2010.

Paul Quinn College began on 4 April 1872 under the AME Church in Waco. Under Bishop William Paul Quinn, the institution expanded, and a curriculum including Latin, mathematics, music, theology, English, sewing, and other craft courses was instituted. Texas chartered the institution as Paul Quinn College in May 1882. The college, which had first been located in Waco, then Austin, was relocated to Dallas on 20 September 1990. In 2008, Paul Quinn remained a SACS-accredited institution with divisions of general studies, arts and sciences, and bachelor's degrees in nine areas including engineering technology, education, and professional studies, all through a general education liberal arts core.

Texas had many competing Negro Baptist factions that sought to locate higher education institutions within their districts. Negro Baptists founded Hearne Academy in Houston in 1881, and the Negro Texas Baptist State Convention and the black Baptist Guadalupe Association opened Guadalupe College in Sequin in 1884. The ABHMS also supported the institution until the Negro Baptists split the state convention in 1893, partly because the ABHMS wanted to centralize its philanthropic efforts into just one of the freedmen schools. The General Baptist State Convention (today's Missionary Baptist General Convention of Texas), which opposed the ABHMS' proposals to downgrade Bishop and make Guadalupe a feeder school, took control of Guadalupe College and relocated it to San Antonio in 1914. Fire destroyed the main building in 1936, and the institution soon closed. Central Texas College, begun in Waco in 1902 as Central Texas Academy under the Negro Baptists, became collegiate in 1907, enrolling more than five hundred students. The school failed financially in 1931, and a federal highway project occupied the site of the campus in the 1950s. The General Missionary Baptist Convention of Texas also operated Richard H. Boyd Industrial Institute from 1913 until a fire destroyed the institution in 1919. Negro Baptists started Butler College in Tyler, and named it the East Texas Normal and Industrial Academy in 1905, but Butler College soon closed.

Texas College (1894–), under the Colored Methodist Episcopal Church (CME), began in Tyler. Texas College became Phillips University in 1909, but resumed as Texas College in 1917, and by 2005, offered sixteen baccalaureate degree programs, associate degree programs in two areas, and alternative teacher certification programs.

Bishop James Steptoe Johnston of the St. Philips Protestant Episcopal Church established, in 1898, the St. Philip's Industrial School as a vocational and liberal arts school for about twenty girls in downtown San Antonio. Artemisia Bowden, a teacher and daughter of a former slave, assumed leadership for the next fifty-two years. The institution moved in 1917 to a location east of downtown. It affiliated with the San Antonio College and the San Antonio Independent School District in 1942. In 1945, the two colleges combined into the San Antonio Union Junior College District. The institution received "A" rating approval from SACS in 1951. In 1987, the southwest campus became St. Philip's College, and included a multi-campus institution of the Alamo Community College District, with an enrollment of more than 8,000 students by 2007.

Jarvis Christian College (1912–) began under the Christian Women's Board of Missions, Christian Church (Disciples of Christ) in Hawkins. The school offered Christian education and industrial courses on 456 acres of land in Wood County, Texas. James N. Ervin of Johnson City, Tennessee, became the first president, in 1914. The school served as a high school until 1927, when it became a junior college. Jarvis Christian chartered as a junior college status in 1928, began upper-level college courses in 1937, and achieved four-year college status by 1941. Oil wells began producing on the property in the 1940s, providing a steady stream of funds. The institution received SACS approval of "A" rating for the "Approved List of Colleges and Universities for Negro Youth" in 1950. The institution had a state approved teacher-education program by 1969. This accredited HBCU offered both bachelor's degrees and dual degrees in engineering, nursing, and mass communications in cooperation with three University of Texas campuses.

In 1878, Prairie View A&M College began in Waller County as the Agricultural and Mechanical College of Texas for Colored Youth, becoming the Alta Vista Agricultural College. In response to the 1890 Morrill Land Grant Act amendment, the legislature attached an agricultural and mechanical department to the normal school, and the school grew to a two-year, teacher-training college. Prairie View State Normal and Industrial College graduated the first four students with a college degree in 1903. However, the college discontinued in favor of the Tuskegee model of industrial education. The president and eight hundred students enthusiastically hosted Booker T. Washington during his Texas tour in 1911.

Four years after Booker T. Washington's death, the college courses restarted at Prairie View. The normal school (junior college) phase ended in 1921 when five students graduated with bachelor's degrees. The senior academy discontinued in 1930, and the institution acquired "A" rating from SACS in 1934. These changes took place under President W. R. Banks (1926–46), who also acquired programs in law, pharmacy, and engineering. The institution became Prairie View A&M. College in 1947, and gained full SACS membership in 1958. The college integrated in 1963 and changed the name to Prairie View A&M University in 1973.

Texas Southern University (1947–) began in response to NAACP lawsuits against Jim Crow states' refusal to admit Negroes into public graduate and professional schools. The state quickly formed Texas Southern University for Negroes on the campus of Houston College.

Houston College began with three hundred students as the Houston Junior College for Negroes after Negro residents petitioned the board of education in 1927 for higher education classes. The first twenty-nine students graduated in 1929. SACS approved the junior college in 1931. The institution became a four-year college in 1934. They began graduate courses in 1943, and separated from the Houston Independent Public School District in 1945. Houston College had divisions of education, fine arts, health, physical education and recreation, home economics, humanities, natural sciences and mathematics, social sciences, pharmacy, vocational education, and law. Houston College had 1,123 students by 1946, and graduated 136 in 1947. In the face of the NAACP lawsuits, the University of Houston, which governed the Negro institution, offered Houston College to the state. On 3 March 1947, the legislature established Texas Southern University for Negroes. After losing the race discrimination case of *Sweatt v. Painter* 339 US 629 (1950), Texas began to enhance programs at TSU in order to discourage Negro applications to the white public colleges. They transferred a one-room law school in Austin to the Houston campus. Texas Southern University was so named on 1 June 1951. The state added a school of pharmacy and a graduate school. The SACS-accredited Texas Southern University grew into eight schools, including some 9,700 ethnically diverse students by 2005.[63]

Meanwhile, in the first quarter of the twentieth century, American colleges and universities continued to set standards and use educational associations to accredit the institutions. However, these early American education associations left the HBCUs out. The National Association of State Universities (founded 1896) excluded Negro schools as members, as did the Land-Grant College Engineering Association (founded 1912). None of the HBCUs had engineering programs, yet. Moreover, Congress passed the Smith-Lever Act in 1914 and the Smith-Hughes Act in 1917 that provided federal grants to the states to support cooperative extension efforts in agriculture, home economics, and vocational education; Jim Crow states, however, discriminated against the HBCUs in the

---

[63] See N. W. Lede, *Mary Allen College: Its Rich History, Pioneering Spirit and Continuing Tradition, 1885–1995* (Houston: Texas Southern University Press, 1995) 1–10; Michael R. Heintze, *Private Black Colleges in Texas, 1865–1954* (College Station: Texas A&M University Press, 1985) 1–21; M. C. Williams, "The History of Tillotson College, 1881–1952" (master's thesis, Texas Southern University, 1967) 1–20; C. F. Toles, "The History of Bishop College" (master's thesis, University of Michigan, 1947) 1–21.

dispensation of these federal funds. Additionally, in 1918, the National Education Association published *Cardinal Principles of Secondary Education,* including health, family life, citizenship, and ethical character in the curriculum. HBCUs met some *Cardinal* standards, but many of them lacked resources.

The early twentieth-century HBCU campuses had few substantial buildings, mainly because builders designed most of the original buildings for short-term use. According to advertisement brochures, physical plants of all the land-grant HBCUs equaled only $2.5 million by 1915. Students at Tennessee A&I built a makeshift gymnasium on the top floor of the Boys' Trades Building and wired lights to the campus power plant. Students had to carry chairs from one classroom to another. Summer session students (mainly adult schoolteachers) raised money to buy classroom chairs. The president of Tennessee A&I explained to the state board in 1943 that the institution tore down the original buildings; he said the construction crews and architects built the four buildings with $86,000. In a door-to-door fund raising campaign, Nashville's community contributed a great deal of the first budget for the institution. Tuskegee Institute students gave sweat equity, in lieu of fees, to help the institution build facilities. Fisk Jubilee Singers and other HBCU student choirs toured and raised money to help build facilities.

From 1921 to 1941 many HBCUs began building new facilities with matching funds provided by northern philanthropic agencies and federal New Deal agencies. Alcorn College received $100,000 from the GEB in 1928, matched by a $200,000 state appropriation for facilities expansion and improvements. The Freedmen's Aid Society of the MEC remained involved with Meharry, and the AMA continued aiding Fisk. The GEB gave Fisk $500,000 toward raising $1 million endowment in 1921, and help also came from the John F. Slater Fund, Carnegie Corporation, and J. C. Penney Foundation. The GEB gave $400,000 to build a library at Fisk, and the Laura Spelman Fund contributed money for annual purchase of books. The GEB and the Rosenwald Fund helped Tennessee A&I build a library, science building, home economics building, industrial arts building, and combination administration, health, and physical education building—doubling the size of the campus between 1927 and 1941. In the 1930s, when selling materials for the Association for the Study of Negro Life and History, Lorenzo J. Greene visited HBCUs and concluded in his diary that the best physical plants existed at Howard University, Tennessee A&I State Teachers College, Langston University, Arkansas AM&N State College, and Hampton Institute.[64]

---

[64] Lorenzo Green (Arvarh E. Strickland, ed.), *Selling Black History for Carter G. Woodson: A Diary, 1930–1933* (Columbia: University of Missouri Press, 1996) 79–83, 338, 351, 353, 356;

Because there were so few public high schools for Negroes, many HBCUs continued to focus on the training of teachers and establishing a *norm* of excepted teaching standards. In many states, for black and white teachers, a high school diploma was sufficient for teaching lower grades. A normal school diploma earned permanent license for the higher grades.

Severe racial disparity between white and black wealth in America oppressed Negro Americans, and this economic disparity kept the HBCUs poor, in debt, and unable to realize the alumni support that many of the nation's white colleges and universities enjoyed. HBCU students came from rural families where 75 percent or more of them were tenants or sharecroppers. Former slaves often headed the families, and they needed financial assistance—mainly because the Negro exited slavery with no real resources in land, possessions, or money. The freedmen's societies passed a resolution in December 1863, asking President Lincoln to give the former slaves "a legal and quiet possession of adequate land for their residence and support, as rapidly and as early as possible."[65] Frederick Douglass wrote,

> The wealth of the master did not attach to the slave, but the reverse. The whites had robbed the slave of the rewards of his labor during more than 200 years. Yet the emancipated slaves and serfs of Egypt and Russian left bondage with tools, implements, and land to make the successful transition from slavery to freedom.[66]

After stripping the slaves of billions derived from their labor, the nation made no real attempt to repair the situation. Congress passed the Southern Homestead Act in 1866 that benefited about 4,000 Negro families—but whites and lumber companies got most of this land. The Freedmen's Bureau (1865–1872) also failed after President Andrew Johnson sabotaged it by not pushing a black Reconstruction agenda held by the radical Republicans. Former slave Benjamin "Pap" Singleton and others led the Black Exodus of twenty-five thousand former slaves from southern states to federal Homestead lands in the West from 1869 to 1881, but Congress held hostile hearings and opposed the exodus. White

---

Henry N. Drewry and Humphrey Doerman, *Stand and Prosper: Private Black Colleges and Their Students* (Princeton: Princeton University Press, 2001) 72–78; Robert J. Booker, *Two Hundred Years of Black Culture in Knoxville, Tennessee, 1791–1991* (Virginia Beach VA: Donning Company, 1993) 42, 44, 45, 46, 57, 163.

[65] US Bureau of Education, *A Study of Private and Higher Education for Colored People in the United States*, Bulletin No. 38, 16.

[66] Frederick Douglass, *Autobiographies of Narratives of the Life, My Bondage and My Freedom,* and *Life and Times* (Library of America Series, New York: Library of America, Penguin Books, 1994) 934.

southern newspapers also opposed the exodus because the whites needed to retain cheap black labor to thwart agricultural recession. Black laborers were needed after Congress passed the Chinese Exclusion Act in 1882. Callie House of Nashville, a former slave, led the National Ex-Slave Mutual Relief, Bounty and Pension Association to gain "A Freedmen's Pension Bill," but federal authorities rejected the idea, and imprisoned Mrs. House in 1917; yet, ex-Confederates received state pensions despite the 14th Amendment of the Constitution, which reads, "Neither the United States nor any State shall assume or pay any debt or obligation incurred in aid of insurrection or rebellion against the United States, or any claim for the loss or emancipation of any slave.... All such debts, obligations, and claims shall be held illegal and void" (article 14, section 4). In September 1883, Frederick Douglass spoke at Louisville:

> This sharp contrast of wealth and poverty [between whites and blacks] ... can exist only in one way, and from one cause, and that is by one getting more than its proper share of the reward of industry, and the other side getting less, and that in some way labor has been defrauded or otherwise denied of its due proportion.... We utterly deny that the colored people of the South are too lazy to work, or that they are indifferent to their physical wants....The trouble is not that the colored people of the South are indolent, but that no matter how hard or how persistent may be their industry, they get barely enough for their labor to support life....[67]

Indeed, the raising of funds by HBCU students became a necessary way of life. The Jubilee Singers toured across the region, nation, and world from 1869 through 1876, bringing money that was critical to the construction of Fisk University's new campus. In letters and reports to the president, the construction chief pleaded with him to pressure the students to pay their bills. Several of the Jubilee Singers became so busy on tour, raising money for the school, that they missed their graduation ceremony in 1874. H. S. Enck said,

> Perhaps nothing was more instrumental in pulling at Northern white hearts and purse strings than the songs of the Tuskegee quartets. These various Tuskegee singing groups scoured the country in search of funds.... Dressed in their white duck pants and blue coats and confining themselves largely to their specialties—old plantation melodies and black folk songs—the quartets were instant successes wherever they appeared.

---

[67] Frederick Douglass, "Address to the People of the United States," 25 September 1883, in Philip S. Foner, ed., *Frederick Douglass: Selected Speeches and Writings* (Chicago: Lawrence Hill Books, 1999) 669–84, 677; Mary F. Berry, *My Face is Black is True: Callie House and the Struggle for Ex-Slave Reparations* (New York: Knopf, 2005) 178; Lester C. Lamon, *Blacks in Tennessee, 1791–1970* (Knoxville: University of Tennessee Press, 1981) 69.

Tuskegee, even though it had one of the best endowment funds among the HBCUs, was in financial need before Washington died. Hampton, Roger Williams, Walden, Storer College, and other HBCUs used choirs and other student groups to raise money. The organizers based the HBCU fundraisers on the premise that the whites held almost all America's wealth.[68]

Frustration and resentment about black deprivation persisting two generations after the end of slavery caused many black students to rise in rebellion against the very people that supported the HBCUs. These educators held a tight rein on black students, partly because they were trying to keep the students within the acceptable rules of southern Jim Crow so as not to draw local Southern hostility or scare northern white donors away. Negro students recognized the arbitrary limitations on their educational progress and human potential, but some of them became critical of conservative white administrations, especially at private black colleges.[69]

At Hampton Institute, the principal, Samuel Chapman Armstrong, was a figure larger than life. A white liberal, he prepared Negroes for equality and even hired them at Hampton. However, the Hampton white teachers refused to dine with Negroes, "our former pupils," and Armstrong's practice of allowing the faculty to segregate themselves from the Negroes during meals drew Negro protest. Hampton, like most HBCUs, was more racially diverse in staff than other colleges in the country. However, in the 1960s, black novelist James Baldwin said to a white audience of his friends who asked what could they do to help in the blacks' civil rights movement: "As long as you insist on being 'white', you make me 'black'." By insisting on separate dining for whites, the faculty members at Hampton Institute failed to realize they insulted the students with racial labels.[70]

A similar student rebellion at Roger Williams University in the late 1880s played into the hands of members of the American Baptist Home Mission Society. The ABHMS members had begun a push to close some freedmen's

---

[68] H. S. Enck, "Tuskegee Institute and Northern White Philanthropy," *Journal of Negro History* 65/4 (Autumn 1980): 336–48. J. B. Roebuck and K. S. Murty, *Historically Black Colleges and Universities: Their Place in American Higher Education* (Westport CT: Praeger, 1993) 99–103.

[69] Raymond Wolters, *The New Negro on Campus: Black College Rebellions of the 1920s* (Princeton NJ: Princeton University Press, 1975) 1–31.

[70] See Hoda M. Zaki, *Civil Rights and Politics at Hampton Institute: the Legacy of Alonzo G. Moron* (Urbana: University of Illinois Press, 2007) for an understanding of the complexities of elite black politics and thought during Jim Crow. See also Robert F. Eng, *Samuel Chapman Armstrong and Hampton Institute, 1839–1893: Educating the Disfranchised and Disinherited* (Knoxville: University of Tennessee Press, 1999) xx, 162–63.

schools and consolidate the students into Atlanta Baptist College (now Morehouse) and other, more central, places to save money. However, black preachers in the American National Baptist Convention resisted the ABHMS plans, and, eventually, the Negro Baptist state convention in Texas split in the debate over Bishop College. In 1892, the black Baptists formed their Baptist Educational Convention with the intent of directing their own educational institutions. However, they had little wealth, and after the National Baptist Convention of the USA (1896–) united the Negro Baptist agencies, there was a spirit of reconciliation with the white northern Baptists. They voted to name Atlanta Baptist College for Henry L. Morehouse, head of the ABHMS. As white contributions dwindled, the ABHMS began to support fewer HBCUs, and they prepared to exit many of their HBCUs by increasing the black faculty/staff members. These northern white Baptists even proposed by 1912 to turn religious education for Southern Negroes over to the white Southern Baptist Convention.[71]

Black-white tensions mounted at Fisk and Meharry. Local Negro leaders, who were upset about the treatment of elite-class Negro visitors who visited the campus, revolted against Fisk's administration in 1912. The blacks felt the contributions and sacrifices of the Jubilee Singers became subordinate to accolades for white financial contributors. They protested the "reserved" seating for whites at Fisk's public events. They anticipated "at least the appointment of a black dean." The president resigned, yet Fisk waited another thirteen years before appointing Negro administrators.[72]

Meharry Medical College was founded in 1874 by George W. Hubbard, who used funds donated by two white brothers in Ohio to train Negro doctors who could minister to people so desperately in need of medical attention after slavery. Hubbard, a northern missionary with a medical education from Vanderbilt, used Meharry graduates for the medical and teaching staff. Meharry built its first hospital, Hubbard Hospital, in 1912. The alumni built him a beautiful home on the South Nashville campus, where Hubbard retired, and he resided there until his death in 1925. They buried him the National Cemetery at

---

[71] Bobby L. Lovett, *The African American History of Nashville, 1780–1930: Elites and Dilemmas* (Fayetteville: University of Arkansas Press, 1999) 150–55; Eugene TeSelle Jr., "The Nashville Institute and Roger Williams University: Benevolence, Paternalism, and Black Consciousness, 1867–1910," *Tennessee Historical Quarterly* 41/4 (Winter 1982): 360–79; Ruth M. Powell, *Ventures in Education with Black Baptists in Tennessee* (New York: Carlton Press, 1979) 27–73.

[72] US Bureau of Education, *A Study of Private and Higher Education for Colored People in the United States*, Bulletin No. 38, 527.

Nashville with a large granite monument.[73]

Hubbard's successor arrived in February 1921 and was engaged in an almost-constant battle with the predominant Negro faculty members and alumni. The situation intensified as the new president pushed Meharry toward upgrading admissions and retention standards to achieve accreditation. Meharry Medical College achieved an "A" rating from the Council on Medical Education and Hospitals in 1923, and in 1931, relocated from south Nashville to north Nashville, adjacent to Fisk University. The GEB, George Eastman Fund, Harkness Foundation, Kellogg Foundation, and Rosenwald Fund helped build the new campus. The deterioration of relations on campus continued into the 1930s, but local black leaders, including J. C. Napier, a part-time teacher at Meharry, helped to quiet things down. Meharry hired white presidents until 1949, and a committee ran the college until a black president was hired in 1952.[74]

In 1924, students started a revolt at Fisk University. The white president Fayette A. McKenzie was pushing hard to improve the quality of students and move the institution toward SACS accreditation. He cultivated financial support among the local elite-class whites by joining their civic clubs and sending his child to a white school (as Tennessee law required), unlike other white faculty at Fisk University who quietly enrolled their children free, on-campus classes. McKenzie made speeches about how Fisk students were prepared for "service" within the existing [Jim Crow] societal structure, and local whites donated $50,000 to the university. McKenzie denied the students a campus NAACP chapter, and he instituted strict student dress codes.

W. E. B. Du Bois, whose daughter matriculated from Fisk, became involved on the students' side. President John Hope sent a message from Atlanta University to his friend, Du Bois, reminding him that a college was a delicate institution easily destroyed by public controversy. Du Bois proceeded to air the campus controversy in *Crisis* magazine: "Suppose we do lose Fisk University; let us never forget that the arch enemy of the Negro race is the false philanthropist who kicks us in the mouth when we cry out in honest and justifiable protest."[75] After McKenzie allowed Nashville police to invade the boys' dormitory and

---

[73] Charles W. Johnson Sr., *The Spirit of a Place Called Meharry: The Strength of Its Past to Shape the Future* (Franklin TN: Hillsboro Press, 2000) 54–55.

[74] Lovett, *The African American History of Nashville*, 100, 101, 109, 124, 128–129, 155–157, 178; "The Tradition of White Presidents at Black Colleges," *Journal of Blacks in Higher Education* 16/1 (Summer 1997): 93–99.

[75] F. McKenzie to Thomas J. Jones, Nashville, October 19, 1924, Fayetter A. McKenzie (1872-1957) Papers 1894-1957, Box 2, MD files, Tennessee State Archives and Library, Nashville; Lester C. Lamon, "The Black Community and Fisk University Student Strike of 1924-25," *Journal of Southern History* 40/2 (May 1974): 225-244.

brutalize the protesters, the black community held mass meetings at local churches, and demanded his resignation. J. C. Napier and elite-class Negroes sided with McKenzie. On 19 February 1925, McKenzie wrote to the chair of the board of trustees, "The future looks very uncertain; internally, I am much depressed. Fisk is gone if I leave now—to stay will be very hard." McKenzie resigned on 16 April 1925. The trustees hired the last of white presidents, Thomas E. Jones, who served until 1946.[76]

Howard University hired its first black president, Mordecai W. Johnson, in 1926, and, although some Negroes objected to his appointment. Most wanted Johnson to succeed. Du Bois argued that since top quality white men would no longer stake their careers as presidents of HBCUs, the trustees should chose highly competent Negroes as president. Some Howard faculty members saw "no good" in the election of a Negro as president and began a movement to remove Mordecai Johnson. Lorenzo J. Greene, a graduate of Howard, said, according to Carter G. Woodson, [The revolt was led by a] "triumvirate of scoundrels—Perry Howard, James A. Cobb, and Emmett Scott (secretary-treasurer at Howard). The latter ... is the smoothest, petty politician in the [Negro] race, a low-down, grafting, crafty, underhanded, suave, scheming, self-inflated egotist."[77] Howard's law school faculty and alumni believed Johnson was weakening the program. The trustees, however, voted confidence in Johnson, and the students celebrated by building a huge bonfire on campus. Howard University enrolled about 1,700 students, and the president of the Association for the Study of Negro Life and History had to resign for his alleged part in the attempt to remove Johnson. The ASNLH founder, Carter G. Woodson, fully supported Johnson, but the intrigue continued into the 1930s. In his *Born to Rebel: An Autobiography*, Benjamin E. Mays, who arrived at Howard in 1934, recalled at a Founders Day Banquet "men looking like thugs darted from the darkness into the light, handing out leaflets entitled "The Case against Mordecai Johnson." The head of the New Deal agency that funneled federal funds to Howard was the guest speaker. The president

---

[76] Ibid., 167.

[77] Greene, *Selling Black History*, 338–39; *Baltimore Afro-American*, 4 July and 2 May 1931; H. A. Boyd, "Fisk U Situation," *Nashville Globe*, August 1924–February 1925; Joe M. Richardson, *A History of Fisk University, 1865–1946* (Tuscaloosa: University of Alabama Press, 1980) 130–13, letters regarding the Fisk revolt, Fayette A. McKenzie Papers, State Library and Archives, Nashville TN; Alrutheus A. Taylor, "Fisk University and the Nashville Community, 1866–1900," *Journal of Negro History* 39/2 (April 1954): 111–26; Thomas E. Davis, "A Study of Fisk University Freshmen from 1928 to 1930," *Journal of Negro Education* 2/4 (October 1933):477–83; Lester C. Lamon, "The Black Community and the Fisk University Strike of 1924–1925," *Journal of Southern History* 40/2 (May 1974): 225–44.

could not allow radicalism and political activism on campus, because such activities could discourage Congress from making annual appropriations to Howard University. Federal appropriations began in 1879 and the powerful chairs of the congressional committees often were Southern white men who could block the appropriations. Intrigue among faculty and staff continued for years, but Johnson "never fired … persons known to be his enemies," said Mays.

Johnson remained close to NAACP secretary Walter White and NAACP board member Eleanor Roosevelt and helped the NAACP raise $20,000 for the legal defense fund. From 1930 to 1960, Congress appropriated $30.7 million for Howard University, compared to just $4.3 million for Howard between 1879 and 1926. Yet, Johnson continued to lobby Congress for more funds. He remained president until 1960, helping to build twenty new buildings and ten schools and colleges.[78]

At the public Negro colleges, Jim Crow state officials ruled with iron fists. The public HBCUs had black presidents from the beginning—men with a mandate from Jim Crow state officials to keep the peace on campus. Black presidents forbade the faculty to get involved in politics, racial matters, or any public controversies. Negro presidents at both public and private institutions knew how to respect Jim Crow, and white supremacy standards did not allow Negroes a class structure or any variations of social privilege. Some Negro college presidents, including Mordecai Johnson, John Hope, and William J. Hale, could be mistaken for white, which, perhaps, drew resentment from their on-campus detractors. Jim Crow treated all non-white persons as subordinate citizens, regardless of the person's self-perceived class status and his appearance of "being as white as a white man" in skin color.

The case of William J. Hale illustrates this bizarre American racial phenomenon of passing for white. At state education meetings, some participants used the words "nigger" and "coons" quite openly, until alerted that the president of Tennessee A&I State College was a Negro. When the board's secretary learned that Hale was a Negro, she refused him a seat until the commissioner of education ordered her to treat Hale equally with the other college presidents. Hale got his revenge: he refused the woman's invitation to have a seat, and stood—

---

[78] Benjamin E. Mays, *Born to Rebel: An Autobiography* (New York: Charles Scribner's Sons, 1971) 139–148; T. C. Battle and C. L. Muse Jr., *Howard in Retrospect: Images of the Capstone* (Washington DC: Howard University, 1995) 1–26; W. D. Dyson, *Howard University: The Capstone of Negro Education, A History: 1867–1940* (Washington DC: Howard University Graduate School, 1941) 1–10; W. W. Patton, *The History of Howard University, 1867–1888* (Washington DC: Howard Industrial Department, 1896) 1–20; S. M. Lloyd Jr., *A Short History of the Howard University* (Washington DC: Howard University, 1973) 1–20; Greene, *Selling Black History*, 61, 104, 110, 111, 118, 133, 164, 338, 351, 353, 356, 367.

with his hat in hand, dignified, looking straight ahead—until the commissioner called for him.

State-controlled curricula at public HBCUs remained greatly restrained by Jim Crow. When Tennessee created its public teacher colleges in 1909, the legislators purposely placed the words "agricultural and industrial" into the name Tennessee State Normal School. These words distinguished the black institution from the white public teacher colleges. The coded words gave assurance to racial conservatives in the General Assembly that there was respect for Jim Crow. One of the legislators still wanted assurance that Tennessee A&I would *not* breed dangerous Negro agitators through an "improper education."[79]

Perhaps the white legislator was referring to Fisk alumnus William E. B. Du Bois, who had recently stirred up the race question and threatened the "Color Line." In *The Souls of Black Folk*, Du Bois said, "The function of the Negro college, then, is clear: it must maintain the standards of popular education, it must seek the social regeneration of the Negro, and it must help in the solution of race contact and co-operation."[80] In 1905, Du Bois met with similar-minded Negro men and formed the Niagara Movement. They issued *The Niagara Resolutions*—demanding voting rights, an end to racial segregation, and the restoration of the Negro's civil rights. "Until we get these rights, we will never cease to protest and assail the ears of America," said the Niagara group.[81]

Black colleges and Negro citizens could expect no real help from the federal government. President Woodrow Wilson (D), former head of Princeton University and former governor of New Jersey, with a doctorate, and raised in the South, came to power in March 1913. He immediately imposed racial segregation in the federal office buildings. Archibald Grimke, head of the DC chapter of the NAACP, sent a letter of protest to Wilson on 29 October 1913. Representative James B. Aswell of Louisiana asserted in 1914 the US was "a white man's country," and it was unjust for the federal government to place a Negro in a position of authority over a white man. Representative Martin Dies of Texas said, "We have solved the question in the South and white supremacy is a fixture." Wilson enjoyed a White House showing of *The Birth of a Nation*, and he

---

[79] B. L. Lovett, *History of Tennessee State University*, manuscript, 2009, 56; *Messages of the Governors of Tennessee, 1899–1907* (Nashville: Tennessee Historical Commission, 1972) 415.

[80] W. E. B. Du Bois, *The Souls of Black Folk* (New York: Penguin Books, 2003) 89–90.

[81] Du Bois, *The Souls of Black Folk*, 89–90; Francis L. Broderick and August Meier, *Negro Protest Thought in the Twentieth Century* (Indianapolis: Bobbs-Merrill Company, 1965) 48–54.

seemed to endorse the movie's sordid racist message. The NAACP launched a protest.[82]

The NAACP and Negro newspapers protested racism in America's WWI military forces. This offended Wilson, who tried to censure the Negro press. After word arrived that black soldiers mingled freely with European women, Wilson sent the president of Tuskegee Institute to tour the soldiers' camps and counsel them that racial segregation remained in America. Du Bois and others were embarrassed, because they had supported Wilson in the 1912 election. But Rayford Logan, historian at Howard University, said Wilson's election did little harm to Negroes:

> Two events opened new vistas, which contemporaries could not adequately evaluate. First in 1911, and more particularly in 1915, the United States Supreme Court began a series of decisions which was to make this branch of the government the most powerful force in changing the legal status and thereby—albeit to a lesser degree—the actual status of the Negro. Second, World War I started a chain of developments which, more than any event since the American Civil War, made it increasingly difficult for die-hard southerners and their northern allies to 'keep the Negro in his place.'"[83]

The US Supreme Court decided in *Buchanan v. Warley*, 245 US 60 (1917) that cities could not segregate Negroes into their own residential districts, yet Wilson did nothing to enforce the decision. A white Mississippi mob burned some Negro veterans in their Army uniforms, and mobs lynched a total of ten Negro veterans without any investigation from Wilson's government. James Weldon Johnson, acting secretary of the NAACP, labeled 1919 "The Red Summer," when mobs terrorized black communities in East St. Louis, Chicago, Detroit, Knoxville, Tulsa, and Elaine, Arkansas. James H. Dillard of the Slater Fund wrote a story in the *New York Times* that sought to allay fears about widespread southern lynching, but Walter White of the NAACP said Dillard's comments represented "idle vaporing of little value."[84]

Several of the HBCU presidents—both black and white—joined efforts with moderate white leaders on the local and state levels and formed the Commission on Interracial Cooperation (CIC) in 1919. Sometimes called "the Committee on

---

[82] Rayford W. Logan, *The Betrayal of the Negro: from Rutherford B. Hayes to Woodrow Wilson* (Toronto: The Macmillan Company, 1965) 365–66.

[83] Ibid., 359.

[84] J. H. Dillard, "Lynching," *New York Times*, 13 April 1919; Kenneth R. Janken, *Walter White: Mr. NAACP* (Chapel Hill: University of North Carolina Press, 2003) 35, 139, 140, 165, 236, 237, 287.

After-the-War Cooperation," it was a racial accommodation movement in the mode of the late Booker T. Washington's ideas. Robert R. Moton, president of Tuskegee Institute; John Hope, president of Morehouse; John M. Gandy, president of Virginia State; and Isaac Fisher, publisher of the *Fisk University News* were among the first Negro members. Negro college women, including Mary McLeod Bethune and Lugenia Burns (Mrs. John Hope), played important roles in the CIC. Margaret Washington was among the Negro women invited to speak on "What it Means to be a Negro" at the October 1920 CIC Southern Women & Race Cooperation meeting in Memphis. Phelps-Stokes, Laura Spelman Memorial, Carnegie, Rosenwald, and Rockefeller funds gave money to improve race relations.

The Oklahoma CIC included thirty-nine blacks and sixteen whites at the 28 November 1920 meeting. They discussed lynching, unfair Jim Crow laws, mistreatment of Negro women by white men, and negative portrayal of Negroes in white newspapers. They talked about the lack of law enforcement on the local and state levels when whites committed crimes against blacks, "growing race hatred" in America, and "a loss of confidence on the part of Negroes in the white man." CIC Papers include blacks' testimonials about the Tulsa Race Riot, 31 May–1 June 1921. Ruth Vance testified, "500 white men and little boys came rushing in on the Negro section and such shooting and killing I never seen ... Troops came to quiet things down ... The Red Cross came to help" the victims. The CIC headquartered in Atlanta, and AU Atlanta stored the CIC Papers.[85]

Not only was the racial situation in American in the 1920s dire, but the poor quality and low availability of public Negro high schools continued to have negative affects on the HBCUs and the pace of their development. The HBCU faculty members often pressured the HBCU presidents not to close the on-campus high schools that fed the freshman enrollment, furnished talent for the collegiate athletic teams, and provided a high school for the local black community. Accreditation of high schools on HBCU campuses sometimes preceded the four-year collegiate accreditation, such as Alcorn in 1924 and Lincoln in 1925. Southern officials did as little as possible to create an adequate number of quality high schools for blacks in the 1920s. Atlanta built its first

---

[85] V. M. Matthews, "University Commission on Southern Race Questions," in Mjagkij, *Organizing Black America*, 683–84; J. Morse, "The University Commission on Southern Race Questions," *The South Atlantic Quarterly* 19 (1920): 302–310; see Jessie C. Smith, ed., *Notable Black American Women* (Westport CT: Greenwood Press, 1992) for profiles of many HBCU women leaders; see Audrey T. McCluskey and E. M. Smith, eds., *Mary McLeod Bethune: Building a Better World* (Bloomington: Indiana University Press, 1999, 2001) 136, 149–54; Mary McLeod Bethune Papers, the Amistad Research Center, Tulane University, New Orleans.

public high school for Negroes in 1924, but by 1926, Georgia still had only two high schools for Negroes and only six by 1927. Morehouse and Spelman continued their high school departments, and 60 percent of Spelman high school students lived on campus. Atlanta University continued its Laboratory School (high school) until 1940. Knoxville College discontinued elementary and high school departments in 1927 and 1931, respectively. In 1934, the city of Knoxville furnished supervisors of art, music, writing, health and safety as well as twelve grades of school for whites, but gave Negro children no equivalents. Nashville public schools upgraded black Pearl High School (1883–) to twelve grades and added an English composition course by 1921. Tennessee A&I continued its high school program until 1936, whereas white public colleges in Tennessee had discontinued their high school programs ten years previously. Alabama maintained few high schools for blacks, whereas, Delaware and South Carolina did nothing.

By the 1920s, some black leaders began to speak out about the condition of race relations in the US. The "New Negro" reflected itself in the graduates and persons affiliated with the HBCUs that began to impact black intellectual life and the forum of ideas in America.

Archibald Grimke, a member of the NAACP's board of directors compared American racial violence to the "Turkish atrocities in Armenia" and to the actions of the Germans in Belgium during the war.[86] More than a million Europeans were the victims of genocide, and, in an attempt to prevent the American racial situation from advancing to such a bloody point, Grimke helped the NAACP with a congressional anti-lynching bill. He teamed with James Weldon Johnson, Walter White, and other NAACP officers to testify before a House Committee about 14th Amendment violations in the Jim Crow states. They asked Congress to invoke Section II of the 14th Amendment, which would reduce, percentage wise, the state's representation in the House according to number of persons [mostly blacks] unlawfully disenfranchised. After Grimke's continuing criticisms of the national office of the NAACP, W. E. B. Du Bois played a major role in denying Grimke reelection to the NAACP's board of directors in 1923, and Grimke retired from the DC branch of the NAACP in 1925. Grimke was an HBCU product; he was a former slave forced to be a house servant and was beaten by his late father's brother. Grimke ran away, worked for the Union Army, attended Charleston's Morris Street School—headed by abolitionist Frances Pillsbury of Massachusetts—completed his bachelor's and

---

[86] Dickson D. Bruce Jr., *Archibald Grimke: Portrait of a Black Independent* (Baton Rouge: LSU Press, 1993) 243.

master's degrees in 1874 at Lincoln University, Pennsylvania, and completed his law degree at Harvard. Grimke died in 1930.[87]

James Weldon Johnson, a product of Atlanta University, became, in 1920, the first Negro secretary of the NAACP. To show no fear of the growing Klan threat, the NAACP held its 1920 Conference in Atlanta around the 14th anniversary of the Atlanta Race Riot of 1906. On 3 July 1923, when black leaders secured one of the federal hospitals to serve veterans and planned for it to become a part of the campus of Tuskegee Institute—with a black staff—some seven hundred Klansmen paraded on the grounds of the hospital, demanding a white-only staff. Johnson demanded federal troops. He sent Walter White to Washington to talk to the FBI. By 1924, the Tuskegee Hospital had a black chief and Negro staff. A modern Ku Klux Klan used violence to work keep blacks in their places. By 1924, thousands of robed Klansmen marched boldly down Pennsylvania Avenue in DC. Jeers and laughter from Negroes, as well as from some whites, greeted many a Klan speech, parade, and cross burning. Mobs lynched nine Negro Americans in 1928, and most southern governments refused to enforce the law if the victims were black and the murderers were white.[88] Ultimately, James Weldon Johnson became a literature professor at Fisk.

The Garvey movement characterized black pride and protest in the 1920s, and to some extent, it also affected people at the black colleges. After arriving from his native Jamaica, Marcus Garvey established his black movement between 1916 and 1925, based upon the racial accommodation ideas of Booker T. Washington and the educational model used at Tuskegee. By 1921, the UNIA (Universal Negro Improvement Association) claimed millions of members engaging Negro uplift, black pride, business enterprise, and racial separatism. By 1925, members had begun introducing UNIA chapters into several Southern towns, including one of the largest in Chattanooga, Tennessee, where a shootout between local police and UNIA members made the national news. Some UNIA ideas likely affected the HBCUs, their students, and graduates. Many learned Negro writers, educated at HBCUs or affiliated with such institutions, took notice of the Garvey movement and its significance in the efforts to uplift the Negro Americans. Garvey and the UNIA drew the attention of Benjamin J.

---

[87] Bruce, *Archibald Grimke*, 22–26, 210–211, 222–23.

[88] Paul H. Bergeron, Stephen V. Ash, and Jeanette Ash, *Tennesseans and Their History* (Knoxville: University of Tennessee Press, 1999) 247–49; Arthur F. Rapier, "The Mob Still Rides," *Southern Changes: Journal of the Southern Regional Council* 22/4 (Spring 2000): 6; Commission on Interracial Cooperation (CIC) Papers, 1942, Atlanta University Library files; David M. Chalmers, *Hooded Americanism: The History of the Ku Klux Klan* (New York: New Viewpoints, 1981) 334; Eugene Levy, *James Weldon Johnson: Black Leader, Black Voice* (Chicago: University of Chicago Press, 1973) 187, 271, 272, 274–75.

Brawley, English professor at Howard University, who included the UNIA in his high school textbook, *A Social History of the American Negro*. Claude McKay, author of *Harlem* devoted a chapter to the UNIA. Although he opposed the Garvey movement because of its black separatist posture, W. E. B. Du Bois included Garvey and the UNIA in *Dusk of Dawn*, and J. A. Rogers book, *World's Great Men of Color*, featured Garvey and the UNIA. Merle Eppse of Tennessee A&I included Garvey in *The Negro, Too, in American History*. Archibald Grimke maintained good relations with Garvey and supported the UNIA *Messenger* newspaper. The *Messenger* began the movement to capitalize respectfully the word Negro, and the idea caught on. Although, in 1925, federal officials sent Garvey to prison in Atlanta, President Coolidge pardoned him in 1927 but exiled him from America. He wrote to his followers:

> My months of forcible removal from among you, being imprisoned as a punishment for advocating the cause of our real emancipation, have not left me hopeless or despondent, but to the contrary, I see a great ray of light and the bursting of a mighty political cloud which will bring you complete freedom.... Hold fast to the Faith. Desert not the ranks, but as brave soldiers march on to victory....[89]

Marcus Garvey died in England in 1940. John Hope Franklin and Alfred A. Moss Jr., said, "Its significance [lays] in the fact that it [the UNIA] was the first mass movement among African Americans and that it indicated the extent to which they entertained doubts concerning the hope for first-class citizenship in the only homeland they knew."[90]

From 1924 to 1931, Du Bois, Charles S. Johnson, James Weldon Johnson, and Alain Locke, among others, launched the Harlem or Black Renaissance. Although there had been a Negro Renaissance in literature and publishing during the period 1890–1915, the new Renaissance was different. Negro

---

[89] M. E. Garvey, "Letter to the Negro World," 10 February 1925, in Robert A. Hill, ed., *The Marcus Garvey and Universal Negro Improvement Association Papers*, vol. 6 (Berkeley: University of California Press, 1989) 96–98; E. David Cronon, *Black Moses: The Story of Marcus Garvey and the Negro Universal Improvement Association* (Madison: University of Wisconsin Press, 1955, 1969) 136.

[90] John Hope Franklin and A. A. Moss Jr., *From Slavery to Freedom*, 322, 323, 326; see Cronon, *Black Moses*, 169, 172, 183, 192, 212, 213, 215; J. A. Rogers, *World's Great Men of Color* (New York: Simon & Schuster, 1947) 415–31; Bruce Jr., *Archibald Grimke*, 253; Benjamin Brawley, *A Social History of the American Negro* (New York: Macmillan, 1921) 370; Merle R. Eppse, *The Negro, Too, in American History* (Washington DC: Associated Negro Universities Press, 1938) 21; Claude McKay, *Harlem: Negro Metropolis* (New York: E. P. Dutton, 1940) 143; W. E. B. Du Bois, *Dusk or Dawn: An Essay toward an Autobiography of a Race Concept* (New York: Harcourt Brace, 1940) 269.

intellectuals purposely organized the Harlem Renaissance to disprove the notion that the Negro had no such a thing as a culture. Many whites believed Negroes had no creative bones in their bodies in relation to history, art, music, painting, theater, dance, sculpture, engineering, or science.[91]

Indubitably, the Harlem Renaissance was a literary battle the Negro and his friends fought against intellectual exclusion, and during this heightened period of black racial consciousness, sociological research into Negro problems increased at the HBCUs. Fisk hired the promising E. Franklin Frazier, former head of a new school of social work at Morehouse College. Morehouse officials had fired Frazier because he had offended a Southern white liberal with a stinging critique of the man's new book, *The Basis of Racial Adjustment*. Du Bois interceded to get Frazier a job at Fisk, and in 1934, Frazier moved to Howard, where he, along with other professors, focused their scholarship on Negro studies. Du Bois's future wife Shirley Graham was a faculty member at Tennessee A&I and published black music ideas in *Crisis*. At Howard University, Alain Locke headed a literary society for students, and Zora Neale Hurston, the most famous of Negro female writers in the Renaissance, began her writings as a student in that literary society. Locke's colleague Benjamin Brawley published *The Negro in Literature and Art* in 1918 and *A Social History of the American Negro* in 1921; J. Emmett Scott published *Negro Migration during the War*; H. J. Seligman and Harper Brothers published *The Negro Faces America*; and Alain Locke published "The Younger Literary Movement" in *Crisis* 28, and *The New Negro*.[92]

Carter G. Woodson and associates in the Howard University community launched Negro History Week crusade in 1926. Some faculty members at Tennessee A&I organized a chapter of Woodson's Association for the Study of Negro Life and History in 1927, and historian Merle Eppse invited Woodson to Nashville to inaugurate the new chapter. Tennessee A&I strengthened its Negro history course that had been camouflaged since 1912 under the course title "Industrial Education with an Emphasis on the Negro." In 1928, Fisk began a social science project of local interviews with former slaves that became the first

---

[91] B. L. Lovett, "From Plantation to the City: William Edmondson and the African-American Community," in Rusty Freeman, ed., *The Art of William Edmondson* (Jackson: University Press of Mississippi, 1999) 15–32.

[92] David L. Lewis, *W. E. B. Du Bois: The Fight for Equality and the American Century, 1919–1963* (New York: Henry Holt, 2000) 206–207, 320, 550; Benjamin Brawley, *The Negro in Literature and Art* (New York: Duffield & Co., 1918) 1–20; Alain Locke, *The New Negro: An Interpretation* (New York: A and C Boni, 1925) 1–21; J. Emmett Scott, *Negro Migration during the War* (New York: Oxford University Press, 1920) 1–10.

volume of the federal *Slave Narratives*.[93] With the help of liberal white benefactors, the Harlem Renaissance reached its height in 1931, but the Negro movement in arts, literature, humanities, social science, and science continued into later decades. The HBCUs affected this movement, and the movement affected the HBCUs.

Unfortunately, however, a terrible HBCU paradox existed as to whether Negroes should study their cultural background or completely assimilate into European-American culture; HBCU presidents focused on remaking the Negro into European culture. They feared loss of white donors if the Negroes became too black on the campuses and did not specifically promote black studies, Negro studies, or African American and African studies. Carter G. Woodson explained, "They [philanthropists] hope to make the Negro conform quickly to the standard of the whites and thus remove the pretext for the barriers between the races." [94]

The racial nature of American society necessitated that Negro scholars and others focus on the Negro problem. W. E. B. Du Bois shared this paradox. In a speech at Fisk University, Du Bois said, "When the southern Negro college changed from a missionary school to a secular college, there was a tendency continually to say: this is not a Negro college; it is a college; we are not teaching Negro science or Negro art, we are teaching Art and Science." [95]

Liberals were willing to soften America's white supremacy system, but they did not have the stamina to dismantle it because many whites objected to higher education for Negroes. Yet, under the leadership of demagogues and anti-intellectuals, the southern states lagged far behind northerners in higher education. Southern scholar, John Egerton said, "By 1938, the prestigious Association of American Universities had only four Southern members."[96]

The US Bureau of Education Report of 1928 reduced the number of HBCUs capable of achieving collegiate status to 130 institutions. Philanthropists continued to pour resources into HBCUs with the best potential for gaining accreditation. HBCU leaders established the National Association of College Deans,

---

[93] See US Federal Writers' Project, *Slave Narratives: A Folk History of Slavery in the United States from Interviews with Former Slaves, Tennessee Narratives* (Washington DC: Library of Congress, 1941); Ophelia S. Egypt, *Unwritten History of Slavery: An Autobiographical Account of Negro Slavery* (Nashville: Fisk University, 1945).

[94] Carter G. Woodson, *The Mis-Education of the Negro* (Washington DC: Association for the Study of Negro Life and History, Inc., 1933) 7.

[95] Eric J. Sundquist, ed., *The Oxford W. E. B. Du Bois Reader* (New York: Oxford University Press, 1996) 409–31.

[96] John Egerton, *Speak Now Against the Day: The Generation before the Civil Rights Movement in the South* (Knoxville: University of Tennessee Press, 1994) 128–29.

Registrars, and Admissions Officers (1925–) to discuss mutual problems and set standards for quality control; CDRAO still functions in this role today. By 1930, HBCUs had 13,860 students enrolled, and had granted 165 bachelor's degrees. During the period 1921–1927 only four of these institutions achieved regional accreditation. In the Southern Association of Colleges and Schools eleven-state territory, where 90 percent of eligible HBCUs resided, SACS had, by 1929, approved none of them.

Negro Republicans continued their protest against this decades-old "lily white" movement; they sent a delegation to confer with Hoover in late summer 1932, but Hoover did not more than accept photo opportunities with them. Most Negroes stayed with the Republican Party in the November 1932 election, although larger numbers than before cast their lot with the Democrats, and Hoover met defeat.

The coming of the liberal New Deal, World War II, and a post-World War II liberal period of American politics profoundly influenced the next stage of development of America's HBCUs. This really would be "the coming out" period of the black colleges and universities.

3

Critical Era of Transformation

With the advent of New Deal liberalism (1933–1953), America's HBCUs benefited greatly. Some Americans came to the realization that the nation could not prosper if they neglected the education of the southern region, which contained 40 percent of the nation's people and a vast store of America's natural resources. Nor could the region be left in the hands of a Jim Crow leadership that rendered the place culturally, economically, and intellectually poor. The South's political and criminal justice systems remained deeply corrupted, and William J. Simmons, Baptist minister and founder of an HBCU, said, "The penitentiary is full of our [black] race, who are sent there by wicked and malicious persecutors, and unjust sentences dealt out by judges, who deem a colored criminal fit only for the severest and longest sentences for trivial offences."[1] These socially isolated white men had an arrogance of power and a commitment to the policies of hatred long ago designed by their grandfathers.

The New Deal helped to usher in a twentieth-century version of the Negro's long-fought Civil Rights Movement, and changes in demographics helped bring about needed changes in the American society. The shifting of the Democratic Party power base from the South to the North helped the party embrace New Deal political liberalism. Northern immigrants, blacks, labor unions, and others now attempted to coexist in this party, and the New Deal's liberal element inspired the federal courts to strengthen enforcement of the 14th Amendment in 1868, which affected the federal government's ability to make economic, international, political, social, and racial progress for America. At this time, almost 90 percent of Negroes still lived in rural parts of the southern states, until the period 1890–1910 when the old plantation system began breaking up, sending a flood of Negroes into southern towns and cities. From southern shantytowns, slums, and cities, Negroes sent a new generation north and west, seeking jobs, better education and training, and no more lynching. The 1930 US Census showed 43.7 percent of Negroes lived in America's urban areas, compared to 10 percent in 1860. Since 1920, the number of Negroes in the North increased by 1,381,545. Negro migrants gained freedom from most of the white

---

[1] William J. Simmons, *Men of Mark: Eminent, Progressive and Rising* (Cleveland OH: G. M. Rewell Company, 1887) 49.

mob violence, but as soon as they were better able to access the American dream, the Great Depression swiftly wiped out any economic gains from the Great Migration. Up to 60 percent of adult Negroes suffered stages of unemployment, and 2,147,044 of them were on relief.[2] However, the Negro was poised to progress forward.

Improved communication among Negroes was another factor in the improvement of black conditions. The number of daily and weekly Negro newspapers increased as the black urban population grew. In the 1930s, the weekly *World* extended publication from Deep South Atlanta into the heart of the heavily black Mississippi Delta. The *Chicago Defender* outright encouraged Negroes to *come north*, and some Negroes actually wrote back asking how they could get there.[3]

The *New York Amsterdam News*, *Kansas City Call*, *Baltimore Afro-American*, *Norfolk Journal and Guide*, *Philadelphia Tribune*, and *Dallas Express* had a total circulation of 132,000, and some fifty black newspapers altogether circulated six hundred thousand copies, meaning about three million papers were read each week. Other newspapers, journals, and quarterlies included *The Crisis*, edited by Du Bois at the NAACP, the National Urban League's *Opportunity*, *Journal of Negro History*, *National Medical Journal*, *Negro Market* of the National Negro Business League, *Colored Hairdresser and Barber*, AMEC *Christian Recorder*, *The National Baptist Union Review* out of Nashville, and other church journals and newsletters. There also existed dailies and weeklies like the *Pittsburgh Courier*, *Oklahoma Black Dispatch*, *Houston Informer*, *Memphis World*, *Atlanta World*, *Nashville Globe*, and quarterlies such as the *Journal of Negro Education*.

In 1942, newspaper editor and publisher P. B. Young said, "the Negro press was holding its place as the articulate voice of the Negro race."[4] Members of A. Philip Randolph's Brotherhood of Sleeping Car Porters Labor Union distributed

---

[2] 14th Census, 1920 (Washington DC: Department of Commerce, Bureau of the Census, 1921); "Number and Distribution of Inhabitants," 15th Census, 1930 (Washington DC: Bureau of the Census, 1932); "Number and Distribution of Inhabitants," 16th Census, 1940 (Washington DC: Bureau of the Census, 1942).

[3] Emmett J. Scott, "Letters of Negro Migrants of 1916–18," *Journal of Negro History* 4 (1919): 1–20; Scott, "More Letters of Negro Migrants of 1916–1918," *Journal of Negro History* 4/4 (October 1919): 412–65; Carole Marks, *Farewell—We're Good and Gone: The Great Black Migration* (Bloomington: Indiana University Press, 1989) 1–35.

[4] P. B. Young Sr., "The Extent and Quality of the Negro Press," Commission on Interracial Cooperation (CIC) Papers, 1919–1944, Pamphlets and Reports, 1942, microfilm, Atlanta Universty, Atlanta GA; Henry L. Suggs, *P. B. Young, Newspaperman: Race, Politics, and Journalism in the New South, 1910–1962* (Charlottesville: University of Virginia Press, 1988) 1–41; Emma L. Thornbrough, "American Negro Newspapers, 1880–1914," *Business History Journal* 40/4 (Winter 1966): 467–78.

Negro newspapers, including the *Defender* and the *Courier*. They threw copies from speeding trains, and Negroes stood by the tracks to rush the papers home to read, distribute, and pass on to others. According to author Paula F. Pfeffer, "Randolph's ideologies and strategies provided the blueprint for the Civil Rights Movement that emerged."[5] In addition, HBCU libraries were a source for newspapers that carried national news, and when Negro migrants began holding better-paying jobs in the industrial North, they sent more of their children to college—mostly to HBCU campuses that served as places of enlightenment and refuge.[6]

The General Education Board (GEB), the Rosenwald Fund, and other philanthropic associations and education reform groups, continued to be agents of change for the HBCUs. Unlike the American Baptist Home Mission Society, which began to back out of the turbulent South by 1913, most of the philanthropic agencies continued to hang on for another decade or two. In their final years as affirmed endowment funds, foundations, and associations, they devised programs and financed facilities to help selected HBCUs gain accredited status. Had it not been for these philanthropic agencies and benevolent foundations, as well as HBCUs and activist Negro leaders, a sizeable number of black and white Southerners would not have been educated at all. Philanthropists pressured Jim Crow states to create more approved public black high schools. Carter G. Woodson said, "This increase in the efficiency of Negro

---

[5] Paula F. Pfeffer, *A. Philip Randolph, Pioneer of the Civil Rights Movement* (Baton Rouge: LSU Press, 1990) 5, 8, 270, 290.

[6] See J. McMahon, *Reconsidering Roosevelt on Race: How the Presidency Paved the Road to Brown* (Chicago: University of Chicago Press, 2003) 1–10; J. B. Kirby, *Black Americans in the Roosevelt Era: Liberalism and Race* (Knoxville: University of Tennessee Press, 1980) 1–20; M. E. Reed, *Seedtime for the Modern Civil Rights Movement: The President's Committee on Fair Employment Practice, 1941–1946* (Baton Rouge: Louisiana State University Press, 1991) 1–20; Harvard Sitkoff, *A New Deal for Blacks: The Emergence of Civil Rights as a National Issue: The Depression Decade* (New York: Oxford University Press, 1978) 1–10; Leslie H. Fishel Jr., "A Case Study: The Negro and the New Deal," in A. L. Hamby, ed., *The New Deal: Analysis and Interpretation* (New York: Longman, 1981) 177–87; D. L. Smith, "Black Communities Mobilize," in David L. Smith, ed., *The New Deal in the Urban South* (Baton Rouge: Louisiana State University Press, 1988) 232–59; C. W. Gower, "The Struggle of Blacks for Leadership Positions in the Civilian Conservation Corps, 1933–1942," *Journal of Negro History* 51 (1976): 123–35; M. H. Little, "The Extra-curricular Activities of Black College Students, 1868–1940," *Journal of Negro History* 65/2 (Spring 1980): 135–48; M. E. Reed, "FEPC and the Federal Agencies in the South," *Journal of Negro History* 65/1 (Winter 1980): 43–51.

rural schools made possible the development of the Negro college [work] separate and distinct from secondary work."[7]

The Rosenwald Fund provided matching funds in fifteen southern states to help build five thousand schoolhouses serving 663,615 Negroes and whites in 883 counties. The Rosenwald Fund made gifts to individual colleges in consultation with Methodist, Congregational, and Episcopal Church boards to concentrate support for the HBCUs deemed worthy of survival. The Rosenwald Fund gave $213,700 to Fisk, $252,000 to Meharry, and $73,530 to Tennessee A&I. The Rosenwald Fund helped Bennett, Bethune-Cookman, Fort Valley Normal in Georgia, Lincoln Institute, Lincoln in Missouri, Livingston, Philander Smith, St. Augustine's, Talladega, Tougaloo, Wiley, Alabama A&M, Alabama State, Fayetteville State, and Virginia State colleges and universities. The Rosenwald Fund also supported the Methodist Church's joint education survey of Negro education and gave funds to help with Negro health projects, the CIC, and fellowships to scholars (blacks and whites) "who wish[ed] to work on some problem distinctive to the South and who expect[ed] to make careers in the South." Rosenwald helped create "Negro University Centers" to foster graduate and professional work at Howard University in Washington, DC; Fisk University and Meharry Medical College in Nashville; Spelman, Atlanta University, Morehouse, Atlanta School of Social Work, and Morris Brown College in Atlanta; and Dillard University in New Orleans.[8]

The Rosenwald Fund, Jeanes Fund, and others still supported some rural Negro high schools because Negroes continued to have limited access to schools. Penn Normal, Industrial and Agricultural School in South Carolina became one of thirty freedmen's schools in the Port Royal Experiment, funded by Quakers, philanthropists, and abolitionists from Pennsylvania. In June 1862, after Union forces took control of the South Carolina Sea Islands, missionaries Laura Towne and Ellen Murray established a freedmen's school in a back room of the Oak Plantation house on St. Helena Island before moving to a Baptist Church. In 1864, donors sent them a prefabricated building and erected it on fifty acres across from the church. Penn School emphasized industrial education and, by 1950, operated as a public school. It later became the Penn Civil Rights Training

---

[7] Carter G. Woodson and Charles H. Wesley, *The Negro in Our History* (Washington DC: Associated Publishers, 1922, 1972) 119.

[8] Alfred Q. Jarrette, *Julius Rosenwald, Son of a Jewish Immigrant, a Builder of Sears, Roebuck & Company, a Benefactor of Mankind: A Biography Documented* (Greenville SC: Southeastern University Press, 1975) 1–40; "Julius Rosenwald (1862–1932)," http://www.searsarchives.com, Sears, 2010; Peter M. Ascoli, *Julius Rosenwald: The Man Who Built Searsh, Roebuck and Advanced the Cause of Black Education in the American South* (Bloomington: Indiana University Press, 2006) 1–21.

Center—a National Historic Landmark. Cardinal Gibbons School began in 1916, and Negroes met with Catholic priests in St. Mary's County, Maryland, to discuss establishment of a reform school, but decided to develop an academic program of agriculture and industrial education instead. Named for Archbishop James Cardinal Gibbons of Baltimore, the school rested on 180 acres on Smith Creek in Ridge. The Knights of Columbus gave $38,000 to erect a two-story brick building, and the school opened in 1924 with twenty-eight students. James H. Dillard of the Slater Fund visited the campus on 30 April 1929. A Jesuit priest and Negroes operated the school, which closed with the last graduating class in 1968.[9]

Since 1913, the accrediting and philanthropic agencies continued working with the Association of Colleges and Secondary Schools for Negroes (ACSSN), which wanted to establish academic ranking mechanisms and accreditation procedures for HBCUs. The Rosenwald Fund, among other agencies, helped finance accreditation visits to the HBCUs, and Carnegie Foundation gave grants to ACSSN and the accreditation associations to help with self-studies. The Middle States Association of Colleges and Schools (MSACS) granted accreditation to Howard University in 1921, Lincoln University in Pennsylvania in 1922, and Morgan State College in 1925. West Virginia Collegiate Institute received North Central Association of Colleges and Schools (NCACS) accreditation in 1927. From 1928 to 1930, the General Education Board (GEB) surveyed Negro education, and made recommendations to specific HBCUs about how to proceed toward accreditation. Many HBCUs needed more library holdings, facilities, science equipment, more college degrees for faculty, and adequate financing.[10]

A hesitant Southern Association of Colleges and Schools (SACS) established, in 1929, a committee to study the HBCU issue. The three-person SACS Committee on Approval of Negro Colleges decided to recognize HBCUs through "Class A" and "Class B" *approval* classifications, which recognized collegiate status, but honored Jim Crow practices by denying full membership with white member institutions. In October 1933, the *Journal of Negro Education*

---

[9] "Penn Center History," http://www.penncenter.com, Penn School National Historic Landmark District, 2010; "Cardinal Gibbons High School," http://www.cardinalgibbons.com; J. Scott McCormick, "The Julius Rosenwald Rund," *Journal of Negro Education* 3/4 (October 1934): 605–26; A. Gilbert Belles, "The College, the Negro Scholar, and the Julius Rosenwald Rund," *Journal of Negro History* 54/4 (October 1969): 383–92; B. C. Caldwell, "The Work of the Jeanes and Slater Funds," *Annals of the American Academy of Political and Social Science* 49/1 (September 1913): 173–76.

[10] See *Survey of Negro Colleges and Universities* (Washington DC: Bureau of Education, 1928) 1–20.

asked, "Why A Class 'B' Negro College?" "This classification is not only confusing to examining officials in higher institutions, but it is misleading to students."

In 1930, Fisk University, which had ended its high school department in 1926, became the first HBCU approved as "Class A" by SACS. SACS approved Talladega College in 1931, Hampton in 1932, LeMoyne, Morehouse, and Spelman college in 1932, Johnson C. Smith, Kentucky State, Tuskegee Institute, Wiley College, and Virginia State in 1933, Prairie View in 1934, Florida A&M and Virginia Union in 1935, and North Carolina Central, Southern A&M, Xavier, and Dillard in 1938. By 1938, two HBCUs achieved North Central accreditation; three achieved Middle States accreditation; sixteen achieved SACS A-approval, and twenty-three received SACS B-approval, for a total of forty-four (36.4 percent) of HBCUs deemed capable of becoming full-fledged four-year colleges. Three HBCUs belonged to the American Association of Teachers Colleges, which the American education community regarded as the highest national recognition for a college. The leading graduate schools readily admitted students from the American Association of Universities that, in 1935, had 285 members including Fisk and Howard.[11] Not many southern white colleges enjoyed such membership. Much of the improvement in the quality of HBCUs had grown out of the aforementioned 1916 report on Negro education, which, for many Negro educators, downgraded most of the Negro schools, saying they would never become "colleges." But the criticism from the 1916 report by Thomas Jessie Jones, from the staff of the Hampton Institute, began an "unprecedented and immediate improvement."[12]

On 6 December 1932, the *Memphis World* proudly announced, "SACS places LeMoyne on Approved List of Institutions of Higher Learning for Negro Youth." The city's mayor and others congratulated President Frank Sweeney, a Harvard graduate, for this achievement since coming to LeMoyne in 1928. Community leaders regretted that LeMoyne had to drop its high school program the previous June in order to be "Rated Class A by the Association of Colleges and Secondary

---

[11] http://www.sacscoc.org, 16 July 2009, list LeMoyne in "1939" for full approval; D. O. Holmes, "The Future Possibilities of Graduate Work in Negro Colleges and Universities," *Journal of Negro Education* 7/1 (January 1938); Horace Mann Bond, "The Evolution and Present Status of Negro Higher and Professional Education in the United States," *Journal of Negro Education* 17/3 (Summer 1948): 224–35; D. O. Holmes, "The Negro College Faces the Depression," *Journal of Negro Education* 2/1 (January 1933): 16–25; "Editorial Comment: Why a Class 'B' Negro College," *Journal of Negro Education* 2/4 (October 1933): 427–431.

[12] Holmes, "The Future Possibilities of Graduate Work in Negro Colleges and Universities," 5–11, 6; E. Franklin Frazier, "Graduate Education in Negro Colleges and Universities," *Journal of Negro Education* 2/2 (July 1933): 329–341.

Schools of the Southern States."[13] The city of Memphis had opened a second black public high school in 1931. LeMoyne had nearly three hundred students, and the new catalog boasted of a "Democratic environment, student participation in government, with view to giving practical training for duties of citizenship," said the *Memphis World* on 16 September 1932. LeMoyne was the result of recent mergers with Roger Williams University and Howe Institute.

Florida Agricultural and Mechanical College received a "B" rating from SACS on 28 December 1931 because the department heads and most faculty members needed more graduate training, salaries were too low, classes were over-sized, and the campus library needed three thousand more books. They earned the "A" rating from SACS in 1935. Florida A&M upgraded to university status by 1951, failed a SACS visit in 1954, but regained accreditation.[14]

Lincoln University in Missouri became a college in 1921. The GEB survey of Negro schools in 1930 recommended it should specialize in teacher education, and move toward regional accreditation, but Lincoln needed to improve teaching and learning. Having tried to achieve North Central Association of Colleges and Schools (NCACS) accreditation since 1924, Lincoln's president reportedly made no further effort to gain accreditation, and the board dismissed him in April 1931. Charles W. Florence, a student at Harvard, then became president. The faculty improved the quality of teaching and learning and, in 1932, required a comprehensive examination of seniors in their major fields. Missouri under-funded the HBCU budget by 9 percent, but the GEB and the Rosenwald Fund awarded scholarships to faculty members to earn more graduate degrees. Lincoln University gained NCACS accreditation in 1934. Said Florence, "There is every reason to think that more will be done in the future to provide equal educational opportunities for Negroes ... It [NCACS] removed one of the stumbling blocks in the way of the school's development."[15]

---

[13] "LeMoyne," *Memphis World*, 6 December 1932, p. 1; Ibid., 16 September 1932.

[14] See L. W. Neyland, *Florida Agricultural and Mechanical University: A Centennial History, 1887–1987* (Tallahassee: FAMU Foundation, Inc., 1987) 1–10; L. W. Neyland and J. W. Riley, *The History of Florida Agricultural and Mechanical University* (Gainesville: University of Florida Press, 1963) 16, 123; Murray D. Laurie, "The Union Academy: A Freedmen's Bureau School in Gainesville, Florida," *Florida Historical Quarterly* 65/2 (October 1986): 165–69; Larry E. Rivers and Canter Brown Jr., "A Monument to Progress of the Race: The Intellectual and Political Origins of the Florida Agricultural and Mechanical University, 1865–1887," *Florida Historical Quarterly* 85/2 (October 2006): 1–41; A. F. Holland, *Nathan B. Young and the Struggle over Black Education* (Columbia MO: University of Missouri Press, 2006) 1–20.

[15] "History of Lincoln University," http://www.lincolnfdn.org, Lincoln University, 2010; W. S. Savage, *The History of Lincoln University* (Springfield IL: Phillips Brothers, 1996) 246, 251.

In the 1930s, of course the status and quality of Negro education remained under debate. Most of HBCUs appeared to continue trades, industrial arts and high school curricula for a longer period compared to their white counterpart institutions. Additionally, although the number of public high schools for Negroes increased, they were not always equal in quality to high schools provided for the whites. In his speech, "Does the Negro Need Separate Schools?" W. E. B. Du Bois said that fewer than half a million of the four million Negroes of school age attended mixed race schools in the North. Blacks needed equal schools as much as separate schools. They needed, he said,

> a separate Negro school, where children are treated like human beings, trained by teachers of their own race, who know what it means to be black in the year of salvation 1935. This is infinitely better than making our boys and girls doormats to be spit and trampled upon and lied to by ignorant social climbers, whose sole claim to superiority is the ability to kick 'niggers' when they are down.... What he needs is Education.

Du Bois spoke to an assembly of faculty, staff, students, and visitors at Fisk University in 1933:

> We suffer a social ostracism, which is so deadening and discouraging that we are compelled either to lie about it or to turn our faces toward the red flag of revolution.... Every step we have made forward has been greeted by a backward step on the part of the American public in caste, intoleration, mob law, and racial hatred.... If this is true, then no matter how much we may dislike the statement, the American Negro problem is and must be the center of the Negro American University.... If the college can pour into the coming age an American Negro who knows himself and his plight and how to protect himself and fight race prejudice, then the world of our dream will come....[16]

Questions concerning the education of Negro women had arisen since 1862 when Mary Jane Patterson became the first black female to graduate from Oberlin. Although some men questioned the right of women to a college education at all, many of the HBCUs admitted men and women on an equal basis. Some all-female HBCUs—Bennett, Spelman, and Tillotson—existed by the 1930s for the exclusive education of Negro women, and women soon outnumbered men in the HBCUs by the late 1930s, comprising the majority of

---

[16] W. E. B. Du Bois, *The Souls of Black Folk* (New York: Penguin Books, 2003) 81; Eric J. Sundquist, ed., *The Oxford W. E. B. Du Bois Reader* (New York: Oxford University Press, 1996) 409, 423–31; Du Bois, "Does the Negro Need Separate Schools?" *Journal of Negro Education* 4 (1935): 328–35; Lucy D. Slowe, "Higher Education of Negro Women," *Journal of Negro Education* 2 (1933): 352–258.

HBCU graduates. Women graduated from the greatest number of HBCU programs—including medicine, but excluding preparation for the ministry.

President Franklin D. Roosevelt (D) held back on enforcing fair allocation of New Deal programs based on race, partly because of the presence of powerful southern congressional representatives in the Democratic Party. Both they and conservatives in the Republican Party tried to block or break his liberal New Deal legislation. After defeating Roosevelt's attempt to add liberal members to the US Supreme Court, the southern congressional representatives issued a *Conservative Manifesto*—similar to the *Southern Manifesto* against the *Brown v. Board of Education*, 347 US 483 (1954) decision. Although "the South" was the poorest region in the United States, the *Conservative Manifesto* repudiated the New Deal and called for strict attention to "states' rights." The congressional representatives did not want to upset the "southern way of life" that favored the white elite-class.

The New Deal liberals took an indirect approach to outmaneuver regressive Southern leaders. The National Emergency Council prepared *The Report on Economic Conditions of the South* in June 1938, which had the help of Southern liberals and progressives. They applauded *The Report* for laying bare the gross social and cultural underdevelopment in the southern US. In Alabama and North Carolina, in 1930, more than 26 percent of Negroes were illiterate, the highest percentages of any other states. White Southerners had the highest illiteracy rates for white Americans, and earned a median income of $1,100 per year compared to $480 a year for the Negroes. In the industrial North, Negroes and whites both averaged higher wages than most Southern whites did. The US census report for 1932 counted fifty Negro architects, 184 engineers, 145 designers and inventors, and 207 chemists. A third of the Southern agricultural workforce was unemployed by 1933, and conservatives argued that lazy Negroes skewed the statistics.

In November 1938, hundreds of invitees met in Birmingham to respond to *The Report on Economic Conditions of the South*. Birmingham was an industrial town, filled with black and white ironworkers and active labor unions. Delegates included labor unions, New Deal administrators, dispossessed Southern whites, Southern progressives, Eleanor Roosevelt, Supreme Court Justice Hugo Black, the NAACP, other civil rights groups, and HBCU representatives such as F. D. Patterson of Tuskegee and Charles S. Johnson of Fisk. The delegates formed the Southern Conference on Human Welfare (SCHW) to abolish the poll tax and to dismantle Jim Crow, writing: "Resolved: That the Conference [expresses] its opposition to and disagreement with the interpretations of the 13th, 14th, and

15th amendments to the Constitution by the Supreme Court."[17] They asked the federal government to expand higher education to help defeat Jim Crow. Race conservatives portrayed the SCHW, the NAACP, and other civil rights groups as communist-inspired organizations, agitators, and outside troublemakers.

During the Great Depression, many HBCUs lost enrollment, cut faculty salaries, and increased work aid to students. State-supported HBCUs suffered more than public, traditionally white institutions (TWIs), but public HBCUs faired better than private HBCUs. About 35,350 students (+5.5 percent over the previous year) enrolled in the HBCUs in fall term 1937–1938; yet, freshman enrollment still fell by 1 percent.[18]

The Great Depression so devastated the South that thousands of Negro teachers lost their jobs. Alabama closed a majority of public schools, and shifted money to white schools. The Works Progress Administration (WPA) instituted a program to rehabilitate unemployed black teachers to assume other jobs. The programs included two-week WPA sessions, including new methods in teaching, use of audiovisuals, interracial relations, readings in black history and culture, and advertising techniques to gain larger school enrollments. HBCUs, including Atlanta University, Livingstone College, and Fisk University, facilitated the sessions and courses, because a great percentage of HBCU graduates were teachers. The WPA lasted until 1943. Negro colleges and county training schools assisted with the National Youth Administration (NYA), including furnishing the sites for Negro camps. The NYA provided jobs and training for Negro youth, and the program enabled students to earn money by performing tasks related to education and continuing studies. NYA youngsters sent money home to help their families. Mary McLeod Bethune, a product of Barber-Scotia College and head of Bethune-Cookman College, headed the Division of Negro Affairs in the NYA. Bethune became a fundraiser and speaker for the Southern Conference on Human Welfare (SCHW). She spoke at Tennessee A&I in April 1943, upon an invitation by the Alpha Kappa Alpha Sorority, while the SCHW held its convention in Nashville.

---

[17] Linda Reed, *Simple Decency & Common Sense: The Southern Conference Movement, 1938–1963* (Bloomington: Indiana University Press, 1991) 5, 94, 97, 181; D. L. Carlton and P. A. Coclanis, eds., *Confronting Southern Poverty in the Great Depression: The Report on Economic Conditions of the South with Related Documents* (New York: Bedford Books, 1996) 151–69; John Egerton, *Speak Now Against the Day: The Generation before the Civil Rights Movement in the South* (Knoxville: University of Tennessee Press, 1994) 187–97; Martin D. Jenkins, "Enrollment in Negro Colleges and Universities, 1937–38," *Journal of Negro Education* 7/2 (April 1938): 118–23.

[18] Holmes, "The Negro College Faces the Depression, 16–25; Jenkins, "Enrollment in Negro Colleges and Universities, 1937–38," 118–23.

Negroes suffered discrimination in the dispensation of New Deal funds and programs, including the Civilian Conservation Corps (CCC). In 1933, writer C. W. Gower said "although Negroes made up 36% of the population of Georgia, only 143 of a total of 3,710 CCC enrollees from that state were Negroes, while in Mississippi with its population slightly over 50% blacks, the selection agents had enrolled only 46 Negroes out of a total of 2,776 men sent to the CCC."[19] Persons from Meharry and Howard served in the Reserve Medical Corps, and along with black chaplains, served in CCC camps. Negroes had to protest to force the federal government to overcome local prejudice against having blacks as camp commanders. George E. Haynes, executive secretary of the Federal Council of the Churches of Christ in America, Walter White, executive secretary of the NAACP, and Edgar G. Brown an officer in the CCC from 1935 to 1942, and writer of an unfinished booklet, *The C.C.C. and Negro Youth,* questioned the Roosevelt administration about persistent racial discrimination in the CCC.[20] Memphis received New Deal money to train Negroes as skilled ironworkers, but upon graduation the blacks received jobs as truck drivers and janitors. Ella Dotson, a female Negro trainee, wrote to FDR in October 1942 complaining that a New Deal agency in Memphis discriminated openly against Negroes, and "I don't want charity. I want work."

By involving the HBCUs, the federal government could better deliver some New Deal relief and training programs to the black community. Grambling State College for Teachers operated a two-hundred-acre farm, wired neighboring homes for electricity, and used a wagon to send teachers into the rural areas of northeast Louisiana to teach poor people new knowledge and skills. The Grambling choir entertained civic and church groups throughout the region. Dillard University administered a penny-a-day health insurance program, combined with Rosenwald Fund grants. The Atlanta School of Social Work obtained New Deal grants to service black communities, and Atlanta University opened a citizenship school to register Negroes to vote. New Deal funds built recreational facilities at Tennessee A&I, and they gave black neighborhoods access to these facilities. Negroes showed their gratitude to the administration when FDR visited Nashville—the local HBCU presidents made sure they were in

---

[19] C. W. Gower, "The Struggle of Blacks for Leadership Positions in the Civilian Conservation Corps, 1933–1942," *Journal of Negro History* 61 (1976): 123–35; McCluskey and Smith, *Mary McLeod Bethune,* 1–20; Darlene Clark Hine, William C. Hine, and Stanley Harrold, *African Americans: A Concise History,* 2nd ed. (Upper Saddle River NJ: Pearson Prentice Hall, 2006) 384–407; Reed, "FEPC and the Federal Agencies in the South," 43–51.

[20] Reed, "FEPC and the Federal Agencies in the South," 43–51; Smith, *The New Deal in the South,* 232-259.

front of Fisk's Jubilee Hall, where FDR sat in the car, listening to the Negro college choirs. The 87-year-old J. C. Napier, a Howard University law school graduate and former US Register of the Treasury (1911–1913), gave the welcome to the presidential party. In 1937, WPA funds assumed work on the slave narratives that Fisk students and the anthropologist professor started in 1928, and now stored and digitized at the Library of Congress. During the Great Depression, the Negro colleges expanded their public service functions, often in conjunction with the National Urban League or the NAACP. LeMoyne College sponsored the NAACP's first youth council in 1938. LeMoyne worked with the Fellowship of Reconciliation (FOR) to try to liberalize race relations in Memphis. Professors at Kentucky State, Southern, and other HBCUs engaged New Deal research projects.[21]

Many Americans had little respect for black intellectual history. The extreme racial prejudice and ignorance of other world cultures that European Americans held—especially for persons of African descent, blinded them against the fact that universities existed in Africa before they appeared in Europe. This European prejudice and ignorance was displayed less by the darker skinned southern Europeans whose land touched the Mediterranean, and who, for hundreds of years, experienced the dominance of the North African culture in Iberia. The southern Europeans, therefore, had not been under the influence of American society's color line, with its prerequisite racial prejudices and Jim Crow practices. Writing in 1942 in the preface of the *National Survey of Higher Education of Negroes,* Ina C. Brown discusses the intellectual problem of race. Brown pointed out that Africans, too, north and south of the Sahara Desert, like other human beings, enjoyed intellectual discourse in their history. Brown said, "Black scholars of Timbuktu visited and lectured at the universities of Fez, Morocco, and Grenada."[22] Black and light-skinned (Arabs) scholars—race had no significance there—enjoyed notoriety for their libraries. Books and salt comprised the chief imports of Timbuktu—but few Europeans ever reached Timbuktu.

Nevertheless, when President Herbert Hoover (R) appointed a Research Committee on Social Trends to survey major aspects of American civilization, Negro scholars and American Negro culture did not seem to matter in the assessments. The Committee produced two volumes of *Recent Social Trends in the*

---

[21] Ibid.

[22] Ina C. Brown, *National Survey of Higher Education of Negroes,* 3 vols. (Washington DC: US Department of Education [USDOE], 1942) 1:1–12.

United States.[23] The Commonwealth Fund, the Rockefeller Foundation, and the Carnegie Corporation helped fund the American Historical Associations' Commission on the Social Studies," which began its work in 1929 and published *A Charter for the Social Sciences in the Schools*.[24] White Americans were trying to discern the idea of "their civilization," and to understand how "American civilization" differed from its root "European civilization" and "western civilization." Historians Charles A., and Mary R. Beard wrote,

> As to ultimates, while rejecting a total determinism, the idea of civilization predicates a partial determinism, such as an irreversible and irrevocable historical heritage, and a partially open and dynamic world in which creative intelligence can and does work; in which character can and does realize ethical values; in which individual and collective efforts, now and in the future, can make the good, the true, and the beautiful prevail more widely, advancing civilization, amid divagations, defeats, and storms, toward its distant, ever-enlarging vision.[25]

Negroes were not included in this federal research about "American civilization," and yet the US Bureau of Education criticized the lack of research at HBCUs. Du Bois said, "Howard, Fisk, and Atlanta are naturally unable to do the type of grade of graduate work, which is done at Columbia, Chicago, and Harvard… Why attribute this to a defect in the Negro race, and not to the fact that the large white colleges have from one hundred to one thousand times the funds for equipment and research that the Negro colleges command?"[26] Since the appearance of Phyllis Wheatley, Benjamin Bannecker, and other Negro writers and scholars in eighteenth-century America, free blacks and even some slaves had been productive in the nation's creative life. Folk tales and music of the slaves had contributed to the richest of American culture. Post-emancipation American Negroes had their first Renaissance, beginning in 1890, opening publishing houses and writing more books.[27] HBCU faculty produced books,

---

[23] See US Research Committee on Social Trends, *Recent Social Trends in the United States* (New York: McGraw Hill, 1933).

[24] See American Historical Commission on the Social Studies, *A Charter for the Social Sciences* (New York: Charles Scribner's Sons, 1932).

[25] Charles and Mary Beard, *The Rise of American Civilization: The American Spirit: A Study of the Idea of Civilization in the United States*, 4 vols. (New York: Macmillan Company, 1942, Collier Books, 1962, 1971) 4:585.

[26] W. E. B. Du Bois, "Does the Negro Need Separate Schools?" in Sundquist, ed., *The Oxford Reader*, 423–31.

[27] Wilson J. Moses, "The Lost World of the Negro, 1895–1919: Black Literary and Intellectual Life before the 'Renaissance,'" *Black American Literature Forum* 21/1–2(Spring–Summer 1987): 61–84.

scholarly articles, and research studies during the Harlem Renaissance, and the productive cultural trend continued after 1931.

While European Americans (whites) wanted to know more about their "civilization," African Americans, shut off from African civilization for up to 314 years, wanted to know about *their* "civilization." The emphasis on Negro/black studies, thus, filled a critical need to know about the American Negro, his problems, and desires. Black studies gave Negro scholars and HBCUs confidence to speak out on Negro issues with a sense of expertise. White scholars at the TWIs also became involved in research and writing on topics about the Negro, but often approached Negro studies from a paternalistic view and many of them viewed this research as "problem studies" they performed on and for the Negro, who was a biological and social inferior. Some foundations favored white institutions and scholars in carrying out black studies. When distributing funding, Rosenwald and Slater funds sometimes gave help to black researchers.

Some HBCUs began journals to facilitate the scholarship of the HBCU faculty. In 1931, Howard instituted the Bureau of Educational Research, where Charles H. Thompson edited the *Journal of Negro Education*. Thompson centered the first articles on New Deal and World War II effects on the Negro. Thompson, among other Negro journalists, saw himself as a civil rights activist, according to historians like Louis Ray, who studied Thompson's editorial thought from 1933 to 1950, and presented it at the 93rd Annual Meeting of the Association for the Study of African American Life and History.[28]

American Negroes held scholarly conferences, formed collegiate associations, and began intellectual networks. Carter G. Woodson began the monthly *Negro History Bulletin* (1933–) to help teachers across America to use *black* materials in their classes. Some newspapers began to recognize Woodson's Negro History Week (today's Black History Month) as a national celebration of Negro life, culture, and history. Woodson and the Association for the Study of Negro Life and History, Inc. (1915–), headquartered in DC near Howard University, directed the national event. They had already published the *Journal of Negro History* quarterly since 1916. In 1935, Ralph Bunche organized a conference to look into the Negro's economic position during the Great Depression, and in 1935, Theophilus McKinney, Sr., dean and registrar at Johnson C. Smith College,

---

[28] Hugh Gloster, "Sutton Griggs: Novelist of the New Negro," *Phylon* 4 (1943) 335–45; see Alfred A. Moss Jr., *The American Negro Academy: Voice of the Talented Tenth* (Baton Rouge: Louisiana State University Press, 1981) 1–20; E. O. Knox, "The Negro as a Subject of University Research in 1942," *Journal of Negro Education* 12/2 (Spring 1943): 199–210; and, see Lawrence Crouchett, "Early Black Studies Movements," *Journal of Black Studies* 2/2 (December 1971): 169–200.

invited social scientists from the HBCUs to attend a conference in order to develop ways to improve the social science offerings. The fifty-two attendees formed the Association of Social Science Teachers—today's Association of Social and Behavioral Scientists (ABSA). They published the 1935 conference proceedings in the *Quarterly Review of Higher Education among Negroes*. The ABSA later published the *Journal of Social Science Teachers*, which became the *Journal of Social and Behavioral Sciences*. Tennessee State University hosted the 70th Annual ABSA Conference. In April 1937, ten English teachers founded the Association of Teachers of English in Negro Colleges (CLA) during a meeting at LeMoyne College, and published the *News-Bulletin* periodical. From 1938 to 1942, Hampton, Tuskegee, Howard, and Atlanta University hosted the Annual National Conference on Negro Adult Education.

With the advent of ethnic conflict, nationalistic, and Fascist forces that started World War II in Europe, the American nation drew criticism for mistreatment of its Negro citizens. Philanthropic agencies increased help to improve American race relations. Edwin R. Embree, in the *Rosenwald Fund Report* of 1938–1940, wrote,

> Among the weaknesses of our democracy is our treatment of Negroes. Our attitude toward this race, which makes up one-tenth of our entire population, more than one quarter of the historic region of the South, is a threat to the whole theory and practice of democracy.... No race or class can be firmly assured of fair play so long as we continue to treat any group unfairly.... We in America are committed to our ideal—but we have never fully realized it.

In 1937, Frederick P. Keppel, president of Carnegie Foundation invited Swedish scholar Gunnar Myrdal to direct "a comprehensive study of race relations in the United States ... in a wholly objective and dispassionate way as a social phenomenon."[29] Keppel and others were reacting to the 1935 race riot in Harlem, where young blacks were angry about their higher unemployment rate as compared to whites, rent gouging by property owners, overcrowding brought on by *de facto* residential segregation, and inequitable shares of New Deal relief money. Myrdal began his sociological study in September 1938 by conducting a two-month tour. "I wanted to see things with my own eyes. I was shocked and

[29] E. R. Embree, *Julius Rosenwald Report for the Two-Year Period 1942–1944* (Chicago: Rosenwald Fund, 1944) 2, 3, 6, 10.

scared ... by all the evils I saw, and by the serious implications of the [racial] problem."[30]

Eleanor Roosevelt, who, along with Keppel, attended that SCHW meeting, spoke out on race issues. She helped the NAACP to lobby Congress for an anti-lynching bill. In 1939, when the Daughters of the Revolution defiantly barred the acclaimed soprano Marian Anderson from performing at their Constitution Hall because she was a Negro, Roosevelt became involved. The school board of Washington, DC, denied use of a high school auditorium for the concert for the same reason. Anderson had won acclaim across Europe, and the concert was an annual affair hosted by Howard University. The head of the Phelps-Stokes Fund published an appeal for the DAR to drop the color line. Roosevelt and the NAACP got permission from the US Secretary of the Interior to move the concert to the Lincoln Memorial, and seventy-five thousand people attended the event on Easter Sunday.[31]

Myrdal returned to Sweden after Nazi Germany invaded adjacent countries in 1940. The Carnegie Corporation received criticism for selecting Myrdal—a white foreign scholar—instead of a black American scholar to lead such a massive study on the Negro. Richard Robbins said they could have selected Charles. S. Johnson, but he did not criticize white American racism as Myrdal dared do.[32] Du Bois, however, was considered to be too far to the left.

Ralph Bunche, an economics professor at Howard University, published *Negro Political Status* in the Myrdal studies, and Eric Williams, professor of social sciences at Howard, published *Capitalism and Slavery* in 1944—a classic that set the standard for the international study of slavery and the economics of slavery. Between 1940 and 1947, Williams wrote twenty articles for the *Journal of Negro History*. The Rosenwald Fund supported James Weldon Johnson, who published scholarly studies in 1933. Charles S. Johnson published Mydral studies in 1943, along with other writers. The Fisk University social science faculty published twenty-three books and monographs.

---

[30] John Hope Franklin and A. A. Moss Jr., *From Slavery to Freedom: A History of Negro Americans*, 6th ed. (New York: Knopf, 1988) 383; Gunnar Myrdal, *An American Dilemma: the Negro Problem and Modern Democracy* (New York: Harper & Row, 1944) 1–42.

[31] Kenneth R. Janken, *Walter White: Mr. NAACP* (Chapel Hill: University of North Carolina Press, 2003) 238, 240–47.

[32] Myrdal, *An American Dilemma*, 167; Erica W. Connell, "Introduction: Symposium on the Life and Wirtings of Eric Williams," *Journal of African-American History* 88/3 (Summer 2003): 291–303; Richard Robbins, *Sidelines Activist: Charles S. Johnson and the Struggle for Civil Rights* (Jackson: University Press of Mississippi, 1996) 124–25; Eugene Levy, *James Weldon Johnson: Black Leader, Black Voice* (Chicago: University of Chicago Press, 1973) 357.

The Rosenwald Fund also sponsored HBCU faculty researchers to travel to Africa and Europe; it also sent Monroe N. Work of Tuskegee Institute, editor of the annual *Negro Year Book,* to the University of Chicago to study research methods. Monroe Work was a prolific scholar since he and his colleagues published articles in several journals.[33]

Negro scholars associated with the HBCUs were quite productive. Alrutheus A. Taylor published a second book after becoming the first Negro dean of Fisk University. Benjamin E. Mays, dean of the School of Religion at Howard, published a pioneering study of black Christianity based on research of 691 churches. Robert E. Martin and Luther P. Jackson at Howard University did political studies in the *JNE,* showing the continuing disenfranchisement of Negro voters and the need for national anti-poll tax legislation. Rayford Logan of Howard published through the University of North Carolina Press, which was promoting Negro studies by black and white scholars. Logan criticized the New Deal's racial inequalities, questioned the progressive credentials of the New Deal Negro advisors, and also questioned Walter White and the NAACP in the fight for black equality. When Du Bois was not available because of his fight with director Walter White, Logan assisted the NAACP to connect the Civil Rights Movement to international human rights movements.[34]

John Hope Franklin, a native of Oklahoma whose family sent him to study at Fisk University in the early 1930s, was part of this excellent crop of professors at Howard University who focused their studies on Negro culture and history. Franklin published *From Slavery to Freedom: A History of Negro Americans* in 1947—the first real textbook on African-American history that endured eight editions into the twenty-first century. Although Howard's Carter G. Woodson, Benjamin Brawley, Tennessee A&I's Merle Eppse, George Washington Williams, and others had attempted general surveys of Negro history, Knopf Publishing Company of Chicago sought a more comprehensive textbook for use in black and white universities in a decade when interest in Negro studies was at its height. Franklin, along with several political scientists, sociologists, and psychologists, especially at Howard, assisted the research staff of the NAACP-Legal Defense Fund in the preparation of the successful legal brief for *Brown v. Board of Education.* He went on to chair the history department at the University

---

33 Monroe Work, Thomas S. Staples, H. A. Wallace, et al., "Some Negro Memebers of Reconstrion Conventions and Legislatures and of Congress," *Journal of Negro History* 5/1 (January 1920): 63–119; Monroe Work, "One Negro in Business and the Professions," *Annals of the American Academy of Political and Social Science* 140/1 (November 1928): 138–44.

34 Janken, *Walter White,* 238; Franklin and Moss, *From Slavery to Freedom,* 351, 368, 482; Woodson and Wesley, *The Negro in Our History,* 879.

of Chicago, later assumed a scholarly chair of excellence at Duke University, and there became Professor Emeritus. His 2005 autobiography, *Mirror to America,* reflects upon his undergraduate days at Fisk University and the rapidity of which his career rocketed after receiving a PhD in history from Harvard University.[35] He became co-winner of the John W. Kluge Prize for the Study of Humanity in 2006, and indubitably enjoyed the status of one of America's foremost scholars, regardless of race.

Meanwhile, Gunnar Myrdal returned to America. He completed the study on race in America: *An American Dilemma the Negro Problem and Modern Democracy*.

Charles S. Johnson convinced the AMA to house the Institute of Race Relations at Fisk University, where he held the first conference in July 1944 for 137 registrants (mostly whites) to discuss America's racial problems. The institute sought practical measures to further equality of opportunity in America. The head of the Nashville *Banner* reportedly pressured Fisk to stop the interracial meeting, and the Nashville *Tennessean* denounced it as a threat to "Western civilization and white culture." Fisk decided to cancel the next conference, but backed down. Upon the resignation of Thomas Elsa Jones, Charles S. Johnson became the first Negro president of Fisk University in 1946. Fisk's most illustrious graduate, Du Bois, to whom the institution awarded an honorary doctorate in 1938, as well as some other Fiskites, doubted Johnson deserved the appointment, but by November 1946, Du Bois believed Johnson, who had "the ear of the foundations," would most likely do a good job. Johnson held a racially integrated presidential inauguration at Nashville's downtown Ryman Auditorium in November 1947, when he said, "I believe in work, justice, freedom, and moral power." Charles S. Johnson was born in Virginia in 1893, attended HBCUs Wayland Academy and Virginia Union University. He attended the University of Chicago for the doctorate in social science, became director of the National Urban League's office of research and founding editor of its periodical, *Opportunity*. He became the "midwife" of the Harlem Renaissance and moved to Fisk University in 1927 to head the social science research program, funded by the Laura Spelman Fund.[36]

American education societies began to admit Negro scholars. E. Franklin Frazier became the first Negro elected president of a major scientific society, the Eastern Sociological Society. In 1943, Atlanta University professor W. E. B. Du Bois became the first Negro elected to the National Institute of Arts and Letters,

---

[35] John Hope Franklin, *Mirror to America: The Autobiography of John Hope Franklin* (New York: Farrar, Straus and Girous, 2005) 1-45.

[36] Robbins, *Sidelines Activist*, 67–68, 124, 140, 161–62.

and he was a member of the Society of American Historians, the Southern Sociological Society, and the American Historical Association, among other learned societies.

In the meantime, the development of enough leaders and practitioners holding graduate and professional degrees remained problematic for the HBCUs. Only three HBCUs had graduate studies by 1932. John H. Burris, graduate of Fisk University, received a master's degree from Dartmouth College in 1879. By 1932, the Negroes, including eight women, who held PhD degrees had graduated from the University of Chicago (13), University of Pennsylvania (9), Yale University (5), Harvard University (4), Boston University (2), Columbia University (4), and Northwestern University (2). Ohio State University, University of Cincinnati, University of London, University of Jena (Germany), University of Michigan, Radcliffe College, La Sorbonne (Paris), Massachusetts Institute of Technology (MIT), University of Southern California, Middlebury College, Wesleyan University, and University of Wisconsin each graduated one Negro PhD. One Negro PhD served as assistant professor at the University of Chicago, and one became associate researcher at MIT. Negro doctorates endured heavy teaching loads, low salaries, and little time for research and writing.[37]

Approximately 5 percent of black, college-age people attended college, and 5.8 percent of eligible Negroes attended high school by 1934; Negro colleges accounted for 92.6 percent of America's black college graduates. Northern TWIs accounted for the remainder of the two thousand Negro college graduates produced in 1937. Texas, DC, North Carolina, Georgia, Tennessee, and Virginia had the most black college graduates. The private HBCUs produced the most, but the public HBCUs and sixteen land-grant HBCUs were gaining ground. Forty-one percent of teachers (all Negroes) at the public HBCUs had college degrees. Sociologist E. Franklin Frazier said, "Over two-thirds of the Negroes who have earned the degree of Doctor of Philosophy have received it since 1917."[38]

America's black colleges and universities only slowly began to offer graduate and professional degrees. Roger Williams, Howard, and Walden

---

[37] Harry W. Greene, "Recent Negro College Graduates," *Nashville World*, 10 May 1932, p. 1.

[38] Charles S. Johnson, "The Negro," *The American Journal of Sociology* 47/6 (May 1942): 854–64; E. P. Davis, "The Negro Liberal Arts College," *Journal of Negro Education* 2/3 (July 1933): 299–311; Martin D. Jenkins, "Graduate Work in Negro Institutions of Higher Education," *Journal of Higher Education* 18/6 (June 1947): 300–306; Jenkins, "Enrollment in Negro Colleges and Universities: 1937–38," 118–23; Ware, "Higher Education of Negroes in the United States," 209; E. Franklin Frazier, "Graduate Education in Negro Colleges and Universities," *Journal of Negro Education* 2/2 (July 1933): 329–41.

universities offered graduate and/or professional degrees by the 1880s. Meharry Medical College, a department of Walden University until 1915, offered dentistry, nursing, pharmacy, and medicine. Howard offered dentistry, law, medicine, pharmacy, social service, and library from 1869 to 1920. A few other Negro medical schools existed, however, new standards in 1910 shut down all but Meharry and Howard by 1924.[39]

In 1921, Howard began offering graduate courses, and organized the Graduate Division in 1927, with its own administration and faculty. Howard offered the Master of Arts and Master of Science degrees in the College of Liberal Arts and the College of Education. Fisk began these degrees in 1927 and 1928, and enrolled twenty-four graduate students in biology, chemistry, education, English, physics, and sociology by 1932. In total, Fisk had trained 570 graduate students and awarded dozens of master's degrees by 1938. Atlanta University discontinued its undergraduate courses in 1931, expanded its graduate courses with the help of a $300,000 grant from the GEB in 1932, and offered programs in social service by 1934. Atlanta University's education department continued the laboratory school, nursery school, kindergarten, elementary school, and high school. From 1928 on, Hampton Institute offered graduate studies in summer session, enrolling thirty-three men and twenty-four women in 1937. A candidate for the Master of Arts degree had to spend 36 weeks in residence and complete the degree within six years at Hampton. Xavier offered social service and library science. Together, these HBCUs enrolled 385 students and conferred 115 master's degrees in 1937.[40]

Jim Crow states financed graduate and professional offerings for whites, only. By 1937, Maryland had admitted two Negroes to a law school, because of NAACP lawsuits. Kentucky, Maryland, Tennessee, Oklahoma, and West Virginia reacted to this threat by offering graduate fellowships for "out-of-town" studies for Negro applicants. Tennessee aided fifty-seven Negro students in business administration, education, engineering, home economics, dentistry, law, medicine, pharmacy, science, and social science by 1941. Three states had commissions studying the graduate/professional school problem related to what to do about the Negroes. The Negro schoolteachers, through their Negro State Teachers Association, were placing pressure on the A&I president, William J. Hale, to begin a graduate program; he announced such courses in the college catalog, but the state board stopped it. Instead, the board ordered a 1936 self-study that recommended A&I first improve its undergraduate program, lighten the teaching load, and improve faculty salaries.

---

[39] Ware, "Higher Education of Negroes in the United States," 209.

[40] Jenkins, "Enrollment in Negro Colleges and Universities," 123.

Seven public HBCUs joined the five private HBCUs in offering graduate studies. Prairie View A&M College organized a division of graduate studies in 1937, offering vocational education, agriculture, home economics, education, and social science. Virginia State offered English, music, social studies, guidance, and science by the 1937–1938 school year. North Carolina A&T cooperated with University of North Carolina and Duke University by 1939 to offer programs in biology, chemistry, education, English, history, home economics, mathematics, and sociology, and on-campus graduate studies in agriculture and rural education. By 1940, twelve HBCUs offered graduate education, enrolling about 1,864 students. The state authorized Tennessee A&I State College to start a Graduate School in June 1942 because of the NAACP-inspired *Michael v. University of Tennessee*, TN (1941) lawsuit. Alabama State, Kentucky State, Lincoln in Missouri, Tennessee A&I, and Tuskegee began graduate offerings, starting 1942–1944.

To help promote the HBCU graduate studies movement, each April issue of the *Journal of Negro Education* featured "The Negro as a Subject of University Research." This issue reported the number and subject matter of master's and doctoral studies in the US. Between 1932 and 1942. The HBCUs produced 46.7 percent of master's degrees with research topics focusing on the Negro in the US. The TWIs in the North and the South produced the remainder of the studies. Nine HBCUs reported 120 black studies master's theses, and fifty-four of these were produced by Atlanta University. North Carolina A&T and North Carolina State reported one master's thesis each in 1942, while Alabama State and Kentucky State reported no completion of theses on Negroes. The number of black studies increased from seventy-six in 1932 to 208 in 1941, with a great deal of them completed in the Southern region. Some sixty-eight institutions—including Atlanta University, Fisk, Hampton, Howard, North Carolina A&T, North Carolina State, Prairie View, Virginia State, and Xavier reported 2,012 graduate studies on Negroes for the years 1932–1942.[41]

Still, racial restrictions, across America, were so confining to Negro citizens that some observers wondered what they really could do with a higher education in the United States. Educated Negroes could not find employment in Europe, and few of them chose to go to Africa, the Caribbean, or South America

---

[41] *A Summary of the Provisions Being Made in Certain States for the Professional and Graduate Education of Negroes* (7 September 1940), Commission on Interracial Cooperation (CIC) Papers, state interracial committees, 1918–1944, R. W. Woodruff Library, Atlanta University, Atlanta GA; Augustus M. Burns III, "Graduate Education for Blacks in North Carolina, 1930–1951," *The Journal of Southern History* 46/2 (May 1980): 195–218; Joe M. Richardson, *A History of Fisk University, 1865–1946* (Tuscaloosa: University of Alabama Press, 1980) 43, 44–45, 188, 193, 117–119.

to work as missionaries and nation-builders. Therefore, the GEB funded Charles S. Johnson and Fisk social scientists in 1932 to study Negro higher education. The intent also was to take note of the experiences of black college graduates as well as give reference to the quality of education received at HBCUs. Additionally, the GEB wanted to know what could Negro college graduates do in a Jim Crow society that other Negroes could not do. Negro college graduates could enter teaching, medicine, law, business, and other professional fields that ordinary Negroes could not. Once again, however, Jim Crow confined almost all of them to jobs and careers wholly within the black communities. More than two-thirds of Negro professionals were teachers or clergy. The survey also revealed the perception that a higher quality of education was received at the private HBCUs than at the younger public black colleges.

To improve the HBCU congressional lobby group, the Negro Land Grant Presidents Association included some *associate* members. These included Atlanta University, Bordentown Manual Training School, Hampton, and Fort Valley Normal, Kansas Vocational School for Negroes in Topeka, and Wilberforce University. The Bordentown School began in 1886, when the Rev. W. A. Rice of the AME Church started Ironsides Normal School. In 1894, New Jersey designated the school for training Negro youth in industrial education and manual training. The state leased land on the outskirts of Bordentown, overlooking the Delaware River, and built new facilities in 1896. In 1903, the state board of education had direct responsibility for Manual Training and Industrial School for Colored Youth at Bordentown. By 1926, the four-hundred-acre campus consisted of thirty buildings and two working farms. After receiving the bachelor's at Amherst College in 1925, William H. Hastie joined the staff at Bordentown until entering Harvard University law school in 1927. Hastie then joined the law school staff at Howard University, became dean, and later a federal judge. In 1948, New Jersey attempted to integrate Bordentown, naming it Manual Training and Industrial School for Youth, but failed. The school paper, *The Ironsides Echo* published until 1953, and New Jersey closed the school in 1954.[42]

It would take more than the Conference of Negro Presidents, more than radio broadcasts downplaying liberal arts education, and more than schools from Kansas and New Jersey added to the HBCU land-grant list to remove the most conservative opposition to black educational progress. During the New Deal, Negroes would have to turn to the US Supreme Court.

---

[42] E. B. Adams, "The Role and Function of the Manual Training and Industrial School at Bordentown as an Alternative School, 1915–1955" (EdD dissertation, Rutgers University, 1977) 1–20.

Howard's law school dean, Charles Hamilton Houston, developed the brilliant legal strategies through which the newest phase of the black Civil Rights Movement could unfold. Houston served as a first lieutenant in the 368th Infantry and judge-advocate in cases involving fellow Negro soldiers. He grew up in racially segregated Washington, DC, and his father, a lawyer, was educated at Howard University. After completing Amherst College, teaching English at Howard, serving in the war, and completing a law degree at Harvard University, Charles Hamilton Houston practiced with his father and began teaching at Howard. He became vice dean of the school of law in 1929, and convinced president Mordecai Johnson to offer a full-time, fully accredited law program. After receiving grant money for its legal activities, the NAACP appointed Houston its chief legal counsel. In the *Tentative Statement Concerning Policy of NAACP in its Program of Attacks on Educational Discrimination*, dated 12 July 1935, Houston wrote:

> The graduate and professional study [program] was selected for attack because a large portion of the leadership of the race should come from Negroes who have had access to graduate and professional schools. The whites are educating their own children for public leadership through graduate and professional study out of taxes in which Negroes contribute, while Negro students are cut off with undergraduate training. In other words, the white system of education is designed to perpetuate the inferior status of Negroes.
>
> Finally, the National Office of the NAACP deems its function in this program to be that of (1) exposing the inequalities and discriminations and (2) wherever requested by the local populace, to render such assistance as it can through its branches and its own staff in making an attack on these evils.[43]

Houston also said, "The masses do need the Negro colleges, because America can never have too much education, and to my mind these colleges, if they are good enough, will have a place on an entirely integrated basis in the permanent scheme of things." Houston's strategy successfully attacked both teacher salaries and admission of Negroes to graduate and professional schools.

---

[43] Thomas C. Holt and Elsa Barkley Brown, eds., *Major Problems in African-American History*, vol. 2, *From Freedom to "Freedom Now," 1860–1990s: Documents and Essays* (Boston: Houghton Mifflin Co., 2000) 256–57; Robert L. Carter, William T. Coleman Jr., Jack Greenberg, et al., "In Tribute: Charles Hamilton Houston," *Harvard Law Review* 111/8 (June 1998): 2148–179.

Houston sent letters to Negro lawyers, asking them to join the movement, and "find suitable plaintiffs" to file the discrimination cases with NAACP help.[44]

A new civil rights era had begun.

The US Supreme Court began to agree with the NAACP lawyers that Jim Crow states had violated *Plessy v. Ferguson* (1896), and had not applied the "separate but equal" doctrine equally. NAACP lawyers won more than a dozen cases. *University of Maryland v. Donald Murray* (1936), and *Missouri ex rel. Lloyd Gaines v. Canada, Registrar of the University, et al.* 305 US 337 (1936) ordered these TWIs to admit the Negro plaintiffs. Houston hired his former law student, Thurgood Marshall, to assist him, and the NAACP launched higher education lawsuits against Jim Crow in Oklahoma, South Carolina, Tennessee, and Texas. In *McLaurin v. Oklahoma State Regents*, 339 US 637 (1950), the US Supreme Court justices wrote, "Our society grows increasingly complex, and our need for trained leaders increases correspondingly.... Self-imposed restrictions [on black citizens] which produce such inequities cannot be sustained." The Jim Crow states attempted to establish law programs for Negro plaintiffs, or they dispensed "out-of-state scholarships." James M. Nabrit established the first course in civil rights law at Howard University in 1938, and in 1939, the NAACP formed the Legal Defense Fund to help finance the expensive legal strategy against Jim Crow.[45]

The US Department of Agriculture shared part of the blame for the limited ability of land-grant HBCUs to offer graduate studies. The USDA employed many Southerners and segregationists on the federal, state, and county levels, and they openly discriminated against black citizens. By 1930, no state had given funds for the establishment of agricultural experimental research stations at HBCUs. Except for those hired through the HBCUs, southern counties did not

---

[44] Holt and Brown, eds., *Major Problems in African-American History*, 2.256–57; NAACP-Legal Defense Educational Fund, *Thirty Years of Building American Justice* (New York: W. W. Norton, 1975) 1–20.

[45] Jacqueline A. Stefkovich and Terrence Leas, "A Legal History of Desegregation in Higher Education," *Journal of Negro Education* 63/3 (Summer 1994): 406–20, *McLaurin v. Oklahoma State Regents*, 339 US 637 (1950) 641; Mark V. Tushnet, *Making Civil Rights Law: Thurgood Marshall and the Supreme Court, 1936–1961* (New York: Oxford University Press, 1994) 11, 26; M. V. Tushnet, *The NAACP's Legal Strategy against Segregated Education, 1925–1950* (Chapel Hill: University of North Carolina Press, 1987) 65–67, 53–54; Jamye Coleman Williams, *The Negro Speaks* (New York: Noble and Noble, 1970) 1–10; Genna R. McNeil, *Groundwork: Charles Hamilton Houston and the Struggle for Civil Rights* (Philadelphia: University of Pennsylvania Press, 1983) 1–32; Juan Williams, *Thurgood Marshall: American Revolutionary* (New York: Random House, 1998) 1–20.

offer Negro extension agents and extension services to black farmers. By 1931, land-grant HBCUs had 5,679 students in regular sessions, 2,995 students enrolled in secondary and high school curricula, and 8,263 students in adult, evening, extension, summer school, and other courses. No HBCU had programs, however, that included all three programs of a bona fide land-grant college: extension, experimental stations, and research programs. Even so, enrollment grew to 6,031 students by 1935. The Conference of Presidents of Negro Land Grant Colleges met at Howard University and asked US Secretary of Agriculture Henry Wallace and President Roosevelt to intervene. Their joint petition on 19 November 1935, said, "Inasmuch as the [land-grant] funds must come through the state universities for white citizens and through administrative boards upon which Negroes have little or no representation, the programs for white citizens may draw upon the funds so heavily as to leave a disproportionately small amount for a program among Negro citizens. [Since 1935, state officials] continued spending $2.8 million less on Negroes than it should be." The 1937 Conference of Presidents of Negro Land Grant Colleges report said, "While they have a separate land-grant college for Negroes, they have not established a graduate or professional school at the institution for Negroes. Land-grant HBCUs received $741,660 (18.32 percent) of the $4.048 million funds allocated to Jim Crow states for cooperative education in 1937." State officials spent $1,199,000 in federal funds at land-grant colleges to train white students in military tactics, but spent no funds at the land-grant HBCUs; yet, three HBCUs continued military training. In 1939, the White House Advisory Committee on Education blamed the USDA for discriminatory practices and limiting Negro access to agricultural education programs.[46]

From 1939 to 1940, the Conference of Presidents continued discussion on the need to develop and expand curricula in business education, consumer education, and adult education. The Conference of Presidents of Negro Land Grant Colleges also discussed the economic condition of black Americans. Blacks made up a large percentage of rural Southerners. Southern landowners in the Mississippi Valley turned thousands of sharecroppers and tenant farmers off the land, because they joined unions and requested higher wages. The New Deal Agricultural Adjustment Act provided cash benefits to farms and grants to help black and white farmers. Many Southern whites, however, misappropriated the money, took advantage of illiterate sharecroppers and tenants, and kept the

---

[46] John W. Davis, "The Participation of Negro Land-Grant Colleges in Permanent Federal Education Funds," *The Journal of Negro Education* 7/3 (July 1938): 282–91; Southern Association of Colleges and Schools, Committee on Approval of Negro Schools, *Enrollment in Negro Colleges, 1934–35* (Atlanta: SACS, 1935) 1–10.

checks meant for the blacks.[47] Robert Weaver, Negro assistant in the Department of Labor, spoke to the Conference of Presidents of Negro Land Grant Colleges about "Education and the National Defense" and high unemployment of Negroes. Weaver was a product of DC's black Dunbar High School and Harvard University's doctoral program in economics. He was concerned about the monopoly of New Deal's agricultural relief programs by property owners, who reduced acreage of cotton and evicted tenant farmers. The HBCU presidents agreed to report on federal programs supposed to benefit Negroes, how HBCUs were involved, and conduct employment and occupation surveys. The 1940 report showed 26.7 percent of the Negroes remained on New Deal relief programs.[48]

Meanwhile, in 1939, the Association of Colleges and Schools for Negroes (ACSSN) pushed the philanthropic agencies and the federal government to finance a study "to determine the areas of specialization upon which the various [Negro] colleges should embark." A proliferation of HBCUs with too little funding continued to be a problem, since the 1916 Bureau of Education study, *Bulletin Nos. 38–39*, and the 1932 study, *Bulletin No. 17*. Not even the ACSSN, the Council of Negro Land-Grant Presidents, or anyone else really knew much about hundreds of Negro schools and the general state of Negro education. Philanthropic agencies helped out.

The National Survey of the Higher Education of Negroes of 1942 appeared in three volumes, including historic photographs documenting HBCUs. The HBCU presidents, Negro scholars, and statisticians from Fisk, Howard, and Alabama A&M helped with the study, which focused on Jim Crow areas with the lowest educational attainment for whites and Negroes, and where 75 percent of blacks resided. The study intended to determine to what extent Negroes go north to study, go south to study at HBCUs, and discuss the basic problems of Negroes accessing higher education in the US. The study intended to develop a profile

---

[47] Franklin and Moss Jr., *From Slavery to Freedom*, 352.

[48] Janken, *Walter White*, 236; John R. Wennersten, "The Travail of Black Land-Grant Schools in the South, 1890–1917," *Agricultural History* 65/2 (Spring 1991): 54–62; Richardson, *History of Fisk University*, 141; James W. Smith, ed., *Leadership and Learning: An Interpretive History of Historically Black Land-Grant Colleges and Universities—A Centennial Study* (Washington DC: National Association of State Universities and Land-Grant Colleges [NASULGC], 1993) 1–7, 9, 33, 100–101; Raymond G. Lloyd, *Tennessee Agricultural and Industrial State University, 1912–1962* (Nashville: Tennessee A. & I., 1962) 1–21; Herman B. Long, "The Negro Public College in Tennessee," *Journal of Negro Education* 31/3 (Summer 1962): 341–48; Embree, *Julius Rosenwald Report for the Two-Year Period 1942–1944*, 2, 6; D. Withrow, *From the Grove to the Stars: West Virginia State College, 1891–1991* (Charleston: West Virginia State College, 1993) 1–30.

against which an institution might place its own educational program and by means of which it might conduct continual appraisal. The site visitors wanted to know how HBCUs compared to TWIs.

According to the report, in 1940 about 118 HBCUs existed, including eighty-five four-year HBCUs—thirty-three public and fifty-two private. Three public and thirty private HBCUs did not offer a four-year curriculum. Thirty-three HBCUs (28 percent) had an "A" approval/accreditation, with 19,920 students, while twenty HBCUs had a "B" approval/accreditation, and enrolled 8,133 students. Forty-nine HBCUs remained non-accredited, with 11,740 students, and 4,207 attended other institutions. These 118 institutions—now more narrowly classified as HBCUs, and separated from other elementary, secondary, and high schools for blacks—had many problems, though not unlike those experienced by some TWIs at the time. The HBCUs depended on funds controlled by whites, "on which are contingent on their interest and good will," said the report. It continued, "The Negro college with an all-Negro faculty provides for the student a certain escape from reality, but the biracial faculty provides the better experience and preparation for the student to function in a multiracial world."

The typical seniors of forty-nine HBCUs were 22.6 years of age, and most of them needed financial aid. "Negro college students typically come from homes which are relatively low in economic status" (p. 30). Yet, both white and black students in the South "suffer economic and cultural deprivations" (p. 48). However, fathers, men with skilled and higher profession jobs, were present in most of their Negro families—a positive factor. Black men outnumbered Negro women two-to-one in some HBCUs and remained the majority of HBCU students as late as 1938. With the advent of World War II, women outnumbered male undergraduates, 57 percent to 47 percent in 1940, and in 1945, there were twice as many black women as black men on the HBCU campus. Negro freshmen at HBCUs generally scored below the national average on standardized test than did freshmen and seniors at white institutions. HBCU freshmen and seniors "sometimes are to be found at the very highest levels" (pp. 57–59). For example, Fisk University freshmen in 1929, 1930, and 1931, made a gross median test score superior to those shown by freshmen at University of Alabama, University of South Carolina, and University of Georgia. Median scores of Negro students at Ohio State University, University of Chicago, and University of Kansas exceeded national averages and outpaced scores of Southern white and black college students. Some 1,469 Negro seniors and 3,050 freshmen scored low on the test on knowledge of black history. Sixty-three percent of black men and 85 percent of Negro women students said they intended to enter the teaching profession, and 74.2 percent of both intended to pursue graduate studies. Indeed, the high motivation of students from HBCUs to enter graduate and professional schools, compared to their black counterparts who attended TWIs, remained a positive fact through the end of century.

Frequently at HBCUs, fewer than 10 percent of faculty members held doctorates, whereas, at the TWIs, fewer than 30 percent of staff held doctorates. Some 78.4 percent of HBCU faculty held master's degrees. Heavy teaching loads accounted partly for "the lack of atmosphere conducive to scholarly activity" (p. 57). Volume 3, page 57, of the 1942 study said,

> Institutions for Negroes are confronted with a series of special problems arising from the racial factor.... The salaries paid to faculty members constitute an important index of the educational quality of an institution because the kind of faculty members an institution can attract and hold depends in large part upon the salaries the institution can offer.

Visiting teams said the HBCU faculty could not prove the success of the graduates, except to list the most outstanding cases, which all colleges can do. "The attitude toward student indifference [toward academic achievement] caused 17 HBCUs, 1939–1940, to drop 506 students because of poor academic performance" (p. 27). The HBCUs developed discipline measures including personal conferences with the advisor, limiting the credit hours of the failing student, no extra activities or Greek membership, supervised study in the dormitories, informing parents of a failing student, denial of financial aid, and requiring precise number of credit hours for graduation. HBCUs also taught etiquette, social relationships, and personal health by appointing hosts for each table in the dining room, serving the meals at tables, careful food selection, and sanitary inspections in the dorms. "A Summary," by Ambrose Caliver, concluded Negroes do not have quality of educational opportunity, but certain "individual educational institutions for Negroes rank high among the best in the country" (p. 59).

In Chapter 6 of "Higher Education of Negroes in Northern Institutions," volume two of the 1942 Bureau study showed fewer than 10 percent of Negroes in northern colleges came directly from the southern states. This survey took into account the ongoing Great Migration. University of Kansas, Ohio State University, University of Chicago, and New York University shared the heaviest enrollment of black graduate students. In all, 110 and ten northern institutions, including five HBCUs there, reported Negro students. Northern states reported 3,893 black undergraduate students, but 2,897 (74 percent) of them attended HBCUs in the South from 1938 into 1939. Again, this was not a burden on southern states, because most HBCUs obtained support from northern missionary and philanthropic groups, and southern Negro organizations and their churches.

The 1942 study also found the northern TWIs often barred Negro students from swimming pools or restricted blacks to swim only at specific times. Blacks had problems scheduling practice teaching, internships, fieldwork, financing, housing, and food procurement, and many had to live off campus. The majority of black northern college students went to the HBCUs for better opportunities for athletic participation, a more normal social life, better access to campus activities, lower cost of tuition and fees, better development of self-esteem, better leadership training opportunities, and better access to professional jobs. The report said, "If you wish to know how far the civilization of a country has advanced, you ask 'How good are its universities?' Social progress and universities development go hand in hand. Any society which neglects to develop its most capable men and women ... fails to take advantage of the important means of social progress" (p. 90). The report quoted Charles Dabney's *Universal Education in the South*: "Simple justice demands that reasonably equal opportunity be assured to the citizens of the United States, regardless of race or place of birth.... Democracies depend on education for their existence."[49]

During WWII, the Commission on Interracial Cooperation (CIC) helped pressure the Jim Crow states to do better about providing equal educational opportunities for blacks. The CIC pushed for improved public education for Negroes as a way of improving race relations, and the CIC cooperated with HBCUs, and waged a campaign to involve the white colleges and universities. The HBCUs cooperated, because they needed improved public schools to feed the HBCUs.

In 1941, the North Carolina Department of Education issued *Education of Negroes in North Carolina, 1914–1925–1939*. Rosenwald, Jeanes, Phelps-Stokes, and the Slater funds were principal contributors. North Carolina appointed a Director of Negro Education in 1913. In 1939, the state approved graduate education provisions and graduate fellowships for Negro citizens, and, in 1941, the CIC report counted eleven private HBCUs: Allen Industrial Home and School, Scotia Seminary (two-year), Bennett College, Immanuel Lutheran (two-year), Palmer Memorial Institute (high school), Biddle (Johnson C. Smith) College, Livingston College, Kittrell College, St. Augustine College, Shaw

---

[49] Ina C. Brown, *National Survey of Higher Education of Negroes*, 3 vols. (Washington DC: USDOE, 1942) 1:90, 1–6, 7, 27, 30, 48, 51, 57, 59, 104, 105; 2:49, 51, 57; 3:7, 27, 59, 90; M. H. Little, "The Extra-curricular Activities of Black College Students, 1868–1940," 135–48; Charles W. Dabney, *Universal Education in the South* (Chapel Hill: University of North Carolina Press, 1936) 1-20.

University, Roanoke Collegiate Institute (high school). Thirty-eight other private schools existed, but public school systems absorbed ten of them. Five schools—including Mary Potter Memorial School at Oxford and Lincoln Academy at Kings Mountain—recently closed. "It should be said, however, that most of these schools did serve their day and generation and kept the light burning even though dimly at times, when there was urgent need for [Negro] education."[50]

In South Carolina, CIC operations heavily depended on the president's office at South Carolina State College. The CIC Papers carried clippings reading "State College Celebrates 45th Birthday." This HBCU enrolled about eight hundred students in the 1940–1941 school year, has matriculated 36,272 students since 1896, and has granted 2,481 certificates, diplomas, and degrees. The South Carolina Federation of Colored Women's Clubs assisted the president's office in directing CIC activities concerned about lawlessness, anarchy, and lynching. *The State* newspaper, dated 26 September 1939, reported "Men in white hoods and robes traveling in automobiles" intimidated the Negro citizens in several towns.[51] They paraded in Spartanburg in June 1941 when a group of hoodlums with KKK hoods herded Negroes off the street just as they were celebrating money gained for picking cotton, pushed them into a barbershop, made them empty their pockets, beat them, and took their pay.

President William J. Hale of Tennessee A&I State College became head of the "Negro Division" of the CIC in Tennessee, which met on his campus during the summer when it was packed with schoolteachers taking courses for certification. They were required to attend the week of CIC workshops and sometimes met with white teachers at George Peabody College for Teachers across town. CIC units also met at Vanderbilt University. Attorney J. C. Napier addressed one of the CIC meetings on justice for the Negro in state courts. Meharry-trained physician Charles V. Roman, a part-time instructor at Fisk and at A&I, spoke about the public health crisis among Negroes and better "training of Negro nurses and doctors." President E. L. Turner of Meharry, along with the state director of Negro education, the state Commissioner of Education, and President Thomas E. Jones of Fisk were among white attendees at the 26 March 1942, CIC meeting. J. Frankie Pierce of the Tennessee Federation of Colored

---

[50] North Carolina Department of Education, *Education of Negroes in North Carolina, 1914–1925–1939* (Raleigh: NC Department of Education, 1941) in CIC Papers, Reports and Minutes, 1941–1942.

[51] CIC Report, "Public School Expenditures: Black and White," 1 June 1941, CIC Papers, 1919–1944; South Carolina Department of Education, *Education of the Negro in South Carolina, 1939–1941* (Columbia: SC Dept. of Education, 1941) in CIC Papers, Reports and Minutes, 1941–1942.

Women Clubs attended the meeting. "The aim of the Inter-Racial Commission is to help to a better understanding and to a truer and wider conception of one of the most important factors in community life today—a program whereby two races can live side by side in peace in the same community," said the minutes of the State Inter-Racial Commission of Tennessee.[52]

The 1941 CIC reports showed great racial discrimination in how Jim Crow states paid the public school teachers. Mississippi remained arrogantly resistant to outside interference and gave little cooperation to assessing the dire situation of black education. However, CIC members at traditionally white Millsap College worked diligently to promote better race relations in Mississippi. The president of Alcorn College led the Negro contingent in Mississippi's CIC, and Ruby E. Stutts, librarian at Alcorn, supplied the state CIC with lists of books on race.[53]

At the Missouri State Conference on Race, a CIC observer reported the contrast between black and white public schools:

> The white school was perfectly beautiful—Negro school on the edge of town. I had to wade thru mud and water, climb over and crawl under barbed wire fences—found them housed in a church—very poor building. They had a dirt floor but when I was there they had a wooden floor—no desks—long benches without backs and a piece of a black board. A man was teaching that school of sixty-seven children ... doing the best he can. One group of black children rode a train to school; another area had no school for Negro children.[54]

Alabama spent $36.03 per white child and $10.65 per black child, and the average expenditure by race from 1938 to 1939 in the twelve Jim Crow states was $45.82 per child for whites and $16.51 per child for blacks. The Alabama report, 1941, said,

> The greatest extremes are found in counties that draw amounts of state school funds because of their many Negro schoolchildren and then invest most of these funds to the education of white children. Thus, one county

---

[52] CIC, "Minutes of the State Inter-Racial Commission of Tennessee," 31 December 1922, 2 January 1923, 26 March 1942, CIC Papers, 1919–1941.

[53] "Minutes of the CIC, Mississippi Council, February 1941–September 1942, CIC Papers, 1919–1944,"; "A Summary of the Provisions Being Made in Certain States for the Professional and Graduate Education of Negroes," 7 September 1940, CIC Papers, 1919–1941.

[54] Missouri Department of Education, *Public School Expenditures: Black and White,* 1 June 1941, Missouri State Convention on Race Relations, 10 May 1926, in CIC, Reports and Minutes, CIC Papers.

> in the black belt reports an average of $91.53 spent on the white schoolchild and $4.45 on the Negro child for a whole year's schooling.

Alabama paid teachers an annual salary of $816 a year for whites and $387 a year for black teachers, while Florida paid an average of $1,133 for white teachers and $569 for black ones. Tennessee paid $887 for white teachers and $580 for black teachers, and Louisiana paid $1,026 for white teachers and $368 per year for black teachers. Officials tried to justify the discriminatory practices by making Negro school sessions a month shorter than white public schools' sessions. They argued that blacks needed less education and money to live.[55]

Tennessee exemplified how some HBCUs engaged in embittered fights with Jim Crow. In the end, the HBCUs and Negro citizens suffered trying to gain equal access to higher education. Charles H. Houston, the NAACP and Tennessee Negro lawyers, Carl Cowan and Z. Alexander Looby, found a suitable plaintiff to file a discrimination suit in the state courts. Looby was a Howard graduate, and completed his master's and doctorates in law at Columbia and New York universities. Redmond was a 1934 graduate of Tennessee A&I. They lost the case because the state court claimed that the inexperienced black Tennesseean filed the case against the wrong defendants. In July 1937, Tennessee implemented an "out-of-state-scholarship program for bona fide Negro residents desiring graduate work and who possesse[d] qualifications, health, character, ability and preparatory education required for admission to University of Tennessee."[56] Houston filed for a *writ of mandamus* in November 1939, but the state court dismissed the case. From 1939 to 1941, six Negro students, who had attended Knoxville College, filed a discrimination suit against the University of Tennessee to gain entrance into public graduate and professional programs. The General Assembly quickly passed legislation to implement a graduate school at Tennessee A&I State College for Negroes, effective 1 June 1942 (*Tennessee Laws, 1941, Chap. 43, Sec. 2*):

> The State Board of Education and the Commissioner of Education are hereby authorized and directed to provide [graduate] educational training and instruction for Negro citizens of Tennessee equivalent to that provided at the University of Tennessee by the State of Tennessee for white citizens of Tennessee. The facilities of the Agricultural and Industrial State College may be used when deemed advisable by the State

---

[55] Alabama Department of Education, *Report on Negro Education*, 1941, CIC Reports and Minutes, 31 December-March 1942, CIC Papers.

[56] Mark V. Tushnet, *The NAACP's Legal Strategy against Segregated Education, 1925–1950* (Chapel Hill: University of North Carolina Press, 1987) 54–55.

> Board of Education and the Commissioner of Education, insofar as the facilities ... are adequate. The cost of providing such facilities shall be paid out of appropriations made to the State Board of Education or from other available funds.[57]

Jim Crow legislatures appropriated no extra funds to start graduate education for Negro citizens. President Hale chaired the committee to develop the graduate school. Only George W. Gore, the dean, had recently, in 1940 completed a PhD degree. Hale took his time, perhaps using the situation to force the state to give adequate funding for Tennessee A&I. Jim Crow officials paced nervously, fearful of additional NAACP suits. Since 1924, Hale had used Rosenwald, GEB, and federal New Deal money to build college-level facilities; Hale decided to use his influence with the philanthropic officials to play against white state officials. When visiting a New York meeting of state departments of education, Tennessee's white director of Negro education, Will Ed Turner, encountered a GEB official, who asked casually about "the condition of Negro education in Tennessee." The GEB official suggested hiring an outside Negro consultant to help implement graduate studies at A&I. Thus, Tennessee officials hired the dean (name not stated) of the Jim Crow law school established in St. Louis in response to the Missouri-NAACP lawsuit.[58] He argued that A&I did not need a law school if Tennessee would increase the amount of the out-of-state scholarships to satisfy the Negro plaintiffs, which effectively stopped A&I's law school plans. State education officials sent a committee of faculty members from the University of Tennessee to visit the Tennessee A&I campus to help with constructing a graduate curriculum, but tension developed between the white committee members and the all-black faculty. Many Negro faculty members had graduate degrees from northern institutions, and respected their curriculum designs instead of the lesser southern universities. State officials told Hale he *must* use the University of Tennessee catalog as a template.

State auditors rushed to the campus but became frustrated because Hale kept the account books in the president's house, and his wife, Harriett, head of the A&I business education program, did the payroll. The Bursar, a Negro lawyer, locked the whites out, declaring the office closed for the day. The state fired the Bursar.

On 7 May 1943, the Commissioner of Education reported to board members and the governor that President Hale still had not submitted the requested graduate school budget, and "If the A&I State College is not brought

---

[57] Tennessee Laws, chap. 43, sec. 2, in *Tennessee Laws* (Nashville: Secretary of State, 1941).

[58] Tushnet, *Legal Strategy against Segregated Education*, 73.

up to a standard that will satisfy the UT, [NAACP] lawsuits will start over again. The question now before the board is, what can be done about it?"[59] The Commissioner telephoned Walter S. Davis, and offered him the acting president's position. Davis began his education at Alcorn State College in his native Mississippi before transferring to A&I's college program in 1927. He earned a bachelor's degree in 1931, completed his master's at Cornell, using Rosenwald/GEB fellowships, and became head of agriculture at A&I. Davis earned a PhD at Cornell University in New York by 1942. The commissioner wrote to W. J. Hale on 28 August 1943: "At the called meeting of the State Board of Education on August 27, 1943, the Board adopted a resolution relieving you of your duties as president of the Agricultural and Industrial State College, effective as of September 1, 1943."[60] He ordered Hale to move his things, vacate the campus, and turn the keys over to Walter Davis. He then wrote to acting president Davis, telling him to select persons on campus to help him proceed.[61]

Shortly after, the Nashville *Globe* reported that former president Hale had died in New York "of a broken heart,[62] in November 1944, state officials appointed Walter S. Davis permanent president. Based on the 1941 legislative mandate, he set out to build new facilities, and even employed rough sketches for a law school and a medical school. Davis met weekly with the white man, Will Ed Turner, state director of Negro education and the man's Negro assistant, Robert E. Clay of the Rosenwald Fund. Both men had offices on the campus. Will Ed Turner, who also had an office downtown in the state department of education, conveyed to the State Board of Education what A&I needed to do to gain SACS "A" approval. The state allowed A&I to have some engineering-type courses, but Will Ed Turner asked, "Who would hire a Negro engineer?" Tennessee officials ignored the 1941 mandate to make A&I equivalent to UT.[63]

During World War II, Negro citizens became angrier with Jim Crow. A. Philip Randolph, head of the Brotherhood of Sleeping Car Porters, threatened a massive march on Washington in 1941. Randolph had attended Cookman Institute (Bethune-Cookman College) before migrating to New York and attending City College. In 1917, he became editor of *Messenger* magazine.

---

[59] Commissioner to Board of Education, 7 May 1943, A&I File, Records of the Board of Education, Record Group 273, State Library and Archives, Nashville.

[60] Commissioner to W. J. Hale, 27 August 1943, A&I File, Records of the Board of Education, Record Group 273, State Library and Archives, Nashville.

[61] Ibid.

[62] H. A. Boyd, "W. J. Hale," *Nashville Globe*, 27 October 1944, 1.

[63] Lovett, "A Touch of Greatness," unpublished manuscript on the history of TSU, 2009; Tushnet, *The NAACP's Legal Strategy*, 54–55.

President Roosevelt agreed to establish the Fair Employment Practices Commission and issue *Executive Order 8802* prohibiting racial discrimination in employment in defense industries and federal agencies. Randolph called off the march. The US Supreme Court decided in *Mitchell v. US,* 313 US 80 (1941) that Negroes who bought first-class tickets for interstate travel had to be provided accommodations equal in comfort and convenience to those for whites. In 1943, students at Howard began sit-in demonstrations at neighborhood Jim Crow restaurants. President Mordecai Johnson persuaded them to suspend the action lest they jeopardize the university's congressional funding. In Chicago, the Congress of Racial Equality (CORE) began in the summer 1942 and soon began sit-ins and freedom rides. In August 1943, the *Monthly Summary of Events and Trends in Race Relations* edited by Charles S. Johnson and sponsored by Rosenwald Fund began publication at Fisk University. The director of the Rosenwald Fund, Edwin R. Embree said,

> Negroes want to help beat Japan and Germany. However, they want democracy to win at home too, and they want it now.... Negroes have been arrested and punished in far greater numbers than white offenders. Galling are the insults and uncertainties [they] face every day ... Resented most of all is the discrimination in the armed forces.[64]

By 1944, two black men served in Congress, two served in state legislatures, and twenty-six black office holders served overall in the country. There was a movement to abolish the poll tax. Despite the President's recommendation, in 1945, Congress failed to provide funds for the federal Fair Employment Practices Commission. After Roosevelt's death on 12 April 1945, Vice President Harry S. Truman succeeded to the presidency. Black leaders pressured him to use executive orders to ban racial discrimination. They demanded that the political parties include civil rights in their political planks. *Morgan v. Virginia,* 328 US 373 (1946) declared unconstitutional state statutes requiring racial segregation on interstate buses.

As the Civil Rights Movement continued to grow, a group of HBCU presidents met with Truman on 22 October 1946 to discuss the importance of HBCUs "to the advancement of ... the nation."[65] On 5 December 1946, Truman signed an executive order creating the Committee on Civil Rights that produced *To Secure These Rights*.[66] Truman appeased those blacks that supported his foreign

---

[64] Embree, *The Rosenwald Fund Report, 1942–1944,* 1–10.

[65] Williams, *Thurgood Marshall,* 160, 169–70.

[66] Kenneth O'Reilly, *Nixon's Piano: Presidents and Racial Politics from Washington to Clinton* (New York: The Free Press, 1995) 155–56; President's Committee on Civil Rights, *To Secure These Rights* (Washington, DC: GPO, 1947).

policies and the anti-communist campaign. Walter White and the NAACP reconsidered *A Statement on the Denial of Human Rights to Minorities in the Case of Citizens of Negro Descent in the U.S.A. and an Appeal to the UN for Address."*[67] The youth chapter NAACP in Houston protested by writing, "The South is Poor. Segregation will make it poorer" and "Not Communism, But Democracy."[68]

HBCUs benefited from the GI Veterans Benefits Bill. In 1946, black veterans comprised 30 percent of students at HBCUs, where student enrollment had increased from forty-four thousand students in 1945 to 58,842 in 1946. More than a million Negro men and women served in America's World War II military forces, yet after the war, whites continued to deny black veterans and other Negro citizens equal access to civil rights and the socioeconomic benefits of the American dream. Even with GI benefits, it remained difficult for Negroes to access post-WWII suburban housing, and, other than low-income projects, few new housing developments were available in black communities, including near the HBCU campuses. HBCUs secured government surplus barracks to house the overflow student body. Later, the HBCUs' enrollment reaped benefits from the Veterans Readjustment Assistance Act. HBCUs produced an estimated 8,050 graduates in 1947 (70 percent of them women). This surge was due to the men being away at war, the success of the NAACP lawsuits against Jim Crow states, the increase in Negro high schools, and the greater production of Negro teachers, said historian Horace Mann Bond.[69]

In 1948 Truman's Committee on Equality of Treatment and Opportunity in the Armed Forces issued *Freedom to Serve.*[70] On 26 July 1948, President Truman

---

[67] *An Appeal to the World: A Statement of Denial of Human Rights to Minorities in the Case of Citizens of Negro Descent in the United States of America an Appeal to the United Nations* (New York: NAACP, 1947), W. E. B. Du Bois Papers, series 9, Petitions, Special Collections and Archives, W. E. B. Du Bois Library, University of Massachusetts, Amherst.

[68] W. C. Berman, *The Politics of Civil Rights in the Truman Administration* (Columbus: Ohio State University Press, 1970); Woodson and Wesley, *The Negro in Our History*, 579–593; D. Clark Foreman, "Should Negro Colleges be Perpetuated or Should There be Integration in Education?" *The Harlem Quarterly* (1950): 317–32; Robert A. Margo, *Race and School in the South, 1880–1950: An Economic History* (Chicago: University of Chicago Press, 1990, 1994) 129–32, 143.

[69] Drewry and Doermann, *Stand and Prosper*, 92–93, 138_[mergers of HBCUs, 95–98, 81–83, WWII and HBCUs; K. O' Reilly, *Nixon's Piano: Presidents and Racial Politics from Washington to Clinton* (New York: Free Press, 1995) 145–65; Bond, "The Evolution and Present Status of Negro Higher Education," 224–35.

[70] H. S. Truman, *Executive Order 9881*, President's Committee on Equality of Treatment and Opportunity in the Armed Services (Washington, DC: GPO, 1948); O' Reilly, *Nixon's Piano*, 160–61; Carl T. Rowan, "Harry Truman and the Negro Was He Our Greatest Civil Rights President?" *Ebony Magazine* 15/1 (November 1959): 44–46.

issued *Executive Order 9981* against racial discrimination and segregation in the armed forces. After winning the closely contested November 1948 election, Truman pushed lightly on civil rights. Blacks continued to push for federal support of higher education for Negroes.[71]

During the Cold War, however, there were new developments in civil rights, and these developments had effects on the history of the HBCUs. In the 1950s and 1960s, European countries began to grant independence to their colonies in Africa, and when African diplomats and their families arrived in America, the nation had to quicken the desegregation of housing, transportation, hotels, restaurants, and public facilities. Blacks and their agencies long held interest in Africa, including the back-to-Africa movements of the 1880s. W. E. B. Du Bois held the first Pan-American Conference in Europe in 1919, when European powers finalized the treaty to end the First World War. Du Bois and his colleagues intended to gain self-determination for the people of Africa, as well as for the African Diaspora. Pan-African movements brought an international dimension to the Civil Rights Movement, and encouraged unity among people of African descent. Marcus Garvey's Universal Negro Improvement Association included an African program. Harlem Renaissance leaders Alain Locke and Aaron Douglass emphasized the African roots. William Leo Hansberry pioneered the teaching and study of African history at Howard and started the history department's African Civilization section. Members of the Howard University community examined, evaluated, and expressed their approval or disapproval of US involvement in international events. Even President Mordecai W. Johnson was critical of western imperialism, because it targeted colored nations for exploitation. Howard University faculty members Rayford Logan and Ralph Bunche, served on US advisory committees on Latin America and did research in Africa. In international achievements, Bunch set the standards, pioneered the concepts, and fought the battles for peace and African independence. Howard sponsored scholarships and exchanges for Virgin Islands and Martinique West Indian students. Howard professors paid close attention to American treatment of Haiti, and made proposals to the State Department to improve that treatment. They argued the issues about Ethiopia and Liberia regarding American foreign policy. By 1944, Howard faculty pushed for American programs to industrialize Africa in preparation for independence. In

---

[71] Alfred B. Bonds Jr., "The President's Commission on Higher Education and Negro Higher Education," and Herbert O. Reid and James M. Nabrit Jr., "Remedies under Statutes Granting Federal Aid to Land Grant Colleges," *Journal of Negro Education* 17/3 (Summer 1948): 426–36; 410–25.

the 1950s, Howard and Lincoln University in Pennsylvania had African studies programs and educational links with Africa. A Ford Foundation grant allowed Hampton to offer courses for US Virgin Islanders on the islands and upon the Hampton main campus. Sixteen percent of the students enrolled at Howard were foreign.[72]

Horace Mann Bond at Lincoln University and scholars at Fisk and Howard made efforts to develop and sustain programs in the study of Africa. Many foundations, however, refused to give support to black-led African Studies programs as opposed to those led by white scholars. Reportedly, the Carnegie Corporation once cut off funding to the Association for the Study of Negro Life and History after Carter G. Woodson criticized a Phelps-Stokes Fund report that advocated the white foundations' support of Negro schools that focused on industrial education instead of liberal arts.[73] Woodson simply wanted to correct the biased black studies by white scholars. Although the GEB failed to support Du Bois' *Encyclopedia of the Negro* project, it sponsored interdisciplinary African Studies programs at Fisk and the University of Pennsylvania, and Carnegie Corporation gave funds for African Studies at Northwestern University, but no HBCUs.

Bond used institutional funds to establish an Institute for the Study of African Affairs in 1950, but the major foundations refused funding. Some 130 Africans attended Lincoln during these years, and the school graduated the heads of state of Ghana and Nigeria. Lincoln University graduate Kwame Nkrumah led the liberation movement against the British and became the first president of his country, Ghana, which gained independence on 6 March 1957. Du Bois, who was harassed by anti-communist forces in the American government and ousted from the NAACP by Walter White and the board, relocated to Ghana in 1960 to assist Nkrumah in building a model socialist society. In 1954, the Ford Foundation gave small support to Howard's African Studies program, but not enough to compete with programs at the TWIs. In May

---

[72] C. L. Muse Jr., "Howard University and US Foreign Affairs during the Franklin D. Roosevelt Administration, 1933–1945," *Journal of African American History* 87 (2002): 403–415; Princeton N. Lyman, "Ralph Bunche's International Legacy: The Middle East, Congo, and United Nations Peacekeeping," *Journal of Negro Education* 73/2 (Spring 2004): 159–70. Mary L. Dudziak, *Cold War Civil Rights: Race and the Image of American Democracy* (Princeton: Princeton University Press, 2000) 38–39, 70, 125; Thomas Borstelmann, *The Cold War and the Color Line: American Race Relations in the Global Arena* (Cambridge MA: Harvard University Press, 2001) 8, 42, 87, 109, 121, 125, 164; Adolph L. Reed Jr., *W. E. B. Du Bois and American Political Thought: Fabianism and the Color Line* (New York: Oxford University Press, 1997) 1–30.

[73] Woodson and Wesley, *The Negro in Our History*, 503, 504–506.

1954, Howard established a master's degree program in African Studies. Ford Foundation increased funding to Howard in 1957. The federal government funded the African Language and Area Center at Howard in 1959 to help with the Cold War. Howard's programs survived the 1960s. By the 1990s, three HBCUs had a pure degree and a separate department in Africana Studies.[74]

From 1933 to 1950, America's black colleges and universities matured into "real colleges." The Negro population percentage in the US had declined to 10 percent from 19 percent in 1800, and during the same time period, the percentage of blacks in the southern population had declined from 35 percent to 21.8 percent.[75]

Most HBCUs remained in the former slave states. The number of land-grant HBCUs increased from three in 1890 to seventeen in 1949; and, would increase to twenty by 1972. The US Bureau of Education, the accreditation agencies, and the philanthropic agencies, along with mergers, conversions to high schools and non-collegiate institutions, and closures helped whittle the 740 schools and HBCU-like institutions in 1913 down to about 119 HBCUs by 1954. Among these clearly identifiable HBCUs were fifty-four private, four-year, eleven two-year, thirty-six public, four-year and five public, two-year institutions. The public institutions enrolled 57 percent of all HBCU students by 1953, and would soon dwarf the private HBCUs in student enrollment and offering of graduate programs. SACS approved additional HBCUs during WWII through 1953: "A" rating for South Carolina State (1941), Alabama A&M (1943), Shaw (1943), Paine (1944), Tennessee A&I (1946), and Bethune-Cookman (1947). SACS approved Winston-Salem (1947), Texas Southern (1948), Alcorn A&M (1948), Grambling (1949), Lane College (1949), Albany State (1951), Florida Memorial (1951), Fort Valley (1951), Savannah State (1951), St. Phillips College (1951), Stillman (1953), and Tougaloo (1953).[76]

By 1954, more than half of the surviving HBCUs had earned regional education association accreditation since 1921, and the pace of HBCU accreditation would quicken during the next forty years, and then falter somewhat at the turn of the twenty-first century. After *Brown* (1954), America's

---

[74] Jerry Gershenhorn, "Not an Academic Affair: African Scholars in the Development of African Studies Programs in the United States, 1942–1960," *Journal of African American History* 94/1 (Winter 2009): 44–68; Roger A. Davidson Jr., "A Question of Freedom: African Americans and Ghanaian Independence," *Negro History Bulletin* 60/3 (July–September 1997): 1–5.

[75] Drewry and Doermann, *Stand and Prosper*, 25.

[76] Ibid., 7, 73, 91–93, 123; SACS, "Membership Directory," www.sacsoc.org, Commission on Colleges, Southern Association of Colleges and Schools, 2010, p. 1.

black colleges and universities were about to enter another critical chapter of their long, arduous history.[77]

[77] "Negro Higher and Professional Education in the United States," *Journal of Negro Education* 17/3 (Summer 1948), included a series of articles: S. O. Roberts, "Negro Higher and Professional Eduation in Tennessee," 361–72; W. E. Anderson, "Negro and Higher Education in Alabama," 249–54; Frank A. DeCosta, "Negro Higher and Professional Education in South Carolina," 350–60; J. B. Cade, Elsie L. Hebert, "Negro Higher and Professional Education in Louisiana," 296–302; Eugene S. Richards, "Negro and Professional Education in Oklahoma," 341–49; Aaron Brown, "Negro Higher an Professional Education in Georgia," 265–71; Helen Harris Bracey, "Negro Higher and Professional Education in Florida," 272–79; William H. Martin, "Negro Higher and Professional Education in Arkansas," 255–64.

4

The Civil Rights Movement

Long before *Brown v. Board of Education*, some black college students wanted to do something about the lack of full citizenship and respect for Negroes. In 1939, under the National Negro Congress, the Southern Negro Youth Congress began at Howard University with the intent of bringing positive socioeconomic and racial change to America. In 1942, some Howard students, including Ruth Powell, Juanita Morrow, and Marianne Musgrave, marched against local Jim Crow eateries in February 1943 and were arrested as "alien agents against the wartime government."[1] By the late 1940s, "[t]he internal political, social, and constitutional readjustments required by the new order of things had for the most part been completed."[2] In reality, however, the Civil Rights Movement was just beginning.

The struggle by black Americans to gain status as equal citizens continued. From 1935 onward, US Supreme court decisions had forced racial modifications in Jim Crow graduate education, equalization of salaries for black and white public school teachers, equal accommodations for the races on railroad trains, and, by the early 1950s, was listening to cases for public school desegregation. In 1953, blacks in Baton Rouge—who made up 70 percent of local bus riders—began a bus boycott because Jim Crow rules forced them to stand behind a line so that half the bus could be devoted to white riders. When Negroes could find no room to stand, the drivers refused to pick up any more blacks, even when seats reserved for whites remained empty. Negroes held a mass meeting and formed a boycott that cost the company $1,600 a day. Black leaders compromised

---

[1] W. H. Turner, "A Critique of Race Relations Theory as Applied to Public Policy: The Case of Historically Black Colleges," presented at 69th Annual Meeting of the American Educational Research Association, Chicago, 31 March–4 April 1985; Darlene Clark Hine, William C. Hine, and Stanley Harrold, *African Americans: A Concise History*, 2nd ed. (Upper Saddle River NJ: Pearson Prentice Hall, 2006) 454–513; Robert Cook, *Sweet Land of Liberty; The Forgotten Struggle for Civil Rights in the North* (New York: Random House, 2008) 87, 144; Vernon E. Jordan, *Vernon Can Read! A Memoir* (New York: Basic Books, 2001) 111–12; Kevin K. Gaines, *Uplifting the Race: Black Leadership, Politics, and Culture in the Twentieth Century* (Chapel Hill: University of North Carolina Press, 1996) 19, 137, 139, 177, 227, 230, 237.

[2] Alfred H. Kelly and Winfred A. Harbison, *The American Constitution: Its Origins and Development*, 4th ed. (New York: W. W. Norton, 1970) 883.

a deal with the city, allowing them to take seats not occupied by whites until whites boarded the bus and demanded those seats. Indeed, some moderate and liberal whites were willing to modify and adjust Jim Crow laws here and there, but they would not dismantle white supremacy.

Other Americans, however, sensed the Civil Rights Movement was intensifying. The United Negro College Fund (UNCF) began a series of meetings about the coming of desegregation. HBCUs had much to lose: their identity per the original mission, the monopoly on black students, the public questioning of their reason for being, and, most of all, the continuing financial support from public, private sources, and especially philanthropic and benevolent help from white sources. In October 1952, the UNCF published the statement, "Why the United Negro College Fund?" The statement said HBCUs would continue to have a main responsibility for the education of Negroes for some time to come because "America's racial problems would be around for a long time."[3] By 1953, twenty-two southern TWIs, mostly religious schools and nine southern seminaries enrolled 453 Negroes. Others engaged discussions about accepting black divinity students. In April 1954, Fisk University held the Twenty-fifth Annual Festival of Music and Art, and John H. Sengstacke, founder of the Chicago *Defender* newspaper syndicate was the honoree. The Sengstacke family paper had defended Negro rights since near the turn of the century and sponsored scholarships, trying to strengthen the HBCUs.

Around noon on 17 May 1954, after reading decisions for other cases scheduled in the morning, chief justice Earl Warren, finally announced, "[b]y the way, we have a decision on *Brown v. Board of Education*." According to Lerone Bennett, the packed court room went completely silent as the US Supreme Court announced the verdict of *Brown v. Board of Education*, 347 US 483 (1954), which declared *Plessy v. Ferguson* (1896) outdated. Thurgood Marshall and his colleagues turned to each other in triumph: "We hit the Jackpot!"[4] Reporters quickly signaled the news to the world, including the communist countries that were awe-struck by such an unexpected American decision. Negroes, who had not been able to find seats in the courtroom, stood on the steps outside, cheering. On May 18, the UNCF said, "The *Brown* decision will allow [HBCUs] to open their doors to all qualified students, and enrollments will continue to grow."[5]

---

[3] Marcus Garvey's UNIA in the 1920s first convinced the news media and others to capitalize the word Negro. The NAACP retained the adjective "Colored" to represent all minorities. The UNCF dropped "Colored" from its charter in 1953.

[4] Lerone Bennett Jr., "The Day Race Relations Changed Forever," *Ebony* 40/7 (May 1985): 108–16.

[5] Ibid.

Tom Brady, a Mississippi circuit judge and a mean-spirited neo-Confederate, said, "We say to the Supreme Court and to the northern world, 'You shall not make us drink from this cup.' We have, through our forefathers died before for our sacred principles. We can, if necessary, die again."[6]

Blacks and whites struggled to interpret the *Brown* decision as it was applied to the wider American society. On 25 May 1954 in Nashville, thirteen social progressive groups, including the Colored Parents and Teachers Association and the League of Women Voters, met to "respond to the challenge" of *Brown*. Among the speakers, Charles S. Johnson, president of Fisk University, said *Brown* was "The most important national mandate in civil rights since the Emancipation Proclamation."[7] In July, Thurgood Marshall, chief legal counsel for the NAACP-Legal Defense Education Fund, speaking at the Eleventh Annual Race Relations Institute at Fisk, said the states ought to make the desegregation process painless.[8] In May 1955, after receiving the requested responses to *Brown* from attorneys general of Jim Crow states, the Court issued *Brown II*, which put forth vague guidelines for school desegregation to unfold "with all deliberate speed."[9] Jim Crow officials took this to mean to move as *slow* as possible to prevent widespread white rebellion. Federal district courts, dominated by local lawyers and politicians beholden to the Republican or Democratic Party, allowed school desegregation, one grade at a time.

It was primarily Southern whites who organized massive resistance movements. More than 100 congressional representatives rebelled against the *Brown* decision, signing the *Southern Manifesto* in 1954 that argued for states rights, and white violence continued in the southern states. In Mississippi, white authorities excluded blacks from juries, and intimidated and even murdered

---

[6] Lerone Bennett Jr., *Before the Mayflower: A History of Black America* 6th rev. ed. (New York: Penguin Books, 1993) 375–76, 549, 551, 554, 556; John Egerton, *Speak Now against the Day: The Generation before the Civil Rights Movement in the South* (Chapel Hill: University of North Carolina Press, 1994) 113–19; Numan V. Bartley, *The Rise of Massive Resistance: Race and Politics in the South During the 1950s* (Baton Rouge: LSU Press, 1969, 1997) 85.

[7] Johnson, *Sidelines Activist*, 13; Editor, "Brown," *Clarksville Leaf Chronicle*, 18, 19, 25 May 1954, p. 1; Patrick J. Gilpin, "Charles S. Johnson and the Race Relations Institutes of Fisk University," *Pylon* 41/3 (Third Quarter 1980): 300–11.

[8] J. B. Roebuck and K. S. Murty, *Historically Black Colleges and Universities: Their Place in American Higher Education* (Westport CT: Praeger, 1993) 37–38; Drewry and Doermann, *Stand and Prosper*, 37, 53, 55, 56, 57–60, 75; Charles S. Johnson, "Some Significant Social and Educational Implications of the US Supreme Court's Decision," *Journal of Negro Education* (1954): 23–29; Lerone Bennett, "The *Brown* announcement," *Ebony* (May 1954); Harold Cruse's classic, *The Crisis of the Negro Intellectual* (New York: Morrow, 2005) acknowledges the Negro intellectual class and their impact on the CRM.

[9] *Brown v. Board of Education*, 349 US 241 (1955).

Negro citizens.[10] Mississippi funneled public funds into the White Citizens Council—the "uptown KKK." White supremacists in Money, Mississippi, murdered a visiting Negro teenager, Emmett Till from Chicago who "whistled at a white woman." Crowds of whites chanted "Two, four, six, eight; hell no, we won't integrate." The issues surrounding the *Brown* decision involved white perceptions of miscegenation and the threat of black boys socializing with white girls in the public schools. Some state legislators supported bills to create gender-based public schools. Prince Edwards County in Virginia closed the public schools in 1954, leaving two thousand black children with no means of education until NAACP plaintiffs won *Griffin v. County School Board of Prince Edward County* 377 US 218 (1964).[11] White politicians won southern elections on anti-integration platforms. Most Jim Crow school systems changed not at all, and more than two-thirds of schools in the nineteen Jim Crow states remained racially segregated *de jure* as late as 1969. In the west and north, *de facto* racial and ethnic segregation of neighborhoods and schools continued without much challenge.

The open neglect of black higher education desegregation and racial discrimination continued in nineteen Jim Crow states long after *Brown*. NAACP plaintiffs and federal court cases forced the Jim Crow states to admit a handful of black graduate and professional students to the public institutions, between 1936 and 1962, but almost all the southern flagships barred undergraduate Negro students, and most did not admit them until after passage of the Civil Rights Act in 1964. Often the first undergraduate blacks admitted to southern flagships were NAACP plaintiffs and badly needed Negro athletes.

The focus of the Civil Rights Movement of the 1950s shifted from public school desegregation to the desegregation of public facilities. This aspect of the twentieth-century Civil Rights Movement added the issue of *class* to the predominant issue of *race*. The authorities and other Americans had refused since antebellum times to recognize a class structure among citizens of African

---

[10] Editor, "Nation Horrified by the Emmett Till Murder," *Jet Magazine*, 15 September 1955, p. 3; Charles M. Payne, *I've Got the Light of Freedom: The Organizing Tradition and the Mississippi Freedom Struggle* (Berkeley: University of California Press, 1995) 39–40; Christopher Metress, *The Lynching of Emmett Till: A Documentary Narrative* (Charlottesville: University of Virginia Press, 2002) 7.

[11] See Numan V. Bartley, *The Rise of Massive Resistance: Race and Politics in the South during the 1950s* (Baton Rouge: Louisiana University Press, 1997) 82–83, 146, 183, 212, 315–19, 342; Wilbur B. Brookover, "Education in Prince Edwards County, Virginia, 30 Years After: 'A Pretty Good Place to Live,'" *Journal of Negro Education* 62/2 (Spring 1993): 146–62; R. C. Smith, *They Closed Their Schools: Prince Edwards County, Virginia 1951–1964* (Chapel Hill: UNC Press, 1965) 1–15.

descent. Upper-class blacks felt equally oppressed as the Negro masses. Poor, working-, middle-, and wealthy upper-class Negroes could shop in the downtown stores and spend their money with white merchants, but they could not sit at a lunch counter, use the public bathroom, drink at the "whites only" water fountain, try on new clothes and shoes, or resist the daily racial insults thrown their way by white employees. Drunken white men in the downtown area could curse, kick, or spit on Negro men, women, and children. The Negroes received unfair treatment and lack of protection from local law authorities, and all classes of Negro citizens were *de facto* and/or *de jure* (by law as in some cities like Atlanta and Indianapolis) ghettoized on the same side of town, where they suffered a lack of paved streets, inadequate water and sewer services, infrequent garbage pickup service, and a shortage of new and better housing. Negroes could not access specified employment, business opportunities, nor enter certain buildings unless as a janitor. These racial conditions hurt Negro college students, who represented the future black elite-class. These youngsters, the offspring of a generation that supplied America with more than a million military personnel, had to use alleyways, back, and side doors to reach the "Colored Section" in the balcony of a downtown movie theater. They had little peace of mind when they retreated to the crowded HBCU campus, where their presidents endured the realities of a Jim Crow society and worked—indeed with sympathy for their students—to keep their young charges *within* the rules of Jim Crow. White Americans, north and south, designed an inhumane social system to *humiliate* the Negro citizen whenever, and wherever, possible.

After *Brown II*, the Montgomery bus boycott began in December 1955. This local movement catapulted into the spotlight Rosa Parks, Edgar D. Nixon, Martin Luther King, Jr., and Jo Ann Robinson. Nixon and Parks were local NAACP officers, and Robinson was an instructor at Alabama State College and head of a local Negro women's action group. King, Jr., was completing his PhD at Boston University and, as a local minister, had just arrived in Montgomery. The president of Alabama State looked the other way while Robinson mobilized students to print and distribute thousand of flyers that read "Stay off the Buses." Alabama officials would retaliate later, but the Montgomery bus boycott continued for nearly a year.

The Fellowship of Reconciliation (FOR) and its Committee for Nonviolent Integration—led by white activist Glenn Smiley—met with King, Jr., and others on the Morehouse College campus on 12 May 1956. They discussed the blossoming Civil Rights Movement. FOR offered their support.[12]

In April 1956, Dillard University held the National Science Institute to encourage more blacks to enter the science fields and persuade Americans to allow black college graduates into such occupations. Southern University claimed to be the largest HBCU with 5,745 students—out of a total of 68,375—and a budget of $4.8 million. Fisk University announced 130 graduates, while Virginia State College listed 250. In November of that year, *Gayle v. Browder*, 352 US 903 (1956) outlawed racial segregation on Montgomery buses, and in January 1957, Martin Luther King, Jr., and others formed the Southern Christian Leadership Conference (SCLC) to coordinate a regional movement. In May, William H. Hastie, former dean at Howard's law school, warned Fisk's graduating class that they face stiff "competition with the increasing growth of public HBCUs and now desegregation." The United Negro College Fund expanded its fundraising efforts to help private HBCUs. The UNCF honored US Senator John F. Kennedy, winner of the Pulitzer Prize, for donating money from his book, *Profiles in Courage*.[13] Kennedy spoke in favor of UNCF and black colleges for political reasons.[14] The UNCF gesture atoned for Kennedy's negative feelings toward black Americans and his fatalistic *Birth of a Nation* interpretation of the history of Reconstruction in *Profiles in Courage*. Students, alumni, and members of UNCF institutions tried to balance the UNCF mission of raising funds, which depended heavily on whites, with support for the Civil Rights Movement. Fisk mourned the loss of Charles S. Johnson, who died from a heart attack in 1956.[15] About a mile down Jefferson Street, Martin Luther King, Jr., the hero of the recent Montgomery bus boycott, was the speaker at a chapel session at Tennessee A&I State University. The students and faculty members were impressed.

Between 1957 and 1958, the Southern Association of Colleges and Schools (SACS) ended the Jim Crow "A" and "B" approval ratings, and accepted eighteen of fifty-nine recent HBCU applicants as *fully accredited* members. SACS

---

[12] See Jo Ann G. Robinson, *The Montgomery Bus Boycott and the Women Who Started It: The Memoir of Jo Ann Robinson Gibson*, ed. David J. Garrow (Knoxville: University of Tennessee Press, 1987) 1–20.

[13] John F. Kennedy, *Profiles in Courage* (New York: Harper and Row, 1950).

[14] Nick Bryant, *The Bystander: John F. Kennedy and the Struggle for Black Equality* (New York: Basic Books, 2006) 78, 92; O' Reilly, *Nixon's Piano*, 190–91.

[15] "1950s," see J. B. Roebuck and K. S. Murty, *Historically Black Colleges and Universities: Their Place in American Higher Education* (Westport CT: Praeger, 1993) 32–34, 35; Cynthia L. Jackson and Eleanor F. Nunn, *Historically Black Colleges and Universities: A Reference Book* (Santa Barbara CA: ABC-Clio, 2003) 41–42, 76, 43, 119–120, 165.

said, "Morehouse is to be highly commended upon the quality of its instruction. The faculty-student ratio is 1 to 15, far more than the minimum standard requested by the Southern Association."[16] Delaware State College received MSACS accreditation in 1957, and Alcorn and Lane completed SACS accreditation in 1961. Mississippi Valley State College achieved SACS accreditation in 1968. Howard L. Simmons, an HBCU administrator and MSACS executive, studied HBCUs in MSACS and concluded that accreditation standards positively forced changes and improvements.

Meanwhile, a group of Spelman College students and their white instructor formed the Social Science Club dedicated to civil rights. In January 1957, the Spelman students attempted to sit in the "whites' only" gallery of the Georgia General Assembly, but the speaker came to the microphone and shouted: "You nigras move over to where you belong! We still got segregation in the state of Georgia!"[17] Howard Zinn, author of *The Southern Mystique,* said "My students and I were ordered out of the gallery of the Georgia General Assembly, the Speaker of the House shouting ... at us."[18] Morehouse conferred an honorary doctorate on Martin Luther King, Jr., at the 1957 commencement, in honor of his role in the Montgomery bus boycott. From the campus next-door, in early 1958, some Spelman students traveled to the Georgia legislature and stood in protest of racial segregation. In 1959, the Social Science Club at Spelman targeted the city's public libraries. They attended a play at Atlanta's Municipal Auditorium, but the management turned out the lights. They also helped with another protest around the Georgia state capitol in 1961. In 1965, the first black since Reconstruction gained election to the Georgia General Assembly, with Spelman students present at the swearing-in ceremony. Howard Zinn said,

> At Spelman, there was always an emphasis on manners and morals ...The Spelman girl was ... the recipient of well-meant advice from her teachers-elders: be nice, be well mannered and lady-like, do not speak loudly, and do not get in trouble. Spelman was pious and sedate, encrusted with the traditions of gentility and moderation. But with the sit-in movement, there began a revolt.[19]

---

[16] Howard L. Simmons, "The Accreditation Process as a Factor in the Improvement of Traditionally Black Institutions," *Journal of Negro Education* 53/4 (May 1984): 400–405.

[17] Harry G. Lefever, *Undaunted by the Fight: Spelman College and the Civil Rights Movement, 1957–1967* (Macon GA: Mercer University Press, 2005) 9.

[18] Ibid., 9, 13.

[19] K. S. Conzett, "Female College Students' Perceptions of their Role in the Civil Rights and Antiwar Movements of the 1960s" (PhD dissertation, University of Iowa, 1994) 1–10; Zinn, *The Southern Mystique* (New York: Alfred A. Knopf, 1964) 4, 5, 8, 82, 108–109, 114, 116,

In Nashville, in January 1958, local Negroes organized the Nashville Christian Leadership Council (NCLC), presided over by Kelly Miller Smith. The organization became an affiliate of King's, SCLC. James M. Lawson, Jr., who was skilled in non-violence tactics and Christian and civil disobedience principles, and who was studying at Oberlin College, heard King, Jr., speak there and was urged by the young minister to come south. Lawson already had spent fifteen months in federal prisons for refusing the military draft. He taught English in India and studied the nonviolence tactics of Gandhi there. The Fellowship of Reconciliation (FOR) hired Lawson in the Nashville office in January 1958. In March, Lawson spoke at First Colored Baptist Church where he and Smith announced the NCLC would begin training students in Christian non-violence tactics. Lawson led the workshops for more than a year. In 1959, near the end of the fall semester, Lawson and Smith yielded to the restless trainees. They sent scouts into the business district, three blocks east of First Colored Baptist Church, to count the lunch counter seats. The group included a white exchange student at Fisk. The Nashville student leaders planned to fill the seats they had counted and keep filling them with reserves if arrests occurred.

In late November 1959, under the guidance of Lawson and with the support of Smith's NCLC, students conducted the first "test demonstrations" on selected restaurants. The owners refused service to the integrated group, which obeyed instructions, kindly said "thank you," and returned to the church, where Lawson and Smith debriefed them. Smith, who was a keen negotiator, tried private negotiations with the shop owners, but without success. The students assumed the activist name Nashville Student Movement (NSM). However, the test demonstrations broke off for the winter college break.[20] Before the Nashville students could resume their demonstrations, sit-in demonstrations took place in Greensboro, home of North Carolina A&T State College. Ezell Blair, Jr., Joseph McNeil, Franklin McCain, and David Richmond carried out unrehearsed, spontaneous demonstrations. Black and white students from local colleges, including Bennett College for women, later joined the protests. The Greensboro student movement remained informal and not well organized.

Thus, on 10 February 1960, the Rev. Douglass Moore, who supported the Greensboro students and knew Nashville had well-trained students, an experienced trainer—Lawson—and a great negotiator—Smith—called Lawson to

---

117; Anthony M. Orum, "Negro College Students and the Civil Rights Movement" (PhD dissertation, University of Chicago, 1967) 1–10.

[20] James M. Lawson, "The Man Who Escaped the Cross," *Fellowship* 25 (1959): 1–12. No biography of Lawson, a visiting professor in Vanderbilt's School of Divinity in 2008–2010, has been published yet.

help spread the protests so that the sit-in movement would not die out. On that Friday afternoon, Lawson called a meeting in the Fisk University auditorium. Two hundred students showed up to hear the plea for help. The students scouted downtown Nashville targets over the weekend and counted lunch counter seats. They planned to implement the sit-ins the following Monday. On that day, despite the snowy weather, Diane Nash, Marion Barry, James Bevel, Barnard Lafayette, John Lewis, and Lawson became leaders in the local sit-in movement.

Like the Civil War, many neo-Confederate officials argued they had the right under states' rights to do as they pleased to Negroes. The white newspapers took pictures of the demonstrators, calling them "outside agitators." Diane Nash and James Bevel were from Chicago, and Barry was a native of Mississippi, a graduate of LeMoyne College, and a graduate student at Fisk. Barry and his mother were part of that Great Migration of Negroes who flooded out of the Delta into the regional capital of Memphis, where they had hoped to find employment and better schools. Lafayette and Lewis were students at American Baptist Theological Seminary. Born in Pennsylvania but raised and educated in Ohio, James M. Lawson was a graduate student, one of a few blacks in Vanderbilt University School of Divinity in 1958. Two-fifths of A&I's five thousand students derived from out-of-state enrollment. All were American citizens.

A few courageous and morally grounded whites, such as Will D. Campbell, immediately joined the black Civil Rights Movement. He was a white minister born in Mississippi who moved to Nashville in 1956. He worked for the National Council of Churches, and was one of a few ministers that assisted Daisy Bates, president of the local NAACP, in the Little Rock, Arkansas, school desegregation process in fall 1957. Campbell assisted Lawson, Smith, and the sit-in demonstrators in Nashville by monitoring police actions during the protests, helping raise money, and negotiating deals. He even joined Smith's church.[21]

Vanderbilt's board of trustees and administration were against any involvement of its students in civil rights activity. The men on the board were wealthy businesspersons, men of power and influence—typical members of the southern white elite-class that sought to keep blacks and the white masses in conformity with "the southern way of life." The vice chair of the board was James "Jimmy" G. Stahlman, editor of the Nashville *Banner* daily evening newspaper. The *Banner* symbolized the vanguard role of southern newspapers in

---

[21] See Will B. Campbell, *Forty Acres and a Goat: A Memoir* (San Francisco CA: Harper and Row, 1989) 1–20; James Talley, "Quick Action Halts Outbreak of Fighting in Downtown Area," *Nashville Tennessean*, 28 February 1960, p. 1.

maintaining the region's racial *status quo*. Based on pressure from the Stahlman faction, the university trustees expelled Lawson. After friendly white sources informed Lawson on 4 March there was a warrant out for his arrest, he fled to the sanctuary of Smith's First Colored Baptist Church. Nashville police officers dragged him from the church sanctuary, while Smith and others observed the arrest to make sure Lawson was not "accidentally shot and killed."[22] He was placed in a van and then jailed. The *Banner* displayed the photographs to show what happens to "troublemakers." Jimmy Stahlman sent a reporter to Ohio to do intelligence on "a flannel mouth" outside agitator.[23] Vanderbilt undergraduates also upheld the "southern way of life"; they voted to continue to keep black undergraduates out of the institution.

An unknown terrorist bombed the home of Z. Alexander Looby, one of the defense lawyers for jailed sit-in demonstrators. In response, some 5,000 people marched from the Tennessee A&I campus to the county courthouse and confronted the city mayor, Beverly Briley. Diane Nash asked him in the front of national television if he thought racial discrimination was wrong, to which he replied, yes. Briley convened the Human Relations Committee to negotiate with white businesses and to decide how to begin racial desegregation, and on 10 May 1960, Nashville announced the beginning of desegregation of its downtown facilities. Many establishments did not participate, and students continued the demonstrations for three more years.[24]

Students in the Atlanta University Center decided that 12 February 1960 would be the day to begin public protests and sit-ins. The student leaders postponed any action in order to talk to the highly respected president of Morehouse College, Benjamin E. Mays, and the council of presidents of Atlanta University Center. As Benjamin Mays recalled,

> Far from being surprised that our students were 'getting into the act,' I would have been dismayed had they not participated in the South-wide

---

[22] David Halberstam, *The Children* (New York: Fawcett Books, 1998) 206–207; Lovett, *The Civil Rights Movement in Tennessee*, 130.

[23] Halberstam, *The Children*, 206–207; Lovett, *The Civil Rights Movement in Tennessee*, 129.

[24] David Halberstam, *The Children* (New York: Fawcett Books, 1998) 92–93; Bobby L. Lovett, *The Civil Rights Movement in Tennessee: A Narrative History* (Knoxville: University of Tennessee Press, 2005) 140; John Lewis, *Walking with the Wind: A Memoir of the Movement* (New York: Simon & Schuster, 1998) 79, 91, 92, 114, 122; Linda T. Wynn, "The Dawning of a New Day: The Nashville Sit-Ins, February 13–May 10, 1960," *Tennessee Historical Quarterly* 50/1 (Spring 1991): 42–54; Jimmie L. Franklin, "Civil Rights Movement," in Carroll Van West, ed., *Tennessee Encyclopedia of History and Culture* (Knoxville: University of Tennessee Press, 1999) 163–68.

> revolution.... They understood perfectly well, however, that I would support them, whatever course they decided to take.... The six presidents in the [AU] Center were in full sympathy with the students, and the Council of Presidents never tried to over-persuade, let along dictate to them.[25]

Mays later wrote, "I never ceased to raise my voice and pen against the injustices of a society that segregated and discriminated against people because God made them black."[26] Similar to the appeals by Du Bois and the 1905 Niagara Movement, the students composed an "Appeal for Human Rights," which was published in Atlanta newspapers on 9 March 1960:

> We, the students of the six affiliated institutions from the Atlanta University Center—Clark, Morehouse, Morris Brown, Spelman Colleges, Atlanta University, and the Interdenominational Theological Center—have joined our hearts, minds, and bodies in the cause of gaining those rights which are inherently ours as members of the human race and as citizens of these United States."

With no acceptable response, the Atlanta demonstrations began on 15 March. Student leaders Julian Bond and Lonnie King dispatched two hundred sit-in students to public, private, and government areas. When Looby journeyed to Atlanta to speak, he told about the bombing of his house and the sit-in demonstrations by the HBCU students in Nashville: "This is not a Negro fight. It is the fight of all right-thinking people."[27]

---

[25] Benjamin E. Mays, *Born to Rebel: An Autobiography* (New York: Charles Scribner's Sons, 1971) 183, 188, 271–74, 287–99.

[26] Ibid.

[27] "The History of Black Student Activism," Special Issue, *The Journal of African American History* 88 (2003): 105–217; Harry G. Lefever, *Undaunted by the Fight*, 1–10, 25, 26, 28, 93, 55, 76, 78, 79, 105, 154, 202; E. A. Jones, *A Candle in the Dark: A History of Morehouse College* (Valley Forge PA: Judson Press, 1967) 189, 273; Stephen G. N. Tuck, *Beyond Atlanta: The Struggle for Racial Equality in Georgia, 1940–1980* (Athens: University of Georgia Press) 49, 51, 56–57, 60, 63, 79, 81, 88, 89, 110, 118, 119, 133, 155, 195–96, 213, 248, 250; Clayborne Carson, ed., *The Papers of Martin Luther King, Jr.: Called to Serve, January 1929-June 1951* (Los Angeles: University of California Press, 1992) vol. 1, 36, 37, 40–46; Benjamin Brawley, *History of Morehouse College* (College Park MD: McGrath Publishing Company, 1970) 117; Clarence A. Bacote, *The Story of Atlanta University: A Century of Service, 1865–1965* (Atlanta: Atlanta University, 1969) 1–10; Lovett, *The Civil Rights Movement in Tennessee*, 140, 141, 129; Hine, Hine, and Harrold, *African Americans: A Concise History*, 2nd ed., 467; Timothy Jenkins and Lonnie King, "SNCC and Kennedy Justice," in Howell Raines, *My Soul Is Rested: The Story of the Civil Rights Movement in the Deep South* (New York: Penguin Books, 1977, 1983) 227–31.

Seventy-seven students, including fourteen enrolled at Spelman, suffered arrests. Some of them had borrowed Professor Zinn's car, saying simply "we are going downtown." A number of white students from Emory University also became involved in the local sit-in movement. Lonnie King and Ralph Moore became notable leaders of the Atlanta student movement, and Ruby Doris Smith participated in the Atlanta Committee on Appeal for Human Rights under the students in the Atlanta University Center. As Doris Smith recalled, "I went through the food line in the restaurant at the State Capitol with six other students, but when we got to the cashier, she would not take our money. She ran upstairs to get the governor. The Lieutenant Governor came and told us to leave. We didn't, and went to ...jail."[28]

In Memphis, in March 1960, students from LeMoyne College and their NAACP chapter provided the "foot soldiers" to begin civil rights demonstrations. LeMoyne graduates helped to man the black schools in Memphis and provided civic, social, and religious leadership throughout the huge black community. Memphis was worse than Atlanta and Nashville; it was a place often described as "the economic and social capital of the Mississippi Delta."[29] Memphis officials strung banners across Main Street reading "Keep Memphis Down in Dixie." During the Civil War occupation by Union troops, Memphis was about 40 percent Negro, and from the 1930s onward, blacks continued flooding the city, pouring out of the impoverished, rural Mississippi Delta where a million of them lived just above slavery conditions.

In the 1930s, Lemoyne College students and a few faculty advisers affiliated themselves with FOR and a NAACP Youth chapter. They became involved in civil rights protests in Memphis, even when the main NAACP branch officers refused to speak against their political ally, the city's political boss, Edward H. Crump—a diehard segregationist from Mississippi. The Youth chapter sent a letter to Crump, protesting the recent police killing of Negro citizens, but Crump convinced the city's NAACP leaders, Robert R. Church and Lt. George W. Lee, to allow the local chapter to become as "dead as a Pharaoh."[30] LeMoyne leaders invited former NAACP secretary James Weldon Johnson, "father of the Harlem Renaissance," and now a faculty member at Fisk University, to journey to

---

[28] Cynthia Griggs Fleming, *Soon We Will Not Cry: The Liberation of Ruby Doris Smith Robinson* (Lanham MD: Rowman and Littlefield, 1998) 1–30; Zinn, *The Southern Mystique*, 4, 5, 8, 82, 108–09, 114, 116, 117; Ruth Searles and J. Allen Williams Jr., "Negro College Students' Participation in Sit-ins," *Social Forces* 40/3 (March 1962): 215–20.

[29] Lovett, *The Civil Rights Movement in Tennessee*, 107–11.

[30] Ibid., 238.

Memphis to speak on an attempt at resurrecting the Memphis branch of the NAACP. LeMoyne, which still had a white president, administration, and faculty, refused to renew the contract for the faculty member who helped lead this community action.

Old "Boss Crump" did not release his political machine's grip on Memphis until he died in August 1954—just after *Brown*. No sooner had Crump died, Negro professionals, many of them HBCU products, began a movement to get blacks registered to vote and run for state and local political offices. The college-educated Negroes (the "young Turks" as they called themselves[31]) included Vasco Smith, a Meharry trained dentist and US Air Force veteran, and his wife, Maxine Atkins-Smith, a Spelman College graduate. In 1959, they and other Negroes formed a political coalition consisting of Republicans and Democrats, and ran a slate of black candidates for city offices, but lost on dismal black voter turnout. Vasco, Maxine, and other college-educated blacks, took control of the NAACP Memphis branch, ousting the preacher leadership.

The task of applying heat directly to Memphis's Jim Crow practices fell to students at LeMoyne College and S. A. Owen Junior College. On 10 March 1960, students from LeMoyne began sit-in demonstrations at segregated public libraries of Memphis, claiming they "need some more books for required term papers."[32] Their arrests inundated the Memphis *World* and the *Tri-State Defender*, and galvanized thousands of citizens. They picketed the jail, attended mass meetings at local churches, and gave money for bail and legal fees. White Memphis withstood the protests and legal siege for four years.[33]

Except for LeMoyne College and the S. A. Owen Junior College in Memphis, the only other HBCU in west Tennessee—where 70 percent of black Tennesseans lived—was Lane College in Jackson. Bishop Isaac Lane and the Colored Methodist Episcopal Church founded the institution and opened it in November 1882 as the CME High School. They changed the name to Lane Institute in 1884 and graduated the first students in 1887. A white, former slave owner and member of the Memphis Conference of the MEC South became the first president. Lane and his son headed the school for several decades, organizing a college department in 1896. In 1914, the school had 218 students, including ten enrolled in college courses. Lane College gained "B" rating from SACS in 1936, "A" rating in 1949, and full SACS membership in 1961. The federal

---

[31] Ibid., 112–18.

[32] Lovett, *The Civil Rights Movement in Tennessee*, 189.

[33] Sherry Hoppe and Bruce W. Speck, *Maxine Smith's Unwilling Pupils: Lessons Learned in Memphis' Civil Rights Classroom* (Knoxville: University of Tennessee Press, 2007) 12, 14, 56, 74–75, 84, 154–55, 158, 259, 263.

government named a WWII merchant marine victory ship in Bishop Lane's honor, and placed its buildings on the National Register of Historic Places.

In spring 1960, the Lane College students and several involved faculty members launched civil rights demonstrations in the city of Jackson. The students, who reactivated the NAACP Youth chapter in April, suffered arrests for challenging segregated buses. Blacks started an economic boycott against downtown white businesses in October. They became involved in the NAACP national voters' registration campaign, and Lane College students were among nearly 150 persons arrested during a voters' rights march in November 1960. Adults from Lane and two nearby TWIs advised the student movement or supported it. Jackson finally began desegregating public schools and downtown restaurants between 1962 and 1965.[34]

Civil rights progress in nearby rural west Tennessee counties was painfully slow. Negroes constituted 60 percent of the Fayette County and Haywood County populations, but owned only 25 percent of the land. Blacks were heavily impoverished, had had no political representation since the 1880s, and fewer than two hundred of them were registered to vote. Vigilantes ran the local NAACP chapter officers out of town, and a number of Negro leaders had been lynched. The situation did not begin to change until 1960 when Negro attorney James F. Estes and others from nearby Memphis helped organize voter registration drives. Later, HBCU students from Memphis, Nashville, and Jackson helped transport tents, clothing, and food supplies to keep destitute black families alive after white landowners retaliated and evicted them from tenant and sharecropping farms in the dead of winter.

The students at Arkansas AM&N State College tried to engage sit-in demonstrations in downtown Pine Bluff. The blacks in rural Arkansas areas were impoverished and not registered to vote, despite comprising 43 percent of the county's population by 1960. The AM& N State College president, Lawrence Davis Sr., stopped the movement. Forty miles away, the governor and the state legislature had closed the Little Rock public school system in defiance of a federal court order to desegregate the all-white Central High School, but the federal courts ordered the system reopened. The Arkansas AM& N State College in Jefferson County had nearly two thousand students drawn also from Memphis high schools. Its students, however, were not civil rights activists. With

---

[34] A. L. Cooke, *Lane College: Its Heritage and Outreach, 1882–1982* (Jackson TN: Lane College, 1987) 22, 49, 57, 81; Arthur L. David, "Lane College," *Tennessee Encyclopedia of History and Culture*, 523.

the president's strong opposition, no effective student sit-in demonstrations were able to march from campus to downtown Pine Bluff at that time.

Young SNCC leaders from Little Rock, which had three HBCUs, including Arkansas Baptist College, Shorter Junior College, and Philander Smith College, came to Pine Bluff and renewed the sit-in effort in February 1963. The same president, Lawrence Davis, Sr., who had taken the heat and invited Martin Luther King, Jr., as the 1958 commencement speaker, was afraid of losing state appropriations and expelled many students and discouraged others from participating. The demonstrations continued, nevertheless, and resulted in the beginning of desegregation in Pine Bluff. Since 1875, the governors of Arkansas had appointed two Negroes on the school's nine-member board of trustees. The pro-segregationist governor Orval E. Faubus appointed only two blacks to the institution's seven-man board trustees. Only after passage of the Civil Rights Acts of 1964 and 1965 did Pine Bluff begin to completely desegregate.[35]

The faculty at the private HBCUs had become increasingly black since the 1920s, while the faculty bodies at the public HBCUs were originally almost all black. After *Brown*, both public and private HBCUs included more non-black faculty members (including a heavy infusion of Indian-Asian and white persons). By the 1960s, the Woodrow Wilson Fellows Program sponsored short-term tenure of young white doctorates and doctoral students at the HBCUs to bolster accreditation efforts. From 1966 to 1967, Morehouse College had twenty-one non-black faculty members. Some faculty members at Knoxville College, including Merrill Proudfoot, a white Presbyterian clergyman, put their careers on the line by supporting student demonstrators against the wishes of the administration. In *Diary of a Sit-in*, Proudfoot captures the plight of students and others who helped to break local Jim Crow laws. Howard Zinn provided leadership in the Atlanta movement.[36] Several Southern University professors resigned in protest over the treatment of student demonstrators, and some white professors at Tennessee A&I State University confronted the governor about the expulsion of sit-in students. A white instructor became a plaintiff in *Geier v. University of Tennessee*

---

[35] *The Lion* (1965), college yearbook, 13; H. Y. McGee, "'It was the Wrong Time, and They Just Weren't Ready': Direct-Action Protest in Pine Bluff, 1963," *Arkansas Historical Quarterly* 66/1 (Spring 2007): 18–42; B. Riffel, "In the Storm: William Hansen and the Student Nonviolent Coordinating Committee in Arkansas, 1962–1967," *Arkansas Historical Quarterly* 63/4 (Winter 2004): 404–19. Randy Finley, "Crossing the White Line: SNCC in Three Delta Towns, 1963–1967," *Arkansas Historical Quarterly* 65/2 (Summer 2006): 122–27.

[36] LeFever, *Undaunted by the Fight*, 52.

(597 F.2d 1056 [1979]) that forced the desegregation of Tennessee public higher education.[37]

In February 1961, Diane Nash, Ruby Doris Smith, Charles Jones of Johnson C. Smith, and Charles Sherrod of Virginia Union joined a protest after authorities arrested nine persons in Rock Hill, South Carolina. Other HBCU students marched in Atlanta and in Lynchburg, Virginia, in support of the "Rock Hill Nine."[38] There was now a need to organize a regional student movement.

Ella Baker, along with Septima P. Clark of the Highlander Folk School in Monteagle, Tennessee, sponsored a black college retreat at Shaw University 15–17 April 1960. The meeting resulted in the formation of the Student Nonviolent Coordinating Committee (SNCC), which aimed to bring focus and discipline to the students' movement. Glenn Smiley and James Lawson of FOR traveled to Raleigh to help with the meeting. The students did not want to be a part of SCLC, CORE, the NAACP, FOR, or any adult organization and did not trust the SCLC leadership. They trusted Lawson. He wrote the SNCC doctrine, and the SCLC, King, Jr., and others pledged to funnel funds to SNCC. SNCC located the headquarters in Atlanta but centered the activist base in Nashville. Marion Barry, a graduate student at Fisk, became the president, and Diane Nash became director of activist programs. Other SNCC leaders represented South Carolina State, Johnson C. Smith, Spelman, Howard, Kentucky State, and American Baptist. Howard Zinn became an adviser to SNCC, which convened one of its first conferences at Morehouse.[39]

The student organization found its best adult supporters among Zinn, Ella Baker, Septima Clark, Lawson, and Highlander Folk School, which helped train the students in summer workshops. Highlander promoted anti-poverty programs in Appalachia and trained pro-Union and community activists. Under Myles Horton, a white progressive educated in America and Europe, Highlander had included racially integrated meetings and workshops since 1932. The staff placed civil rights on the agenda soon after Horton attended the Supreme Court session that announced *Brown*. The governors and state attorneys general of Arkansas, Georgia, and Tennessee attacked Highlander as an "outside agitator" and center of communist influence.[40] In 1961, despite help from Eleanor Roosevelt and other liberals, Highlander lost its state charter. Tennessee

---

[37] See Merrill Proudfoot, *Diary of a Sit-in* (Urbana: University of Illinois Press, 1990) 1–10.

[38] Ibid., 86–88, 90, 107.

[39] Ibid., 161–64.

[40] Lovett, *The Civil Rights Movement in Tennessee*, 134–36.

governor Buford Ellington (D), who acknowledged his Mississippi roots as "an old fashioned segregationist," led the charge.[41] The state auctioned the Highlander properties, but Highlander obtained another state charter under a slightly altered name, moved to Knoxville, and continued its operations. Septima P. Clark was the sole Negro staff member at Highlander. She continued through the summer of 1961, holding workshops for the student activists. She was a graduate of Avery Institute and former teacher in South Carolina schools and got started in civil rights activism after meeting Thomas E. Miller, former president of South Carolina State College. Miller was one of the men who organized the Charleston branch NAACP. Clark was a strong advocate for complete independence of SNCC. Ella Baker worked with Clark to push the student movement as an alternative to the more conservative approaches of the SCLC and the NAACP. Baker completed Shaw University, migrated north, and became an ally of George Schuyler of the Pittsburg *Courier*. Baker worked as a field secretary to organize NAACP branches; she headed the education committee for the New York City NAACP by 1957. She then went south to help organize SCLC, believing the leadership for the Civil Rights Movement should be in the South.[42] Baker, Clark, and Zinn abhorred the chauvinistic practices carried out within the movement by the male leadership, especially within the preacher-dominated SCLC, and even within SNCC itself. When invited to a private meeting along with Martin Luther King, Jr., and other SCLC officers at the home of the president of Shaw University, Baker refused to participate in their plans to ensure prevention of any SNCC radicalism. Despite the oppression of sexism and chauvinism, black women, like Baker, Clark, Nash, and others took on leadership roles, helping the movement become successful. [43]

The black college student activists also had ideological problems with the NAACP, which preferred voter registration drives, and a barrage of federal court

---

[41] Ibid., 136; John M. Glen, "Myles Horton and the Highlander Idea: A Different Kind of Education," in Larry H. Whitaker and W. Calvin Dickinson, ed., *Tennessee: State of the Nation* (Mason OH: Thompson, 2006) 227–35.

[42] Frank Adams and Myles Horton, *Unearthing Seeds of Fire: the Idea of Highlander* (Charlotte NC: John F. Blair Company, 1975) 1–35; C. Alvin Hughes, "A New Agenda for the South: The Role and Influence of the Highlander Folk School, 1953–1961," *Phylon* 46/3 (Third Quarter 1985): 242–50.

[43] Barbara Ransby, *Ella Baker and the Black Freedom Movement: A Radical Democratic Vision* (Chapel Hill: University of North Carolina Press, 2003) 189–92; Joan C. Elliott, "Ella Jo Baker: A Civil Rights Warrior," *Griot* 11 (1982): 42–48. Glenda E. Gilmore, *Gender and Jim Crow: Women and the Politics of White Supremacy in North Carolina, 1896–1920* (Chapel Hill: University of North Carolina Press, 1996) 12, 38, 139. Bettye Collier-Thomas and V. P. Franklin, eds., *Sisters in Struggle: African American Women in the Civil Rights-Black Power Movement* (New York: New York University Press, 2001) 43, 112, 116.

cases to dismantle Jim Crow. NAACP officers, including Roy Wilkins, believed the sit-in tactics distracted attention from the legal tactics, and the students' public demonstrations could provoke white violence and turn public opinion against the blacks' Civil Rights Movement. However, by 1961, the successful demonstrations by HBCU students changed the mind of the NAACP, which supplied lawyers and helped contribute money. The NAACP-LDEF filed a successful federal case to protect peaceful civil rights demonstrators.

Many American intellectuals—including some black ones who benefited from the integration of TWIs—picked up their pens and published essays in newspapers and journals that castigated the black colleges. They questioned the need for HBCUs to exist within a newly desegregated American society.[44] Benjamin Mays, Howard Zinn, and others responded, defending HBCUs as valuable to America's higher education system. At the time, barely one percent of the faculty/staff at the TWIs were blacks, but some of these blacks heartily defended white colleges and white culture. Mays said, "It is discouraging and disturbing to me that there are indications of a subtle move afoot to abolish black colleges."[45] Indeed, some students and faculty members on the HBCU campuses dared to challenge the nation's racial practices and boldly brought to the outside world's attention this embarrassing and taboo subject in the midst of America's war of propaganda against Communism. HBCUs were supposed to serve black students in Jim Crow days, send them out to "work and serve," but not give leadership and certainly not challenge white leadership.

Perhaps the black and white intellectuals at the TWIs did not know that civil rights activism was not a new phenomenon at HBCUs. Students at Talladega College staged a strike to challenge white paternalism and mistreatment of black students by white faculty members in 1914. A host of student revolts against Jim Crow-related issues took place on HBCU campuses in the 1880s and again between 1924 and 1931. Students at Oakwood College, Alabama, staged a strike in the 1930s; they felt oppressed under the paternalist white administration, and asked for a black president, black faculty members, and more emphasis on liberal arts education. The white Seventh-day Adventist Church, which had operated Oakwood since 1896, hired a black president, and elevated the school to four-year college status in 1944. Talladega College had a reputation for resistance to Jim Crow, and its white president Buell G. Gallagher, who presided from 1937 to 1943 opposed racial prejudice. Gallagher

[44] C. Jenkins and D. Riesman, "The American Negro College," *Harvard Educational Review* 37/1 (Spring 1967): 3–50.

[45] Mays, *Born to Rebel*, 192–95.

commissioned Hale Woodruff of Atlanta University to paint a militant black resistance mural, *Amistad,* in the new library. Gallagher published several books and scholarly articles, saying the college must include the community as an integral part of its curricula, and colleges must engage social change and improvement in that part of society. Gallagher left the presidency in 1943. Students at Georgia's Fort Valley State College had a NAACP chapter by 1944 and were largely responsible for the success of local black voter registration campaigns. At Savannah State, near coastal Georgia, in the late 1940s, some fifty students, including members of the NAACP youth chapter, went to jail for trying to desegregate city buses. Howard University students and others continued their civil rights demonstrations in DC from 1948 to 1949.[46]

Meanwhile, in 1961, the HBCU students' Civil Rights Movement shifted from sit-ins to a strategy of Freedom Rides. The Congress of Racial Equality developed this civil rights strategy during the 1940s. CORE attracted older and professional-class blacks and whites who devoted themselves to nonviolent tactics in transforming a racist and sexist America into a true Democracy for *all* its citizens. CORE reflected the Quakers' nonviolence philosophy at a time when the US Supreme Court became supportive of the Negroes' ongoing Civil Rights Movement. *Mitchell v. United States,* 313 US 80 (1941) decided that segregation of a Negro in a passenger train violated the Interstate Commerce Act of 1887. *Morgan v. Virginia,* 328 US 373 (1946) invalidated a state statue that required the segregation of black and white passengers on interstate buses. Bayard Rustin, who attended Cheyney State College and Wilberforce University, became involved with the members of the Society of Friends and their school of nonviolence in 1942 when he was arrested in Nashville during a Freedom Ride. Rustin became a theoretician in the Civil Rights Movement and helped develop strategies for the movement. CORE conducted the Journey of Reconciliation, using trains and buses from 9–23 April 1947. Persons affiliated with HBCUs were

---

[46] See D. D. Bellamy, *Light in the Valley: A Pictorial History of Fort Valley State College since 1895* (Fort Valley: FVSC, 1996) 1–10; Holly Fisher, "Oakwood College Students' Quest for Social Justice before and During the Civil Rights Era," *Journal of African American History* 88/2 (Spring 2003): 110–125. Drewry and Doermann, *Stand and Prosper,* 146,147, 148, 159; Buell G. Gallagher, "Reorganize the College to Discharge Its Social Function," *Journal of Negro Education* 5/3 (July 1936): 464–73; B. G. Gallagher, "The Impact of the War Upon Privately-Conrolled Colleges and Universities for Negroes," *Journal of Negro Education* 11/3 (July 1942); James M. McPherson, "White Liberals and Black Power in Negro Education, 1865–1915," *American Historical Review* 75/5 (June 1970): 1357–86.

among the sixteen participants.[47] *Henderson v. United States*, 39 US 816 (1950) invalidated racial discrimination in railroad dining cars, and in November 1955, a month before the Montgomery bus boycott began, the ICC ordered racial discrimination to stop in all buses, railroads, and terminals in interstate commerce. The federal court ruled against segregated street buses in November 1956, and several southern cities began voluntary desegregation of streetcars and buses by 1957. While some local governments began to ignore the Jim Crow seating laws, others enforced the rules.

CORE director James Farmer intended for the 1961 Freedom Ride to pressure newly elected President John F. Kennedy (D) to protect the civil rights of citizens on the nation's interstate routes. Kennedy had barely won the 1960 presidential election, with black votes serving as the margin, and he was afraid to upset the southern Democrats who could derail his reelection. Farmer launched the Freedom Rides, anyway, in May 1961, to commemorate the seventh anniversary of *Brown*. The Freedom Rides teamed up pairs of black and white citizens to ride together on carriers requiring separate racial seating. However, after officials allowed Klansmen to burn a bus outside Anniston, Alabama, and administer severe beatings to the riders, CORE supporters used automobiles to transport the riders to the airport and fly them to New Orleans, where the project was to end on 17 May.

As soon as the student activists in Nashville heard about the disaster, they turned their attention to this crisis. SNCC member John Lewis had signed up to ride with the first group out of Washington, DC, but had left the rides midway to take care of personal and college business. Diane Nash notified James Farmer that the students were going to continue the Freedom Rides. The Civil Rights Movement would die if a few racists could stop it now, she said. Farmer exclaimed that Diane was going to get somebody killed.[48] During an intense, late-night meeting, Nash and her colleagues gained the financial support of Kelly Miller Smith and the NCLC board members. They gave $900 to SNCC, and Nash recruited ten local college students to ride a bus from Nashville to Birmingham: two whites—one of whom was an exchange student at Fisk, the other from George Peabody College; two blacks from American Baptist, and six blacks from

[47] See Raymond Arsenault, *Freedom Riders: 1961 and the Struggle for Racial Justice* (New York: Oxford University Press, 2006) 533–87; Searles and Williams, Jr., "Negro College Students' Participation in Sit-ins," 215–20.

[48] Lewis, *Walking with the Wind*, 113–115; Belinda Robnett, "Women in the Student Nonviolent Coordinating Committee: Ideology, Organizational Structure, and Leadership," in Peter J. Ling and S. Monteith, eds., *Gender and the Civil Rights Movement* (New Brunswick NJ: Rutgers University Press, 1999) 131–68.

Tennessee A&I. She telephoned the Rev. Fred Shuttlesworth, head of an SCLC affiliate in Birmingham, speaking in code: "The chickens are being shipped."[49] The students began the dangerous journey around 6:45 in the morning. Birmingham police arrested the students as soon as they arrived at the bus station, and the police telephoned the white students' parents to take them home. They placed the black ones in three cars and delivered them north to the Alabama-Tennessee border, putting them out in the darkness of night, saying, "Cross that line into Tennessee and save all of us a lot of trouble."[50] One freedom rider from Tennessee A&I, Catherine Burks, smiled teasingly at the police commissioner, and like a swan song said, "We'll be back."[51]

Perhaps the governor of Alabama, John Patterson, had alerted his friend, Buford Ellington, governor of Tennessee, to be on the lookout for these "troublemakers." The two men had become friends and fellow quail hunters at the Southern Governors' Conference meetings. Alabama's governor asked Ellington to do something about the freedom riders, who "invaded the sovereign state of Alabama."[52] However, in the middle of nowhere, the students turned away from the Tennessee line and made their way to some isolated rural houses—careful—like the Underground Railroad—to select the "safe houses." They found a telephone and called Nash, who told them: "Stay put. Someone will be there from Nashville to pick you up and take you *back* to Birmingham."[53] Leo (Kwame) Lillard, a senior at Tennessee A&I, drove from Nashville to pick up the students—taking back roads for fear of being stopped by the police. Lillard said to the author, Bobby L. Lovett, "I chose the oldest house, and knocked on the door. That was the right house!"[54] The students came out of hiding, crammed into the automobile, and returned to Birmingham. Lillard graduated in 1961, completed his graduate work up north in urban planning, and worked in New York before moving back to Nashville to become a city planner, a city council member, community activist, and head of local African Cultural Alliance and the popular Annual African Street Festival.[55]

The Rev. Fred Shuttlesworth, a product of Selma University and Alabama State College, despite threats of arrest from Birmingham police, sheltered the

---

[49] Lovett, *The Civil Rights Movement in Tennessee*, 160–62; Andrew Manis, *A Fire You Can't Put Out: The Civil Rights Life of Birmingham's Reverend Fred Shuttlesworth* (Tuscaloosa: University of Alabama Press, 1999) 270–71; Arsenault, *Freedom Riders*, 186.

[50] Arsenault, *Freedom Riders*, 198.

[51] Ibid.

[52] Lovett, *The Civil Rights Movement in Tennessee*, 164, 169.

[53] Ibid., 162.

[54] Ibid., 161.

[55] Lovett, *The Civil Rights Movement in Tennessee*, 159–173.

people and transported them back to the bus station. Reinforcements arrived by train, enlarging the group to nineteen riders. The city held the buses, so the students sat on the benches at the depot, singing freedom songs to commemorate the anniversary of *Brown*. Students at Talladega College went to nearby Anniston to protest the burning of the freedom riders' bus. They started protests in Talladega that lasted into 1962.[56]

There was threat of war led by white race radicals. King, Jr., Farmer, and other leaders rushed to Birmingham. Nash proposed a march through downtown, but the older leaders vetoed the idea as too dangerous. John Seigenthaler and envoys from the Kennedy administration hoped to get the college students to call off the project. They refused, so Kennedy sent six hundred US Marshals to Alabama and continued negotiations with the governor; Patterson believed Kennedy was afraid to stand up to the Negroes. Federal envoys negotiated a deal to allow the buses to continue to Montgomery. On 19 April 1961, escorts accompanied the bus toward Montgomery. Just outside town, they suddenly turned away and left the bus unprotected. It seemed a setup to allow Klansmen and white race radicals to attack the Negro demonstrators. White mobs rushed the riders at the Montgomery bus terminal, beating them to a bloody mess. The black leaders, including King, Jr., gathered with Ralph Abernathy at his church for a mass meeting. A crowd of whites surrounded the church on 20 May and threatened to burn it and the occupants. Governor Patterson refused a rescue, and federal marshals fought against the mob with tear gas while some of the blacks managed to slip out the church to safety. Kennedy kept negotiating with Patterson. Early the next morning, state troops and trucks arrived to deliver the church attendees to their homes.

On 24 May, the buses prepared to leave Montgomery under armed guard and continue the trip into adjacent Mississippi. Just as the buses prepared to leave the bus terminal, the SNCC members pressured Martin Luther King, Jr., to ride with them, but King refused. One cynical student mocked King as acting like "De Lawd,"[57] but King, Jr., was already on probation for his recent demonstrations in Georgia. The more aggressive radicals among SNCC members did not trust SCLC preacher-leaders and believed that SCLC staff had withheld some donations meant for SNCC activities. Nor did they trust the Kennedy administration, believing Kennedy had made political deals with segregationist state officials. James Farmer had excuses for not taking the ride, but Farmer

---

[56] Vincent P. Franklin, "Patterns of Student Activism at Historically Black Universities in the United States and South Africa, 1960–1977," *Journal of African American History* 88/2 (Spring 2003): 204–17; Manis, *A Fire You Can't Put Out*, 252, 253, 262–280, 287, 303, 320, 336.

[57] Lovett, *The Civil Rights Movement in Tennessee*, 166; Arsenault, *Freedom Riders*, 250.

avoided the students' stinging criticism, changed his mind, and made a last-minute dash onto one of the buses.

When the buses arrived in Jackson, Mississippi, state authorities arrested the freedom riders, issued huge fines, and sent the riders to jails. The students remained angry with Kennedy for agreeing to this arrangement to save face for racist Mississippi. The local white judge turned his back when the lawyers argued the Freedom Ride defendants' pleas, then turned to the audience in the court and arrogantly announced, "Guilty!"[58] New SNCC recruits kept a steady stream of freedom riders on buses and trains, but at least 350 freedom riders, both black and white, crowded the Hinds County jail before many of them ended up on the notorious Parchman Penitentiary work crews.

In support of the spreading Civil Rights Movement, about two hundred persons left the Mount Zion Baptist Church and marched to the state capitol in Charleston, South Carolina. Upon failing to obey police orders to disperse, they were arrested for being "loud, boisterous and flamboyant."[59]

At Southern University, sit-in demonstrations took place on campus on 7 March 1960, and on 28 March, seven students held a sit-in at a downtown lunch counter—although Louisiana recently had issued an order to college presidents to punish students for such engagements. On 30 March, three thousand students marched through downtown and held a rally and prayer, sixteen of whom suffered arrest by local police. Upon their boycotting of classes, Southern expelled seventeen students and hundreds more left in protest. Later, in *Edwards v. South Carolina*, 372 US 229 (1963), the US Supreme Court, by a vote of 8–1, upheld the right to demonstrate on public property. The First Amendment guaranteed free speech, free assembly, and freedom to petition government, while the 14th Amendment protected civil rights protests.[60]

One way in which many whites retaliated against the blacks' Civil Rights Movement was to use news media to identify the "trouble makers" and "outside agitators." Many newspapers published the faces, names, occupations, and addresses of civil rights protestors as a way to single them out for retaliation by employers, law enforcement, and government agencies. In May and June 1961, after some freedom riders had been bailed out of Mississippi jails and arrived by bus in Memphis prior to transferring to Nashville-bound buses, some newspaper reporters in Memphis took their pictures and shared the photographs with other

---

[58] Ibid., 168.

[59] Franklin, "Patterns of Student Activism," 204–27.

[60] Ibid., 204–17.

newspapers. Some of these journalists, such as the ones at the Nashville *Banner*, became the first to use pictures and newspaper files to publish articles and books to stamp their claim on "the Civil Rights Movement."[61]

The black press had been helping HBCUs squeeze their ordinary stories into the public forum since the nineteenth century. Black reporters transmitted the brutal aspects of the 1960s Civil Rights Movement beyond the Cotton Curtain. This especially was true of the Chicago *Defender*, Memphis *World* and *Tri-State Defender*, Pittsburgh *Courier*, and *Jet* and *Ebony*. Many of the reporters had been trained at the HBCUs' journalism programs, and these blacks made a positive impact on civil rights reporting. Whereas much of southern white media served as a vanguard for white society, the Negro press served to protect and promote black interests. Both sides found it hard to abandon these traditional journalistic roles. The national television networks concluded documentaries on the 1956 Clinton High School desegregation crisis, the Little Rock school integration crisis of 1957, and the Nashville sit-in demonstrations of 1960, but hardly any of those networks employed Negro professionals to lead the production of such stories and films.

In the case of Tennessee A&I State, three of its former graduates and students served the American news media well during the movement in the 1950s and 1960s. One, Theodore R. A. Poston, played basketball at Tennessee A&I State Normal Teachers College. He was born in Hopkinsville, Kentucky, and after completing Tennessee State in 1928, moved to New York to perform odd jobs before writing for the Pittsburgh *Courier*, the *Amsterdam News* in Harlem, and later—as a nationally celebrated journalist—in the New York *Post*. From 1959 to 1960, Poston covered the struggle of Negro citizens trying to register to vote in two predominantly black counties of West Tennessee. The West Tennessee *Fayette County Falcon* wrote, "The eyes of the Nation [sic] were on Fayette County Wednesday."[62] Poston won journalism awards in 1949 and a nomination for the Pulitzer Prize. Nathaniel D. Williams, Poston's classmate at Tennessee A&I., became "the voice of Beale Street." Soon after announcement of *Brown*, Williams and his all-black panel of local educators on the WDIA radio station discussed "Should the Negro Ease up in His Push for Integration?" [63] Williams developed a program on WDIA Radio Station called "Brown American Speaks," which included issues that discussed the burgeoning Civil Rights Movement, police brutality, education of black youth, and local politics. Poston

[61] Lovett, *The Civil Rights Movement in Tennessee*, 128.

[62] Editor, "Eyes of the Nation," *Fayette County Falcon*, 4 August 1960, 1.

[63] Ernestine Jenkins, "The Voice of Memphis: WDIA, Nat D. Williams, and Black Radio Culture in the Early Civil Rights Era," *Tennessee Historical Quarterly* (2006): 254–67.

and acclaimed journalist Carl T. Rowan trained under George W. Gore, dean of Tennessee A&I who later [64] became president of Florida A&M University. Rowan worked for the Minneapolis *Tribune* and convinced the editor in 1951 to send him south to see if things had changed since he left his home in McMinnville, Tennessee. He published *South of Freedom* (1952) that showed Jim Crow alive and well in the South.[65]

In response to the Freedom Rides, Tennessee copied Louisiana's example and instituted several punitive laws and regulations intended to retaliate against civil rights demonstrators. Based on an April 1960 Tennessee Board of Education regulation, state authorities ordered the expulsion of Tennessee A&I University students for participating in the Freedom Rides. In late May 1961, A&I students and faculty members stood outside Kean Hall, refusing to march inside for the spring graduation ceremony unless *all* of the students eligible for graduation could receive their degrees. The president persuaded Governor Buford Ellington that he could not prevent any students who had met all requirements according to the catalog from graduating. With a loud cheer and the casting of mortarboards into the air, the processional moved into the arena to listen to the speaker—Ted Poston.

When the A&I campus emptied for the summer, state authorities pressured the A&I administrators to expel the freedom riders. On 1 June 1961, the disciplinary committee met; they sent letters to students in Mississippi jails and letters to their homes, informing them of their expulsion. Rowan, the Deputy Assistant Secretary of State for Public Affairs in the Kennedy administration, rejected the invitation to speak at Tennessee A&I's 1961 commencement, saying,

> There is no secret about it—we all know they expelled fourteen Tennessee State students for participating in the Freedom Rides. I attended school there for one year, but I disagree with their policy. My views are known—I felt no useful purpose could be served at such a time by a speech, which would have embarrassed the administration.[66]

In fall 1961, local NAACP lawyers and Tennessee A&I students successfully sued in district federal court for reinstatement. They won the case of *Knight v.*

---

[64] Ernestine Jenkins, "The Voice of Memphis: WDIA, Nat D. Williams, and Black Radio Culture in the Early Civil Rights Era," *Tennessee Historical Quarterly* 65/3 (Fall 2006): 254–67.

[65] Carl T. Rowan, *South of Freedom* (Baton Rouge: Louisiana State University Press, 1952, 1997); C. T. Rowan, *Go South to Sorrow* (New York: Random House, 1957).

[66] Lovett, *The Civil Rights Movement in Tennessee*, 172; Carl T. Rowan, *The Coming Race War in America: A Wake-Up Call* (Boston: Little, Brown and Co., 1996) 282–98; Editor, "TSU: Major Event Will Honor Students," *Nashville Tennessean*, 29 March 2008, 1.

State Board of Education, 200 F.Supp. 174 (1961). Even so, some of the students refused to return to Tennessee A&I State University, and most of the original fourteen freedom riders did not complete their college careers.

Total costs in lost careers and monetary damages suffered by civil rights workers and their communities remain uncalculated, unaccounted, and unapologized for, said James Mapp, longtime Chattanooga NAACP director in 2004.[67] Untold numbers of college students ended their careers because of the Civil Rights Movement. Southern governors cooperated with each other to block civil rights activities upon public HBCU campuses. At the 1961 Southern Governors' Conference, the members even requested the federal government hold off on plans to reorganize the National Guard under closer federal control.[68]

Racial conservatives, student militants, financial benefactors, and others went after HBCU presidents. At the University of Maryland Eastern Shore, student civil rights protesters figured into the resignation of the president. Stephen J. Wright of Fisk University spoke out in favor of a peaceful student movement and publicly backed the student sit-in demonstrations. When hundreds of Nashville college students were bailed out of the local jails in spring 1960, they marched to the Fisk auditorium, allegedly into the custody of President Wright. John Lewis, author of *Walking with the Wind,* said that Wright was the only local college president to support the student sit-ins.[69] Wright allowed civil rights speakers access to the Fisk podium. The speaker at the 1961, commencement exercise said students need to resort to "strong measures needed to disturb the complacency" about racial discrimination in America. Many students reacted "with dismay, concern, and general unhappiness" in June 1966 when Wright resigned.[70]

Morehouse College president Benjamin E. Mays received twenty-eight honorary doctorate degrees, but he was the first Morehouse president with an earned doctorate degree. He said, "A college is no stronger than its faculty. The buildings may be ever so fine, but if the faculty isn't strong, the college is weak."[71] He increased salaries, improved the quality of faculty, and convinced Phi Beta Kappa to charter the Delta Chapter at Morehouse on 17 May 1968. By that time, more than 50 percent of Morehouse graduates entered graduate school,

---

[67] B. L. Lovett, Interview with J. Mapp, Chattanooga, 21 March 2003.

[68] Governor Buford Ellington's Papers, Southern Governors' Conference, Correspondence, 1959–1962, TSLA, Nashville.

[69] John Lewis with Michael D'Orso, *Walking with the Wind: A Memoir of the Movement* (New York: Simon and Schuster, 1998) 109, 113.

[70] Lewis, *Walking with the Wind,* 109; Editor, "Fisk Commencement,"*Nashville Tennessean,* 5 June 1961.

[71] Mays, *Born to Rebel,* 181.

studying in 45 of the best schools in the nation. Morehouse was second among Georgia colleges in production of Woodrow Wilson Fellows. Since 1932, 129 Morehouse graduates had received doctorates. Said Mays:

> After Martin Luther King, Jr. received the Nobel Peace Prize, I was eager to do two things: To see to it that Morehouse would be the first to honor Dr. King on his return from Oslo, and do all that I could to get the city of Atlanta to honor this distinguished native son.... The Morehouse Convocation in Archer Hall in January 1965 recognized the great honor that had come to one of her sons.... Martin Luther King, Jr., Morehouse alumnus, Nobel Peace Prize winner, delivered a brilliant address on the civil rights situation in this country.... The State of Georgia and the city of Atlanta had never produced a Nobel Peace Prize winner....[72]

In Mississippi, white supremacists controlled state and local governments. They took pride in keeping Negroes under proper behavior and respectful of the state's white-supremacy policies. In 1890, the state Democratic Party adopted a slogan of white supremacy and pledged it would never die in Mississippi, and the legislature refused to ratify the 13th Amendment to the Constitution. At Jackson State College, the administrators seemed afraid to speak out as defiantly as Mays did at Morehouse. SNCC leaders, who had arrived from Nashville, argued that unless local Negroes became involved there would be no civil rights progress in Mississippi. James Lawson was so frustrated about the inaction of black Mississippians that he proposed forcing the local Negroes to start *intrastate* freedom rides.

However, a handful of students at private Tougaloo College, on the outskirts of Jackson, marched in support of the sit-in demonstrations sweeping the southern region. Students tried to desegregate local parks and a bus terminal. Some students at Jackson State started a boycott on campus, and when that did not work, they marched on the jail in support of the "Tougaloo nine" who tried to integrate a public library. Mississippi authorities turned back the march and kept the lid on Jackson State. The governor toured Jackson State College to show a group of "outsiders" the progress made by "our Negroes." The Mississippi State Sovereignty Commission, a state agency funded by the legislature and partly by a wealthy New York philanthropist to defend white supremacy, threatened to revoke the Tougaloo charter after students from Tougaloo were

---

[72] Mays, *Born to Rebel*, 188, 265–74, 271–73; Jones, *A Candle in the Dark*, 189, 273; Brawley, *History of Morehouse College*, 117.

arrested for attempting a Freedom Ride from Jackson to New Orleans. The president of Tougaloo College resigned, and some black Mississippians opened their homes to the freedom riders, providing food and shelter until their court dates in Mississippi.[73]

By August 1961, Diane Nash and others had returned from the Mississippi jails and Freedom Ride court trials to the Nashville SNCC office. SNCC members attended another workshop at Highlander in August. Once they were back in Nashville, the youngsters were so committed to the movement that they conducted one more downtown Nashville demonstration. Often the judges in Nashville—embarrassed in front of the nation and the world—reduced the fines to $5 or dismissed the charges completely. The hardcore activists still refused bail and insisted on serving their sentences as protest against an unfair, corrupt, and racist criminal justice system. Eventually, SNCC members headed back to Mississippi.[74]

What did the Freedom Rides accomplish? The insistence of HBCU college students on continuing the Freedom Rides had given a critical infusion to a public version of the Civil Rights Movement. The rides provided a reason to continue the activist nature of the Civil Rights Movement; otherwise, the movement was in danger of dying. The Nashville HBCU students' courageous actions caused CORE to return to the Freedom Rides project. The Nashville *Commentator* (Oct. 28, 1961) said CORE assisted 186 Freedom Riders, mostly students, returning to Jackson for the 14 August 1961 trials. Both the sit-in demonstrations and the Freedom Rides spread the Civil Rights Movement among the Negro masses and into ordinary black homes, beauty and barbershops, local civic and social clubs, local high schools, and among faculty and staff members at local HBCUs. Ordinary property owners, black businesspersons, sororities, and fraternities helped bail students out of jails and gave money to provide bus fares for students to return for the Mississippi court trials. President John F. Kennedy gained credit for diffusing a potential racial war in Alabama and Mississippi. The US Attorney General met with SNCC leaders in summer 1961, and Kennedy met with Negro lawyers, education and union leaders to get their input, before making a major radio address on race relations. In November 1961, the federal Interstate Commerce Commission forbade segregated interstate facilities.

---

[73] Arsenault, *Freedom Riders*, 332–34, 370, 379, 389–90, 428, 433, 466, 518, 629.

[74] See Kelly Miller Smith Papers, boxes 78–81, Nashville Christian Leadership Conference Records, Special Collections, Heard Library, Vanderbilt University; Dale A. Johnson, ed., *Vanderbilt Divinity School: Education, Contest, and Change* (Nashville: Vanderbilt University Press, 2001) 131–77, 234–62, 239–45.

The last of the Freedom Rides ended on 10 December 1961. Among the HBCUs, Tennessee A&I supplied the largest number of riders, followed by Howard, Fisk, American Baptist, Central State, Johnson Smith, Virginia Union, Tougaloo, Claflin, Southern, Morehouse, Dillard, Morris, Spelman, Alabama State, and Florida A&M. Several riders were affiliated with white institutions. The freedom riders won commendations and recognitions for their bravery, including a near-week-long Freedom Rides conference convened at Tougaloo in 1991. Several other reunion programs took place, including one in Nashville in 2006. In January 2007, a group of them, including the Rev. James M. Lawson, Jr., then a visiting professor at Vanderbilt University, joined with a new generation of students from Fisk, American Baptist, and Tennessee State to take another ride south to Birmingham. In March, the Atlanta University Center commemorated the fiftieth anniversary of the Atlanta student movement.[75]

Carl T. Rowan spoke at Tennessee State University's May 1992 commencement, addressing more than seven hundred graduates. His anger over the expulsion of the freedom riders in 1961 had dissipated. In 2008, the Melvin N. Johnson administration agreed to honor fourteen of the freedom riders expelled from Tennessee A&I in 1961 and grant them honorary degrees. However, the Tennessee Board of Regents rejected the proposal by a vote of 7 to 5. Some black members of the Board had benefited from the accomplishments of the Civil Rights Movement, but they, too, did not see the contributions of the TSU freedom riders as invaluable. Persons across Tennessee were so outraged they mounted an intense campaign to reverse the board's decision. The Regents reconvened through a telephone conference call, open to the public, per state "Sunshine Laws." They reversed their decision in a unanimous vote. On 25 April, TSU released the statement: "Today, it gives me much pleasure to report that the Tennessee Board of Regents has joined the community in support of awarding honorary Doctor of Humane Letters degrees to 14 students, who were expelled from TSU in 1961.... They are individuals who have demonstrated extraordinary achievements, setting standards that merit distinction."[76] Tennessee State University awarded the degrees to twelve persons at Fall Convocation. Family members of two of the fourteen Freedom Riders accepted their honorary doctorate degrees.

---

[75] Editor, "Freedom Riders," *The Journal of Blacks in Higher Education, Weekly Bulletin*, 11, 15 March 2010.

[76] Office of Public Relations, "Freedom Riders," news release, 25 April 2008, Tennessee State University.

In August 1961, after the leaders of SNCC went back to Mississippi, Kelly Miller Smith and other NCLC officers worried about the lack of communications with Diane Nash and about the near empty SNCC office where some students camped out. Kennedy administrators breathed a sigh of relief about the shift in SNCC priorities and helped form a legal defense non-governmental agency called the Voters Education Project, headquartered in Atlanta.

However, in 1962, all hell broke out.[77] A shootout occurred when President Kennedy sent federal troops from Memphis to the University of Mississippi in Oxford to enforce a 1962 federal court decision to allow James H. Meredith of Mississippi, a black US Air Force veteran, to enroll. Ole Miss had been admitting foreigners of color, but since opening in 1848, the institution had barred American blacks. Meredith attended the HBCU Jackson State College, and his wife was enrolled there. NAACP-affiliated lawyer A. W. Willis, Jr., handled Meredith's case. Willis was a graduate of Talladega College and received a law degree from the University of Wisconsin.

Federal officials accompanied Meredith ninety miles to Oxford on the morning of 20 September. Governor Ross Burnett blocked the entrance to the University of Mississippi, saying, "I do hereby deny you ... admittance to the University."[78] The officials regrouped in Memphis and returned Meredith to Oxford by airplane. In Oxford, the federal law enforcement agents met an army of neo-Confederates. Some of them were still arriving in pickup trucks, asking observers where the fighting was. Deaths and casualties occurred on the campus before federal marshals could escort Meredith to the registrar and then to his dormitory room. Students, faculty, and their families welcomed the US forces, including black soldiers, to bring control to the battle-scarred campus. After Meredith took his seat in class, neo-Confederates occupied the Oxford town square with rebellious Confederate flags, allowing whites to pass, but throwing bricks and bottles at blacks and federal vehicles. Meredith graduated in 1963. He donated his papers to Ole Miss in 1997.[79]

Meanwhile, SNCC survived the Freedom Rides, but registering blacks to vote in Mississippi remained dangerous. On 12 June 1963, a white man shot down Medgar Evers, the head of the state NAACP, in front of his home in Jackson, Mississippi. His wife recalled Medgar "would sit and pound the desk or

---

[77] William Doyle, *An American Insurrection: The Battle of Oxford, Mississippi, 1962* (New York: Doubleday, 2001) 1–3.

[78] Ibid., 75.

[79] Doyle, *An American Insurrection*, 75, 217, 266, 300; Payne, *I've Got the Light of Freedom*, 153, 178–79, 220, 233, 285; Kenneth Goings, "Archie Walter Willis Jr. (1925–1988)," *Tennessee Encyclopedia of Culture and History*, 1064–65.

the chair … in utter despair and grief and anger that so many people's lives had been snuffed out like this." Evers was a US military veteran. Andrew Young of the SCLC said,

> We tried to warn SNCC. We were all southerners and we knew the depth of the depravity of southern racism. We knew better than to try and take Mississippi. I had several misgivings about the Freedom Summer strategy. First, I thought that it was unnecessarily dangerous. There were no protections for civil rights workers and none could be expected for the idealistic students who were fanning out across Mississippi.[80]

SNCC sent envoys to northern campuses and recruited white students to come south. These "foot soldiers" increased to nearly a thousand, and John F. McClymer said,

> An army invaded Mississippi during the Freedom Summer of 1964. Hundreds of volunteers—white and black, many of them college students—fanned out across the state. Working with SNCC field-workers and local volunteers, they helped organize voting registration drives, opened schools and health clinics, attracted enormous attention from the national media … and bitter hostility from local whites.[81]

Confederate-flag-wavers in Mississippi lived up to Andrew Young's expectations. Twentieth-century Mississippi was a place *within* America but not *of* America. Some white Mississippi supremacists, with deep ignorance and hatred, reflected Nazi Germany in their use of terror, fear, intimidation, a corrupted criminal injustice system, economic blackballing, personal assaults, exile, and brutal murders against the state's black population. Fewer than four hundred Negroes registered and dared to vote in a state that had a high number of all-Negro towns, but where nearly 100 percent of eligible voters could not vote. During the Freedom Summer, many white supremacists jailed and brutalized hundreds of blacks, and murdered three voter-registration volunteers, one black, and two white: James Chaney, Andrew Goodman, and Mickey Schwerner. Despite a preponderance of evidence of the defendants' guilt, all-white Mississippi juries acquitted the murderers in October 1967. Most white Mississippi murderers went to their graves unpunished.

A persistent bombardment by the Freedom Summer army of 1964, the Civil Rights Act of 1964, the Voting Rights Act of 1965, and federal, civil, and criminal

---

[80] Payne, *I've Got the Light*, 103.

[81] Andrew Young, *An Easy Burden: the Civil Rights Movement and the Transformation of America* (New York: Harper Collins, 1993) 302–305, 307–308; John F. McClymer, *Mississippi Freedom Summer* (Belmont CA: Thomson Wadsworth, 2004) 1–8, 9–13.

court trials finally softened Mississippi officials to the point where they allowed black Mississippians to register and vote peaceably—although Negroes never gained complete political parity in Mississippi. However, when Ross Barnett's successor, Governor Paul B. Johnson, Jr., cut off state funding of the White Citizens Council, Jackson began to desegregate and comply with the Civil Rights Act of 1964. Black voter participation increased from 7 percent to 67 percent between 1964 and 1970. Black Mississippians, including other graduates of HBCUs, such as Mississippi Valley State College, won seats to the legislature. In 1992, the black legislators successfully pushed a resolution to get Mississippi to ratify the 13th Amendment. Blacks represented Mississippi in the Congress for the first time since Reconstruction. They won elections to local city councils, county commissions, and Harvey Johnson, a graduate of Tennessee State University, became mayor of Jackson.

On 14 December 1961, in Louisiana, home of many of the neo-Confederate reinforcements who rushed into battle in Oxford, Mississippi, police arrested twenty-three black students demonstrating against Jim Crow stores in Baton Rouge—home of Southern University. Ronnie Moore, student president of the local CORE chapter, organized two thousand students from the campus to take buses or walk five miles to downtown to protest the arrests. A CORE field secretary took up the lead to keep the protestors at the State Capitol building continuing the protest against "the evil of discrimination." Students sang freedom songs and displayed signs calling for boycott of stores. Police arrested the Rev. B. Elton Cox, the leader, and others, for obstructing public passages and breaching the peace.

CORE lawyers got the case appealed from the supreme court of Louisiana to the US Supreme Court, which affirmed *Edwards v. South Carolina,* 372 US 229 (1963) through *Cox v. Louisiana,* 379 US 536 (1965). The decision said the officials denied Cox rights of free speech and free assembly in violation of the First and the 14th amendments of the US Constitution. Southern University in Baton Rouge and its branch campus in New Orleans became sites of resistance against Jim Crow. Students replaced the American flag with a Black Liberation flag on the New Orleans campus. In May 1969, the governor sent state troops to occupy both campuses for the remainder of the semester. On 22 February 1985, Southern held a commemoration program titled: "They Refused to be refused: the 25th Anniversary of Student Protest at Southern University."[82]

Next door, in Alabama, blacks continued to have a hard time dislodging Jim Crow. Some of the students at Alabama A&M State College, assisted by Oakwood College students, started lunch counter sit-ins in Huntsville, but the police arrested forty-nine persons. The state under-funded Alabama State so badly that it lost SACS accreditation. In 1962, Alabama State's president for the previous thirty-seven years took ill and resigned.[83]

In 1963, Governor George Wallace (D) tried to block a court order to admit two Negro students to the University of Alabama, saying "Segregation now, Segregation tomorrow, and Segregation forever!" Wallace made his speech, and submitted to the power of the US Marshall, allowing the black students to enroll in college. Kennedy addressed the nation by radio and television on 11 June 1963:

> This afternoon ... the presence of Alabama National Guardsmen was required on the University of Alabama to carry out the final and unequivocal order of the United States District Court.... This nation was founded on the principle that all men are created equal, and that the rights of every man are diminished when the rights of one man are threatened.... When Americans are sent to Vietnam and West Berlin [to defend America], we do not ask for whites only.... We are confronted primarily with a moral issue.[84]

Kennedy asked for the cooperation of the American people to "move ahead" in granting equal rights to all citizens.[85]

Between 1965 and 1966, the war in Vietnam raged. At home, white reactionaries had decided to bring their ethnic power to bear on stopping the Civil Rights Movement, and black communities reacted with greater resentment, anger, and

---

[82] Franklin, "Patterns of Student Activism at Historically Black Universities in the United States and South Africa," 204–17; Vincent P. Franklin, "Education for Life: Adult Education Programs for African Americans in Northern Cities, 1900–1942," in Harvey G. Neufeldt and Leo McGee, eds., *Education of African American Adult: An Historical Overview* (Westport CT: Greenwood Press, 1990) 113–34.

[83] R. Norrell, *Reaping the Whirlwind: The Civil Rights Movement in Tuskeegee* (New York: Random House, 1985) 1–20; M. Thrasher, *Tuskeegee: Its Story and Its Works* (Manchester NH: Ayer Company, 2000) 1–10.

[84] Bryant, *The Bystander*, 422.

[85] Ibid., 417–24.

militancy. One activist in particular, Malcolm X, the chief minister for the black separatist Nation of Islam, denounced nonviolent resistance tactics.[86]

When the interstate highways were under construction in middle Tennessee, a Tennessee A&I State University group of faculty members and nearby citizens represented black neighborhoods in suing the state government in *Nashville I-40 Steering Committee v. Ellington*, 387 F.2d 197 (1967). The Federal Highway Act of 1956 allowed billions of dollars to be spent on building interstate roads, making America more accessible for travel and commerce. The completion of America's interstate highway system generally spared black citizens the indignities once suffered on the narrow two-lane highways, where small-town and county law officers reserved speed traps, verbal or physical abuse, and denial of hotel, restaurant, and restroom services. However, American racial politics guided decisions made about where to locate the new billion-dollar interstate highways, decisions that frequently left black citizens, their neighborhoods, colleges and schools without real convenience or benefits. Black plaintiffs argued that the planners of Interstate 40 diverted the noisy, smoky road away from Vanderbilt University, skirting white neighborhoods west of TSU. The planners brought the highway directly through the heart of the black business district on Jefferson Street, and this section of the four-lane interstate had no noise barriers. The federal court refused to force the state to relocate I-40 along the banks of the Cumberland River, which ran behind Tennessee State's campus, and the highway planners wiped out hundreds of black homes and businesses in the Fisk-TSU-Meharry community. In addition, the planners gave the Fisk-TSU-Meharry complex no I-40 access; the nearest ramp was three miles away. However, the court did force the planners to build an I-40 interstate ramp at 28th Avenue North—an awkward ramp that entered near the A&I campus—but vehicles had to travel another mile on a narrow two-lane street to access Fisk University and Meharry Medical College. Although the four-lane highway passed over Jefferson Street, the construction crews piled dirt under what, ordinarily, would be overpasses. This created dead end streets that disrupted the black business district and split the black community in half.[87]

---

[86] Malcolm X's words appear in Francis L. Broderick and August Meier, eds., *Negro Protest Thought in the Twentieth Century* (New York: Bobbs-Merrill, 1965) 381–83. Malcolm X was chief spokesman for Elijah Muhammad's militant Nation of Islam, a black Muslim organization. Malcolm X was the most outspoken of civil rights leaders in the 1960s.

[87] Devin M. Barbee, "The Causes and Effects of Interstate 40 through North Nashville" (senior thesis, Tennessee State University, 2005) 1–51; and see Hubert Ford Jr., "Interstate 40 through North Nashville, Tennessee: A Case Study in Highway Location Decision-Making" (master's thesis, University of Tennessee, 1970) 1–31.

This action isolated Fisk University, Tennessee State University, and Meharry Medical College from the rest of the city. A railroad gulch blocked the only direct approach to Meharry Hubbard Hospital facility. The black community in south Nashville could reach nearby white hospitals more easily than trying to drive to Meharry in an emergency. Hubbard Hospital nearly closed down. After years of black protest, the state unloaded the dirt from one overpass, which created another through street into Jefferson Street. The city built an overpass over the railroad gulch, allowing better street connections to Meharry and Fisk.[88] For the Atlanta University Center, access to the interstate also remained awkward and dangerous.

High casualties and deaths among black soldiers became one of the issues that generated new activism among many black college students. Many of the local draft boards in southern states, like Draft Board 105 in Memphis, tended to exclude black members, making it harder for them—and easier for whites—to gain deferments and exemptions, particularly since new rules took into account high school and college grades for those males over 18 seeking to avoid the draft. With fewer blacks being granted deferments, American casualties in Vietnam included 25 percent of the black soldiers. SNCC officers adopted an anti-Vietnam position that opposed the fight against people of color in Asia while America continued to oppress citizens of color at home. Some SNCC members traveled to North Vietnam as part of the peace movement led by pacifist groups.

In 1966, Stokely Carmichael, a Howard University student, replaced the mild-mannered John Lewis as head of SNCC. Carmichael had experienced the awful black slums in his native West Indies. He proclaimed the "Black Power" slogan during summer 1966 civil rights marches. The slogan, and Carmichael's raising clenched fists for the "black power salute" in Mississippi irritated Martin Luther King, Jr., and many of the older civil rights leaders. Adam Clayton Powell, the black congressional representative from Harlem, used the phrase "Black Power" during a rally in Chicago in May 1966, then used the term again that same month during his commencement speech at Howard University. By fall 1966, some students at Tennessee A&I began verbally attacking some professors as "Uncle Toms" for their persistent use of "Negro" and "Colored People" instead of "Black" in the classrooms.[89]

---

[88] Barbee, "The Causes and Effects."

[89] Harold Cruse, *The Crisis of the Negro Intellectual* (New York: New York Review Books, 1967, 2005) 545; Y. R. Williams, "American Exported Black Nationalism: The Student Nonviolent Coordinating Committee, the Black Panther Party, and the Worldwide Freedom Struggle, 1967–1972," *Negro History Bulletin* 60/3 (September 1997): 13–19;

Carmichael toured HBCU campuses, including Dillard University, trying to rekindle student involvement in the Civil Rights Movement that the passage of the Civil Rights Act and the Voters Rights Act had weakened. At Morgan State, Carmichael told the students to stop being passive and be willing to go to jail for their freedom. Many newspapers were following Carmichael, and the FBI and local law-enforcement authorities reportedly paid hundreds of black informants. Tennessee A&I State University student Frederick Brooks headed the revived SNCC chapter in Nashville. A 1966 SNCC flyer circulated on the campus of Tennessee State read:

> White people who desire change in this country should go where that problem [of racism] is most manifest. The problem is not in the Black community. Thus, an all-Black project is needed in order for the people to free their selves. Black Power [will] emphasize color consciousness among blacks and bring the Civil Rights Movement's decision-making process to the local [neighborhood] level.[90]

George Ware, Tennessee A&I State University Campus Coordinator for SNCC, explained in *The Meter*:

> To SNCC, Black Power means that Negroes must begin to develop methods of exerting influence over their own lives. The first thing which must be done is that black people begin to become unified, because we are oppressed as a group and we must oppose our oppressors as a group. There is power in numbers and we must use this power to develop political influence through which we may develop the economic power, which we do not have now.... Black Power is given an erroneous definition by the American white press. Whites have power, and since we are ... black, then that power would be Black Power.[91]

Ware denied reports by white newspapers that SNCC put whites out of the organization:

> They left. We say to white people that instead of trying to organize the black communities, they should go into the white communities and work

---

Howard Zinn, *SNCC: The New Abolitionists* (Boston: Beacon Press, 1965) 1–10; C. Sellers and R. Terrell, *The River of No Return: The Autobiography of a Black Militant and the Life and Death of SNCC* (New York: W. Morrow Press, 1973) 1–10; see: Phillip Foner, *The Black Panthers Speak* (New York: Da Cappo Books, 1995) 1-20; Charles V. Hamilton, *Black Power* (New York: Vintage Books, 1967) 1–29; V. P. Franklin, "The History of Black Student Activism," Special Issue, *The Journal of African American History* 88/2 (Spring 2003): 105–217.

[90] SNCC, "Black Power," flyer, campus of Tennessee State University, 1967.

[91] George W. Ware, SNCC, "Black Power," *The Meter*, 13 December 1966, Tennessee State University Library, Special Collections, Nashville.

> to remove the deeply rooted racism, which is where the problem is. We are just pro-black.... Black Power is a call, perhaps, the last call, to the black middle class to come home... and make common cause with the black have-nots.[92]

Young white civil rights activists formed the Students for a Democratic Society (SDS) to protest the Vietnam War and oppose gradual erosion of American Democracy. They protested social inequalities and started a free-speech movement on college campuses. They demanded a new, less restricted culture.

Indeed, in 1967, the Vanderbilt University Annual Spring Symposium scheduled Carmichael to speak, along with US Senator Strom Thurmond (D) and Martin Luther King, Jr. The Vanderbilt forum consisted of several days of speakers, usually two or three per day. The list of speakers for the 8 April session meant to create a sensation, featuring Thurmond (the avowed racial conservative), King, Jr. (the moderate, non-violent advocate), and Carmichael (the black militant). Thurmond, who had been the Dixiecrat Party presidential candidate opposed to President Truman's reelection in 1948, was among the southern members of Congress in 1966 determined to stop King, Jr., and the Civil Rights Movement. The Tennessee General Assembly responded with a resolution for the federal government to deport Carmichael to Trinidad. They asked Vanderbilt University to cancel Carmichael's invitation. Some of them claimed "communism" was behind the Negroes' Civil Rights Movement. The four black legislators, who only joined the body in 1964, objected to the resolutions, but had insufficient influence to defeat them. The editor of the *Banner* censored Vanderbilt officials for inviting Carmichael to speak.[93]

Carmichael took time to speak at Fisk and Tennessee State. The Fisk administration—perhaps believing the event would be bad publicity for the institution's fund raising among whites—almost succeeded in forcing Carmichael's speech to a nearby church, but yielded to student protest. Carmichael tried to incite the students to increased militancy against white power and criticized Fisk students for "trying to be damned near white."[94] He claimed the white donors controlled Fisk University. He accused local black college administrators of allowing whites to dictate who could or could not speak at the HBCUs. Tennessee State's vice president of student affairs brazenly said Carmichael dared not set foot in a campus facility. The Student Government

---

[92] Ibid.

[93] Editor, "Carmichael," *Nashville Banner*, 4 April 1967; "John Birch Society," *Nashville Tennessean*, 7 April 1967.

[94] Lovett, *The Civil Rights Movement in Tennessee*, 206.

Association invited Carmichael and held the rally *outside* the Student Union Building. They then demanded the university pay Carmichael a $300 honorarium from the SGA accounts. The president refused, but the Alumni Association officers persuaded him to allow the payment from the Alumni Association account.

A city police car stopped a SNCC station wagon, arrested the occupants, and found the check. They turned a copy over to the editor of the *Banner*, James Stahlman, who claimed to be "a friend of President Davis." Stahlman covered the lauded sports program at A&I, claimed to have helped save Meharry Medical College in a recent financial crisis, and claimed he was one of the powers behind the decision to grant A&I university status in 1951.[95] The *Banner* advertised the Carmichael payment, but absolved President Davis of the blame, saying radical students and outsiders were to blame.

On 8 April, despite a bomb threat at Vanderbilt, Carmichael did speak:

> I am nonviolent right now. If a white man tries to put his arm on me, I am going to break his arm. I am now and never have been a pacifist. I will not bow down my head and let them beat me until *they* become civilized. Segregated schools and the ghetto are products not of Black Power but of the absence of a group with the power to organize their community.[96]

A SNCC-inspired black power rally took place on the night of 8 April near Fisk. The event turned into a riot, perhaps inspired, or induced by external racists, police officers, federal, state, and local government intelligence agents. Rioting soon extended a mile down (west) Jefferson Street to Tennessee A&I. Law enforcement and young blacks continued to oppose one another for two nights, and Governor Buford Ellington sent troops and tanks to occupy the Tennessee A&I campus. A delegation of faculty, administrators, and the student government president visited the governor's office, where he agreed to withdraw the troops if the delegation persuaded students to stay in the dormitories.

After calm came to the campus, the governor said, "There is going to be some changes at Tennessee State."[97] The state targeted eighty-three of Tennessee A&I's students for expulsion, believing that out-of-state "troublemakers" were behind the turmoil. State officials created a 15 percent out-of-state student enrollment cap for fall 1967. Tennessee A&I had grown to about six thousand students, with nearly 40 percent of them coming from out of state. A&I was in the last phases of a building boom, and the out-of-state measure caused a huge

---

[95] Ibid., 210.

[96] Ibid., 207.

[97] Ibid., 210.

budget deficit, crippling A&I's ability to retire the debt on the buildings. Tennessee State was paying about two percentage points more interest on capital projects debt than public TWIs paid. Tennessee's TWIs were lesser known, and they did not have national reputations, international recognition, Olympic medals, or large, out-of-state and international student enrollments like Tennessee A&I and other HBCUs. President Davis begged the governor for a temporary variance on athletes and the marching band members already had been recruited. The officials agreed.

Carmichael and King had warned the whites that young blacks would make the summer of 1967 a "hot summer."[98] King, Jr., had asked the Vanderbilt audience "How can a [black] man raise himself up by the bootstraps when he has no bootstraps?"[99] Urban race riots hit America that summer, with blacks on the offensive. President Lyndon B. Johnson (D) convened a National Advisory Commission on Civil Disorders, whose report blamed the riots on "… ignorance, discrimination, slums, poverty, disease, not enough jobs…. We should attack them because there is simply no other way to achieve a decent and orderly [American] society."[100]

The Civil Rights Movement had caused much stress among HBCU presidents; in December 1967, President Walter S. Davis took sick leave. In January, he announced he was too sick to return to work.

On 4 April 1968, the murder of Martin Luther King, Jr., caused another round of urban riots across America. Some students ran through the graduate men's dormitory at the University of Arkansas screaming, "They finally got that black bastard." They forgot there were a few black students quietly studying in their rooms who had not received the news. The president of the University of Arkansas made amends by sending a delegation of students to King's funeral. To quell the riots, troops invaded the black communities; the governor's troops blocked entrances to Tennessee State's campus, but his action angered a group of young black and white faculty members so much that they filed a federal lawsuit, *Sanders v. Ellington,* 288 F. Supp. 937 (1968) to dismantle all aspects of Jim Crow public higher education throughout Tennessee. President Davis announced his retirement from A&I, effective 1 September 1968, his twenty-fifth year.[101]

---

[98] Ibid.

[99] Ibid., 207.

[100] Ibid., 209–11.

[101] See Lovett, *The Civil Rights Movement in Tennessee,* 201–14.

In 1968, student protests against the lingering practices of Jim Crow in South Carolina led to a police massacre of students. On 8 February 1968, President M. Maceo Nance had just arrived home when word came that three students had been killed about two blocks away where 150 to three hundred persons engaged a week-long demonstration at a "Whites' Only" bowling alley, which refused to admit a black Vietnam War military veteran. Heavily armed white officers entered the downtown area, and some of them entered the campus to help firefighters extinguish a student bonfire. In less than ten seconds, Samuel Hammond, Delano Middleton, and Henry Smith lost their lives. Nearly thirty students suffered shotgun pellet wounds, most shot in the back, by some of the police forces. Dozens of students were arrested; President Nance went to the jail, but the police refused to release any students into his custody. He went to the bowling alley, but the authorities refused to talk to him. He called the governor, who claimed the police fired in self-defense. They found no weapons among the students. "I was frightened and angry," said Nance.[102] On campus, he found hundreds of students milling around the auditorium, angry about the badly beaten male and female students resting in the campus infirmary. Nance convinced the students to go into the dormitories. Cleveland Sellers, former SNCC organizer, was arrested, tried, and convicted to one year in jail for "inciting a riot" as an "outside agitator." State officials closed the campus. When South Carolina State College reopened, Nance honored a previous commitment to host speaker Roy Wilkins of the NAACP, and approved a campus charter for the Black Awareness Coordinating Committee. Nance recalled, "There wasn't any precedent for us to call upon to assist us in making judgments. In this business [of being an HBCU president in a racially ingrained South] you have to make hard decisions."[103] The US Department of Justice later charged nine police officers with the shooting of the students. However, as in Mississippi, the local all-white juries rejected the charges. Nance served as president until June 1985, and Cleveland Sellers became president of Voorhees College in South Carolina. Not until 8 February 2001 did the governor of South Carolina officially apologize to the survivors of the Orangeburg Massacre.

---

[102] M. Maceo Nance recounted the Orangeburg Massacre in "South Carolina State College," in James W. Smith, ed., *Leadership and Learning: An Interpretive History of Historically Black Land-Grant Colleges and Universities—A Centennial Study* (Washington DC: National Association of State Universities and Land-Grant Colleges [NASULGC], 1993) 131–37.

[103] Ibid.; see the film *Scarred Justice: The Orangeburg Massacre 1968* (Northern Light Productions, 2008), dir. Bestor Cam, Judy Richardson; J. Bass and J. Nelson, *The Orangeburg Massacre* (Macon GA: Mercer University Press, 1984, 1996) 121–26, 170–73, 133–34, 212.

At Mississippi Valley State College, the growth of militancy among the student body in part accounted for the institution's troubles for nearly a generation into the future. Blacks were no longer 57 percent of the state's population, and Negroes continued to exit Mississippi, headed north on the Great Migration. Yet, the southern states continued to expand black higher education in the face of lawsuits.

On 5 April 1946, the state authorized the Mississippi Vocational College for Negroes. The Delta Council, founded in 1929, to promote better education access in Mississippi, pushed for black state supported schools. The Council wanted to expand "its program in the study of race or race relationships and the maintenance of harmonious understanding between the two races of the Delta."[104] Some legislators objected to the bill because Coahoma Junior College already served the Negroes. The state delayed the project for two years. The new school focused on training Negro teachers and classes in trades and industry, and in 1948, the legislature appropriated the money. In December, they selected the site on an Itta Bena plantation. The board of trustees recommended James H. White as president—the man who earlier failed to get the job of president at Alcorn A&M State College.

James White was a 1924 normal school graduate of Tennessee A&I State Normal College. He worked in the Sumner County schools for the next two years then taught school in Indiana until appointed principal of Hardeman County Training School in September 1928, upon the recommendation of the president of Tennessee A&I State Teachers College. The brick, one-story school for Negroes in Hardeman County began in 1920, with a $4,000 note from the county and matching money from the Rosenwald Fund. White succeeded principal George W. Thomas, a graduate of Roger Williams University, who had been unable to raise the money to retire the county note. White paid the note and raised additional funds to start a student band, publish a monthly school paper, *The Allen-White Voice,* and become a campus newsletter from 1936 to 1941 for the National Youth Administration. He received master's degrees from Fisk University and Tennessee A&I , and in 1948, White became president of Lane College, which gained SACS accreditation on 6 December 1949. White then resigned and headed to Mississippi.

James H. White and state officials, before a small crowd, broke ground at the Itta Bena site on 10 February 1950. The institution opened its doors on 19 February 1950 on 450 acres of what had been a cotton plantation. This vocational

---

[104] James H. White, *Up from a Cotton Patch: the Development of Mississippi Valley State College* (Itta Bena MS: J. H. White, 1979) 38, 32–41.

school sat in the middle of nowhere, surrounded by flat, rich delta land and cotton fields as far as one could see. The school had eleven faculty members, all blacks, including two women. They inaugurated White as president on 6 December 1953. Mississippi Vocational College issued its first twelve diplomas in 1953. By 1962, the institution included six academic divisions, including the liberal arts and the sciences, and gained authorization to offer the Bachelor of Arts degree in 1962—the year of "insurrection" at "Ole Miss." The state renamed Mississippi Vocational College as the Mississippi Valley State College in 1964. The institution began a self-study for SACS accreditation. In April 1968, a nine-person SACS committee visited the campus. MVSC had 2,483 students, 105 fulltime faculty members, and 10 percent of the faculty held PhD degrees. MSVSC needed library improvements, a faculty senate, and more doctorates on the staff. Upon clearing up most of the problems, SACS granted MVSC accreditation on 4 December 1968.

In 1969, student rebellions broke out on campus. White had not organized a student government association to allow students to express their opinions. The students protested the inferior campus conditions, shabby buildings, and archaic dress codes and curfews. MVSC revolts, said J. H. White, demonstrated the infectious pattern of black college student unrest in the region.[105]

White agreed with the governor to arrest ninety students and jail them in the college gymnasium. They were later taken to Jackson, then released to return to their homes. Though expelled from MVSC, the students said, "We spoke our minds, and peace was sometimes shattered."[106] In spring term of 1969–1970, President White still refused the student demands, and a boycott of classes took place. Only four of the 2,500 students showed up. The governor telephoned White about a Jackson newspaper report that said MVC was a white elephant for the state, and the students had to wear boots in buildings covered by water. White said to the governor, "Let me worry about the College. Where there is mud, we will have grass and flower beds."[107] They decided to bus 886 students to the Mississippi State Penitentiary. White ordered the campus closed, with "re-registration" scheduled for 13 February 1970. Ninety-three black students also suffered arrest at the University of Mississippi, while participating in a joint protest against MVSC and White. Students filed a lawsuit against the college. All

---

[105] Ibid., 153.

[106] Harvey G. Hudspeth, "Mississippi Valley State University at the Millennium: A Sixty-Year History, 1943–2003," *The Griot* 23/1 (1 April 2004): 1–17.

[107] White, *Up from a Cotton Patch*, 164.

the MSVC students gained release from prison. White said, "Some students want an education."[108]

Enrollment dropped from 2,310 to 972 students in the spring of 1970, helping to cause a budget deficit. The legislature passed an extra appropriation to help MVSC, and on 22 March 1971 White wrote a memorandum to the campus community, saying, "Under no circumstances will the College be closed because of financial status."[109] In July 1971, White resigned. The state eventually dropped the charges against the students in 1973, but MVSC took years to recover from the riots.

The institution organized a student government association so students could voice their opinions. The school relaxed the hard rules about visiting "off-campus," student manners, and student discipline. White said, these changes "reflected the anxiety of an older man with high standards faced with the laxity of a permissive society."[110]

Although retired, White watched the changes from nearby. In his book he said, someone in Greenwood wrote, "Students object to an administration which has not bothered to deny, that is, have sold out their birthright as beautiful Black Afro-Americans for the sake of money which has purchased buildings and facilities which are more of an insult than benefit."[111] White, who envisioned himself as a HBCU missionary, said, "You know sunshine brings out the adders—the snakes crawl when the sun shines. Fighters talk about you when you have done something.... The Negro will never make the progress that is his to make until he stops trying to follow false leadership." He and his wife, Augusta Charter (a Tennessee A&I graduate), died in 1974 and 1993 and are interred on the campus.

Enrollment at MVSC reached 3,100 in 1977, but dropped to 2,238 by 1982, and rose again to 2,575 in 1983. The college faced a number of challenges over the years, included budget deficits, tax fraud, and the threat of closure. The desegregation case of *Ayers v. Mississippi* threatened to merge MVSU with nearby Delta State University, but the idea faded away. Harvey G. Hudspeth said, "It was clearly seen as a shameless attempt by white leaders to deliberately destroy an HBCU through 'merger' with a predominantly white college whose higher financial and educational standards would ultimately result in forcing all Valley applicants out, thus destroying MVSC altogether."[112] A scandal about fraud in

---

[108] Ibid., 158, 154–55.

[109] Ibid., 164.

[110] Ibid., 168.

[111] Ibid., 154.

[112] Hudspeth, "Mississippi State University," 1–17.

ACT scores and the athletic program also hit the university, but the problem ended with the dismissal of three faculty/staff members and several student athletes. In 2003 and 2004, MVSU had 129 faculty members, a staff of forty-nine, and more than four thousand students.[113]

In 1969, SNCC had all but disappeared. However, Wiley College students, some of whom had led protests in the early 60s, re-invoked former SNCC strategies to protest on-campus conditions. Some Morehouse students stormed a trustees' meeting, held them hostage, demanded the white trustees resign, and directed others to rename Morehouse for the late Martin Luther King, Jr. Also in 1969, Congress recommended the 26th Amendment, lowering the voting age from 21 to 18, amid the protest of "[I am old enough to] die for Democracy in Vietnam but cannot vote in America." In January 1969, the US had begun peace talks with North Vietnam, but the new American president, Richard M. Nixon (R), expanded the war into neighboring Southeast Asian countries. His decision caused an intensification of anti-war demonstrations on college campuses. On 4 May 1970, several students died at the hands of state troops on the TWI Kent State University's campus in Ohio, and students shut down many American college campuses in protest.

On May 14 and 15, 1970, a riot began along Lynch Street in Jackson, Mississippi, that traveled through the HBCU Jackson State University campus. The school had about four thousand students, and four hundred were scheduled to graduate the following week. There were reports of students throwing objects at passing cars, and university president James A. Peoples, Jr., agreed to police entering the campus. Claiming a response to gunfire, police poured hundreds of shots into the building and windows, then they picked up their shell casings before calling for medical assistance for the victims. Those murdered were Phillip L. Gibbs and James E. Green, and twelve other students were wounded. Witnesses' testimony to FBI agents said the police fired on the crowd and the dormitory without provocation. One police officer reportedly said to a passing student beforehand, "you better get in a ditch, there is going to be shooting up there."[114] On 13 June 1970, Nixon established a commission to investigate unrest

[113] White, *Up from a Cotton Patch,* 11–29, 32–45, 107, 110, 112, 114, 154, 161–71; Hudspeth, "Mississippi Valley State University at the Millennium," 1–17.

[114] Cynara K. Robinson, "FBI Records Documenting HBCU Campus Rebellions, 1968–1972," 93rd Annual Meeting of the ASAALH (4 October 2008) used FBI Record Group 65 of the National Archives and Record Service to show a more accurate version of what law authorities did to the students.

on the nation's college campuses, and on 25 June, the commission held public hearings in Jackson. Today, a black granite monument, donated by the class of 1971, the closing of Lynch Street, and a university plaza mark the site of the massacre.[115]

Black protest upon the black college campuses was not over. In 1972, students at Southern University protested bad treatment at the institution, and their protest drew police forces to the campus. FBI reports for 16 November include photographs of two hundred students around the administration building, police arriving, and tear gas canisters being fired on the crowd. Some participants threw the canisters back at the police, who fled, only to return with more force. The campus closed for ten days, with only international and out-of-state students being allowed to remain in the dormitories.[116] However, there was no racial massacre.

Richard D. Morrison recalled, "Most campuses in the 1960s and early 1970s experienced turmoil as students and others supported the Civil Rights Movement, protested the war in Vietnam, and advocated other social causes. Alabama A&M University was not immune to these trends." A student movement at A&M in 1972 tried to toss the Reserve Officers Training Corps (ROTC) off campus. He said it was "a reflection of the anti-military mood sweeping America's campuses at the time." Morrison and Governor Wallace closed the campus for a week. "You come back when you decide you want to go to class," Morrison said. The institution expelled the leader of the student revolt. "I don't know what ever became of him," said Morrison. The student activists labeled R. D. Morrison an Uncle Tom.[117]

The Vietnam War ended in January 1973. The two sides signed the American-Vietnam treaty in 1975. However, for HBCUs and constituents, the end of the Vietnam War was not as beneficial to them compared with the end of World War II. A large number of black Vietnam veterans received dishonorable and less-than-honorable discharges, and federal guidelines for colleges restricted their financial aid. The 1970s seemed to spell the end of the intensity of the 1960s Civil Rights Movement. Irwin Unger said, "Since the late sixties a backlash—a powerful negative reaction—to that decades' social and political liberalism had been emerging. Angry backlash voters, generally middle-aged and white, felt

---

[115] In March 1996, JSU hosted a conference that published *From Tragedy to Triumph: Perspectives on the Jackson State University Gibbs/Green Experience* and *Lynch Street: The May 1970 Slayings at Jackson State College*.

[116] Ibid.

[117] R. D. Morrison, "Alabama A&M University," in James Smith, ed., *Leadership and Learning*, 128–31.

traditional institutions and values were being destroyed."[118] Nixon asked Congress to halt forced busing of schoolchildren. However, he and Vice President Spiro Agnew of Maryland had to resign for corruption, felonies and other crimes.

In conclusion, racial desegregation introduced new black competitors for HBCUs. These competitors were predominantly black colleges and universities (PBCUs) that resulted from "white flight" to the suburbs, the concentration of minority and poor populations left in the core of the inner cities, and community colleges that had been opened recently in heavily black counties in some states. PBCUs included Cuyahoga Community College in Ohio, Compton Community College in California, Denmark Technical College in South Carolina, J. F. Drake Technical College in Alabama, Lawson State Community College, also in Alabama, and Kennedy-King College in New York. Others were Lewis College of Business in Detroit, Martin University in Indianapolis, Medgar Evers College in New York City, New York City Technical College, Shelton State Community College in Alabama, Sojourner-Douglass College in Baltimore, Southwestern Christian College, H. Council Trenholm State Technical College in Alabama, and York College in New York. PBCUs and other minority colleges/ universities outnumbered HBCUs that comprised 2.5 percent of America's colleges and universities by 2009.[119]

Zion College began in the white Highland Park Baptist Church in Chattanooga in 1947 as a Bible Institute for training Negro ministers and church workers. There was no Negro college close to Chattanooga except Morristown Junior College and Knoxville College that existed far to the east, and Tennessee A&I State University, which was two hours west by car. The southern, white, progressive University of Chattanooga, although a church affiliated institution, did not admit Negroes. Lee Robertson and other ministers chartered Zion College in 1949, with about seventeen students. Zion participated in dual-degree programs with Tennessee Temple College, a white Baptist institution. In 1953, Zion graduated its first student, Horace Traylor, a graduate of Howard High School, "the first member of his race ever to receive a college diploma in

[118] Irwin Unger, *These United States: The Questions of Our Past* (New York: Prentice Hall, 1989) 837.

[119] Woodson and Wesley, *The Negro in Our History*, 780; Michael T. Nettles and Laura W. Perna, *The African American Education Data Book*, 3 vols. (Atlanta: Frederick D. Patterson Research Institute of the UNCF, 1997) 3.58; National Association for Equal Opportunity in Higher Education, *2004 Profiles of Member Institutions, Presidents and Chancellors* (Washington DC: NAFEO, 2004) 1–10.

Chattanooga" said the Chattanooga *Times*.[120] Traylor next completed Gamma Theological Seminary in nearby Atlanta. However, the officials at Zion College saw desegregation coming.[121] With the announcement of *Brown*, the founders abandoned the Zion concept. Others continued the operations that fall. Zion College became a four-year school in 1957, offering BA and BS degrees. The institution downgraded to junior college status in 1958. Horace Traylor became the first black president in 1959 and was able to solicit the support of local leaders. The faculty consisted of graduates of Boston University, Tennessee A&I, Columbia University, Clark College, and Atlanta University. Some faculty members at the University of Chattanooga also taught part-time at Zion. In July 1964, the trustees changed the name to Chattanooga City College. They had some 100 students by December 1965. By 1967, there was talk of the University of Tennessee opening a branch campus in Chattanooga, and the University of Chattanooga was talking about merging with the University of Tennessee. Traylor and other black leaders decided that it was best to be a part of that merger. On 1 July 1969, the state assumed the University of Chattanooga as the new University of Tennessee-Chattanooga campus, and Chattanooga City College merged into UTC. Traylor became a staff member at University of Tennessee-Chattanooga.[122]

The US Department of Education defined HBCUs as colleges established for blacks *before* 1964. Thereafter, Morehouse School of Medicine and Charles R. Drew University of Medicine and Science in California joined the government's list of HBCUs, and Congress added three HBCU land-grant colleges. Financial problems and mergers reduced the number of HBCUs from 119 to 106 by 2001. Through accreditation losses and closures, the number of HBCUs fell to 103 by 2003. Yet, between 1920 and 1954, the percentage decline in the number of HBCUs slowed. Some 26.2 percent of Negro college students attended TWIs when Congress passed the Civil Rights Act in 1964. Then, HBCUs had 93 percent

---

[120] Editor, "Zion College," 30 August 1959, *Chattanooga Times*; "Zion College," *Chattanooga Times* 8 August 1959; Editor, "Zion College," *Chattanooga Times*, 29 March 1952; Editor, "Zion College Renamed; Now Chattanooga City," *Chattanooga Times*, 23 July 1964; Editor, "Approval Given for UTC, CCC to Consolidate," *Chattanooga Times*, 4 February 1969.

[121] Telephone interview with former Chattanooga City College president Horace Taylor, 12 March 2008, Miami Gardens, Florida; "Zion College Newspaper Clipping File," Historical Collection, Chattanooga Public Library, 2008. I thank Chattanooga Public Library as well as Chrystal Partridge, professor of education at UT-Chattanooga and former Tennessee State faculty member, for the leads on Zion College.

[122] "Zion College," 30 August 1959.

of enrolled black college students. By 1999, HBCUs enrolled 16 percent of black college students.[123]

Lastly, the philanthropic agencies that helped finance the HBCUs in the last half of the nineteenth century and through the first forty years of the twentieth century had mostly closed their doors. Several of them merged into the Southern Education Foundation, which now served as lobbyist, advocate for HBCUs, and promoter of access to quality education for minorities in the southern states, and a research group on minority issues in education. However, the SEF did not have large sums of money to infuse into the black institutions, and foundations such as Carnegie and Rockefeller's General Education Board had shifted their priorities to influencing reform and major changes in all of education and tackling other lingering problems in American society. *Brown*, and especially the Civil Rights Movement of the 1960s and 1970s, brought some foundations, education associations, US presidents, and federal agencies to the aid of the HBCUs.

On the one hand, some of the changes caused by the intensification of the Civil Rights Movement in post-World War II American society strengthened many HBCUs; on the other hand, some factors weakened and even closed down a few of them, such as Zion College. Despite the turmoil of the modern Civil Rights Movement, the black colleges and universities, many of their students, faculty members, former students, and alumni proved to be an asset, not a liability, to American Democracy and the history of American education. Over the last three decades of the twentieth century, these historic, minority colleges and universities have had to face the complexities of an American society that, although reluctant, was fast-becoming racially integrated, yet remained deeply tainted by the persistence of racial discrimination *de facto*.

---

[123] Mike Loftin, "Grasp Opportunity: CCC Graduates Told," *Chattanooga Times*, 2 August 1969.

5

Facing the Complexities of Integration

Within the social and political complexities between 1975 and 2000, HBCUs faced many new challenges and dilemmas: the conversion from federal grants in the 1960s to loans in the 1980s; HBCUs had to adjust enrollment management to include more adult and evening students, including whites; some colleges became predominantly minority or black (PBCUs), and began to compete with HBCUs for resources to educate low-income students. Writers Juan Williams and Dwayne Ashley, said, "The 1970s found HBCU administrations searching for ways to heal the psychological and financial wounds caused by the radicalism and sweeping changes of the previous decade. Almost overnight, public black colleges found themselves grappling with issues of cultural identity."[1]

Additionally, the problem of economic disparity between the races and the continuing racial discrimination that had plagued American society since emancipation continued to have an adverse influence on African Americans and their institutions. In 1942, when nearly fifty thousand former slaves were still alive in the US, researcher Ina C. Brown said,

> Negroes in the South will face all the problems, which confront the southern people as a whole. Unless drastic and far-reaching changes occur in our total economy, the South will still be a colonial, extractive, agricultural region with all the problems that such an economy implies in an industrial age.... The majority of students in many of the Negro colleges come from homes ... economically and culturally impoverished.[2]

America's HBCUs and PBCUs still had a heavy load of such students in 2010. All of this affected the history and development of the late twentieth-century HBCUs.

By the 1980s, conservative politicians in both major political parties began to dismantle the War on Poverty programs left by President Lyndon B. Johnson (D).

---

[1] Juan Williams and Dwayne Ashley, *I'll Find a Way or Make One: A Tribute to Historically Black Colleges and Universities* (New York: HarperCollins, 2004) 265.

[2] Ina C. Brown, "The National Survey of Negro Higher Education and Post-War Reconstruction: The Place of the Negro College in Negro Life," *Journal of Negro Education* 11/3 (July 1942): 375–81.

They attempted to reduce Social Security benefits left from the liberal New Deal, but instead cracked down on the spread of socialism national health care and the conservatives' welfare queens (poor mothers) while cutting taxes and taking home more of the profits for themselves and their campaign contributors. Between 1980 and 2009, the number of millionaires tripled, and soon there were hundreds of billionaires. America's poor, working class grew larger and middle-class citizens struggled to keep from being poor again. From 1964 to 1970, two-thirds of black American families had two-head households, but by 2009 that number had dropped to only 38 percent. America's black families on average had less than one-tenth of the wealth of American families. Black per capita income remained at 63 percent of the per capita income for whites.[3]

Even professed "conservative," President Richard M. Nixon (R) feared the immediate consequences of the ever-widening economic disparity in America. He sought advice from Daniel Patrick Moynihan, former U.S. Assistant Secretary of Labor and a sociologist who completed *The Negro Family: The Case for National Action* in 1965. The "Moynihan Report" concluded that civil rights legislation would not adequately address the problems of blacks in the inner city because their family structure had disintegrated, allowing a pathology of juvenile delinquency, illegitimacy, drug addiction, poverty, and poor academic performance in schools. Indeed, these forces weakened the role of the black man and resulted in a disproportionate number of dysfunctional, female-headed families.[4] Nixon asked Moynihan to develop a "Family Assistance Plan" in summer 1969 to give each poor family an annual payment and food stamps, but Congress defeated the plan. A leading conservative Republican who worked with the Nixon administration, Patrick Buchanan, author of *The Death of the West*, bitterly recalled, "Where I fault him is that Nixon was not a conservative. Lyndon Johnson laid the foundations of the Great Society, and Nixon built the skyscraper. If you take a look at all those social programs of the Great Society, they were all funded ... under Nixon."[5]

---

[3] See Anne K. Walters, "At the Mercy of Federal Loan Policy: A Fight in Congress over Interest Rates Leaves Many on Campuses not Knowing what They Will Owe," *The Chronicle of Higher Education* 52/17 (16 December 2005): A26.

[4] United States, *The Negro Family: The Case for National Action* (Washington, DC: Office of Policy Planning, US Department of Labor, 1965).

[5] Hine, Hine, and Harrold, *The African-American Odyssey*, vol. 2, 552–53; see Patrick Buchanan, *The Death of the West: How Dying Populations and Immigrant Invasions Imperil Our Country and Civilization* (New York: St. Martin's Press, 2002) 1–30; Kenneth O'Reilly, *Nixon's Piano: Presidents and Racial Politics from Washington to Clinton* (New York: The Free Press, 1995) 277–330.

The failure of the War on Poverty not only hurt the blacks, who had exited slavery just five generations previously—mostly penniless, landless, and illiterate—and, who then endured 100 years of brutal Jim Crow, but it likely hurt the HBCUs' ability to recruit good students and maintain endowments.

Moreover, the War on Drugs began in the 1970s to deal with the problem of Vietnam veterans returning home as drug and alcohol addicts. The "War on Crime" started in the 1980s and, thereafter, the federal, state, and local law authorities—overwhelmingly composed of whites—focused their attentions on people of color, even though the white Americans constituted the majority of blue *and* white-collar criminal offenders. America's criminal justice system became a profitable business that protected white Americans and their children from frequent arrests and long terms of imprisonment, but created jobs and wealth from the arrest and incarceration of minority Americans. Defendants of color were also more likely than whites to get maximum penalties for capital offenses. Only after protest and petition from black congressional representatives did the Congress and the US Justice Department develop guidelines to study "Driving While Black," the phenomenon of white law-enforcement agents targeting Americans of color on the nation's highways.[6]

The Tennessee Supreme Court established the Commission on Racial and Ethnic Fairness on 27 September 1994, which was part of the National Conference on Eliminating Racial and Ethnic Bias in the Courts and the National Consortium of Task Forces and Commissions on Racial and Ethnic Biases in the Courts. The Tennessee Commission's final report in February 1997 found "significant perceptions of bias and discrimination do exist in some aspects of our judicial system."[7] By 2009, America had 2.2 million imprisoned people—nearly 25 percent of the world's prisoners. Blacks made up 12 percent of the American population, constituted 12.4 percent of drug users and dealers, but made up 90 percent of all drug arrests. More than half of America's prisoners were minorities, although blacks comprised 13 percent of Americans; Hispanics, 14 percent; Asians, Pacific Islanders, and Native Americans, 6 percent by 2009.[8]

The national attack on black men under the War on Drugs and the War on Crime naturally concerned the HBCUs. Black male enrollments plunged once many black men had records that barred their admission or negatively affected their ability to gain government education funds, veteran's education benefits,

---

[6] Jesse Jackson, Jesse L. Jackson Jr., and Bruce Shapiro, *Legal Lynching: The Death Penalty and America's Future* (New York: Random House, 2001) ix–xv.

[7] Tennessee, *Final Report of the Tennessee Supreme Court Commission on Racial and Ethnic Fairness* (Nashville: Tennessee Supreme Court, 1997) 185–87.

[8] John Hope Franklin and A. A. Moss Jr., *From Slavery to Freedom,* 6th ed., 490–91.

and bank loans. In the late 1940s, after World War II, there was a time when black men outnumbered black women on the HBCU campuses. However, by 2007, of the nation's 16.7 million black adult males, 22 percent of them had no high school diploma, and a third of black men were not in the full-time labor force. The states consigned marginally prepared students to the two-year public colleges, until half of black college students attended less-than-four-year bachelor's degree granting institutions, but about 90 percent of the HBCUs were four-year institutions by 2009.[9]

America's black male problem negatively affected black male enrollment in all colleges and universities. The situation became so critical in Tennessee that the leaders of the Tennessee senate sent a letter to the head of the Tennessee Higher Education Commission urging him and others to "do everything we can to turn this trend around." [10] The president of Tennessee State University, Otis L. Floyd, made black male enrollment a priority in 1990, but his initiative died with his resignation in June. In 2003, students at Howard University held forums on the gender and racial disparity issues. On November 14, 2003, the "State of the African American Male Conference" met at the Library of Congress under the Congressional Black Caucus. Fort Valley State University hosted a national conference on the problem.

African American congressional representative Danny K. Davis said,

> In America, the poor and people of color are more likely to be incarcerated.... Significant remnants of the legacy of slavery and social, economic and political discrimination still pervade American society today. Given this information, if we don't respond to this problem soon, many African American Males will disappear from mainstream society.[11]

Congressman Davis founded the State of African American Males (SAAM) to conduct a historic national dialogue, and establish networks to improve the conditions of black men. Central State, Johnson C. Smith, North Carolina Central, South Carolina State, Spelman, Wilberforce, and Virginia State, along with Ohio University, formed The Interlink Alliance in October 2008, working

---

[9] See Bell, *Faces at the Bottom of the Well: The Permanence of Racism* (New York: Basic Books, 1992) 1–20; Derrick Bell, *Silent Covenants: Brown v. Board of Education and the Unfulfilled Hopes for Racial Reform* (New York: Oxford University Press, 2004) 78, 145–46, 148–49; Darlene Clark Hine, William C. Hine, and Stanley Harrold, *African Americans: A Concise History*, 2nd ed. (Upper Saddle River NJ: Pearson Prentice Hall, 2006) 553.

[10] Avon Williams to Lt. Governor John Wilder, 7 April 1988, Avon N. Williams Jr. Papers (1922–1994), Special Collections, Tennessee State University Library, Nashville.

[11] Danny K. Davis, "Young African American Males at the Crossroads," Joint Center for Political and Economic Studies, *Focus* 36 (2007): 3–4.

cooperatively on a black male initiative that engaged and motivated college bound students as early as middle school. James M. Lawson, speaking in Nashville, said, "Racism is more pervasive today than ever before. Some two million white people of color are in American prisons for things that two million white people are not in jail for. It is one example of how white supremacy continues to dominate our American society.... It [America] is flirting with disaster."[12]

After *Brown*, some modern education foundations began to infuse resources into HBCUs, similar to what some of their predecessors had done in the first fifty years of the century. The W. K. Kellogg Foundation sponsored a National Taskforce on African American Men and Boys. Private agencies began to invest in building the infrastructure for science, mathematics, technology, and graduate studies at the black colleges, with intentions of producing more black PhD degree holders and improving the diversification of the nation's science corps. The National Association of Land Grant Colleges and State Universities (AALGSU), which admitted black land-grant colleges as members in 1955, began to help direct national attention and aid to HBCUs to help solve their problems and make them more competitive with TWIs.

In 1956, the Ford Foundation gave Dillard University and Florida Normal and Industrial Memorial College large grants to help improve endowments and salaries, and gave grants to Cornell University to train HBCU science instructors. The Woodrow Wilson Teaching Internship Program placed young PhD candidates at HBCUs for one year to teach, supervise special projects, promote more intellectual discourse, and work with exceptional students (i.e., help start Honors Programs) capable of entering the nation's top graduate schools. Since 1946, the Wilson Foundation had offered fellowship programs to help the nation produce mostly white PhD graduates. In 1963, the Rockefeller Foundation began an equal opportunity program, giving $2.5 million to UNCF, $8.3 million to individual HBCUs, and funding grants to help TWIs to recruit top minority students. A 1967 Ford Foundation study found 2,280 black PhD holders, compared to 60 in 1932, but the 1967 total represented just 1 percent of all PhD

---

[12] Ibid.; author's notes from a lecture by Rev. Lawson at a civil rights symposium at the Nashville Public Library, 15 February 2004. I had the honor of introducing Lawson, the main speaker, for the Civil Rights Conference, University of Tennessee-Martin, February 2009; USG, *Summary and Final Recommendations of the University of Georgia's African-American Male Initiative* (Athens GA: Board of Regents of the University of Georgia, 2003) 1, 2, 12–13.

holders in the US. The National Science Foundation (NSF) started giving limited, but targeted money to HBCUs in 1967.

The Carnegie Foundation funded the Harvard-Yale-Columbia Summer Intensive Study Program (ISSP) that allowed one top, post-junior student from each of the HBCUs to enroll in regularly scheduled courses on these Ivy League campuses during the summer session. They transferred the credits back to the home institution, and Carnegie paid the tuition and fees for the student at the home institution for the next two semesters (the senior year). The ISSP exposed the participants to the idea of going on to graduate schools and pursuing PhD degrees and college teaching. Blacks represented 3.4 percent (30,751 students) of the graduate student enrollment in the United States in 1970. Blacks, who comprised 11 percent of America's people, represented 6 percent of US medical enrollment in 1972–1973; 3.8 percent of students enrolled in dental school; and 3.9 percent of law school enrollment in the United States.[13]

American presidents began to lend more aid to higher education, and some of this aid trickled down to the black colleges. Under President Dwight D. Eisenhower (R), the National Defense Education Act of 1958 allocated $280 million for state universities to upgrade science facilities, and created $300 million in low-interest student loans. The US Commission on Civil Rights recommended federal funds only to institutions as do not discriminate.

The John F. Kennedy (D) administration was so short, from 20 January 1961 to 22 November 1963, that no major legislation or presidential orders seemed to affect the HBCUs. However, the Higher Education Act of 1963 gave grants and loans to help colleges build facilities, and Kennedy's donation of *Profiles in Courage* profits to the UNCF in 1957 helped others view HBCUs favorably. Kennedy said, "It should be clear by now that a nation can be no stronger abroad than she is at home. Only an America which practices what it preaches about

---

[13] C. V. Willie, "Philanthropic and Foundation for Blacks: A Case study from the 1960s," *Journal of Negro Education* 50/2 (Summer 1981): 270–84; F. Brown and M. D. Stent, "Black Graduate and Professional School Enrollment: A Struggle for Equality," *Journal of Black Studies* 6/1 (September 1975): 23–34; Frank Brown and Madelon D. Stent, "Black College Undergraduates, Enrollment, and Earned Degrees: Parity or Underrepresentation?" *Journal of Black Studies* 6/1 (September 1975): 5–21, part of *JBS*'s "The Black University: Assimilation or Survival." The foundation programs at the HBCUs were not elitist. Dorothy Granberry (Tennessee A. & I. State University), Andrew Jackson (Amiri Al-Hadid) (Alabama State University), Bobby Lovett (Arkansas A. M. & N. State College), and Jacqueline Mitchell (Howard University) constituted the Harvard-Yale-Columbia ISSP alumni who joined the faculty at Tennessee State University. Many of the black participants originated from poor and working-class backgrounds.

equal rights and social justice will be respected by those whose choice affects our future."[14]

Under President Lyndon B. Johnson (D), the National Defense Education Act Amendments of 1964 gave grants and loans to help with construction of higher education facilities. The Housing and Urban Development Act (1965) established a low interest rate for the College Housing Loan Program. The National Sea Grant College Act (1966) enhanced teaching and education in marine and coastal sciences. Hampton Institute favored marine/costal studies. The Higher Education Act (1965) included student aid, outlawed discrimination in education access, and included Title III that designated funds to help improve the infrastructure of institutions with a predominance of financially needy students.

The HBCUs received Title III funds through the US Department of Education in five-year cycles. They expanded the program to help eligible institutions become self-sufficient and expand their capacity to serve low-income students by providing funds to improve and strengthen academic quality, institutional management, and fiscal stability. The Department of Education allowed the HBCUs to use the funds for planning, faculty development, establishing endowment funds, administrative management, development and improvement of academic programs, joint use of instructional facilities, construction and maintenance, support of graduate programs, and student services. Tennessee State used part of the funds to allow faculty members to complete their PhD degrees. HBCUs, by 2006, had received millions of Title III dollars per year.

These federally funded programs included Upward Bound, which allowed disadvantaged high school students to spend several weeks at college campuses, retooling their academic skills and preparing for college; Talent Search programs worked with pre-high school students, and Special Services programs helped effect retention once the students entered college. The "Trio Programs" continued on college campuses, especially HBCUs and colleges with substantial minority students or located near large minority populations in need of pre-college programs, until the government began cutting back in 2007. Seventy-seven HBCUs lost funding for one or more of their Trio programs that year.

The land-grant HBCUs continued lobbying, as they had done since 1921, to gain equitable shares of agricultural and land-grant federal funding, and their efforts proved successful. Richard D. Morrison led the effort to interact with Nixon and

---

[14] William A. DeGregorio, *The Complete Book of U.S. Presidents: From George Washington to George Bush* (New York: Barricade Books, 1991) 527, 563, 581, 603, 639, 637, 667, 561.

secure equitable federal funds for land-grant HBCUs. Morrison was a 1927 graduate of a small Mississippi boarding school. He earned a bachelor's in agriculture from Tuskegee Institute in 1931, and worked in Talladega for five years, before becoming head of agriculture at Alabama A&M in 1937. Morrison and colleagues built a barn; he taught courses in farm mechanics, and sent food from the college farm to the cafeteria to feed students and local poor people. He said, "I had to build [A&M] [almost] from scratch." [15] Morrison completed a PhD in agricultural science at Michigan State University. He was president of Alabama A&M from 1962 to 1984. Morrison served on a key government relations committee in the National Association of State Universities and Land Grant Colleges (NASULGC). He formed a committee with two other presidents, and visited the US Secretary of Agriculture. In 1967, Congress appropriated $283,000 for each HBCU. Morrison said, "It is too little; but it does permit us [HBCU land-grant institutions] to get a foot in the door."[16] NAACP plaintiffs filed a desegregation suit against the federal government in 1970 for failure to force the Jim Crow states to complete desegregation in higher education.

The 109 HBCUs began to engage more cooperation and unity among themselves. The National Association for the Advancement of Education (NAFEO) began in 1969 with office and lobby activities in DC to promote public *and* private minority colleges and universities. NAFEO and the college delegations meet annually to discuss institutional achievements, topics of common interests, and strategies to solicit more support from corporations, foundations, public, alumni, and government agencies. On 20 May 1970, twelve HBCU presidents visited Nixon to discuss additional needs of black colleges. He agreed to support more federal grants to the HBCUs for research, training and community improvement projects. In 1971, HBCU land-grant institutions formed the Association of Research Coordinators to represent their interests before the National Experiment Station Committee on Organization and Public Policy through NASULGC. They wrote letters to congressional representatives asking for funds for extension and cooperative extension work to "help them assume a role in social and economic development."[17] Morrison said the campuses realized that facilities needed upgrades to carry out their research mandate, "So we kept hammering on the fact that we had money for research now we needed some laboratories." Congress appropriated some $8.6 million for HBCUs.[18]

---

[15] Richard D. Morrison, *History of Alabama A. & M. University, 1875–1992* (Huntsville AL: R. Morrison, 1993) 15–16, 329–35.

[16] Ibid.

[17] Ibid.

[18] Ibid.

Congress also added University of District of Columbia, Pacific Territories, and College of the Virgin Islands to the list of land-grant institutions, and HBCU presidents agreed to include Tuskegee as a land-grant institution, which justified more money for the HBCUs. The University of the Virgin Islands (UVI) chartered on 16 March 1962 as the College of the Virgin Islands and ended efforts by Hampton Institute to provide courses on St. Croix and St. Thomas. UVI maintained articulation agreements with mainland institutions. The first UVI campus opened in July 1963 on St. Thomas, with another campus opening on St. Croix in 1964. Land-grant status led to creation of the Reichhold Center for the Arts and Eastern Caribbean Center of the Virgin Islands. UVI earned MSACS accreditation, and offered degrees in business, education, humanities, nursing, science and mathematics, marine science, and environmental studies. The DC Post Secondary Education Reorganization Act of 1967 gave 1890 land-grant status to Federal City College. In 1975, Federal College, Washington Technical Institute, and District of Columbia Teachers College began consolidation into the University of District of Columbia by 1 August 1977. UDC had 5,456 students by 2001, and seventy-five undergraduate and graduate programs by 2006.[19]

On 9 April 1974, Nixon visited Central State University, just six days after a tornado had ripped through the campus, forcing the school to close until the following fall. Although the governor of Ohio had signaled that the state had no certain plans to rebuild the institution, Nixon directed federal officials to cut the red tape and bring federal disaster aid immediately, and the following fall all but 45 students reenrolled in Central State University.

Upon the resignation of Nixon on 4 August 1974, Vice President Gerald R. Ford (R) succeeded to the presidency. Forty-four HBCU presidents, under the auspices of NAFEO and UNCF, appeared at the offices of the Secretary of Health, Education, and Welfare in November 1975. They asked for increased funding to help the HBCUs reach parity with other institutions. Title XII Amendment (1975) to the Foreign Assistance Act (1961) included the HBCUs in US government programs to provide assistance to foreign countries through the US Agency for International Development. HBCUs began to benefit from the Smith-Hughes Act (1917) augmented by the National Vocational Education Act (1968; 1976), adding technological and scientific development in industry to improve the quality of American life.

---

[19] US Department of Education (USDOE), National Center for Education Statistics (NCES), fall enrollment in degree-granting HBCUs, 1976–2001, Washington, DC: USDOE, 2001).

In December 1976, President Ford chartered the National Advisory Committee on Black Higher Education and Black Colleges and Universities to assess the status of higher education of black Americans as well as the needs of HBCUs. The committee's charge was to recommend to the US Secretary of Education ways to raise the participation of blacks in postsecondary education, aid development of educational alternatives for black youths, ensure continued operation of HBCUs, and increase access, retention and graduation of blacks in higher education.

Jimmy Carter (D) succeeded Ford on 20 January 1977. The USDA increased *permanent* funding for land-grant HBCUs to $13 million, allowing HBCUs to hire research faculty and conduct high-quality research projects. By 1977, they had received $71.7 million in research and $37.9 million in federal extension grants. Carter signed *Executive Order 12232* in 1980, formally establishing the White House Initiative on HBCUs, and providing for thirty federal departments to assist HBCUs through grants, contracts, and agreements, and preparation of an annual report on how federal agencies had assisted the HBCUs. Carter's administration made efforts to protect busing as a mechanism for school desegregation, prosecuted discrimination cases under the Fair Housing Act, reinforced the Equal Employment Opportunity Commission, and approved congressional strengthening of the Higher Education Act of 1965.[20]

Ronald Reagan (R) succeeded Carter, becoming president on 20 January 1981. He issued *Executive Order 12320*, the first presidential action to establish a meaningful framework for federal agency accountability to HBCUs. By 1981, half of federal funding for HBCUs went to Howard, Meharry, Tuskegee, Southern, North Carolina A&T, Tennessee State, Jackson State, Prairie View, Florida A&M, and UDC. Ninety-four percent of all federal funds obligated to the HBCUs came from the departments of Education, Health and Human Services, and Agriculture. In 1982, Reagan signed legislation to extend the Civil Rights Act of 1965. He extended the White House Initiative on HBCUs' beyond 30 June 1982. On 2 November 1983, he signed the bill to make the birthday of Martin Luther

---

[20] L. E. Gary, in "The Significance of Research for the Survival of Black Colleges," *Journal of Black Studies* 6/1 (September 1975): 35–54, wrote that the lack of researchers among blacks created a dependence on white researchers who often centered on the weaknesses of blacks. See also James W. Smith, ed., *Leadership and Learning: An Interpretive History of Historically Black Land-Grant Colleges and Universities*, 80–85, 90–98, 26–137; Leonard H. O. Spearman, "Federal Roles and Responsibilities Relative to the Higher Education of Blacks Since 1967," *Journal of Negro Education* 50/3 (Summer 1981): 285–98; *First Annual Report—Higher Education Equity: The Crisis of Appearance versus Reality* (Washington DC: GPO, 1977) 1–21; Nina Mjagkij, ed., *Organizing Black America: An Encyclopedia of African American Associations* (New York: Garland Publishing, 2001) 363–64.

King, Jr., a national holiday. The USDOE, Office of Civil Rights ordered a new round of five-year plans to continue to dismantle the vestiges of racial discrimination in public higher education systems. The OCR guidelines included "Commitments [so] that traditionally black institutions have resources comparable to those of system institutions having similar missions."[21]

The continuing Civil Rights Movement also increased student demands for diversification of the HBCU curricula. The HBCUs needed to shift more resources into graduate programs to compete with the TWIs in attracting students, blacks, whites, and others. The Association of Research Coordinators pushed the Council of Presidents of 1890 Institutions to ask Congress for money to build more research facilities on HBCU campuses. Congress passed such a bill on 22 December 1981. By 1983, the USDA money was upgrading research facilities at HBCU land grants, including allocating $1.7 million to Delaware State to upgrade research facilities. Cooperative Agriculture Research Programs (CARP) allowed USDA money to flow to non-agricultural departments, helping to broaden research and graduate program capabilities across the institution. Congress gave $100 million for HBCUs in Part B of Title III of the Higher Education Act in 1986. A 1983 USDOE study, *The Traditionally Black Institutions of Higher Education, 1860–1982*, had input from HBCU advocates, UNCF, NASLGC, and NAFEO. By the early 1980s, thirteen of the twenty land-grant HBCUs were offering master's degree programs.

President George H. W. Bush (R) issued an *Executive Order* on 28 April 1989. The *Executive Order* emphasized technology, planning, and development advice for HBCUs. Bush's order also created the President's Board of Advisors on HBCUs to strengthen their capacity.[22] The Board recommended all federal agencies establish dedicated programs to strengthen HBCUs. They aided capacity building, and established a long-term goal of giving HBCUs 10 percent of money the federal agencies sent to colleges.

William J. Clinton (D) became president on 20 January 1993, and his *Executive Order 12876* increased funding from federal agencies to HBCUs by 21 percent, and reaffirmed the mandate that established the White House Initiative on HBCUs. The advisory committee said,

> Conceived out of social need … for many denied access to opportunities, HBCUs have always operated with a mission beyond that of just

---

[21] See US Commission on Civil Rights, *The Black/White Colleges* (Washington DC: Civil Rights Commission, 1981) 1–10; L. L. Haynes III, *A Critical Analysis of the Adams Case: A Sourcebook* (DC: Institute for Services to Education 1979) 1–10.

[22] President's Board of Advisors, "President G. W. Bush," White House Initiative on HBCUs, Washington, DC, White House, 28 April 1989, 1.

> educating young people. Their expanded mission has included serving as beacons of light and anchors of stability in the neighborhoods and communities in which they are located; providing significant professional and leadership opportunities for African Americans and other viability of local communities.[23]

From 1993 to 1999, federal obligations to HBCUs for science and engineering increased from $232,667 to $326,427. The NSF gave 1 percent of its grants to HBCUs.[24] Seventy-one of 106 HBCUs, public and private, shared in these kinds of federal funding sources.

The federal appropriations, especially Title III, helped HBCUs keep tuition and fees from rising too fast, and helped renovate classrooms, build new facilities, install new technology, and upgrade equipment for teaching, learning, research, and public and community service projects. With state and institutional funds, the University of Arkansas at Pine Bluff embarked on a construction program in the late 1990s, completing Caine-Gilleland Hall for the sciences for $7.4 million, Dawson-Hicks Hall for the social sciences for $6 million, and Henderson-Young Hall for $6.3 million, and using Title III funds to help furnish the facilities with computer technology. The US Department of Education recognized eighteen HBCUs, including six private ones, for making substantial contributions to legal, medical, dental, veterinary medicine, and other graduate opportunities for blacks, and declared these institutions eligible for special Title III funding. President Norman Francis of Xavier University in New Orleans, the longest-tenured HBCU president, said, "It was the best kind of money. It still serves that important flexible function."[25]

Federal agencies provided $404 million to HBCUs in fiscal year (FY) 2001 in support of science and engineering, compared to $214.2 million in 1991. The 2001 contributing agencies included the USDA, Department of Defense, Department of Energy, Health and Human Services, NASA, NSF, and others. The top ten recipients, respectively, were Howard University, Morehouse School of Medicine, Meharry Medical College, Florida A&M University, Hampton

---

[23] W. J. Clinton, *Executive Order 12876* on HBCUs, Washington, DC, White House, 1 November 1993, 1; W. J. Clinton, "Remarks by the President to the National Association for Equal Opportunity in Higher Education Leadership Banquets," Washington, DC, White House, 16 February 2000, 1.

[24] See the Southern Education Foundation report, *Igniting Potential: HBCUs and Science, Technology, Engineering and Mathematics* (Atlanta GA: Southern Education Foundation [SEF], 2005).

[25] Henry N. Drewry and Humphrey Doermann, *Stand and Prosper: Private Black Colleges and Their Students* (Princeton: Princeton University Press, 2001) 258–259, 37, 53, 55, 56, 57–60, 72, 75, 100–101.

University, Tuskegee, North Carolina A&T State University, Xavier University (Louisiana), Tennessee State University, and Southern University A&M. The increase from FY 1991 through FY 2001 represented a 7 percent average annual increase. Morehouse expanded its dual-degree programs with the Georgia Institute of Technology, and launched the Center for Excellence in Science, Engineering and Mathematics with a $6.7 million US Department of Defense grant. Morehouse teamed with the Department of Defense, Babson College, and Carnegie Mellon University to establish the entrepreneurship Center in the development of minority entrepreneurship.[26]

President George W. Bush, Jr., (R) and Congress increased the appropriations for aid to HBCUs beyond the president's cuts and requests for these institutions for FY 2004. Nearly ninety percent of HBCU students required financial aid, but federal Pell Grant awards covered less than 30 percent of the costs. Fifty percent of students at minority institutions relied on Pell Grants, compared to 28 percent of students at all colleges and universities. For FY 2005, the USDOE requested a $24 million increase for HBCUs. The HBCU Capital Financing Program authorized USDOE to select a private for-profit Designated Bonding Authority (DBA). It could issue up to $375 million in bonds, and use the corpus to make loans to creditworthy HBCUs for capital projects related to instruction, research, or housing of students, faculty or staff, The DBA intended to establish the HBCU Capital Financing Advisory Board to advise the secretary and the DBA how to implement construction, renovation, or maintenance financing. After some sort of disagreements in the executive director of the White House Initiative on HBCUs' office, the administration appointed a new director in 2007. The FY 2009, as submitted by President Bush's administration, was down 35.7 percent (-$153 million) for aid to HBCUs.

The 1890 land-grant HBCUs used their Cooperative Agricultural Research Program resources and federal grants to help rehabilitate minority communities, engage cooperative initiatives with themselves, and involve more minorities and other citizens in agricultural, consumer, and food sciences. The USDA Rural Development Program and the HBCU land-grant institutions began working together to support the development of businesses that create quality jobs in HBCU communities. The USDA statement said, "The 1890 institutions have some of the best agricultural science and business education programs in the nation," and they need help to begin to remove the "persistent barrier to full and

[26] Newsletters for the White House Initiatives on HBCUs, 1995–2002, Special Collections, Tennessee State University Library, Nashville TN. Many HBCU land grants serve as depositories for federal documents and reports.

equal participation of blacks in higher education in the nineteen states that previously operated segregated colleges and universities."[27]

President Barack Obama issued *Executive Order 13532* on 26 February 1010 to help strengthen the capacity of HBCUs to provide the highest quality education. The order recognized 105 HBCUs in 20 states, DC, and the US Virgin Islands.[28]

Again, in the new era of integration the HBCUs had new competitors—the TWIs and the PBCUs. Many of the small TWIs redirected their enrollment management strategy to include black students; low-income and inner city students could bring federal grants to the institution. Small private liberal arts Eureka College had had no Negro students, faculty/staff members, or residents living in the area. However, Eureka College, from where President Reagan graduated in 1931, had 14 percent black students, a black faculty member, and an Upward Bound program between 1971 and 1974. Eureka enrolled black students from cities like Bloomington, Chicago, Memphis, and Peoria; and, offered black history courses and a "Black Cultural House" for the students.[29]

Most of the nineteen Southern Regional Education Board (SREB) flagship institutions remained hostile to enrolling a large percentage of blacks. Southern institutions changed entrance requirements, but not enough to restrict the regional whites that lagged behind national test standards. These TWIs often soft-pedaled affirmative action programs to minimize the on-campus presence of ordinary black students and maximize the use of black athletes. Some TWI students, administrators, and faculty members often assigned negative stereotype images upon campus blacks. Very few SREB flagship institutions had 10 percent black students, even though the 2004 US census counted blacks as comprising nearly 30 percent of the population in some SREB states.

Although America's intense racial situation of the 1960s led to student revolts on some TWI campuses, the Civil Rights Movement only marginally affected those areas. Again, the era of Integration affected traditionally white institutions (TWIs) in terms of student diversity efforts, but some of the TWIs—not only the ones in the southern US—had difficulties in absorbing more black students. Many northern whites were just as prejudiced as a lot of those in the

---

[27] Smith, ed., *Leadership and Learning*, 126–37; Jackson and Nunn, *Historically Black Colleges and Universities: A Reference Book*, 85–110.

[28] US Department of Education, White House Initiative on HBCUs, Executive Order 13532, Washington, DC, White House, 26 February 2010, 1–2.

[29] I was the sole black professor at Eureka College, August 1970–August 1973.

South, but they had insulated themselves against interaction with blacks since antebellum times.

As the anger of black students on white campuses in the North and the West grew more intense, the national Black Student Union was formed in 1967. Black students and their white supporters made demands for black studies programs. Asian, Hispanic, and Women's groups, and other minority groups also demanded ethnic studies and degree programs. When the TWI administrations did not immediately meet their demands, the students often engaged sit-in demonstrations. The upheaval caused the implementation of some racial reforms on TWI campuses. This was true even at some southern TWI campuses, such as Memphis State University in the 1960s. At the University of Illinois-Urbana, Rutgers, and Columbia, black students shouted "Black Power," and demanded fundamental changes to make the university more racially inclusive, more diverse, and with shared student power. Harvard University also established an Afro-American studies program, and Temple University offered a PhD degree in the field of Africana studies.[30]

The demand for "more black studies" at TWIs spilled over to some HBCU campuses. Public and private HBCUs often had minimized emphasis of black studies because the curriculum often reflected black problems and concerns. Thus, generally, most HBCUs had no organized curriculum and no degree programs dedicated to studies of black people. Indeed, although black faculty members maintained courses and research focusing on the black experience and problems in almost every department, HBCUs did not use the term "Black Studies" to describe courses so smoothly integrated into the departmental and university curricula. Tennessee A&I State Normal School faculty slipped the first black studies course into the curriculum in 1912, and disguised it as Industrial Education "with an emphasis on the Negro."[31] At Howard University, Carter G. Woodson, his associates, and the Association for the Study of Negro Life and History (1915–) developed a Negro history journal (1916–), a *Negro History Bulletin* (1933–), organized conferences, printed books, taught the subject matter in courses at Howard, and pushed for the inclusion of black studies in all America's colleges and high schools. The study of black history, culture, and

---

[30] Jo Ann Williamson, *Black Power on Campus, The University of Illinois, 1965–75* (Urbana: University of Illinois Press, 2003) 1–10; Richard P. McCormick, *The Black Student Protest Movement at Rutgers* (New Brunswick: Rutgers University Press, 1985) 1–10; Stefan Bradley, "'Gym Crow Must Go!' Black Student Activism at Columbia University, 1967–1968," *Journal of African American History* 88/2 (Spring 2003): 163–181.

[31] Tennessee A&I State Normal School, *The Bulletin, 1913*, Tennessee State University Library, Special Collections, Nashville, 1–10.

Negro problems became popular in the 1920s and 1930s, and such studies took on new meaning during the New Deal period of American history, particularly when there was a need to find out the socio-economic condition of the Negro community. In the 1940s, Howard University, Lincoln University in Pennsylvania, and other HBCUs, as well as several TWIs, competed for funding from the foundations for black studies programs. Half-a-dozen or so HBCUs began to organize their decades-old black studies courses into Black Studies or African American Studies programs.[32]

By 1994, eleven HBCUs—led by Howard University and Atlanta University—had full departments and/or Africana or African studies degree programs, but, by 2009, these HBCU programs did not enjoy heavy enrollment of majors. HBCU students enrolled in the elective black studies courses, but they chose other major degree programs to prepare them to find a job. At the Ninety-third Annual Meeting of the Association for the Study of African American Life and History, held in Birmingham, in 2008, one speaker estimated about 150 black studies and Afro studies programs existed, but few of them were at HBCUs. The Ford Foundation gave a grant to the National Council of Black Studies to look at use of information technology in the field and to build cooperative research networks to link black studies programs and the community.

The modern HBCU student had a greater need to maintain full-time jobs *off campus*, whereas the old HBCU work-aid programs occurred almost exclusively *on campus*. Many HBCUs that once had been predominantly residential became commuter colleges, which attracted adult white students. Off-campus jobs seemed to diminish the average semester hour load carried by the students, their focus on academics, quality of study time, and access to faculty members after class hours. This situation adversely affected the full-time equivalent (FTE) versus the headcount (HC) enrollment figures at public HBCUs. They usually calculated a FTE as 12 semester hours of course load. A public HBCU could have 8,000 HC, but only a 5,600 FTE that counted for state funding formulas. The average funding per FTE in the SREB area, where most HBCUs existed, was about $10,000. More white college students held jobs than black college students by 2010.[33]

---

[32] Hine, Hine, and Harrold, *The African-American Odyssey*, vol. 2, 402–403.

[33] SREB, *The Fact Book* (Atlanta: Southern Regional Education Board, 2004); SREB, *SREB Fact Book on Higher Education* (Atlanta: SREB, 2009) tables 3, 4, 18, 27, 34; Southern Education Foundation (SEF), *A Report on Black Students and Postsecondary Education in the South* (Atlanta GA: Southern Education Foundation, 1998) 1–10; SEF, *In Redeeming the*

Yet, black college students, including the ones at HBCUs, were no less in debt than white college students. Since 2000, the number of undergraduates using loans to help pay for college has more than doubled at Bowie State University. Seventy-eight percent of all black college students had to borrow money in 2000, leaving 40 percent of them more in debt than other similar college groups. Recent graduates had an average $17,947 debt. The cost of college constituted a larger percentage of the black family's budget than for white families. The *SREB Fact Book on Higher Education*[34] said the costs of one year of public college tuition, fees, room and board represented 26 percent of income for middle-income households with earnings of $43,000, 44 percent for families in the $25,700 income range, and 113 percent of income for students in the lowest fifth ($10,000 annual income). By 1995, in twelve SREB states, thirty percent of black families had incomes under $10,000, and by 2010 the average American black family enjoyed less than 65 percent of the annual income of a white family.[35]

Thus, compared with TWIs, HBCUs had a greater percentage of students who were poor, heavily indebted, and working, despite being not as widely employed and well paid as white college students. HBCU students needed more financial aid that made the admission and registration process at the HBCUs slow, cumbersome, complex, and highly criticized by outside observers.[36]

By end of century, the HBCUs represented a minority group in itself among some 465 minority colleges and universities serving mostly Native Americans, Hispanics, and African Americans. These institutions constituted 22.7 percent of America's total number of minority colleges and universities, but served 35 percent of America's minority college students by 2004. About 90 percent of the 106 HBCUs, which comprised approximately 2.5 percent of all America's colleges and universities, were four-year institutions of higher education. A large part of the PBCUs were not four-year colleges and universities. "The claims we [HBCUs] had on resources are going to be challenged by predominantly black colleges and universities (PBCUs)," said NAFEO president Frederick S. Humphries, who also warned the audience that many PBCUs were community colleges for now, but

---

American Promise (Atlanta: SEF, 1995) 1–10; SEF, *Unintended Consequences: Perspectives on Teacher Testing and Historically Black Colleges and Universities* (Atlanta: SEF, 2003) 1–10.

[34] SREB, *Fact Book on Higher Education* (Atlanta: SREB, 1005).

[35] SREB, *College Completion and Affordability: Perspectives from the 2009 SREB Fact Book on Higher Education* (Atlanta: SREB, 2009) 1–15.

[36] SREB, States' Future Economic Standing if Current Education Levels Remain the Same (St. Petersburg FL: State Leaders Forum, 17 November 2004) 1–5, 8, 21, 23–25.

they, too, could become four-year colleges.[37] In 2008, 720,366 students enrolled at predominantly black colleges, including 309,855 (43 percent) at the HBCUs.[38] The advent of PBCUs and the increasing re-segregation of American society were only a few of the problems that confronted America's historically black colleges and universities in the last decades of the twentieth century. The filing of numerous state and federal court lawsuits involved the HBCUs, affecting these institutions negatively and positively.

Within these social and political complexities between 1968 and 2010, the HBCUs faced many new challenges and dilemmas. Desegregation helped create hundreds of predominantly black colleges and universities (PBCUs) that began to compete with the HBCUs for students and government support. Some modern foundations began to infuse resources and other support into selected HBCUs, especially to help improve access and quality in engineering, science, technology, and teacher education programs. These agencies included the Ford Foundation, the Rockefeller Foundation, the Carnegie Corporation, and the Southern Education Foundation that became an advocate and cheerleader for the nation's black colleges and universities. And United States presidents such as Richard Nixon, Gerald Ford, Jimmy Carter, Ronald Reagan, George Bush, George Bush Jr., and Barack Obama supported the White House initiatives on HBCUs. Within such a supportive environment during 1972–2010, a few HBCUs did not survive, but 103 HBCUs did.

---

[37] As dean of the College of Arts and Sciences at Tennessee State University (1988–2000), I attended the NAFEO meeting over the years. I wrote notes of some of the speeches, including the one by F. S. Humphries, 6 March 2004, at the NAFEO annual meeting in Washington, DC.

[38] SREB, "Enrollment in Predominantly Black and Historically Black Colleges," *SREB Fact Book on Higher Education*, 2009, table 34.

6

Desegregation of State Higher Education Systems

Due to the success of massive resistance against *Brown v. Board of Education*, America remained a society that was spurious, not fair and equal, and full of systemic discrimination based on skin color. The nineteen former Jim Crow states refused to address inequality, unfairness and continuing racial discrimination.

African Americans had few other choices except to sue government officials. In major decisions, the federal courts ruled that state-imposed racial segregation had no place in American society. State governments had to comply with the equal protection clause of the 14th Amendment and develop meaningful, long-range plans to desegregate all public higher education. Still, some state officials doubted the value, quality, and the need for HBCUs; and, thus some state desegregation plans found ways to compel the HBCUs to alter their missions, limit the number of academic programs, and, in practice, remain subordinate to the traditionally white institutions (TWIs).[1]

In 1969, the Office of Civil Rights (OCR) in the Department of Health, Education, and Welfare concluded that racially segregated higher education systems still existed in several states. OCR began developing guidelines for former Jim Crow states to submit their plans for higher education desegregation. However, they were very slow in soliciting five-year plans from these states. The NAACP-LDEF and others filed *Adams v. Richardson*, 351 F. Supp 636 (1970, 1972)—a class action suit by college students, black students, tax payers, and

---

[1] J. B. Roebuck and K. S. Murty, *Historically Black Colleges and Universities: Their Place in American Higher Education* (Westport CT: Praeger, 1993) 16, 45–46, 46–47; John Matlock, "The Effect of Desegregation Policies on Historically Black Public Colleges and Universities" in Antoine Garibaldi, ed., *Black Colleges and Universities* (New York: Praeger Publishers, 1984) 199–218; Mary F. Berry and John W. Blassingame, *Long Memory: The Black Experience in America* (New York: Oxford University Press, 1982) 264, 266, 279, 287, 292; Richard L. Plaut, "Racial Integration in Public Higher Education in the North," *Journal of Negro Education* 23/3 (Summer 1954): 310–16; R. M. Hendrickson, *The Colleges, Their Constituencies and the Courts* (Dayton OH: Education Law Association, 1999) 1–10; Jean L. Preer, *Lawyers vs. Educators: Black Colleges and Desegregation in Public Higher Education* (Westport CT: Greenwood Press, 1982) 1–10; Albert L. Samuel, *Is Separate Unequal? Black Colleges and the Challenge to Desegregation* (Kansas City: University Press of Kansas, 2004) 1–10.

citizens against the US Secretary of Health, Education, and Welfare (HEW). The plaintiffs insisted the US Justice Department take direct steps to end the dual system of higher education in all states that continued to ignore Title VI. In 1973, the National Association for the Advancement of Equal Opportunity in Education (NAFEO) intervened as a friend of the court, arguing HBCUs should not be on the losing end of desegregation of higher education because these institutions had not committed racial discrimination like TWIs. HBCUs provided valuable education to students who, along with their ancestors, historically had suffered from American Jim Crow practices [*de facto* and *de jure*]. The court agreed, "The process of desegregation ... should take into account the unequal status of the black colleges and the real danger that desegregation will diminish higher education opportunities for blacks."[2] The court ordered the HEW to work with the NAACP-LDEF to draft an order for acceptable desegregation plans that must comply with Title VI of the 1964 Civil Rights Act, which forbids discrimination by agencies that received federal funds. The plans had to help increase minority access and graduation rates, strengthen and enhance the HBCUs rather than dismantle them; desegregate faculty and staff, and monitor and evaluate the effectiveness of ongoing plans. HEW released new desegregation guidelines on 5 July 1977 and revised the guidelines again in 1978. In March 1979 North Carolina sued the US Department of HEW for rejecting the state's plan and threatening to cut federal education funds to North Carolina, but HEW won the case.[3]

More than 150 persons participated in a forum on "The Impact of Desegregation on Higher Education," held at North Carolina Central University from 18–20 July 1979. In 1981, the proceedings were published, expressing fear that current OCR officials may not be there when a new set of federal officials become less committed to desegregation plans. In 1987, Judge John H. Pratt of the US District Court for DC found no reason to continue *Adams v. Richardson*. He dismissed the case in December. In March 1988, Congress rejected a presidential veto of the Civil Rights Restoration Act that intended to reverse a 1984 Supreme Court decision that placed limits on enforcement of previous civil rights legislation.[4] In 1989, OCR declared Arkansas, Georgia, Mississippi, North

---

[2] *Adams v. Richardson*, 356 F.Supp 92 (D.D.C.), aff'd, 48F.2d, 480 F.d 1159 (DC Cir., 1973).

[3] US Department of Education, Office of Civil Rights, "Revised Criteria Specifying the Ingredients of Acceptable Plans to Desegregate State Systems of Higher Education," *Federal Register*, 12 February 1978 (43 FR 6658) ("Revised Criteria"); *North Carolina v. US Department of Education*, mem. op. no. 79-217-CIV-5 (E.D. NC, 17 July 1981).

[4] David S. Tatel, "Southern Colleges Still Segregated," *New York Times*, 2 November 1988, 31.

Carolina, Oklahoma, South Carolina, and West Virginia adequately desegregated. Plans expired in Delaware, Florida, Kentucky, Maryland, Pennsylvania, Texas, and Virginia. By 1990, the NAACP, NAFEO and others lost the appeal for *Adams* to remain open.

However, on 31 January 1994, in light of the US Supreme Court decision *United States v. Fordice,* US 1125 Ct. 2727 (1992), the Office of Civil Rights published a notice[5] outlining new procedures and analysis that the agency planned to follow in future reviews of states with a history of *de jure* segregated systems of higher education. OCR planned to examine a wide range of factors to consider as well as factors addressed in *Fordice* and reflected in the criteria for acceptable desegregation plans specified in USDOE, "Revised Criteria" of 1978. The principal focus was on the SREB states, where 53.4 percent of the nation's 41 million African Americans lived by 2008.

Tennessee was one of the worst Jim Crow states for denying equal access to higher education for black citizens. Tennessee's HBCUs consisted of sixteen academies, institutes, colleges, and universities by 1908. The AME Zion Church operated Greenville Industrial College, with eighty-nine students, but the school did not survive, along with the Academy of Athens, Bristol Normal Institute, Warner Institute in Jonesboro, and Turner Normal College in Shelbyville. The largest enrollments among Tennessee HBCUs were Walden University (925), Howe Bible and Normal Institute (729), LeMoyne Normal Institute (725), Fisk University (571), Knoxville College (507), Meharry Medical College (480), and Lane College (298). HBCUs enrolled 5,592 students in 1908–1909, but few studied college courses. Eight HBCUs—American Baptist College, Zion College (Chattanooga City College), Fisk University, Knoxville College, Lane College, Meharry Medical College, Morristown Junior College, and Tennessee A&I State College—survived *Brown.*

Since 1912, state officials had discriminated against Tennessee A&I State College for Negroes, yet by 1954 the college's leaders and supporters had made the HBCU the fourth largest in enrollment among Tennessee's seven public institutions of higher education.[6] In the 1960s, when black citizens and others

---

[5] US Department of Education, Office of Civil Rights, "Notice of Application of Supreme Court Decision," 31 January 1994; *Norma v. Cantu,* Asst. Sec. of Civil Rights, 26 January 1994, Washington, DC.

[6] George N. Redd, "Educational Desegregation in Tennessee—One Year Afterward," *Journal of Negro Education* 24 (1955): 333–47. Reed was the dean at Fisk University. Also see Anders Walker, *The Ghost of Jim Crow: How Southern Moderates Used Brown v. Board of Education to Stall Civil Rights* (New York: Oxford University Press, 2009) 1–241.

protested against Jim Crow, the governor and other state officials retaliated against Tennessee A&I, expelling dozens of student civil rights leaders. After local black power students rioted in 1967, state officials approved guidelines that limited out-of-state student population. The measure was a punitive one; it devastated the enrollment, cut income from tuition and fees, and left Tennessee A&I State University financially crippled.

Rita Sanders (Geier), an instructor of history at Tennessee A&I State University, made up her mind to sue. She recalled that, while trying to get to her Vanderbilt University law classes, troops surrounding the A&I campus blocked her path. Out of anger, frustration, and a need for someone to do something about Tennessee's Jim Crow officials, she filed *Sanders v. Ellington*, 288 F. Supp. 937 (1968) in the Middle Tennessee Federal District Court. Patrick Gilpin a white Woodrow Fellow history professor serving at Tennessee A&I joined her in the lawsuit. A black parent in Wilson County whose child intended to attend Tennessee A&I joined the lawsuit. Sanders (Geier), a graduate of Fisk University, had gone north to complete her masters. The plaintiffs retained a white labor lawyer, George E. Barrett.

Sanders v. Ellington (1968) represented a bold move to stop the construction of a University Tennessee branch campus a few miles from Tennessee A&I. Rather than encourage everyone to attend Tennessee A&I, the local Chamber of Commerce and some other white officials had invited the University of Tennessee to expand in Nashville. State officials intended to make UT the "flagship" with branch campuses in the major cities of Chattanooga, Knoxville, Memphis, and Nashville. The other six public, four-year institutions of higher education remained under the control of the Tennessee Board of Education until the General Assembly created the State Board of Regents to govern these schools in 1972. To file *Sanders* in 1968 in the South was no easy task. Since Jim Crow days, civil rights plaintiffs and lawyers encountered racially conservative federal judges that gained their federal appointments through state and local political spoils systems. The South belonged solidly to the Democratic Party into the 1960s, and southern Democrats represented primarily the racially conservative wing of the party. No black men or women served on the federal court bench in Tennessee.

Judge Frank Gray, Jr., of the Federal District Court of Middle Tennessee, was a former mayor of Franklin, a town thirty miles south of Nashville. Franklin rested in Williamson County, where in antebellum times slaves constituted 43 percent of the population. Busing and other factors caused white flight from Nashville-Davidson County into Williamson and surrounding counties. Franklin built predominantly white, middle- and upper-class suburban developments.

Blacks continued to migrate to Nashville and northern industrial centers, and they soon represented less than 10 percent of Williamson County's population, down from 43 percent. The area became a racially conservative Republican Party stronghold, with a Confederate statue standing in Franklin's town square.[7]

As expected, Frank Gray ruled in August 1968 that the completion of University of Tennessee's downtown Nashville campus did not foster segregation. Gray sat on the case for 18 months, and state officials continued the construction of the downtown UTN campus one interstate exit away from Tennessee A&I. *Sanders* defendants argued the solution was to place Tennessee A&I under the Board of Trustees of the University of Tennessee because Tennessee A&I needed to hire a predominantly white faculty and attract more white students. Naturally, these white supremacy advocates did not suggest that TWIs recruit enough black faculty, staff, and student members to mirror the state's 16 percent black population. The defendants and local daily newspapers launched a public campaign to discredit Tennessee's only public HBCU, using words that played on whites' racial prejudices and their ignorance about blacks and Tennessee A&I's history.

Tennessee A&I State University (TSU), like several other HBCUs, had engaged a long struggle to obtain engineering programs. In 1944, Walter S. Davis, the president of what was then named Tennessee A&I State College, asked for engineering programs; however, the state failed to approve engineering for the black college. Soon after the end of World War II, while southern white officials, like those in Tennessee, purposefully impeded the Negro citizen's access to engineering programs, the President's Council of Land-Grant HBCUs began promoting engineering programs. Soon after six Negro students sued to enter programs at the all-white University of Tennessee in Knoxville in August 1951, the state renamed Tennessee A&I State College the Tennessee A&I State University. The institution organized a school of engineering in 1951, and built an engineering building in 1962.

Without adequate resources and enough doctoral faculty members, HBCU engineering programs, including the one at TSU, struggled to gain accreditation by the 1960s. Despite the passage of *Brown*, the state's engineering program at University of Tennessee remained exclusively for whites. UT admitted no undergraduate black students until passage of the Civil Rights Act in 1964. Thereafter, UT-Knoxville had twice the student enrollment of TSU, but black faculty members and students remained marginalized at under 3 percent. TSU had nearly six thousand students, including white faculty and students, and had

---

[7] Lovett, *The Civil Rights Movement in Tennessee*, 9, 96, 97, 351, 355, 358–59, 363, 370–80, 399.

no racial discrimination history. It was one of the five largest of the HBCUs, drawing students from across America and the world and TSU student athletes had consistently won more Olympic medals since 1948 than any other Tennessee college. The local white press, the daily *Tennessean* and the *Banner,* still played the role as the vanguard of the white South, supporting segregationist state officials. On 23 December 1969, Gray finally ordered plaintiffs and defendants to present desegregation plans by 1 April, 1970.[8] State defendants continued to take their time, stall, and play a waiting game.

Arguments in the *Sanders v. Ellington* case went nowhere until 1972, when a group of all-black plaintiffs—separate from the Rita Sanders (Geier) group—gained the court's permission to join the lawsuit. They consisted of HBCU graduates and 100 black citizens, who formed Tennesseans for Justice in Higher Education (TFJHE)—a statewide organization designed to stop the threat by state officials to merge the HBCU and TSU, under the auspices of the historic Jim Crow UT. Raymond Richardson, TSU professor of mathematics and a graduate of Rust College, who had earned a PhD in mathematics at Vanderbilt University, became co-leader of the TFJHE along with Sterlin Adams—mathematics professor and head of the TSU faculty senate, who was a graduate of LeMoyne College and Atlanta University.

Adams and Richardson, along with other members of TFJHE, did not trust the Rita Sanders (Geier) white attorney George Barrett as one who would protect black interests. At times he seemed to be willing to compromise with the state and local white power brokers. Thus, the TFJHE hired the civil rights attorney, Avon N. Williams, Jr., a graduate of the HBCU Johnson C. Smith College. After serving in America's Jim Crow army during World War II and being barred from attending either the UT law school in his hometown of Knoxville or the state's only other law school, Vanderbilt University, Williams completed his bachelor's and master's degrees in law at Boston University from 1946 to 1948. He interned in the Nashville law office of Z. A. Looby and affiliated with the NAACP-Legal Defense Fund from 1949 to 1951 at his practice in Knoxville. Williams filed the Clinton high school desegregation case for Negro families in nearby Anderson County and the UT desegregation for six black students, in 1950, eventually winning both cases. After moving to Nashville and joining Z. Alexander Lobby's law office in 1951, Williams became an officer in the Nashville branch NAACP. In 1968, he won election to the state senate, where he served for twenty-four years. Before his death in 1994, he filed eighty-five civil rights cases.

Williams and the Tennesseans for Justice in Higher Education enlisted help from experts at HBCUs and civil rights agencies to help handle the *Geier-UT* case.

---

[8] Ibid., 334–401.

The Race Relations Information Center (RRIC) in Nashville gave support to efforts to desegregate American higher education. The RRIC gathered and distributed information about civil rights activity, and maintained the Southern Reporting Service library, a remnant of the Southern Conference on Human Welfare. The RRIC board included Luther H. Foster (President of Tuskegee), Andrew Billingsley (VP of academic affairs at Howard), Vernon Jordan (director of UNCF), James R. Lawson (President of Fisk), and Herman H. Long (President of Talladega). A noted white author, John Egerton, wrote, "As long as the Negro public colleges remain black-led, black-populated institutions, it would appear from the record that white-dominated state governments and higher education systems do not intend to bring them to full equity."[9] Tennesseans for Justice in Higher Education and colleagues tried to make the federal court aware of the damaging effects of Jim Crow, the present effects and the future prognosis. They argued that a court order for immediate desegregation without long-term goals, precise objectives and benchmarks, supportive programs and adequate financing would not be fair and effective in dismantling *all* vestiges of discrimination. They did not want a *Brown*-like gradualism plan. The state of Tennessee submitted weak plans that placed a heavier burden of desegregation on Tennessee State University. They became alarmed when the TFJHE plan insisted that the more nationally recognized TSU should absorb the newly built UT-Nashville campus, public TWIs should be desegregated fully, and effective long-range plans should be monitored by a third party—not by state officials. Students at TSU also feared "white power" would take control of the HBCU.

In 1976, local newspapers and the TSU campus paper, *The Meter*, pictured TSU students marching in front of the Federal Court Office Building. One of the signs said, "UTN plus TSU=TSU." UT alumni responded with a demonstration favoring retention of the University of Tennessee-Nashville (UT-N) name. Whites continued to make negative public remarks about TSU's "quality," and the UT-N chancellor made mean-spirited remarks about TSU, which the *Tennessean* readily publicized.

In January 1977, after nine years of litigation, Judge Gray seemed to tire of the state of Tennessee toying with half-hearted desegregation plans. Gray ordered the merger of the UT-N campus with TSU, effective 1 July 1979, under State Board of Regents (1972–), not UT.

After Gray retired, Thomas A. Wiseman, Jr., a Democrat from rural Tennessee and a former state treasurer, became the new judge. Wiseman did not believe an institution could remain predominantly black and call itself an

---

[9] John Egerton, *The Public Black Colleges: Integration and Disintegration* (Nashville: Race Relations Information Center, 1971) 1–3.

integrated institution. He expressed a profound irritation with TSU alumni and others calling the merged institution "an HBCU." Like many other white Tennessee officials, and much of the general white public, it was difficult for this judge to imagine that anything black could be equal to anything white and/or be of high quality. Whites expected black officials to think the same way. The president of UT complained in a letter to the governor, "One of the defendants" was "not singing the same tune with the rest of us."[10] They were angry with TSU President Frederick S. Humphries for not going along with their position during testimony in the *Geier-UT* court trial. Humphries admitted that TSU was under-funded and historically treated unequally by the state, and at a board meeting, the governor and some of other Board of Regents members cornered Humphries in a bathroom and battered him about his remarks. They "[tongue] lashed him like a slave," Williams recalled in his memoirs.[11]

Rumors circulated that the governor intended to fire Humphries, TSU's president since January 1975. The board had selected him by a 6–4 decision to succeed Andrew P. Torrence, who resigned abruptly in April 1974. Torrence believed white state officials, the state's persistent under-funding of this public HBCU, the 1968 law that limited out-of-state enrollment, and now the turmoil of the *Geier-UT* case constrained his ability to move TSU forward.

The Humphries supporters, including Sterlin Adams, others in Tennesseans for Justice in Higher Education, and the eleven members of the Tennessee Caucus of Black State Legislators organized a caravan to the next State Board of Regents (TBR) meeting. They packed the meeting place, startling state officials. Thus, Governor Ray Blanton (D) backed off from an immediate firing, but convinced the board members to place Humphries on probation for one year. Next, Humphries' supporters solicited letters from a friendly SACS official in Atlanta, who frightened Blanton with a letter of inquiry about what was going on at TSU. The governor returned a letter to SACS saying there was no intent to fire the president, but merely an effort to get him to clean up some problems at TSU. Indeed, Humphries received some complaints and confrontation from student leaders who felt some problems at TSU were not being addressed fast enough, especially conditions in dormitories and other facilities. Avon Williams

---

[10] Lovett, *The Civil Rights Movement in Tennessee*, 373–74.

[11] Avon N. Williams Jr. Papers, Special Collections, Tennessee State University, Nashville TN. The TSU Library staff is processing the papers for public access. The author thanks Cindy Williams, the late Senator Williams's only surviving child and a Nashville schoolteacher, for working with me in her father's office to retrieve the papers from the attic. Workers from TSU graciously transported the boxes to the TSU Library. Ms. Williams initiated the offer of the papers to TSU, whose downtown campus (former UT-Nashville) honors the name of *Avon N. Williams Jr.* on the building.

petitioned the Sixth Circuit Court of Appeals, but the justices remanded the issue back to the district court, saying the district federal judge had authority to protect Humphries' position. Williams did not trust Judge Wiseman, and Wiseman, in turn, seemed to have no love for Williams. Blanton's term ended in January 1979 when he went to prison for selling pardons.

Under the next governor, the *Geier-UT* case became *Geier v. Alexander*, 801 F.2d 799 (1986). Although Wiseman had to protect Humphries' position, strangely, he allowed former UT-Nashville faculty members (mostly whites) to enter the case as "plaintiffs." Some of these people had continued, since the 1979 merger, to harass Humphries and his predominantly black administration with a persistent list of complaints and concerns. They had the ear of Roy Nicks, chancellor of the Board of Regents, who seemed to have a particular dislike of Humphries. These dissident plaintiffs, supported by the local daily newspapers and seemingly members of the Nashville Chamber of Commerce, wanted more of "a white presence" at TSU. Otherwise, predominantly white Nashville could never claim Tennessee State University as the city's "public university." With Wiseman's support, the parties agreed to a *Stipulation of Settlement* that imposed 50-percent-white-student and faculty quotas on TSU.[12] They suggested use of the racial makeup of the "service-mix area" for further desegregation of the state's TWIs. This meant that Nashville was 76 percent non-black and that TSU should reflect that racial makeup. However, Memphis was predominantly black, and the white officials backed off this formula that threatened predominantly white Memphis State University. Black student activists opposed the Settlement's grants ("scholarships) to attract white ("minority") residential students to the main campus. After all, since the Civil Rights Act white officials had failed to use this "scholarship" method to enroll more blacks at UT and other public colleges. Simply put, many activists in the black community, especially the student leaders at Tennessee State University, believed state officials did not want a predominantly black TSU to persist in Nashville, the state capital.

The *Geier Settlement* remained full of contradictions—ones advantageous to whites. Provision IV-C and (D) of the *Geier Settlement* required "a Physical Facilities Plan" for TSU to make its physical plant more comparable to the TWIs and to enhance TSU's urban regional mission, but the Tennessee Board of Regents staff issued a report that recommended only a twelfth of the money needed. State officials later allocated inadequate capital funding, allowing facilities to deteriorate, and forcing Tennessee State University to return some

---

[12] Lovett, *The Civil Rights Movement in Tennessee*, 380–81; *Geier v. Alexander* 801 F2d 799, 6th Circuit, 1986; *Geier v. Alexander* 593 F Supp 1263 (MD Tenn., 1984); TSU, "The Stipulation of Settlement" file, Tennessee State University, Special Collections, Nashville.

state funds based on the charge they allowed enrollment of academically suspended students.[13] Provision IV-A of the 1985 *Geier Settlement* required the higher education governing agencies to develop a comprehensive plan to enhance TSU as "the regional urban university for Middle Tennessee"[14] and provide funding in support of this plan. But state officials allowed the public TWIs near TSU to duplicate programs offered at Tennessee State University. Adams-Richardson *Geier* plaintiffs appealed to the Sixth Circuit Court of Appeals, but the court said the *Settlement* was an agreement between parties.

Wiseman, the Chamber of Commerce, the city's white newspapers, and the officials at the State Board of Regents, among other whites, remained anti-TSU. In measured words, they declared TSU was too black. Humphries held a luncheon for the local media, hoping to improve relations with them, but he changed few minds among the overwhelmingly white staff members of the local newspapers and television stations. The faculty dissidents formed a caucus with an integrated façade and planned to write a list of complaints against the Humphries administration. First, the dissidents tried to win over the Student Government Association. SGA president-elect Augusto Macedo came to their meeting, listened, and then wrote a letter, dated 22 April 1985, to the chair of the "Caucus for Excellence and Integrity in Higher Education." The letter read,

> I was nominated to serve on your Executive Committee, which I declined. I was deeply disturbed and highly dissatisfied with your organization, which is composed of Neo-Nazis. Your only goals are to condemn [TSU] and return society to the 'Good Old Days' of white supremacy. I submit to you that, we the students of TSU will not allow your organization of educated Klansmen to direct or distort the future of Black Americans.[15]

Finally worn down by Chancellor Nicks, the lack of support for TSU from the local white community, the constant sabotage and complaints from the campus dissidents, and the mounting difficulties of governing the institution, Humphries privately notified his closest advisers and supporters he was leaving. He resigned 30 June 1985, to become president of Florida A&M. Upon returning to TSU in 2002 to have a campus building named in his honor, Humphries recalled how he survived for more than ten years: Chancellor Nicks "hardly missed a day" sending a letter about this or that. "At the end of the day I often arrived home to merely lie across the bed and let the heat escape from my

---

[13] Lovett, *The Civil Rights Movement in Tennessee*, 382–84.

[14] TSU, "The Stipulation of Settlement," 3.

[15] Agustus Macedo, "Letter," *The Meter*, 17 November 1985, Tennessee State University Library, Special Collections, Nashville.

body."[16] HBCU leadership was destabilized this way. Judge Gray had refused to cooperate, and he handed them a defeat through the 1979 merger, but the pro-Jim Crow officials kept fighting to break the predominantly black TSU.

TSU had four presidents and acting presidents between 1 July 1985 and 30 April 1991. During this period, state officials limited the budget, forced severe personnel cuts, and allowed the campus facilities to grossly deteriorate. The local news media frightened away many students, both black and white, with negative reports, while the *Geier Settlement* allowed local and state officials and on-campus white dissidents to toy with the HBCU.

It was the black Student Government Association (SGA), however, that played a major role in fighting off state officials and the dissidents on campus. Through the student newspaper, they criticized the obvious bias of Judge Wiseman.

After Governor Lamar Alexander (R) and the Board of Regents appointed Roy P. Peterson, a minor black official with the Kentucky higher education commission, as interim president at TSU on 1 July 1985, the SGA leaders and the student newspaper, *The Meter*, declared "war."[17] They circulated the word in the black community that Peterson insulted them, calling them "a bunch of silly children," after the students demanded the new interim president give his position about the *Geier Settlement* and whether or not TSU should retain its HBCU label and its "black heritage." Organizations of local black women cleverly invited Peterson to a "community forum" at historic First Baptist Church, Capitol Hill and were not pleased at his responses to questions about reported student dissatisfactions. Because of questions about how Peterson was giving on-campus construction contracts to white companies but not to black firms, and because of the student rebellion on campus, state senator Avon Williams and other black leaders persuaded the governor and the Board of Regents to dismiss interim president Peterson less than a year later.

The governor and the Board of Regents quickly picked Otis L. Floyd, the lone black vice president at nearby Middle Tennessee State University to serve as

---

[16] The author attended the TSU dedication ceremony and recorded remarks by Humphries; *Report of Findings of the 25th Anniversary Legislative Retreat and Training Conference: "Securing Prosperity for our Children in the 21st Century" Annual Report* (Nashville: Office of Minority Affairs, and Political Research Group at TSU, 1985–2001); *Annual Desegregating Monitoring Report* (Nashville: Tennessee Higher Education Commission, 1985–2001) 1–31; "Tennessee Public School Systems American College Test—ACT," *Tennessee Report Card 2002: A Summary of Tennessee's Public School Systems* (Nashville TN: State Department of Education, 2002) 39, 93; Boxes 30–40, Geier documents in the Avon Williams Papers, Special Collections, Tennessee State University Library, Nashville TN.

[17] Lovett, *The Civil Rights Movement in Tennessee*, 385.

interim president at Tennessee State University. Still suspicious about this appointment, a few hundred students took over Floyd's administrative office space and held a sit-in, with students taking turns in between classes sitting on the floor and studying their books. The students—and some faculty members—were not happy that Floyd had been appointed with no real credentials in the Civil Rights Movement. As rumors predicted, the Board appointed Floyd permanently in early 1988, without much campus input. The student leaders distrusted Floyd's commitment to TSU as an HBCU, and they believed he was one of the "good ole' boys" in Tennessee's networks of white officials. Students renewed their protests.

The student leaders drove downtown to see the new governor, Ned R. McWherter (D), to protest the miserable physical conditions on the campus. Even though Williams and other Black Caucus members had secured several million dollars to repair dormitories and campus facilities, the money had been used ineffectively through, what many believed, was the usual state corruption in construction contracts and perhaps the cooperation of weak black officials. Surprisingly, McWherter drove out to the campus with the students, secretly toured the facilities, and met with state officials, Avon Williams, and other black state legislators to decide on a *Master Facilities Plan* (1989), costing $122 million intended to upgrade, renovate, or tear down, and build new facilities, bringing the HBCU campus up to par.

McWherter and the Board of Regents rescued President Floyd, appointing him the first black chancellor of the Board of Regents in July 1990. Prior to leaving TSU, Floyd officiated at the ceremony to name the TSU downtown campus (former UT-N campus) in honor of retired attorney Avon N. Williams, Jr. George W. Cox, a TSU vice president, served as interim president from July 1990 to April 1991, until the next president was appointed.

James A. Hefner was the embattled president of Jackson State University. To the surprise of the campus community, he was placed on the list of presidential finalists at the last moment. This move caused one of Jackson State's vice presidents, a former TSU dean, to step aside as a finalist, although he was a favorite among TSU constituents. Reportedly, the governor, who perhaps had conferred with the governor of Mississippi, sent Chancellor Floyd to Mississippi to personally interview Hefner. The TSU council of deans and others interviewed him on the TSU campus with pointed questions such as, why was he leaving Jackson State so suddenly to come to TSU? Hefner replied he wanted a larger university like Tennessee State. Instead of waiting until 30 June to leave his Jackson State position, Hefner surprised the TSU campus by coming to the office in April, before the Jackson State graduation.

Naturally, the student leaders, especially SGA President Jeff Car, quietly eyed Hefner and remained vigilant. The SGA worried that the *Master Plan* (1989) was a pretext for running more blacks away from TSU. The students publicly protested when Hefner and the Board placed Otis L. Floyd's name on the new Campus Center in 1993. Hefner carefully measured his words that TSU remained an integrated "HBCU," and remained president until 2005.

The strong black student leaders of 1986 to 1991 were instrumental in guarding the HBCU, Tennessee State University. Macedo completed law school after graduating from TSU; Greg Carr completed a PhD in black studies at Temple University and became a member of the faculty at Howard University; Jeff Carr graduated from TSU and became a community leader and founder of a theater company in Nashville.

The TSU-UTN *Geier* merger state desegregation case remained under the watchful eye of other former Jim Crow states. On 11 May 1994, the *Tennessee Desegregation Monitoring Committee Minutes* showed there were fifty-seven black students admitted to the two public medical schools, eleven of them graduated and thirty-nine remained in the *Geier* pre-professional summer program. One official admitted, "It is not as high as we would like."[18] The reports for 1996 showed TSU, which had nearly nine thousand students, spent $924,000 for white minority scholarships, and UT-Knoxville, with twenty-four thousand students, spent $1.3 million on scholarships for blacks. UT now had fewer than 5 percent black students, while TSU had 24 percent white students.

Two years after Avon N. Williams, Jr., passed away in July 1996, Tennessee officials filed for dismissal of *Rita Sanders Geier Plaintiffs, USA, Plaintiff-Intervener, Raymond Richardson, Jr. et al., Plaintiffs-Interveners, H. Coleman McGinnis, et al. Plaintiffs-Interveners vs. Governor Don Sundquist, et al. Defendants*, Civil Action No. 5077. On 4 January 2001, the federal court allowed Tennessee to end the 32-year-old *Geier* lawsuit. State officials agreed to appropriate $75 million for further desegregation efforts over the next five years. TSU would receive about $400,000 for an "image-building campaign, " as well as $750,000 for white student scholarships, and TSU could start a School of Public Affairs. TSU would also receive $1 million per year for ten years and one-to-one matching funds, up to another $1 million per year, for a total of $30 million for the "TSU Endowment and Educational Excellence Fund." In addition, TSU would receive $10 million to develop a law school, "if one is established in Middle Tennessee." In the TSU faculty senate minutes of 19 September 2002, Lewis Laska, a white faculty member of the College of Business, said the settlement really "abolished

[18] Ibid., 394.

affirmative action in Tennessee."[19] The plaintiffs' lawyers did not actually win *Geier*; instead, they abandoned and settled the case, then asked for $10 million in fees. Hefner saw the settlement as a great opportunity for TSU to become the city's premier public university. The Nashville *Tennessean*-wrote,

> Many factors have held back [TSU] through the years, racism being among them. Also high on that list was attitude. Whether real or perceived, TSU developed the reputation through the years as being inefficient, undisciplined and unfriendly, particularly to non-minority students. That reputation not only held back TSU's ability to thrive, it hurt Nashville. When people in this city, including working adults, contemplated returning to college for a degree or just for a few courses, TSU was not an inviting option. Since it is the only public four-year in Nashville, potential students who marked it off their list would have either to drive farther or pay more to fulfill their educational dreams. Over the last few months, however, TSU had confronted its perception and turned it around.... Now the contagion needs to spread beyond the TSU campus. TSU's transformation into the region's premier public university will require willingness from business, political and civic leaders to see the new TSU. If ... community leaders have avoided TSU in the past, for whatever reason, they need to change their habits. [TSU] already has.[20]

White racial attitudes in Tennessee toward a predominately-black Tennessee State University had not, in fact, changed much. Wiseman seemed pleased to dismiss the *Geier* desegregation case in 2005. President Hefmer resigned in 2005, and TSU had to find new leadership to affect the new direction.[21]

North Carolina was a trendsetter in white southern education reform.[22] North Carolina had a large number of HBCUs because the state's population centers,

---

[19] Ibid., 397, 398, 400; see Lewis L. Laska, "A Legal and Constitutional History of Tennessee, 1772–1972," *Memphis State University Law Review* 6/1 (Summer 1976): 563–672.

[20] Editor, "TSU," *The Tennessean*, Nashville, 14 August 2002, 1; Brad Schrade and Jaime Sarrio, "Settlement of Desegregation Suit Brings $200 Million Mixed Opinions," *The Tennessean*, Nashville, 11 July 2010.

[21] Editor, "Tennessee Higher ED Desegregation Case Comes to an End," *Diverse: Issues in Higher Education* 23/17 (5 May 2006): 18; Julianne Basinger, "Tennessee State U's President Is Accused of Misusing Funds and Lying about Gifts," *Chronicle of Higher Education* 50/33 (23 April 2004): A32.

[22] H. Leon Prather, *Resurgent Politics and Educational Progressivism in the New South, North Carolina, 1890–1913* (Rutherford NJ: Fairleigh Dickson University Press, 1979) 45.

such as Durham, Raleigh, and Winston-Salem maintained large Negro populations—the descendants of large numbers of slaves. Black higher education in North Carolina started with private missionary groups. The American Missionary Association opened six institutions between 1867 and 1900. The Board of Missions for Freedmen of the Presbyterian Church opened seven freedmen's schools between 1867 and 1904. The Freedmen's Aid Society of the MEC opened an HBCU. Individuals, black church groups, and northern philanthropists established dozens of other schools to extend education to Negroes, including Biddle Memorial Institute (1867–1925); Johnson C. Smith University (1923–); Shaw University (1865–); Saint Augustine's College (1867–); Zion Wesley Institute (1879–; it became Livingstone College in 1887); and Bennett College (1873–).

In the history of higher education in North Carolina, although "the majority of rural whites were opposed to educational equality for blacks,"[23] North Carolina supported five public HBCUs. (1) Fayetteville State University began as the Howard School in 1867, became State Colored Normal School in 1877, then Normal State School in 1926, graduating its first four-year college class in 1939. The institution became Fayetteville State College in 1963, a university in 1969, and part of the UNC system since 1972. (2) In 1891, the state established North Carolina Agricultural and Technical State University, the HBCU land grant institution. First named the A&T College for Negroes, the school temporarily located in Raleigh, and moved to Greensboro in 1893. It added a master's program in 1939, and the North Carolina A&T became a part of the UNC system in 1972. (3) Winston-Salem State University began as the Slater Industrial Academy, a one-room school, in 1892. The state chartered it in 1897 as the Slater Industrial and State Normal School. The school then became Winston-Salem Teachers College in 1925, Winston-Salem State College (1963), Winston-Salem State University (1969), and part of the UNC system in 1972. (4) North Carolina Central University chartered in 1909 and opened in 1910 as the National Religious Training School and Chautauqua under James E. Shepard. In 1923, the state made the institution into the Durham State Normal School for Negroes. It was renamed North Carolina College for Negroes in 1925. State and private gifts made by B. N. Duke, citizens of Durham, and federal grants helped expand the physical plant. SACS approved the institution, and the college began the library science school in 1941. The name changed to North Carolina College at Durham in 1947, then North Carolina Central University in 1969. NCCU has been in the UNC system since 1972. (5) Elizabeth City State University began on 3 March 1891 by an act of the General Assembly. The school started in January 1892 with

[23] Ibid., 107–14, 255.

twenty-three students. The institution became a two-year school in 1937 and took the name Elizabeth City Teachers College in 1939, awarding its first bachelor's degree, and achieving SACS accreditation, in 1961. The curriculum expanded from an elementary education major in 1959–1963 to twelve more majors. It became Elizabeth City State University in 1969, and part of the UNC system since 1972. ECSU enrolled 2,577 students on its two-hundred-acre campus, had 862 acres of land, new buildings and a pharmacy program, and graduated sixteen thousand students by 2007.

When the modern movement to desegregate higher education in the former Jim Crow states began in the 1970s, it was easy for plaintiffs to show that North Carolina had a jaded Jim Crow history of mistreating its Negro citizens when it came to equal access to quality higher education. Like their neighbors in Tennessee, North Carolina white officials felt it was part of their public mandate to ensure unequal education for Negro citizens. In this regard, officials created the five public HBCUs to keep blacks out of the higher-quality white institutions.

In February 1933, Thomas R. Hocutt, a graduate of North Carolina College in Durham, unsuccessfully applied for admission to the University of North Carolina. He followed with an unsuccessful lawsuit. However, *University of Maryland v. Murray*, 169 Md. 478 (1936), which forced white officials to admit Donald G. Murray to the school, encouraged the North Carolina civil rights activists. In March 1936, the North Carolina Committee on Negro Affairs developed a list of improvements needed for black education. White officials appealed to conservative blacks to shun the NAACP's legal approach, and work *within* the state to develop a compromise. The NAACP won *Missouri ex rel. Gains v. Canada*, 305 US 337 (1938), and this sent additional fears through white North Carolina. In order to show compliance with *Plessy v. Ferguson* (1896) "separate but equal" principle, North Carolina spent $800,000 between 1939 and 1942 to build new facilities and buy equipment at North Carolina College and North Carolina A&T, including a law school and graduate program. However, Negro women insisted on applying to the white law school. In June 1951, the University of North Carolina law school, like University of Tennessee's law school, admitted Negroes.[24] But this was not enough.

Negro leaders continued to press North Carolina to desegregate all higher education in the state. In the first desegregation of higher education plan of 1972, the University of North Carolina system, which consisted of eleven other

---

[24] Augustus M. Burns III, "Graduate Education for Blacks in North Carolina, 1930–1951," *Journal of Southern History* 46/2 (May 1980): 195–218; Nelson H. Harris, "Desegregation in North Carolina Institutions of Higher Learning," *Journal of Negro Education* 27/3 (Summer 1958): 295–99.

institutions, absorbed the five public HBCUs. President Ronald Reagan (R) and his conservative administration allowed North Carolina and five others to go slow on higher education desegregation. One NAACP lawyer labeled the desegregation plan as a "sellout."[25] Some believed the large number of black colleges increased North Carolina's resistance to desegregation of higher learning. Neo-Confederates would base the resistance on the old Civil War call for states's rights. Some federal officials were surprised that North Carolina failed to embody its progressive image.[26]

The TWIs continued to have better graduate and professional degree programs, more funding for teaching, research, and public service programming than the HBCUs. In 1983, when the OCR forced the states to submit stronger higher education desegregation plans, the North Carolina plan improved. That improvement continued over 25 years. In 2002, 32,575 black college students (25.1 percent of the total) attended institutions of higher education in North Carolina. That included 19,276 of black students enrolled at the five public HBCUs, or 59 percent of enrolled black college students in the UNC system. Some 129,543 students enrolled in the UNC system. Local adult whites enrolled at HBCUs, but few of the white, first-time freshmen chose to attend the HBCUs.

Besides ingrained racial prejudices among white first-time freshmen, was there, perhaps, racial disparity in assignment of curricula among the public HBCU and TWI institutions. The desegregation plan did not completely stop this discrimination, but diminished it somewhat. North Carolina Central already offered a law degree as a result of NAACP efforts to force desegregation of graduate education in the Jim Crow states, and once offered a doctorate in 1952, graduating five students, but discontinuing the doctorate program in education in 1964. Instead, in the era of desegregation, NCC created some hybrids, combining law with master's degrees in library science and business administration. Elizabeth City had a pharmacy program in collaboration with UNC-Chapel Hill, four master's programs, and a center of excellence in remote sensor research. Winston-Salem State offered master's programs in physical therapy, education, nursing, business administration, and computer science. North Carolina A&T, one of the state's three public engineering colleges, had a doctoral program in three areas of engineering. Most PhD and professional degree seekers still had to access major programs at North Carolina's

---

[25] Reginald Stuart, "New Trend in College Desegregation Emerges," *New York Times*, 3 September 1981, 1–5.

[26] William Link, oral history interview with Joseph Califano, 5 April 1991, Southern Oral History Program Collection, Southern Historical Collection, Wilson Library, University of North Carolina, Chapel Hill.

traditionally white institutions (TWIs). By 2007, the state listed five of the TWIs as "Doctoral/Research University-Extensive." They upgraded UNC-Charlotte to "Doctoral/Research Intensive" status. They confined all five public HBCUs to lower tiers: "Master's (Comprehensive) Colleges and Universities" or "Baccalaureate Colleges-General."[27]

The North Carolina state desegregation plan also did not provide financial resources to address the poorer students at North Carolina's five HBCUs. They required more financial and academic assistance compared with students overall at the public TWIs. Students at the HBCUs were mostly female (74 percent at Elizabeth City State; 52 percent at North Carolina A&T). The latter institution had the highest percentage of black students (91 percent), and Elizabeth City the least at 78 percent. Winston-Salem State University had 3,396 students in fall 2002. North Carolina A&T reported 11,093 students for fall 2006, with 92 percent of the students receiving some kind of financial aid to pay tuition, fees, and other expenses that totaled $14,016 for in-state students and $23,458 for out-of-state students. North Carolina A&T had colleges of engineering and arts sciences, and six schools under agriculture and environmental sciences, business and economics, education, nursing, technology, and graduate studies. A&T began offering the PhD in 1993. A&T had a graduation rate of 38 percent for 2000–2006. Of the faculty, 328 of the 425 members held doctorates or professional degrees.[28]

Racism, a lack of equal educational and economical opportunities for black citizens, and the northern migration of many blacks caused South Carolina's black population to plummet from 58 percent in 1865 to 30 percent in 2000. Blacks comprised the majority of inhabitants in twelve counties, including 61 percent in Orangeburg County, the home of the state's only public four-year university. After the OCR cited South Carolina in 1980 as one of the states still not adequately desegregated, the state made a concerted effort to desegregate higher education. The effort included programs to enhance HBCUs Denmark

---

[27] North Carolina A&T State University, *10-Year Report to the Chancellor, 1981–1991* (Greensboro: Office of University Relations, 1991) 1–24; University of NC System, *Academic Program Inventory: North Carolina Senoir Colleges and Universities* (Chapel Hill: UNC, 1998) 1–31.

[28] North Carolina A&T., *Data Book* (Greensboro: North Carolina A&T University, 2008) 10–11; US Department of Education (USDOE), *Historically Black Colleges and Universities, 1976–2001* (Washington DC: GPO, 2004) 6; L. E. Murphy, F. R. Coble, and S. A. Allen, *The History of Winston-Salem State University, 1892–1992* (Virginia Beach VA: Donning Company, 1993) 1–15; Sylvia M. Jacobs, "Standing on the Shoulders of a Giant: Personal Reflections on a Great American," *Journal of African American History* 94/3 (Summer 2009): 377–90; Southern Regional Education Board, *2005 Fact Book* (Atlanta: SREB, 2005) 1–40.

Technical College and South Carolina State. The state created a scholarship database, web integration of services, fifteen academic programs, fifteen retention programs, eighteen leadership programs, data collection, and a publication about successful retention programs, and responded to the Southern Education Foundation *Miles to Go* report, which criticized the state's low percentage of black faculty and black retention/graduation rates.[29]

However, considering the devastation 115 years of Jim Crow education had heaped on black South Carolinians, the efforts to make public HBCUs equal to public TWIs seemed too slow. Younger blacks, especially students, displayed anger about the pace of plans to enhance South Carolina State University (SCSU). On 28 February 2004, Andrew Hugine, Jr., became the ninth president of South Carolina State University. Less than a month later, forty-five students, along with the president, other administrators, and staff members met with the legislative Black Caucus. The officials informed the university delegation the state increased the 2004–2005 budgets for South Carolina State by recommendation of the governor from $20.9 million to $21.4 million; other institutions were not receiving an increase. It seemed odd that the delegation came to the meeting to announce a $500,000 increase. Some students had refused to attend the meeting at the state capitol, and student leaders who attended the meeting believed students could not express real concerns openly. The black leaders kindly thanked the white officials for the $500,000, but student leader Joshua Alexander later expressed concern about the process and about SCSU maintaining focus on providing a quality education for black students.[30]

At the University of South Carolina (USC), where Negro students had been thrown out of the public institution in 1876, since being readmitted in the 1960s, blacks comprised 10.8 percent of graduate students and 8.5 percent of professional students (medicine, pharmacy, and law) in fall 1999. On the graduate and professional levels, the USC was in line with other SREB institutions. In fall 2000, blacks comprised 30 percent of the 116,982 students in state research universities, teaching colleges and universities, regional campuses, and technical colleges in South Carolina. By fall 2004, blacks were 34 percent of students at two-year institutions, and 14 percent of 25,596 students at USC—higher than most of the SREB flagships.

---

[29] Southern Education Foundation (SEF), *Miles to Go: A Report on Black Students and Postsecondary Education in the South* (Atlanta: SEF, 1998) 1–20; Peter Wallenstein, ed., *Higher Education and the Civil Rights Movement: White Supremacy, Black Southerners, and College Campuses* (Gainesville: University Press of Florida, 2008) 1–298.

[30] South Carolina State University, "Concerns by Joshua Alexander," *The Collegian*, Spring 2004, 1.

The number of predominantly black colleges in South Carolina increased from two to four institutions. Calhoun Technical College and Williamsburg Technical College were predominantly black colleges and universities (PBCUs). South Carolina State University had a headcount of 4,466 students for fiscal year 2004–2005, ranking it fifth in enrollment among the state's ten "Teaching Universities;" and had 98 percent black students in fall 2004 compared to 92.09 percent blacks in fall 2000. Williamsburg Technical College enrolled 1,093 students, 65.3 percent of whom were black. Enrollments at Denmark Technical College and at Orangeburg-Calhoun Technical College were, respectively, 94.3 percent and 55.1 percent black. The South Carolina General Assembly established Denmark Technical College in 1947, which opened in March 1948 as the Denmark branch of the South Carolina Trade School System. SACS accredited the institution in 1979 as Denmark Technical College in rural Bamberg County offering associate degrees, diplomas, and certificates.

Although they comprised more than 30 percent of the population and 30 percent of enrolled college students, African Americans in 2002–2003 received a smaller proportion of the degrees awarded by South Carolina's public institutions: associates (26.6 percent); bachelors (20.8 percent); masters (15.2 percent); and doctoral (14.3 percent). The six-year minority retention and graduation rates in fall 1999 were five percentage points lower than for white undergraduates. Only 20 percent of blacks transferred from two-year colleges to four-year institutions in fall 2003 compared to a 70-percent transfer rate for whites. Among a total of 103 seats for public colleges and universities board of trustees, blacks constituted 20.3 percent. Nearly half of them sat on the board of South Carolina State. At two-year public colleges, blacks comprised 24.5 percent of 151 trustee members, and black faculty members comprised 9 percent at public institutions. USC employed 71 (4.9 percent) black faculty members among 1,447. Most black faculty worked at two-year institutions, at SCSU or at Denmark Technical College (84.8 percent black staff/faculty).[31]

By 2004, the desegregation plan focused on statistical achievements rather than on equity and quality in academic programs for blacks, whites, and HBCUs. South Carolina seemed to be approaching the parity of 33.1 percent minority students enrolled in the higher education system. But it was not likely that white students would prefer to enroll at public HBCUs. Compared to nearby TWIs, SCSU was located in a predominantly black county, had fewer desirable degree programs, no doctoral programs and just a few master's programs in limited fields of education, agribusiness, nutritional science, and transportation. The

[31] SREB, *South Carolina Featured Facts from the SREB Fact Book on Higher Education, 2009* (Atlanta: Southern Education Foundation, 2009) 1–31, 20.

white USC campuses had all of the doctoral programs, most of the master's degree programs, and all of the professional programs among state institutions. The Commission on Higher Education approved South Carolina State's BS degree in nuclear engineering in September 2002, placed the MS degree in nuclear engineering at USC, and provided exchanges for students and faculty in nuclear engineering to compensate for faculty deficits at SCSU. South Carolina remained near the bottom of SREB states in recruiting and retaining minority (i.e., African-American) students and faculty.[32]

Pennsylvania developed plans to eliminate racial discrimination within its system of higher education. Pennsylvania was nearly 86 percent white in 2000, compared to 69.1 percent white population overall in the US. Blacks comprised little over 10 percent of the 12.2 million people in Pennsylvania. The state had a low number of adults holding high diplomas and college and professional degrees. Pennsylvania, in other words, had a large working-class white population. However, the graduation rate at Pennsylvania's four-year institutions was high.

In a state where anti-slavery and abolitionist groups had thrived, Pennsylvania had two HBCUs: Cheyney University of Pennsylvania—a state university—and Lincoln University—a *state-related* Commonwealth university developed out of the anti-slavery movement. Cheyney University enrolled 1,536 students—55 percent women, 15 percent out-of-state, and 18.6 percent graduate students studying in four master's programs in education. Ninety percent of the 292 degrees awarded by Cheyney in 2002–2003 went to blacks, compared to 6 percent (136 of 2,259) of degrees awarded to blacks at West Chester University of Pennsylvania. Among the "state-related Commonwealth universities," Lincoln University, which included an Urban Center in Philadelphia to attract adult white students, awarded 373 degrees including master's degrees, with 80.7

---

[32] Southern Education Foundation (SEF), *Black Faculty in Traditional White Institutions in Selected Adams States: Characteristics, Experiences and Perceptions* (Atlanta: SEF, 1988); Y. A. Robinson, "The Federal Commitment to Historically Black Colleges and Universities: The Dollars and Sense of Title III of the Higher Education Act of 1965" (PhD dissertation, Claremont Graduate School, 1997) 1–20; Roebuck and Murty, *Black Colleges and Universities*, 45–47; J. Matlock, "The Effect of Desegregation Policies on Historically Black Public Colleges and Universities," Garibaldi, *Black Colleges*, 199–218; National Center for Higher Education Management Systems and Center for Public Trusteeship and Governance of the Association of Governing Boards of Universities and Colleges, *Foundations for the Future: A Report to the South Carolina Commission on Higher Education*, 4 December 2003, San Jose CA, 4–6; National Center for Public Policy and Higher Education, *Measuring Up: The State Report on Higher Education, South Carolina* (San Jose CA: National Center on Higher Education, 2004) 1–11; South Carolina Commission on Higher Education, *South Carolina Higher Education Statistical Abstract, 2009* (Columbia: SCCHE, 2009).

percent of degrees going to blacks. Cheyney and Lincoln had a dozen master's degree programs, but did not have doctoral programs to compete with the TWIs. In the 1983 plan, the state did little to enhance the two HBCUs, except to allow them to continue to exist, and created the Horace Mann Bond-Lesley Pinckney Scholarship annually awarded to graduates at Cheyney and Lincoln to pursue master's degrees at three white state universities.

In 1998–1999, blacks received 754 degrees, including a few doctorate degrees, or about 4.3 percent of total degrees in Pennsylvania. However, in 2003, Temple University in heavily black Philadelphia graduated 1,050 blacks including 198 masters, and 99 doctorate and professional degrees—17 percent of Temple's 6,190 degrees. The "private state-aided institutions" awarded 645 (6.1 percent) of their degrees to blacks. Carnegie Mellon University awarded three of 158 doctorate degrees to blacks, 33 of 984 master's degrees, and 51 of 1,020 bachelor's degrees. The Pennsylvania College of Medicine awarded 9 degrees to blacks. In 2004, state and private institutions granted 7 percent of all degrees to blacks.

By 2008, black higher education attainment had improved, but the gap between black and white Pennsylvanians remained as wide as it was ten years ago. Compared to 7.9 percent in 1996, blacks comprised 8.9 percent of fall college enrollments in 2005. The fall 2008 enrollment was 2,073 students, including 374 graduate students, at Lincoln University. Cheyney University enrolled 1,233 students, including 48 graduate students. The two HBCUs awarded 635 bachelors and graduate degrees in 2007–2008.[33] Cheyney and Lincoln made major contributions to the Pennsylvania higher education system, but by 2010, the HBCUs were not growing; enrollment and number of graduates stagnated.

Louisiana developed two public colleges for blacks: Grambling University and Southern A&M University. Louisiana had a 50-percent black population during slavery, but lost 17 percent of its Negro population after slavery ended. Northern philanthropists and missionary church groups entered Louisiana, 1865–1935, and established freedmen and colored schools. Two private HBCUs, Dillard University and Xavier University, both in New Orleans, survived the twentieth

[33] PDE, *Reports of State Universities of Pennsylvania* (Harrisburg: Pennsylvania State Department of Education, 2004); Pennsylvania Department of Education, Office of Postsecondary and Higher Education, *A Rising Tide: The Current State of Higher Education in the Commonwealth of Pennsylvania* (Harrisburg PA: PSDE, April 2006) 9–15, 36, 50, *Colleges and Universities Education Digest, 2005–06*, and *Profiles*, 19 June 2009; Pennsylvania State Department of Education, *Education in Pennsylvania: A Statistical Summary, 2005* (Harrisburg PA: PSDE, 2005) 1–25; PDE, *College Enrollment, University Enrollment* (Harrisburg PA: Office of Postsecondary Higher Education, 2003) 1–14.

century. Black Lt. Governor, P. B. S. Pinchback, pushed for a Negro university equal to those in Europe.

Legislative Act No. 87 (1880) established Southern University. The legislation even included a provision for a department of law and of medicine in New Orleans. The Louisiana General Assembly funded the institution on 10 April 1880, as a university for the education of persons of color, and the school opened in New Orleans on 7 March 1881, but state funding was inadequate. The state sold the first site and bought a new building in 1883. The early classes consisted of grammar through high school, with some college work. Agricultural and industrial subjects dominated the curricula. Southern became an 1890 land-grant college. In 1912, the state authorized the institution to move to Baton Rouge, where it reopened on 9 March 1914, offering study from sixth grade through normal school, which was extended to four years of college in the 1920s. Baton Rouge College, which was already in existence and which black Baptists first named the Baton Rouge Academy, was an institution that supplied high school students to Southern. By the 1940s, SU had divisions of agriculture, liberal arts, business education, teacher education, health and physical education, home economics, mechanical arts, and music. The state established the law school in 1947. In the 1970s, the state created the SU System: Baton Rouge campus, the law center, New Orleans campus, and the Shreveport campus.

Grambling University began around 1901 when Charles P. Adams came to this southwest Louisiana lumber mill community at the request of a group of farmers who wanted to open a school for Negro children. The Colored Farmers Association helped Adams raise money to complete an existing elementary school building consisting of two stories with classrooms and a ten-room dormitory upstairs. Adams started the classes in November 1901 for the Louisiana Agriculture and Industrial Institute. He, his wife, and a friend comprised the beginning faculty. A white woman, Fidelia Jewett, made a large donation, and by 1914, five whites from nearby Ruston and three blacks from Grambling served on the board of trustees. The Parish government contributed funds to the "Lincoln Parish Training School." The state assumed control of Grambling in 1928 as a two-year college, and it became Louisiana Negro Normal and Industrial Institute, and a four-year institution, in 1940, achieving SACS accreditation in 1949. Grambling remained an independent campus, however, sitting almost next door to a growing public TWI.

Blacks comprised 32.5 percent of the people in Louisiana in the US Census of 2000, when 18.7 percent of Louisianans had a college education compared to

24.4 percent for the nation. The percentage of black college graduates was lower than the state average.[34]

On 14 March 1974, the federal government filed a lawsuit against the state of Louisiana and its higher education boards for violations of Title VI of the Civil Rights Act (1964) and the Fourteenth Amendment of the US Constitution. Beginning with *US v. Louisiana* 527 F. Supp 509 (E.D.La.1981), during 1981–1987, the federal government began forcing the state to desegregate its higher education system. In Shreveport, New Orleans, and Lincoln parish, HBCU and TWI campuses existed in close vicinity to one another. There was a 1981 consent decree about open admissions, student attrition, program duplication, the allocation of curricular offerings, roles for the public HBCUs, and balancing the racial diversity of staff, faculty, and governing board memberships. The four public HBCUs—Grambling, Southern University-Baton Rouge, Southern-New Orleans, and Southern University-Shreveport—remained heavily black. They suffered a scarcity of graduate programs to attract non-blacks by 1987.

The court ordered Louisiana to develop new remedies, including getting rid of program duplication. Then, the court vacated its decision in the face of opposition from whites, and remanded the case in light of the pending *Ayers v. Mabus* (US, 111 S.Ct. 1579, 113 L.Ed.2d 664 [1991]) case in neighboring Mississippi. *The United States v. Fordice* (SOS U.S. 717 [1992]) decision held that Mississippi had to desegregate its higher education system. Not until the 1994 desegregation agreement with the federal government did Louisiana faithfully promise to enhance the HBCUs and hire more other-race faculty, staff, and students at the TWI and HBCU campuses. The plan also included some curriculum changes including adding master's degrees in physics, urban forestry, and doctorates in public policy and science and mathematics education at the HBCUs. The state plans aimed to make further improvements in HBCU facilities of at least $93 million.

White students enrolled in Louisiana public higher education declined by 4.3 percent between 1993 and 1998. At public two-year colleges, white enrollment fell 58.6 percent to 51 percent, and other-race students increased 13.6 percent for the same period. The black student percentage of Louisiana's two-year college enrollment was 33 percent by 1998. In the restoration of the 1981 consent decree, the community college that Louisiana promised in the agreement became part of

---

[34] SREB, *Louisiana Featured Facts from the SREB Fact Book on Higher Education, 2009* (Atlanta: Southern Regional Education Board, 2009) 2, 4, 10, 11, 14, 15, 19, 20; Louisiana Board of Regents, *Statewide Student Profile System*, "Fall 2001–2002 through Fall 2009–2010 Data" (Baton Rouge: LBR, 2001–2010); and "20-Year Enrollment History—Fall 1980 through Fall 1999–2000," LBR Statewide Student Profile System.

Southern University at Baton Rouge. Black enrollment in the two-year program placed in the Southern University System was 92 percent. Blacks comprised 26.4 percent of students in Louisiana public colleges and universities and 25.7 percent in the public four-year colleges and universities. Blacks averaged 94 percent of students at Louisiana's four-year HBCUs.

In the state of Louisiana's 1994 settlement with the US Department of Justice, Southern at Baton Rouge received master's degree programs in criminal justice, physics, urban forestry, environmental chemistry, professional accounting, public administration, and rehabilitation counseling, Southern University upgraded the department of architectural engineering and the School of Architecture. Additionally, Southern University got a School of Nursing, School of Accountancy, and a School of Public Policy and Urban Affairs. The state added doctoral programs in public policy, science, and mathematics education. A program review in 1999, however, forced Southern to reduce the number of academic programs from 130 to 70. By 2008, Southern University's colleges and schools consisted of agriculture, family and consumer sciences, arts and humanities, business, engineering, sciences, graduate school, school of public policy and public affairs, school of architecture, school of nursing, and Army and Navy ROTC. By 2008, the university achieved accreditation for 83 percent of eligible programs. Since 1990, the university completed fifteen construction projects at a cost of $30 million, a facilities master plan, and another $93 million in construction projects were underway or planned. The Louisiana State Commission of Higher Education monitored the progress at Southern as part of monitoring the desegregation plans.[35]

However, the HBCUs in Louisiana continued to struggle. In particular, Grambling University entered a period of instability due to poor leadership selected at the institution, the actions, or lack thereof, by its governing board. Lack of institutional vision, and personal politics played by blacks, whites, and alumni constrained Grambling. SACS placed the institution on probation, but within a year, Grambling gained reaffirmation of accreditation. Nevertheless, Louisiana's educational outlook was sinking and not rising. Among the state's 4.4 million people, fewer than 20 percent of adults had a bachelor's degree and 0.8 percent had a professional degree. Blacks comprised 32 percent of the population, and the state's poverty rate was 16.5 percent—twice that percentage

---

[35] John B. Williams, *Race Discrimination in Public Higher Education: Interpreting Federal Civil Rights Enforcement* (Westport CT: Praeger, 1997) 133–34; Southern University at Baton Rouge, "University Accrediting Agency," http://www.subr.edu, 1; *The Chronicle of Higher Education* 65/1, Almanac Issue 2008–2009 (29 August 2008): 76–77.

was poor in New Orleans districts. By 2020, Louisiana's projected high school graduates were expected to *decline* by seven thousand persons.[36]

Next door to Louisiana, Alabama also had a consistent, lengthy and malevolent history of denying its black citizens equal justice, economic opportunity, and access to quality public education. Since that southeast American territory had been admitted into the Union on 14 December 1819, slaves and free Negroes endured brutal treatment. The expansion of cotton agriculture and the extension of slavery went hand-in-hand between 1820 and 1860, when settlers moved westward from Georgia and South Carolina into Alabama to do subsistence farming, harvest timber, mine and manufacture iron, and grow cotton. The number of slaves in 1820 numbered from 10 percent in some areas to 50 percent or more in the state's cotton belt. President Andrew Jackson, a Tennessee slaveholder who also owned plantation lands in Alabama, ignored the US Constitution and refused to enforce a US Supreme Court decision in favor of the native people who occupied much of the Alabama land. In 1830, President Jackson signed the Indian Removal Bill that allowed the removal of the Creek Indians from Alabama lands so the expansion of white settlers and slavery could continue. By 1850, more than fifty thousand South Carolina natives had moved into Alabama, and slaves comprised 45 percent of Alabamians. Political power, socioeconomic influence, land, and slaves concentrated in the minority slaveholding class, the slavocracy, who did everything possible to realize more wealth and keep the Negroes enslaved: "Then, there was the hope on the part of most of the non-slaveholders that they would some day become owners of slaves; and consequently, they, too, took on the habits and patterns of [racial] thought of the slaveholders."[37]

---

[36] *Normal Observer*, 20 September 1990; Franklin, "Education for Life: Adult Education Programs for African Americans in Northern Cities," in Harvey G. Neufeldt and Leo McGee, eds., *Education of African American Adult: An Historical Overview* (Westport CT: Greenwood Press, 1990) 113–34; Blake Clark, "Common Sense College," Grambling College for Teachers, *Survey Graphic* (April 1948), reprinted in *Reader's Digest* (January 1950): 131–133; M. B. Gallott, *A History of Grambling State University* (New York: University Press of America, 1985) 1–20; USDOE, National Center for Education Statistics (NCES) tables, i.e., "Fall enrollment in degree-granting institutions, by race/ethnicity of student and state of jurisdiction, 2000" (Washington, DC: NCES, 2000) table 213.

[37] Franklin and Moss Jr., *From Slavery to Freedom*, 113, 237; Carol Berkin, Christopher L. Miller, Robert W. Cherny, and James L. Gormly, *Making America: A History of the United States* (Boston: Houghton Mifflin, 1995) 226, 261–62, 288, 396, 532, 685–86, 907.

Indeed, when the slavocracy and southern nationalists started the Civil War in 1861, the yeoman farmers—poor, landless whites—also fought, bled, and died to keep the Negro enslaved. Thousands of Negro men from Alabama left the farms to serve in the Union Army that won the Civil War. During Reconstruction, several Negroes served in state government, and James T. Rapier, a Negro, represented Alabama in Congress.[38] Between 1868 and 1874, however, the white Democrats committed violence at every major election, murdered white and Negro Republicans, and redeemed the government. Of the 181,471 Negro men eligible to vote, only three thousand were registered to vote in Alabama in 1900. Of 8.84 million American Negroes, 84 percent lived in the southern states.[39]

Like elsewhere in the America's Jim Crow South, white Alabamians of all classes used lynching, murder, intimidation, fear, open racial discrimination, and naked power to deal with Negro civil rights activists and to retain white supremacy. By the early twentieth century, some of Alabama's Negro schools looked worst than animal stables. In Wilcox County, in 1912, Negro children outnumbered white school age children, but the county spent more money on schools for the whites than for the black schools. The state provided $2.5 million for white teachers but only $372,177 (13 percent) for Negro teachers. Many of the Alabama counties, almost all of them 25–30 percent black, had no public schools for Negroes. The educational conditions were so terrible in Alabama that Julius Rosenwald of Chicago gave $25,000 to Booker T. Washington at Tuskegee in order to begin building "Rosenwald schools" in Alabama, beginning in 1912.[40]

Negroes in Alabama, except those receiving help from northern philanthropists and churches, had to rely on creation of their own high schools and colleges. Black Alabamians had seventy-two private schools and two public schools in 1915. The Tuscumbia Colored High School included three years of curriculum. Snow Hill Institute became one of the Tuskegee-like schools founded by former Tuskegee graduates such as William J. Edwards. Snow Hill began in deeply impoverished Wilcox County in 1893 in a log cabin, had 293 students and a budget of $12,883 in 1915, became a public school in 1936, and closed in 1973 because of desegregation. Black leaders such as Carrie A. Tuggle of Birmingham,

---

[38] Loren Schweninger, *James. T. Rapier and Reconstruction* (Chicago: University of Chicago Press, 1978) 1–23.

[39] Franklin and Moss Jr., *From Slavery to Freedom*, 6th ed., 237; John M. Faragher, Mari J. Buhle, Daniel Czitrom, and Susan H. Armtage, *Out of Many: A History of the American People*, 2nd ed. (Upper Saddle River NJ: Prentice Hall, 1997, 1994) 318–19, 334.

[40] Prather, *Resurgent Politics and Educational Progressivism in the New South*, 263; Cynthia Griggs Fleming, *In the Shadow of Selma: Struggle for Civil Rights in the Rural South* (Lanham MD: Rowman and Littlefield, 2004) 43–45, 240–41.

assisted by Negro fraternal groups and churches, organized and financed private high schools. Tuggle Institute was "A loosely organized elementary school with a few secondary students" maintained by women of the Court of Calanthe and Daughters of the Rising Sun, with 146 students, including boarders, and six Negro teachers in 1914.[41] Ten HBCUs that began in Alabama survived into the twenty-first century. The private HBCUs that survived include Barber Memorial Seminary (1896–); Selma University (1878–); Payne University (1888–); Tuskegee University (1881–); Oakwood College (1896–); Talladega College (1865–); Miles Memorial College (1905–); and Stillman College (1876–).[42]

Alabama supported two public HBCUs: Alabama A&M State University and Alabama State University. The latter school began in 1867 as Lincoln Normal School at Marion, and by 1868 gained support from the American Missionary Association. The state assumed Lincoln Normal in 1873 for Negroes. The state authorized Alabama Colored People's University in 1887, and the institution moved to a black church in Montgomery. Whites opposed it, the state court declared the 1887 act unconstitutional, and the school lingered until 1889. In that year, the state clarified its support and sanctioned a new campus for the "Normal School for Colored Students." In 1914, the school had 714 elementary and secondary students, two white and twenty-nine black teachers. Women comprised twenty-three of the teachers. Slater Fund helped support the school, which had a four-year program and a normal department by 1928, when it became State Teachers College. It conferred the bachelor's degree in 1931, gained "B" approval from SACS in 1935, the "A" rating in 1943, became Alabama State College in 1948, and gained university status in 1969.

Alabama officials continued to oppress the Negro citizens after *Brown v. Board of Education*. Alabama lost the Montgomery bus boycott battle in 1955–1956. In 1960, the officials kept sit-in demonstrations and the NAACP out of the state and forced public HBCUs to expel student civil rights activists. In 1961, the governor allowed the brutalization of the freedom riders, while a succeeding governor stood in the doorways of schools and colleges, blocking federal court orders to admit Negro students. By 1963, terrorists blew up three little black girls in their Sunday school; so many bombs ripped across Birmingham, it was dubbed "Bombingham."

---

[41] US Bureau of Education, *A Study of Private and Higher Education for Colored People in the United States*, Bulletin No. 38 (Washington DC: General Printing Office, 1917) 95; Alabama Women's Hall of Fame "Carrie A. Tuggle (1858–1924)," http://www.awhf.org/tuggle.html.

[42] Leland S. Cozart, *A Venture of Faith: Barber-Scotia College, 1867–1967* (Charlotte NC: Heritage Printers, 1976) 1–20.

Prior to the Voting Rights Act of 1965, Alabama reached a low point in democracy: fewer than 20 percent of all eligible Alabamians participated in elections. Alabama used poll taxes, the "grandfather clause," literacy test, lynching, murder, mob violence, and a racist criminal justice system to continue to disenfranchise Negro citizens. When *Adams v. Richardson* ordered the US Department of Education and the Office of Civil Rights to enforce Title VI of the 1964 Civil Rights Act, white Alabama officials continued, with a high sense of confidence and neo-Confederate arrogance to deny black citizens equal access to quality higher education. Most white voters seemed to support the state officials' stance against desegregation and no advancement for black citizens.

It comes as no surprise, then, that Alabama was one of the toughest cases for desegregation of higher education in the 1970s and 1980s. The US Office of Civil Rights (OCR) wrote to the governor of Alabama on 7 January 1981 to submit a statewide desegregation within 60 days. He called a meeting of all public college presidents on 19 January 1981 but the meeting degenerated into ways to pick apart the OCR report. The whites at the meeting ignored the presence of the black higher education officials when openly discussing ways in which to declare unconstitutional the federal government's demand that Alabama desegregate its higher education system. Alabama officials formed a committee and tried to develop a statewide desegregation plan to appease OCR and white Alabamians. One proposal suggested merging University of Alabama-Huntsville with Alabama A&M. The HBCU opted out of this plan by arguing its unique 1890 land-grant status would be incompatible with the TWI. By December 1981, the committee completed *A Desegregation Plan for Public Higher Education in the State of Alabama* that included limited enhancements for the HBCUs.[43] The Alabama Council on Higher Education rejected Alabama A&M's proposal for a graduate program in food science in December 1981. President R. D. Morrison, who had been accused by students of being against the sit-ins, placed his career on the line and sent a respectful but lengthy letter to the governor saying Alabama's desegregation plan needed more details and specific sources of funding.

The Office of Civil Rights sued Alabama in district federal court on 11 July 1983. A black federal judge presided over the case. Alabama A&M moved to

---

[43] USDOE Office of Civil Rights, *Historically Black Colleges and Universities and Higher Education Desegregation* (Washington, DC: OCR, 1991) 1–4; Edwin H. Litolff III, "Higher Education Desegregation: An Analysis of State Efforts in Systems Formerly Operating Segregated Systems of Higher Education," PhD diss., Louisiana State University, 1–124; Reginald Stuart, "New Trend in College Desegregation Emerges," *New York Times*, 3 September 1981, 1–5.

become a plaintiff in 1983. Alabama petitioned the US Eleventh Circuit Court of Appeals to have the black judge removed from the case, but the move failed. The judge ruled against the state's plan and ordered a new plan be sent to his court by 14 February 1986, requiring comment by the parties fifteen days thereafter. Upon appeal by the state, a three-judge panel in the Court of Appeals suggested settlement between the parties and declared that the district judge had a conflict of interest. When Alabama officials refused settlement, the appeals court assigned the case to the chief judge of the federal district of northern Alabama. He scheduled the trial to begin 29 October 1990.

A settlement cut Alabama's original plan from a $74.6 million commitment for desegregation of higher education to $10 million over ten years. The state could divert no money from the HBCUs. Alabama A&M had first choice for new programs in Huntsville. Auburn University—the TWI—got all the cooperative extension funds. Alabama A&M, with fewer than five thousand students, was 77 percent black compared to just 4 percent black students at flagship Auburn University. Alabama A&M had schools of agriculture, environmental science and home economics, arts and sciences, business, education, school of technology, and graduate studies.

In *Knight v. Alabama* (1991),[44] the court ordered Alabama State, which was 97 percent blacks, to increase white enrollment. Alabama State included colleges of business administration, education, health sciences, arts and sciences, University College, graduate studies, school of music, AFROTC, and a doctoral program in educational leadership, policy and law. So far, blacks have received only 4 percent of the doctorate degrees awarded by all Alabama institutions.

President Morrison resigned. The governor appointed Alan Keys, without consulting Alabama A&M's faculty or staff. Keys, a notable black conservative Republican with a PhD from Harvard, seemed to be a rhetorician who fine-tuned his political arts through conservative radio, television, and print media. Keys had no in-depth experience as a college administrator. He promptly began removing the current leadership and appointing new but inexperienced administrators from within the institution. While the campus constituents divided against each other, Keys, during his one-year tenure (1991–1992), was busy engaging politics near DC.[45]

Alabama, with a 26 percent black population among 4.5 million, seemed confident it was moving toward parity for blacks in higher education. In fall

---

[44] *John F. Knight Jr. and Alease S. Sims et al. v. the State of Alabama et al.*, Civil Action no. CV83-M-1676, US District Court, Northern District of Alabama, Birmingham.

[45] Richard D. Morrison, *History of Alabama A&M University* (Huntsville: Alabama A&M University, 1993) 1–31.

2003, 24.6 percent of students in four-year public institutions were black and they comprised 26 percent of students in public two-year colleges. Blacks comprised the majority of students in several of the Alabama technical and community colleges: Bishop State Community College (59.9 percent), Drake State Technical College (79.5 percent), Ingram State Technical College (63.7 percent), Lawson State Community College (96.8 percent), Patterson State Technical College (55.5 percent), Reed State Technical College (58.3 percent), and Trenholm State Technical College (75.7 percent). Blacks comprised majorities at Alabama State University (91.2 percent), Alabama A&M University (87 percent), Concordia College (66 percent), Miles College (98.3 percent), Oakwood College (88.2 percent), Stillman College (97.6 percent), and Talladega College (96.4 percent). Alabama A&M and Alabama State had 33.7 percent of black students attending four-year public colleges in Alabama. By 2007, college enrollment trends looked promising, but alarming gaps remain.[46]

By fall 2006, Alabama State's enrollment grew from 91.2 percent to 95 percent black. From 1993 to 2003, black enrollment at Alabama's TWIs ranged from 7.7 percent at the land-grant Auburn University to 12.8 percent at the University of Alabama. Black enrollment was 16.2 percent at the University of South Alabama, 33.4 percent at Auburn University-Montgomery, 40.6 percent at University of West Alabama, and 41.3 percent at Faulkner University. In 2005, Alabama State and Alabama A&M jointly asked a federal judge to continue the twenty-four-year-old desegregation case. Lawyers for these two universities filed objections to the scheduled termination of judicial orders that provided money for new programs, facilities, and scholarships at the HBCU. They objected to limitations placed on HBCU academic programming. The twenty-five-year-old desegregation case ended in December 2006, when US District Judge Harold Murphy approved the agreements, which had provided $210 million in state funds to Alabama A&M and Alabama State University.[47] Alabama State Representative John Knight, a key plaintiff in the case, said he was pleased.[48]

---

[46] SREB, *Alabama Featured Facts from the SREB Fact Book on Higher Education, 2007* (Atlanta: Southern Regional Education Board, 2007) 4, 10, 11–38; UAS Minority Participation Task Force, *The University of Alabama System 2007 Minority Participation Report*, 14 September 2007 (Tuscaloosa: University of Alabama, 2007) 3, 124–25.

[47] Alabama Commission on Higher Education, *Statistical Abstracts*, 2001–2002 through 2010–2011 (Montgomery: ACHE, 2001–2010), http://www.ache.alabama.gov; Alabama Commision on Higher Education, "Headcount Enrollment, All Alabama Higher Education Institutions, Fall 1989–1999," *Statistical Abstract: Higher Education in Alabama, 1999–2000* (Montgomery: ACHE, June 2000) 1.

[48] Associated Press, "25-year-old Alabama College Desegregation Case Ends," 12 December 2006, Montgomery.

Georgia, like its next-door neighbor, Alabama, was not receptive to civil rights for non-whites. In 1733, English philanthropists established Georgia, the last of the original Thirteen Colonies. They received land from the English Crown to house, work, and rehabilitate English convicts transported from England. They barred slaves and English women (including prostitutes) from the Georgia experiment for nearly a generation. The introduction of African slaves came around 1760. President Jackson and Congress approved the Indian Removal Act (1830) and forced the Cherokee Indian Nation on the Trail of Tears out of Georgia and into Oklahoma. White settlers took over the Indian's lands and expanded cultivation of rice, cotton, and plantations. Negroes soon comprised a third of the population, and made up 44 percent of the people in Georgia by 1860. Blacks outnumbered whites in the low country near Savannah.

In 1865, after the end of slavery, some members of the US Colored Troops (USCT) settled in the Savannah area. William and Ellen Craft established freedmen schools, and other blacks formed the Georgia Colored Equal Rights and Education Association, held conventions, and pushed for public education and land. The Union Army settled forty thousand freedmen on forty-acre plots. However, in late 1865, the landowners and former Confederates returned, militarily defeated, angry, broke, and persistently hateful of the blacks. President Andrew Johnson restored their rights and gave all the land to the whites. Many landholders worked the blacks against their will, ignored labor contracts required by the federal Freedmen's Bureau, and seldom gave Negroes due process of law as required by the 14th Amendment. Georgia's black elite failed to dominate Negro society, or acquire much out of Reconstruction, while Georgia whites easily imposed a rigid Jim Crow system. In 1897, white school officials in Augusta closed the Negro Ware High School, and transferred its budget to the Negro primary school.[49]

In 1910, Negroes still comprised 40 percent of Georgia's population and resided mostly in rural areas. Some 36.5 percent of Negroes suffered illiteracy. Georgia spent an average of $9.58 on white students and $1.76 on Negro pupils in the last decade. There were dozens of private schools for Negroes, but only one black public school—the Georgia State Industrial College at Savannah. Forty-nine private schools, including seven Catholic parish schools, eleven Episcopalian, thirteen Seventh Day Adventist, two CME, and fifteen independent institutions served black Georgians by 1913. By 1915, fewer than

[49] Hine, Hine, and Harrold, *The African-American Odyssey*, 2:334–36.

two hundred black Georgians studied on the college level. Some 149 of them studied in private HBCUs in Atlanta.[50]

Georgia's state capital became the center of Negro higher education. The Freedmen's Aid Society of the Methodist Episcopal Church (MEC) began Clark University in 1870. By 1914, Clark had 304 students, including thirty-two college students, and enrolled students from forty-nine other states. Bishop W. P. Thirkield organized Gammon Theological Seminary in 1882 under the Stewart Missionary Foundation and the MEC to interest black churches in African missionary work, and the American Baptist Home Society (ABHMS) began the Baptist College in 1867, in Augusta, moving it to Atlanta in 1869. Its name was changed in 1913 to honor Henry L. Morehouse, head of the ABHMS. Morehouse College had 277 students in 1914, including eleven college students, and nineteen teachers, including fourteen males and seventeen blacks. Morris Brown College began in the basement of Bethel AME Church in 1885. The AMEC again chartered the school in 1906, but the institution struggled under an unwieldy board of trustees, elected annually by the AME Conference. Each trustee had to give a certain amount of money each year. By 1914, Morris Brown had 508 students, half from Atlanta, including ten enrolled in college courses, fifty-eight from other states, 186 boarders and twenty-nine, mostly male, teachers. Spelman Seminary for Negro girls began in 1881 under the ABHMS to train teachers. Spelman had a hospital to train nurses and received support from the GEB, the Slater Fund, and Woman's auxiliary of the ABHMS. Spelman had 595 students by 1914, eleven in college courses, and 385 boarders, eighty-three from other states.[51]

Paine College enrolled fourteen students in college-level classes. Paine College began under the Colored Methodist Episcopal Church in 1882 in Augusta, issued the bachelor's degree as early as 1885, and by 1914, the school had 202 students, including fourteen in college courses, and the rest enrolled in elementary, secondary, theology, and industrial programs. Negro teacher Charlotte Hawkins Brown (1883–1961) founded Palmer Memorial Institute around 1901 in Augusta. In 1915, with the help of Boston philanthropist Galen L. Stone, she turned Palmer into a junior college and served as president until 1952.

---

[50] Henry A. Bullock, *A History of Negro Education in the South, from 1619 to the Present* (New York: Praeger, 1970) 1–30; US Office of Education, *National Survey of the Higher Education of Negroes* (Washington, DC: GPO, 1942) 1–20; Office of the Interior , Bureau of Education, *Negro Education: A Study of the Private and Higher Schools for Colored People in the United States* (New York: Negro Universities Press, 1969) 1–50.

[51] Thomas Jessie Jones, Bureau of Education, *Negro Education: A Study of the Private and Higher Schools for Colored People in the United States* (New York: Arno Press, 1969) 1–50.

Small schools like Palmer Institute and Baptist Central College in Macon closed after desegregation.[52]

Georgia supported three public HBCUs: Savannah State University (1890–), land grant Fort Valley State University (1895–), and Albany State University (1903–). Albany began as the Training Institution for industrial education in southwest Georgia. It became a college in 1932 and a university in 1966. Atlanta University remained the top graduate-level HBCU in Georgia.

The exclusion of black Georgians in the real participation of quality public higher education persisted by the time of *Adams v. Richardson* (1970, 1972). Georgia's all-white congressional delegation, which enjoyed electoral support from the same kind of voters as in adjacent Alabama, joined with others to approve the "Declaration of Constitutional Principles" (called the "Southern Manifesto") that denounced the Supreme Court's *Brown* school desegregation decision. Only by 1961 did Georgia's race system suffer some cracks, and soon thereafter, the Civil Rights Act of 1964 forced public and private institutions to end racial exclusion.

On 11 June 1973 an insufficient desegregation plan for the Georgia university system arrived at the Office of Civil Rights. In July, Georgia submitted a revised plan that included Fort Valley State College. On 20 May 1974, the Board of Regents of Georgia completed a revised plan that answered all of HEW's suggested actions. A federal district court in DC ruled that the Georgia plan was not adequate to comply with Title VI of the Civil Rights Act of 1964. Georgia's revised plan of 26 August to satisfy the OCR request for effective plans. Thus, Georgia had to submit revised plans for 1983, inclusive of the OCR 1979 guidelines.[53]

In the 1970s, blacks made up about 28 percent of Georgians. After the Great Migration to the North slowed from 1960 to 1970, the southern black population began to grow. The US Bureau of the Census projected blacks as making up 30.2

---

[52] For profiles of early Georgia freedmen's schools, see US Bureau of Education, *A Study of Private and Higher Education for Colored People in the United States*, Bulletin No. 38 (Washington DC: General Printing Office, 1917) 221. Jeffrey Robert Young, "Slavery in Antebellum Georgia," *New Georgia Encyclopedia*, http://www.georgiaencyclopedia.org/nge/Article.jsp?id=h-1019&hl=y (20 October 2003).

[53] Juan A. McGruder, "The Impact of Institutional Collaboration on Mission, Character, and Financial Stability: The Case of the Atlanta University Center" (PhD dissertation, Vanderbilt University, 1999) 1–21; Donnie D. Bellamy, "Whites Sue for Desegregation in Georgia: The Fort Valley State College Case," *Journal of Negro History* 64/4 (Autumn 1979): 316–41.

to 34 percent of Georgians.[54] Black college enrollment grew in Georgia and across southern states, and by 2002, Southern Regional Education Board (SREB) reports showed that 41 percent of whites and 31 percent of blacks attended college in Georgia. Georgia State University and Georgia Institute of Technology in Atlanta, respectively, had 28.0 percent and 7.4 percent black students for a total combined 8,880 black students in 2004. Black students at Georgia State University had increased by 5 percent since 1995. Blacks had declined 1.6 percent at Georgia Institute of Technology. They increased by three points at Medical College of Georgia to 226 students (10.8 percent of total students) by 2004. Including public HBCUs, the Georgia state four-year college and university system enrolled 58,757 black students (23.4 percent). Black students comprised 16,619 (30.7 percent) in the two-year institutions by 2004. At the four major universities, blacks comprised 13.8 percent of students. They comprised 28.9 percent of students at regional universities, including at the three HBCUs; 21.6 percent at two small, state city colleges; 30.7 percent at two-year state colleges; and 23.4 percent for the system. The University of Georgia's major athletic teams appeared to be heavily, if not predominantly, black, but the flagship campus enrolled few other black students. In 2001, only 294 black students were fourth year or beyond at the University of Georgia. Blacks declined 1.6 points there to 1,854 students or 5.6 percent in 2004. Georgia changed rules, regulations, admission policies, and lottery scholarship guidelines that kept University of Georgia overwhelmingly white.[55]

Students could not access high-demand, modern, degree graduate programs at public HBCUs. Private HBCUs had more students than Georgia's public HBCUs combined. The Atlanta University Center had more to offer in undergraduate, graduate, and professional degree programs, and had more regional, national, and international appeal. Some 89 to 98 percent of the students at the state's three public HBCUs were Georgia residents. The three public HBCUs had lower percentages of HOPE lottery scholarship students than other Georgia institutions. Savannah State had 2,900 black students (90.3 percent) by 1995, but declined to 2,648 black students (94.6 percent) by 2004, and remained 95 percent black by fall 2006. In the same city, TWI Armstrong Atlantic

---

[54] US Census Bureau, *People Quick Facts: Georgia* (Washington, DC: Census Bureau, 2000) 1.

[55] J. P. Reidy, "Aaron A. Bradley: Voice of Black Labor in Georgia Low Country," and J. M. Russell and J. Thornberry, "William Finch of Atlanta: The Black Politician as Civil Leader," in H. N. Rabinowitz, ed., *Southern Black Leaders of the Reconstruction Era* (Urbana: University of Illinois Press, 1982) 281–308, 309–34; Bellamy, "Whites Sue for Desegregation in Georgia," 316–41; Manis, *Macon Black and White*, 49, 51, 187.

State University had 1,540 black students (22 percent—a 3 percent increase over 1995) in 2004. Armstrong State received much more state funding because ASU generated 60 percent more credit hours than Savannah State. While Armstrong State had more than seven thousand students, Savannah State had 47 percent fewer students (90.1 percent black) and offered just over a dozen programs in social sciences, education, nursing and business. Fort Valley enrolled fewer than three thousand students, a decline of total students since 1995, including a loss of non-black (white) students.[56]

Delaware, another original member of the Thirteen Colonies, was nearly 25 percent slaves, and maintained slavery until ratification of the 13th Amendment (1865). Delaware then maintained a Jim Crow system. In January 1948, in fear of NAACP lawsuits, Delaware said Negroes could pursue courses of study at the TWIs not offered at the HBCU. At the same time, Delaware became a part of the Southern Regional Education Board (SREB) to protect Jim Crow.[57]

According to *Adams v. Richardson* (480 F2d 1159 156 US App. DC 267 [1973]) and the OCR guidelines (1979), Delaware's higher education desegregation plans only marginally improved education opportunities for black citizens. Flagship University of Delaware had 5.7 percent black students enrolled. The community college and Wesley College had 20.3 and 22.5 percent black students. Delaware State had a 30 percent graduation rate between 1996 and 2002; Wesley College, 38 percent rate; University of Delaware, 70 percent—all increases since 1995. Blacks comprised 19.2 percent of Delaware's 783,600 people in 2000. Some 26.7 percent of white adults and 14.4 percent of black adults had at least bachelor's degrees, compared to 14.2 percent of all black adults in the US. Delaware intended to enhance the HBCU, Delaware State University, but DSU enrollment declined from 3,381 students in 1994 to 3,178, which represented 6.52 percent of Delaware's total 49,354 students in degree, diploma, and certificate programs in 2003. A new president came aboard in 2003 to turn things around. DSU had 16.2 percent white enrollment and 4.3 percent Hispanics, Asians, and others, a 400-acre main campus in Dover, and offered sixty-six undergraduate degrees, sixteen

---

[56] The University System of Georgia, *Strategic Plan: Transforming the System, Changing Lives, Strengthening the State* (Atlanta: USG, September 2007) 1–20; The USG, *University System of Georgia Headcount Enrollment, Fall 1995–2004* (Atlanta: USG, 2004) 1–15; USG, *University System of Georgia African-American Enrollment, Fall 1995–2004* (Atlanta: USG, 2004) 12–13.

[57] William H. Williams, *Slavery and Freedom in Delaware, 1639–1865* (Wilmington DE: SR Books, 1996) xiv; SREB, *Delaware Featured Facts from the SREB Fact Book on Higher Education 2009* (Atlanta: SREB, 2009) 1–10; Delaware Department of Education, Higher Education, *Measuring Up 2008: The State Report Card on Higher Education*, 1–10.

graduate degrees, the EdD, and, by 2005, a PhD degree in mathematical physics and applied mathematics. The students originated from twenty-eight states and thirty-one countries; eighty-three of 168 faculty members held doctorates. DSU had seventeen formal international partnerships by 2005. This institution had 10 percent white students by 2010, and some of them threatened to sue DSU when the administration planned to cut men's tennis and women's equestrian sports that had mostly white team members.[58]

The Border State of Kentucky remained in the Union and exempted from the Emancipation Proclamation, even though some 225,000 slaves lived there. As in Delaware, Missouri, and West Virginia, Kentucky maintained slavery until ratification of the 13th Amendment in 1865.

Kentucky State Normal School for Colored Persons celebrated dedication on 22 October 1887. It had 152 students by 1900, eight hundred students by 1917, and changed its name to Kentucky State Industrial College for Colored Persons in 1926 and to Kentucky State College for Negroes in 1938. The institution received NCATE accreditation in 1956 and SACS accreditation in 1958. Citing *Adams v. Richardson*, Kentucky officials claimed that as early as 1968 they had attempted to strengthen Kentucky State University by giving the HBCU extra funding. Kentucky State did build several facilities between 1964 and 1969, when the enrollment reached 1,600 students. The institution became Kentucky State University in 1972, and graduated the first master's degree students in 1974. The state claimed it spent $20.3 million to renovate buildings and build one new facility in 1976–1977, while developing a new mission for the state's only public HBCU. That mission, however, was a focus on liberal studies, interdisciplinary, and multicultural education—fields not in great demand for many of today's students.

A letter dated 15 January 1981 from the US Office of Civil Rights, USDOE, designated Kentucky one of ten states still operating a racially segregated system of higher education in violation of Title VI of the Civil Rights Act of 1964. The complaint focused on Kentucky State University in Frankfort. The public TWIs had no meaningful affirmative plans to hire black professionals and recruit black students. Kentucky developed a new plan in January 1982, and OCR formally accepted the comprehensive five-year plan, *Enhancement of Kentucky's Historically Black University* read: "The Commonwealth will strengthen Kentucky State University by giving the university a state appropriation amounting to a minimum number of dollars for special enhancements including new academic

---

[58] "Delaware State," *Journal of Blacks in Higher Education* 67/1 (4 February 2010): 1–2.

programs in transportation management and microcomputers by 1984–1985."[59] Kentucky State was to receive more faculty, revisions of curriculum, improvement of library and research facilities, improved or additional equipment, a graduate center, enhancement of land-grant activities, and development of cooperative programs with other state institutions/agencies. "The Governor will direct state agencies to look to the State Governmental Services Center at Kentucky State to provide personnel training and certification programs, applied research assistance, program evaluations and technical assistance."[60]

After expiration of that plan in 1987, state officials developed *The Kentucky Plan for Equal Opportunities in Higher Education, 1990–1995*, and extended it for one year to allow time to develop *Partnership Agreement: the Commonwealth of Kentucky and the US Department of Education, Office of Civil Rights*.[61] OCR officials made separate visits to Kentucky's TWIs in spring of 1999 and identified several areas that needed addressing to ensure access and equity for African-American students and the enhancement of Kentucky State University. As part of the Partnership process, Kentucky and OCR examined the status of blacks regarding access, enrollment, retention, and graduation at the state's eight four-year universities, fourteen community colleges, and fifteen technical colleges. Kentucky was committed, through the state's Council on Postsecondary Education, to keep OCR informed of any proposed major changes in the mission of any institution of higher education, although OCR allowed revisions "consistent with sound educational practices."[62] The agreement acknowledged "*Fordice* ... allowed such changes, and the court urged an examination of a wide range of factors to determine whether [a] state has perpetuated...*de jure* segregation in any facet of its institutional system."[63]

Kentucky State University suffered much instability between 1982 and 2004; the school had at least eight presidents and interims. By 2004, KSU had 65 percent non-blacks among 130 full-time faculty members. Whites comprised most of the student enrollment of 2,335. Some 17.1 percent of Kentuckians had a bachelor's degree or higher. Enrollment grew from 2,254 in 2000 to 2,834 in 2009. KSU's 1890 land-grant program addressed agricultural, educational, economic,

---

[59] USDOE, Office of Civil Rights, *Partnership Agreement: The Commonwealth of Kentucky and the US Department of Education, Office of Civil Rights* (Washington, DC: OCR, 1999) 2, 1–18.

[60] Ibid., 3–5, 8.

[61] Ibid., 2–3, 7, 11.

[62] Ibid., 11–13.

[63] Ibid., 11–14.

and social problems of the people of Kentucky, especially limited [disadvantaged] persons and families. KSU gained a graduate program in aquaculture, in cooperation with the University of Kentucky. Kentucky State University had 196 total graduate students in 2009. The December 2007 KSU website said, "...It is unusual for such an institution to serve a state that persistently lost its black population. It is also unusual for what [an HBCU] to thrive and prosper despite repeated efforts to close it." In 2000, blacks comprised 7.3 percent of Kentucky's 4,041,769 people.[64]

Maryland, as in next-door Virginia, introduced many African slaves to help grow the cash crop of tobacco, but white indentured servants outnumbered black slaves in the beginning. The bondage of whites faded through the eighteenth and the early nineteenth centuries. President Lincoln exempted Maryland, another of the original Thirteen Colonies and a Border State, from the Emancipation Proclamation; however, he persuaded Maryland to abolish slavery in late 1864. Maryland maintained a rigid racial system that denied black citizens equal access to public institutions. In 1935, Donald Murray, through a NAACP lawsuit, gained admission to the law school at the University of Maryland. The state moved toward greater inclusion of Negroes in the higher education system. However, blacks constituted about 25 percent of the state's population, and socioeconomic disparity by race—partly based on difficulties blacks encountered in accessing equal quality education—was a fact in Maryland. When the sit-in demonstrations broke out in the Deep and Upper South in 1960–1961, they occurred in Baltimore, too, often involving students at the HBCUs.[65] Thus, when *Adams v. Richardson* (1970, 1972) requested higher education plans from the Jim Crow states, Maryland had an obligation under federal law to do more to remedy past discrimination and remove vestiges of the Jim Crow system of higher education.

Maryland was one of the ten states notified by OCR that it was in violation of Title VI of the Civil Rights Act (1964). The Maryland plan for desegregation was rejected in 1970. The plan was revised and implemented, but OCR rejected it

---

[64] Clair Drake, "The Black University in the American Social Order," *Daedalus* 100/3 (Summer 1971): 833–97; Kentucky Council on Postsecondary Education, *Total Headcount Enrollment by Level, Public Institutions, 2000–2009* (Frankfort KY: Council on Postsecondary Education Comprehensive Database, 16 September 2010) 1; KCPE, *Diversity and Demographics, 1995–2008* (Frankfort KY: Council on Postsecondary Education, 2010); "Enrollment by Level, Institution, and Race over Time," and "Six-year Graduation Rates at Four-year Public Institutions by Race, Gender, and Residency, Entering Class, 2002, 2001, 2000, 1999."

[65] Franklin and Moss Jr., *From Slavery to Freedom*, 6th ed., 364–65.

in 1973. OCR and Maryland agreed to a 1974 plan, but OCR began enforcement proceedings in 1975 because Maryland was not implementing the plan rapidly enough. Maryland sued and received an injunction against OCR proceedings. After the initial five-year OCR plans, 1972–1989, Maryland entered a partnership agreement with the USDOE to advance equal educational opportunity in the state regardless of race. The Maryland Higher Education Commission continued working to address the legacy and effects of decades of "separate but unequal" higher education. The *2004 Maryland State Plan for Postsecondary Education* partly read,

> The State's commitment to its agreement to the US Department of Education Office for Civil Rights remains a priority. The State must continue its efforts to ensure that the Historically Black Institutions are comparable to and competitive with the traditionally white institutions with respect to all operations and programmatic characteristics. In addition to enhancing Historically Black Institutions, they must pay attention to reducing the achievement gap between African American students and white students, as well as recruiting more African American students into advanced degree programs. Every effort must be made to ensure that [black] students have an equal chance of success.[66]

Maryland and OCR, on 6 December 2000, agreed to a "Five-year Report and Partnership." Maryland intended to evaluate its progress through an ongoing basis, and adjust policies, practices, and programs as needed to enhance and strengthen diversity and other goals. African Americans, Asian Americans, Hispanics, and Native Americans represented 35 percent of all students and 38 percent of undergraduates at Maryland colleges and universities in 2003. Blacks alone comprised 26 percent of students in Maryland's campuses. One of the objectives of the agreement with OCR was to make the HBCU campuses comparable to other institutions with respect to the physical characteristics of landscape, ambiance, and appearance, as well as to the availability, quality, and adequacy of facilities necessary to support the missions and programs of the institutions. The state spent $30 million in operating funds for HBCU enhancement between fiscal years 2002 and 2004, including funding the Access and Success grant program, funds for enhancing management functions, to service debt service, assist Coppin State in capital projects, provide state matching funds, and eliminate duplicative academic programs. The state committed to raise the match for the Private Donation Incentive Grant Program for every $1 raised by the HBCUs up to a certain level. FY 2003 budget included

---

[66] Maryland Higher Education Commission, *2004 Maryland State Plan for Postsecondary Education* (Annapolis MD: MHEC, 2004) ii–iv, 24–28.

$112 million for new higher education capital projects, including enhancing the campus infrastructure and the quality of facilities at HBCUs. The total five-year amount of capital funds ($75 million) budgeted for the three public HBCUs was part of $1 billion Maryland planned to spend in higher education. Blacks comprised 28 percent of Maryland's population in the 2000 US Census. The Maryland Task Force to Study College Readiness for Disadvantaged and Capable Students made recommendations about providing minority students adequate opportunities to matriculate and successfully graduate from colleges. Reminded of *Fordice*, the Task Force also made recommendations on state financial aid. The, said, "The State must ... remain committed to enhancing historically black colleges and universities."[67]

Even though black students still had a lower six-year graduation rate than whites, Hispanics, and Asian Americans, they began to make progress. African Americans had a 98 percent positive change in their enrollment in Maryland's independent college and universities from 1994 to 2004. At Maryland institutions in 2004, blacks comprised more than 26 percent of the student body, compared to 21 percent in 1994. At the community colleges, blacks increased from 22.6 percent to 29 percent of total enrollment between 1994 and 2004, compared to a 2 percent drop for all other students. By 2006, enrollment of black students at the HBCUs ranged from a high of 92 percent to a low of 77 percent. Coppin State had the highest percentage of blacks, and Eastern Shore the lowest. Both these public HBCUs feared threat of closure or merger, but only with OCR approval.[68]

In November 2005, Morgan State University protested when the Higher Education Commission granted a joint master's program in business to two TWIs. Boards of higher education in former Jim Crow states routinely allowed white institutions to duplicate degree programs offered at nearby HBCUs, despite the recent desegregation plans. Such duplicity could bleed the HBCU of top undergraduate students as well as of black and white graduate students. The former chair of the US Commission on Civil Rights, Mary Frances Berry said, "This is a clear case of an undermining of desegregation efforts."[69] Some blacks, dismissed Morgan's protest by saying, "Higher Education is becoming increasingly competitive."[70] Raymond Pierce, dean of law at North Carolina Central University said, "The current administration is not upholding civil rights

[67] MHEC, *2004 Maryland State Plan*, 24–28.

[68] "Race and Ethnicity of Students at 1,400 Colleges and Universities," *The Chronicle of Higher Education* (26 September 2008): B30.

[69] Sam Latham, "Morgan State," *The Nashville Pride*, 25 November 2005, 1.

[70] Ibid.

laws."[71] Berry and Pierce agreed blacks must take concerted steps to stop political efforts to constrain HBCU programs and weaken their ability to exist. The Maryland Senate approved a bill intended to protect the state's HBCUs from having their students drawn away by new programs at other colleges that duplicated HBCU degree programs. NAFEO appealed to the Black Congressional Caucus and the new chair of the House Judiciary Committee, asking them to hold hearings on congressional legislation to protect HBCUs from state actions that leave them with inadequate financial support or hinder their ability to compete against TWIs. By 2007, 19,933 students enrolled at the state's four HBCUs—now with graduate and doctoral programs. The HBCUs often had to rely on area public TWIs for collaborative programs in critical disciplines. Blacks comprised 29.4 percent of Maryland's people in 2009.[72]

Virginia, founded in 1607, was the first of the English colonies. Jamestown was the place where the first few African slaves arrived in 1619. In the seventeenth century, white indentured servants outnumbered African slaves in Virginia, however, by 1790, Virginia had the largest number of slaves among the states. Like it's neighbor, Maryland, Virginia used its slaves mostly in cultivating, "worming," and harvesting tobacco. The whites ruled the black workers through the fear—they whipped them in front of the other slaves as an example of what happens when a Negro misses a worm on the tobacco plants. Whether they were slaves, free Negroes, white indentured servants, or free whites, Africans and Europeans together had hewed a nation out of the Virginian wilderness. Nevertheless, over the next two centuries, European Americans sought to exclude the African Americans from exploiting America's riches. Blacks increased from 20 percent to 40 percent of Virginians, but lack of socioeconomic opportunity, lynching, white mob violence, and impoverished conditions sent them elsewhere. Blacks represented 18.8 percent of Virginia's people by 1970.

In 1970, Virginia received $3.97 million in federal land-grant funds, giving $3.783 million to the TWI land grant and $195,563 (4.9 percent) to the HBCU land

[71] Ibid.

[72] J. Joseph Curran Jr. and Robert N. McDonald, memo to MHEC, Calvin W. Burnett, "Civil Rights Discrimination, Race—Higher Education—Standards for Measuring the State's Success in Dismantling the Past System of *De Jure* Segregation in Public Higher Education" (Annapolis MD: State Attorney General, 8 November 2005) 153–83; Peter Schmidt, Josh Keller, and Sara Hebel, "State Digest: Move to Protect Programs at Historically Black Colleges in Maryland," *Chronicle of Higher Education*, 16 March 2007, A1; MHEC, "Trends in the Percentage of African Americans Enrolled at Maryland Campuses, 1995–2005" (Annapolis MD: MHEC Information System, 2010); MHEC, "Academic Program Proposals under Review, 2009–2010" (Annapolis MD: MHEC, 2010) 1.

grant, Virginia State College. Like those in Tennessee, blacks were tired of the arrogant white Jim Crow state officials. Some citizens filed *Norris v. State Council of Higher Education of Virgini*a US (327 F Supp. 1368 [E.D. Va 1971]), which sought to block the plans Virginia had for upgrading the TWI Richard Bland College in Petersburg to four-year status. However, a few miles away the HBCU Virginia State College remained neglected by the state. Virginia State received very little in the way of federal funds for cooperative education that were sent to Virginia. It was not until 1972 that the TWI got $2,743,617, and Virginia State received $600,000. Between 1963 and 1973, only fifty blacks—among 1,800 graduates—received M.D. degrees from Virginia's medical schools. Blacks seeking graduate and professional degrees continued to leave Virginia, as in Jim Crow days.[73]

Virginia responded in 1973 to the US Education Department, Office of Civil Rights (OCR) requests for plans. The state planned to appoint blacks to higher education governing boards, hire black recruiters at the public TWIs, institute equal employment programs in these institutions, and broaden financial aid but state officials simply continued Jim Crow practices. HEW rejected the Virginia plan in November 1973 on grounds of insufficient specificity about the process of further desegregation and warned Virginia against closing or downgrading Virginia State. OCR restrained Virginia from doing anything that would place a greater burden on black citizens than upon the white ones. Virginia had to have a new plan to begin the full desegregation of higher education by 10 February 1974. Virginia's plans gradually included the two public HBCUs: Norfolk State and Virginia State universities.

Norfolk State University (1935–) began as a unit of Virginia Union University. It became the independent Norfolk Polytechnic College in 1942 and a part of Virginia State College in 1944. Norfolk State offered its first bachelor's degree in 1956, became a completely independent state supported institution in 1969, and achieved university status by 1979.

Norfolk State reported to the State Council of Higher Education for Virginia that renovation and maintenance projects were currently funded and underway to provide the capacity to support a target enrollment of eight thousand students. In 1999, Norfolk State had a freshmen cohort six-year graduation rate of 29.2 percent, much lower than Virginia's TWIs, and by 2005, had about seven thousand students (64 percent women, 86 percent blacks, and 27 percent out-of-state), doctoral programs in psychology and social work, and seventeen master's degrees, including engineering.

---

[73] Trimika M. Yates, "The Impact of *Adams v. Richardson* on Select Universities in the Commonwealth of Virginia," PhD diss., University of Virginia, 2004, 30–78.

Virginia State University (1872–) placed greater emphasis on sponsored research, increasing the six-year student retention rate beyond the current 42 percent, implementing new degree programs, and increasing accreditation of its programs from 80 percent to 100 percent. Virginia State University grew into a 236-acre campus, 416-acre agricultural research facility, with fifty buildings on the main campus, $96 million annual budget, forty-five baccalaureate degree programs, and master's degrees in schools of agriculture, business, engineering, science and technology, liberal arts and education, graduate studies, research, and outreach. They approved a doctorate program in education in 2003.[74]

Virginia officials did not make Virginia State equally competitive with the TWIs. Among SREB member states, the number of blacks attending college and earning bachelor's degrees increased in Virginia between 1993 and 2003. Black enrollment in public, two-year institutions increased as in the SREB states. By fall 2006, among 7,986 new black freshmen in Virginia's public institutions, 80 percent were in-state students. By 2007, black enrollment lagged behind foreign students in engineering/sciences in Virginia. The three largest HBCUs remained heavily black by fall 2006: Hampton (88 percent), Norfolk State (86 percent), and VSU (94 percent). In fall 2009, students of color comprised 29 percent of enrollment in Virginia's colleges and universities.[75]

By 1970, 378,000 blacks enrolled in America's HBCUs. By 1977, 1.1 million blacks enrolled in all colleges and universities, representing 9.3 percent of all students.[76]

---

[74] State Council of Higher Education for Virginia, "Fall Enrollment Headcount, 2009," SHEV, Richmond VA, 2010; SCHEV, "Fall Headcount Enrollments, 2006–2007," SHEV, Richmond VA, 2010; VSU, *Virginia State University Magazine* 7/2 (Winter 2008): 1–28.

[75] Smith, ed., *Leadership and Learning*, 80–85, 90–98. See the following reports of the State Council of Higher Education for Virginia: "Enrollment Trends at Virginia's Public Colleges and Universities" (19 March 2003), "A Status Report on Advancing Virginia Through Higher Education: The System wide Strategic Plan for Higher Education in Virginia" (3 October 2006); "Revised Enrollment Demand and Service Projections through 2012" (2008); "Fall Headcount Enrollment by Race/Ethnicity, Gender and Program Detail, Sector Summary Totals for Science, Technology, Engineering and Mathematics" (2006); "Fall Headcount by Domicile/Race-Ethnicity of New Undergraduates-E12NR Non-Resident (2006); "Graduation Rates, 4-year Public Institutions, First-time, Full-time Freshmen Cohorts" (2006); "Admissions: Public Four-Year Institutions Profile" (2005). "Rising to the Challenge" (19 July 2005). See also *Virginia State University 2004–2008 Strategic Plan* (July 2003); Lyman B. Brooks, *Upward: A History of Norfolk State University, 1935–1975* (Washington DC: National Publishing Co., 1973) 1–10; A. H. Grundman, "Northern Baptists and the Founding of Virginia Union University: The Perils of Paternalism," *Journal of Negro History* 63 (1978): 26–41.

[76] Franklin and Moss Jr., *From Slavery to Freedom*, 6th ed., 362–364.

Since the white supremacy state Democrat Party took control of Mississippi in 1890, the state remained at the bottom of almost every cultural, educational, economic, and social statistic among the fifty American states. As previously discussed, Mississippi officials reflected the trend in the southern states, imposing a rigid Jim Crow system and doing as little as possible for blacks.

Black higher education had advanced in Mississippi, depending on outside help, more than upon state support. From 1866 through the 1940s, northern missionaries and the church groups created ten Negro Schools in Mississippi. (1) St. Augustine Seminary at Bay St. Louis was the only training school for Negro Episcopalian priests in the United States by the 1940s. (2) Mary Holmes Seminary started in 1892 under the Board of Missions for Freedom of the Presbyterian Church, USA, and existed as a two-year junior college until it closed with about three hundred students in the summer of 2004 because of bankruptcy after losing SACS accreditation in December 2002. (3) Okolona Industrial School began in 1902 and associated with the Protestant Episcopal Church's American Church Institute for Negroes; Prentiss Normal and Industrial Institute was founded in 1907 as a Christian non-denomination institution. (4) The General Christian Missionary Society founded Southern Christian Institute in 1873, in Edwards. (5) Piney Woods Country Life School began in 1909–1910, and included academic, grammar, high school, and junior college departments within a twenty-acre campus, two-hundred-acre farm, and 1,300 acres of wooded land by 1946. The state supported a department for blind persons, and the GEB in 1943 gave $10,000 for buildings. Piney Woods became a boarding high school for inner city students by 2005. (6) Campbell College in Jackson existed by the 1940s under the African Methodist Episcopal Church. The school offered high school and a four-year college program with four hundred students and ten faculty members. The school did not have state department of education or SACS approval. (7) Natchez College began in 1885 under the Negro Baptist Convention of Mississippi. The institution had a faculty of twelve and a student body of three hundred in high school and college courses by 1946. Natchez College did not have SACS or state approval. (8) Mississippi Industrial College at Holly Springs opened in 1905 under the Colored Methodist Episcopal Church, and gained approval by the state to train teachers and Christian workers. (9) Rust College, formerly "Shaw University" named after the Reverend S. O. Shaw in 1870, began in 1866 under the Freedmen's Aid Society of the Methodist Episcopal Church. The Rev. Richard S. Rust of Cincinnati and the Methodist Episcopal Church chartered the school in 1868. The school became Rust College in 1915. Rust, a liberal arts college offered the bachelor's degree by 1936 with 416 students, continued into the twenty-first century with eventual SACS accreditation, and became the oldest of eleven HBCUs supported by the United Methodists. (10) The American Missionary Association founded Tougaloo College (1869–), which gained a charter from the legislature in 1871, became a teacher training college by 1892, offered liberal arts college courses by 1897, and granted the first bachelor's degree in 1901. Tougaloo gained SACS approval of its high school department in 1931, and "B" approval of the college program in 1932.[77]

Mississippi eventually had three public HBCUs: Jackson State, Alcorn State, and Mississippi Valley. The American Baptist Home Mission Society (ABHMS) established Jackson State College as a seminary for twenty students at Natchez in 1876 before moving to Jackson in 1882 and then to Lynch Street in 1903. The first Negro president took over the institution in 1911 and raised it to college level work by 1927. The GEB issued faculty scholarships, helped furnish buildings, and gave funds for summer institutes to help upgrade the school toward SACS approval. The ABHMS discontinued support, and the state took control in 1934. It adopted the name Mississippi Training School for Negroes. The Rosenwald Fund gave $10,000 a year to upgrade the school, and the R. H. Green Foundation of Mississippi gave $5,000 for equipment. After the state took over in 1940, Jackson State was offering the third year of college by 1943, and the fourth year in 1944, when the alumni petitioned the state to change the name to Jackson State College. By 2006, the institution would be designated Mississippi's "urban university" and listed by Carnegie as "doctoral-research intensive" university. Jackson State created the Jake Ayers Institute for Research in Urban Higher Education, including an executive PhD program.[78]

Despite *Brown*, Mississippi continued *de jure* segregation in its public higher education system, maintaining five white institutions and three black colleges. In 1969, the US Department of HEW requested Mississippi submit a plan for desegregation of higher education. In June 1973, the Board of Trustees of State Institutions of Higher Learning submitted a plan of compliance that aimed to improve educational opportunities for all state citizens, set numerical goals on the enrollment of other-race students at state universities, hire other-race faculty members, and institute remedial programs and special recruitment efforts to

---

[77] Tougaloo College, "Our History," http://www.tougaloo.edu/content/history/index.htm, 2010; Jackson State University, "History," http://www.sums.edu/about; Rust College, "About Rust College," http://www.rustcollege.edu/about_rust.html; Editor, "Historic Mary Holmes College Closes after More than a Century of Service," *Presbyterian Voice* 16/2 (April 2005): 1.

[78] Lelia G. Rhodes, *Jackson State University: The First Hundred Years, 1877–1977* (Jackson: University Press of Mississippi, 1979) 1–20.

achieve the goals. HEW rejected the plan as failing to comply with Title VI of the 1964 Civil Rights Act and the 14th Amendment. The Mississippi legislature refused to fund a new plan; Ole Miss required an ACT entrance score of 15, and the HBCUs required a 13. By 1975, black students comprised 4.1 percent of students at University of Mississippi, but 96.6 percent at HBCUs Jackson State, 99.9 percent at Alcorn State, and 100 percent at Mississippi Valley State.

Jake Ayers, Sr., a parent of a Jackson State University student, filed his case in 1975 claiming Mississippi had, for decades, under-funded its three black public universities. The United States intervened against Mississippi. After twelve years of failed attempts to resolve their differences over a voluntary desegregation plan, the parties went to trial under *Ayers v. Allain* (674 F. Supp. 1523 [1987]). Plaintiffs, including the federal government, argued that Mississippi's higher education system was in violation of the fifth, 9th, 13th, and 14th Amendments and Title VI of the Civil Rights Act (1964). The US Fifth Circuit Court of Appeals in 1990 reversed part of the lower court's decision, which held that Mississippi had no *de jure* segregation practices, but the appeals court allowed most of the district court ruling to stand, saying Mississippi had carried out its duty to implement racially neutral policies and procedures for its public higher education system since students "seeking higher education had 'real freedom' to choose the institution of their choice." Upon plaintiffs' appeal in *US v. Governor Mabus,* 499 US (1991), the US Supreme Court in 1992 said, discrimination still could exist under proposed race neutral admission policies even when *de jure* segregation had been removed.[79]

US v. Fordice, Governor of Mississippi, et al, 505 US 717 (1992) was argued 13 November 1991 and decided 26 June 1992. The Court said,

> The courts below did not apply the correct legal standard in ruling that Mississippi has brought itself into compliance with the Equal Protection Clause...There are several surviving aspects of Mississippi's prior dual system which are constitutionally suspected.... Though certainly closure of one or more institutions would decrease the system's discriminatory effects, the present record is inadequate to demonstrate whether such action is constitutionally required.... The full range of the State's higher educational activities, including its funding of the three historically black schools, must be examined on remand under the proper standard to determine whether the State is taking the necessary steps to dismantle its prior [segregated] system.

---

[79] Curan and McDonald, "Civil Rights and Discrimination," 160, 172.

US Supreme Court Justice Clarence Thomas concurred: "I agree with the Court that a State does not satisfy its obligation to dismantle a dual system of higher education merely by adopting race-neutral policies of for the future administration of that system." The concurring opinion said,

> [There may be] sound educational justification for maintaining historically black colleges as such. Despite the shameful history of state-enforced segregation, these institutions have survived and flourished. Indeed, they have expanded as opportunities for blacks to enter historically white institutions have expanded. Between 1954 and 1980, for example, enrollment at historically black colleges increased from 70,000 to 200,000 students, while degrees awarded increased from 13,000 to 32,000.[80]

The Court remanded *Ayers v. Fordice* to the Circuit Court, which ordered the district court to take action, and which directed the parties to make an agreement. The trial version of *Fordice* had enforced the rumors about sacrifice of at least one HBCU, Mississippi Valley, in the name of desegregation. From next door, while they grappled with the *Geier* case and ways in which to subordinate predominantly black Tennessee State University, white Tennessee officials Charles W. Burson, Attorney General, John K. Walkup, Solicitor General, and Christine Modisher, Assistant Attorney General of Tennessee, filed friend-of-the-court briefs.

In *Ayers v. Fordice* (879 F. Supp. 1419, 1494 [N.D. Miss. 1995]) the judge rejected the closing of one of the HBCUs—Mississippi Valley State University—and he ordered the state to spend more money to improve Alcorn, Jackson State, and Mississippi Valley. The state would allocate funds to enhance HBCU endowments, add graduate programs, and grant scholarships to attract whites to public HBCUs and blacks to TWIs. All eight public universities had to begin uniform admissions standards. HBCUs had to implement higher admissions standards, drop remedial courses, and attract 10 percent white students to tap the state's matching endowment funds. The judge did not order a merger of TWI Delta State with MVSU. He ordered the evaluation of each challenged policy or practice to determine whether it was traceable prior to *de jure* Jim Crow and whether it continued to foster segregation, whether it lacked sound educational justification, whether its elimination was practicable, and that Mississippi had dismantled its prior dual system of higher education based on race. He ordered a desegregation monitoring committee to oversee compliance. Mississippi

---

[80] Susan T. Hill, *The Traditionally Black Institutions of Higher Education, 1860–1982* (Washington DC: US Department of Education [USDOE], National Center for Education Statistics [NCES], 1983) xiv–xv; *United States v. Fordice*, 505 US 717 (1992), US Supreme Court (6 June 1992), decision and majority and dissenting opinions.

transformed its student admissions policies from the standardized test-driven system rejected by the Court to a uniform statewide standard.[81]

In April 1997, the US Court of Appeals for the Fifth Circuit upheld the district judge's ruling, and on 20 January 1998, the US Supreme Court refused a stay. The full-time black freshman enrollment at public universities had dropped, and there was a fear of further decline in enrollment of black college students at Mississippi's public colleges because of new universal admission standards. During a status conference in June 1998, the federal district court ordered the universities to monitor the various elements that affect freshman enrollment and advise the court of its findings. The state colleges implemented summer remedial programs for pre-college students. Mississippi had 37.2 percent blacks compared to 12.9 percent for the United States. They comprised 28 percent of the state's college students. Only 16.9 percent of Mississippi's population had a bachelor's degree or higher, compared to nearly 25 percent per the national average. Some 62 percent of black college students attended the public and private four-year HBCUs, which enrolled 92 to 99 percent black students.[82]

Ayers v. Fordice case and its conclusions were truly instructive for the Deep South. The decision concluded that mere adoption of race-neutral policies did not fulfill the state's affirmative duty to dismantle segregated systems of higher education.[83] Critics said *Ayers v. Fordice* merely tinkered with the real issues of desegregation of higher education. In 2002, plaintiffs appealed to the Supreme Court, but they lost the appeal in 2004. No mergers resulted, but *Fordice* set the precedents for desegregating state higher systems. The decisions held that lack of black studies programs and waivers for children of alumni were not traceable to *de jure* segregation. The states' predominantly black public HBCUs continued their historic designation. The United States Department of Education, Office of Civil Rights, based its guidelines for higher education desegregation mainly on *Fordice.*[84] HBCU supporters packed a committee room at the Mississippi legislature to hear the proposal by Republican Governor Haley Barbour to merge the three black state universities into one because of state budget cuts. The governor offered to merge two predominantly white state universities, too. The controversial issue went nowhere by summer 2010.

---

[81] Curran and McDonald, "Civil Rights and Discrimination," 165.

[82] US Census Bureau, *State and County Quick Facts: Mississippi* (Washington, DC: Census Bureau, 2010) 1.

[83] Stefkovich, "A Legal History of Desegregation in Higher Education," 406–20.

[84] Curran and McDonald, "Civil Rights and Discrimination."

Texas, in the law school case of *Sweatt v. Painter*, 339 US 629 (1950) had resisted desegregation of higher education. University of Texas accepted black graduate students in 1950, but it was not until 1956, that public colleges in Texas began to accept black undergraduates. Thirty-eight of 57 colleges in Texas admitted 820 blacks. Only eleven of the institutions considered Negroes eligible for faculty and staff positions. The largest number of Negro college students attended TWIs in east Texas, where many blacks resided.

One HBCU officer predicted that the black colleges "will probably be affected adversely [by *Brown* and desegregation] in their enrollment and rate of growth—a decline in the enrollment of some, a slower rate of growth in others. Such schools will also be under greater pressure to meet accreditation standards and to improve their curricula." Only one of the six private Negro colleges in Texas was on the SACS Approved List of Colleges for Negro Youth. These minority institutions had to gain accreditation and "drop their racial designation and become an undifferentiated part of the whole of private higher education in Texas."[85]

The OCR guideline, resulting from *Adams v. Richardson* (1972–1977), required white and black public institutions to function as part of a unitary higher education system. The Texas Higher Education Coordinating Board developed and monitored four successive plans. OCR approved *Texas Equal Educational Opportunity Plan for Higher Education* (1981). Texas submitted a second plan in 1989, and *Access and Equity 2000* (1994). Beginning in 1997, OCR reviewed Texas public higher education, and the fourth plan was approved in May 2000 as the *Texas Commitment*. All the plans focused on the public HBCUs, Prairie View A&M University and Texas Southern University, and a host of measures to improve the two institutions. The state committed to $379 million dollars in these regards. In 2003–2004, PVAMU had 7,808 students, including 392 (5 percent) whites, and TSU had 10,888 including 256 (2.4 percent) whites.[86]

The University of Texas System's report, *Service to Texas in the New Century: A Long Range Plan for the University of Texas System* (December 2000) said "Unless the educational attainments of the state's Hispanic and African American populations are increased, the Texas workforce for 2030 will be less well educated than it is today … If current educational trends continue, average household income in Texas will decline by $3,000 in real dollars by 2030." Texas projected a 52 percent non-white population by 2010. However, the Texas plan of

---

[85] Kirk and King, "Desegregation of the Negro College," 323.

[86] William C. Bednar, "Desegregation of Higher Education in Texas: What Does the Future Hold?" Paper, 11th Annual Texas Higher Education Law Conference, University of North Texas, Denton, 2–3 April 2007, 1–7.

"Closing the Gaps 2015" seemed to be on track in 2006 when the population enrolled in higher education was up 5.3 percent compared to 5.0 percent in 2000. The gap between white and black participation in higher education all but closed during that period. However, unless Texas stopped allowing TWIs to duplicate programs at the HBCUs, it seemed Prairie View and Texas Southern would not reach 24–30 percent white enrollment, as Tennessee State University.[87]

Florida A&M University sat almost side-by-side with Florida State University. Both sides feared the HBCU or the TWI would merge into the other institution. Former dean of Tennessee A&I State College, George W. Gore, Jr., president of FAMU (1950–1968), said,

> I think many black people want integration, but they want black institutions, too. They are ambivalent about it. And when integration is offered to them only on the white man's terms, then it is not attractive. If it means killing off black leadership and giving whites complete control of everything, that is no good.... [I]t is absurd to think of duplicating university facilities in Tallahassee from now into the indefinite future, but a merger now would leave thousands of blacks without a school, and that would be tragic. It would not be true integration; it would not be equitable—and we would be suspicious of any effort that was not based on equity.[88]

Some persons proposed that FAMU move to another part of the state where it could retain its name and black leadership. Speaking at the opening convocation in August 1988, after a letter arrived in the president's office at Florida A&M saying graduates of an institution and their ultimate performance determined if an institution was of quality, Frederick S. Humphries urged faculty, staff, and students to help him dispel the notion that the HBCU was not of quality:

> The students must never be better than the faculty, because ... if the faculty is not really good they can guarantee that the graduates won't be. If we are not teaching much, the students cannot learn much. Therefore,

---

[87] Ibid.

[88] Egerton, *Public Black Colleges*, 120; "UF Facts," www.ufl.edu/facts (21 June 2010); B. L. Perry Jr., "Black Colleges and Universities in Florida: Past, Present, and Future," *Journal of Black Studies* 6/1 (September 1975): 69–78.

students will either progress or retrogress, based on what we offer. And if we are not offering quality then there won't be quality.[89]

The issue of *access* was the focus of the blacks' argument for keeping HBCUs open for *all*. Blacks comprised 14.6 percent of Florida's 17,019,068 people, compared to 16.8 percent for Hispanics and less than 2 percent for Asians and Native Americans, and in fall 2002, blacks comprised 14.26 percent of 261,667 part-time and full-time public college students, including 4,593 or 10.1 percent of the system's graduate students. At the University of Florida, blacks comprised 7.4 percent of the students, and a total of 637 (4.98 percent) of the 12,784 graduate students. The University of Florida claimed third place in degrees awarded to African Americans in 2000–2001. The University of Florida had the fourth-largest student enrollment of all US universities by 2002, with more than 48,000 students. Just down the street from FAMU, Florida State University had 12.7 percent black students, including 623 (9.4 percent) black graduate students in fall 2002. Florida Atlantic University had the highest black enrollment percentage (15.1 percent) among TWIs, and New College of Florida had the lowest black student enrollment (1.59 percent). In fall 2004, blacks made up 14 percent of the students in Florida's public colleges and universities, or about 40,175 students. About 32.25 percent of them enrolled at FAMU.

Florida did away with the affirmative admission policy. The replacement policy granted seats in the public universities to students in the top 20 percent of their high school graduating class. This lowered the percentage of black students at the University of Florida. The new policies sent many unprepared minorities to the four-year institutions from failing inner city schools, where re-segregation had become reality, and, thus, the Hispanic and black students often did not have the true academic background. The desegregation plans enforced the admission of more minority students, but did not include effective *remediation*, *retention* and *graduation* plans.[90]

Many black students entered community colleges or ended up transferring from the senior institutions to the junior colleges, while reverse transfers were not so encouraging. From 1963 to 1967, Florida merged its twelve black

---

[89] M. F. Wilson and N. E. Gaymon, eds., *A Century of Wisdom: Selected Speeches of Presidents of Florida A. & M. University, 1887–1987* (Winter Park FL: Four-G Publishers, 1990) 179.

[90] Florida A&M University, "University History," http://www.famu.edu/index.cfm?universityhistory, 2010; FAMU, "University Strategic Plan," http://www.famu.edu/index.cfm?aboutFAMU&strategicplan, 2010; State University System of Florida, "Fall Student Enrollment," 1991–2010 (Tallahassee FL: SUSF, 2010); SREB, *Featured Facts on Higher Education in Florida, 2010* (Atlanta: SREB, 2010) 1–24.

community colleges (founded between 1949 and 1962) into the Florida Community College System. In 2001, several community colleges gained permission to offer the four-year baccalaureate degree to ease general enrollment pressure on Florida's existing four-year universities. In Florida's twenty-eight community colleges, the minority students comprised 39 percent (147,245 of 357,050) of the enrollment. In fall 2004–2005, blacks comprised more than 40 percent of community college minority group enrollment.[91]

Florida A&M received more black students, partly because FAMU improved the quality and expansion of its programs. They improved retention and graduation rates. This success gave the institution a good reputation for educating minorities. Humphries struck out on a vigorous recruitment of students that were national scholars and top academic achievers, which helped quiet some criticism about "lack of quality." Florida A&M had the largest enrollment among 103 HBCUs, with 13,070 students, including 1,569 graduate students, 1,036 faculty members, and awarded 1,604 bachelors, 401 masters, 109 professional, and twenty-four doctoral degrees in 2003–2004. FAMU was 94.4 percent black in 2004 and 91 percent black by fall 2006–07.[92]

Arkansas public and private college education for Negro citizens started slowly. The Southland College in Helena opened in 1864 as an orphan home, moved to a rural area in 1866, and became Southland College in 1872. The Indiana Society of Friends operated the institution with 352 students, including two hundred boarders, and sixteen teachers by 1915. The institution offered a normal school curriculum, but closed in 1925. Besides public Arkansas AM&N State College, the state included four other HBCUs by 1946: Arkansas Baptist College, Dunbar Junior College, Philander Smith College, and Shorter-Flipper-Curry College. Altogether, the five HBCUs in Arkansas had budgets totaling $258,600 in 1942, and enrolled 916 students by 1945–1946. Whites had seventeen institutions of higher learning, including eight public TWIs, enrolling seven times as many students as the state's HBCUs.[93] Five Arkansas HBCUs survived *Brown*.

---

[91] Ibid.

[92] Ibid.

[93] William H. Martin, "The Education of Negroes in Arkansas," *The Journal of Negro Education* 16/3 (Summer 1947): 317–24; Thomas C. Kennedy, *A History of Southland College: The Society of Friends and Black Education in Arkansas* (Fayetteville: University of Arkansas Press, 2009) 263; Robert A. Leflar, "Legal Education in Arkansas: A Brief History of the Law School," *Arkansas Historical Quarterly* 21/2 (Summer 1962): 99–131; William H. Martin, "Negro Higher and Professional Education in Arkansas," *Journal of Negro Education* 17/3 (Summer 1948): 255–64; Bobby L. Lovett, "African Americans, Civil War, and Aftermath in Arkansas," *Arkansas Historical Quarterly* 54/3 (Autumn 1995): 304–58.

Shorter College, located in North Little Rock, began in 1886 as Bethel University by the AME Church. The name changed to Shorter College in 1903. Since 1955, Shorter has provided a two-year college education in general education, an associate degree, and paraprofessional certificate programs. About twenty-four faculty/staff members teach and train 120 students, mostly from the local area. Shorter, with residential spaces for fifty students, was accredited by the North Central Association of Colleges and Schools (NCACS). Philander Smith College was the largest of the Arkansas privates and accredited by NCACS, NCATE, Council on Social Work Education, and the Association of Collegiate and Business Schools. The institution remained related to the United Methodist Church, and offered twenty-two programs in Christian education, business and economics, arts and humanities, natural and physical sciences, and education as well as an Honors Academy, Management Institute, and centers of excellence. The new mission statement for Philander Smith College included the preparation of students of life in this pluralistic, complex, and technological society; and enabling students to understand other cultures. Like many of the HBCUs, Philander Smith College also intended to develop leadership skills in her students. In 2004, Philander Smith's new president began raising funds to build new facilities and revamp the curriculum. Arkansas Baptist College, located in North Little Rock, began in 1884 as the Minister's Institute. Today, it is the only black Baptist higher education institution west of the Mississippi River. Accredited by the NCACS, the institution's curriculum includes Christian philosophy of life, school of business and applied science and technology, school of liberal arts and social science, and a scholars' college. Arkansas Baptist College had two hundred students by 2005. The institution held its 123rd commencement exercise on 12 May 2007. Shorter, Arkansas Baptist, and Philander Smith formed a cooperative center of higher education.

In 1972, in response to *Adams* and the OCR request for compliance with Title VI of the Civil Rights Act, Arkansas placed Arkansas AM&N State College in the University of Arkansas system, changing the name to University of Arkansas at Pine Bluff. UABP got new programs, including a Center of Excellence in Fisheries and Biology. However, the University of Arkansas established a Graduate Center in Pine Bluff, among other places, and this hampered the growth of graduate studies at the public HBCU. UAPB started a University Museum and Cultural Center to keep university archives and artifacts and to serve the Arkansas Delta region, including a facility that opened in 2005, but the center depended on private funds.

The state had 27 percent black residents in 1920, and 15.8 percent in 2007. Enrollment in Arkansas higher education institutions increased 2.2 percent between 2005 and 2007. UAPB remained relatively small compared to 17,926 students at the University of Arkansas at Fayetteville in 2006. UAPB had the third-smallest enrollment among eleven public universities in the state in 2006, but the largest percentage increase among those institutions. The headcount enrollment at UAPB increased 8.7 percent from 3,040 students in 1999–2000 to 3,303 students in 2003–2004. UAPB enrollment slightly exceeded Arkansas AM&N State College's 1967 enrollment. By 2007, blacks constituted 17.9 percent of the 180,938 students enrolled in Arkansas higher education institutions, but the black-white graduation rate gap widened.[94]

Oklahoma had 7.6 percent blacks in the 2000 census. In the state's higher education desegregation plan, the lone predominantly black public institution, Langston Agricultural and Normal University (1897–) became a part of the Oklahoma A&M System. The institution honored the name of civil rights pioneer John Mercer Langston, who died in 1897. The institution maintained accreditation through the NACAS. The institution included urban campus centers in Tulsa and Oklahoma City as well as the main campus in rural Langston.

State desegregation plans assigned an urban mission with schools of arts and sciences, business, agriculture and applied sciences, nursing and health professions, physical therapy, honors program center for international development, and graduate programs limited to master's degrees in education and rehabilitation counseling, and a master's and doctorate in physical therapy. Oklahoma invested at least $70 million in capital developments, including faculty and classroom facilities in Tulsa, which helped attract adult white students. No blacks served on Oklahoma's board of regents for the higher education system, and the state's lone HBCU remained low in priority. Langston University had a headcount of 3,922 students in 2006, and enrolled 3,447 students in 2007–2008. Langston graduated thirty-six masters including nineteen "blacks-African Americans" and 305 bachelors including 217 "blacks-African Americans" in 2007–2008. State institutions graduated 22,594 students including 1,420 blacks-African Americans.[95]

---

[94] Arkansas Department of Education, "Arkansas Total 5-Year Enrollment," 2004–2009 (Little Rock: ADHE, 2010) 1; US Census Bureau, *State and County Quickfacts: Arkansas, 2009 Estimate* (Washington, DC: Census Bureau, 2010); ADHE, 2009 Higher Education Annual Comprehensive Report, Little Rock AR, 2009, 6-63-103, 6-61-122.

[95] *2008 Annual Report of the State of Higher Education in Oklahoma: Degrees of Progress*, 96, 219, 254; *Degrees Conferred in Oklahoma Higher Education, 2007–08*, Oklahoma State Regents for Higher Education, April 2009; OSRHE, 2009 Annual Report, *The State of Higher Education in Oklahoma, Degrees of Progress* (Oklahoma City: OSRHE, 2009) 31, 1–42.

For many decades, Missouri, a slave state until 1865, had resisted black movements to gain equal access to public higher education on par with white citizens. The NAACP helped Lloyd Gaines win the case of *Ex. Rel. Gaines v. Canada* 305 US 337 (1938), forcing Missouri to recognize the state had to obey the equal protection clause of the Fourteenth Amendment to the US Constitution. To prevent any more Negroes from having excuses to attend professional and graduate programs with the white citizens, Missouri created a bogus law school for Negroes in a rented building in St. Louis, with space for a library and a handful of students. The school eventually closed, especially after opposition from the NAACP. With such a small Negro population, except in its cities, Missouri pretty much maintained racial segregation *de jure* and *de facto* into the twenty-first century. In Missouri, the blacks comprised 11.2 percent of the 5.7 million people in 2000. There were two HBCUs in Missouri by 2005. Lincoln University now had 56 percent white students.

Harris-Stowe State University listed as an HBCU by 2005. The institution resulted from the merger of two normal schools, Harris Teacher's College (white) and Stowe Teacher's College (Negro), in 1954. Both institutions had been a part of the city public school system. The state of Missouri assumed the merged institution in 1979 and authorized the Bachelor of Science degree in 1981. By 2005, the merged city-state college was predominantly black and African American. Harris-Stowe College conferred bachelor's degrees in education until the state authorized the institution to confer degrees in other subjects in June 1993. By 2000, Harris-Stowe State University had 1,800 students, 102 faculty members (38 full-time; 62 percent doctorates), and four departments, but no schools, colleges, or graduate programs within the institution. Within the Missouri plan to integrate higher education, Harris-Stowe received a mission in urban education to serve the entire St. Louis metropolitan area in applied professional disciplines. By 2005, Harris-Stowe offered twelve bachelor degree programs, including new ones in business administration, education, criminal justice, health care management, accounting, information computer technology, and hospitality/tourism management; and they planned other programs.[96]

In Ohio, where blacks comprised 11.5 percent of 11.4 million people in 2000, the state did not make Central State University a desegregation priority. Urban schools in Ohio had *de facto* segregation along lines of socioeconomic class and

---

[96] Missouri Department of Higher Education, *Strategic Plan 2006* (Jefferson City MO: Missouri Department of Education, 2008) 1–14.

race, and Ohio reduced the appropriations to Central State University by 19.5 percent below the 2001 level.

The Central State University administration instituted a fund raising campaign with the help of the "Evening with Bill Cosby" program held at the Schuster Center in Dayton, 25 April 2001. The program helped raised $1.4 million dollars toward an endowment fund. By fall 2004, CSU had 1,820 students (up 12.3 percent since 2000). In Dayton, the state, in 1967, established Wright State University, which by 2005 had 17,074 students (10.5 percent blacks), 775 faculty members, a $348 million budget of $348, an endowment of $73 million, and 109 undergraduate and forty-six graduate and professional programs. By 2005, nearby Central State University advertised itself as "...a premier historically black university that nurtures students within a value-based environment focused on excellence in teaching and learning, research, and public service."[97]

West Virginia resulted from sixty-eight western counties seceding from the rebellious state of Virginia in June 1862. Located in mountainous terrain, West Virginia had little slavery and few Negroes. After coalmines and manual labor jobs all but dried up, Negroes left for other places, and with so few blacks, West Virginia made the decision to desegregate public higher education after the announcement of *Brown*.

The two state HBCUs eventually became predominantly white. The opening of two public colleges for Negroes in West Virginia already had hurt the private HBCU, Storer College, and with integration, Storer College no longer could survive. Storer College (1865–1955) began as a freedmen's school in Harper's Ferry, West Virginia, the site of John Brown's 1859 raid. The Freewill Baptist Home Mission Society of New England established the school on Camp Hill, in Union Army barracks. They named the school for John Storer, a philanthropist from Maine, who gave $10,000 to match an equal amount from the Freewill Baptist Church. Storer Normal School admitted its first students on 2 October 1867. Whites in the neighborhood opposed the school and often harassed the white teachers. The school had a liberal leaning, and it advocated freedom and civil rights for blacks in the tradition of John Brown. In 1918, the alumni had a stone tablet embedded in a cornerstone of "John Brown's Fort," and Frederick Douglass visited the school in 1881 to give his famous John Brown speech. The Storer student singing group toured to raise money in 1878. Storer Normal

---

[97] US Census Bureau, *Quickfacts: Ohio* (Washington, DC: Census Bureau, 2009) 1; Ohio Board of Regents, *Higher Education Fact Book* (Columbus OH: Ohio Board of Regents, 2009) 1–¡4; Ohio Board of Regents, *Preliminary Headcount Report, 1951–2007* (Columbus OH: OBR, 2010) 1–8; OBR, *Statistical Profiles* (Columbus OH: Ohio Board of Regents, 2010) 1–10.

School hosted the second Niagara Movement Conference, headed by W. E. B. Du Bois. Storer became a college in 1938 and grew to four hundred students, preparing teachers and ministers. In the 1940s, the college was in financial trouble and seeking $300,000 additional endowment, though Storer "has no debt" with assets of $500,000.[98] The college had exhibits at the Northern Baptist Convention meeting in Wichita, Kansas, in May 1941, trying to draw support. "The men and women of limited means, who came here, need your help."[99] On 1 May 1942, Storer College inaugurated the Iota Chapter of Beta Kappa Chi Scientific Honor Society, founded at Lincoln University, Pennsylvania, in 1924. Two black men served among the presidents of Storer College. With the announcement of *Brown*, the state of West Virginia withdrew support from the institution. Storer College closed, and Virginia Union University and Howard University stored the Storer College records.

West Virginia State University (1891–) began as West Virginia Colored Institute offering high school curricula. In 1915, the named changed to West Virginia Collegiate Institute, and the school offered college degrees. In 1929, it became West Virginia State College. The state established the West Virginia State Community and Technical College at WVSC in 1953. The student body, in the 1960s, became 90 percent white commuters, but blacks predominated as on-campus residents. West Virginia State College remained under a black administration, but the state continued to chip away its most competitive programs. The state gave up the land-grant status and transferred the funds to TWI West Virginia University. The school lost its graduate program, the West Virginia Graduate College to TWI Marshall University. The community college gained separate accreditation in 2003 and fully separated from WVSU in 2008. West Virginia State College became West Virginia State University in 2004. In 2009, the Community and Technical College became Kanawha Valley Community and Technical College, which shared the WVSU campus. Hazo W. Carter, Jr., former president at Philander Smith College in Arkansas, serves as the ninth president. His father taught at, and retired from, Tennessee State University. Carter, Jr., lobbied for many years to have the 1890 land-grant status restored. In 2001, land-grant status and funds were returned to WVSU—the smallest of the land-grant HBCUs. The WVSU website says, "West Virginia State

---

[98] Henry T. M'Donald, "Storer College," *History of Education in West Virginia* (Charleston WV: Tribune Printing Co., 1904) 1–23; West Virginia University Libraries West Virginia and Regional History Collection, "Storer College: A Photographic Exhibit of the First African American College in West Virginia," www.libraries.wvu.edu/exhibits/storer (2002).

[99] Ibid.

University is a historically black university, which has evolved into a fully accessible, racially diverse, and multi-generational institution."[100] The institution had 3,214 students in 2007.

Bluefield State College (1895–) began as a black teachers college. In 1954, when West Virginia integrated its institutions of higher education, Bluefield State had 354 students, including three whites. By 1965, the institution was a four-year teacher-education college, with predominantly white students. Black alumni complained about the institution's failure to display the real history of the college. In November 1968, after black student protest against the release of black faculty and staff, someone threw a brick through the president's window, and a bomb ripped through the gymnasium. The state closed the dormitories, displacing much of the black student body, and moved the black historic documents, pictures, and artifacts into a small room. BSC had 2,768 mostly white students in 2001; today, few black faculty and administrators work at Bluefield State. Under West Virginia plans for desegregation of higher education, the strategic planning for Bluefield State aims to increase black faculty/staff and students. Given the isolation and poverty of the area, and the anti-black attitudes of many whites in West Virginia, those institutional goals will be tough for Bluefield State College to achieve. Bluefield enrolled only 1,887 students in 2007. West Virginia had 3.2 percent blacks in 2008.[101]

Kansas, a free state, had an HBCU. The institution closed eleven years before *Brown*, although Negroes attended the major public universities in Kansas long before *Brown*. The state's sole HBCU, Western University (1865–1944) began as a freedmen's school at Quindaro. The town on the Missouri River was, reportedly, an Underground Railroad site and a haven for anti-slavery whites and other abolitionists. The state began supporting the institution in 1867 just before thousands of Negroes moved into Kansas in the Black Exodus of 1869–1881, led

---

[100] West Virginia State Archives, "A Brief History of African Americans in West Virginia," West Virginia Division of Culture and History (Charleston WV: West Virginia State Archives, 2009).

[101] West Virginia University Libraries West Virginia and Regional History Collection, "Storer College: A Photographic Exhibit of the First African American College in West Virginia," www.libraries.wvu.edu/exhibits/storer (2002); Charles H. Amber, *A History of Education in West Virginia: From Early Colonial Times to 1949* (Huntington WV: Standard Printing and Publishing Company, 1951) 1–10; West Virginia Higher Policy Commission, *Higher Education Report Card 2008* (Charleston WV: WVHE Policy Commission, 2009) 1–20; SREB, *Featured Facts on Higher Education in West Virginia 2009* (Atlanta: Southern Education Regional Board, 2010) 1–10; A. Paul Bradley, *Promoting a Culture of Student Success: How Colleges and Universities Are Improving Degree Completion* (Atlanta: SREB, 2010) 1–46.

by Benjamin "Pap" Singleton and others. After the school's namesake, the Rev. Eben Blachley, a Presbyterian minister, died in 1877, the freedmen's school became inactive. In 1881, the African Methodist Episcopal Church (AMEC) revived this school, named it Western University, and hired William T. Vernon, former US Register of the Treasury to run the institution, which housed and educated several hundred students. Vernon retired in 1910. The next year, AME Bishop Abraham Grant raised $2,000, and had a marble statue to John Brown carved in Italy. Besides trying to find a way to put Quindaro, Kansas, on the map, the AMEC hired H. T. Kealing, a former editor at the AMEC Publishing House in Nashville to head Western University. The school thrived over the next several decades; it taught industrial trades, including blacksmithing, wheel righting, tailoring, carpentry, printing, shoemaking, and included trades for girls, such as millinery and sewing. The state of Kansas financed the construction of several facilities—including a boys' trade building in 1907 and a girls' dormitory in 1914—and appropriated money for other facilities as late as 1924. Western University reached the status of a junior college, but the Great Depression forced the school to close by 1943. The AMEC moved Douglass Hospital into one of the buildings in 1945; the hospital closed in 1978.[102]

Although there was the beginning of desegregation of higher education in the Jim Crow states, 1968–2005, affirmative action in higher education admissions met sharp resistance. The white population in America dropped from 85 percent to about 69 percent by 2009. In the SREB states, whites comprised 34 percent of the nation's white population; southern blacks made up 53 percent of all blacks in America.[103]

In *Hopwood v. State of Texas*, 78 F.3d 932 (1996), the Fifth US Circuit Court of Appeals struck down an affirmative action admissions policy at University of Texas Law School. In 1997, state officials declared "race-neutral criteria" for university admission policies. *Hopwood* advanced a new white concept of "color blindness." Ian F. H. Lopez said, "We find ourselves now in the midst of a racial era marked by what I term 'colorblind white dominance' in which a public consensus committed to formal antiracism deters effective remediation of racial inequality, protecting the racial status quo while insulating new forms of racism and xenophobia."[104] Alvin Chambliss, Jr., of *Fordice* tried to allay fears about

---

[102] Thaddeus T. Smith, "Western University: A Ghost College in Kansas" (master's thesis, Pittsburg State College, Pittsburg KS, 1966) 1–10.

[103] US Census Bureau, *Fast Facts, 2009* (Washington, DC: Census Bureau, 2010) 1.

[104] Ian F. H. Lopez, "How Colorblindness Perpetuates White Dominance," *The Chronicle Review* (3 November 2003): B6–9.

Hopwood.[105] On 24 April 2001, the US Supreme Court decision *Alexander v. Sandoval*, 532 US 275 (2001), limited the scope of Title VI to exclude private citizens from challenging discrimination based on disparate impact. After Alabama amended its constitution to declare English the "official language" in 1990, Martha Sandoval sued the Alabama department of safety under Title VI of the Civil Rights Act of 1964, but the justices allowed arguments based on *intentional* discrimination only.

On 1 April, 2003, college students caravanned by buses and cars to Washington, DC, to show support for the University of Michigan, whose affirmative action policy was being challenged by three white students. Students took buses from Tennessee State University and other HBCUs because they were concerned that an adverse ruling by the US Supreme Court could stop affirmative admission programs for blacks seeking professional/graduate programs at TWIs. At least three hundred organizations submitted sixty friend-of-the-court briefs to the court on Michigan's side. The federal administration entered the case, saying quotas for minorities embodied racial discrimination against whites. On 23 June 2003, in *Grutter v. Bollinger*, 539 US 306 (2003) and *Gratz v.* Bollinger, 539 US 244 (2003), the court said race could *not* be the *definitive* element in admissions policy, especially when the policy assigned a numerical weight to race and seemed to be a quota system. Admissions decisions, including race, became a permissible element in a complex of many elements including ones that relate to the educational benefits of diversity.[106]

During 1954 to 2010, America's historically black colleges and universities underwent difficult times because of complexities created with the new integrated American society. In particular, the public HBCUs, which now, among the 105 black colleges and universities, enrolled the majority of the HBCU students, got caught up in the vicious educational policies of desegregation of higher education in nineteen states. The *Geier* case in Tennessee in 1968, and then the *Adams* case in DC in 1970, began a host of state and federal lawsuits to dismantle the last vestiges of the Jim Crow state higher education systems. Almost all these cases centered in the Southern Regional Education Board (SREB) states.

---

[105] Hill, *The Traditionally Black Institutions of Higher Education*, 58, Table 3.6.

[106] J. W. Wilson, *The Declining Significance of Race* (Chicago: University of Chicago Press, 1978) 1–19; Neil J. Smelser, William J. Wilson, and Faith Mitchell, eds., *America Becoming: Racial Trends and Their Consequences*, 2 vols. (Washington DC: National Academy Press, 2001) 1.208–210; Sara Hebel, "Desegregation Lawsuit Nears End in Tenn.," *Chronicle of Higher Education* 53/5 (22 September 2006) A24.

Some northern areas, including Delaware, Ohio, and Pennsylvania yet had separate colleges for blacks, and these minority institutions, too, needed to receive more attention and resources from the state governments. Although the US Department of Education (USDOE) was a reluctant player in the early lawsuits to force the states to comply with Title VI of the Civil Rights Act (1964), the Office of Civil Rights (OCR) within the USDOE was aggressive in forcing the affected states to develop five-year plans for desegregation of higher education. These cases and plans dominated thirty-five years of black public higher education until 2010 and yielded great enhancements to the public HBCUs. Meanwhile, the prestigious private HBCUs lurked in the shadows of the larger public HBCUs, and, except for some federal grants and entitlements like Title III funds, these private historic colleges and universities suffered financial neglect and thus enrollment stagnation or decline in enrollment.

The public HBCUs, through the new state desegregation funds, gained new programs, mostly graduate programs, which allowed them to add many more graduate students and white adult students than the private HBCUs. At the same time, the relations between public HBCUs and the conservative white state officials were antagonized for some time to come. Thus, during the long decades of desegregation of state higher education systems, 1968–2005, the HBCUs—all 105 of them public and private—sort of limped into the twenty-first century, and all of them would be hard pressed to survive and prosper.

7

Moving into the Twenty-first Century

Frederick S. Humphries, president of the National Association for Equal Opportunity in Education (NAFEO), said,

> Black colleges ... are sort of waddling and don't seem self-assured about their direction. Part of the difficulty rests with the need to do an assessment where they are and what direction they should take, given the shifts in society and the world. They need to ask the question of whether the structures that have supported them in the past are the correct vehicles to support them in the future. Governing boards are marginalizing their schools, selecting poorly trained leaders and paring back things ...won in the days of segregation. Very few schools are advancing into graduate education.... They [HBCUs] have not come to grips with the kind of people [needed] in the twenty-first century.[1]]

HBCUs weathered the storms of a turbulent history, but they had to navigate history while charting a road map into the future. Most HBCUs met that challenge by continuing to make adjustments in their mission, goals, and objectives by using mergers and cooperative agreements, extending the majors into fields of business, engineering, and science, integrating the faculty and student bodies, forming associations, and increasing their fund-raising efforts.

The first decade of the twenty-first century appeared hostile to the HBCUs, and did not look promising to predominantly white public and private institutions of higher education either. In 2001, there existed 103 HBCUs: fifty-three private, fifty public, 89 four-year, and fourteen two-year colleges. They slowed their attrition rate relative to the 1920–1960 decades, and constituted nearly 3 percent of America's colleges and universities. Forty-nine of the private HBCUs remained affiliated with religious groups. The HBCUs awarded 20–30 percent of all bachelor's degrees earned by blacks, and enrolled about 16 percent of America's black college students. Public HBCUs enrolled 72 percent of the students attending HBCUs. The Atlanta complex enrolled 3.8 percent of all

[1] Reginald Stuart, "A Decade of Turbulence: A Report on Historically Black Colleges and Universities," *Crisis* 114/5 (September–October 2007): 16–18.

HBCU students. Some 90.6 percent of HBCU enrollment was on the four-year level and majority female.[2]

HBCUs depended more and more on tuition, fees, private, federal, and state funds, while money and race, relative to higher education attainment, continued to matter. Public and private HBCUs suffered budget problems in the first decade of the twenty-first century. Tennessee State University faced a 9 percent budget decrease and the resignation of its president after five years on the job. The state of Tennessee seemed to be abandoning its public colleges, imposing a 35 percent decrease in state funding in the last five years. Private-not-for-profit HBCUs in 1996–97 derived 22 percent of their revenue from student tuition and fees, and by 2000–01 the proportion had increased to 25 percent. In 2001, the combined initial spending associated with 101 HBCUs totaled $6.6 billion. Public HBCUs accounted for 62 percent of the total amount. The economic impact of the nation's HBCUs was $10.2 billion with 35 percent due to the multiplier effect. This amount would rank the collective economic impact of the nation's HBCUs 232nd on the Forbes Fortune 500 list of the United States' largest companies. Additionally, the employment impact of the 101 HBCUs included 180,142 (initial and induced) full- and part-time jobs in 2001.[3]

For 145 years since the end of slavery, American wealth disparity based on race remained a factor that negatively affected the HBCUs and African Americans. HBCU students and graduates had lower black family median income than the white counterparts, and HBCU students had a median family income of 40 percent of the national median income for all college students. By 2006, white families had a median wealth eleven times the average wealth held by black families. College-educated citizens earned higher incomes. In

---

[2] Michael T. Nettles, "Racial Similarities and Differences in the Predictors of College Student Achievement," in W. R. Allen, E. G. Epps, and N. Z. Hanffreds, eds., *College in Black and White: African American Students in Predominantly White and Historically Black Public Universities* (Albany NY: University of New York Press, 1991) 75–91; J. B. Roebuck and K. S. Murty, *Historically Black Colleges and Universities: Their Place in American Higher Education* (Westport CT: Praeger, 1993) 4, 7, 19; see A. W. Astin, L. Tsui, and J. Avalos, *Degree Attainment Rates at American Colleges and Universities: Effects of Race, Gender, and Institution Type* (Los Angeles: Higher Education Institute, 1996) 1–20.

[3] NCES, "National Longitudinal Study of High School Class of 1972: High School and Beyond Longitudinal Study," "Institutional Characteristics" (November 2002), *Digest of Education Statistics 2002* (Washington, DC: USDOE, 2002); Catherine Millett, "How Undergraduate Loan Debt Affects Application and Enrollment in Graduate or First Professional School," *Journal of Higher Education* 74/4 (July–August 2003): 386–427; Institute of Education Sciences, National Center for Education Statistics, *Economic Impact of the Nation's Historically Black Colleges and Universities: Technical Report* (Washington, DC: US Department of Education, October 2006) 1–6.

percentages, twice as many whites as blacks held college degrees, and black graduates earned 92 percent of the median earnings of white college graduates. A greater percentage of black high school graduates suffered unemployment than white high school dropouts. The USDOE reported in 2008 that nearly half of all white, full-time college students held a job compared to 34 percent of black college students.[4]

The poor black constituents served by HBCUs seemed to correspondingly affect the HBCU's lesser ability to build endowments and reserve funds. Most HBCUs had a giving rate of 10 percent or less compared to 25–60 percent of alumni at many TWIs. In 2005–2006, the HBCU with the largest endowment ($397,877,000) was Howard University. Spelman College for women ranked second in total endowments among the 103 HBCUs. With 99 percent black students, Spelman increased alumnae-giving participation to "31 percent, and raised $12,912,547" in 2008–2009, increasing that to $13 million and a 36 percent giving rate in 2010. A quarter of the HBCUs had endowments of less than $6 million. Four had less than $1 million by 2007. Harvard had a $24–38 billion endowment. The UNCF raised $2 billion since 1944. Several TWIs had $1 billion endowment funds.[5] Few agencies gave grants for enhancing HBCU endowments, but some higher education desegregation plans gave state funds to help build endowments at HBCUs.[6]

Part of the problem was a missing tradition of "giving" in the black middle-class community. However, Reginald Lewis, a graduate of Virginia State and CEO of TLC Beatrice International, gave more than $4.4 million to Harvard and Virginia State. Oprah Winfrey, a graduate of Tennessee State University, contributed several million dollars to Morehouse, TSU, and other HBCUs. Morehouse gained two gifts totaling $3 million from alumni, and held the Robert E. Johnson Scholarship Fund endowed by a gift from William H. "Bill" and

---

[4] US Census Bureau, *Family Net Worth—Mean and Median Net Worth in Constant (2007) Dollars by Selected Family Characteristics: 1998 to 2007* (Washington, DC: US Census Bureau, 2007) 1, table 705; Steven C. Riggert, Mike Boyle, Joseph M. Petrosko, Daniel Ash, and Carolyn Rude-Perkins, "Student Employment and Higher Education: Empiricism and Contradiction," *Review of Educational Research* 76/1 (Spring 2006): 62–63.

[5] NCES, *Historically Black Colleges and Universities, 1976 to 2001* (Washington DC: USDOE, NCES, IPEDS, 2004) NCES2004–062, "Staff and Salaries," "Finance," "Student financial aid," 4–7, "Completions, 2000–01," "Finance, 1999–2000" surveys, "Fall Enrollment in Degree-granting HBCUs, Type and Control of Institution: 1976–2000," table 222.

[6] Drewry and Doermann, *Private Black Colleges*, 37, 53, 55, 56, 57–60, 72, 75, 101–108, 205, 256; Susan T. Hill, *The Traditionally Black Institutions of Higher Education, 1860–1982* (Washington DC: US Department of Education [USDOE], National Center for Education Statistics [NCES], 1983) 73.

Camille Olivia Hanks Cosby. With a generous grant from the Coca-Cola Foundation, Morehouse established the Leadership Center in 1995, and in 1996, with students from forty states and eighteen countries, launched "The Campaign for a New Century," with a goal of $105 million. Tennessee State University announced that former Tigerbelle and Olympic gold medalist Edith McGuire-Duvall, a 1966 graduate, gave $1 million to the TSU Foundation for certain programs and to help foster greater alumni giving.[7] Howard University asked the alumni "to raise the bar on fund raising." President H. P. Swygert, increased annual alumni giving from 4 percent in 1995 to 17 percent by 2008. He swelled the endowment fund from $144 million in 1995 to $510 million. Congress and federal agencies granted $233 million for programs and operations in 2008. Swygert, an alumnus, gave more than $2 million: "People give to students, they give to ideas, [and] they give to memory."[8]

Many persons believed that college education generally translated into quality citizens for a democracy. Compared to a lower percentage for high school dropouts, 77 percent of college graduates participated as voters in late twentieth-century elections. College-educated blacks had higher voter participation rates than other blacks. One report estimated the value added in future wages from attending HBCUs was 38 percent higher than for the average black person. TWIs had the majority of black students, but TWIs had lower graduation rates for blacks than for white students.[9]

---

[7] Tennessee State University, "McGuire Gives Million Dollars," *The Blue Notes* 1/1 (October 2008): 1.

[8] *The Chronicle of Higher Education*, "Searchable Database: College and University Endowments," 2010, http://chronicle.com/premium/stats/endowments/results, 1–25; G. Washington to President J. A. Hefner, "Requested Response to Audit Findings," 23 February 2004, Special Collections, Tennessee State University Library, Nashville TN; TSU Foundation Board Minutes, "Awarding of Scholarships by the President, 2004," copy to B. L. Lovett files.

[9] NCES, Higher Education Statistics for 1980–1990, 1990–2000, 1995–2000); see Harold Wenglinsky, *Students at Historically Black Colleges and Universities: Their Aspirations and Accomplishments* (Princeton: ETS, Policy Information Center, 2000) 1–20; Piper P. Aheron, Elaine Johnson Copeland, et al., *Clinton Junior College* (Charleston SC: Arcadia Company, 2004) 1–10; C. Hoffman, M. T. Snyder, and B. Sonnenberg, *Historically Black Colleges and Universities, 1976–1990* (Washington DC: USDOE, 1992) 1–10. The reports refer to African Americans. Although a few researchers lump all "blacks" (dark-skinned Americans of African origins) together, recent African immigrants, especially in Houston and Nashville, attained college degrees at a rate twice that of native born African Americans by 2009; M. Christopher Brown, "The Historically Black College as Social Contract, Social Capital, and Social Equalizer," *Peabody Journal of Education* 76/1 (2001): 31–49.

Some public and private HBCUs also struggled with the graduation rate problem (the following number are in percentages): Southern at New Orleans (11.7), Stillman (12.0), Allen University (12.5), LeMoyne-Owen (14.0), Texas Southern (14.7), St. Paul's (15.4), Huston-Tillotson (15.8), Texas College (17.8), and Edward Waters (17.9). Several HBCUs outdistanced the national median college graduation rate of 54 percent: Spelman (77.0), Miles (72.4), Claflin (67.7), and Fisk (63.8). Others came close to the national rate: South Carolina State (52.8), North Carolina Central (50.5), Morehouse (50.1), and Oakwood College (50.1). Several HBCUs were making great strides to close on the national college graduation rate: Dillard (49.7), Tougaloo (49.5), Xavier (48.4), Tuskegee (47.7), Florida A&M (45.6), Elizabeth City State (45.5), Lincoln, Pa. (44.4), Tennessee State (44.3), Winston-Salem State (43.7), and Alcorn State (42.4). Both Tennessee State and Alcorn once had graduation rates in the 20 percent range, but these institutions, and many other HBCUs, developed more effective teaching and learning strategies and attracted more of the high-achieving high school graduates while continuing open admission for low-achieving high school students. This was a dilemma for the HBCUs: Should they abandon the HBCU's original mission of helping the less fortunate students, and focus on recruiting only the top students as the TWIs did? The average graduation rate for blacks at HBCUs was 34 percent and climbing. In 2004, SREB TWIs had a 50 percent or lower graduation rate for all students for the six-year period. The Ivy League schools, each with their billion dollar endowment funds and restricted admission of the "cream of the crop" students, had 95–96 percent graduation rates for all race students.[10]

In part because of attending failing schools, half of America's black students had to attend community and two-year colleges. Their graduation rate was about 14 percent in 2009. The HBCUs did a good job with the same type students, graduating them at nearly three times the community college graduation rate. By investing more time and money in remedial courses, developmental programs, scholarships, counseling, and advisement the HBCUs continued to serve diverse populations and less wealthy students. But this approach strained HBCU budgets.

Lane College (1882–) focused on recruitment, maturation, and graduation of black male students. The administration imposed a dress code, a curfew, prohibition of profanity, drugs and weapons, and re-instituted compulsory attendance at Wednesday chapel. The enrollment since 2000 has doubled to 1,500 students. Reginald Stuart said, "Lane's story of growth, expansion and rising

---

[10] Nancy King, "Graduation Rates are up Again," *The University Faculty Voice* 8 (October 2003): 7.

endowment is rare these days. Historically Black colleges, the second-class citizens in American higher education...have faced challenges since the end of legalized segregation in higher education."[11] "It's been a turbulent decade," said the president of Lane College, Wesley McClure. "Public funds for higher education are shrinking. Corporate and philanthropic support of HBCUs remains small, and in some cases, is shrinking."[12] Phil W. Petrie, interim editor-in-chief for *Crisis* magazine said, "Our HBCUs need us.... HBCUs are facing a turbulent decade. For some of us, 'Alma mater, how we love thee' is a melancholy, funereal refrain reminding us that our schools have already moved from homecoming to 'home going' status...."[13]

Spelman College (1881–) continued to be a success story, with a 77 percent graduation rate, in the twenty-first century. Two white Baptist missionaries, Sophia B. Packard and Harriett E. Giles, started the school with $100 and, later, with donations from John D. Rockefeller and his mother-in-law, Laura H. Spelman. Although located on just thirty-two acres within the Atlanta University complex, Spelman College has more than 2,100 students from forty-one states and fifteen countries, and, by 2007, 84 percent of full-time faculty held PhDs or other terminal degrees. Spelman College has a Women's Research and Resources Center—the first of its kind on an HBCU campus. In addition to a host of Bachelor of Arts degree programs, Spelman offers BS degrees in biochemistry, biology, chemistry, computer and information sciences, engineering (dual degree with Georgia Tech Institute), mathematics, environmental science, and physics. Spelman has emphasis and precise programs on development of leadership skills. A number of special programs funded by federal and corporate grants reflected this Spelman concept.

Spelman College was one of eight HBCUs, along with Ohio University, to announce in October 2006 a new educational partnership, the Interlink Alliance, to work cooperatively in faculty development, student leadership, and an African-American male initiative that engages and motivates prospective college students as early as middle school. The Cosby family financed an entire building at Spelman with a multi-million dollar gift to endow professorships in the fine arts, humanities, and the social sciences to enhance the intellectual, cultural and creative life of Spelman College and its surrounding community. Spelman awarded honorary doctorates to Bill and Camille Cosby. In 2008, Spelman

---

[11] Stuart, "A Decade of Turbulence," 16.

[12] Ibid., "Editor's Note," 1.

[13] Stuart, "A Report on Historically Black Colleges and Universities," 16–18.

sponsored a Faculty Research Day for faculty to present their research on the campus.[14]

Some private HBCUs, such as Xavier (1915–), endured financial challenges by making "chicken salad out of chicken feathers," while instituting high quality programs. Operating by 2004 with a $78 million budget and an endowment of about $27 million, Xavier University in New Orleans remained the only historically black Catholic university among 253 Catholic schools in the United States. Katherine Drexel and the Sisters of the Blessed Sacrament founded Xavier University in 1915. The college of liberal arts and sciences formed in 1925, and awarded the first college degrees in 1928. The institution gained SACS accreditation in 1938, and has maintained re-accreditation. Since 1986, the institution's student enrollment (85 percent black) more than doubled to 3,994, with half the students coming from Louisiana and others coming from forty-one other states, DC, Virgin Islands, and fourteen countries. Xavier's mission aimed to promote a more just and humane society, and prepare students to assume roles of leadership and service in society. Toward those academic goals, Xavier continued using pluralistic teaching and a learning environment that incorporated all relevant educational means, including research and community service. Pope John Paul II canonized the founder of Xavier in October 2000. The Sisters of the Blessed Sacrament continue to help staff and finance the institution.

Xavier ranked number one in placing blacks in medical schools, with an average of 80 percent acceptance of its students into the nation's medical schools, placing seventy-seven students in medical schools in 1996 alone, and, thus, was number one in undergraduate blacks receiving degrees in biology and life sciences. In 2002, Xavier awarded 660 degrees, including 473 undergraduate, seventy-six masters, and 111 pharmacy degrees. By 2004, Xavier University ranked number one in the nation in the number of Doctor of Pharmacy degrees awarded to African Americans, training 25 percent of America's African-American pharmacists. Xavier maintained a Center for Student Leadership and Services, and began development of centers for The Advancement of Teaching and for Intercultural Studies. Xavier University, despite limited resources (under $30 million endowment, with about four thousand students), had nearly 91 percent doctorates and equivalents among the full-time faculty. The summer sessions filled with students seeking to keep on track with accumulated credits

[14] Spelman College, *The Report on Philanthropy, 2007–2008, 2008–2009* (Atlanta: Spelman College Library, 2008) 1–10; Spelman College, *Five-Year Report* (Atlanta: SC, 2007) 1–11; http://www.spelman.edu/about_us/news/publications, 2010.

needed in pre-professional programs.[15] However, Xavier suffered financial strains, forcing cuts in programs and faculty by 2005.

In 2005, a series of hurricanes hit the Gulf States, and the biggest one, Katrina, forced Xavier University, along with HBCUs Dillard University, Southern University-New Orleans, and local TWIs to cancel fall 2005 semester. HBCUs and TWIs suffered hundreds of millions of dollars in physical plant damage. When Katrina released its fury, Dillard and Xavier both were reaching graduation rates that nearly mirrored the national median, but because of Katrina, the HBCUs once again had to prove their resilience, fitness for survival, and the will to win. In January 2006, Dillard welcomed back more than 50 percent of its two thousand students, housing them in local hotels and holding classes there and in other local colleges' facilities. About 59 percent of the laid-off Dillard faculty members returned to their jobs.[16]

Dillard University was the result of a merger of several local, former freedmen's colleges. The AMA founded Straight University in June 1869, and the next month the MEC opened Union Normal School for the freedmen. These schools became Straight College and New Orleans University, offering grammar, high school, and college studies. Straight had a law department from 1874–1886. New Orleans University had Flint Medical College, the Sarah Goodridge Hospital, and a Nurse Training School. The medical school discontinued in 1911, while the hospital and nursing school continued as Flint-Goodridge Hospital. New Orleans University and Straight College merged as Dillard University on 6 June 1930, in honor of James H. Dillard. They moved to a new site in 1935, and Dillard University continued to operate the hospital until 1983.

By 2007, the HBCUs had to operate in a city devastated by the floods, and with only 65 percent of its population back in the city. New Orleans had crime and poverty rates among the highest in the nation. Xavier received $165 million in low-interest federal loans to help retire debt incurred by the storm and to rebuild the campus. Freshman enrollment grew 40 percent in 2007. Southern

---

[15] "A Nationally Recognized Power House in the Sciences," Xavier University, 2010, http://www.xula.edu/mediarelations/quickfacts.php;; J. W. Carmichael, Jr., and Deidre Labat, "Minorities in the Biological Sciences, the Xavier Success Story, and Some Implications," *Bioscience* 43/8 (September 1993) 564–69; "Fiscal Strains Force Xavier University to Cut Programs, Faculty," *Diverse: Issues in Higher Education* 22/20 (17 November 2005): 16.

[16] Diana Chandler, "Dillard University Overcomes Katrina," 28 October 2010, United Methodist News Service, New Orleans. The Black College Board of the United Methodist Church also supports other HBCUs: Clark Atlanta, Huston-Tillotson, Meharry, Paine, Philander Smith, Rust, and Wiley.

University-New Orleans, which never had residence halls, operated out of a series of trailers after having all of its buildings inundated by fifteen feet of water. The federal government awarded Southern $44 million to build dormitories and renovate buildings. By early 2008, SUNO prepared to move back into five of its eleven buildings. Enrollment declines damaged TWIS like Tulane and Loyola, but they were bouncing back, too.[17]

The HBCUs were among the nation's oldest institutions. In many cases, some of the nation's architectural and historic structures were located on HBCU campuses. In September 1991, the US Department of Interior began a project to preserve select buildings on HBCU campuses. One public HBCU, Delaware State, was included in the group of eleven.[18] A federal report said, "The Department of Interior recognizes the existence of highly significant historic properties on Historically Black College and University (HBCU) campuses. These are important national historic treasures worthy of our care and attention."[19] Restoration costs for these nationally significant buildings were $755,002,942 as of 1 June 1997. HBCUs became eligible under the Omnibus Parks and Public Lands Management Act (1996) for federal aid to rehabilitate properties on the National Registry of Historic Places. On the HBCU campuses, it was not uncommon to find facilities designed by notable black architects, such as E. C. Miller or McKissack and McKissack. Eighty percent of HBCUs had properties eligible for the National Registry of Historic Places, but many had no funds or personnel to submit nominations or to rehabilitate crumbling buildings. At the request of the Congressional Black Caucus, the US General Accounting Office published a *Historic Preservation: Cost to Restore Historic Properties at Historically Black Colleges and Universities* including photographs of these national treasures.[20] There were 712 properties at twenty-eight HBCUs needing $755 million dollars for restoration. US Senator Joseph I. Lieberman said, "Despite

---

[17] Barack Obama, "Remarks by the President on the Fifth Anniversary of Hurricane Katrina in new Orleans, Louisiana," 29 August 2010, Xavier University (Washington, DC: White House Press Office, 2010) 1–3; Xavier University of Louisiana, "Hurricane Katrina 5 Years Later: Reflections from the Xavier Family," *Katrina Memorial Electronic Journal*, 2010, http://www.xula.edu/katrina/katrina; Xavier University of Louisiana, 2010, Bill Barrow, "Southern University at New Orleans Gets Long-awaited Rebuilding Grant," New Orleans *The Times-Picayune*, 17 August 2009, 1.

[18] NPS, "NPS and HBCUs: Preserving Our Heritage," *Cultural Resources Management* 16/1 (1993): 1–33.

[19] *Historic Preservation: Cost to Restore Historic Properties at Historically Black Colleges and Universities* (Washington DC: General Accounting Office, February 1998) 1–10.

[20] Ibid.

playing a central role in our economy, society, and culture, HBCUs have been physically eroding for years. The architectural beauty of these historic sites is a sign of something deeper—the fact that HBCUs have served as critical portals of opportunity for African Americans throughout our history. That's why they deserve our protection and sensitive preservation."[21]

Several HBCUs earned listings on the National Register of Historic Places. These listings included important structures at Shaw University, Lane College, and historic districts at Fisk and Tennessee State. From 1995 to 1998, federal appropriations to the Interior Department provided more than $5.7 million in matching grants to the UNCF to help HBCUs repair historic structures listed on the National Register of Historic Places. In January 1999, the Interior Department awarded $4.9 million in historic preservation grants to HBCUs that needed the most help: Allen University, Claflin University, Concordia College, Fisk University, Hampton University, Knoxville College, Miles College, Rust College, Spelman College, Stillman College, Talladega College, and Voorhees College.

Many local communities left an uncounted number of Rosenwald schools and the buildings remaining from recently closed HBCUs like Morristown College to rot. When drawing up its new Master Plan from 1989 to 2002, Tennessee State University tore down the last of the original four buildings dating back to the school's opening in 1912. They tore down a building then on the Register of National Historic Places, but built a replica of the building—Goodwill Manor. TSU secured a National Historic District listing for five of the oldest remaining buildings, dating back to 1927, when the northern foundations gave money to Tennessee A&I State Teachers College to build facilities suitable for a college. In some cases, the historic buildings of HBCUs that closed long ago survived in the African-American community as schools, community centers, and church facilities. Federal, state, local, and private and community agencies usually did not identify all these historic structures.[22]

With America's severe shortage of teachers looming on the horizon, the HBCUs came under the spotlight for failing to continue to produce a large supply of minority teachers. At one time blacks comprised 15 percent of the nation's

---

[21] Ibid.; US Department of the Interior, National Park Service, "Ken Salazar, Secretary of the Interior, Announced 20 HBCUs to Receive Historic Preservation Grants," 18 September 2009, Washington, DC, 1.

[22] TSU, "Application for Historic District Nomination," Tennessee State University to State Review Board of Tennessee, Tennessee Historical Commission, 15 January 1998, TSU Library, Special Collections, Lovett Collection, Nashville.

teaching corps, but, unless the downward trend stopped, blacks were predicted to constitute only 5 percent of the nation's teaching corps by 2007.

After the National Council for the Accreditation of Teacher Education's (NCATE) responded with higher standards in the late 1980s and early 1990s, a few of the teacher-education programs at the HBCUs, especially the small private ones, became at risk. The test-taking requirements of the 1998 amendment of the Higher Education Act (1965) and the Education Act (2001) increased pressure on states to rely on standardized tests as the gatekeeper to teacher-education licensure, thus placing even greater pressure on the HBCUs. Sixteen southern states averaged 93 percent for the passing rate on certification tests in 1999–2000, when the average for HBCUs was 79 percent. Most HBCU teacher-education programs maintained the required minimum of at least a 70 percent passage rate under state guidelines. Some HBCUs that once produced qualified teachers failed to meet new NCATE and state standards, mainly due to financing problems.

Many HBCUs responded to the teacher-education challenges. HBCUs gave more attention to teacher education, which was the original mission for many of the black colleges. By 2001, 10.6 percent of black males and 28.2 percent of black females entered teaching compared to 5.4 percent of white males and 17.5 percent of white females. By 2003, whites commanded 90 percent of the teaching jobs, and nearly 90 percent of all American children still attended public schools by 2004. Forty percent of the children in the nation's public schools were of color. By 2005, HBCUs awarded 55 percent of their master's degrees in the field of education. Florida Memorial College added the master's in several fields of education. Several HBCUs including Tennessee State and Alabama A&M offered the PhD and EdD. HBCUs still produced a higher proportion of their bachelor's degrees in education fields than other institutions.[23]

The HBCUs also remained important for steering more African Americans and women into agriculture, business, engineering, home economics, and science. Between 1991 and 2003, the American Assembly of Collegiate Schools and

---

[23] Hill, *The Traditionally Black Institutions of Higher Education*, 35; see Michael T. Nettles and K. Millett, *Preparing HBCUs to Address the Crisis of African American Education through Higher Standards in Teacher Education* (Atlanta: Southern Education Foundation [SEF], 2002) 1–10; Gwendolyn V. Holmes, "A Descriptive Study of Reform in Teacher Education at Historically Black Colleges and Universities" (EdD dissertation, Virginia Polytechnic Institution and State University, 1997) 1–20; SEF, *Unintended Consequences: Perspectives on Teacher Testing and Historically Black Colleges and Universities* (Atlanta: SEF, 2003) 1-10; C. Emily Feistritizer, *The Making of a Teacher: A Report on Teacher Preparation in the U.S.* (Washington DC: Center for Education Information, 1999) 1–20.

Colleges of Business Programs increased the number of HBCUs receiving accreditation from seven to eighteen institutions, including Morehouse College—one of few liberal arts colleges in that prestigious membership. The land-grant HBCUs offered some 874 programs, enrolled 70,382 students taught by 3,724 faculty members and offered dozens of master's degrees. They enrolled 35 percent of minorities in agriculture science, graduated 63 percent of blacks with bachelors in agriculture, and offered sixty bachelor's degrees in home economics, including child and family development, clothing and textiles, early childhood education, food management, and hotel and restaurant management. By 2000, Tuskegee University produced 90 percent of blacks holding degrees in veterinarian medicine.[24]

The engineering/science aspect of black education, once purposely constrained by the Jim Crow system and racial discrimination elsewhere, developed slowly in America. Since the 1920s, the land grant HBCU college presidents pushed the federal government to support their efforts to establish industrial arts, engineering, and science programs. On 26 October 1943, at the Conference of Presidents of Land Grant Colleges in Chicago, eight science professors organized the Association of Science Teachers at Negro Colleges and Affiliated Institutions, which became the National Institute of Science to stimulate interest and improve teaching of science at the institutions. The land-grant HBCUs expanded the movement at the end of World War II and, partly due to pressures made by a significant part of the HBCU post-war student enrollment, the WWII veterans comprised as much as 30 percent of HBCU enrollment between 1946 and 1953. The HBCU presidents spoke to the president of the US about their problems in 1946. At the Presidents' Twenty-sixth Annual Conference of Negro Land-grant Colleges, 19-21 October 1948, the delegates approved a program to survey the HBCUs offerings in engineering and mechanical arts. They approved a resolution to ask the USDOE to help the HBCUs establish and expand programs in engineering. They asked for help to remove the discrimination and disparity existing for seventy-five years. By 1949, seven land-grant HBCUs were offering engineering courses: architectural (4), civil (2), electrical (4), mechanical (4), and industrial or general (1). Prairie View

[24] Richard J. Bennof, "What Is the Level of Federal Science and Engineering Support to Historically Black Colleges and Universities?" issue brief, NSF99-356, 26 August 1999, National Science Foundation, Division of Science Resources Studies, Washington, DC, 1–4; Joan Burreli and Alan Rapoport, *Role of HBCUs as Baccalaureate-Origin Institutions of Black SLE Doctorate Recipients*, NSF publication, 08-319 (Washington, DC: Division of Science Resources Studies, 2008) 1–6.

was the only HBCU land grant offering four programs. Howard became the first HBCU to offer graduate programs and doctorates in engineering fields.[25]

In 1986, twenty-four blacks earned PhD degrees in engineering from American colleges and universities. This was not enough. By 1993, nine HBCUs offered degrees in engineering, and by 2000, 325,416 blacks enrolled in undergraduate engineering and science programs. Between 1994 and 2001, black recipients of master's degrees increased from 6.1 percent to 8.9 percent in all fields of study and from 4.9 percent to 9.7 percent in science and engineering fields. HBCUs produced 15 percent of master's degrees held by blacks in technical fields. Bowie State, Clark Atlanta, Southern at Baton Rouge, North Carolina A&T, Tennessee State, Alabama A&M, and Tuskegee were among America's top 26 producers of master's degrees awarded to blacks in computer science, engineering, and mathematics. Howard University produced 21.4 percent of doctorates awarded to blacks in computer science, engineering, and mathematics.[26]

Among the top fifty-one baccalaureate-institutions-of-origin for black science and engineering doctorate recipients for 1997–2001, nearly a third of the institutions were HBCUs: Howard, Spelman, Hampton, Morehouse, Southern, Xavier, Jackson State, Tuskegee, FAMU, Alabama A&M, Prairie View, Tougaloo, Fisk, Morgan, and Tennessee State. Tennessee State, with nine thousand students and a $160 million budget, produced fifteen of these baccalaureates that went on to earn doctorates compared to sixteen for the overwhelmingly white University of Tennessee with 25,000 students and a billion-dollar-plus budget. TWIs University of Georgia and Georgia Institute of Technology produced thirty black students who went on to earn doctorates in science and engineering at various institutions, while Spelman College, Morehouse College, and Clark Atlanta University alone produced 143 students who went on to earn doctorates in science and engineering. For 1997–2001, Mississippi had no TWIs listed among America's top fifty-one colleges and universities as producing black students that

---

[25] Burreli and Rapoport, *Role of HBCUs*, 1–6; William M. King, "Hubert Branch Crouch and the Origins of the National Institute of Science," *Journal of Negro History* 79/1 (Winter 1994): 18–33; R. B. Atwood, "The Future of Negro Land-Grant College," *Journal of Negro Education* 27/3 (Summer 1958): 381–91.

[26] Roebuck and Murty, *Black Colleges and Universities*, 102–104, A-64, C-2, C-3; James W. Smith, ed., *Leadership and Learning: An Interpretive History of Historically Black Land-Grant Colleges and Universities—A Centennial Study* (Washington DC: National Association of State Universities and Land-Grant Colleges [NASULGC], 1993) 35–40; Cynthia L. Jackson and Eleanor F. Nunn, *Historically Black Colleges and Universities: A Reference Book* (Santa Barbara CA: ABC-Clio, 2003) 103; *Proceedings of the Negro Land-Grant Colleges*, 1944–1951 (Washington DC: Howard University, 1951) 1–25.

went on to earn doctorates in science or engineering, but Jackson State University produced twenty-eight students who became doctoral recipients in these fields. TWIs in the nineteen former Jim Crow states listed among the top fifty-one producers of black doctorate recipients in science and engineering accounted for 170 such students. Indeed, the HBCUs produced 628 doctoral students in the period 1997 to 2000. The private HBCUs outperformed the public HBCUs in this role.[27]

In its 2005 science, technology, engineering, and mathematics (STEM) report on HBCUs, the Southern Education Foundation tried to expose donors and policymakers to information about the importance and disproportionately large contribution that HBCUs were making to human capital development in these vital fields. SEF challenged TWIs to do more to enhance the number of blacks pursuing STEM training. SEF believed fairness and excellence are crucial challenges in southern education. The report showed how HBCUs are producing a fourth of the entire nation's African-American college graduates in the sciences and even much higher percentages in some fields such as natural sciences. STEM focused on Clark, Spelman, Morehouse, Xavier, Tennessee State, and Morgan State to demonstrate "best practices" with good results.[28]

Twenty-first-century HBCUs increased their number of technical programs. Tennessee State added PhD degrees in biological sciences, including an emphasis in agricultural sciences, and in computer engineering—graduating its first student with the PhD in biological sciences in May 2002. Maryland Eastern Shore added the PhD in food science and technology, while Delaware State developed the PhD in mathematics. The Minority Institution Astrobiology Collaboratory began after the Astrobiology Science Conference held at NASA's Ames Apace Center in 2002, where less than one percent of the eight hundred attendees were blacks. This collaboration between North Carolina Central, Tennessee State, South Carolina State, Norfolk State, Benedict College, Houston Community College, and Bennett College introduced HBCU students and minority youngsters in outreach programs to the field of astrobiology that studies both life existing in space and the life humans would take there. The Nashville *Scene* announced one such HBCU graduate was "working on a Mars projects at Fisk

---

[27] Burreli and Rapoport, *Role of HBCUs*, 1–6.

[28] Southern Education Foundation (SEF), *Miles to Go: A Report on Black Students and Postsecondary Education in the South* (Atlanta GA: SEF, 1998) 1–139; SEF, *Igniting Potential: Historically Black Colleges and Universities in Science, Technology, Engineering, and Mathematics* (Atlanta GA: SEF, 2005) 1-10.

University and enrolled as a graduate student in the Science and Technical Communication Department at the University of Washington."[29]

A coalition of industry, government agencies, and HBCUs forged corporate-academic alliances to continue to extend quality engineering and technology programs to minorities. In 2004, Alabama A&M, Florida A&M., Hampton, Howard, Jackson State, Morgan State, North Carolina A&I, Prairie View A&M, Southern, Tennessee State, and Tuskegee maintained accredited engineering and technology schools. HBCUs continued to graduate nearly 30 percent of black engineers in the US, and offered a wide range of degrees in aeronautical and industrial technology, architectural, bioenvironmental, chemical, civil, computer, electrical, industrial, manufacturing, material sciences, mechanical, and transportation, and offered bachelor, masters, and PhD degrees. Howard offered five masters and three PhD degree programs in engineering. Tennessee State, Florida A&M, and Morgan offered PhD programs in engineering. Fisk's Molecular Spectroscopy Research Laboratory was internationally recognized, and the American Chemical Society (ACS) continuously approved its chemistry program. After fifteen years of rebuilding its chemistry program, Tennessee State won ACS approval by 2007.

Title III and other federal and state grants helped with money, equipment, and faculty and student training. Help also came from IBM Corporation, AT&T, Boeing Co., Lockheed Martin Co., Office of Naval Research, and Raytheon. American business and industry tapped *all* the nation's human resources in order for America to remain competitive with other nations. Boeing awarded millions of dollars in contracts to HBCUs. Various companies sponsored fellowships to help fine tune HBCU engineering and technology faculty. IBM hired nearly 100 students from the HBCUs. By 2005, Norfolk State had graduate programs in optical engineering, computer science, criminal justice, clinical psychology, and social work. Alabama A&M, by 2007, was offering the PhD in applied physics, plant and soil science, food science, and reading/literacy, and masters' degrees in art, social work, and biology. Hampton and Tuskegee implemented doctoral programs in science.[30]

HBCUs increased their competitiveness in research activities far beyond the abilities they had in the 1930s. Wilberforce secured external funds for a computer

---

[29] S. Latham, "Fisk University Science," *The Nashville Scene*, 15 March 2007, 1.

[30] USDOE, National Center for Education Statistics, "Degrees Conferred by HBCUs in 2001–02," table 2, A-16, A-20; USDOE, NCES, "Characteristics of Minority-serving Institutions and Minority Undergraduates Enrolled in These Institutions," NCES Publication 2008156, Statisical Analysis Program, November 2007, Washington, DC, i–6, 33–36.

science and engineering program—a Teaching Collaboration and Research Center, and participation in the Minority Male Health Consortium and Cooperative Education. Tuskegee, which enrolled more than three thousand students in 2003, continued to be a leader in research and public service in the impoverished Black Belt. In 2004, Tuskegee hosted the National Technical Association's conference on "Science and Technology: Research, Business, and Impact on HBCUs/Minority Institutions," and the 2004 Southeastern Conference on Theoretical and Applied Mechanics. Tuskegee's Center of Excellence in Minority Veterinary Medical Education housed outreach programs to affect the South and the African continent. Alabama A&M, Jackson State, and Tennessee State co-sponsored the Tri-State Research Collaboration Conference in Nashville in 2004 to leverage their resources and synergy in research expertise, pursue collaborative research activities and projects in nanoscale science and technology, computational science, environmental science (bioremediation, plant science, etc), homeland security, health research and health science, and teacher education and learning science. Howard University was one of America's top institutions in federal research and development revenues received from the federal government from 2005–2006.[31]

HBCU graduates overall had a higher retention rate in graduate schools compared to black students originating at TWIs. Black females at HBCUs selected business, engineering, and science as majors at greater rates compared to their counterparts attending TWIs. Tranquil racial relations on the HBCU campus and excellent social-support networks improved minority students' academic achievement. Students attending church-affiliated HBCUs developed higher self-ratings in domains of self-concept-psychosocial wellness, academic, and achievement than students attending many TWIs did. Ashley McDonald, a Tennessee State University student, said she transferred from the University of Kentucky, where students were "treated as nothing more than numbers as they walked into lecture halls with 200–300 students." McDonald said,

> At TSU, instructors ... do teach a subject that some are forced to learn the hard way. That subject is life. It is true that life at an HBCU is not a representation of the real world. Black people do not make up the majority of this society. But life at an HBCU does teach you that nothing comes without hard work.... Overcoming the odds makes for a more determined spirit. It gives you a clearer picture of where you want to be. That is an experience I was not able to get at the University of Kentucky.

---

[31] NCES, "Current-fund Revenue Received from the Federal Government by the 120 Degree-granting Institutions, 2005–06," *Digest of Education Statistics: 2009* 1/1 (April 2010): table 357.

> They remind you constantly that you are black.... I thank TSU and other schools that strive to give their students a sense of [positive self-] identity and the motivation to excel in life.[32]

---

[32] Ashley McDonald, "HBCUs Nurture Blacks in a Way Like No Other," *The Meter* (17 March 2008): 5. Carter G. Woodson, *The Mis-Education of the Negro* (Washington DC: The Associated Publishers, 1933, 2005) 16, 71–72, 88–89; Mikyong Minsumkim and Clifton F. Conrad, "The Impact of Historically Black Colleges and Universities on the Academic Success of African American Students," *Research in Higher Education* 47/4 (June 2006): 399–427; Laura W. Perna, "The Contribution of Black Colleges and Universities to the Preparation of African Americans for Faculty Careers," *Research in Higher Education* 42/3 (June 2001): 267–94.

8

New Challenges

When they faced the first decade of the twenty-first century, some of the HBCUs still had many problems, mainly financial difficulties, a dearth of quality leadership, and inadequate alumni support of endowment funds. Noting the history of the HBCUs, Arne Duncan, speaking at the National Historically Black Colleges and Universities Conference, 2 September 2009, said President Barack Obama's budget included increased funds for HBCU students and ways to fix the high school-college pipeline:

> ...one of the biggest problems facing the HBCUs [is that]...Students so often receive an inadequate education in high school and arrive on campus with poor skills. HBCUs in particular need more funding to be successful. Today, schools of education at HBCUs face a new challenge—to turn out this next generation of African American teachers to serve in high-poverty urban and rural schools.[1]

Duncan mentioned Philander Smith College's Black Male Initiative Program that doubled the graduation rate for black men on campus. Elizabeth City State University had a 51 percent graduation rate over six years, but several HBCUs graduated fewer than 20 percent of their students. "That is an unacceptable outcome for students," said Duncan.[2]

The HBCUs had an added problem not mentioned by the US Secretary of Education: the state practice of giving TWIs better resources and duplicative programs that rivaled those at nearby public HBCU was an externally imposed problem that impeded the expansion of graduate offerings at public HBCUs and efforts to attract more non-black enrollments. The HBCUs had struggled since the 1930s to compete in America's graduate and professional education degree arena. After 1942, the historically black colleges and universities (HBCUs) started conferring a larger share of master's degrees, and after 1951 doctorate degrees. HBCUs produced 44 percent of blacks with master's degrees by 1977. Between 1993 and1997, Howard University awarded 156 doctorate degrees (12.5 percent),

---

[1] USDOE, "Remarks of Secretary Arne Duncan at the 2009 HBCU Conference," White House Initiative on Historically Black Colleges and Universities, 2 September 2009 (Washington, DC: The White House, 2009) 1–4.

[2] Ibid.

while the top twenty-two US institutions altogether awarded 1,244 doctorates to blacks. Atlanta University, Howard, Prairie View, Jackson State, Texas Southern, Southern University, Alabama A&M, and Tennessee State each annually awarded more than two hundred master's degrees. In 1999–2000, HBCUs granted 3,433 associate, 28,976 bachelors, 6,575 masters, and 337 doctorate degrees—including degrees in natural sciences, computer science, education, and technical fields, and 1,509 professional degrees. The four largest HBCUs, enrolling more than eight thousand students and holding Carnegie Corporation designations of level 1, doctoral institutions, were FAMU (93 percent blacks), Southern at Baton Rouge (94 percent blacks), Howard (83 percent blacks), and Tennessee State (76 percent blacks), and each annually produced one-thousand-plus undergraduate and graduate degrees. As bachelor's-institutions-of-origin, HBCUs produced students that earned doctorates in science and mathematics, and who became judges, attorneys, and military leaders at higher rates than black students at most traditionally white institutions (TWIs).

As a feeder, the HBCUs also produced more black baccalaureates in biophysical and physical sciences, business/management, computer science, engineering, and mathematics than the 673 other institutions in the Southern Regional Education Board (SREB) states. Some 35 percent of blacks holding graduate and professional degrees had HBCU origins from 1990 to 2001. The minority schools in the SREB states had 36.1 percent of the area's black graduate student enrollment.[3] Perhaps the expansion in science, social science, and technical areas could have been greater, but state education agencies granted additional graduate programs to HBCUs often confined to fields of teacher education and low-demand fields, and this practice likely drove students to the TWIs.

The nation's production of black graduate students as well as the lower faculty salaries at the HBCUs contributed to the small percentage of black faculty employed at America's HBCUs and working at the TWIs. The proportion of US doctorates earned, in all fields, by minority students peaked in 2004, but continued to grow between 1994 and 2006. Blacks led the minority group with 1,659 doctorates earned in 2006. Women increased their share to 45 percent. Meanwhile, blacks comprised less than 6 percent of full-time faculty members in the USA, but made up 13 percent of the American population. Nine HBCUs, including Bluefield State College, had majority white faculty by 2001. Whites represented 74 percent of faculty members at Xavier University in 1997. By 1999,

[3] Southern Education Foundation (SEF), *Miles to Go*, 15; USDOE, "Enrollment in the degree-granting HBCUs, 2000–2001," table 9; Roebuck and Murty, *Historically Black Colleges and Universities*, 102–104, A-64, C-2, C-3.

Spelman College, which once had all-white faculty, had 76.5 percent non-white faculty. After 1969, when the TWIs began to hire black faculty and staff, the percentage of black faculty members stagnated and declined on HBCU campuses. Tennessee State University had 100 percent black faculty in 1912, and in 1999 had a faculty of 43.5 percent blacks, 44.3 percent whites, and 12.2 percent "other race" (Asian, Asian-Indian, Native American, and Hispanic). In 2001, at HBCUs blacks averaged 58 percent of faculty: 4,411 male and 3,890 female.[4]

The American racial situation—including benign but anti-black racial attitudes among non-black (white and other) faculty as well as heavily white male resistance to affirmative action made it difficult to develop an adequate supply of black PhD holders in content areas other than education and teachers/administrators for secondary schools and community colleges. Even though 84 percent of black college students attended TWIs, community and junior colleges in America, these institutions maintained a low production of black graduates that entered graduate and professional programs. Yet, America still needed more blacks holding quality PhD degrees.

By 1978, 1,200 blacks received doctorates from American institutions, including a few black graduates from southern universities. In 1999, blacks received 5.9 percent of all doctorate degrees, but only 2.8 percent of doctorates earned in the physical sciences Again, no HBCU offered doctorate degrees before 1951. The 2005 Woodrow Wilson National Fellowship Foundation, *Diversity & the Ph.D.: A Review of Efforts to Broaden Race & Ethnicity in U.S. Doctoral Education*, focused on blacks and Hispanics, "because they are the largest underrepresented groups in higher education relative to their presence in the nation's population."[5] African Americans and Hispanics had 32 percent of doctoral-age citizens, but by 2003, only 7 percent of all doctoral recipients were African Americans or Hispanic. The Wilson Foundation report said, "It's getting worse. Despite extraordinary support within and beyond academic for affirmative action admissions programs—as evidence by the University of Michigan case—court challenges have had a significant chilling effect, resulting in a dilution of

---

[4] Joseph O. Jewell, "To Set an Example: The Tradition of Diversity at Historically Black Colleges and Universities," *Urban Education* 37/1 (January 2002) 7–21; "Employees in Degree-granting Historically Black Colleges and Universities, by Employment Status and Sex, and by Primary Occupation and Type of Institution: Fall 2001," in NCES, *Historically Black Colleges and Universities 1976 to 2001* (Washington, DC: National Center for Education Statistics, 2001) iii, 73.

[5] The Woodrow Wilson National Fellowship Foundation, *Diversity and the Ph.D.: A Review of Efforts to Broaden Race and Ethnicity in U.S. Doctoral Education* (Princeton NJ: Woodrow Wilson National Fellowship Foundation, 2005) 1.

resources and weakening of institutional will."[6] There has been a decline in fellowships offered to minority students, a decline in offering financial help to minority doctoral students, changes in support programs for minority students, and aid packages that focus less on under-representation issues. "The dearth of minorities [in TWIs] is even greater in dean, provost, and vice president positions," said a 2004 American Council on Education report.[7] The racial discrimination remained unchanged said former US Civil Rights Commission chair Mary Frances Berry.[8]

White faculty members continued to increase at the HBCUs. Regional accreditation association standards demanded more doctoral holders. However, the hiring of the TWI's surplus non-black PhDs—many of whom never developed teaching skills of quality—sometimes brought to the HBCU campuses some individuals who seemed discontented with their personal career fate and did not appreciate placement in the predominantly black environment. Some of them had low expectations of HBCU students; in frustration and resentment, some publicly criticized the institution *and* the students; a few other displaced, non-white professors did not take too seriously their professorial responsibilities and their own self-improvement. An HBCU newspaper said having non-black faculty members did not necessarily translate into higher quality: "We need individuals with competence and dedication, not simply credentials, to fill the teaching positions at the HBCUs, if we are to maintain our relevancy."[9] Often, however, the HBCU got what it paid for. Faculty salary disparity between public HBCUs and public TWIs remained a problem, even after the desegregation of higher education cases were settled by 2005, because the federal court avoided the complex issue of wage discrimination in the former Jim Crow states, and the

---

[6] Ibid.

[7] *Minorities in Higher Education Twenty-first Annual Status Report, 2003–2004.*

[8] Woodrow Wilson National Fellowship Foundation (WWF), *Diversity & the PhD: A Review of Efforts to Broaden Race & Ethnicity in U.S. Doctoral Education* (Washington DC: WWF, 2005) 1–10; Mary Frances Berry, "Kerner Commission's Work Remains Unfinished," *Focus* 36 (2008): 14–15; SEF, *Black Faculty in Traditional White Institutions in Selected Adams States: Characteristics, Experiences and Perceptions* (Atlanta GA: Southern Education Foundation, 1988) 1–19; see National Advisory Commission on Black Higher Education and Black Colleges and Universities, *A Losing Battle: the Decline in Black Participation in Graduate and Professional Education* (Washington DC: American Council on Education, 2004) 1–30; Center for Advancement of Racial and Ethnic Equity, *Minorities in Higher Education Twenty-first Annual Status Report 2003–2004* (Washington DC: American Council in Education, 2004); *The Chronicle of Higher Education* (9 December 2005); *The Chronicle of Higher Education* (25 February 2005):

[9] Editor, "Racial Problems and the Recruitment of Academic Staff at Southern Colleges and Universities," *American Sociological Review* 26/6 (December 1961): 960–70.

SREB states and college and university boards, therefore, made no real uniform efforts to deal with the disparities of salary by race at institutions of higher education.

According to the USDOE data, in 2001–2002, average salaries of full-time instructional faculty on nine-month contracts at HBCUs were 81 percent of the average of all American institutions of higher education. Again, the average income for an African-American family was only 63 percent of the income for European-American families. Thus, racial disparities in salaries plagued almost all American blacks. Average HBCU faculty salaries lagged behind faculty salaries at TWIs. In 2002–2003, the average salary at HBCUs was $67,400 for a professor. Howard, the top doctoral research level HBCU, reported average salaries of $92,500 for professors, $68,000 associate professors, $58,000 assistant professors, and $48,000 instructors in 2005. Average faculty salaries at Morehouse College were $73,100 for professors, $60,400 for associates, and $44,900 for assistants; Spelman College: $81,500, $59,700, and $48,500. Salaries at the instructor level at HBCUs and TWIs came closest to matching each other.[10]

Despite problems in faculty recruitment, salaries, endowments, and making the annual budgets, America's black colleges and universities had to intensify their efforts to salvage as many minority college students as possible. Once they recruited, retained, educated and trained, then graduated them, the HBCUs had to provide their students with avenues to employment and give them the armor to survive in America's hostile racial environment. HBCUs, thus, since 1837, continued to serve as academies of last resort for many economically disadvantaged students. The HBCU faculty and staff established missions, purposes, goals and objectives intended to provide an environment of emotional support for students, as repositories for black heritage and culture, and foster self-pride and self-esteem. HBCUs aimed to enhance opportunities for leadership and development skills and continue as exemplary institutions for diversity. HBCUs offered programs designed to meet unique needs of students and minority communities.

Talladega College, among small HBCUs, struggled to survive in the new century. Talladega began on 20 November 1865 when a freedmen's convention met in

---

[10] NCES, "Employees in Degree-granting Institutions, by Race, Ethnicity, Sex, Employment Status, Control and Type of Institution, and Primary Occupation: Fall 2007" and "Average Salary of Full-time Instructional Faculty on 9-month Contracts in 4-year Degree-granting Institutions, by Control and Type, 2008–09," table 259, in *Digest of Education Statistics* (Washington, DC: National Center for Education Statistics, 2009).

Mobile, Alabama. Two former slaves, William Savery and Thomas Tarrant, made a commitment to the education of our children and youth as vital to the preservation of our liberties. They, along with the American Missionary Association and others, bought twenty acres of land and the old Baptist Academy for whites, and opened the school for 140 students. The institution gained its charter in 1869. By 1928, Du Bois and *Crisis* magazine considered Talladega one of the best HBCUs. The state's oldest black college had about 350 students. By 2001, Talladega enrolled 540, and in 2003 some 468 students from twenty-nine states, five foreign countries, and 39 percent from outside Alabama. Some 341 of the students were residents, while the institution had campus housing capacity for 660 persons. The average high school grade point average for the students was 2.6, and the average ACT composite score was 17. Some 98 percent of the students required financial aid to pay the academic year costs of $11,548. According to the Office of Institutional Effectiveness, the results for fall 2003 were quite satisfactory.[11] Some 70 percent of the freshmen indicated they would return, and indicators in acquisition of academic skills and academic competencies were 60–95 percent in various areas including listening, writing, communication, scientific inquiry, and mastery in various literary works. The "Matrix" included action steps and precise plans for academic achievement and increased enrollments.[12]

In order to maintain a competitive twenty-first-century academic agenda, Talladega employed forty-five faculty members to educate, train, and graduate students in biology, business administration (accounting, economics, and management), chemistry, computer science, education, English, finance and banking, history, marketing, mathematics, music, physics, psychology, public administration, social work, and sociology. Budget problems affected the institution's re-accreditation efforts. However, Talladega installed the twentieth president in January 2008, who increased enrollment, restored SACS accreditation, expanded academic and athletic programs, raised millions of dollars, added buildings, and advanced the institution's mission and vision. Talladega maintained SACS accreditation in 2009, and is providing quality

---

[11] Talladega College, *Student Learning Outcomes Matrix for General Education at Talladega* (Talladega AL: Talladega College, Office of Institutional Effectiveness, 2004) 1–20.

[12] Maxine D. Jones and Joe M. Richardson, *Talladega College: The First Century* (Tuscaloosa: University of Alabama Press, 1990); Roebuck and Murty, *Historically Black Colleges*, 35, 37; Drewry and Doermann, *Stand and Prosper*, 70, 92–93, 123, 140, 146, 238, 239, 241–242; Jackson and Nunn, *Historically Black Colleges and Universities*, 11, 44, 112–14, 118, 119.

education through liberal arts. The institution reported about 600 students by 2010.[13]

Mary McLeod Bethune founded Bethune-Cookman College. Former slave parents gave birth to Bethune in South Carolina in 1875. She was a product of Barber-Scotia College, and attended Dwight Moody's Institute for Home and Foreign Missions in Chicago. She taught school in Georgia and South Carolina. Her husband, Albertus McLeod, attended Avery Institute. After the family moved to Daytona in 1904, Bethune founded the Daytona Educational and Industrial School for Negro Girls. She sent a letter to the *Daytona Morning Journal* in 1915, emphasizing that local people should not perceive it as a threat to whites; the school was in their best interests, and deserved white financial support. Bethune wrote a letter to Julius Rosenwald:

> My work is very much in need of help. We have lost two crops this year from heavy rains.... We are six hundred dollars behind with our November expenses.... We have one hundred seventy seven dollars in treasure, which will not carry us a week. Will you give us two thousand dollars toward our running expenses? Will you help us now?[14]

The school became Daytona Normal and Industrial School, merging with the Methodist Episcopal Church's Cookman Institute of Jacksonville, Florida, in 1923, achieving junior college status in the 1930s, and becoming a four-year institution under Bethune's leadership.

Bethune was one of the few female college founder-presidents in the world. She served on various assignments under Presidents Calvin Coolidge (R), Herbert Hoover (R) and Franklin Roosevelt (D), formed the National Council of Negro Women, directed the Negro Youth Administration during the New Deal, and continued as Bethune-Cookman College president until 1947. She died in 1955. In 1975, the National Park Services designated her home a National Historical Landmark. Some of the press dubbed her the female Booker T. Washington.

---

[13] Talladega College, *Talladega College Strategic Plan: 2000 and Beyond* (Talladega AL: Talladega College, 2000) 1–20; Talladega College, "Talladega College History," 2010, http://www.talladega.edu/history.asp.

[14] Audrey T. McCluskey and E. M. Smith, *Mary McLeod Bethune, Building a Better World, Essays and Selected Documents* (Bloomington: Indiana University Press, 1999) 58–61, 70, 80, 166; Mary McLeod Bethune Papers are stored at the Amistad Research Center, Tulane University, New Orleans LA; see R. Holt, *Mary McLeod Bethune: A Biography* (Garden City NY: Doubleday Co., 1964) 1–20.

By 2005, Bethune-Cookman College had 2,900 students, a solid reputation for academic excellence and community service, with schools of business, education, general studies, arts and humanities, nursing, social science, and science, engineering, and mathematics, a Renewing Ethical Values Program and religious programs for the students. Bethune-Cookman remained an athletic power.[15] The institution remained SACS accredited.

Fisk University, which thrived as an intellectual center for black scholars from 1927 to 1957, was examining itself in order to find a new fit in the twenty-first century. An extensive in-house study revealed some valuable data for use in Fisk's strategic planning. Roughly 75 percent of the respondents (faculty, administrators, staff members, and students) agreed they were proud of historic Fisk. Some 56 percent of the student respondents agreed that Fisk was a good value for the education students received, but that Fisk University needed to do more to secure the inner-city campus, expand student enrollment, and bring more diversity into the student body, which was mostly black, female, and residential. Fisk maintained accreditation by SACS, had state approval for its teacher-education program, and continued to be the first private HBCU to gain accreditation from the National Association of Schools of Music. By 2001, the enrollment dipped under one thousand to about 845 students, and the endowment had slipped badly in recent decades.

Fisk University got busy under its newest president Hazel O'Leary in charting new strategies, goals, and objectives for a viable twenty-first century institution. In 2006, Fisk agonized over plans to sell part of its international art collection to make ends meet and pump $15-$20 million back into the endowment; however, several million-dollar grants and contributions materialized. President O'Leary canvassed community organizations, preaching the history and value of Fisk University. By 2007, Fisk had an economic impact of $42 million on the local community. Fisk ranked high in graduation rates for low-income students and had cooperative programs and partnerships with Vanderbilt University and next-door Meharry Medical College. Larger donations began to flow, and Fisk University completed a major, $750,000 upgrade to the art gallery facility open to the public.

Fisk University, as many other private HBCUs, had spent its endowment principal. The donations from its thousands of alumni only trickled in. Moreover, after 1980, in America's *de facto* re-segregated society, Fisk and other minority institutions seemed to receive smaller donations from the whites that held most

---

[15] Shelia Y. Fleming, *Bethune-Cookman College, 1904–1994: The Answered Prayer to a Dream* (Daytona Beach: Bethune-Cookman College, 1995) 1–30.

of the nation's surplus wealth. Additionally, the 105 HBCUs commanded only 16 percent of the blacks enrolled in the nation's colleges and universities, and the public HBCUs, with cheaper tuition and fees, better campus facilities, and more graduate and technical degree programs, made it difficult for private HBCUs, like Fisk, to compete in the pool of black college students. Fisk University was deep in debt, trying to make payrolls, maintain old buildings, and pay for daily operations. By 2010, Fisk University was still trying to sell one of its precious art collections for $30 million, but the state attorney general and a local court blocked the sale in order to keep the treasured collection in Tennessee. The money would only bandage Fisk's financial wounds, because the institution needed to build its endowment fund to about $150 million to survive the future. The endowment was gone, and the buildings on campus were mortgaged to close annual budget shortfalls. By November 2010, Fisk University's financial situation again seemed to improve through large donations, but the permanent fix to this private HBCU still escaped Fisk University administrators, faculty, and students.

In the early 1940s, private higher education for blacks was in crisis. Contributions from foundations and colleges dwindled, partly due to America's Great Depression (1929–1939) and World War II. Some foundations, such as the Rosenwald Fund in 1948, shut down.[16]

In 1943, a group of private HBCUs met and reflected on a bleak article forecasting financial troubles for these institutions in the Pittsburgh *Courier*. Frederick D. Patterson, president of Tuskegee Institute, wrote the article on 30 January 1943. They agreed to pool solicitation of resources by organizing the "United College Drive"—the United Negro College Fund (UNCF). Patterson proposed that each institution give up separate campaigns and pool the names of annual donors. They met in Atlanta on 27 September 27 1943, and twenty-seven accredited, private HBCUs agreed to begin the campaign by May 1944. The members met on 27 June 27 1944 and agreed to set a goal of $1.5 million, with 45 percent divided equally, 45 percent based on previous five-year average income

---

[16] See Emma D. Cody-Mitchell, "The Economic Health of Private Historically Black Colleges and Universities: 1986–1995" (PhD dissertation, University of Tennessee, 2000) 1–20; Cynthia L. Jackson and Eleanor F. Nunn, *Historically Black Colleges and Universities: A Reference Book* (Santa Barbara CA: ABC-Clio, 2003) 111–25; Eric Anderson and Alfred A. Moss Jr., *Dangerous Donations: Northern Philanthropy and Southern Black Education, 1902–1930* (Columbia: University of Missouri Press, 1999) 1–21; Evelyn C. J. Carroll, "Priorities in Philanthropic Support for Private Negro Colleges and Universities, 1930–1973" (PhD dissertation, University of Michigan, 1982) 1–20.

from endowment funds, gifts and grants, and 10 percent based on the five-year enrollment.

Philanthropists including the GEB, John D. Rockefeller, Jr., Walter Hoving, Thomas A. Morgan, and the Rosenwald Fund, helped with fundraisers. Negro soldiers, states, labor unions, corporations, other businesses, and the black community contributed. Rockefeller, Jr., worked on other wealthy whites to become involved, because "Next to the war, and the problems immediately growing out of it, I think it is not an overstatement to say that the Negro problem is the most important problem, which confronts our nation."[17] UNCF gained a permanent head in 1948. By 1960, the HBCUs, which depended on tuition, lost their monopoly on black students.[18] But the UNCF raised funds through nationally televised telethons, mass mailings, students, and solicitation of corporations and according to its 13 June 2003 report, thirty-nine UNCF members enrolled 65,000 students. UNCF had liabilities and net assets of $183,768,523. The report said,

> Financial need is rising, even as historic budget deficits and economic uncertainty are forcing colleges to raise tuition. The congressional Advisory Committee on Student Financial Assistance, in 2002, said almost half of all qualified low- and moderate-income high school graduates could not afford a four-year college. By 2010, cost alone could prevent 4.4 million qualified students from attending a four-year college.[19]

In February 2004, under new leadership, UNCF intended to increase the endowment to $1 billion, position UNCF to become a greater advocate for members' interests in DC and corporate boardrooms, change the UNCF agenda to help improve members' operations, and help them with capacity building, financial management, governance, curriculum development, and facilities needs. In March 2008, the UNCF capacity-building program announced nearly $6 million dollars in grants to Benedict, Claflin, Jarvis Christian, Morehouse, Philander Smith, and Wiley colleges to help hire consultants for fund-raising campaigns.[20]

---

[17] F. D. Patterson, "Would It Not Be Wise for Some Negro Schools to Make Joint Appeal to Public for Funds?" *Pittsburgh Courier*, 30 January 1943, 1.

[18] S. K. Tucker, "The Early Years of the United Negro College Fund, 1943–1960," *Journal of African American History* 87/1 (2002): 416–32; Caroline S. V. Turner, "Envisioning Black Colleges: A History of the United Negro College Fund," *Oral History Review* 37/1 (January 2010): 152–55.

[19] United Negro College Fund, *Annual Report*, 13 June 2003, Fairfax VA, 1–10.

[20] Marybeth Grasman, *Envisioning Black Colleges: A History of the United Negro College Fund* (Baltimore: Johns Hopkins University Press, 2007) 1–288.

The compassionate capitalism version, proposed by former president George Bush (R) in the late 1980s, never kicked in. By 2008, under unrestrained capitalism, America's financial markets and the economy collapsed, college endowments plunged, and the pension funds lost a large amount of money within 18 months. Students increasingly failed to access the student-loan credit markets, unemployment rose to 9.5 percent, and community college enrollments increased dramatically as the unemployed sought more education and training; state and college budgets, however, declined. Between 1994 and 2009, 224 American colleges and universities closed their doors, and among them were several HBCUs. The Southern Association of Colleges and Schools (SACS), the accrediting agency for most HBCUs, wanted to see three consistent years of financial solvency. Since the 1965 Higher Education Act, accrediting agencies had acted as gatekeepers for issuance of federal higher-education funds. The loss of accreditation denied federal funds to the institution and its students.

Eight private HBCUs lost accreditation: Daniel Payne College (Birmingham) in 1977, Virginia College (Lynchburg) in 1980, Friendship College (South Carolina) in 1981, Mississippi Industrial College (Holly Springs) in 1982, Natchez Junior College (Mississippi) in 1983, Bishop College (Texas) in 1988, and Morristown Junior College (Tennessee) in 1995. By 2002–2004, the new list of HBCUs that lost accreditation included Knoxville College (Tennessee), Barber-Scotia College, and Morris Brown College (Georgia). The latter three institutions, continued to operate as unaccredited colleges.

In 2002, SACS voted to deny reaffirmation of accreditation to Knoxville College, mostly due to financial insolvency that prevented the institution from maintaining certain standards. Alumni, friends, and donors seemed incapable of saving Knoxville College (1875) that was a result of efforts by the Freedmen's Mission under Presbyterian missionaries from the North establishing a freedmen's school in Nashville on 13 October 13 1863. They named the school for white missionary John G. McKee, who worked tirelessly raising money. Nashville assumed the McKee School for Negroes in fall 1867. The missionaries moved their operations to Knoxville, and opened Knoxville College in 1875. KC thrived, becoming a liberal arts college in 1877, and graduating two students in 1883. KC briefly operated a medical school during the 1890s. Tennessee used Knoxville College as the recipient of federal 1890 land-grant funds for the Negro portion for twenty years. The institution sold the farm and timberlands by the 1950s and became one of the first HBCUs that earned *full* SACS membership in 1958. The school declined for a while, but rebounded under new leadership by the 1980s. Knoxville College, however, was adversely affected by absorbing a neighboring HBCU, Morristown College.[21]

On a site just adjacent to an old east Tennessee slave market and a former Civil War military hospital, Judson S. Hill, a Methodist minister from the New Jersey Conference, founded Morristown Normal and Industrial College in 1881 as a grammar school. Andrew F. Fulton, a former slave, helped Judson build the school. Fulton graduated from the school, and stayed to teach and establish a musical legacy in the community. The school had 258 students by 1914, including 150 boarders, and fifty-four students from other states. Judson Hill remained president until 1931. Three Negroes served on the faculty of seventeen members. For almost 120 years, Morristown College was a center of education for Negroes in rural Hamblen County, northeast Tennessee. The school included curricula in business, domestic science for women, trades, and printing, among other subjects, with a mission of serving disadvantaged students who might not be admitted to more traditional institutions. By 1935, the motto was "Ambition knows no Limits." Morristown College hired the first Negro president in 1937 when the school was increasing in debt. The school included courses for World War II veterans, and in 1948, after the debts were paid, Morristown Junior College gained its first SACS approval, became a member of the American Association of Junior Colleges, and flourished in the 1950s. Mary G. Boyd became Morristown College's president when her husband, president D. M. Boyd, died in 1952. She directed the college until a new president came aboard in 1953. Morristown College High School graduated its last class in 1959, and the institution's high school became public. In 1963, Morristown College received funds from the National Science Foundation, the Board of Education of the United Methodist Church, and other donors to improve facilities and equipment. The school gained SACS accreditation in 1981, but had fewer than two hundred students. The US Department of Interior in 1983 designated Morristown College a Historical District. In 1984, the UMC ended its support of Morristown College. In 1987, the trustees announced the closing of this HBCU because of a loss of SACS accreditation.

Knoxville College absorbed Morristown Junior College as a second campus in 1988–1989. However, financial hard times hit Knoxville College, which had to close the Morristown campus by December 1995. Knoxville College's enrollment was no more than 300 students by 2002, and nearly 100 percent of the students needed financial aid. After losing accreditation in 2002–2003, a new mission statement kept Knoxville College open as a work college to serve students of

---

[21] Julie Nicklin, "Knoxville College May Lose Accreditation: Barber-Scotia Is Taken Off Probation," *Chronicle of Higher Education* 43/20 (24 January 1997): A29.

diverse backgrounds and cultures, among other goals. The institution required the students to work a minimum of ten hours per week on campus, give work and service in the community, and engage in a series of internships. KC now offered a Bachelor of Science degree in liberal studies in four concentrations and a two-year college degree. KC admitted students with a minimum 2.0 high school GPA, and used ACT/SAT scores to award scholarships. The annual cost for a residential student was $9,982; students received financial aid from college, work-aid, and scholarships, but not federal funds.[22]

According to the 1917 US Bureau of Education report, the board of trustees at Morris Brown in Atlanta seemed notable for being "unwieldy" and fussy. In 2002, the federal government made accusations of financial fraud and misuse of funds against certain administrators. SACS initially denied Morris Brown College reaffirmation of accreditation in December 2002. On 7 April, the SACS denied the institution's appeal. Morris Brown had nearly three thousand students, but had $27 million in debt. The news sent shock waves through the community. Howard University's *Hilltop* student newspaper staff started a "Save Morris Brown College" website. Some radio stations that catered to the black community started fundraisers. The president resigned in February 2002, and the new president installed in September, resigned in April 2003. Morris Brown lost half of its 2,500 students and UNCF membership. By 2003, MBC had raised $5 million toward the $27 million debt.

One strategy was to join another accreditation agency. But the Atlanta *Journal-Constitution* said, "Morris Brown is on life support, and its leaders need to pull the plug.... At this point, the best thing they can do is plan a graceful exit for the school and its students."[23] Morris Brown College graduated forty-two students in May 2004, and continued to operate in 2009, with endorsements from some Georgia elected officials. But Frederick Douglass Jordan Hall came into foreclosure, and the creditor sold the building. Two hundred students continued classes, and faculty and staff reported to work. A community effort was being

[22] Lovett, *The African American History of Nashville*, 133–34; B. H. Hammond, "A Historical Analysis of Selected Forces and Events which influenced the Founding, Growth and Development of Morristown College, a Historically Black Two-Year College, from 1881 to 1981" (PhD diss., George Washington University, 1983) 1–10; Jovita Wells, *A School for Freedom: Morristown College and Five Generations of Education for Blacks, 1868–1985* (Morristown TN: Morristown College, 1986) 1–10; W. P. and C. L. Osborne and Luie Hargraves, eds., *Contributions of Blacks in Hamblen County, 1796 to 1996* (Morristown TN: Historical Project by Progressive Business Association, 1995) 331–73.

[23] Editor, "Morris Brown on Life Support," *Atlanta Journal*, 21 May 2004, 1.

launched for the "Yes we care" campaign to raise money and save Morris Brown, but the institution continued to die.[24]

By 2003–2004, Mary Holmes College, which had shrunk from 624 students in 1980 to 305 by 2001, closed. Fifteen percent of 103 HBCUs were on warning status with various accreditation agencies. Texas College survived probation, but, in 2005, SACS denied Bethune-Cookman College and Oakwood College approval to offer master's degrees. SACS continued Talladega on warning for failure to comply with standards in financial resources. Other HBCUs were struggling.[25]

On 24 June 2004, Barber-Scotia College, North Carolina, with fewer than six hundred students, learned that it had lost accreditation. Ninety percent of the students depended on federally funded aid. SACS said Barber-Scotia College failed to comply with SACS principles and philosophy of accreditation (integrity) and that the school had awarded degrees to nearly thirty students in the adult program whom, SACS determined, had not fulfilled the proper requirements. The enrollment dropped from 600 students in 2004 to ninety-one in 2005. The General Assembly Council of the Presbyterian Church, USA, voted to continue the denomination's financial support of Barber-Scotia College. To help out, another HBCU, St. Augustine College, rented space on the Barber-Scotia College campus in fall 2006. But, the Barber-Scotia enrollment dropped to just twenty full-time students by 2009. Barber-Scotia reapplied for SACS accreditation in 2010.[26]

SACS placed LeMoyne-Owen College on one-year probation for 2006 because of its need to reduce debt and improve academic qualifications of its business-school faculty. The president hired a new chief advancement officer for institutional advancement to plan and implement major giving campaigns and increase alumni giving. No one wanted this historic college to close.

Beginning in 1864, Negro and white northern missionaries in the American Missionary Association conducted elementary classes for fugitive slaves in contraband Camp Shiloh near Fort Pickering in Memphis. Rioters, consisting of

---

[24] Editor, "Morris Brown," Nashville *Tennessee Tribune* 12 March 2009, 1; Beth McMurtrie, "Southern Association Upholds Loss of Accreditation for Morris Brown College," *Chronicle of Higher Education* 49/32 (18 April 2003): A35.

[25] Editor, "Southern Association Strips 2 Black Colleges of Accreditation," *Chronicle of Higher Education* 49/17 (3 January 2003): A34.

[26] Julia Nicklin, "Barber-Scotia Gets Warning from Accreditation," *Chronicle of Higher Education* 40/44 (6 July 1994): A28.

downtown business owners, Irish immigrants, police and firefighters destroyed this freedmen's school, Lincoln Chapel, along with all other freedmen's schools and churches on 1–3 May 1866. Dozens of Negroes lost their lives to roving white mobs that retaliated after the Union Army mustered out of service the US Colored Troops Regiments (USCT), which had controlled the streets and allowed fugitive slaves to populate the city. The rioters ran thousands of Negroes out of town, but they drifted back into the city as soon as the Union Army restored peace. AMA missionaries rebuilt Lincoln Chapel in 1867 at the original site near Beale Street.[27] In 1871, the freedmen's school became a higher-education institution, and northern philanthropist Francis Julius LeMoyne denoted $20,000 to the AMA. Lemoyne Institute provided the only high school and normal school education for black Memphians. The college moved to its present site on Walker Avenue in 1914. LeMoyne affiliated with the Tennessee Negro Baptists by 1929, when Roger Williams University closed and sent the remainder of its students from Nashville to Howe Institute. It merged with LeMoyne, and the Tennessee Negro Baptists sold the Howe buildings in 1937. LeMoyne College was one of the earliest SACS-approved HBCUs in the early 1930s, and even had a football program until the 1940s. The institution became one of the largest producers of Negro teachers, and in 1968, LeMoyne merged with local S. A. Owen Junior College, which began in 1954 under the black Tennessee Baptist Missionary and Educational Convention. Lemoyne-Owen College indeed had advantages in Memphis-Shelby County where 40 percent of black Tennesseans resided.

However, a federal court desegregation lawsuit forced the city's public TWI, Memphis State University, to accept black students in 1961. The Civil Rights Act of 1964 forced all the TWIs to desegregate. The downtown Shelby State Community College had, since 1972 become 72 percent black after "white flight" to the eastern suburbs. By 1997, state officials combined Shelby State Community College with predominantly white Memphis Technical Institute in east Memphis to form Southwest State Community College. Also by 2006, the University of Memphis' enrollment of 22,000 included 24 percent black students, and this TWI had begun to rival Tennessee State University, 210 miles to the east, in the number of black students who graduated each year. To revitalize the heavily black, south Memphis area, across Walker Avenue from LeMoyne-Owen College, the city tore down the LeMoyne Gardens low-income federal housing project that had housed Negroes since WWII, and replaced it with a new housing development, including single-family dwellings, using federal and local funds. The LeMoyne-Owen College Community Development Corporation moved into

[27] B. L. Lovett, "Memphis Riots: White Reaction to Blacks in Memphis, May 1865–July 1866," *Tennessee Historical Quarterly* 38/1 (Spring 1979): 9–33.

a new building there, and began to invest in the rehabilitation of housing in order to raise the economic, health, and educational levels of people who lived in the community surrounding the college. This program included the Economic Development Venture Initiative to help develop and strengthen businesses in the area, with the goals of creating well-paying jobs for neighborhood residents and stimulating economic growth. The Community Development Corporation also operated through the for-profit affiliate Tennessee Capital and Development Company and the Small Business Administration for Shelby County. Tennessee Construction, a for-profit construction company, created affordable homes near LeMoyne-Owen College. The LeMoyne Family Life Center offered violence prevention programming and activities to low-income boys at Cummings Elementary School next door, by 2006. LeMoyne believed solving youth violence diminished neighborhood violence.

Despite the revitalization efforts, another problem for an urban HBCU like LeMoyne-Owen College was the dire socioeconomic depression that continued to plague twenty-first-century black Americans. In Memphis, 34 percent of the black families lived below the poverty level—two points above the poverty rate for New Orleans. One Memphis zip code had an average family income below $10,000, whereas the poverty rate for a family of four in America was $21,000 in 2009. The city had had a black mayor since 1992, but dominant black political leadership seemed disjointed, distracted, and deeply corrupted. By 2006, Lemoyne-Owen College's student body, that consisted largely those of working- and low-income class origin, as well as a small number of whites, had decreased by half. Without dormitories, LeMoyne could hardly raise student enrollment, and with less money from tuition and fees the endowment soon declined from $10.5 million to almost nothing. The city tried to help by placing "The Middle College" on the LeMoyne-Owen campus to serve public high school students, who also could enroll in college classes. Some Memphis leaders, who were themselves LeMoyne alumni, launched fundraisers, but many faculty members fled when the budget deficits became worse in 2006–2007. Efforts to give faculty raises helped run the school's debt up while the physical plant deteriorated. By January 2007, newspapers reported that LeMoyne-Owen expected to run out of money by the following March. The Memphis community donated money, and LeMoyne-Owen College continued offering undergraduate degrees in business and economic development, education, fine arts and humanities, natural sciences, mathematics, computer science, and social and behavioral sciences.[28]

---

[28] www.loc.edu (Nashville: LCAAHC, 1996); P. M. Magness, "Le Moyne-Owen College (1871–)," B. Lovett and L. T. Wynn, *Profiles of Americans in Tennessee*, 74–75; Miriam

While LeMoyne Owen College wrestled with SACS and the HBCU's ongoing problems, other HBCUs were in trouble in the first decade of the twenty-first century. Compton College in California lost its Western Association of Colleges and Schools accreditation in June 2005. Compton began in 1927 as a component of Compton Union High Schools District until separated in 1950, and classes began at a separate junior college site in 1953. When whites migrated out of Compton, the student body became predominantly black in the 1960s. The trustees elected the first black president in 1970. By the 1990s, Hispanics comprised nearly half the student body. The institution earned accreditation, with about 10,000 students. However, the trustees lost the ability to guide, govern, and advance the institution. Compton could not achieve re-accreditation. Compton College had to merge with another public community college. In 2006, the campus became the Compton Community Educational Center of El Camino College in order to stay open.[29]

The Charles R. Drew University of Medicine and Science in Los Angeles sprouted out of the ashes of the black Watts riots in 1966, which illustrated the gross inadequacies in health care suffered by minority citizens in Los Angeles. Drew University trained nearly a third of black and Hispanic physicians in Los Angeles County until 2007. The Los Angeles County drastically cut funding for the Martin Luther King/Charles R. Drew Medical Center, leaving the medical school with no training site for residents and clinical students. The matter ended up with the school suing the county. Charles Drew, meantime, lost accreditation and stopped its residency programs. Some 32 percent of the students were black, 31 percent Hispanic, and 37 percent others. The University had about $55 million in endowment, but with the loss of accreditation, federal support was lost. A new president, a female Australian, came aboard in 2006 to try to turn things around. The minority community was not happy about the choice. Drew University continued operations and offered a single interdisciplinary biomedical sciences department. The clinical students took training in doctors' offices, clinics, and a few hospitals. The Western Association of Schools and Colleges (WASC) accredited the institution through 2011.[30]

DeCosta-Willis, editor, *The Memphis Diary of Ida B. Wells: An Intimate Portrait of the Activist as a Young Woman* (Boston: Beacon Press, 1995) 21, 33, 34, 51, 60, 62, 110, 111, 137, 146.

[29] "El Camino College, Compton Community Educational Center History," www.compton.edu/campusinformation/campushistory.aspx, 2010, 1; Marla Fisher, "Embattled Community Compton College Loses Accreditation," *Community College Week* 17/24 (4 July 2005): 3–14.

[30] Charles Drew University, "About CDU," www.cdrewu.edu/about-cdu, 2010, 1.

North Central Association of Colleges and Schools' Higher Learning Commission (NCACS) placed Lewis College of Business in Detroit on "show cause" and withdrawal of accreditation, effective 30 June 2007, or until the resolution of appeal. Violet T. Lewis founded Lewis College in 1928–1929. It became Detroit's first black-owned business school in 1938, when Violet Lewis opened the Detroit branch, because black leaders in Detroit appealed to her that no local vocational schools would accept Negro students. They gained NCACS accreditation in 1978, when the Indianapolis branch merged with the Detroit branch. Lewis College continued as a two-year, coed institution offering degrees in business and liberal arts. The federal government designated Lewis College an HBCU in 1987. By 2007, the student enrollment was under two hundred with thirty-six faculty members. Like several HBCUs, Lewis College suffered a failure to attract quality leadership on the boards and the administration. Although the Lewis College website acknowledged the NCACS accreditation situation, no explanation was printed; however, Lewis College lost accreditation because of administrative and financial problems. Moreover, Detroit declined economically, and white flight set in. But the Lewis College continued to solicit donors and students.[31]

In Texas ninety-three private colleges (black and white) began between 1837 and 1900. About twenty existed by the late 1980s. Many of these survivors were the results of mergers, name changes, location changes, revisions of mission, and three were two-year colleges. HBCUs were among these institutions. Bishop College (1867–1988) surprised many when it suddenly closed. The alumni association continued reunions through 2010.[32] To increase their chances of survival, other small, private HBCUs in Texas formed a non-profit consortium, the Texas Association of Developing Colleges, to pool resources and jointly recruit and register new students. The consortium included Huston-Tillotson, Jarvis Christian, Paul Quinn, Texas College, and Wiley College. The TADC administered the Urban Scholarship Fund established by the Texas legislature. TADC served as a parent corporation for the East Texas Education Opportunity

---

[31] Lewis College of Business, "Welcome," http://www.lewiscollege.edu/index.html, 2010.

[32] Bishop College Alumni Association, "Bishop Events," BCAA, 2010, http://www.bishopcollegealumni.com; B. L. Lovett, *A Black Man's Dream: The First Hundred Years, The Story of R. H. Boyd* (Nashville: Mega Publishing, 1993) 22–23.

Center. That organization administered programs funded by state, federal, and private sources.[33]

SACS removed probation for Texas College in 2006. President Billy C. Hawkins engaged an aggressive fund-raising campaign. He raised enrollment from 281 students in 2000 to 807 in 2005. Texas College (1894–) recruited national leaders like Willie Brown, a former mayor of San Francisco whose sisters graduated from Texas College, and baseball Hall of Fame personality Hank Aaron, a Texas College alumnus. Texas College, in 2006, offered sixteen baccalaureate degree programs, two associate degrees, and alternative certification in teacher education. President Hawkins attracted many students back to the college by reinstituting intercollegiate competition in volleyball, basketball, football, softball, and baseball. The institution also supported an academic development center, a career planning and placement center, and a counseling center. Students at Texas College participated in the National Pre-Alumni Council to help UNCF member institutions in fundraising initiatives.

Both Edward Waters College in Jacksonville, Florida, and Hiawassee College (a TWI) in Tennessee lost their SACS accreditation in 2005 but sued in federal court, charging the accrediting agency did not grant them a meaningful opportunity to respond to accusations before imposing the harshest penalty. Hiawassee College felt its financial situation did not warrant the loss of accreditation. A district judge said, "I find that the college has shown a substantial likelihood that it will prove at the trial that the association denied the college due process [under the Fourteenth Amendment to the Constitution]."[34] The courts ordered reinstatement until the trial was held. The UNCF filed a friend-of-the-court brief in support of Edward Waters College's lawsuit, saying the removal of accreditation from Edward Waters was the latest in a consistent and persistent series of adverse actions that SACS has taken against HBCUs. Paul Quinn College also secured a court injunction against SACS action to deny re-accreditation.[35]

---

[33] "HBCU Leaders Meet to Plan Financial Futures," *Black Issues in Higher Education* 20/13 (14 August 2003): 16.

[34] Burton Bollag, "Federal Judge Rules Against Accreditor," *Chronicle of Higher Education* 53/25 (23 February 2007): A26.

[35] L. E. Rivers and C. Brown Jr., *Laborers in the Vineyard of the Lord: The Beginning of the AME Church in Florida, 1865–1895* (Gainesville: The University of Florida Press, 2001) 1–30; SACS, "News Release, August 27, 2009, Updated Notification to the Public Regarding the Revised Accreditation Status of Paul Quinn College," Commission on Colleges (Atlanta: Southern Association of Colleges and Schools, 2009) 1; Jimmy Jenkins, "Edward Waters Loses Accreditation After Plagiarism Scandal," *Chronicle of Higher Education* 21/24 (30 December 2004) 24.

Edward Waters College began under AME Church missionaries in 1866 to educate former slaves. The first AME pastor in Florida, William G. Steward, named the institution Brown Theological Institute. The state granted a charter to the institution in 1872, but it closed for nearly a decade because of financial difficulties. The institution reopened in 1883 as East Florida Conference High School, extended the program to divinity studies, and renamed Edward Waters College for Bishop Edwards Waters in 1892. The institution had difficult times in 1901 after a fire destroyed the facilities, and there were discussions in 1903 to merge with Morris Brown College in Atlanta. Edward Waters College built on a new site in Jacksonville in 1904 with money raised by local Negro leaders. Edward Waters College gained accreditation on the junior college level in 1955. They developed the four-year college curriculum in 1960, and gained SACS accreditation as a four-year college in 1979. In 2005, SACS settled with Edward Waters and granted accreditation. In 2008, the institution counted 839 students, 51 percent males, and 90 percent on financial aid.

Bennett College (1873–) in Greensboro survived probation by SACS. Bennett was placed on probation in part because it had a $3.8 million deficit. In July 2002, Johnnetta B. Cole, the retired president (1987–1997) of Spelman College and then professor at Emory University, arrived to take control. The enrollment had declined, buildings were in disrepair, and some persons expected Bennett to close down. On 14 April 2005, Cole announced a 10 percent cut in faculty and staff. A few faculty members raised a loud protest. Cole believed a group of faculty members were trying to hinder her ability to lead Bennett in the direction it should be going. On 27 April, Cole announced her resignation effective 15 July 2005. However, she was persuaded to stay.[36]

On 18 May 2005, President Cole called a press conference surrounded by officers of the college and supporters, including Yvonne Johnson—alumnae, mayor pro-tempore of Greensboro, and chair of Bennett's board of trustees. Cole listed her administration's accomplishments: full SACS approval, erasure of the deficit, a balanced budget for the current year, the raising of $24 million dollars under the "Revitalization of Bennett College" campaign chaired by US Senator Bob Dole (R), and a recent gift of $600,000 by Bill Cosby's family. Bennett survived the crisis.

By 2005, Bennett College offered twenty-four majors on the undergraduate level. The curriculum emphasized preparing students for leadership roles, life-

---

[36] Bennett, Grambling, Morris Brown, and Talladega were penalized by SACS for financial audit problems (Beth McMurtrie, "Southern Accrediting Group Penalizes 21 Colleges," *Chronicle of Higher Education* 48/18 (11 January 2002): A37.

long learning, morally grounded maturation, intellectual honesty, purposeful public service, and responsible civic action through an interdisciplinary, learner-centered residential environment. The College included programs in African Women's Studies, Womanist Religious Beliefs, and summer institutes on Global Diversity and Inclusion for young girls. Bennett remained affiliated with the United Methodist Church, with about six hundred students coming from twenty-nine states and eleven foreign countries, and ranked fourth among HBCUs in percentage of alumnae earning doctoral degrees. Nearly 80 percent of the faculty had terminal and doctoral degrees. President Cole turned Bennett over to a new president in 2007.

In June 2007, SACS issued a warning to Dillard University about its financial health and budget management. SACS placed Dillard, along with three TWIs, on probation in 2008. Paul Quinn, Florida Memorial, Hinds Community College, and FAMU drew SACS probation or warning by 2007–2008. SACS removed Florida A&M from the list in fall 2008. In 2009, SACS listed 4 HBCUs, including two public institutions, on probation or warning.[37]

Presidential and vice presidential candidates for the HBCUs seemed to suffer a lack of quality in some cases, and there existed a dearth of high-quality candidates by the early twenty-first century. Of course, there were plenty of good-looking resumes and "doctors," but not all of them had records of *doctoring* on the subject as highly trained PhD researchers, publishers in content areas, and leadership/people skills.

Without the ability of the administrative leadership to research, plan, and carry out an effective strategy for institutional problems, some of the HBCUs could not forge an effective strategic plan. Without a sound vision, these institutions failed to attract large investors. They suffered program stagnation and deteriorating facilities. There were plenty of persons in line with doctorates. They met the minimal qualifications; they had nice resumes; however, often they had lackluster training in real research methods, problem-solving, organizational experiences, human relations, people, and leadership skills. They could not "walk the walk" and truly *perform* on the job.

---

[37]Terrance MacTaggart, "The Realities of Rescuing Colleges in Distress," *Chronicle of Higher Education* 54/17 (12 October 2007): A2; CHE, "The Almanac Issue 2007–2008," *Chronicle of Higher Education* 54/1 (31 August 2007): 1–36; Marisa Lopez-Rivera, "Update on Accreditation Actions Taken by Regional Organizations," *Chronicle of Higher Education* 55/7 (6 January 2006): A41; Burton Bullag, "Update on Accreditation Actions Taken by Regional Organizations," *Chronicle of Higher Education* 53/17 (5 January 2007): A27.

Some state desegregation plans integrated the institutional and state boards. However, minority board members and vice versus white board members not always gained appointment because they had great leadership and fundraising abilities. Incompetent boards could not strategically lead an institution into the future, especially against a backdrop of personal bickering, egotism, and political and religious intrigue. Egotistical members often savored the presidency for themselves, but failed to perform once they got the coveted position. Some board members who were alumni interfered daily with on-campus operations and the internal decision-making processes. They were persistently nostalgic about how it used to be when they were students on campus; however, now, they were not active, effective fundraisers.

In April 2007, the governor of Texas fired the entire Board of Regents that governed the HBCU Texas Southern University. They charged board members with ineffectiveness in fund raising and failure to give adequate oversight to university operations. Texas Southern had suffered instability of leadership in the 1990s. The president (1999–2005) resigned over the misspending of institutional funds, but a deadlocked jury trial saved her in October 2007. In December 2007, SACS placed Texas Southern on probation for financial management and governance issues. A permanent president came aboard in early 2008. The legislature threatened to give no extra money to bail Texas Southern out until the university had a reorganization plan.[38]

At Tennessee State University, the president addressed the university community with a letter dated 7 October 2008 announcing a $10 million deficit, and the firing of several administrators, including the vice president/provost. He did this because poor leadership had helped to cause a crisis, which, in addition to a recent consultant's study, revealed the university was failing to serve students in an effective and customer-focused manner. Tennessee State lost about four hundred newly enrolled students in September 2008 because of this personnel problem. The faculty, staff, and friends donated enough funds to the TSU Foundation to save the enrollment of another 1,200 students caught in the fiscal mess. The out-of-state enrollment so critical to the HBCU's revenues dropped dramatically. This large HBCUs SACS reaffirmation of accreditation for 2010 seemed to be in jeopardy of warning or probation. In response to inquiries by local newspaper reporters, president Melvin N. Johnson held the State of the University Town Hall Meeting, and answered questions about the crisis. In July

---

[38] P. F. "President Fired for Lavish Spending at Texas Southern University," *Chronicle of Higher Education* 54/34 (28 April 2006): A39; P. Healy, "Backers of Texas Southern Fear State May Try to End Its Autonomy," *Chronicle of Higher Education* 44/16 (12 December 1997): A35.

2010, Johnson, under tremendous faculty pressure, announced his resignation, effective December 2010.

Yes, many HBCUs were in trouble, but besides the issues of leadership and maintaining accreditation standards, the integration of technology into classroom instruction became another priority for twenty-first-century HBCUs. By 2003, one-in-thirteen students enrolled in distance education courses across America. Similar enrollment through HBCUs was off-pace, but steadily growing. Most minority colleges used technology to enhance administrative and student service functions, though they lagged in computer services and faculty use of information technology for teaching and learning. The HBCUs were slow to deliver electronic instruction because of cost, staffing deficiencies, lack of procedures for accountability for such instruction, and the need to continue traditional classroom instruction for a highly academically diverse student body.

Some HBCUs used grants to develop technical programs to assist nearby minority communities and low-income schools to gain access to the Internet. Several HBCUs offered on-line degrees, electronic classrooms, and universal computer access. Hampton, Norfolk State, St. Paul's, Virginia State, and Virginia Union joined the Virginia High-Technology Partnership Program. Johnson C. Smith University engaged imaging technology research. In December 2005, Duke Energy Foundation granted funds for the Women in Technology Program, and JCSU was the only HBCU ThinkPad University where students regularly received an IBM Laptop computer and the latest software. "The Vision" statement (2006) said,

> In the 21st century, technology as it is infused into a dynamic liberal arts education is a pathway at the core of change. We use technology as a tool for developing and assessing students continuously and as a tool for faculty to provide an innovative, sound liberal arts knowledge base through effective instructional delivery.[39]

Johnson C. Smith University (JCSU) made the Templeton Foundation Honor Roll for Character Building Colleges in 1997–1998. Community service was a requirement for graduation, and JCSU implemented the Daniel J. Sanders Development Institute in 1995 to train student leaders in developing leadership skills. The renaissance at Johnson C. Smith began in 1994, when the board of trustees elected President Dorothy Yancey. In 1998, she led JSU in completing the "Vision Shared," $63.8 million capital campaign drive, and implementing new majors in liberal arts, criminal justice, and computer engineering. Yancy secured

---

[39] Johnson C. Smith University, *The Vision Statement* (Charlotte NC: JCSU, 2006) 1–2.

funds for new facilities, and by 2005, JSC had a budget of $31.9 million and an endowment of $39.4 million—compared to $14.9 million in 1994—ninety-one full time faculty members, and 1,500 students. By 2006, JCSU was located on a 100-acre campus, offering thirty majors and undergraduate degrees through colleges of arts and science, professional studies, and honors, a liberal studies program, and military programs, including AFROTC and the Army ROTC.[40]

Though they encountered many problems and complexities in the first decade of the twenty-first century, America's black colleges and universities continued their progress into the future. To help ensure a continuation of a strong liberal-arts legacy, the National Endowment for the Humanities, by 2007, offered the Humanities Initiatives for Faculty grant competition at HBCUs and other institutions. The program served to promote collaborative work among faculty, help develop new humanities programs or resources, and/or train staff and faculty members in the use of diverse humanities materials. Indeed, in the HBCU's quest to meet the challenges of twenty-first-century society and its technological economy, the liberal arts tended to suffer as more resources went into business, engineering, science, health care, and computer programs. Six HBCUs met the Carnegie category of Doctoral-Research Extensive Level University; Carnegie listed twenty-five as master's-level institutions. Lane College's president Wesley McClure recognized that HBCUs exhibited historical, unique, and effective approaches to addressing major problems in an increasingly diverse society. Some HBCUs formed partnerships with government agencies and private investors to repair, improve, and build family dwellings and apartments in nearby communities. Howard University made plans to build apartments, condominiums, retail outlets, and parking facilities near the campus. Winston-Salem State University made plans to overhaul nearby vacant houses and sell them to low-income families. Southern University-New

---

[40] K. Redd, "Historically Black Colleges and Universities: Making a Comeback," *New Directions for Higher Education* 102 (1998): 33–44; NCES, 1995–96 National Postsecondary Student Aid Study, Undergraduate Data Analysis System (Washington DC: USDOE, 1996); ETS Policy Information Center, *What Jobs Require: Literacy, Education, and Training, 1940–2006* (Princeton: Educational Testing Service, 2000); "Distance Education: Challenges for Minority-Serving Institutions and Implications for Federal Education Policy," Subcommittee on Select Education, Committee on Education and the Workforce, US House of Representatives (6 October 2003), Release of Testimony (Washington DC: GPO, 2003) 1–10; *The Alliance for Equity in Higher Education Serving the Nation: Opportunities and Challenges in the Use of Information Technology at Minority-Serving Colleges and Universities* (Washington DC: The Institute for Higher Education Policy, 2004); Inez M. Parker, *The Biddle-Johnson C. Smith University* (Charlotte: Fortress Press, 1985) 1–20.

Orleans launched the 2003 *Journal of Urban Education* to publish articles about "what works" in increasing educational access for inner city and poor people.

The globalization of the society and the economy also challenged the HBCUs to become more involved in world affairs through their students, programs, and faculty members. In the 1950s, students from Africa flooded many HBCUs, and soon comprised the largest contingent of international students at the HBCUs. Southern University, Johnson C. Smith, and Howard University, among other HBCUs, signed education memorandums of understanding with Ghana, South Africa, and other African nations in the 1990s. The 2000 International African Youth Leadership Summit met at Lincoln University and eighty HBCUs and the University of Ghana sent representatives, including student government officers. The Council of Engineering Deans of the HBCUs recognized the value of greater involvement of the US in Africa. The US Agency for International Development and the UNCF supported the collaboration of HBCUs with colleges and universities throughout the world, including Africa. The USAID supported the Global Health Initiative to strengthen the capacity and participation of HBCUs in the USAID international population and health programs. In 2002, Hampton University received a $5.9 million federal grant to increase access to basic educational materials for a sub-Saharan African children project shared with three private and three public HBCUs. The program intended to affect Benin, Ethiopia, Guinea, Mali, Senegal, and South Africa. In January 2005, Dillard and Xavier co-hosted the meeting for HBCUs on study-abroad programs. HBCUs participated in a collaborative on how Africans in the Diaspora could contribute and collaborate with the African Union and its member states in implementing Africa's Consolidated Science and Technology Plan of Action in 2006. HBCUs were expected to play a significant role in building capacity for science and technology in Africa.

Despite overcoming great odds during the past 172 years, the future of many of America's HBCUs was, at times, uncertain. Even so, the nation's HBCUs held fast to their mission of equipping the black leaders of tomorrow.

Epilogue

To America: Gifts from Black Colleges and Universities

Throughout their history, HBCUs have been valuable to America's development. The HBCUs contributed to American culture and society, music, religion, science, social sciences, sports and athletics, patriotism, war, and peace.

Military Commitment to America

HBCUs made critical and positive responses to America's war efforts and to the preservation of democracy at home and its extension abroad. One-hundred-and-seventy-nine thousand US Colored Troops (USCT) in the Union Army and twenty thousand Negroes in the Union Navy helped preserve the American Union and end slavery. After the Civil War, some of these USCT comprised the four Negro units ("Buffalo Soldiers") of the American Army that guarded the Great Plains. In 1873, while a freshman at Atlanta University, Henry O. Flipper (1856–1940) received his appointment to West Point and became the institution's first Negro graduate on 14 June 1877. HBCU communities appreciated military pomp and pageantry. Wilberforce University established a student military program in 1894, and there already was such a program at Roger Williams University. Negro men and women maintained post-Civil War private militia, like the Douglass Guards. The West Virginia State principal and six students became officers during the Spanish-American War, 1898–1899.

HBCUs contributed students and faculty members to the armed services during WWI. Meharry Medical College contributed to the Medical Corps, and Fisk and Walden provided dormitory space for newly recruited WWI trainees. Several HBCUs had Reserve Officers Training Corps (ROTC) units along with brass bands after passage of the National Defense Act (1916). Many graduates from West Virginia State College went to Officers Reserve Training camp at Des Moines, Iowa. The National Baptist Publishing Board, led by former Bishop College student R. H. Boyd, organized Boy Cadets dressed in military-like uniforms to "march for Jesus"[1] at the annual National Baptist Sunday Congress parades in support of America's war effort. The Negro Press Association supported the war effort, but criticized Jim Crow practices at home.[2]

---

[1] Bobby L. Lovett, *Black Man's Dream The Story of R. H. Boyd and the* NBPB (Nashville: Mega Pulbisihing, 1993) 121.

[2] B. L. Lovett, *How It Came to Be: The Boyd Family's Contribution to African American Religious Publishing from the 19th to the 21st Century* (Nashville: Mega, 2007) 65–66.

President Woodrow Wilson threatened to censor the black press, and made it clear that Jim Crow would remain in place after the war. Many white Americans, including the Mormon Church, opposed arming black people and stationing Negro recruits in white areas. After World War I, whites continued their racist practices. Rayford Logan of Howard University said, "At the end of World War I, none of the seventeen Negro land-grant colleges provided military training as required by the First Morrill Act of 1862."[3] Some Negro veterans led ROTC-like units on HBCU campuses, including West Virginia State, but whites tried to minimize the Negro's contribution to the nation's war effort. Historian Darlene Clark Hine said, "A 1925 study by the American War College concluded that African Americans were physically unqualified for combat duty. [They] were by nature subservient and mentally inferior, believed themselves to be inferior to white people, were susceptible to the influence of crowd psychology, could not control themselves in the face of danger, and did not have the initiative and resourcefulness of white people."[4]

After the war, black aviation pioneers Eugene Bullard and Bessie Coleman paved the way for Negroes to fly airplanes. At least a hundred black pilots existed by the end of the 1920s. John W. Greene, a 1922 graduate of Hampton, received his commercial pilot's license in 1933, and served as an aircraft mechanic for the US Army during WWII. The first all-black air show occurred in 1931 in Los Angeles. By 1939, the Challenger Air Pilot Association existed under Negro leadership. Janet W. Bragg, a Chicago nurse who attended Spelman College, purchased the first aircraft for the black Challenger Air Pilots Association at the Harlem Airport. In April 1939, a new law authorized the secretary of war to lend materials for instruction and training of Negroes to accredited civilian aviation schools, and West Virginia State College became the only HBCU to have a Civilian Pilot Training Program. The Rosenwald Fund helped with construction of flight-training facilities outside Tuskegee, and Janet Bragg became a commercial pilot in 1943 through the Tuskegee Institute Civilian Training School.

Still, the American military insisted there was no need to train blacks to fly combat airplanes. Black leaders solicited the support of Eleanor Roosevelt. The experiment to train Negroes as military pilots began on 1 July 1940 when

---

[3] Rayford W. Logan, *The Betrayal of the Negro: from Rutherford B. Hayes to Woodrow Wilson* (Toronto: The Macmillan Company, 1965) 394; Gregory Hunter, "Howard University: 'Capstone' of Negro Education during World War II," *Journal of Negro Education* 79/1 (Winter 1994): 54–70.

[4] Darlene Clark Hine, William C. Hine, and Stanley Harrold, *African Americans: A Concise History*, 2nd ed. (Upper Saddle River NJ: Pearson Prentice Hall, 2006) 435.

Tuskegee Institute gained approval for combat aviation training. In September 1940, A. Philip Randolph and other Negro leaders drafted a memorandum to President Roosevelt and recommended the use of Negro officers, professionals, and nurses. On 25 October 1940, Roosevelt promoted Colonel Benjamin O. Davis, Sr., to brigadier general, and in March 1941, the Army Air Force officially established separate training facilities at Tuskegee for Negro pilots, though he NAACP opposed it as Jim Crowism. Eleanor Roosevelt visited the facility and took a photograph in a two-seater plane with a black pilot at the controls. By the summer, two airfields existed at Tuskegee. The 32nd Fighter Group (100th, 301st, and 302nd fighter squadron) organized on October 1942 at Tuskegee. General Davis's son, B. O Davis, Jr., later headed the unit. However, the limited number of units left many trained black pilots to linger around Tuskegee with little to do. After some protest, in April 1943, the 99th Pursuit Squadron shipped overseas to the war zone, and saw their first action against enemy planes on 2 June. The Tuskegee Airmen flew more than 15,500 sorties, completed 1,578 missions, destroyed 409 enemy aircraft, and never lost a bomber they escorted in Europe. The US conceived the 477th Bombardment Group on paper, but the unit never entered combat, and some of these restless black men mutinied against tyrannical white officers. About six hundred Negro pilots received training and certification by war's end. West Virginia State College students served in the 99th and 332nd fighter groups in larger numbers than any other HBCU.[5]

In April 1942, the Navy announced acceptance of Negroes for general service and as noncommissioned officers. They trained at Camp Robert Smalls, at the Great Lakes Naval Training Station. From there, they traveled to a training station near Hampton Institute. Carl T. Rowan left Tennessee State in 1942 after passing the Navy officers' candidate school test, and became an officer. After the war, Rowan completed his education at Oberlin and University of Minnesota and became one of America's most notable journalists. Samuel Lee Gravely, Jr., left Virginia Union University in his second year and entered the Navy's college V-12 program, becoming, in 1944, the first black commissioned officer in the US Navy Reserve Office Training Course. He later became Rear Admiral in command of a Navy warship. By October 1944, the Navy had five hundred black enlisted men and petty officers—including fifty Negroes as ensigns, lieutenants, medical and dental officers, nurses, WAVES officers, and chaplains. The US military named some Liberty ships for Negroes, including one for John Hope, former president of Atlanta University, and Bishop Isaac Lane, founder of Lane College. But the US Navy enrolled many poorly educated southern whites that

---

[5] Hine, Hine, and Harrold, *African Americans*, 440–41; Hunter, "Howard University: 'Capstone' of Negro Education during World War II," 54–70.

continually practiced racism. The American Navy had a 10 percent quota on black enrollees.[6]

In 1943, WVSC became a site for the Army Specialized Training Program (ASTP). Howard, Prairie View, Wilberforce, North Carolina A&T, and Meharry also became ASTP sties. The Association of Colored and Secondary Schools for Negroes protested because 221 white colleges had ASTP sites. The six HBCUs handled 1,400 trainees, who completed their courses in April 1943, went to further training, and then into the European theater of the war.[7] Negro officers began to oppose Jim Crow in the military, and some riots broke out in camps. In March 1943, the army prohibited the designation of recreational facilities by race. Southern officers cleverly replaced the signs "White" and "Colored" with the designations "No 1" and "No. 2," and continued to punish soldiers who disobeyed Jim Crow practices. The American Council on Race Relations grew out of the Chicago mayor's Committee on Race Relations to advance racial equality during the war. A military advisory committee published a study to improve racial understanding and prevent more race riots.[8]

By February 1945, 497,000 Negroes served overseas. Twenty-two Negro combat units engaged ground operations in the European theater of the war, and many black units served in the Mediterranean, Pacific, and North African theaters. The marines and the Coast Guard also commissioned a few Negro officers. More than a million Negro men and women served in various branches of the American armed services during the Second World War, 1941–1945.

The Allied Forces convened a conference to create the United Nations to replace the defunct League of Nations. The US State Department approved HBCU presidents Mordecai W. Johnson and Mary McLeod Bethune to attend the organizational meeting. Charles S. Johnson of Fisk University attended the first meeting of the UN Economic and Social Council. Ralph Bunche, professor at Howard, served on the official US staff at the meeting in San Francisco in April 1945. He won the Nobel Peace Prize in 1950 for his contributions to world peace.

Sixty-three HBCUs participated in the Engineering, Science, and Management War Defense Training Program; these programs enrolled fifty-

---

[6] John Hope Franklin and A. A. Moss Jr., *From Slavery to Freedom: A History of Negro Americans*, 6th ed. (New York: Knopf, 1988) 390–91.

[7] Harlan, *History of West Virginia State College*, 3; Withrow, *West Virginia State College*, 1–10; Charles H. Houston, "The Negro Soldier," *Nation* 159/17 (21 October 1944): 496–97; Ensign Wesley A. Brown, "The First Negro Graduate of Annapolis Tells His Story," *Saturday Evening Post* 221/52 (25 June 1949): 26–114; Benjamin E. Mays, "The Achievements of the Negro Colleges," *Atlantic* 217/2 (February 1966): 90.

[8] Center of Military History, *Ulysses Lee and the Empowerment of Negro Troops* (Washington, DC: GPO, 1965) 1-30.

thousand students in pre-employment courses that prepared students for work in aircraft industries, shipbuilding, welding, automotive mechanics, electricity and radio, among other defense industries. Moreover, they boosted the HBCUs' argument for engineering programs, and helped recruit thousands of students after the war.[9]

Because of World War II, HBCUs became the sites of many of America's ROTC units. In 1942, Prairie View Agricultural and Mechanical College established the first Reserve Officers Training Corps in a Negro land-grant college. West Virginia State received an Artillery ROTC unit. ROTC units also existed at Hampton and North Carolina A&T. WVSC counted at least eleven former students who gained the rank of general in the US armed forces. After World War II, Negro officers in active service took charge of ROTC units on HBCU campuses. By 1950, ROTC units existed at ten HBCUs, and their graduates held commissions in the Korean War. Eighty percent of black officers in the American military were former HBCU students. On 16 April 1965, President Lyndon B. Johnson appointed Benjamin O. Davis, Jr., lieutenant general and chief of staff of US and UN forces in Korea. Daniel "Chappie" James, a graduate of Tuskegee gained appointment as a four-star general in the US Air Force in 1975. He directed AFROTC units, including the one at Tennessee State, during his illustrative career. Among 350 colleges with ROTC programs, twenty ROTC programs (nearly 6 percent) existed at HBCUs. By 2005, Norfolk State had one of the largest of naval ROTC units. Southern produced twelve generals.

Black soldiers met the challenges of racism in the American military. Officers, especially white southerners, openly practiced racial discrimination, and not a single man among a million Negro soldiers received the highest award, the Medal of Honor. In addition, during the First World War, out of nearly half a million Negro soldiers, none of them won the Medal of Honor, although France graciously awarded their highest honor, the *Croix de Guerre*, for bravery to several American Negro soldiers. Yet, some twenty-two Negroes won the Medal of Honor during the American Civil War.

In 1993, a five-man team of researchers at Shaw University investigated why black WWII veterans did not receive the Medal of Honor. The team's findings resulted in seven former soldiers (one survivor, Vernon J. Baker) being awarded the Medal of Honor on 13 January 1997. In 1997, HBCU researchers, including Daniel K. Gibran, published *The Exclusion of Black Soldiers from the*

---

[9] Hine, Hine, and Harrold, *African Americans*, 2nd ed., 438–41; Henry F. and Katherine Pringle, "America's Leading Negro University," *Saturday Evening Post* 221/34 (19 February 1949): 36.

Medal of Honor in World II.[10] Julius W. Becton, Jr., Lt. General, US Army (Retired) and former president of Prairie View A&M University, said,

> We black soldiers hungered for action. We wanted our chance to fight directly against that enemy abroad in order to help defeat the enemy at home. We knew that men who risked their lives for their country, some of whom would pay the ultimate price, would help establish the claim to equal citizenship [for blacks].... Despite the barriers of segregation ... [w]e went into combat and by our deeds helped to battle the racial discrimination that so crippled our country.[11]

Black colleges are the primary source of African American Army officers.[12] In 1995, the US Army awarded 3,963 commissions to students who had gone through ROTC programs while in college, including 436 commissions (11 percent) to African Americans. Of those 436 commissions, nearly half went to students at HBCUs." Twenty-eight HBCUs continued ROTC programs. Alabama A&M, Florida A&M, Hampton, Howard, Jackson State, Norfolk State, Prairie View, South Carolina State, and Tuskegee had the largest military programs.[13]

Tennessee State, Florida Memorial, Hampton, and Texas Southern joined with Western Michigan University, Tuskegee Airmen, Inc., and the Organization of Black Airline Pilots in 2004 to form a coalition to address shortages of blacks in the airline industry. Blacks comprised only 2 percent of commercial pilots. *Aviation Week and Space Technology* named Tennessee State University a top aeronautical engineering school. The 6 December 2005 Nashville *City Paper* reported professors and engineering students at Tennessee State University were developing technology to help the American military gather information about troop movement and insurgent activities in combat zones. The research was collaboration between TSU's Center of Excellence for Battlefield Sensor Fusion, Pennsylvania State University, and the US Army Research Laboratory. The TSU Center had capabilities to work with the NASA Jet Propulsion Laboratory. In January 2006, Tennessee State announced the opening of its Center for Excellence and Intelligence Studies in cooperation with military-related agencies.[14]

---

[10] E. V. Converse III, Daniel K. Gibran, J. A. Cash et al., *The Exclusion of Black Soldiers from the Medal of Honor in World II* (Jefferson NC: McFarland and Company, 1997) 1–50.

[11] Converse III, Gibran, and Cash, *The Exclusion of Black Soldiers*, 1–50.

[12] Dyer Scott, "A Few Good Officers: HBCUs Seek Ways to Boost ROTC Pipeline," *Black Issues in Higher Education* 17/3 (30 March 2000): 18; Keven Chappell, "ROTC on Campus Leadership Development for a Lifetime," *Ebony* 63/11 (September 2008): 170–76.

[13] Converse III, Gibran, and Cash, *The Exclusion of Black Soldiers*, 1–50.

[14] Henry O. Flipper, *The Colored Cadet at West Point: Autobiography of Henry Ossian Flipper, U.S.A.* (Lincoln: University of Nebraska Press, 1978, 1998) i–xxi; A. Russell Buchanan, *Black Americans in World War II* (Santa Barbara CA: Clio Books, 1977) 1–31;

Legal Education Programs at HBCUs

Deep racial discrimination in America compelled HBCUS to enter the field of legal education. Former slaves became citizens with all the rights thereof by the Civil Rights Act of 1866, which the 14th Amendment (1868) made permanent. When the all-white US Supreme Court declared the 1875 act unconstitutional in 1883, there were no Negro lawyers present to argue for their people. The few black attorneys that existed after the emancipation seldom gained admission into courtrooms unless accompanied by a white attorney. Negro lawyers represented clients who had less wealth, and, thus, black lawyers earned less money than their white counterparts. Negro lawyers could not join local bar associations, yet, the state-sanctioned bar associations could disbar them. Many white court officers, including judges, repeatedly used racist terms when Negro lawyers and clients were present in courtrooms. The Jim Crow system discouraged Negroes from even entering the courthouse, but some southern courtrooms had balconies for the Negroes. No Negro, not even a black lawyer, alone, could stand on the main floor, though they paid taxes to support the facility, operations, and personnel.

Howard University became the first HBCU to open a school to train lawyers. The federal agencies, particularly the Union Army and the Freedman's Bureau, placed special interest in Howard University. Howard University started a law school in 1869. The Board of Trustees elected John Mercer Langston dean of the law department on 6 January. Langston graduated from Oberlin College, studied some law under a local judge, and became the first college-trained Negro to become a lawyer by 1855. Upon his appointment at Howard, Langston traveled the country recruiting bright students for the first law class, as he and other black graduates similarly recruited Negro students to attend biracial Oberlin College.

Franklin and Moss Jr., *From Slavery to Freedom*, 6th ed., 339–410; R. B. Edgerton, *Hidden Heroism: Black Soldiers in America's Wars* (Boulder CO: Westview Press, 2002) 141–44; T. G. Oliver, "Historical Black Colleges and Universities: Civilian and Military Leadership," *Education* 117 (1996): 202; Charles Johnson, *African-Americans and ROTC: Military, Naval, and Aeroscience Programs at Historically Black Colleges* (Westport CT: Greenwood Press, 2002) 1–30; S. Sandler, *Segregated Skies: All-Black Combat Squadrons of World War II* (Washington DC: Smithsonian Institution Press, 1992) 1–25; C. E. Francis and A. Caso, *The Tuskegee Airmen: The Men Who Changed a Nation*, 4th ed. (Boston: Braden Publishing Company, 1997) 29–33; "Tennessee State University," *Columbia Electronic Encyclopedia*, 6th ed., New York, Columbia University, 1 December 2009.

Howard University graduated its first class of ten lawyers in 1871. Eight of Langston's students from the first law school class gained admission to practice in the DC courts. D. Augusta Straker entered the law school in 1870 after listening to Langston's recruitment speech. Straker graduated in June 1871, became a lawyer in Orangeburg County, South Carolina, by 1876, and gained election to the state legislature. Straker became dean of law at Allen University in Columbia, South Carolina, and graduated seven students in law by 1887. In 1872, Charlotte E. Ray—the first Negro woman lawyer—graduated from Howard's law program. James Carroll Napier graduated in that class, won election to the Nashville city council in September 1878, and, on the same night traveled to DC to marry Dean Langston's daughter, Nettie DeElla. J. C. Napier became US Register of the Treasury (1911–1913). Langston became Howard University acting president upon the resignation of Oliver O. Howard. The trustees chose a white man as permanent president. Langston left the university in June 1875, with fifty-eight law-school graduates to his credit, practiced law, became a member of the DC board of health, minister to Haiti, president of Virginia Normal and Collegiate Institute, and US Congressman from his native Virginia.[15]

The Howard law program classes met in the four instructor's homes and offices, in various downtown buildings, Lincoln Hall, and other places until the university purchased a house on Fifth Street, N.W., by 1887. The program consisted of evening classes three times a week. Around 1925, Howard University hired Charles Hamilton Houston, a graduate of Amherst College. He was a teacher of English for two years at Howard, an army officer in World War I, a graduate of Harvard University School of Law (1922) and the first black editor of the *Harvard Law Review*. He received the doctorate of judicial science from Harvard in 1923.

In 1925, Houston convinced the president and Howard's trustees to keep the program open, provide more resources, and improve it into a quality program. Houston told them he counted only 100 practicing Negro attorneys out of about 1,000 Negroes claiming to be lawyers compared to 160,000 white lawyers. With his plans to make Howard's law program into "a West Point of Negro leadership,"[16] Houston trained the students by having them focus on cases argued at the nearby US Supreme Court, visiting local legal offices, and by accompanying the students to National Bar Association meetings. He taught students to do research and avoid academic "sloppiness" in briefs, by which

---

[15] William J. Simmons, *Men of Mark: Eminent, Progressive and Rising* (Cleveland OH: G. M. Rewell Company, 1887) 512, 744, 752.

[16] Douglass O. Linder, "Before *Brown*: Charles H. Houston and the Gaines Case," *Famous Trials* (Kansas City: University of Missouri at Kansas City School of Law, 2010) 1–7.

some whites characterized Negro lawyers. The American Bar Association, since the 1880s, had refused to admit Negro members. Howard graduate George H. Woodson led efforts to found the National Bar Association in 1925. In 1931, the American Bar Association approved Howard's law program, which moved to the main campus in 1936. The law school now is located on its own twenty-two-acre campus, publishes the *Howard Law Journal* and *The New Barrister*, and in 2006, conferred 185 doctorate and master's degrees.

Charles Hamilton Houston became chief legal counsel for the NAACP in 1936. The NAACP hired Thurgood Marshall, a 1933 graduate of Howard's law program, to assist him. The NAACP formed the Legal Defense Education Fund in 1939 to help fund the lawsuits. Houston died 22 April 1950, and Howard University named the law facility in his honor. The Harvard University Law School created the Charles Hamilton Houston Institute for Race and Justice. Thurgood Marshall, a graduate of Lincoln University, Pennsylvania, recalled how he and fellow law students at Howard contemplated "What we would do to Jim Crow"? once they became lawyers. Houston's successor at the LDEF, Marshall became a notable twentieth-century's architect of American race relations, and the first black member of the US Supreme Court, serving from 1967 to 1993.[17]

Several other HBCUs had legal education programs at a time when a college degree was not required to enter a law program. Jonathan J. Wright, the first Negro justice on a state supreme court (South Carolina), established the law department at Claflin College between 1877 and 1881. He conducted the classes at his office on Queen Street in Charleston. Central Tennessee College (Walden University) established a law school in 1877, matriculating its first law student in 1879. The faculty revised the program in 1882, and graduated the last student in 1911. Lincoln University, Pennsylvania, operated a law program from 1870–1873. Straight University in New Orleans had a law school in 1881–1886, and graduated about fifty students, including thirty-five whites. Shaw University had a law school from 1890 until 1918. Allen University produced fourteen lawyers under Dean Straker. Virginia Union Law School existed between 1922 and 1931.[18]

The dearth of Negro lawyers was so bad that West Indies native Z. Alexander Looby chartered Kent School of Law (1933–1947) in Nashville. Looby received his bachelor's at Howard University, Bachelor of Law at Columbia University, and doctor of juristic science at New York University. He moved to Nashville in 1926–1927 to practice law and teach part-time at Fisk University and

---

[17] Brian Gilmore, "American Racial and Legal History According to Derrick Bell," *Crisis* 112/5 (September/October 2005): 40.

[18] *The Ledger*, Straight University Law Department, 24 September 1881.

down the street at Tennessee A&I State Teachers College. Looby moved to Memphis in 1928. However, he found that the Edward H. Crump political machine in Memphis was acutely anti-black. He recalled when he was sitting up front to represent a client, a Memphis court officer told Looby "You must sit back there." Looby said, "Sit where?" The poorly educated white man said, "Back there with the other niggers." Looby said, "Like hell I will!" The judge reminded the officer that Looby, a Negro, really was a lawyer and could sit up front. In the midst of the Great Depression, which gripped black Memphis, Looby moved back to Nashville, the state capitol. In 1940, Looby lost his first election for the city council, and in 1943 he presided over the local Negro lawyers' association, the James C. Napier Bar Association. After a Looby survey claimed that Nashville had only "four good Negro lawyers," he organized the Kent School of Law and held classes in the downtown Colored YMCA; they trained more than ninety students in 1947–1948. Looby helped Houston, Marshall, and other NAACP lawyers to file a higher-education desegregation case (1937–1939), win a Negro teacher pay-equity case (1942), and gain acquittal for twenty-three of twenty-five Negroes in the Columbia race riot case in 1947. Looby won a city council seat in 1950, helped file Nashville's school desegregation in 1955, forced the integration of local public parks in 1956, defended the Nashville sit-in demonstrators and survived his house being bombed in 1960. In 1972, having barely retired, Looby died.[19]

After forming the LDEF in 1939, the NAACP filed a barrage of suits against Jim Crow graduate schools. Hamilton and Marshall argued that whites had full access to graduate programs and schools of law, medicine, engineering, and other professional studies while Jim Crow states denied Negroes such access in violation of the equal protection clause of the 14th Amendment and *Plessy v. Ferguson*'s (1896) "separate but equal" provision. They won approximately fifteen cases.

Several states hurriedly created law schools on HBCU campuses to comply with *Plessy*. Missouri created a law school in St. Louis with a Negro dean to teach three Negro students. Perhaps because the NAACP considered the school a sham, the Lincoln University Law School in Missouri publicized its existence with a bunch of photographs, showing roughly twenty students and a small cage

---

[19] B. L. Lovett and L. T. Wynn, eds., *Profiles of African Americans in Tennessee* (Nashville: Local Conference for African American History and Culture, 1996) 78–79; Will Sarvis, "Leaders in the Court and Community: Z. Alexander Zooby, Avon N. Williams, Jr., and the Fight for Civil Rights in Tennessee, 1940–1970," *Journal of African American History* 88/1 (Winter 2003): 42–58; James Barron, "Avon Williams, 72, Lawyer who Fought to End Segregation," *New York Times*, 31 August 1994, 18.

of books for the library. South Carolina briefly established a law program at South Carolina State A&M Institute, calling the program "a chair of law." The NAACP appealed these Jim Crow situations without success. The state formed a law school at North Carolina Central University in 1939, and opened it in 1940 under the dean at the University of North Carolina, who served until 1942. NCCU law school Dean Janice L. Mills said, "For sixty years, our [law] school has surmounted incredible odds. It has a rich and brilliant history: one of racial segregation, adversity, triumph, transition, growth and development."[20] As she spoke, the NCCU School of Law enrolled four hundred students by 2004. The Tennessee General Assembly authorized a graduate school and programs at Tennessee A&I State College "equivalent to University of Tennessee for white students,"[21] including a law school, but the Negro consultant, the dean of the St. Louis law school for Negroes, advised Tennessee officials to grant increases in the out-of-state-scholarships to the Negro plaintiffs. The officials took his advice.

In September 1947, the Texas legislature changed the name of Prairie View Normal and Industrial School to Prairie View College, with courses of study "equivalent to those offered at the [white] Agricultural and Mechanical College of Texas."[22] The Texas legislature appropriated $2.6 million to create a Negro law school as an adjunct to the University of Texas, with five UT faculty members teaching part-time at the Negro school in Austin. The legislature then created Texas Southern University for Negroes (1947–), and incorporated the one-room Negro law school into the university, which they established on the campus of the Houston City College for Negroes. The law program produced its first JD degree in 1950. The law school earned American Bar Association accreditation in 1967, and TSU reported 2,585 law graduates since 1947. In February 1976, the TSU law school became the Thurgood Marshall School of Law, and became a top producer also of Hispanic-American graduates.

The School of Law at Southern University in Baton Rouge began in September 1947. Southern University had its beginnings from state legislation passed on 10 April 1880, and was later reorganized into college, normal, high school, grammar, girls' industrial, agricultural and mechanical, and a music department in order to receive 1890 land-grant funds. The institution relocated from New Orleans to Baton Rouge. In the 1980s, Louisiana upgraded the program. In July 1985, the law program at Southern University became the

---

[20] North Carolina Central University School of Law, *So Far: Sixty Years of Helping People Help Others* (Durham NC: NCCU School of Law, 1999) 1–20.

[21] Lovett, *The Civil Rights Movement in Tennessee*, 340.

[22] Prairie View A&M University, "History of Prairie View A&M Univesity," http://www.pvamu.edu/pages/605asp.

Southern Law Center. Florida established a law school at Florida A&M on 21 December 1949. The first classes began in 1950. The law program discontinued when the Florida Board of Control withdrew approval in 1966, about the time that the latest civil rights acts forced Florida to desegregate all colleges and universities. The FAMU law school graduated fifty-seven students from 1954 to 1968. NAACP lawsuits forced some states to admit black law students to the white schools, and the trend of erecting law schools on HBCU campuses came to an end by 1951.

The University of Arkansas admitted its first black citizen, Silas H. Hunt, a graduate of Arkansas AM&N State College and a WWII veteran, to the law program in 1948. Arkansas admitted five other Negro students to the law school by 1950. They were former students of HBCUs Arkansas AM&N, Wilberforce University, Morehouse College, and Lincoln University in Missouri. They could not use student dormitories, student restrooms, or sit in any but their assigned seats in the back corner of the classrooms at the University of Arkansas. Arkansas at first built a picket fence in the back corner of the classroom to separate the Negro student from the white students, otherwise, the instructor taught the black man at home or on another site. Some white students began attending the small classes for Negroes, because they included more attention from the professor. Most of the Negroes completed the program; but from 1955–1968, no Negro students attended the law school.[23]

NAACP lawsuits forced Oklahoma to accept two qualified Negro students into the public law school by 1949, but the officials required the men to sit in the hallway and listen to the lectures through the open classroom door. They sued again, and got access to the classroom. By 1950, two more TWIs admitted black law students. Houston died just before *Sweatt v. Painter* 399 US 629 (1946) forced the desegregation of the University of Texas law school in June 1950. They admitted Heman Marion Sweatt, a product of Wiley College. *Gray v. University of Tennessee* 97 F. Supp. 463 (1951) forced the officials to accept six Negro graduate and law students in 1951.

After the movement to desegregate higher education in the former Jim Crow states, 1970 to 2005, Africans Americans pushed for more access to legal education at the HBCUs. In 2000, Florida reestablished a College of Law under FAMU. Frederick S. Humphries, retired FAMU president, assisted in opening the new law school campus in Orlando. The school gained a three-to-five-year provisional accreditation from the American Bar Association in June 2004 when the first class was graduated. In 2005, the school graduated fifty-seven students.

[23] Judith Kilpatrick, "Desegregating the University of Arkansas School of Law: L. Clifford Davis and Six Pioneers," *Arkansas Historical Quarterly* 68/2 (Summer 2009): 123–56.

Enrollment in 2005–2006 reached 410 students, including 49 percent blacks, 14.6 percent Hispanics, and majority women. The 2005 brochure read, "FAMU will continue its mission of meeting the educational needs of African Americans and other ethnic minorities, while maintaining its leadership in racial diversity." FAMU College of Law received full ABA accreditation in 2009.[24]

The *Geier et al. v. Sundquist et al.* US 5077 (2002) higher-education desegregation case settlement granted Tennessee State University permission to seek a merger with the Nashville School of Law (an evening school). This was part of the *Geier* final settlement. The TSU president was not able to implement the law school because discussions collapsed due to opposition from Nashville School of Law's officials, faculty (local judges and lawyers), and alumni who originated mostly from white, working-class and middle-class backgrounds and wanted nothing to do with a predominantly black TSU. The Nashville School of Law was not accredited by ABA, and, thus, needed affiliation with a fully accredited institution like Tennessee State University; however, state law allowed Nashville School of Law graduates to pass the state bar and become local practicing attorneys, and even judges and court officers. TSU could not afford establishment of a law school on its own, and many faculty members did not welcome a law school that used up institutional resources to pay high salaries, but produced little revenue. Law programs at the HBCUs intended to enroll "students from groups under-represented in the American bar."[25]

The David A. Clarke School of Law at the University of District of Columbia (UDC) received ABA accreditation in April 2005, had 55 percent minority students, 61 percent female students, and included the sixth-highest percentage of African-American law students enrolled in the 190 ABA-accredited law schools. By 2020, the US Department of Education continues to maintain the Thurgood Marshall Legal Educational Opportunity Program to provide low-income, minority, or disadvantaged secondary school students and college

---

[24] S. Latham, "FAMU College of Law receives full accreditation from ABA," *Nashville Pride*, 7 August 2009, 1; Gabrielle Finley, "Florida A&M University's College of Law Will Enroll First Class in August," *Black Issues in Higher Education* 19/9 (20 June 2002): 21.

[25] Jack Greenberg, *Crusaders in the Court: How a Dedicated Band of Lawyers Fought for the Civil Rights Revolution* (New York: Harper-Collins, 1994) 1–30; M. V. Tushnet, *The NAACP's Legal Strategy against Segregated Education, 1925–1950* (Chapel Hill: University of North Carolina Press, 1987) 1–30; Juan Williams, *Thurgood Marshall: American Revolutionary* (New York: Random House, 1998) 1–25; W. E. Terry, *Origins and Development of Texas Southern University, 1927–1967* (Houston, 1978) 1–40. D. D. Bruce Jr., *Archibald Grimke: Portrait of a Black Independent* (Baton Rouge: Louisiana State University Press, 1993) 22–26.

students with information, preparation, and financial assistance to gain access to and complete law school study.[26]

In 2010, America had six ABA-approved HBCU law programs: Howard University, North Carolina Central University, Southern University, Texas Southern University, Florida A&M University, and University of DC among some two hundred ABA schools of law. These HBCUs produced many of the nation's minority lawyers. For 2007–2008, the ABA reported 9,631 minority students earned JD degrees, 23 percent of the 43,588 degrees awarded. The total attrition rate was 6,460 for that year, and minority students had high attrition rates among 31,368 students enrolled in JD programs in 2008–2009.[27] More black lawyers were needed.

Medical and Health Programs at HBCUs

HBCUs played a critical role in the expansion of medical education in the United States. The Negro population suffered not only from tuberculosis, but also from many diseases caused by malnutrition and poor environmental conditions during, and after, slavery days. The slave masters often provided minimal health care, according to nineteenth-century standards, for slaves. However, by the 1850s, the masters often purchased death and accident insurance policies on slaves. Some of the insurance companies, and their successors, that benefited from the profits on slave insurance still exist in American business. After emancipation in 1865, the former slaves had little or no access to health care, except "root doctors" and home remedies, and no place to bury their dead except in church yards, freedmen's and pauper cemeteries, and newly formed cemeteries their leaders formed through proprietary and stock companies. Untrained undertakers got a lucrative start during the years of high black mortality rates. From the cradle to the grave the African Americans faced Jim Crow and racial discrimination across America.[28]

The Jim Crow states and even places in the North imposed racial segregation by law and *de facto* racial discrimination in medicine, health facilities, doctors' offices, hospitals and cemeteries. Most private white physicians refused to treat Negro patients, partly because their white customers would not approve

---

[26] See Williams, *Thurgood Marshall: American Revolutionary*, 1–30; USOE, www2.ed.gov/programs/legal.

[27] "Enrollment," "Graduates," American Bar Association, www.aba.org., July 2010; Darryl C. Wilson, "'Black' Law Schools Face Challenges of a New Day," *Black Issues in Higher Education* 18/4 (12 April 2001): 50.

[28] Darlene Clark Hine, "The Anatomy of Failure: Medical Education Reform and the Leonard School of Shaw University, 1882–1920," *Journal of Negro Education* 54/4 (Autumn 1985): 512–25.

of sharing offices, equipment, and services with Negroes. There were few medical schools in the North accepting Negro applicants, and no southern medical schools and hospitals admitted Negroes. Health care was almost non-existent during slavery, and the post-emancipation health condition of the freedmen was shamefully pitiful. Indeed, some people believed the former slaves would die out.

Women were barred from medical schools until 1849, when Elizabeth Blackwell graduated from Geneva Medical College in upstate New York. Howard University's medical program (1868–) admitted black and white women from the first, and graduated the first woman in 1872. In 1876, the first Negro woman to graduate from a white medical school, Sarah Loguen (Fraser), the daughter of a fugitive slave, graduated in a class of nine men and four women from Medical College of Syracuse University, and established practice in DC. Medical colleges sprang up for women, who were expected to attend females in childbirth. By 1890, women represented 15–20 percent of medical students in American institutions. In 1890, there were 909 Negro doctors to serve 7.5 million African Americans.[29]

Negro leaders, northern philanthropists, and federal agencies created and operated a host of Negro medical and nursing schools from 1876 to 1924. The federal Freedmen's Bureau, 1865–1872, established nearly fifty hospitals, clinics, and even cemeteries for the former slaves. Early schools included Howard University Medical School (1868), Meharry Medical Department at Central Tennessee College (1876), Leonard Medical School (1882) at Shaw University, Louisville National Medical College (1888), Flint Medical College (1889) at New Orleans University, Dixie Hospital Training School in Hampton (1891), Knoxville Medical College (1895), Flint-Goodridge Hospital School of Nursing in New Orleans (1896), University of West Tennessee Medical School (1900), Hubbard Hospital at Meharry (1912), and Tuskegee Hospital for Veterans (1924). A Meharry graduate reportedly founded a medical school in Jackson, Tennessee, and edited the *Medical and Surgical Observer* (1892) medical journal. Tuskegee offered nursing since 1892, and Shaw University issued its first pharmacy degree in 1893.[30]

---

[29] Ellen Carol DuBois and Lynn Dumenil, *Through Women's Eyes: An American History*, vol. 1, 2nd ed. (Boston MA: Bedford/St. Martin's, 2009) 276–78; D. C. Hine, W. E. Hine, and Stanley Harrold, *The African Odyssey*, 3rd ed. (Upper Saddle River NJ: Pearson Prentice Hall, 2006) 385–87; Todd L. Savitt, "Straight University Medical Department: The Short Life of a Black Medical School in Reconstruction New Orleans," *Louisiana History* 41/2 (Spring 2000): 175–201.

[30] David H. Jackson, *Booker T. Washington and the Struggle against White Supremacy: The Southern Educational Tours, 1908–1912* (New York: Palgrave Macmillan, 2008) 93–94; W.

Charles B. Purvis, among others, helped form the National Medical Society (NMS), which was chartered in the District of Columbia, in 1925. Purvis attended Oberlin College in 1860–1862, and graduated from the Western Reserve medical college in 1865. For two years he served as a lieutenant and assistant surgeon in the Union Army and worked in the Freedmen's Hospital in 1868; he became secretary of the medical faculty. The program enrolled whites, too. When serving as speaker to the graduating class of 1883, Purvis said, "Gentlemen: Medicine is a science, a progressive one. In some of its branches, it is almost an exact one. Each year, however, brings us new ideas, new experiences, and new successes. Therefore, I want to enjoin upon you the importance of keeping abreast with the daily growth of your profession."[31]

The expense of medical education for a people who recently exited slavery was too much, however.[32] Thus, the 1910 report by Abraham Flexner, *Medical Education in the United States and Canada* helped close all of the HBCU medical schools except Howard and Meharry. The Carnegie Foundation, of which Flexner became general secretary in 1912, funded the report, and the American Medical Association adopted the report, which imposed new standards for medical education. Approval of the Flexner Report almost immediately began to raise the standard of medical education in the US. It set new standards and helped reduce the number of medical schools by half by 1930. The report's section on "The Medical Education of the Negro" (pp. 180–84) noted the black medical schools. Charles W. Johnson, Sr., in *The Spirit of a Place Called Meharry*, said the Flexner Report "painted a picture of inferiority" on Negroes and caused graduates of black medical schools to be treated not as "complete physicians but as something less, with peculiar qualifications for providing service only to the "Negro people."[33] Part of chapter fourteen of *Flexner*,

> The practice of the Negro doctor will be limited to his own race, which in turn will be cared for better by good Negro physicians than by poor white ones. The Negro must be educated not only for his sake, but for ours. He has his rights and due and value as an individual; but he has, besides, the tremendous importance that belongs to a potential source of infection and contagion. A well taught Negro sanitarian would be immensely useful; an essential untrained Negro wearing a MD badge is dangerous. The Negro

---

Dyson, *Howard University* (Washington DC: Howard University, 1971) 1–10; Daniel L. Lamb, *Howard University Medical Department: A Historical Biography and Statistical Souvenir* (Washington DC: Howard University, 1900) 1–21.

[31] Simmons, *Men of Mark*, 692.

[32] Abraham Flexner, *Medical Education in the United States and Canada*, bulletin 4 (New York: Carnegie Foundation for the Advancement of Teaching, 1910, 1960, 1972).

[33] Charles W. Johnson Sr., *The Spirit of a Place Called Meharry* (Nashville, 2000) 24–25.

needs good schools rather than many schools ... so that they ... may play an important role in the sanitation and civilization of the whole nation.[34]

By the first quarter of the twentieth century, the Negro and death rates threatened to spiral out of control. A white patient had a fourteen-times better chance of hospitalization, and in the case of tuberculosis, the Negro had one chance out of twenty-five for survival. When black leaders secured one of the federal hospitals to serve veterans, whites objected, even opposing the location of the facility on the campus of Tuskegee Institute. They did not want a Negro staff serving whites. On 3 July 3 1923, some seven hundred Klansmen paraded on the grounds of the hospital demanding a white-only staff. The NAACP appealed to the president, and asked him to send troops to Alabama. By 1928, Fisk teamed with the Tennessee department of public health to study death rates of black and white citizens. The 1930 study, Elbridge Sibley, *Differential Mortality in Tennessee*, showed Negroes had a death rate twice that of whites from pneumonia, typhoid, pellagra, and tuberculosis.[35]

In 1908, fifty-two Negro nurses met in New York, and formed the National Association of Colored Nurses, which had 560 members by 1920. The number of Negro dentists increased from 1,109 in 1920 to 1,773, including twenty-seven females, by 1930. Mississippi, with more than 40 percent blacks, had twenty-nine black dentists. Tennessee, with more than 20 percent Negroes, had sixty-nine black dentists. Yet, Pennsylvania, with a smaller percentage of Negroes, had 176 Negro dentists. The National Dental Association was formed in 1940.[36]

The 1930 census showed 3,805 Negro physicians, including ninety-two women. The greatest number of black doctors practiced in Illinois, New York, New Jersey, Missouri, Pennsylvania, and Tennessee. Tennessee had 285 black doctors, Mississippi had sixty-nine, and South Carolina had sixty-four. In North Carolina, 129 Negro physicians served all the Negroes. Whites had a physician for every five hundred people. Negroes—who often lived in the poorest of housing—wooden shacks, tenement houses, and poorly ventilated one-stories on low ground—had one doctor for every 3,200 people.

---

[34] Johnson, *The Spirit of a Place Called Meharry*, 25; Charles Victor Roman, *Meharry Medical College, A History* (Nashville: Meharry Medical College, 1934) 1–30. Black physicians Johnson and Roman served on Meharry's staff; Flexner, *Medical Education in the United States and Canada*, 180–82; Clark Hine, "The Anatomy of Failure," 512–25.

[35] Hine, Hine, and Harrold, *American Odyssey*, 385–87; Elbridge Sibley, *Differential Mortality in Tennessee, 1917–1928* (Washington, DC: Negro Universities Press, 1930, 1969) 1–20.

[36] Ibid.; Booker T. Washington, "Training Colored Nurses at Tuskegee," *American Journal of Nursing* 11/3 (December 1910): 167–71.

With help from the Rosenwald Fund, Fisk, Meharry, and Tennessee A&I formulated plans to employ health education to address health problems among Negroes. The increase of Negro health practitioners was deliberate. In 1931, the American Medical Association approved thirty-one HBCUs to offer "premedical courses." On 15–16 October 1932, Hampton Institute's School of Nursing and the US Public Health Service hosted the first Public Health Conference on the Negro. Conferees concluded that 60 percent of Negro children suffered a variety of diseases, most of which could be prevented and cured if the Negro families had proper access to public health programs. Failure to prevent or cure these diseases negatively affected the life expectancy of Negro adults and curtailed their potential as grown men and women, including a high percentage of Negroes rejected for the World War II draft for health reasons. A high rate of illiteracy among many Negro citizens hindered the spread of health education. The social science team at Fisk University did surveys on economic, social, and political problems of Negroes that helped lead to New Deal programs to address some Negro problems. Following the war, in 1946, Fisk and Tennessee A&I, among other HBCUs, teamed up with the US Office of Education to administer health education programs for the "functionally illiterate." Historians Woodson and Wesley said, "With such ill adapted education as Negroes have had it is little wonder that their health has been neglected."[37]

Fortunately, many white employers became concerned about the constant contact with their Negro workers, and the situation caused some of them at least to provide minimal health care for blacks. The Jim Crow states also contemplated how to train a few Negroes in medicine and health fields without desegregation of TWIs. Tennessee began making contractual arrangements with Meharry Medical College in 1941–1942, formally signing an agreement on 18 April 1945. Meharry soon found that the $75 per student per quarter was not acceptable. The fee increased to $100 per quarter in 1946. Tennessee later authorized an increase to $166.66 per quarter plus a differential between cost at HBCU Meharry and white University of Tennessee.

In 1947, Tennessee officials led a group of southern states in forming the Southern Regional Education Board (SREB) to contract with Meharry, Clark Atlanta School of Social Work and others to produce Negro health professionals. In his January 1949 legislative message, Governor James N. McCord of Tennessee said,

[37] Carter G. Woodson and Charles H. Wesley, *The Negro in Our History* (Washington DC: Associated Publishers, 1922, 1972) 576–93.

> This compact was not intended as a subterfuge designed to perpetuate segregation, or to avoid the civil obligations of the states in the field of education as the professional leaders of the NAACP whom reside in the North would have you believe. As it [relates] to Meharry it was, and now is, an honest and sincere effort to preserve for the Negro boy and girl, (sic) in both the South and elsewhere, their only real opportunity for an education in medicine, dentistry, and nursing.[38]

McCord warned fellow southern governors to cooperate, because they "could not afford to let the federal government take over this domain."[39] Robert Churchwell, a Negro reporter for the black Nashville *Commentator* newspaper, said, "The plan to make Meharry a regional school will enable southern governments to put off democratizing ... [It] is designed to hold back the wheels of progress [for Negroes]."[40]

Meharry even had an SREB-like contract with New York. In 1950, the SREB arrangement included nineteen institutions and 1,069 students. The University of Arkansas admitted the first Negro into its medical school in 1948. There were just ninety-three Negroes in twenty white medical schools in 1950. Some 216 Negro students attended forty-eight white medical schools by 1956. Negro doctors constituted 2.2 percent of all physicians—one for every 4,567 Negroes. The SREB arrangements continued through 1960 until congressional passage of the Civil Rights Bill in 1964.[41]

The General Education Board invested heavily in Howard and Meharry, which trained 83 percent of America's black physicians. Meharry produced more

---

[38] Jim N. McCord, "Message to the Tennessee General Assembly," January 1949, Jim Nance McCord Papers, Governor's Papers, letters and messages for 1946–1949, SREB letters and messages from McCord, Speeches to the Legislature, 1949, Box 17, subject files, folders, microfilm, Manuscripts Division, Tennessee State Library and Archives, Nashville TN, GP45

[39] Ibid.

[40] Robert Churchwell, "Meharry," *Nashville Commentator*, 1 January 1949, 1. Note: Robert Churchwell retired as the first black reporter for the *Nashville Banner*. He died in 2009. Three of his four sons practice medicine, and one heads a department at Vanderbilt University Medical School.

[41] John H. Franklin and Loren Schweninger, *In Search of the Promise Land: A Slave Family in the Old South* (New York: Oxford University Press, 2006) 209–34; Johnson, *The Negro College Graduate*, 3, 9, 23; Joe W. Trotter Jr., *The African American Experience* (New York: Houghton Mifflin Company, 2001) 330–31; Booker, *And There Was Light: The 120-Year History of Knoxville College, 1875–1995*, "The Medical Department;" Joe M. Richardson, *A History of Fisk University, 1865–1946* (Tuscaloosa: University of Alabama Press, 1980) 126–27; Johnson, *The Spirit of a Place Called Meharry*, 10–11; Thomas J. Ward Jr., *Black Physicians in the Jim Crow South* (Fayetteville: University of Arkansas Press, 2009) 1–20.

black physicians than any white medical school in the country. Meharry had 40 percent of black physicians and dentists practicing in the US, 40 percent of black faculty in American medical schools, and several founders of hospitals. Negro historians Woodson and Wesley said,

> The rise of the Negro physicians has ... advanced the cause of health by their close contact with Negro patients who more freely disclose to them the origin and history of their complaints than they would to the physicians of another race. Negro physicians ... have demonstrated the capacity to interpret and apply the principles of advanced medicine with special reference to laboratory work and institutional service."[42]

The School of Medicine at Howard began in 1868 but dated back to 1862 when the Union Army established a hospital to administer to former slaves in the Washington, DC, contraband camps. Alexander T. Augusta was in charge of the hospital for freedmen in 1863, after being educated in Trinity Medical College in Toronto, Canada. Augusta later became the first Negro on the faculty at Howard University. Anderson R. Abbott helped set up the hospital. He had completed studies at Oberlin College and at a medical school in Toronto. Jermone Riley, another free black Canadian, helped establish the hospital. Both of these men and John Rapier, Jr., gained appointments as Union Army surgeons to work in the frame building in northwest DC. Congress chartered Howard University on 2 March 1867, which opened on 1 May 1867, and included five white female students, the daughters of the founders. The Medical Department opened on 5 November 1868 and included the hospital for freedmen. The medical classes began the following Monday with seven Negroes and one white student. The medical department had five faculty members including one Negro, Augusta. Charles Purvis joined the faculty, and he became a member of the Howard University board of trustees. In 1869, a separate building housed the medical department and the Freedman's [Freedmen's] Hospital. The first medical curriculum required three years of study. The pharmacy program required two years. One student graduated from the pharmacy program in 1870, and five medical students graduated in 1871. The first female graduated in 1872. Dentistry began in the early 1880s, and the hospital served five thousand patients in 1886. A high school diploma was required for admittance in 1903. The program used evening classes until 1910 when it became a four-year day program. The faculty required two years of college for admission by 1914. The federal government transferred the Freedmen's Hospital to Howard in 1867. The university built Howard University Hospital in 1975, and opened the Cancer

---

[42] Woodson and Wesley, *The Negro in Our History*, 570–78.

Center (1980), Ambulatory Care Tower (1991), and Health Sciences Library (2001).[43]

Meharry Medical College began at Central Tennessee College as the Medical Department under the auspices of the Freedmen's Aid Society of the Methodist Episcopal Church (North). Nashville was inundated by thousands of former slaves living in the remnants of three large, former-contraband camps. George W. Hubbard, a Union Army veteran, a missionary from New Hampshire, and recent graduate of the University of Nashville medical program founded Meharry. A white benefactor from Ohio Samuel Meharry and his four brothers donated the first funds. The first class graduated in 1878. The College added programs in dentistry (1886), pharmacy (1889), and nursing (1910). Robert F. Boyd, a Meharry medical and dental graduate, formed Nashville's Mercy Hospital for Negroes in 1893. Boyd became the first president of the National Medical Association, which included pharmacists and dentists, and has published its journal since 1909, focusing on solving health disparities for blacks and the underserved. Charles V. Roman, an 1890 graduate of Meharry, edited the *Journal*. The NMA raised awareness of health problems faced by blacks, and united Negro doctors to solve the problems. Hubbard Hospital opened in 1912, and succeeded the small clinics operated by Boyd and others.[44]

On 13 October 1915, Meharry Medical College received a state charter separate from Walden University that was having severe financial problems. Meharry gained "A" rating from the AMA in 1923, and, with financial help from several northern philanthropic associations, including Rosenwald, Eastman, Carnegie, and the General Education Board, Meharry abandoned its old buildings on First Avenue North, and moved to a new campus on Eighteenth Avenue North, opposite the Fisk University campus. Financial problems plagued the school through the 1940s, and the last white president, M. D. Clawson, served from 1945 to 1950. A committee directed the institution until 1952, when Harold D. West became the first black president. Meharry redefined itself in 1962, dropping nursing and dental technology. Tennessee State University assumed these programs. Meharry experienced another administrative committee in 1966–1968. Presidents Lloyd Elam, Richard Lester, David Satcher,

---

[43] Sterling M. Lloyd Jr., *A Short History of Howard University College of Medicine* (Washington DC: Howard University, 2006) 1–20; William M. Cobb, "The First Hundred Years of the Howard University College of Medicine," *Journal of the National Medical Association* 57 (1967): 409–20.

[44] Todd L. Savitt, "The Journal of the National Medical Association 100 Years Ago: A New Voice of and for African American Physicians," *Journal of the National Medical Association* 102/1 (Spring 2010): 734–44.

John Maupin, and Wayne J. Riley headed Meharry through 2010. Meharry has 218 faculty and 786 students in twenty buildings.[45]

The medical schools at Howard and Meharry offered other degrees beside the MD degree. Meharry Medical College, in addition to its MD and DDS, became notable for its research doctorate degrees: MPhD and PhD degrees in biochemistry, biomedical sciences, microbiology, pharmacology, and physiology. Meharry achieved SACS accreditation for these programs in December 1972—in addition to accreditation of its medical programs by medical associations—in order to authenticate its School of Graduate Studies and Research (1972). This allowed Meharry to become the third HBCU, behind Howard and Atlanta University, in offering PhD degrees in the biomedical sciences. Howard's original mission of direct service to communities having a shortage of health personnel continued in many demonstrative programs, and its College of Medicine (1868–) offered anatomy, biochemistry and molecular biology, microbiology, pharmacology, and physiology and biophysics in the basic sciences. Howard's College of Medicine had four clinical departments, eleven institutes and centers, and the University Hospital. Morehouse School of Medicine offered a PhD in biomedical science, MPH in public health, and the MD degree. The school gained SACS accreditation.

HBCUs served the local black communities when no other health-care facility was available to blacks. Howard, Meharry Medical College, and Tuskegee Institute sponsored hospitals with about nine hundred beds catering mostly to minority and poor patients (both whites and blacks). Meharry turned its Hubbard Hospital (1912–) over to the city as Nashville-Davidson County's General Hospital in the 1990s. Meharry and Howard continued sponsoring large community clinical programs, with help from the National Cancer Institute and other state and federal agencies. These HBCUs focused on eliminating racial disparities in health care and better ways to serve poor and minority citizens. Hubbard Hospital also served whites in the city of Nashville.

Outreach initiatives at Meharry included programs in sickle-cell disease, tropical diseases, and summer biomedical sciences programs to help expand minority applicants in the field. Nearby Tennessee State and Meharry developed

[45] Reavis L. Mitchell Jr., "Meharry Medical College (1876–)," in B. L. Lovett and L. T. Wynn, eds., *Profiles of African Americans in Tennessee* (Nashville: Local Conference on African American History and Culture, 1996) 89–91; Edward Jones, "Morehouse in Business Ninety Years—Building Men," *Phylon* 18/3 (Third Quarter 1957): 231–45; Editor, "The Coming Shortage of Black Medical School Graduates," *Journal of Blacks in Higher Education* 28/1 (Summer 2000): 44–46; Editor, "The New President of the Morehouse School of Medicine," *Journal of Blacks in Higher Education* 36/1 (Summer 2002): 103.

a joint School of Allied Health Professions, eventually including graduate and undergraduate degrees in health information management, dental hygiene, cardio-respiratory care sciences, health-care administration, medical technology, occupational therapy, speech pathology and audiology, and physical therapy. There was a joint Fisk-Meharry program in clinical psychology. In March 2005, Meharry announced a new Research Center to Combat Health Disparities among Women of Color, the first such center in the world, scheduled to open in 2006. Black women were twice as likely to die of cervical cancer as white women were. Blacks and Hispanics were twice as likely as Caucasians to develop diabetes and suffer complications such as blindness and amputations. Similar differences persisted even when taken into account income and education for heart disease, sexually transmitted diseases, and a host of other conditions. The new center would attempt to understand the genetic, education, income, health practices, and cultural factors that contribute to such disparities especially among women of color. David Satcher, former US Surgeon General and a former president of Meharry Medical College, concluded that while overall longevity for black and white Americans had improved over the last forty years, the gap between these American racial groups had narrowed little.[46]

To help bear the burden of training black doctors and health specialists, two new black medical schools came on line after *Brown*. The Charles R. Drew University of Medicine and Science in Los Angeles sprouted out of the ashes of the black Watts riots in 1966, which illustrated the gross inadequacies in health care suffered by twentieth-century minority citizens in Los Angeles. Charles R. Drew, Percy Julian, and Hildrus A. Poindexter at Howard University's School of Medicine, Elmer S. Imes in physics at Fisk University, and N.O. Calloway and George Washington Carver at Tuskegee Institute made monumental contributions to research in medicine and science. Drew in particular developed techniques for preserving blood plasma and became director of the American Red Cross Blood Bank during World War II.

The Morehouse School of Medicine started, in 1975, to train students in basic medical sciences with students transferring to four-year schools to complete their medical education. The Liaison Committee on Medical Education, a joint committee of the Association of American Medical Colleges and the American Medical Association, granted a Letter of Reasonable Assurance in summer 1977. This school opened as a two-year program in 1978, became independent of Morehouse College in 1981, and graduated the first class of doctors on 17 May 1985. Morehouse School of Medicine attracted 70 percent of its

---

[46] David Satcher, "The Initiative to Eliminate Racial and Ethnic Health Disparities Is Moving Forward," *Public Health Reports* 114/3 (May–June 1999): 283–87.

students from Georgia. The institution enrolled 212 students by 2001. By 2009, the MSM offered the MD, master of public health, graduate education in biomedical sciences, and Master of Science in clinical research.[47]

Other HBCUs played vital roles in addressing health and medical problems among African Americans. The private HBCUs, especially Xavier, became the major producers of black students going to medical schools, while the public HBCUs, which had most of the graduate programs, handled the task of sending African-American graduates to PhD programs at the nation's larger universities. The Southern Education Foundation, United Negro College Fund and others helped promote and finance several programs to increase black applicants to health and medical programs. Xavier University (1915–) opened a college of Pharmacy in 1927. By the late twentieth century, pharmacy programs also existed at FAMU, Hampton, and Texas Southern. Hampton offered PhD degrees in nursing, pharmacy, and physical therapy by 2004. Twelve HBCUs offered nursing, related medical programs, and offered social work and programs in mental health research and substance abuse. Tennessee State University developed a School of Nursing in 1966 that had a student passage rate of 93–100 percent on state board examinations by 1990. TSU graduated 118 undergraduate and eighteen master's degrees in nursing in 2007 alone.[48]

Religious Education at HBCUs

Since 1837, the HBCUs, public and private taught morality, religion, service, respect of human rights, and working with the hands and head. Into the 1960s, public HBCUs required weekly chapel, including religious music. Sunday schools and church services existed on HBCU campuses. Catholic-affiliated Xavier University continues to have a strong campus ministry. Howard

---

[47] US Department of Education (USDOE), National Center for Education Statistics (NCES), Table A-9, "Fall enrollment in degree-granting HBCUs, 1976–2001"; Editor, "Surge on General David Satcher Takes a Post at Morehouse School of Medicine," *Journal of Blacks in Higher Education* 35/1 (Spring 2002): 132.

[48] D. A. Johnson, *Vanderbilt Divinity School: Education, Contest, and Change* (Nashville: Vanderbilt University Press, 2001) 131–77; Cynthia L. Jackson and Eleanor F. Nunn, *Historically Black Colleges and Universities: A Reference Book* (Santa Barbara CA: ABC-Clio, 2003) 40, 46–47, 75, 186–87, 201; Woodson and Wesley, *The Negro in Our History*, 579–93; M. Morris, *The History of the Negro in Medicine* (New York: Macmillan, 1969) 1–20; James Summerville, *Educating Black Doctors: A History of Meharry Medical College* (Knoxville: University of Tennessee Press, 1983) 1–31; T. L. Savitt, "The Education of Black Physicians at Shaw University, 1882–1918," in J. J. Crow and F. Hatley, eds., *Black Americans in North Carolina and the South* (Chapel Hill: University of North Carolina Press, 1984) 160–88; Editor, "Hampton's Pharmacy School Receives $2 Million to Study Ecstasy," *Black Issues in Higher Education* 20/8 (5 June 2003): 15.

University had its beginning as the Theological and Normal Institute in a missionary prayer meeting on 20 November 1866, at the First Congregational Church of Washington, DC. Mainly through support of the American Missionary Association, Howard opened a theological department on 15 September 1871, and was accredited by the American Association of Theological Schools on 15 December 1939, offering, by 1940, bachelors' and masters' degrees in religious education. Northern Methodists opened Claflin and Bennett. Baptists opened Spelman, Benedict, Leland, Shaw, and Morehouse. The Protestant Episcopal Church established a Commission on Home Missions to Colored People, the American Church Institute for Negroes, Payne Divinity School at Virginia Theological Seminary, St. Paul's, Voorhees, St. Augustine, and Hoffman Hall (1890–1907) at Fisk. The latter theological program moved to Mason, Tennessee, to become Hoffman-St. Mary's Industrial School for secondary students. The AME Church opened Allen, Morris Brown, Edward Waters, and Paul Quinn. The Presbyterians founded Barber-Scotia. The New England Congregationalists founded nearly twenty schools and colleges for Negroes, including Fisk, Howard, Atlanta, Talladega, Hampton, and Tougaloo. Tuskegee Institute affiliated with no specific religious denomination, but it had the Phelps Hall Bible Training School, which prepared students for the ministry and other Christian work during Booker T. Washington's time. The black National Baptist Convention of America operated the National Baptist Theological Seminary and Training School (1918–1934) in Nashville, but closed in favor of the school at Virginia Union. The rival National Baptist Convention, USA, opened American Baptist Theological Seminary (1924–) partly supported by the white Southern Baptist Convention until 1996.

Between 1959 and 1969, several black schools of theology and religion merged and formed the Interdenominational Theological Center, a Christian and ecumenical center, and a graduate professional school of theology. The GEB gave Gammon Theological Seminary $15,000 to study the situation in Atlanta in 1956, and to determine if a new seminary could accommodate the Atlanta Center (AUC). They chartered the Interdenominational Theological Center on 14 March 1958. The Phillips School of Theology (1944–) of Lane College and its affiliated Christian Methodist Episcopal Church became the founding member in August 1959. The ITC began operations on the Gammon campus in September, and built a new ITC facility on Beckwith Street in December with GEB matching funds. The ITC also included Morehouse School of Religion (1867–) originally sponsored by the ABHMS. The Morehouse School of Religion produced notable preachers and theologians including Howard Thurman, Dillard H. Brown, Kelly Miller Smith, Sr., and Martin Luther King, Jr., among many others. Gammon

Theological Seminary (1869–) at Clark Atlanta joined the ITC. Turner Theological Seminary, which began in 1894 at Morris Brown College, sponsored by the AMEC, also joined. The Presbyterian Church, USA, sponsored the Johnson C. Smith Theological Seminary, which moved to AUC in 1969. The Charles C. Mason Theological Seminary, sponsored by the Church of God in Christ, joined the ITC. Absalom Jones Theological Institute to train black Episcopal priests became a part of ITC in 1971, but closed in 1979. By 1984, ITC gained accreditation from the American Association of Theological Schools and the SACS. ITC had 450 students, and offered graduate degrees on a ten-acre campus. ITC admitted students from other denominations.

Morris College (1908–), Livingston College (1879–), Shaw University (1865–), and Johnson C. Smith (1867–) intermittently awarded theology degrees through the 1970s. Shaw University separated the religion department out as an independent institution in 1976. Morris College closed in 1981. Howard (20), ITC (58), and Virginia Union (26) awarded 104 theology degrees in 1982. By 2004, the American Baptist Churches—the most racially integrated of Baptist denominations—supported sixteen colleges, including four HBCUs: Benedict College, Florida Memorial College, Shaw University, and Virginia Union University. Virginia Union displayed its eminent former students: Adam Clayton Powell, Sr., Charles S. Johnson, and Lawrence Douglas Wilder (recent governor of Virginia). Wilberforce created the Ray Charles Distinguished Chair of Sacred and Choral Music through a $2 million gift from the Rhythm and Blues singer.[49]

Liberal Arts and Social Science Education at HBCUs

Most HBCUs grounded their curricula in liberal arts, including classics of Western civilization. Thus, the black colleges gave their students formative exposure to Victorian culture and ideals and a strong background in the knowledge and ideas shared widely among middle-class Americans.[50] Consequently, the works of black authors and artists showed a high level of agreement about the values of American culture and about American values in general. HBCU scholars displayed the complex and contradictory relationship between blacks and whites.

---

[49] Benjamin E. Mays, *Born to Rebel: An Autobiography* (New York: Charles Scribner's Sons, 1971) 234–40.

[50] R. M. Story, *And So I Sing: African American Divas of Opera and Concert* (New York: Amistad, 1990, 1993) 105, 128, 139, 174, 202. See R. Abdul, *Blacks in Classical Music* (New York: Dodd, Mead & Company, 1977) 1–20; Daniel Payne, *Recollections of Seventy Years* (New York: Arno Press, 1968) 1–20; Henrietta White, *Nashville's Holy Trinity Episcopal Church: The Early Years* (Nashville TN: Holy Trinity Church, 2002) 110–15.

The HBCUs included many notable, liberal-arts and social-science scholars. Islay Walden, born a slave and educated at Howard University, was one of America's earliest poets focusing on religious devotion. William S. Scarborough, a linguist and the president (1908–1920) at Wilberforce University, published *First Lessons in Greek* (1881). W. E. B. Du Bois taught classics at Wilberforce University from 1894 to 1896, and taught history and economics at Atlanta University from 1897 to 1910 and again from 1934 to 1944. George M. McClellan, a product of Fisk University, published in 1906 *Old Greenbottom Inn*, a collection of fiction. James Weldon Johnson published his heralded *The Autobiography of an Ex-Colored Man* in 1912.[51] A product of Bishop College and Richmond Theological Seminary (Virginia Union University), Sutton E. Griggs had a great impact on early American literature, publishing thirty-three books, novels and tracts between 1899 and 1931. E. Franklin Frazier, a graduate of Howard University, did graduate work in sociology at the University of Chicago and taught at Howard for twenty-five years, influencing generations of students and the black leadership class. Frazier said, "Negro education in the past, to characterize it briefly, has been too much inspiration and too little information."[52] In 1957, Frazier published *The Negro in the United States*.[53] The notable Negro names in the humanities included John Hope, president of Morehouse College; William H. Crogman, professor at Clark University. Benjamin Brawley of

---

[51] James W. Johnson, *The Autobiography of an Ex-Colored Man* (Boston: French & Co., 1912); George M. McClelland, *Old Green Bottom Inn and Other Stories* (New York: AMS, 1975); William S. Scarborough, *Lessons in Greek* (New York: Barnes & Co., 1881).

[52] John T. Biggers, C. Simms, and J. E. Weems, *Black Art in Houston: The Texas Southern University Experience* (College Station TX: Texas A. & M. University Press, 1978) 1–10; Cary D. Wintz, *The Harlem Renaissance: A History and an Anthology* (Maplecrest NY: Brandywine Press, 2003) 1–20; Eugene Levy, *James Weldon Johnson: Black Leader, Black Voice* (Chicago: University of Chicago Press, 1973) 1–20; Richard Robbins, *Sidelines Activist: Charles S. Johnson and the Struggle for Civil Rights* (Jackson: University Press of Mississippi, 1996) 1–10; Steven Watson, *The Harlem Renaissance: Hub of African American Culture, 1920–1930* (New York: Pantheon Books, 1995) 18, 22, 24, 58, 70, 146, 158–59; Dickson D. Bruce Jr., *Black American Writing from the Nadir: The Evolution of a Literary Tradition, 1877–1915* (Baton Rouge: Louisiana State University Press, 1989) 6, 7, 22, 23, 33, 111, 140, 142, 156, 187, 202, 203, 232, 253; J. Lee Greene, *Blacks in Eden: The African American Novel's First Century* (Charlottesville: University of Virginia Press, 1996) 272; J. V. Gabbin, *The Furious Flowering of African American Poetry* (Charlottesville: The University of Virginia Press, 2000) 169–81, 233, 261; T. M. Davis, *Nella Larsen: Novelist of the Harlem Renaissance, A Woman's Life Unveiled* (Baton Rouge: Louisiana State University Press, 1994) 8, 25, 50–66; Nathan I. Huggins, *Harlem Renaissance* (London: Oxford University Press, 1971) 17, 19, 74, 229; Benjamin G. Brawley, *The Negro Genius: A New Appraisal of the Achievement of the American Negro in Literature and the Fine Arts* (New York: Dodd, Mead, and Company, 1937) 1–10.

[53] E. Franklin, *The Negro in the United States* (New York: MacMillan, 1957).

Morehouse published *The Negro in Literature and Art in the United States* in 1929, the first comprehensive discussion of the topic.[54] The National Endowment for the Humanities supported the strengthening of the liberal arts and humanities at the HBCUs into the twenty-first century.

Painting, Sculpture, Arts and Crafts at HBCUs

In the field of art, the HBCUs contributed immensely to America's cultural development. *African-American Artists, 1929–1945* credits the HBCUs and Works Progress Administration centers for helping nurture Negro artists, many of whom were born, educated, and worked in the South.[55] Art stored at these minority institutions concertedly documented that Negroes, too, were creators of the world's finest art. When Alain Locke published *The Negro in Art* in 1940, he did so to make accessible to the public the work of Negro artists beyond that of "music, dance, drama, and poetry."[56] Locke, who used many of his art pieces in the book's photographs, said, "As an individual, the Negro artist's task, today, is merely that of expressing his modern self in contemporary idioms, those of his adopted culture."

Many of America's early Negro artists traveled to France to study painting, and at least four of these artists returned to teach and build departments of art at the HBCUs, including at Atlanta University, Fisk University, and Cheyney State Teachers College. Henry O. Tanner offered classes in painting at Clark University in Atlanta in the late 1880s before extending his career and base to the racially liberal environment of Paris, France. Tanner later won medals for his art. His famous painting, *The Banjo Lesson* (1893), ended up in the College Museum at Hampton University. Negro sculptor Edmonia Lewis, a product of Oberlin College, preceded Tanner, but her work displayed European classical influence with no hints of Negro or African background.

In 1890 to 1915, a Negro Renaissance sprouted in the South when Negro migrants to urban areas turned their creative energy loose in art, dance, music, and literature. Although these works originated through untrained hands, several HBCUs preserved them in collections of Negro art, crafts, and artifacts.

---

[54] Benjamin Brawley, *The Negro in Literature and Art in the United States* (New York: Duffield & Co., 1921).

[55] Metropolitan Museum of Art, *African-American Artists, 1929–1945* (New York: MMA, 2003) 1–90.

[56] Alain Locke, *The Negro in Art: A Pictorial Record of the Negro Artist* (New York: Hacker Art Books, 1968).

They displayed some in the Negro Building at the Atlanta Exposition (1895), Tennessee Centennial Exposition (1897), and Jamestown Exposition (1907).

In art, literature, theater, music, and writing Negro artists attempted to recapture the Negro past. They included both its rural, southern roots and its African heritage. William H. Sheppard was a missionary to Africa and a collector of African art. Sheppard was a church pastor in Montgomery in the 1880s after completing the Presbyterian Theological Institute (Stillman College). He and others operated the American Presbyterian Congo Mission from 1891 to 1910, when Sheppard collected African art at a time when the American art community gave no recognition to black art. Sheppard noted the fine artisanship of Africans in architecture, woodcarving, cloth-making, the making of boxes and baskets, clay pots, decorative motifs, embroidery, and metalwork. His huge collection resided in the museum at Hampton Institute.[57]

The *Journal of American Folklore* published folktales gathered from students in Tuskegee Institute and other persons elsewhere in the South as early as 1919.[58] Thomas W. Talley, a chemistry professor at Fisk University and the son of former slaves, began a series of writings that became a collection and analysis of Negro folk songs and rhymes.[59] Charles W. Wolfe and Laura C. Jarmon published one of Talley's 1923 manuscripts discovered in the Fisk library; they titled it *The Negro Traditions* (1993), which consisted of stories, songs, and music.[60] The Hampton journal, *The Southern Workman*, kept the old plantation melodies alive when many former slaves and their children preferred to trash these old tunes.[61] Famed Negro musician John Wesley Work said, "One would be as likely to hear Negro folk songs in St. Peter's at Rome as in Fisk University."[62] John Work, Jr., became a faculty member at Fisk in 1898. He published *Folk Songs of the American Negro* (1915), and helped compose and preserve old Negro music, including the spirituals arranged by his father, John Work.[63] John W. Work III taught at Fisk, and began taking notes and recordings of American black vernacular music,

---

[57] Harold G. Cureau, "William H. Sheppard: Missionary to the Congo, and Collector of African Art," *Journal of Negro History* 67/4 (Winter 1982): 340–52.

[58] Editor, "Folk-Tales in Tuskegee Institute, Alabama," *Journal of American Folklore* 32/125 (July–September 1919): 397–401.

[59] Thomas Talley, *Negro Folk Rhymes Wise and Otherwise* (New York: MacMillan, 1922).

[60] C. W. Wolfe and L. C. Jarmon, eds., Thomas Talley, *The Negro Traditions* (Knoxville: University of Tennessee Press, 1993).

[61] Hampton Normal and Agricultural Institute, *The Southern Workman* 61/1 (December 1912): 546.

[62] Linda T. Wynn, "John W. Work III (1901–1967)," in B. L. Lovett and L. T. Wynn, eds., *Profiles of African Americans in Tennessee* (Nashville: LCAAHC, 1996) 147–48.

[63] Ibid.

including the Delta blues, in the late 1930s. The Library of Congress took up the project as part of its American Folk Song collection. Work published more than fifty-nine compositions, and, until he died in 1967, "the origins of black folk music and folkways remained his life vocation."

Between 1868 and 1972, several HBCUs opened art galleries. Many of those galleries remain open today, and open to faculty, students, community groups, and other visitors. Lack of funding, inadequate gallery space and a scarcity of curators and art historians kept many of these national treasures hidden away in storage rooms. However, through a national tour of selected art pieces from the HBCU collections, in the 1990s, the country became aware of this rich legacy of culture and art. The works included ones by John Biggers, James Weeks, Henry O. Tanner, and Aaron Douglass. The Ford Motor Company and AT&T Company financed a tour of samples of the great art treasures held by the black colleges. *To Conserve a Legacy: American Art from Historically Black Colleges and Universities* (1999) featured 260 art pieces from the collections at Clark, Fisk, Hampton, Howard, North Carolina Central, and Tuskegee. Additionally, the Ford Foundation, which wanted to know about results, sponsored the Margaret Walker Digitization HBCU Partnership for Black Studies. Andrew Mellon Foundation gave $850,000 in 2005–2009 to help digitize almost five thousand images for about 20 HBCUs and their special collections to be shared on the Internet. Among this group, Dillard University included materials from Straight College and New Orleans University. HBCUs were great depositories for unexplored scholarly resources. Indeed, the HBCUs helped to centralize the development of black culture after slavery, and demonstrate how these minority institutions in particular remained central to the intellectual and social life of the black community. Many in the black community showed up to hear and see famous speakers and performers seldom seen by black folk, dance bands, art exhibitions, dazzling parades, explosive athletic contests, and to shake the hands of the major personalities and leaders in black culture.[64]

---

[64] H. G. Cureau, "The Art Gallery, Museum: Their Availability as Educational Resources in the Historically Negro College," *Journal of Negro Education* 42/4 (Autumn 1973): 452–61, demonstrated their importance; Arna Bontemps, *The Great Slave Narratives* (Boston: Beacon Press, 1969) x, xi; J. M. Spencer, *The New Negroes and Their Music: The Success of the Harlem Renaissance* (Knoxville: University of Tennessee Press, 1997); Marcia M. Mathews, *Henry Ossawa Tanner: American Artist* (Chicago: University of Chicago Press, 1969) 388–89; Franklin and Moss Jr., *From Slavery to Freedom*, 6th ed., 360–69; Sterling Stuckey, *Going Through the Storm: The Influence of African American Art in History* (New York: Oxford University Press, 1994) 1–32; J. M. Vlach, *By The Work of Their Hands: Studies in Afro-American Folklife* (Charlottesville: University of Virginia Press, 1991) 1–15; Randy Freeman, ed., *The Art of William Edmondson* (Jackson: University of Mississippi Press, 1999); see R. J.

HBCUs and the Black Cultural Renaissance

At the same time, indubitably intellectuals associated with the HBCUs provided the leadership for the Harlem [Black] Renaissance (1924–1931). Juan Williams and Dwayne Ashley said, "A cultural and artistic legacy had come into its own during the 1920s, due in large part to the educational efforts and influence of HBCUs. That legacy would continue in coming decades."[65] When Alain Leroy Locke, a Harvard graduate and Rhodes Scholar, began teaching philosophy at Howard University in 1912, there were few Negro artists recognized by the whites. Trained white artists were Eurocentric: they felt they were the originators of science, mathematics, history, and the arts, that there was no such a thing as "a field of black art." But Negroes, too, had creative minds. Many of the HBCU campuses included literary clubs, art collections, museum pieces, and art classes. In the first quarter of the twentieth century, minority business and city directories listed many literary clubs, art clubs, and garden clubs in the Negro neighborhoods. This was especially true in cities like Nashville and Atlanta where several HBCUs wielded influence. These clubs served to promote gatherings and discussions in Negro homes, local schools, and on HBCU campus facilities at a time when blacks often had no access to libraries and other public facilities.[66]

Out of this cultural tradition, Locke started *The Stylus* for the campus literary society in 1916. Zora Neale Hurston published her first literary piece in *The Stylus* while she was a student at Howard University before heading to Harlem and publishing her first short story in the Urban League's *Opportunity* magazine. Locke recognized the Negro's hidden cultural history, and he published *The New Negro: An Interpretation* (1925).[67] He wrote, "We have enough

---

Powell and J. Reynolds, *To Conserve a Legacy: American Art from Historically Black Colleges and Universities* (Cambridge: Massachusetts Institute of Technology Press, 1999); Alain Locke, *The Negro in Art: A Pictorial Record of the Negro Artist and the Negro Theme in Art* (Washington DC: Associates in Negro Folk Art Education, 1940) 1–8; Theresa Leininger-Miller, *New Negro Artists in Paris* (New Brunswick NJ: Rutgers University Press, 2001) 247–49; Lisa M. Messinger, L. G. Collins, and R. Mustalish, *African-American Artists, 1929–1945: Prints, Drawings and Paintings in the Metropolitan Museum of Art* (New York: MMOA and Princeton University Press, 2003) 35.

[65] Juan Williams and Dwayne Ashley, *I'll Find a Way or Make One: A Tribute to Historically Black Colleges and Universities* (New York: HarperCollins, 2004) 193; "Art from HBCUs on Exhibit at Fisk, Tennessee State Universities," *Black Issues in Higher Education* 17/25 (1 February 2001): 19.

[66] Editor, "The Negro in Periodical Literature, 1973–1974," *Journal of Negro History* 68/2 (Spring 1983): 232–82.

[67] Alain Locke, *The New Negro: An Interpretation* (New York: Albert & Charles Boni, 1925) 1-31.

talent now to begin to have a movement and to express a school of thought."[68] This was a call to inspire the beginning of the Harlem Renaissance. Negro artists included racial consciousness and the African origins in their artwork. They visualized the blacks' civil rights agenda, and through their works, eschewed overt protest against American racism. Charles S. Johnson, founding editor of the *Opportunity* magazine and W.E.B. Du Bois, founding editor of the NAACP's *Crisis* magazine, played crucial roles in the movement. Their publications served the budding young black artists and writers, like Zora Neale Hurston, and the black American's cultural legacy to the nation and world. While teaching at Howard, Benjamin Brawley, who wanted to show positive images of the Negro, published *A Social History of the American Negro* (1921). New Deal agencies in the 1930s recognized the black artists, and the Works Progress Administration hired some of them and gave grants to others to operate Negro art schools. Then the maturing of the HBCUs colleges in the 1920s and 1930s gave Negro Americans a greater stage upon which to play their role in the development of American intellectual history. Charles H. Thompson began editing the *Journal of Negro Education* at Howard University in 1931. Between 1924 and 1944, Negro writers produced many scholarly books.[69]

In 1940, W. E. B. Du Bois became editor-in-chief of a new publication, *Phylon: A Journal of Race and Culture* at Atlanta University. *Phylon* meant race translated from Greek. The front pages devoted an "Apology" to the continuing use of the older concept of the word "race," but discussed how important the concept was to understanding current world society, its dynamics and problems. The top Negro PhD degree holders in the field—including Ira De A. Reid, Stanley Braithwaite, W. Mercer Cook, Rayford Logan, Horace Mann Bond, and Rushton Coulborn—served on the editorial board. They intended to revive the spirit of the old *Atlanta University Publication*s (1897–1914), "which formed the first scientific basis for factual study of the condition and relations of one racial group in the United States, and was the beginning in America of applied Sociology and Anthropology to group problems."[70] According to Du Bois,

> This pioneer work has been supplemented widely since 1914 by institutions like Fisk University and the University of North Carolina, and by individual students in such investigations. Frazier's Negro Family in

---

[68] Eugene C. Holmes, "Alain Locke and the New Negro Movement," *Negro American Literature Forum* 2/3 (Autumn 1969): 60–68; Alain Locke, "The Negro's Contribution to American Culture," *Journal of Negro Education* 8/3 (July 1939): 521–29.

[69] See Benjamin Brawley, "The Negro in Contemporary Literature," *The English Journal* 18/3 (March 1929): 194–202.

[70] *Phylon* 1 (January 1940) I–ix.

> the United States, Johnson's Negro College Graduate, Caroline Bond Day's Negro-White Families, Abram Harris' The Negro as Capitalist, Cayton and Mitchell's Black Workers and the New Unions, Reid's studies of Pittsburgh and New Jersey, and Bond's Negro Education in Alabama, not to mention an increasing volume of government reports."[71]

While *Phylon* does not duplicate the *Journal of Negro History*, *Journal of Negro Education*, and the Negro press, Du Bois wrote,

> [W]e feel ...a new view of the social sciences is necessary, as comprehending the actions of men and reducing them to systematic study and understanding.... We shall strive to abolish the present economic illiteracy and paralysis, and openly hold up to frank criticism that widespread assumption that the industrial organization of the nineteenth century was something permanent and sacred and furnished a final world, which stops the twentieth century from facing the problem of abolishing poverty as a first step toward real freedom, democracy and art among men, through the use of industrial technique and planned economy.[72]

Several other HBCUs sponsored journals to serve as an outlet for faculty research and to help with accreditation standards requiring faculty publications. Johnson C. Smith sponsored the *Quarterly Review of Higher Education among Negroes*. Wilberforce issued the *Negro College Quarterly*. Lorenzo Greene succeeded the Lincoln University, Missouri, *Research Journal* with the *Midwest Journal* (1947–1956). Tennessee State had an annual *Faculty Research Journal*.

Fisk University scholars especially were quite productive in the early development of black intellectual history. A product of Virginia Union, Charles S. Johnson, left Harlem to become head of the social science division at Fisk in 1928, and remained there until his death in 1956. Aaron Douglass, the most noted of Harlem Renaissance artists, came to Fisk in 1937, and gained recognition for creating some of America's most spectacular murals with deep African and Afro-American traits. A product of Atlanta University, James Weldon Johnson, the "father of the Harlem Renaissance," left his post at the NAACP and assumed the Adam K. Spence Chair in Creative Literature at Fisk in 1931, where he remained until his death six years later. Nella Larsen, the "novelist of the Harlem Renaissance," matriculated in Fisk's normal program, and returned to live on campus with her husband in the 1930s after she already was famous for

[71] Ibid.

[72] Ibid.

publishing *Quicksand* (1928).[73] Flournoy Miller and Aubrey Lyles, who had begun writing plays at Fisk, wrote about Eubie Blake and Noble Sissle's famous music in the Jazz Age. Arna Bontemps, another refugee of the Harlem Renaissance, came to Fisk and ended his career there as the librarian and prolific publisher of many books. Arthur A. Schomburg stayed a few years at Fisk University before returning to New York and helping to create the nation's all-important Schomburg Collection of African-American culture, art, and research now at the Harlem branch of the New York Public Library. Charles S. Johnson, Aaron Douglass and others began the Fisk University Annual Festival of the Arts, which involved the Negro masses and extended the Renaissance into the urban South. During the 1947 Festival of Arts, they included the work of William Edmondson, a local Negro stone sculptor whose sculptures were exhibited in Paris and across America in the late 1930s and 1940s. Today his works form the subject of several books including *The Art of William Edmondson* (2002).[74] Scholarly articles recognize the importance of this illiterate sculptor, the son of former Tennessee slaves. His work constitutes a permanent exhibit at the Cheekwood Galleries in Nashville. Besides recognizing the importance of Edmondson's works in Negro culture, President Johnson and faculty visited and brought back exhibits of primitive art from Haiti. Langston Hughes, the most prolific writer of the Black Renaissance period and a product of Lincoln University in Pennsylvania, spent time at Fisk, and the papers of Jean Toomer, author of *Cane* (1923), a man called "the most brilliant of the Harlem Renaissance writers," rest at Fisk University's Special Collections Library.[75] Negroes indeed had many creative bones in their bodies.

This cultural revival of the 1920s and 1930s had begun among southern Negroes during and after slavery. Their African ancestors had glorified art and had, for thousands of years, expressed their creativity in ebony, bronze, gold, iron, wood, and stone objects. From the time of the African griot (storyteller/historian) to modern Negro writers, blacks expressed their human feelings, if not through the written word, then through oral memory and history. And like their ancestors, American Negroes, slaves, and free persons, crafted objects of iron, wood, leather, stone, and made some wonderful pieces of

---

[73] Thadious Davis, *Nella Larsen, Novelist of the Harlem Renaissance* (Baton Rouge: Louisiana State University Press, 1994) 1–21; Nella Larsen, *Quicksand* (New York: Penguin Books, 2002).

[74] Rusty Freeman, ed., *The Art of William Edmundson* (Jackson: University Press of Mississippi, 1999).

[75] Jean Toomer, *Cane* (New York: Boni and Liveright, 1923); Genevieve Fabre and Michael Feith, eds., *Jean Toomer and the Harlem Renaissance* (Piscataway NJ: Rutgers University Press, 2001) 1–21.

furniture. Once freed from enslavement, that artistic urge of self-expression intensified around 1890–1915. Shortly after the end of World War I, the Great Migration spread the Negro Renaissance, like dandelion seeds, into northern Negro centers such as Harlem.

Indubitably, some of America's greatest collections of art continued to exist off the beaten path in small HBCU galleries, libraries, and archives. The oldest of HBCU art galleries at Howard University included collections in European, Baroque, South American, African American, and African art. Howard's African Art Collection began with the 365 pieces donated by the estate of Alain L. Locke (1886–1954). The many pieces of African art and artifacts collected by officials at Walden University's school of African missions in Nashville became neglected with the closure of the school in 1929. At Fisk University's Carl Van Vechten Gallery, visitors may still see some of America's richest art treasures. Fisk named its famous art gallery for Vechten, the wealthy white patron and novelist, because he befriended struggling Negro artists during the Harlem Renaissance. Fisk upgraded the gallery facility in 2009. Neighboring Tennessee State moved its Hiram Van Gordon Memorial Art Galley from a basement to a new space and used Title III funds to expand and upgrade the facility. At other HBCUs, the visitor might see real Negro folk art: basketry, ironwork, stone sculpture, banjos and fiddles made of wood, as well as photos of shotgun houses descended from the West African architectural tradition, work by slave furniture artisans and cabinetmakers, pottery and iron vessels made by slave artisans, and jewelry-like ornaments carved in wood by slaves. At Talladega, one still may see the Amistad murals painted by artist Hale Woodruff under commission by the board of trustees in 1939 in commemoration of the 100th Anniversary of the infamous Amistad slave-ship rebellion. The Spelman College Museum of Fine Art became the premier institution in Atlanta emphasizing works by and about women of the African Diaspora.

Theatre, Speech, and Drama at HBCUs

HBCUs contributed to the history and evolution of theatre, drama, and speech in the United States. The early freedmen schools had debate and oratory clubs, which naturally led to the performance of plays and dramas. Howard University had a Drama Club as early as 1909. They formed their own association in the 1920s, and promoted the Little Theater movement for children, starting in 1921. This movement led to the formation of the Collegiate Dramatic Association by the HBCUs in 1930. The Southeastern Association of Dramatic and Theatre Arts existed by 1936, holding its annual conferences on various HBCU campuses. The HBCUs competed with one another in the dramatic arts through the Theatre Festival of the Southern Association of Dramatic and Speech Arts by the late 1940s. Humanities Clubs since the 1920s, Players' Guilds, and traveling theater and musical groups enhanced the culture on HBCU campuses. And for the benefit of the adjacent communities, many HBCUs observed annual arts festivals and Negro Art Week.

In 1951, the eighteen-member Collegiate Dramatic Association became the National Association of Dramatic and Speech Arts. Howard, Morgan State, and Florida A&M built new theater facilities by the 1960s. Howard had a 1,508-seat auditorium plus the 314-seat Ira Aldridge Theatre in a new Fine Arts Building. The Charles Winter Wood Theatre seated seven hundred people in the new FAMU fine arts facility. By the 1960s, the HBCUs would join integrated regional and national theater, speech arts, forensics, and debating associations and societies. Tougaloo College organized the Free Southern Theater to dramatize the Civil Rights Movement during the 1960s. Also during the 1950s and 1960s, HBCU groups—including FAMU, Howard, and Tennessee State—traveled the country and performed in foreign countries at the invitation of US agencies.

Music, Orchestras, Marching Bands, Dance, Entertainment Arts, & Journalism

HBCUs helped transform music into something truly American, changed American culture and world culture, and was a great part of African and African-American history. Music was a natural and integral part of African-American life, even during 246 years of enslavement in America. African ancestors mastered melodic instruments including gongs, rattles, zithers, flutes, fiddles, lutes, harps, bow-lutes, musical bows, mirlitons, whistles, the kakaki, the alghaita, and clarinets, as well as the drums. People of African descent smoothly sang the melodies.

Most HBCUs had choral groups that toured the country, raising funds and attracting students. Often, their first directors were white men, who tried to preserve, especially for white listeners, the old slave spirituals in the late 1860s and early 1870s. They also performed contemporary compositions such as European-American songs. The Fisk Singers began local and regional concerts as early as 1869, entertaining audiences in Nashville and surrounding towns. They began touring the country to help raise money for the building program in 1871. When Frederick Douglass visited Nashville in September 1873, he did not get to meet the Jubilee Singers, who were touring Europe. The singers later visited Douglass at his home in Washington, DC.[76] Marilyn Thompson said, "In its 110-year existence, the choral program [of Hampton University] has asserted itself as

[76] Andrew Ward, *Dark Midnight When I Rise: The Story of the Fisk Jubilee Singers, How Black Music Changed America and the World* (New York: HarperCollins, 2000) 1–30, 36.

a major force, greatly shaping the institution's destiny." The first choral group left the campus in 1873, led by a white director, Thomas P. Fenner of Rhode Island, to raise money to build a dormitory. They gave a concert at the White House for President U. S. Grant and at Steinway Hall in New York. Into recent years, the choir traveled annually, and the department of music at Hampton remained one of the top ones in the nation. [77] Blues, jazz, gospel, popular American compositions, and Negro spirituals pricked the interest of Americans and foreigners alike. In some parts of Europe, such as in Caen, France, local choirs in 2006 reproduced concerts of black spiritual and gospel music during the Christmas season to a packed audience. Europeans had picked up the tradition of singing Negro songs from visits by HBCU choirs.

HBCUs helped give birth to ragtime and its more sophisticated urban cousin, jazz. Scott Joplin, the father of ragtime music sharpened his musical skills by composing songs for the Negro Queen City Band in Sedalia, Missouri. Tuskegee Institute had a sizeable band wearing military-like uniforms by 1890, and Florida A&M had a large band by 1892. William C. Handy had a marching band of eleven pieces at Alabama A&M State College by 1900. The administration, like many middle- and upper-class Negroes, did not approve of students playing ragtime and jazz. Handy moved to Memphis and gained fame by composing jazzy campaign tunes for one of the mayoral candidates in 1909, and this jingle became the popular tune "The Memphis Blues." Handy relocated to New York to form the W. C. Handy Music Publishing Company. He became "the father of the blues." The pure form of ragtime music all but died soon after World War I ended. However, black commercial bands and other Negro composers were combining orchestras with choirs and dance performances for the benefit of patrons in Harlem nightclubs.

Students at the HBCUs helped transform ragtime into urban jazz. Thirty-eight HBCUs had outstanding jazz, swing, and dance orchestras. They formed, managed, and even composed the music of the early ragtime and jazz bands at the HBCUs. James "Jimmie" M. Lunceford, who graduated from Fisk University in 1926 and became a schoolteacher in Memphis public schools, organized a student group called the "Chickasaw Syncopators" and toured the country with their popularized "Gentleman Swing." Clark Atlanta had one of the first touring jazz bands, the ten-piece "Collegian Rambles." Morehouse College had a large orchestra that performed with the Morehouse Choir. Alabama State had three orchestras—"The Bama State Collegians," "The Revelers," and the "Cavaliers"—that performed jazz during the period 1925–1935. Tennessee A&I State College

---

[77] Marilyn Thompson, "The Hampton University Choir," *The Western Journal of Black Studies* 12 (1988): 215–17.

jazz group, "The Collegians," toured the country in their own bus. A Pittsburgh *Courier* poll in 1949 voted the Tennessee A&I State College "Collegians" the top college orchestra in the country. Their bus crashed on tour on 14 June 1949, killing two members and injuring others. Andrew L. Goodrich, an authority on jazz at HBCUS, credits presidents of Alabama State College and Tennessee State for promoting and financing student jazz- and dance-band development. Professional bands under Duke Ellington, Count Basie, Ray Charles, Louis Armstrong, and others recruited new members from HBCU campuses. Many jazz band players, soloists, and singers got their start on HBCU campuses. However, Tennessee A&I State University discontinued its touring dance band in 1952. Moreover, the HBCUs almost lost their jazz heritage after allowing the bands to die out following *Brown* and desegregation of the TWIs. This vacuum allowed white universities to assume jazz bands larger than any of the ones at the HBCUs. But the Spelman Jazz Ensemble began in 1983 under Joe Jennings, and over the next twenty-five years they toured the country and performed with jazz greats, including Nancy Wilson and Wynton Marsalis. Only gradually did the HBCUs reenter jazz/big band fields. In the 1990s, they even formed an association to push the jazz revival among the HBCUs. Tennessee State University reorganized its jazz band in the 1990s and had three groups by 2005.

Marching bands in the black community began with the US Colored Troops Regiments, such as the 11th USCT Infantry Regiment, during the Civil War. With a handful of brass instruments and a drum, the USCT bands helped to recruit rural slaves into the Union Army. Until 1866, they marched during parades and Emancipation Proclamation Day celebrations. When the US Regular Army formed the 9th and 10th Calvary and the two Negro infantry regiments in 1866, they, too, had marching bands. In civilian life, Negro men kept up the tradition through their Grand Army of the Republic (GAR) units and local Negro Militia units. They pleased the crowd with brass buttons, buff and blue uniforms, and lively music. The tradition continued at the HBCUs, including Roger Williams University, in the 1880s and 1890s. Kentucky State College had a fourteen-piece marching band at the start of the First World War. The tradition of marching bands took off at the HBCUs especially from 1944 to 1946, when intercollegiate football and other male-dominated sports restarted at many HBCU campuses. Tuskegee and Florida A&M had marching bands the crowds admired, and these marching units overshadowed the jazz bands and traveling orchestras. The marching bands could impress the masses while marching in street parades. Thus, the HBCU marching bands, especially the ones at Tennessee State and FAMU, caught on with the American public. They performed at professional football games and in Presidential Inaugural Parades. Only the smallest of 103

HBCUs and some poor inner-city high schools had no marching bands by 2009. However, marching bands were terribly expensive, costing thousands of dollars to transport the band, equipment, and personnel. Even though some inner-city high schools lost the ability to maintain large marching bands, some HBCUs kept the tradition alive and produced band directors for the large city school systems, which received invitations to perform at the "Battle of the Bands" at the HBCU football classics and homecoming parades. The creative field of music simply was a long tradition among blacks.[78]

The HBCUs and blacks affiliated with them contributed to American concert music, opera, and church music. The National Baptist Publishing Board under Richard H. Boyd, a former Bishop College student, published at least a half dozen religious songbooks by 1915. From the 1930s into the 1950s, Roland Hayes, Marian Anderson, and Paul Robeson took the spirituals into the concert halls. John R. Johnson and brother James Weldon Johnson, composed "Lift Every Voice and Sing, often referred to as "the Negro National Anthem."

Modern African-American divas of opera and concert often had their beginnings and connections at the HBCUs. Charlotte Holloman, a gifted soprano, traveled Europe and performed in American theaters from 1954 through the 1960s. She was a graduate of Howard University and the daughter of the president of Central State University, Charles Wesley, who was a former Fisk Jubilee singer, along with his classmate Roland Hayes, an internationally acclaimed tenor. Felicia Weathers, who attend Lincoln University in Missouri before studying voice at Indiana University, debuted at the Metropolitan Opera House in 1965. Betty Allen, who attended Wilberforce University with classmate Leontyne Price, toured and performed in Europe. Margaret Tynes, a Virginia born soprano, who attended North Carolina A&T, made her debut in opera as Lady Macbeth in 1952. Mattiwilda Dobbs, a valedictorian graduate of Spelman, helped desegregate the San Francisco Opera. Dobbs became a regular in the New York Metropolitan Opera Company, and began teaching at Howard University.[79]

---

[78] Eric Kelderman, "William P. Foster, Who Led Florida A&M's Famed Marching 100, Dies at 91," *Chronicle of Higher Education* 57/5 (24 September 2010): A4.

[79] Ben Sidran, *Black Talk: How the Music of Black America created a Radical Alternative to the Values of Western Literary Tradition* (New York: Holt, Rinehart, and Winston, 1971) x–xvii; A. L. Goodrich, "Jazz in Historically Black Colleges," lecture at Tennessee State University, 25 February 2005; S. Curtis, *Dancing to a Black Man's Tune: A Life of Scott Joplin* (Columbia: University of Missouri Press, 1994) 1–30; L. F. Emery, *Black Dance in the United States from 1619 to 1970* (Palo Alto CA: National Press Books, 1972) 243, 244, 245, 264; B. W. Peretti, *Jazz in American Culture* (Chicago: Ivan R. Dee, 1997) 1–10; J. W. Holland, *Black Recreation: A Historical Perspective* (Chicago: Burnham, Inc. Publishers, 2002); John Lovell Jr., *Black Song: The Forge and the Flame* (New York: Paragon House, 1972) 1–10.

HBCUs made contributions in the field of dance. The communities that surrounded the black colleges accommodated a mixture of rural and urban black culture, including the dances performed by Negro patrons in the local cafes and "juke joints." Negro dancing dated back to their ancestors in Africa, and the slaves continued the tradition, dancing in circles, counter-clockwise in harmony with the natural rotation of the earth. They often allowed an individual or a couple to take the center of the circle, while other participants clapped, stamped their feet, and kept up the rhythm. Slave dances transformed into dances that characterized black urban culture. When millions of Negroes went to northern cities during the Great Migration, they took their dance styles and mixed them into new dances. Near Fisk and Tennessee State, the "Black Bottom" neighborhood originated the dance called "do the black bottoms." During her stay with her brother John Hurston, a Meharry Medical College student, 1913–1915, Zora Neale Hurston visited the nearby black cafes and joints, and saw firsthand these urban black dances. The "big apple" dance started in a Negro dance hall in Columbia, South Carolina, home of HBCU Allen University.

The first Negro dance companies started in Harlem with emphasis on African and African-American styled dances, which became favorite performances in the ballrooms and nightclubs frequented by whites during the Harlem Renaissance. Unlike southern whites, who were surrounded by black culture, northern whites were amazed to see and hear black music and Negro dances for the first time. Black dance companies sprouted at Atlanta University, Fisk, Howard, Spelman, Tuskegee, and other HBCUs. In 1948, after seeing her performing African dances at Fisk University, the president of the Rosenwald Fund, Edwin Embree, gave one of its last grants to Pearl Primus for her to tour and perform in Africa. Du Bois's wife, Shirley Graham, whom he met at Tennessee A&I, left the faculty, and directed black drama in northern cities.

The HBCUs continued to produce students and former students who made great contributions to the arts. Phylicia Rashad, a graduate of Howard University, became the first black woman actor to receive the Tony Award. Oprah Winfrey, a graduate of Tennessee State University, became America's most successful talk-show host, winning many awards in the field of performing arts. Fisk produced Nikki Giovanni, a world-renowned poet. Alex Haley, author of *Roots*, was a product of Alcorn State University. The award-winning journalist Carl T. Rowan was a former student at Tennessee State, as was Theodore Poston, who won awards as early as the late 1940s. Even through the "hip-hop generation," the HBCU campuses would remain centers for African-American culture. In the 1970s, Toni Morrison, once a student at Howard and teacher at Howard and Texas Southern, won major prizes in literature. Alice Walker, a former student at Spelman College, won the Pulitzer Prize for poetry and the American Book Award for *The Color Purple,* which Oprah Winfrey, a Tennessee State University graduate, converted into a popular movie. In 1993, Toni Morrison became the first African American to win the Nobel Prize for Literature. In 2008, the Black College Communication Association reported forty programs at the HBCUs. Howard University had the largest School of Communication among the black colleges and universities.[80]

HBCUs, Sports & Athletics: "A Will to Win"

In sports, the HBCUs gave a treasured gift to America. As early as the 1870s, the HBCUs included physical education. Competitiveness among the students led to their challenging nearby HBCUs in football, baseball, and track and field. Biddle University (Johnson C. Smith) and Livingston College challenged each other in football in 1892, while Tuskegee Institute and Atlanta University engaged a football game in 1897. Florida A&M State Normal College placed intramural sports under faculty supervision in 1899, and began its athletic program in baseball and football, followed in 1901 by tennis and basketball, and varsity competition with Alabama State and Tuskegee in 1906.

When sports competition became more organized, students on all the different kind of teams had to buy their own equipment and uniforms. The seniors often served as the coaches and assistant coaches. By 1912, student newspapers began to cover HBCU collegiate competition. In the 1920s, for baseball, basketball, and football, HBCUs began hiring coaches. Cleve Abbott started the Tuskegee Relays in 1927. These coaches—including Amelia C. Roberts in track at Tuskegee and Edward Hunt legendary football and basketball coach at Morgan State—also served as head of physical education and taught classes. Given their heavy teaching loads and low salaries, the early HBCU coaches excelled in winning athletic contests.

Negro schools had no facilities, resources, or collegiate status to compete in most college sports venues. The "Tuskegee Relays" became the top event in track and field among HBCUs by the 1940s. Tennessee A&I built a rough football stadium, nicknamed "the hole," in 1927, and later improved it with New Deal funds. Knoxville College and other HBCUs began building such facilities.

---

[80] F. G. Yerby, "The Little Theatre in the Negro College" (master's thesis, Fisk University, 1938) 1–10; E. J. Fisher, "The Improvement of Speech and Drama Facilities in Negro Colleges and Universities from 1952–1962" (master's thesis, Tennessee A. & I. State University, 1963) 1–30; Jon M. Spencer, *The New Negro and Their Music: The Success of the Harlem Renaissance* (Knoxville: University of Tennessee Press, 1997) 1–30; J. M. Spencer, *As the Black School Sings: Black Music Collections at Black Universities and Colleges* (New York: Greenwood Press, 1987) 1–10; Hine, Hine, and Harrold, *African Americans*, 542, 546.

A group of players organized the National Association of Baseball Players in 1858. Baseball's popularity spread into the South with the arrival of Union Army soldiers. The National League of Baseball Clubs began in 1876, and the American Baseball League began in 1899. The World Series began in 1903.

HBCU communities represented an elite class of Negroes who had the leisure time and some resources to engage in recreation and spectator sports. Thus, the black colleges and universities often served as a reflection of American cultural trends. Baseball, in particular, was popular as it required little equipment and no costly facilities. With plenty of open spaces, rural Negro communities took up baseball. Alcorn State College fielded its first baseball team in 1875. The sport was popular by the 1880s, and the HBCUs in Atlanta formed a collegiate baseball league in 1896.

Five professional Negro baseball teams existed in 1900, and eight teams formed the Negro Baseball League in 1920. From then until 1960, the professional Negro Baseball League thrived. When the professional Negro teams barnstormed the country, they often played against baseball teams at the HBCUs. During the winter months, some professional players returned to classes at the HBCUs, recruiting players on campus. Since many HBCUs had high school departments well into the 1930s and 1940s, the pool of athletes on campus was deep. John "Buck" O'Neil, the manager of the famous Kansas City Monarchs before joining the Chicago Cubs as a scout and coach, was a product of Edward Waters College. The black colleges had a thriving baseball tradition including rivalries such as Howard University and Lincoln in Pennsylvania, Fisk University and Tuskegee, and Wiley College and Prairie View. The baseball prowess of the HBCUs increased after thousands of veterans hit the campuses in 1946.

In 1947, Jackie Robinson, a former student athlete at University of California, Los Angeles, and a member of a professional Negro League team, became the first black hired by a white professional league.[81] Thereafter, television captured the Negro spectators, who watched their black baseball heroes winning contests against white players. The black baseball stadiums, like Martin Stadium in Memphis, owned by three black physicians, closed down. The Negro Baseball League folded in 1960. Urban black youngsters could not play baseball in the streets. They lost interest in baseball, while increasing interest in basketball and football. A decreasing number of HBCUs could afford to continue

[81] Hine, Hine, and Harrold, *African Americans*, 330, 321, 322, 424, 425. Robinson retired in 1957 and died of diabetes in 1972; Carol Berkin, Christopher L. Miller, Robert W. Cherny, and James L. Gormly, *Making America: A History of the United States* (Boston: Houghton Mifflin, 1995) 570.

baseball competition after the Civil Rights Act encouraged the TWIs to give scholarships to black players.

Football became the favorite American spectator sport, and many HBCUs had football teams. Biddle University and Livingston College played each other on December 27, 1892. Fisk played football by 1894. Howard played Harvard University in 1898. West Virginia State College fielded its first football team in 1901. However, football was so rough and deadly that President Theodore Roosevelt summoned white college athletic leaders to a couple of White House conferences to encourage reforms. In 1906, 62 members formed the Intercollegiate Athletic Association, which became the National Collegiate Athletic Association (NCAA) in 1910. The NCAA did not accept black members; however, Hampton, Howard, Virginia Union, and Shaw formed the Central Intercollegiate Athletic Association (CIAA) in 1912. Morehouse, Fisk, Florida A. & M., and Tuskegee formed the Southeastern Conference in 1913. Prairie View, Bishop, Paul Quinn, Wiley, and Sam Houston colleges formed the Southwestern Athletic Conference (SWAC) in 1920. Others formed the Mid-Eastern Athletic Conference.

The Tennessee A&I State Teachers College football schedule for 1925–1937 included Alabama State College, the Elks Club of Chattanooga, Kentucky State College, Knoxville College, Lemoyne College, Miles Memorial College, Morris Brown College, Philander Smith College, Walden College, West Virginia State College, Wilberforce of Ohio, Rust College, Simmons University (KY), Lincoln University (MO), Fisk University and occasionally Meharry Medical College. Howard and Lincoln (PA) universities played before 18,000 spectators in 1925. Hampton and Lincoln (PA) played in a classic in New York in 1929.[82] The Pittsburgh *Courier* (September 2, 1933) and *Time* magazine (October 28, 1941) featured outstanding HBCU teams.

Between 1941 and 1945, many HBCU football teams discontinued football and some other sports partly due to the dearth of men on the campuses. Some of the schools, like LeMoyne College, which discontinued the sport in 1941, never resumed football. Large HBCUs, like Fisk, Hampton, Howard, and Bethune-Cookman, resumed playing football after World War II. In 1944, the students, many of them veterans, demanded that Walter S. Davis, the acting president, reinstitute A&I football. Davis, who played football at A&I during his undergraduate years, 1927–1931, and coached the team in 1931–1933, obliged. He hired Arthur Kean from Kentucky. Tennessee A&I State and Arkansas A. M. & N. State College met each other in the "Memphis Classic" on the Booker T.

---

[82] Hine, Hine, and Harrold, *African Americans*, 330, 331, 322, 379, 380, 424, 425.

Washington High School football field in Memphis in November 1944. The "Memphis Classic" continues today between TSU and Jackson State University. The Southern Intercollegiate Athletic Conference (SIAC) began sponsoring the Vulcan Bowl in Birmingham to determine the black college football champion. Florida A. & M. won its first black college national title in football in 1938, and dominated the sport for a time.

Among the HBCUs that placed hundreds of former players in the professional football leagues, Tennessee State University placed "Jefferson Street Joe" Gilliam with the Pittsburgh Steelers as one of the first black players to start as quarterback. Gilliam's coach, John S. Merritt, placed more than 150 players in the NFL, and received congratulations from US President Jimmy Carter for winning 200 college football games by 1980. He had 30 straight winning seasons, 4 undefeated seasons, 6 national championships, and 4 black college football titles before his death in 1983. Twenty-three Merritt-coached pro players distinguished themselves, including six who played in NFL Super Bowls. One of them, Claude Humphreys, gained admission into the NFL Hall of Fame. Between 1952 and 1992, Alcorn A. & M. had 72 football players drafted to professional teams, 8 in baseball 1981–1990, and 6 in basketball 1969–1985.

Grambling became a powerhouse under football Coach Eddie Robinson, who placed Doug Williams as the first black quarterback in the NFL in 1978. In the 1971 season, Grambling State University had a school record of 43 former Grambling players admitted to NFL training camps at one time. Eddie Robinson of Grambling University was among America's great football coaches, holding the most wins. Between 1961 and 2004, Grambling had 216 former players who played in the professional football leagues. Twenty-one former Grambling players performed in the National Football League's Super Bowl, and Doug Williams was starter and "most valuable player" in Super Bowl XXII, which his team, the Washington Redskins, won the game.

On the state level, the HBCUs had heavy representation by student athletes in the halls of fame. HBCU football programs continued to supply the national, Canadian, and European football leagues with players. In 1996, HBCUs had 17 players selected by fourteen of the NFL teams. For the 2004–2005 NFL rosters, there were 47 NFL players from 19 HBCUs: Grambling University (5), North Carolina A. & T. University (5), Alcorn University (4), Hampton University (4), University of Arkansas at Pine Bluff (4), South Carolina State University (3), Tennessee State (3), Texas Southern (3), and Bethune-Cookman led the list. Clark Atlanta had 17 former players in the NFL between 1967 and 1999. Jerry Rice of Mississippi Valley State became the NFL's greatest, record-breaking wide receiver. Steve McNair of Alcorn State led the Tennessee Titans (Houston Oilers) in 2002 to the NFL Super Bowl. Walter Payton of Jackson State became the greatest running back, playing for the Chicago Bears NFL team. The 2006 NFL rosters listed 44 players from some 22 HBCUs with Howard (5) and Hampton (7) supplying the most players.

Basketball began early at the HBCUs. FAMU began playing basketball in 1901, and by 1905, blacks played basketball in newly founded YMCA gymnasiums. By 1910, other HBCUs, including Howard and Hampton engaged basketball games. The New York Rens, a Negro team beat the Boston Celtics in 1932. Unlike their white counterparts, the HBCUs were not always equipped with gymnasiums, but Knoxville College proudly showed off its new brick gymnasium in 1927. At the same time, the Tennessee A&I State Normal School Student Athletic Association had to play games outside until the students outfitted a space on the top floor of the Boys Industrial Building, and installed electric lights for playing basketball. Tennessee built its first physical education and recreation building in 1934, but the basketball floor was the stage of the auditorium with a few bleachers on the stage, while others sat in the seats on the auditorium floor. The state had refused the request to build a facility separate from the administration and classroom building, and did not allow Tennessee A&I State University to have a modern facility four-thousand-seat basketball arena until 1952.

The highly respected John B. McLendon of Tennessee A&I State University was a key to the rise of HBCU basketball. After leaving Kansas, the young McLendon brokered private games between his North Carolina College team and white teams in Durham in the late 1940s. Born and educated in Kansas, McLendon was a descendant of blacks and Indians who made the exodus to the west, and, thus, he had experienced first-hand racial discrimination in the Midwest and the North. While the Negro's Civil Rights Movement gathered steam after Negro soldiers returned from World War II, McClendon smartly recognized the time had come to move against segregated basketball. In 1948, when President Harry S. Truman (D) abolished segregation in the American armed forces, McLendon organized the HBCU basketball coaches into a committee to petition the all-white basketball associations to include HBCU conferences and black teams in the regional and national championship tournaments. McLendon and his associates created the National Athletic Steering Committee in August 1951 and placed further pressure on the two white national athletic associations. Indiana State University broke the ice in 1948 by playing a black basketball player in the National Association of Intercollegiate Basketball (NAIB) tournament in Kansas City. Four years later, the NAIB became the

National Association of Intercollegiate Athletics (NAIA), and accepted all teams regardless of race. Some thirty-six HBCUs eventually joined this association.

Tennessee A&I State University, with its new basketball arena, Kean Hall, became the first HBCU to play in the NAIA on 10 March 1953. In 1954, Tennessee A&I hired John B. McLendon, who was brought to Tennessee by President Walter S. Davis not only to help build a top sports program but also to help continue the HBCU process of racial integration and build teams equal to those at white colleges. Davis did not like losing, and he wanted the whites to respect Tennessee A&I State University as a serious contender. In December 1954, the Tennessee A&I State University Tigers gained an invitation to the NAIA Tournament. At the District Tournament in 1955, Tennessee State met defeat by another HBCU, Texas Southern, under coach Edward Adams—the first black coach inducted into the Helms Athletic Hall of Fame. In 1956, Texas Southern, Tennessee State, and Central State made it to the NAIA tournament at Kansas City. Texas Southern became the first HBCU to play in the championship game, losing to McNeese State in 1956.

With their "run-and-gun" fast offense and firepower, perfected by McLendon, one of the HBCUs was bound to win a National Championship. In 1957, Tennessee State beat Southeastern Oklahoma, and won the NAIA championship. Tennessee A&I State University repeated the NAIA championship in 1958, beating Western Illinois 85–73, at Kansas City, and again winning the coveted James A. Naismith Trophy. McLendon became NAIA Coach of the Year.

McLendon entered in 1997 the Memorial Basketball Hall of Fame, and the National Collegiate Basketball Hall of Fame in 2007 and the NAIA Hall of Fame. The HBCU student athletic teams helped destroy myths about white superiority and black inferiority, and America's white professional and collegiate teams began recruiting HBCU athletes. Bradley University of Peoria, Illinois, became one of the first TWIs to use black players to compete with southern white college teams in the 1950s. After the Civil Rights Act of 1964 forced school systems and the National Collegiate Athletic Association (NCAA) to begin desegregation, the NCAA divided its membership into divisions to accommodate all sizes (enrollments) of colleges and universities, including the HBCUs. The smaller NAIA continued to include several small HBCUs by 2009: Fisk, Huston-Tillotson, Jarvis Christian, Texas College, Wiley, Allen, Morris, Langston, Wilberforce, Harris-Stowe, Tougaloo, and Dillard, Southern at New Orleans, Xavier, Edward Waters, Philander Smith, and Talladega.

In 1966, Texas Western College (University of Texas at El Paso) was the first TWI to field five black starters on a basketball team. They beat the University of

Kentucky for the national championship. "That game was the beginning of the end of segregated colleges and universities. What Texas Western did that day opened the door to a new level of consciousness across the country in sports," said a commentator in *The Chronicle of Higher Education.* Black athletes began to dominate some of the largest TWI teams, while blacks in the general student body often represented smaller percentages. America's TWIs seemed willing to invest in what they perceived as superior black bodies, but too often, the TWIs gave much less financial aid and educational programming in developing black minds. Black athletes at the TWIs had academic support systems to keep them in school and remain eligible to play sports, while ordinary black students suffered high dropout rates, low graduation rates, and no support. The nation's community colleges, where half of black college students enrolled, became athletic farms and athletic recruiting pools for the large TWIs.

Nevertheless, the coaches at the HBCUs maintained a competitive spirit even in America's new athletic system. Dave Robbins at Virginia Union, Clarence "Big" Gaines at Winston-Salem, Ben Jobe at Southern University, Harold "Hal" Hunter at Tennessee State, and others rated as top basketball coaches. In 1967, under Coach Clarence Gaines, Winston-Salem State University was the first black basketball team to win the NCAA II championship. Beginning in the 1950s, Florida A&M excelled in NCAA Division II men's basketball competition, winning more than seven hundred games, thirteen conference titles, and advancing six FAMU teams to NCAA postseason play.

After passage of the Civil Rights Act of 1964, America's colleges and universities began giving more recognition to women's basketball. Cheyney State, under coach Vivian Stringer, was the first HBCU women's basketball team to participate in a women's national basketball championship in 1982. In 1986, Tennessee State became the only HBCU member of the formerly all-white Ohio Valley Conference; the women won championships in basketball. FAMU women's basketball team produced seven all-Americans between 1977 and 1990, advancing to NCAA tournament play in 1995. Several other HBCUs advanced to NCAA tournament play. Southern University became recognized force in intercollegiate athletics, winning multiple Southwest Athletic Association Conference championships.

Track and field competition heavily involved blacks in America. Since slavery days, running and jumping competition had been popular in the black communities. The earliest of nationally recognized Negro athletes originated from the northern universities and the nation's private athletic associations and teams. Blacks played football for a few northern colleges, such as Amherst and

Harvard, in the 1890s. DeHart Hubbard, a student at the University of Michigan, became the first African American to win an Olympic gold medal for the broad jump at the Paris games in 1924. Negro college athletes won medals in the 1932 Olympics. Jesse Owens of the University of Southern California won four gold medals at the 1936 Olympics in Berlin, where eight other black athletes, including Ralph Metcalfe and Matthew Robinson, won nine medals. Then, the famous Tuskegee relays in track and field helped develop HBCU teams into national and international powerhouses.

From 1948 to 1984, men's and women's track and field teams at Tennessee State won thirty gold, silver, and bronze medals in the Olympics, thirty-four national titles, and thirty medals in the Pan American Games. Tennessee A&I State University Tigerbelles Women's Track and Field Team coach Edward S. Temple took over the team in 1950. He was a recent graduate and track star from Pennsylvania. The president promised a small salary and the chance to complete his masters at A&I. He recruited Mae H. Faggs, a high school student in Chicago, who already had participated in her first Olympics. Faggs won gold in the women's relay in the 1952 Olympics, along with three other black women. Faggs then won the bronze in 1956, along with Temple's Tigerbelle relay team—the first women's track team to originate from one organization or one university: Tennessee A&I State University. The 1956 team consisted of Faggs, Isabella F. Daniels, Margaret R. Matthews, and Wilma G. Rudolph. The latter student, a former victim of polio, still attended a nearby high school. After enrolling at Tennessee State, Rudolph became the first American woman to win three gold medals in the 1960 Olympics. Temple became the most internationally recognized track and field coach in the history of American sports, and trained the American Olympic teams in 1958 and 1975. TSU inaugurated the Annual Edward S. Temple Seminars on Sports and Society in 1993–1994. Wilma Rudolph was the speaker.

The HBCUs produced Olympic stars in men's track and field as well. Tennessee State's Ralph Boston won gold, silver, and bronze medals for the long jump in the 1960, 1964, and 1968 Olympics. Robert "Bullet Bob" Hayes, a star halfback at Florida A&M University, won Olympic Gold Medals in the 100-yard dash and 100-meters men's relay team in 1964. Gerald H. Ashworth, Otis P. Drayton, and Richard V. Stebbins were his teammates on the 100-meter relay. Edwin Moses of Morehouse won the gold medal for the 400-meter hurdles in the 1976 Olympics. After NAIA women's indoor track and field championships started, HBCU teams won eight championships between 1981 and 1997. Between 1966 and 1977, Southern (Baton Rouge), Prairie View, Texas Southern, and Jackson State won the NAIA men's indoor track and field championships on seven occasions. Jackson State won three consecutive crowns in 1975, 1976, and 1977. In 1996, Lincoln University in Pennsylvania won its second straight Division III NCAA men's indoor track championship; Lincoln women took second place.

Other sports gained the attention of the HBCUs. In the "roaring twenties," "[s]ports became a national mania... as people found more leisure time. Golf boomed.... Boxing drew huge crowds... Baseball attendance soared. More than twenty million fans attended games in 1927... On college campuses, football became more popular than ever. Universities vied with each other in building massive stadiums, seating upward of seventy thousand people."[83] In the Negro communities, people stretched their meager resources to engage the same kind of sports.

Negro communities did not have swimming pools, but Negro youngsters had engaged swimming since slavery, using ponds, lakes, and rivers. By 1940, many HBCUs had swimming facilities. From 1934 until 1980, the swimming pool for the Tennessee A&I Tiger Sharks was under the basketball court (stage) in the Administration, Health, and Physical Education building. During the Jim Crow era, Negroes could not use municipal swimming facilities until after the "swim-in" protests of the 1960s and after the desegregation ordered by federal courts. Even then, many southern municipalities, including Memphis and Nashville, shut all the public pools down, depriving a generation of black youngsters of swimming lessons and experiences. Swimming pools went private; wealthier whites built pools in their backyards, and cities stopped the expansion, and sometimes the maintenance, of public swimming pools. Nevertheless, America's HBCUs competed against one another in swimming, and, by the late 1960s, competed against TWI teams.

In boxing, Jack Johnson and Joe Louis dominated the World Heavyweight Championship into the 1950s. Jack Johnson beat a white man in 1908, and the black communities went crazy with pride and joy. The whites yearned for a "white hope" to beat Johnson, but he remained Heavyweight Champion of the World until the federal authorities brought charges against him for having a white wife. A white, Jess Willard, finally beat Johnson; however, in the 1930s, Joe Louis of Detroit became Heavyweight Champion of the World. Negroes crowded the radios in the stores, homes, and streets to cheer every time Louis

---

[83] Robert A. Devine, T. H. Breen, George M. Frederickson, and R. Hal Williams, *America Past and Present*, 6th ed. (New York: Longman, 2002) 742; Irwin Unger, *These United States: The Questions of Our Past* (New York: Prentice Hall, 1989) 594.

defeated his challengers. When inducted into military service during World War II, Louis toured army camps, giving boxing exhibitions. Boxing teams became popular because of Joe Louis' popularity, and the HBCUs held their own boxing tournaments by 1940. Louis's mother toured HBCU campuses helping to raise war bonds. However, because of the liability of the sport, many institutions discontinued boxing, and the NCAA abolished national collegiate boxing championships in 1961.

In the period 1990 through 2005, the HBCU athletic programs found it very difficult to recruit the region's top athletes and win national championships. The TWIs, as a part of America's wealthiest segment of society, had the money, the facilities, and the leadership to outdo most of the less financially fortunate HBCUs. Teams at TWIs became heavily black, and the racial shift in the recruitment of black college students caused HBCU athletic teams to lose their monopoly on that vast pool of athletes. American collegiate sports appeared unfair, unequal, and discriminatory by gender, race, and economic class. John S. Merritt, the acclaimed football coach at Tennessee State from 1961 to 1982, said the coaches in the integrated high schools often would discourage top black athletes from talking to him and other HBCU recruiters. The high school coaches sometimes "took the boy to lunch" knowing well HBCU recruiters could not afford a second or third trip to see the youngster. These high school coaches (including some black ones) seemed to be feeding the best black athletes to their alma maters and TWIs that had agreements [monetary, perks and otherwise] to support them and the student recruits. The NCAA seldom caught and punished TWI officials for extending such illegal and closely disguised legal benefits to young black athletes and their parents.

This American TWI network developed a farming system, sending star high school black athletes to private boarding schools in the east to improve their discipline and academics in order to become minimally accepted for junior college and then four-year college admission. This grow-your-own system for white sports produced ready-to-play collegiate-level black athletes. Of course, America's multi-billion dollar business of college sports became too expensive for HBCUs to compete on the top levels. Florida A&M attempted to enter the top level of NCAA competition, but backed out of the expensive proposition in 2004, and the disappointment was perhaps part of the reason for the release of the institution's president. The nation's HBCUs could do little about the situation except continue to compete with each other and engage occasional contests against small TWIs in their NCAA division. None of the HBCUs could compete for the major NCAA championships within the new system of American capitalism and sports.

The large HBCU powerhouses, like Tennessee State, FAMU, Grambling, Hampton, Howard, Jackson State, Southern, and others, however, played their football contests in huge municipal arenas in "city classics" to raise large amounts of money for athletic programs. These "classics" had started at the HBCUs in the 1940s, such as the "Memphis Class" begun in 1944 the Vulcan Bowl played in Alabama, and the Howard versus Lincoln game played in 1945.[84]

Many HBCUs yet continue their annual "classics" in various cities today, especially in Atlanta, Cincinnati, and New Orleans, drawing crowds of more than fifty thousand. The HBCU athletic galas often take place in late summer and early fall when time is right for the traditional family reunion time among African Americans. HBCUs used the occasions to carry out elaborate receptions, student recruitment sessions on Friday evenings and Saturday mornings, and visits by huge, colorful, high-stepping marching high school bands in "Battle of the Bands," preceding the football game.

New NCAA rules forced colleges and universities to raise the graduation rates for their athletes.[85] From 1996 to 2003, graduation rates of athletes increased from an average low of 22 percent to a high of 95 percent. HBCUs had a 35 percent graduation rate for all students compared to 51 percent for black athletes. National Collegiate Athletic Association (NCAA), Division I HBCUs had 41 percent and 52 percent graduation rates for black students and black student athletes. Division III HBCUs had 47 percent and 46 percent graduation rates for all black students and black athletes. The graduation rate for all college athletes was 59 percent up from 56 percent in 1996, while for black athletes as a whole the graduation rate was 52 percent up from 48 percent. Tennessee State University won the Ohio Valley Conference honors for the highest graduation rate. Hampton, Howard, and South Carolina State had graduation rates for student athletes/general students of 60/52, 58/62, 51/46, respectively. The number of minority coaches leading the nation's largest collegiate football programs remains low.[86]

---

[84] D. Rogosin, *Invisible Men: Life in Baseball's Negro Leagues* (New York: Kodansha International, 1983,1995), 47–49; Josephine Posey, *Against Great Odds: The History of Alcorn State University* (Jackson: University Press of Mississippi, 1994) 1–20; Dwight Lewis and S. Thomas, *A Will to Win* (Nashville: Cumberland Press, 1983); Williams and Ashley, *I'll Find a Way or Make One*, 248, 251, 252, 254, 258, 262, 271, 273, 276, 292.

[85] Scott Wright, "Black Basketball Player's Graduation Rates Sink," *Black Issues in Higher Education* 16/15 (16 September 1999): 27.

[86] Gerald Eskenazi, "Colleges: Athletes Lead Nonathletes in Graduating, Survey Says," *New York Times*, 28 March 1991; Welch Suggs, "'Report Card' Grades Colleges on Hiring Minority Candidates as Football Coaches," *Chronicle of Higher Education* 51/11 (5

November 2004): 33; Libby Sander, "Minority Coaches Are Still Scarce in Big-time College Football," *Chronicle of Higher Education* 54/8 (19 November 2007): A32.

Conclusion

Beginning with the establishment of Cheney Institute in Pennsylvania in 1837, the history of America's black colleges and universities continued into 2010 as a complex story. Overall, the HBCUs and blacks in general reaped many benefits from changes brought about by the desegregation of higher education from 1968–2005. This history was slow to develop. By the time the Civil War began in 1861, only three institutions of higher education existed exclusively to serve African Americans. These institutions were in their infancy and not places where bachelor's and advanced degrees could be earned. American Negroes who received such degrees relied on a few predominantly white colleges, and foremost among them was Oberlin College of Ohio. When the Civil War ended and the Thirteenth Amendment freed the slaves, lower and higher education that had been expressly withheld from African Americans became a priority of black Americans and concerned white Americans. Northern white benevolent associations and especially church and religious organizations invested heavily in human capital and money, with the support of the Christian community in the North, to expand public and private education in the southern states.

Thus, the period from 1865 to 1900 included the founding of hundreds of schools and colleges for Negro American citizens. There were about 800 institutions of learning for Negroes within America's existing Jim Crow (racial segregation) system, 240 of which sought to provide higher learning. In this age of education reform in America, mainly northern agencies intervened to upgrade the Negro's access to secondary and higher education in the southern states, and help selected Negro institutions of higher learning to become accredited colleges.

With the advent of New Deal liberalism (1933–1953), America's black colleges changed positively. The Negro's civil rights movement began during that period of transformation for the black colleges and universities. The HBCUs were affected by the liberal changes, with Howard University and some other HBCUs exhibiting the New Negro attitude about black Americans willing to compete publicly with white Americans for equal rights in their country. The HBCUs contributed to the nation's World War II efforts, while at the same time demanding action from the White House in order to secure constitutional rights for blacks and stop racial discrimination in America. These years were highly productive years in the intellectual history of the HBCUs. Faculty and staff members, especially at Howard University, Fisk University, and Atlanta University, wrote articles and books, published monographs, organized scholarly journals and professional academic associations, and lent their expertise to the nation. That was a time when the nation's black colleges and universities realized their true image and personality.

By the time the Second World War began in 1939, about 109 HBCUs were recognized as colleges, and dozens of them achieved accreditation from their regional associations of higher education. By 1942, nearly a dozen HBCUs offered graduate degree programs. By 1950, nursing and pharmacy programs, religion and theological seminaries, two medical schools, and six law schools existed on HBCU campuses. The students were expected to think, work, and then go out and serve humanity. Most HBCUs focused on the liberal arts and sciences and stressed preparation of leaders. Indubitably, the development of Negro leadership through the HBCUs' educational process was crucial to the development and advancement of African-American communities throughout the country. Considering the brutality of *de jure* racial segregation systems in the southern region and the benign neglect of Negro opportunities in the northern region's *de facto* racial discrimination system, America's black colleges and universities served herculean tasks in helping to hurry the socioeconomic advancement of millions of former slaves, their descendants, and the African-American community as a whole.

By 1948, when President Harry S. Truman issued presidential orders to stop racial discrimination in federal agencies, America's constitutional adjustments declared by the US Supreme Court for the most part had been completed in terms of equal rights for all Americans. The philanthropic agencies that helped the HBCUs in the last eighty-five years had closed their doors or shifted priorities from grants and benevolence to more pressing needs, including education reform and enhancement of quality. The federal government agencies, presidents, and few modern-day foundations took up the burden of helping improve the HBCUs after the war. Many HBCUs advanced from college to university standard, including several schools/colleges on campus, and expanding graduate programs. In particular, the seventeen land-grant HBCUs began developing engineering programs, determined to prepare their students to compete in America's postwar technological economy. They invested agricultural resources into urban landscaping, agricultural marketing, and local community development.

In retrospect, when *Brown v. Board of Education of Topeka*, 347 US 483 (1954) culminated the early civil rights movement to which Charles Hamilton Houston and other Howard University-affiliated persons, including Thurgood Marshall, had lent their leadership, the public protest aspect of that movement heavily involved the HBCUs—especially the ones in urban areas. Such urban HBCUs mostly provided the foot soldiers for the movement, and presidents on black college and university campuses tried to manage the difficult situations that student demonstrators imposed on the black institutions of higher education. The clear examples of such complexities and dilemmas for black college presidents occurred at Mississippi Valley State College, Southern University, Tennessee A & I State University, and Arkansas AM & N State College. The movement helped bring about the Civil Rights Acts of 1964, 1965, and 1968, and perhaps influenced more of the nation's foundations, benevolent societies, and federal presidents to provide aid for the improvement of America's black colleges and universities. By 1980, some 109 HBCUs still existed, but integration soon led 84 percent of black college students to enroll in traditionally white institutions (TWIs), often those conveniently near their homes.

But the civil rights movement did not enhance the public HBCUs, their facilities, equipment, personnel, and expand their programming ability to compete with the TWIs in the new era of integration. There were examples, as at Tennessee State University, where state officials placed duplicative degree programs on the public HBCU campus, but mostly to deter black students from enrolling at the segregated white public colleges and universities. However, when black citizens continued to enroll at the TWIs, government officials reinstituted benign neglect of local HBCUs. Therefore, beginning in 1968 and through 2005, blacks sued the federal and state governments to force the desegregation of public higher education and force government officials to grant to HBCUs the resources needed to continue to become quality institutions of higher education, which they needed to compete in America's higher education system of more than 4,000 colleges and universities.

Within these social and political complexities during 1968 and 2010, HBCUs faced many new challenges and dilemmas. Desegregation helped create hundreds of predominantly black colleges and universities (PBCUs) that began to compete with the HBCUs for students and government support. Some modern foundations began to infuse resources and other support into selected HBCUs, especially to help improve access and quality in engineering, science, technology, and teacher education programs. These agencies included the Ford Foundation, the Rockefeller Foundation, the Carnegie Corporation, and the Southern Education Foundation that became an advocate and cheerleader for the nation's black colleges and universities. Additionally, US presidents like Richard Nixon, Gerald Ford, Jimmy Carter, Ronald Reagan, George Bush, Bill Clinton, George Bush Jr., and Barak Obama supported the White House Initiatives on HBCUs.

Within such a seemingly supportive environment in 1972–2010, a few HBCUs did not survive. But 103 HBCUs did survive by 2010. Meanwhile, by 2002, federal and state court cases and orders from the US Department of

Education Office of Civil Rights had forced the beginning of meaningful desegregation of higher education in nineteen states. Again, public HBCUs gained enhancements as a result of these actions, but the private HBCUs, which once had constituted the majority of the black colleges and universities, did not directly benefit. Thus, of the HBCUs that closed or suffered loss of regional accreditation in 2000–2010, almost all of them were private institutions. This situation placed a heavier burden on the United Negro College Fund (1944–), which had to develop new programs to address leadership, management, and budget issues at its member institutions. Even once prestigious HBCUs, including Morris Brown College, Fisk University, Clark Atlanta University, and Howard University, felt the financial squeezes that threatened cutbacks and even closure from 1995–2010. Indeed, the advent of the twenty-first century was not kind to the private HBCUs, although they were among the oldest black colleges in America upon whose campuses some of America's precious historic buildings faced disrepair and even demolition.

But all the HBCUs, including the public ones, began to see difficult times in the first decade of the twentieth century. Indeed, surely since the 1990s, American society became more racially polarized, urban school systems resegregated *de facto*, and conservative federal court judges issued rulings that supported white resistance to affirmative action programs that could lift the descendants of slaves to par with other Americans. It seemed to be a repeat of the end of Reconstruction in the 1890s.

However, the nation's black colleges and universities had weathered the storms from 1837–2010, and they seemed prepared to navigate safely into the future. The 103 HBCUs integrated their faculty and student body, added graduate and doctoral programs, expanded their science and technology programs, enhanced their teacher education programs (the original mission), continued serving disadvantaged populations, and increased access to federal, state, and local financial support. The HBCUs, public and private, depended more on tuition, fees, and auxiliary enterprise funds, while the economy declined and the poorer students suffered adversely from America's racial disparity in income and wealth. The future of American higher education was in crisis, but the HBCUs were not doing any worse than many of the TWIs. Certainly, the black colleges and universities could look back 137 years and recognize their will to survive.

Finally, the advancement of the access and quality of higher education for black Americans had come a long way since 1837, and, indeed, the HBCUs played a major role in this human story. The number of blacks enrolled in America's colleges and universities exceeded 2.3 million (12.6 percent) out of 18.2

million college students by 2007–2010. Blacks comprised 12.5 percent of the American population and 14 percent of American college students. The percentages of blacks who held bachelor's degrees, masters degrees, and doctorate degrees had significantly increased since 1900, even though the 2010 percentage was below the percentage of white Americans. The number of black faculty remained below 6 percent at the nation's colleges and universities, and most of the black faculty were employed at the nation's HBCUs and PBCUs. The number of black Americans earning PhD degrees, especially in critical areas of engineering, mathematics, science, social science, humanities, and technology generally remained static since 1954, and this situation not only slowed the diversification of faculty/staff at the TWIs, but made it difficult for the nation's black colleges and universities to maintain much-needed black faculty members—surely in the critical areas aforementioned.

Indubitably, racial violence, a hundred years of post-slavery Jim Crow laws and practices, massive white resistance to *Brown* (1954), more than a generation of whites fighting against full desegregation of state higher education systems, and white opposition to affirmative action for blacks in higher education had impeded the steady progress of African Americans to achieve parity in American higher education. These negative phenomena in American history had taken a terrible toll on America's black citizens and their institutions. Indeed, relative to Jim Crow and racial discrimination, the HBCU story demonstrates that the evil men do while they live continues long after they have died. On the positive side, student enrollment grew at HBCU campuses until more than 300,000 students, blacks, whites, and persons of other races and ethnicities attended these minority institutions. HBCUs were gifts to America and a valuable part of the higher education system of the United States of America.

Selected Bibliography

Adams, Francis D., and Barry Sanders. *Alienable Rights: The Exclusion of African Americans in a White Man's Land, 1619–2000*. New York: HarperCollins, 2003.

Anderson, Eric, and Alfred A. Moss, Jr. *Dangerous Donations: Northern Philanthropy and Southern Black Education, 1902–1930*. Columbia: University of Missouri Press, 1999.

Asenault, Raymond. *Freedom Riders: 1961 and the Struggle for Racial Justice*. New York: Oxford University Press, 2009.

Bacote, Clarence A. *The Story of Atlanta University: A Century of Service, 1865–1965*. Atlanta: Atlanta University, 1969.

Bartley, Numan V. *The Rise of Massive Resistance: Race and Politics in the South during the 1950s.* Baton Rouge: Louisiana State University Press, 1969, 1997.

Bass, J., and J. Nelson. The *Orangeburg Massacre*. Cleveland OH: World Publishing Company, 1970.

Bellamy, D. D. *Light in the Valley: A Pictorial History of Fort Valley State College since 1895.* Fort Valley GA: Fort Valley State University, 1996.

Bennett, Lerone, Jr. *Before the Mayflower: A History of Black America*. 6th edition. New York: Penguin Books, 1993.

Blight, David W. *Frederick Douglass' Civil War: Keeping Faith in Jubilee*. Baton Rouge: Louisiana University Press, 1989.

Booker, Robert J. *And There Was Light: The 120-Year History of Knoxville College, Knoxville, Tennessee 1875–1995*. Virginia Beach: Donning Company, 1994.

Brawley, Benjamin. *History of Morehouse College*. College Park MD: McGrath Publishing Company, 1970.

Brooks, Lyman B. *Upward: A History of Norfolk State University, 1935–1975*. Washington, DC: National Publishing Company, 1973.

Brown II, Christopher M. *Quest to Define Collegiate Desegregation: Black Colleges, Title VI Compliance, and Post-Adams Litigation*. Dayton OH: Education Law Association, 1999.

Bullock, Henry A. *A History of Negro Education in the South, from 1619 to the Present*. New York: Praeger, 1970.

Cooke, A. L. *Lane College: Its Heritage and Outreach, 1882–1982*. Jackson TN: Lane College, 1987.

Copeland, Elaine Johnson, et al. *Clinton Junior College* (Charleston SC: Arcadia Publishing Company, 2004.

Cozart, Leland S. *A Venture of Faith: Barber-Scotia College, 1867–1967*. Charlotte NC: Heritage Printers, 1976.

Davis, L. *A Clashing of the Soul: John Hope and the Dilemma of African American Leadership and Black Higher Education in the Early Twentieth Century*. Athens: University of Georgia Press, 1998.

Du Bois, William E. B. *The Souls of Black Folk*. New York: Penguin Books, 1903, 2003.

Dison, W. D. *Howard University: the Capstone of Negro Education*. Washington, DC: Howard University, 1941.

Drewry, Henry N. and Humphrey Doerman. *Stand and Prosper: Private Black Colleges and Their Students*. Princeton NJ: Princeton University Press, 2001.

Egerton, John. *Speak Now Against the Day: The Generation before the Civil Rights Movement in the South*. Chapel Hill: University of North Carolina Press, 1994.

Egerton, John. *The Public Black Colleges: Integration and Disintegration*. Nashville: Race Relations Information Center, 1971.

Embree, E. R. *Julius Rosenwald Report for the Two-Year Period 1942–1944*. Chicago: Rosenwald Fund, 1944.

Eng, Robert F. *Samuel Chapman Armstrong and Hampton Institute, 1839–1893: Educating the Disfranchised and Disinherited*. Knoxville: University of Tennessee Press, 1999.

Fairclough, A. *Race and Democracy: The Civil Rights Struggle in Louisiana, 1915–1972*. Athens: University of Georgia Press, 1995.

Franklin, John Hope, and Alfred A. Moss, Jr. *From Slavery to Freedom: A History of Negro Americans*. Chicago: Knopf, 1988.

Garibaldi, Antoine, editor. *Black Colleges and Universities*. New York: Praeger Publishers, 1984.

Rockefeller Foundation, General Education Board. *The General Education Board: An Account of Its Activities, 1902–1914*. New York: GEB, 1915.

Goldstone, Lawrence. *Dark Bargain: Slavery, Profits and the Struggle for the Constitution*. New York: Walker and Company, 2009.

Jones, Maxine D., and J. M. Richardson. *Talladega College: the First Century*. Tuscaloosa: University of Alabama Press, 1990.

Harlan, J. C. *History of West Virginia State College: 1890–1965*. Dubuque IA: W. C. Brown, 1968.

Harlan, Louis R. *Booker T. Washington: The Wizard of Tuskegee, 1901–1915*. New York: Oxford University Press, 1983.

Harris, Leonard, editor. *The Philosophy of Alain Locke: Harlem Renaissance and Beyond*. Philadelphia: Temple University Press, 1989.

Heintze, Michael R. *Private Black Colleges in Texas, 1865–1954*. College Station: Texas A&M University Press, 1985.

Hill, Johnny R. *A Study of the Public Assisted Black College Presidency*. New York: Carlton Press, Inc., 1974.

Hill, Susan T. *The Traditionally Black Institutions of Higher Education, 1860–1982*. Washington, DC: US Department of Education, National Center for Education Statistics, 1983.

Holmes, Dwight O. W. *The Evolution of the Negro College*. College Park MD: McGrath Publishing, 1969.

Jackson, David H. *Booker T. Washington and the Struggle against White Supremacy: The Southern Educational Tours, 1908–1912*. New York: Palgrave Macmillan, 2008.

Jarrett, Alfred Q. *Julius Rosenwald, Son of a Jewish Immigrant, A Builder of Sears, Roebuck and Company, A Benefactor of Mankind: A Biography Documented*. Greenville SC: Southeastern University Press, 1975.

Johnson, Charles. *African-Americans and ROTC: Military, Naval, and Aero Science Programs at Historically Black Colleges*. Westport CT: Greenwood Press, 2002.

John, Charles S., Sr. *The Spirit of a Place Called Meharry*. Nashville: Self-published, 2000.

Jones, E. A. *Candle in the Dark: A History of Morehouse College*. Valley Forge PA: Judson Press, 1967.

Kannerstein, Greg, editor. *The Spirit of the Intellect: Haverford College, 1883–1983*. Haverford PA: Haverford College, 1983.

Katz, Milton S. *Breaking Through: John B. McLendon, Basketball Legend and Civil Rights Pioneer*. Fayetteville: University of Arkansas Press, 2007.

Kennedy, Thomas C. *A History of Southland College: The Society of Friends and Black Education in Arkansas*. Fayetteville: University of Arkansas Press, 2009.

Lede, N. W. *Mary Allen College: Its Rich History, Pioneering Spirit and Continuing Tradition, 1885–1995*. Houston: Texas Southern University, 1995.

LeFever, H. G. *Undaunted by the Fight: Spelman College and the Civil Rights Movement 1957–1967*. Macon GA: Mercer University Press, 2005.

Litwack, Leone. *North of Slavery: the Free Blacks in the Free States, 1790–1860*. Chicago: University of Chicago Press, 1961.

Logan, Rayford. *The Betrayal of the Negro: from Rutherford B. Hayes to Woodrow Wilson*. Toronto, Canada: Macmillan, 1965.

Lloyd, Raymond G. *Tennessee Agricultural and Industrial State University, 1912–1962*. Nashville: Tennessee A&I State University, 1962.

Lovett, Bobby L. *The Civil Rights Movement in Tennessee: A Narrative History*. Knoxville: University of Tennessee Press, 2005.

McCluskey, Audrey T., and E. M. Smith. *Mary McLeod Bethune: Building a Better World*. Bloomington: Indiana University Press, 2001.

McNeil, Genna R. *Groundwork: Charles Hamilton Houston and the Struggle for Civil Rights*. Philadelphia: University of Pennsylvania Press, 1983.

Mays, Benjamin E. *Born to Rebel: an Autobiography*. New York: Charles Scribner's Sons, 1971.

Morrison, Richard D. *History of Alabama A. & M. University, 1875–1992*. Huntsville: Alabama A & M University, 1993.

Murphy, L. E., F. R. Coble, and S. A. Allen. *The History of Winston-Salem State University, 1892–1992*. Virginia Beach: Donning Company, 1993.

Nettles, Michael, and K. Millett. *Preparing HBCUs to Address the Crisis of African American Education Through Higher Standards in Teacher Education*. Atlanta GA: Southern Education Foundation, 2002.

Neyland, L. W., and J. W. Riley. *The History of Florida Agricultural and Mechanical University*. Gainesville: University of Florida Press, 1963.

Payne, Daniel A. *Recollections of Seventy Years*. New York: Arno Press, 1968.

Payne, Daniel A. *The History of the Origin and Development of Wilberforce University*. Xenia OH: Wilberforce University, 1891, 1999.

Peabody, Francis G. *Education for Life: The Story of Hampton Institute*. New York: Doubleday Books, 1920.

Posey, Josephine. *Against Great Odds: The History of Alcorn State University*. Jackson: University Press of Mississippi, 1994.

Powell, R. J., and J. Reynolds. *To Conserve a Legacy: American Art from Historically Black Colleges and Universities*. Cambridge: Massachusetts Institute of Technology Press, 1999.

Powell, Ruth M. *Ventures in Education with Black Baptists in Tennessee*. New York: Carlton Press, 1979.

Newton, W. N., and G. W. Penniman, editors. *An Era of Progress and Promise: the Religious, Moral, and Educational Development of the American Negro since His Emancipation*. Boston: Priscilla Publishing Co, 1910.

Rawick, George P., editor. *The American Slave: A Composite Autobiography*. 41 volumes. Westport CT: Greenwood Press, 1972–1979.

Read, Florence. *The Story of Spelman College*. Princeton NJ: Princeton University Press, 1961.

Rhodes, Lelia G. *Jackson State University: The First Hundred Years, 1877–1977*. Jackson: University Press of Mississippi, 1979.

Richardson, Joe M. *A History of Fisk University, 1865–1946*. Tuscaloosa: University of Alabama Press, 1980.

Robbins, Richard. *Sidelines Activist: Charles A. Johnson and the Struggle for Civil Rights*. Jackson: University Press of Mississippi, 1996.

Roebuck, J. B., and K. S. Murty. *Historically Black Colleges and Universities: Their Place in American Higher Education*. Westport CT: Praeger, 1993.

Sadler S. *Segregated Skies: All-Black Combat Squadrons of World War II*. Washington, DC: Smithsonian Institution, 1992.

Samuel, Albert L. *Is Separate Unequal? Black Colleges and the Challenge to Desegregation*. Kansas City: University Press of Kansas, 2004.

Simmons, William J. *Men of Mark: Eminent, Progressive and Rising*. Cleveland OH: G. M. Rewell Company, 1887.

Sitkoff, Harvard. *A New Deal for Blacks: The Emergence of Civil Rights as a National Issue: The Depression Decade*. New York: Oxford University Press, 1978.

Smith, James W., editor. *Leadership and Learning: An Interpretive History of Historically Black Land-Grant Universities—A Centennial Study*. Washington, DC: National Association of State Universities and Land-Grant Colleges, 1993.

Smith, Jessie C., editor. *Notable Black American Women*. Westport CT: Greenwood Press, 1992.

Southern Education Foundation, *Unintended Consequences: Perspectives on Teacher Testing and Historically Black Colleges and Universities*. Atlanta GA: SEF, 2003.

Southern Education Foundation. *Igniting Potential: Historically Black Colleges and Universities in Science, Technology, Engineering and Mathematics*. Atlanta GA: SEF, 2005.

Strickland, A. E., editor. *Lorenzo J. Greene, Selling Black History for Carter G. Woodson: A Diary, 1930–1933*. Columbia: University of Missouri Press, 1996.

Summerville, James. *Educating Black Doctors: A History of Meharry Medical College*. Knoxville: University of Tennessee Press, 1983.

Terry, W. E. *Origins and Development of Texas Southern University, 1927–1967*. Houston: Texas Southern University, 1978.

Tushnet, Mark V. *NAACP: Legal Strategy against Segregated Education 1925–1950*. Chapel Hill: University of North Carolina Press, 1987.

US Civil Rights Commission. *The Black/White Colleges*. Washington, DC: Civil Rights Commission, 1981.

US, Department of Interior, National Park Service. *Historic Preservation: Cost to Restore Historic Properties at Historically Black Colleges and Universities*. Washington, DC: General Accounting Office, 1998.

US Bureau of Education. *A Study of Private and Higher Education for Colored People in the United States*. Bulletin 38. Washington, DC: General Printing Office, 1917.

US Bureau of Education. *National Survey of the Higher Education of Negroes*. Washington, DC: General Printing Office, 1942.

Ward, Andrew. *Dark Midnight when I Rise: The Story of the Fisk Jubilee Singers, How Black Music Changed America and the World*. New York: HarperCollins, 2000.

Ward Jr., Thomas J. *Black Physicians in the Jim Crow South*. Fayetteville: University of Arkansas Press, 2009.

Williams, George Washington. *History of the Negro Race in America, 1619–1880*. New York: G. P. Putnam Sons, 1883.

Williams, John B. *Race Discrimination in Public Higher Education: Interpreting Federal Civil Rights Enforcement*. Westport CT: Praeger, 1997.

Wolters, Raymond. *The New Negro on Campus: Black College Rebellions of the 1920s*. Princeton NJ: Princeton University Press, 1975.

Ward, Brian. *Radio and the Struggle for Civil Rights in the South*. Gainesville: University of Florida Press, 2004.

Wells, Jovita. *A School for Freedom: Morristown College and Five Generations of Education for Blacks*. Morristown TN: Morristown College, 1986.

White, James H. *Up from a Cotton Patch: J. H. White and the Development of Mississippi Valley State College*. Itta Bena MS: Self-published, 1979.

Williamson, Jay A. *Radicalizing the Ebony Tower: Black Colleges and the Black Freedom Struggle in Mississippi*. New York: Teachers College Press, 2008.

Withrow, D. *From the Grove to the Stars: West Virginia State College, 1891–1991*. Charleston: West Virginia State College, 1993.

Woodson, Carter G. *The Mis-Education of the Negro*. Washington, DC: Associated Universities Publishers, 1933.

Woodson, Carter G., and Charles H. Wesley. *The Negro in Our History*. Washington, DC: Associated Universities Publishers, 1972.

Woodward, C. Vann. *The Strange Career of Jim Crow*. New York: Oxford University Press, 1966.

Wiggins, David K., and Patrick B. Miller, *The Unlevel Playing Field: A Documentary History of the African American Experience in Sports*. Urbana: University of Illinois Press, 2003.

Williams, Juan, and D. Ashley. *I'll Find a Way or Make One: A Tribute to Historically Black Colleges and Universities*. New York: HarperCollins, 2004.

Zaki, Hoda M. *Civil Rights and Politics at Hampton Institute: the Legacy of Alonzo G. Moron*. Urbana: University of Illinois Press, 2007.

Appendix

Founding Years

Name of Institution	Status Year	Founded
Alabama A&M University	Public	1875
Alabama State University	Public	1874
Albany State University	Public	1903
Alcorn State University	Public	1871
Allen University	Private	1870
American Baptist College	Private	1924
Arkansas Baptist College	Private	1884
Atlanta University	Private	1929
Barber Scotia College	Private	1867
Benedict College	Private	1870
Bennett College	Private	1873
Bethune-Cookman College	Private	1904
Bishop State Community College	Public	1936
Bluefield State College	Public	1895
Bowie State University	Public	1865
Central State University	Public	1887
Charles R. Drew Univ. of Science & Medicine	Public	1966
Cheyney State University	Public	1837
Chicago State University	Public	1867
Claflin University	Private	1869
Clark University of Atlanta	Private	1865
Clinton Junior College	Public	1894
Coahoma Community College	Public	1949
Compton Community College	Public	1927
Concordia College	Private	1922
Coppin State College	Public	1900
Delaware State University	Public	1891
Denmark Technical College	Private	1948
Dillard University	Private	1869
Edward Waters College	Private	1866
Elizabeth City State University	Public	1891
Fayetteville State University	Public	1867
Fisk University	Private	1867

Florida A&M University	Public	1887
Florida Memorial College	Private	1879
Fort Valley State University	Public	1895
Grambling State University	Public	1901
Hampton University	Private	1868
Harris-Stowe State College	Public	1954
Hinds Community College	Public	1903
Howard University	Public	1867
Huston Tillotson College	Private	1876
Interdenominational Theological Center	Private	1958
L.F. Drake State Technical College	Public	1961
Jackson State University	Public	1877
Jarvis Christian College	Private	1912
Johnson C. Smith University	Private	1867
Kentucky State University	Public	1886
Knoxville College	Private	1875
Lane College	Private	1882
Langston University	Public	1897
LeMoyne-Owen College	Private	1871
Lewis College of Business	Private	1929
Lincoln University, MO	Public	1866
Lincoln University, PA	Public	1854
Livingstone College	Private	1879
Mary Holmes College	Private	1866
Meharry Medical College	Private	1876
Miles College	Private	1905
Mississippi Valley State University	Public	1950
Morehouse College	Private	1867
Morehouse School of Medicine	Private	1975
Morgan State University	Public	1867
Morris College	Private	1908
Morris Brown College	Private	1881
Morristown Junior College	Private	1881
Norfolk State University	Public	1935
North Carolina A&T State University	Public	1891
North Carolina Central University	Public	1910
Oakwood College	Private	1896
Paine College	Private	1882
Paul Quinn College	Private	1872

Philander Smith College	Private	1877
Prairie View A&M University	Public	1878
Rust College	Private	1866
St. Augustine's College	Private	1867
St. Paul's College	Private	1888
St. Philip's College	Private	1889
Savannah State University	Public	1890
Selma University	Private	1872
Shaw University	Private	1865
Shelton State Community College	Public	1953
Shorter College	Private	1886
Simmons Bible College	Private	1873
South Carolina State University	Public	1896
Southern University and A&M College	Public	1880
Southern University at Shreveport	Public	1964
Southern University at New Orleans	Public	1956
Southwestern Christian College	Private	1949
Spelman College	Private	1881
Stillman College	Private	1876
Talladega College	Private	1867
Tennessee State University	Public	1912
Texas College	Private	1894
Texas Southern University	Public	1947
Tougaloo College	Private	1869
Tuskegee University	Private	1881
University of Arkansas at Pine Bluff	Public	1875
University of District of Columbia	Public	1977
University of Maryland, Eastern Shore	Public	1886
University of the Virgin Islands	Public	1962
Virginia State University	Public	1882
Virginia Union University	Private	1865
Voorhees College	Private	1897
West Virginia State College	Public	1891
Wilberforce University	Private	1856
Wiley College	Private	1873
Winston Salem State University	Public	1892
Xavier University (La.)	Private	1915

HBCU Historical Chronology

1819 Maryville College admits Negro student
1824 Dartmouth College admits Negro students
1835 Oberlin College admits Negro students
1837 Cheyney State University founded for Negroes
1854 Lincoln University, Pennsylvania, for Negroes founded
1855 Berea College admits black and white students
1856 Wilberforce University for Negroes founded
1862 Congress approves Morrill Land-Grant Act
1863 Total of 209,000 Negroes would serve in Union Army and Navy
1865 AME Church buys Wilberforce; Daniel Payne becomes America's first Negro president
1866 Northern missionary agencies established more Negro colleges and schools
1869 First HBCU Medical School, Howard University, opens
1870 US approved 13th (1865), 14th (1868), and 15th (1870) Amendments.
1871 First Negro land grant, Alcorn A&M State College, created
1872 First HBCU law school, Howard University, graduates class
1876 Meharry Medical Department founded at Central Tennessee College
1877 Compromise begins the end of Reconstruction
1881 First of anti-Reconstruction Jim Crow laws passed by southern states; Spelman Seminary, first HBCU for women in US founded
1882 John F. Slater Fund created
1883 US Supreme Court declares 1875 Civil Rights Act unconstitutional
1889 Middle States Association of Colleges and Schools (MSACS) founded
1890 Morrill Land-Grant Amendment allows racial segregation in colleges
1895 Southern Association of Colleges and Schools (SACS) and North Central Association of Colleges and Schools (NCACS) established
1896 US Supreme Court affirms Jim Crow laws in *Plessy v. Ferguson* decision
1899 US Supreme Court backs up *Plessy* decision in case of *Cummings v. Georgia*
1900 W.C. Handy forms eleven-piece marching band at Alabama A&M.
1903 General Education Board created
1907 Anna T. Jeanes Fund created
1908 *Berea College v. Kentucky* affirms Jim Crow laws
1909 Seven HBCU medical schools exist
1912 Total of seventeen Negro land-grant colleges now exists

1913	Association of Colleges and Secondary Schools (ACSSN) for Negroes created
1914	Congress passed Smith-Lever Act
1917	Julius Rosenwald Fund formally created; Smith-Hughes Act passed
1918	*Cardinal Principles of Secondary Education* by National Education Association published
1920	First HBCU to offer graduate studies, Howard University
1921	Howard University accredited by MSACS; HBCUs enroll 11,527 students
1922	Annual Conference of Presidents of Negro Land-Grant Colleges begins
1923	Several HBCUs begin mergers for survival
1924	Harlem Renaissance begins
1925	Northern universities accept more HBCU graduates
1927	NCACS accredits West Virginia State College
1928	US *Survey of Negro Education* report issued; 13,860 students in seventy-seven HBCUs
1929	Beginning of ten-year Great Depression
1930	SACS begins approval of selected HBCUs for college certification; only two HBCU medical schools remain
1931	American Association of Teachers Colleges begins to approve selected HBCUs
1934	Lincoln University, Missouri, approved by NCACS
1935	Howard's Charles Hamilton Houston and the NAACP launched three-prong federal court attack on Jim Crow education
1937	Involvement of HBCUs in New Deal reform and relief programs
1938	More than two thousand Negro college graduates produced by all institutions
1939	MSACS, NWACS, SACS have approved twenty-seven HBCUs
1940	Howard University's Alain Locke published *The Negro in Art: A Pictorial Record of the Negro Artist and of the Negro Theme in Art* (1940).
1941	America enters World War II with heavy support from HBCUs
1942	Atlanta University, Fisk, Howard, and Tennessee State offering graduate degrees; US, *A Public Survey of Higher Education of Negroes* published
1944	United Negro College Fund (UNCF) founded
1945	HBCUs begin development of marching bands, sports programs, and engineering
1946	58,842 students in HBCUs, 30 percent are WWII veterans; HBCU presidential delegation meet with President Truman about HBCU needs

1947 *To Secure These Rights*, presidential committee report on civil rights; Southern Regional Education Board created for Jim Crow education

1948 Rosenwald Fund closes; President Truman issues *Executive Order 9981* against racial discrimination in US armed services

1949 Conference of Presidents for Land-Grant Negro Colleges encourages development of engineering and mechanical arts degree programs at HBCUs

1953 Since 1940, SACS has approved another seventeen HBCUs; National Association of Intercollegiate Athletics accepts HBCUs as members

1954 Supreme Court nullifies *Plessy* in *Brown v. Board of Education* decision; HBCUs admitted to Association of Land Grant Colleges and State Universities

1955 About 68,375 students enrolled in HBCUs

1957 Tennessee A&I State University wins the NAIA basketball championship; SACS accepted eighteen HBCUs for full membership

1958 National Council for Accreditation of Teacher Education (NCATE) accepts HBCUs for full accreditation

1959 Interdenominational Theological Center created by HBCU schools of religion and theology Nashville practice sit-in demonstrations downtown

1960 February, students at North Carolina A&T State College and Tennessee A&I State University begin sit-in demonstrations that spread across region; April, Student Nonviolent Coordinating Committee (SNCC) organized at Shaw University

1961 CORE Freedom Rides project assumed by Nashville Student Movement and SNCC

1964 Comprehensive Civil Rights Act and the Higher Education Act passed by Congress

1968 Tennessee State faculty member files *Geier et al. v. Ellington* higher education desegregation case

1969 National Association for Advancement of Equal Opportunity in Education (NAFEO) founded

1970 NAACP files *Adams v. Richardson* against federal government to force former Jim Crow states to desegregate higher education

1971 Several HBCU presidents resign after civil rights turmoil on campuses

1975 Number of black Americans enrolled in colleges and universities 213,000

1977 Federal court orders merger of Tennessee State with predominantly white UT-Nashville

1979 US Department of Education created; USDOE Office of Civil Rights issues new guidelines for desegregation of higher education
1981 President Ronald Regan issues *Executive Order 12320* to assist HBCUs
1982 Eight HBCUs annually issue more than two hundred master's degrees each
1983 USDA funds upgrading research facilities at HBCU land grants
1985 Five HBCUs close since 1976, leaving 10 USDOE approved institutions
1987 National Association of State Universities and Land Grant Colleges establishes programs to help HBCUs solve their problems
1988 HBCUs: 37.8 percent of bachelor's, 30.2 percent of master's, 15 percent of doctorates, and 31 percent of professional degrees earned by blacks
1989 HBCU white student enrollment reaches 26,962.
1990 HBCU fall full-time enrollment 257,152; 187,046 public; 70,106 private
1991 HBCUs top producers of students that entered doctoral programs in engineering
1992 *Ayers v. Fordice* (1975–2000) begins trial
1994 One and a half million African Americans enrolled in all colleges and universities, 16 percent enrolled in the HBCUs
1996 US Fifth Circuit Court strikes down University of Texas affirmative action admissions policy
1997 Black faculty members at TWIs rise to 5.2 percent; white faculty/staff 25 percent at HBCUs
1998 SEF publishes *Miles to Go: A Report on Black Students and Postsecondary Education in the South;* US GAO publishes *Historic Preservation: Cost to Restore Historic Properties at HBCUs*
2000 Black male enrollment in HBCUs falls from 37 to 31 percent; HBCUs enrolling 18 percent of black students and producing 29 percent of black college graduates
2001 103 HBCUs in nineteen states, including fifty-three privates, fifty publics, eighty-nine four-year, and fourteen two-year colleges
2002 Enrollment of blacks in engineering increased 27 percent since 1993
2003 Minority institutions awarded more than half of the teacher-education degrees and certificates to blacks, Hispanics, and Native Americans
2003 Howard University, a comprehensive doctoral extensive level 1 HBCU, produced 21.4 percent of doctorates awarded to blacks in engineering, computer science, and mathematics
2004 Eighty-seven percent of HBCU degrees awarded to black students
2005 Ninety-five percent of HBCUs maintained accreditation
2006 Affirmative Action Programs under attack in the federal courts.

2007 HBCU fall full-time enrollment 306,774 (83.5 percent blacks); Degrees conferred: 3,763 Associates; 31,070 Bachelor's; 7,129 Master's; 1,778 Professional; 495 Doctor's

2010 Severe economic recession adversely affects American higher education

Index